AN EXEGETICAL SUMMARY OF
1 CORINTHIANS 1–9

AN EXEGETICAL SUMMARY OF 1 CORINTHIANS 1–9

Second Edition

Ronald L. Trail

SIL International

Second Edition

Library of Congress Catalog Card Number: 2008923530
ISBN: 978-155671-204-3

Printed in the United States of America

Copies of this and other publications of SIL International may be obtained from

International Academic Bookstore
SIL International
7500 West Camp Wisdom Road
Dallas, TX 75236-5699, USA

Voice: 972-708-7404
Fax: 972-708-7363
academic_books@sil.org
www.ethnologue.com

PREFACE

Exegesis is concerned with the interpretation of a text. Exegesis of the New Testament involves determining the meaning of the Greek text. Translators must be especially careful and thorough in their exegesis of the New Testament in order to accurately communicate its message in the vocabulary, grammar, and literary devices of another language. Questions occurring to translators as they study the Greek text are answered by summarizing how scholars have interpreted the text. This is information that should be considered by translators as they make their own exegetical decisions regarding the message they will communicate in their translations.

The Semi-Literal Translation

As a basis for discussion, a semi-literal translation of the Greek text is given so that the reasons for different interpretations can best be seen. When one Greek word is translated into English by several words, these words are joined by hyphens. There are a few times when clarity requires that a string of words joined by hyphens have a separate word, such as "not" (μή), inserted in their midst. In this case, the separate word is surrounded by spaces between the hyphens. When alternate translations of a Greek word are given, these are separated by slashes.

The Text

Variations in the Greek text are noted under the heading TEXT. The base text for the summary is the text of the fourth revised edition of *The Greek New Testament,* published by the United Bible Societies, which has the same text as the twenty-sixth edition of the *Novum Testamentum Graece* (Nestle-Aland). Dr. J. Harold Greenlee researched the variants and has written the notes for this part of the summary. The versions that follow different variations are listed without evaluating their choices.

The Lexicon

The meaning of a key word in context is the first question to be answered. Words marked with a raised letter in the semi-literal translation are treated separately under the heading LEXICON. First, the lexicon form of the Greek word is given. Within the parentheses following the Greek word is the location number where, in the author's judgment, this word is defined in the *Greek-English Lexicon of the New Testament Based on Semantic Domains* (Louw and Nida 1988). When a semantic domain includes a translation of the particular verse being treated, **LN** in bold type indicates that specific translation. If the specific reference for the verse is listed in *A Greek-English Lexicon of the New Testament and Other Early Christian Literature* (Bauer, Arndt, Gingrich, and Danker 1979), the outline location and page number is given. Then English equivalents of the Greek word are given to show how it is translated by commentators who offer their own translations of the whole text and, after a semicolon, all the versions in the list of abbreviations for translations. When reference is made to "all versions," it refers to only the versions in the list of translations. Sometimes further comments are made about the meaning of the word or the significance of a verb's tense, voice, or mood.

The Questions

Under the heading QUESTION, a question is asked that comes from examining the Greek text under consideration. Typical questions concern the identity of an implied actor or object of an event word, the antecedent of a pronominal reference, the connection indicated by a relational word, the meaning of a genitive construction, the meaning of figurative language, the function of a rhetorical question, the identification of an ambiguity, and the presence of implied information that is needed to understand the passage correctly. Background information is also considered for a proper understanding of a passage. Although not all implied information and background information is made explicit in a translation, it is important to consider it so that the translation will not be stated in such a way that prevents a reader from arriving at the proper interpretation. The question is answered with a summary of what commentators have said. If there are contrasting differences of opinion, the different interpretations are numbered and the commentaries that support each are listed. Differences that are not treated by many of the commentaries often are not numbered, but are introduced with a contrastive 'Or' at the beginning of the sentence. No attempt has been made to select which interpretation is best.

In listing support for various statements of interpretation, the author is often faced with the difficult task of matching the different terminologies used in commentaries with the terminology he has adopted. Sometimes he can only infer the position of a commentary from incidental remarks. This book, then, includes the author's interpretation of the views taken in the various commentaries. General statements are followed by specific statements, which indicate the author's understanding of the pertinent relationships, actors, events, and objects implied by that interpretation.

The Use of This Book

This book does not replace the commentaries that it summarizes. Commentaries contain much more information about the meaning of words and passages. They often contain arguments for the interpretations that are taken and they may have important discussions about the discourse features of the text. In addition, they have information about the historical, geographical, and cultural setting. Translators will want to refer to at least four commentaries as they exegete a passage. However, since no one commentary contains all the answers translators need, this book will be a valuable supplement. It makes more sources of exegetical help available than most translators have access to. Even if they had all the books available, few would have the time to search through all of them for the answers.

When many commentaries are studied, it soon becomes apparent that they frequently disagree in their interpretations. That is the reason why so many answers in this book are divided into two or more interpretations. The reader's initial reaction may be that all of these different interpretations complicate exegesis rather than help it. However, before translating a passage, a translator needs to know exactly where there is a problem of interpretation and what the exegetical options are.

Acknowledgments

Richard C. Blight edited this volume for its content and its presentation. Faith Blight has carefully edited the material to prepare it for publication.

ABBREVIATIONS

COMMENTARIES AND REFERENCE BOOKS

AB Orr, William F., and James Arthur Walther. *1 Corinthians.* The Anchor Bible, edited by W. F. Albright and D. N. Freedman. Garden City, N.Y.: Doubleday, 1976.

Alf Alford, Henry. The Greek Testament. Vol. 2. 1865. Reprint. Chicago: Moody, 1968.

BAGD Bauer, Walter. *A Greek-English Lexicon of the New Testament and Other Early Christian Literature*. Translated and adapted from the 5th ed., 1958 by William F. Arndt and F. Wilbur Gingrich. 2d English ed. revised and augmented by F. Wilbur Gingrich and Frederick W. Danker. Chicago: University of Chicago Press, 1979.

EBC Mare, W. Harold. *1 Corinthians*. In the Expositor's Bible Commentary, edited by Frank E. Gaebelein. Vol. 10. Grand Rapids: Zondervan, 1976.

Ed Edwards, Thomas Charles. *A Commentary on the First Epistle to the Corinthians*. 1885. Reprint. Minneapolis: Klock and Klock, 1979.

EGT Findlay, G. G. St. *Paul's First Epistle to the Corinthians*. In the Expositor's Greek Testament, edited by W. Robertson Nicoll. Vol. 2. 1900. Reprint. Grand Rapids: Eerdmans, 1980.

Gdt Godet, F. L. *The First Epistle to the Corinthians.* Translated by A. Cusin. 1886. Reprint. Grand Rapids: Zondervan, 1971.

He Héring, Jean. *The First Epistle of Saint Paul to the Corinthians*. 2d ed. Translated by A. W. Heathcote and P. J. Allcock. London: Epworth Press, 1962.

Herm Conzelmann, Hans. *1 Corinthians*. Hermeneia—A Critical and Historical Commentary on the Bible. 1969. Translated by James W. Leitch. Philadelphia: Fortress Press, 1975.

HNTC Barrett, C. K. *A Commentary on the First Epistle to the Corinthians.* Harper's New Testament Commentaries, edited by Henry Chadwick. New York: Harper & Row, 1968.

Ho Hodge, Charles. *An Exposition of the First Epistle to the Corinthians.* Thornapple Commentaries. 1857. Reprint. Grand Rapids: Baker, 1980.

ICC Robertson, Archibald, and Alford Plummer. *A Critical and Exegetical Commentary on the First Epistle of St Paul to the Corinthians*. 2d ed. The International Critical Commentary, edited by S. R. Driver, A. Plummer, and C. A. Briggs. 1914. Reprint. Edinburgh: T. & T. Clark, 1971.

LN Louw, Johannes P., and Eugene A. Nida. *Greek-English Lexicon of the New Testament Based on Semantic Domains*. New York: United Bible Societies, 1988.

Lns Lenski, R. C. H. *The Interpretation of St. Paul's First and Second Epistles to the Corinthians*. Minneapolis: Augsburg, 1963.

My Meyer, Heinrich August Wilhelm. *Critical and Exegetical Handbook to the Epistles to the Corinthians*. Translated from the 5th ed. by D. Douglas Bannerman. Revised and edited by William P. Dickson. Meyer's Commentary on the New Testament. New York: Funk & Wagnalls, 1890.

NCBC Bruce, F. F. *1 and 2 Corinthians*. New Century Bible Commentary, edited by M. Black. Grand Rapids: Eerdmans, 1971.

NIC Grosheide, F. W. *Commentary on the First Epistle to the Corinthians*. The New International Commentary on the New Testament, edited by F. F. Bruce. Grand Rapids: Eerdmans, 1953.

NIC2 Fee, Gordon D. *The First Epistle to the Corinthians*. The New International Commentary on the New Testament, edited by F. F. Bruce. Grand Rapids: Eerdmans, 1987.

NTC Kistemaker, Simon J. *Exposition of the Epistle of James and the Epistles of John*. New Testament Commentary. Grand Rapids: Baker, 1986.

Rb Robertson, Archibald Thomas. *The Epistles of Paul*. Word Pictures in the New Testament. Vol. 4. Nashville, Tenn.: Broadman, 1931.

TG Bratcher, Robert G. *A Translator's Guide to Paul's First Letter to the Corinthians*. Helps for Translators. London: United Bible Societies, 1982.

TH Ellingworth, Paul, and Howard Hatton. *A Translator's Handbook on Paul's First Letter to the Corinthians*. Helps for Translators. London: United Bible Societies, 1985.

TNTC Morris, Leon. *The First Epistle of Paul to the Corinthians*. 2d ed. The Tyndale New Testament Commentaries. Grand Rapids: Eerdmans, 1985.

Vn Vine, W. E. *1 Corinthians*. N.d. Reprint. Grand Rapids: Zondervan, 1965.

GREEK TEXT AND TRANSLATIONS

GNT The Greek New Testament. Edited by B. Aland, K Aland, J. Karavidopoulos, C. Martini, and B. Metzger. 4th ed. London, New York: United Bible Societies, 1993.

KJV The Holy Bible. Authorized (or King James) Version. 1611.

LB The Living Bible. Wheaton, Ill.: Tyndale, 1971.

NAB The New American Bible. Camden, New Jersey: Thomas Nelson, 1971.

NASB The New American Standard Bible. Nashville, Tennessee: Holman. 1977.

NIV The Holy Bible, New International Version. Grand Rapids: Zondervan, 1984.

NJB The New Jerusalem Bible. Garden City, New York: Doubleday, 1985.

NRSV The Holy Bible: New Revised Standard Version. New York: Oxford University Press, 1989.

REB The Revised English Bible. Oxford: Oxford University Press and Cambridge University Press, 1989.

TEV Good News Bible, Today's English Version. 2d ed. New York: American Bible Society, 1992.

TNT The Translator's New Testament. London: British and Foreign Bible Society, 1973.

GRAMMATICAL TERMS

act.	active
fut.	future
impera.	imperative
indic.	indicative
infin.	infinitive
mid.	middle
opt.	optative
pass.	passive
perf.	perfect
pres.	present
subj.	subjunctive

EXEGETICAL SUMMARY OF 1 CORINTHIANS

DISCOURSE UNIT: 1:1–9 [AB, Ed, Gdt, GNT, HNTC, Ho, ICC, NCBC, NIC2, TG, TH, TNTC]. The topic is the introduction [AB, Ed, HNTC, Ho, ICC, NIC2, TG, TH, TNTC], prologue [NCBC], preface [Gdt], greeting and thanksgiving [GNT].

DISCOURSE UNIT: 1:1–3 [AB, Alf, EBC, Ed, EGT, Gdt, Herm, HNTC, Ho, ICC, Lns, My, NCBC, NIC, NIC2, TG, TH, TNTC]. The topic is the salutation [Ed, EGT, Ho, ICC, NCBC, NIC, NIC2, TNTC], greetings [AB, EBC, Lns], address [Gdt, HNTC], opening [Herm], address and greeting [Alf, My]. This unit follows Paul's usual way of opening letters: A to B: greetings [Gdt, Herm, HNTC, ICC, Lns, NIC, NIC2, TH, TNTC].

1:1 Paul (a) called[a] apostle[b] of-Christ Jesus by[c] (the) will[d] of-God,

TEXT—Instead of Χριστοῦ Ἰησοῦ 'Christ Jesus', some manuscripts have Ἰησοῦ Χριστοῦ 'Jesus Christ'. GNT selects the reading 'Christ Jesus' with a B rating, indicating that the text is almost certain. The reading 'Jesus Christ' is taken by He, KJV, LB, and NASB.

LEXICON—a. κλητός (LN 33.314) (BAGD p. 436): 'called' [BAGD, LN]. This adjective is also translated as a verb: 'to be called' [AB, He, HNTC, ICC, Lns, NCBC, NIC2, TH, TNTC; all versions except LB, REB], 'to be appointed' [Ho], 'to be chosen (by God)' [LB], 'to be called (by God as an apostle)' [BAGD]. It is also translated as a noun: '(by God's) call' [REB].

b. ἀπόστολος (LN 53.74) (BAGD 3. p. 99): 'apostle' [AB, BAGD, He, HNTC, ICC, LN, Lns; all versions except LB], 'ambassador' [BAGD], 'messenger' [BAGD, LN], 'missionary' [LB]. This refers to the office of apostle held only by the original twelve disciples and Paul [Ho, ICC, Lns]. Some take it to be a more general term for one who is sent on a mission [Herm, TH].

c. διά with genitive object (LN 89.76) (BAGD A.III.1.d. p. 180): 'by' [AB, BAGD, ICC, LN; all versions except KJV], 'by means of' [BAGD, LN], 'through' [BAGD, EBC, Gdt, He, HNTC, LN, Lns, NIC; KJV]. Here it indicates the efficient cause: 'by the will of God' [BAGD].

d. θέλημα (LN 30.59) (BAGD 2.b. p. 354): 'will' [AB, BAGD, He, HNTC, LN, Lns; all versions except LB], 'intent, purpose' [LN]. It is also taken to indicate the agent: '(by) God' [LB], 'divine summons' [ICC].

QUESTION—What is the function of the nominative case Παῦλος 'Paul'?

The nominative case indicates the writer of the letter [Gdt, Herm, HNTC, ICC, Lns, NIC, NIC2, TH, TNTC]. Some translations show this by adding a preposition: 'from Paul' [REB, TEV]; or a complete phrase: 'this letter is from Paul' [TNT].

QUESTION—What verb is implied with ‘a called apostle’?

The words ‘to be’ are implied: ‘called to be an apostle’ [He, HNTC, Ho, ICC, NCBC, NIC2, TH, TNTC; all versions except LB, NASB, REB]. Note the contrast between this usage and 15:9 where Paul is called an apostle [NIC2].

QUESTION: Who is the actor of the event κλητός ‘called’?

1. God is the actor [AB, EGT, ICC, NIC2, Rb, TG, TH; LB, REB]: God called me to be an apostle of Christ Jesus because he himself willed to do so. It was by God’s command that Paul became an apostle [Rb].
2. Christ Jesus is the actor [He, Herm, Lns, My, NIC]: Christ Jesus called me to be his apostle in accordance with God’s will. Christ called Paul to be an apostle because it was what God willed [NIC]. This happened on the way to Damascus (Acts 26:12–19) [Herm].

QUESTION—How are the two nouns related in the genitive construction ἀπόστολος Χριστοῦ Ἰησοῦ ‘apostle of Christ Jesus’?

1. This means an apostle who was appointed by Christ Jesus [He, Herm, NIC, NIC2].
2. This means an apostle who belongs to Christ Jesus [Gdt; LB].
3. This means both of the above interpretations [Ed, Lns]; an apostle whom Christ Jesus appointed to belong to him as his apostle.
4. This means an apostle who represents Christ Jesus or who was sent out by Christ Jesus [TG].

QUESTION—Why did Paul mention his role as an apostle?

Some Corinthians were at odds with Paul regarding his apostleship (9:1–23). Paul therefore begins by stating that his apostleship is of divine origin [NIC2].

and Sosthenes the brother[a]

LEXICON—a. ἀδελφός (LN 11.23) (BAGD 2. p. 16): ‘brother’ [AB, BAGD, He, LN, Lns; all versions except REB], ‘Christian brother’ [HNTC, LN], ‘colleague’ [REB], ‘fellow believer’ [LN], not explicit [ICC]. ‘Brother’ is used figuratively since Jesus calls everyone who is devoted to him ‘brother’. Here it is used to indicate membership in the Church [BAGD], It represents the relationship between believers, all having God as their Father [HNTC, ICC].

QUESTION—What relationship is indicated by καί ‘and’?

1. This associates Sosthenes with the contents of the whole letter [EGT, Gdt, Lns, My]: this letter is from Paul and Sosthenes. Perhaps Paul discussed the contents of the letter with him [Lns, My] and Sosthenes gave his approval [EGT, Lns].
2. It merely associates Sosthenes with the greeting [Herm, Ho, NIC, NIC2, Rb]: Paul and Sosthenes greet you. Sosthenes was not a co-author of the letter [Herm, Rb].

QUESTION—What is the significance of the definite article in the phrase ὁ ἀδελφός '*the* brother'?

It indicates that he was well-known to the Corinthians [EBC, Ho, ICC, NIC]: Sosthenes, the brother whom you know. It indicates that he was Paul's co-worker [NIC2].

1:2 To-the church[a] of God, the-one being in Corinth,

LEXICON—a. ἐκκλησία (LN **11.32**) (BAGD 4.b. p. 241): 'church' [AB, BAGD, He, HNTC, **LN**, Lns; all versions except LB], 'congregation' [BAGD, LN], 'body of (Corinthian) Christians' [ICC], 'the Christians' [LB]. Specifically, the Christian church is meant, and refers to the totality of Christians living in one place. In the NT this term indicates an assembly of God's people [LN, TG].

QUESTION—What is the function of the dative case of τῇ ἐκκλησίᾳ 'to the church'?

The dative case indicates the recipients of the greeting and of the letter [Gdt, Herm, HNTC, ICC, Lns, NIC, NIC2, TH, TNTC]. This is indicated in translations by adding a preposition: 'to the church' [all versions]; or a complete phrase: 'we send greetings to the church' [NAB], 'we give greetings to the church' [ICC].

QUESTION—How are the two nouns related in the genitive construction τῇ ἐκκλησίᾳ τοῦ θεοῦ 'the church of God'?

1. This means the church which belongs to God [Ed, Ho, ICC, My, NIC2, TG; REB].
2. This means the church which was called by God and which belongs to God [Gdt, Lns].
3. This means the church which worships God [TG].

QUESTION—Was Corinth a small village, a town, or a city?

Corinth was an important seaport city of Greece, located in the Roman province of Achaia [TG].

having-been-sanctified[a] in[b] Christ Jesus,

LEXICON—a. perf. pass. participle of ἁγιάζω (LN **53.44**; 88.26) (BAGD 2.4. p. 8, 9): 'to be sanctified' [AB, BAGD, He, HNTC, Lns; KJV, NASB, NIV, NRSV], 'to be consecrated' [BAGD; NAB, NJB], 'to be consecrated to God' [ICC, **LN**], 'to be dedicated' [BAGD], 'to be dedicated to God' [LN (53.44); REB], 'to be set apart as sacred to God' [Vn], 'to be set apart' [TNT], 'to be made acceptable to him' [LB], 'to be cleansed' [Ho], 'to be made holy' [BAGD, LN (88.26)], 'to be purified' [BAGD], 'to be God's holy people' [TEV]. The perfect participle indicates a completed work which continues in a state of present sanctification [EBC, Gdt, ICC, Lns, NIC, TH].

b. ἐν with dative object (LN 89.119; 90.6) (BAGD I.5.d. p. 259): 'in' [AB, BAGD, He, HNTC, ICC, LN (89.119), Lns; all versions except LB, TEV], 'in union with' [LN (80.119); TEV], 'by' [LN (90.6); LB].

QUESTION—What is meant by ἡγιασμένοις 'having been sanctified'?

It means that they have been set apart for God [EBC, HNTC, Ho, LN, Lns, NCBC, TNTC; REB, TNT]. It denotes dedication to God's service and commitment to be loyal to him [LN (53.44)]. Basic to the meaning of sanctify is the concept of belonging to God [AB, TG, TH], and being set apart for his purposes alone [TH]. It means to be included within the inner circle of what is considered to be holy in both a religious and a moral sense. This is accomplished by contact with what is holy. [BAGD]. It also includes being separated from everything that is ungodly [Ho, Lns, NIC2, TNTC]. It can be translated 'God's holy people', combining the ideas of belonging to God and bearing his character [NIC2; TEV].

QUESTION—What relationship is indicated by ἐν 'in'?

1. It indicates that Christ Jesus is the agent of the verb 'to sanctify' [AB; LB]: whom Christ Jesus has sanctified.
2. It indicates the means by which God sanctifies people [Herm, NIC, NIC2]: whom God has sanctified through/by Christ Jesus.
3. It indicates the person in association with whom the event takes place and refers to a spiritual union with Christ [Alf, BAGD, EBC, Ed, Gdt, Ho, Lns, NCBC, Rb, TG, TH, Vn; TEV]: who are sanctified because of their union with Christ Jesus/who belong to God in union with Christ Jesus. It implies that this relationship is the reason they are sanctified [Ed, Gdt, Ho, Lns, My, NCBC, Vn] or the means by which they are sanctified [Alf, Ed].

called[a] saints,[b]

LEXICON—a. κλητός (LN 33.314) (BAGD p. 436): 'called' [AB, BAGD, He, ICC, LN, Lns; all versions except LB, NASB], 'invited' [LB]. This adjective is also translated as a noun phrase: 'by calling' [NASB], 'by divine call' [HNTC]. See this word at 1:1.

b. ἅγιος (LN **11:27**; 53.46) (BAGD 2.d.β. p. 10): 'saints' [AB, BAGD, HNTC, Lns; KJV, NASB, NRSV], 'a holy people' [NAB], 'God's people' [**LN**; LB, REB, TNT], 'God's holy people' [EBC, NIC2; NJB]. This adjective is also rendered as an adjective: '(to be) holy' [NIV]; as a prepositional phrase: 'into the inner society of the Church' [ICC]; as a verb: 'to be consecrated' [He], 'to belong to' [LN, TG; TEV].

QUESTION—What is meant by ἅγιοι 'saints'?

1. It refers primarily to their being set apart to be God's people [AB, EBC, HNTC, LN, Lns, TG, TH, TNTC; LB, REB, TNT]. Both 'saints' and 'sanctified' remind us of the people of Israel whom God chose to be his people for his special purpose [HNTC, TH]. Therefore the main focus of these terms is that Christians belong to God, rather than that they are sinless [TH]. They belong to the holy God and thus are holy ones [AB]. The concept that people belong to God entails the idea that they are set apart to serve God's purposes [TH]. High moral character implied by such separation is not in focus, but it is not out of mind [TNTC].

2. It refers to their holy characters [Vn; NAB, NIV]. They are sanctified positionally in Christ Jesus and are then responsible to lead a life of holiness into which they are called [Vn].
3. It refers both to their being set apart to God and to their holy characters [Ho, NIC2; NJB, TEV]: called to be God's holy people. They are inwardly renewed as well as outwardly consecrated to God [Ho].

QUESTION—Who is the implied actor of κλητός 'called'?

God is the actor [BAGD, EBC, Ed, EGT, He, Herm, ICC, Lns, My, NIC, NIC2, TG; LB]: called by God to be saints. God called them through his messengers [My, TG] and by the preaching of the gospel [ICC, NIC]. The actor is either God or Christ [Herm]. The Holy Spirit is the actor [Ho]. This is more than an invitation, it is an effective call [Ho, Lns, My].

QUESTION—What is the purpose of repeating the idea of holiness or sanctification: ἡγιασμένοις…ἁγίοις 'having been sanctified ... saints'?

The use of related words together has the function of emphasizing the idea [Lns, TH].

QUESTION—To what are they called?

1. They are called to be saints [AB, Ho, ICC, Lns, NIC2; all versions].
2. They are saints who are called into God's kingdom [BAGD, My].

with all the-ones calling-on[a] the name[b] of our Lord Jesus Christ in every place,[c] theirs and ours;

LEXICON—a. pres. mid. participle of ἐπικαλέω (LN 33.176) (BAGD 2.b. p. 294): 'to call on' [BAGD, HNTC, LN, Lns; KJV, LB, NAB, NASB, NIV, NJB, NRSV, TNT], 'to invoke' [He; REB], 'to appeal to' [AB, LN], 'to ask for help' [LN]. The phrase ἐπικαλουμένοις τὸ ὄνομα 'calling on the name' is translated 'to worship' [TEV], 'Christian worshippers' [ICC]. The middle voice indicates 'to call on someone for aid' [BAGD]. The present tense refers not so much to a specific act as a habitual state of mind [EBC, Ho].

b. ὄνομα (LN 9:19) (BAGD I.4.b. p. 571): 'name' [AB, BAGD, He, HNTC, LN, Lns; all versions except TEV], not explicit [ICC; TEV]. The word 'name' signifies the character of the person addressed [EBC], or the person himself [EBC, LN]. In the OT (Joel 2:32) people call on the name of Yahweh, so in this place Paul is giving Jesus the highest possible designation [Alf, Herm, Ho, TNTC].

c. τόπος (LN 80.1) (BAGD 1.a. p. 822): 'place' [AB, BAGD, ICC, LN, Lns; all versions except KJV, NAB, NASB, NRSV, TNT], 'meeting-place' [HNTC], 'position, region' [BAGD]. This word is also joined with 'every' and translated 'everywhere' [BAGD; LB, NIV, NJB, TEV], 'wherever (they may be)' [He; REB]. Here it is used literally as an inhabited 'place,' that is, a city or village. Ἐν παντὶ τόπῳ means 'everywhere' that men or Christians live [BAGD]

QUESTION—What is meant by 'calling on the name of the Lord Jesus Christ'? This is a technical term used by early Christians to designate those who believe in Christ [Herm, NIC2], who worship Christ [ICC, TG, TH; TEV], and designates people who are Christians [He]. It means to address Christ in prayer [EGT, HNTC], to invoke Christ's aid [AB, BAGD, Ed, HNTC, Ho, Lns], to ask for forgiveness of sins [AB], to confess faith in Christ [AB, HNTC, NCBC, NIC], or to worship Christ [Gdt, HNTC, ICC, Lns, Vn; TEV].

QUESTION—With what is the clause 'with all the ones calling on the name of our Lord Jesus Christ' to be connected?

1. It is connected with the phrase 'to the church of God in Corinth' [Alf, Ed, EGT, Herm, HNTC, Ho, My, NIC2, TH; LB, NAB, TEV]: Paul and Sosthenes write to the church of God in Corinth, and to all those who call on the name of our Lord. This implies that Paul is addressing two groups, one in Corinth, the other in a larger area. From 2 Cor. 1:1 we can conclude that this is not to be taken as a general letter to all Christians everywhere, but a letter to the Christians in Corinth and its surrounding area of Achaia [Ho, My]. Some think that just the greeting is addressed to both groups, while the letter itself is addressed specifically to the Corinthians [EGT, Herm, HNTC].
2. It is connected with the words 'called to be saints' [Gdt, ICC, NIC, Rb, TNTC; NJB]: the church in Corinth is called to be saints along with all the others who are called to be saints, that is, with all those who call on the name of our Lord. This implies that the letter is addressed to only one group, the Corinthians, but that they are described as saints just as are all those who call on the name of the Lord in all other places [NIC]. The letter is addressed to the Corinthian church and this clause is added to remind them of the unity of the Christian brotherhood [ICC].
3. It is connected with both 'called to be saints' and 'made holy' [Vn; TNT]. This indicates that the others share a common calling and sanctification with the Corinthians but that the letter is addressed only to the Corinthians [Vn].

QUESTION—What is meant by τόπος 'place'?

1. It means a location [BAGD; all versions]: in every location.
2. It is a Jewish technical term meaning 'meeting place' [HNTC, Ho, NIC2, TH]: in every place of worship [Ho], or in every Christian place of worship [HNTC, TH].

QUESTION—What do the words αὐτῶν και ἡμῶν 'theirs and ours' modify?

1. They modify the words 'our Lord' [AB, EBC, EGT, Gdt, He, HNTC, ICC, NIC2, Rb, TG, TH, Vn; all versions except possibly KJV]: their Lord and ours. Paul is correcting the previous too limited phrase 'our Lord' [EGT, Gdt]: calling on the name of our Lord, that is, their Lord *and* our Lord.
2. They modify the word 'place' [Alf, Ed, Herm, Ho, Lns, My, NIC]: their places and ours. It means every place where those who call on the name of

the Lord live and also the place where we who send the letter live [Alf, Lns]. This stresses the unity of the universal church [NIC2].

1:3 Grace[a] to you and peace[b] from[c] God our Father and (the) Lord[d] Jesus Christ.

LEXICON—a. χάρις (LN 88.66; 57.103) (BAGD 2.c p. 877): 'grace' [AB, BAGD, He, HNTC, Lns; all versions except LB], 'favor' [BAGD, Herm, Ho], 'all his blessings' [LB], 'gracious care or help' [BAGD], 'good will' [BAGD, Gdt], 'free and unmerited favor' [ICC], 'gift' [Herm, LN]. It is derived from χαρίζομαι 'to give generously' with the resultant meaning of 'gift', and from χαριτόω 'to show kindness to someone' with the resultant meaning of 'kindness' [LN]. The customary Greek greeting was χαίρειν 'greetings' but with the primary meaning, 'to rejoice' [NIC2] and is related to χάρις 'grace' [NIC, NIC2, TH]. Paul has taken a common greeting word and invested it with new meaning [NIC, NIC2]. 'Grace' refers to God's free gift in Christ [TNTC], or to God's gifts as a whole [TH], or to God's undeserved favor [Lns].

b. εἰρήνη (LN 22.42; 25.248) (BAGD 1.2. p. 227): 'peace' [AB, BAGD, He, HNTC, LN (22.42, 25.248), Lns; all versions except LB], 'great peace of heart and mind' [LB], 'the peace which comes from reconciliation with him' [ICC], 'welfare' [BAGD, NIC2], 'health' [BAGD], 'well-being, wholeness' [NIC2], 'tranquillity' [LN (22.42)], 'freedom from worry' [LN (25.248)]. Εἰρήνη is used here with the meaning of the Hebrew word *shalom* 'welfare, health'. Paul joins the customary Greek epistolary greeting χαίρειν with a Hebrew expression [BAGD]. The primary meaning of the Hebrew *shalom* was 'material well-being', whereas Greek εἰρήνη had the meaning of 'rest' [Herm]. The usual Hebrew greeting was *shalom* 'peace' [HNTC, NIC2, TNTC]. The Hebrew word for peace indicated positive blessings, especially spiritual, and not the absence of strife [TNTC].

c. ἀπό with genitive object (LN 90.15) (BAGD V.4. p. 88): 'from' [AB, BAGD, He, HNTC, LN, Lns; all versions except LB, TEV]. This preposition is also translated as a verbal phrase: 'May God grant/give' [ICC; LB, TEV]. This word indicates the originator of the action: 'peace that comes from God, the Father' [BAGD].

d. κύριος: (LN **12:9**) (BAGD 2.c.γ. p. 459): 'Lord' [AB, BAGD, He, HNTC, ICC, LN, Lns; all versions], 'lord, master' [BAGD]. The term is used for one who has supernatural authority over men, 'Lord, Ruler, One who commands' [LN].

QUESTION—What verb is implied in this greeting?

1. The verb 'to be' is implied: [BAGD, Gdt, ICC; KJV]: May grace and peace *be* yours.
2. The verb 'give' is implied with God and Jesus Christ as the giver [ICC; LB, TEV]: May God and Jesus Christ *give* you grace and peace.

3. The verbal phrase 'I wish' is implied [Herm, NIC]: *I wish* you grace and peace.
4. The verbal phrase 'I pray that God will give' is implied [TG]: I pray that God and Jesus Christ will give you grace and peace.

QUESTION—What is meant by εἰρήνη 'peace'?

1. It refers primarily to a person's objective relationship with God in which enmity has ceased, resulting in a state of peace between that person and God [EBC, Herm, Lns]: may you have a loving relationship with God and the Lord Jesus Christ.
2. It refers primarily to the state of well-being or spiritual good health as a result of God's blessings [HNTC, NIC2, TH, TNTC]: may you have a sense of well-being in your spirits.
3. It refers primarily to the tranquillity of a person's mind [Gdt, ICC, NIC; LB]: may you feel tranquillity in your minds.

DISCOURSE UNIT: 1:4–9 [AB, Alf, EBC, Ed, EGT, Gdt, Herm, HNTC, Ho, ICC, Lns, My, NCBC, NIC, NIC2, TG, TH, TNTC]. The topic is thanksgiving [AB, Alf, EGT, Gdt, Herm, HNTC, NCBC, NIC, NIC2, TNTC], Paul's thanksgiving for God's work in the lives of the saints [EBC], introduction [Ho, Lns], preamble of thanksgiving and hope [ICC], conciliatory preamble [My].

1:4 I-give-thanks[a] to my God always[b] for[c] you

TEXT—The word μου 'my' does not occur in some manuscripts. It is included by GNT with an A rating, indicating that the text is certain. It is also included by AB, Alf, Ed, Gdt, Lns, My, NIC, NIC2, Rb; KJV, NAB, NASB, TEV, TNT. It is omitted or not translated by all other versions.

LEXICON—a. pres. act. indic. of εὐχαριστέω (LN 33.349; 25.100) (BAGD 2. p. 328): 'to give thanks' [BAGD, HNTC; NRSV, TEV], 'to thank' [LN (33.349); all other versions], 'to be thankful, to be grateful' [LN (25.100)]. It has the basic meaning of expressing gratitude for benefits or blessings. [LN (33.349)]. The present tense is a customary present indicating habitual action, especially with the adverb 'always' [AB, EBC, ICC; NJB].

b. πάντοτε (LN 67.88) (BAGD p. 609): 'always' [AB, BAGD, LN, Lns; all versions except LB, NAB, NJB], 'at all times' [BAGD, LN], 'on every occasion' [LN], 'continually' [NAB, NJB], 'constantly' [HNTC]. This adverb is also translated as a negative verbal phrase: 'to never cease' [He, ICC], 'to never be able to stop' [LB].

c. περί with genitive object (LN 89.36; 89.6): 'for' [AB, He, HNTC, ICC, LN (89.36), Lns; all versions except KJV, NASB, NJB], 'on account of' [AB, LN (89.36)], 'concerning' [LN (89.6), Lns, TH; NASB], 'about' [TH; NJB], 'on your behalf' [KJV], not explicit [ICC; LB]. It means 'about' or 'concerning' them, not 'on behalf of' them [TH]. Paul thanks God for his working in the lives of the Corinthians [NIC2]. All virtues possessed by the Corinthians are gifts of God's grace [Ho, NIC].

QUESTION—Is the word πάντοτε 'always' intended to be taken literally or figuratively?

This is an hyperbole (overstatement for effect) [My, NIC], and means 'regularly' [EBC], 'habitually' [EBC, NIC, NIC2], 'very often', or 'repeatedly' [TH]. He never forgets them [NIC2].

QUESTION—How are the nouns related in the genitive construction τῷ θεῷ μου 'my God'?

It may be expressed 'the God whom I worship' [TG, TH]. Paul changes from 'our' to the singular 'my' because this involves his personal relationship with God [Gdt].

because-of/for[a] the grace[b] of God

LEXICON—a. ἐπί with dative object (LN 89.27; 90.23) (BAGD II.1.b.γ. p. 287): 'because of' [AB, He, HNTC, ICC, LN (89.27), TH; NAB, NIV, NRSV, TEV], 'on the basis of' [LN (89.27), Lns], 'for' [BAGD; KJV, LB, NASB, NJB, REB, TNT], 'concerning, about' [LN (90.23)].

b. χάρις (BAGD 3.b. p. 878): 'grace' [AB, BAGD, He, HNTC, Lns; all versions except LB, NAB], 'favor' [Ho; NAB], 'wonderful gifts' [LB], 'favors' [ICC]. See this word at 1:3.

QUESTION—What relationship is indicated by ἐπί 'because of'?

1. It indicates the reason for thanking God [AB, BAGD, He, Herm, ICC, NIC, NIC2, TG, TH; NAB, NIV, NRSV, TEV]: I thank God because he has given his grace to you.
2. It indicates the content of what he thanks God for [BAGD, Gdt; KJV, NASB, NJB, REB, TNT]: I thank God that he has given his grace to you. This specifies what Paul was thankful about when he said 'I thank God for you' [Gdt].

QUESTION—What does the word χάρις 'grace' imply in this context?

It refers to the outworking of his grace [Ho, My, NIC, TG, Vn]: good things, blessings [TG], free gifts [Herm, NIC2]. Some commentaries think that the expressions of God's grace are defined by the following verses 1:5–7 [Alf, Lns, My, NIC] or in the immediately following context: their being enriched in speech and knowledge [My, NIC2, Vn]. Others think that the reference is more general [Gdt, ICC, TNTC], such as spiritual gifts [NCBC, NIC2, TG; LB], the fruits of the Spirit [Ho], salvation and the resulting new life [BAGD, Gdt], God's work in their daily lives [EBC, ICC].

which was-given to-you in[a] Christ Jesus,

LEXICON—a. ἐν with dative object: 'in' [AB, He, HNTC, Lns; all versions except KJV, TEV], 'by' [KJV], 'through' [TEV]. This word is also translated as a phrase: 'through your union with' [EBC, Ho, ICC], 'as members of' [Alf], 'in your fellowship with' [My]. It is also translated as a clause: 'now that you are (Christ's)' [LB]. See this word at 1:2.

QUESTION—Who is the implied actor of the verb δοθείσῃ 'was given'?

God is the implied actor [EBC, ICC, Lns, NIC2, TH; LB, NAB, TEV]: for God's grace which he gave you in Christ Jesus.

QUESTION—To what should the prepositional phrase ἐν Χριστοῦ Ἰησοῦ 'in Christ Jesus' be connected and what is the relationship indicated by ἐν 'in'?

1. The phrase should be connected with the pronoun ὑμῖν 'you' [AB, Alf, EBC, Ed, HNTC, Ho, ICC, My, Vn]: grace which was given to you who are in Christ Jesus. The preposition ἐν 'in' indicates the person in association with whom the grace was given [Alf, EBC, HNTC, Ho, ICC, Lns, Rb]: grace given to you who are in union with Christ Jesus. This carries with it the inference that grace was given because of the fact that they were in Christ [Alf, EBC, Ed, Ho, ICC].
2. The phrase should be connected with the verb δοθείσῃ 'was given' [Herm, Lns, Rb, TH; KJV, NJB, TEV]: grace which was given in Christ Jesus to you. The preposition ἐν 'in' indicates the instrument or the agent through which grace was given [TH; KJV, TEV]: grace given to you through/by Christ Jesus.
3. The preposition ἐν 'in' indicates both the person in association with whom the grace was given, and the instrument through which the grace was given [He, NIC]: grace given through Jesus Christ to you who are in union with him.

1:5 that/because[a] in everything[b] you-were-enriched[c] in[d] him,

LEXICON—a. ὅτι (LN 90.21; 89.33; 91.15): 'that' [LN (90.21), Lns; KJV, NASB], 'namely that' [LN (91.15)], 'because' [AB, LN (89.33)], 'for' [He, HNTC, LN (89.33); NIV, NRSV, REB, TEV, TNT], 'whereby' [ICC], not explicit [LB, NAB, NJB].

b. πᾶς (LN 58.28) (BAGD 2.a.β. p. 632): 'everything' [BAGD, Lns; KJV, NASB], 'all things' [TEV], 'all gifts' [He], '(your) whole life' [LB], 'every respect' [BAGD, HNTC; TNT], 'every way' [AB, BAGD; NIV, NRSV], 'every kind of, all sorts of' [LN]. This pronominal adjective is also translated as an adjective: '(riches) of every kind' [ICC], 'all (the enrichment)' [REB]; and as an adverb: 'richly (endowed)' [NAB, NJB].

c. aorist pass. indic. of πλουτίζω (LN **59.59**) (BAGD 2. p. 674): 'to be enriched' [AB, He, Lns; KJV, NASB, NIV, NRSV], 'to be made rich' [BAGD, HNTC, LN; TNT], 'to be endowed' [NAB, NJB], 'to receive riches' [ICC], 'to become rich' [TEV]. This verb is also translated actively: 'to enrich' [AB; LB], 'to cause to have an abundance of' [LN]. It is also translated as a noun: 'enrichment (that has come to you)' [REB]. It is used figuratively here of spiritual riches [BAGD]. It means to receive an abundance of good things [TH]. The aorist refers to the point in time that the action took place in the past [Gdt, Lns, NIC]. The aorist sums up God's work in making them rich and views it as a single act: God made them rich [EBC].

d. ἐν: 'in' [AB, BAGD, He, HNTC, Lns; all versions except KJV, LB, TEV], 'as immanent in' [ICC], 'by' [KJV], 'in union with' [TEV], not explicit [LB]. See this word at 1:2 and 4.

QUESTION—What relationship is indicated by ὅτι 'that/because'?

1. It indicates more specifically what aspects of 'grace' that Paul was thankful for [EGT, Herm, Ho, Lns, My, NIC, NIC2, Rb, TG, TH, TNTC, Vn]: I thank my God for the grace given you, specifically that you were enriched in speech and knowledge. These were just two of the gifts they were given [TNTC].
2. It indicates the grounds for stating that the grace of God was given to them [Gdt, He, HNTC]: I thank my God for the grace given you. I know that he has given grace to you because you were enriched in speech and knowledge.
3. It indicates the content of Paul's thanksgiving (1:4) [Vn; NASB, REB]: I thank my God ... that you were enriched in him.

QUESTION—What is the extent of ἐν παντί 'in everything'?

It means that they have been enriched in all that is now under discussion: all the gifts of grace that they now possess [NIC], all that is relevant as exemplified by the two named gifts [EBC], or limited by them [Alf, Lns].

QUESTION—Were the words 'you were enriched' stated with irony or sincerity?

The words were stated with sincerity [AB, Alf, EBC, EGT, Gdt, He, Herm, HNTC, Ho, ICC, Lns, My, NCBC, NIC, NIC2, TNTC, Vn]. Paul is glad for the gifts they have received, but he does not approve of the way they have used them. Although Paul is sincere here, he uses 'rich' ironically in 4:8 [He].

QUESTION—Who is the antecedent to the pronoun ἐν αὐτῷ 'in him'?

The antecedent is Christ Jesus [AB, NIC2, TH, Vn; REB, TEV]: you were enriched in Christ.

QUESTION—Who is the agent of the passive verb ἐπλουτίσθητε 'you were enriched'?

1. The agent is God [AB, EBC, HNTC, Lns, TG, TH, Vn]: God enriched you in every way. The passive reflects an Aramaic tendency to avoid using God's name [AB].
2. The agent is Christ [KJV]: Christ enriched you in every way.

in[a] all[b] speech[c] and all knowledge,[d]

LEXICON—a. ἐν (LN 89.5): 'in' [AB, HNTC, ICC, Lns; KJV, NASB, NIV, NJB, NRSV], 'with' [He; NAB], 'including' [TEV], not explicit [LB]. Some translations begin a new sentence here: 'You possess' [REB], 'You have' [TNT].

b. πᾶς (LN 58.28) (BAGD 1.a.β. p. 631): 'all' [AB, He, LN, Lns; KJV, NASB, NIV, NRSV, TEV], 'every' [NAB], 'every kind of' [BAGD, HNTC, LN, NIC2; NJB], 'every form of' [ICC], 'all sorts of' [BAGD, LN], 'full' [REB], not explicit [LB]. This adjective is also translated as an adverb: 'fully' [TNT]. Πᾶς usually has the meaning 'every kind of' when used with abstract nouns [NIC2].

c. λόγος (LN 33.99; 33.98) (BAGD 1.a.α. p.477): 'speech' [AB, He, HNTC, LN (33.99); NASB, NRSV, TEV], 'speaking' [BAGD, LN (33.99); NIV], 'utterance' [Lns, NIC; KJV, NJB], 'gift of speech' [NAB], 'inspired utterance' [ICC], 'word' [BAGD, LN (33.98)], 'saying, message, statement' [LN (33.98)]. This noun is also expressed as a verb: 'to give expression to' [REB], 'to express' [TNT], 'to speak out' [LB].

d. γνῶσις (LN 28.17; 32.16) (BAGD 2. p. 163): 'knowledge' [AB, BAGD, He, HNTC, LN, Lns; all versions except LB], 'Christian knowledge' [BAGD, Gdt], 'spiritual illumination, for the giving and receiving of instruction' [ICC], 'understanding' [LB].

QUESTION—What relationship is indicated by ἐν 'in'?

1. It indicates the specific meaning of the words 'enriched in everything' [Alf, EGT, Gdt, HNTC, Lns, My, NIC, NIC2, TG]: you were enriched in everything, that is, you were enriched in all speech and all knowledge.
2. It indicates two examples of the many ways in which they were enriched [EBC, Herm, Rb, TNTC; TEV]: you were enriched in everything. For example, you were enriched in all speech and in all knowledge. These are especially pertinent to their spiritual condition and will be discussed later in the letter [Herm].

QUESTION—What is meant by λόγος 'speech'?

It means all kinds of Christian speaking [EGT, HNTC, Ho, Lns, TH, Vn]. It means the ability to express to others the knowledge one has [EGT, NIC, Vn]. Some think it is speaking about the gospel [AB, Ed, TG], Christian truth [Ed, Lns], and the Christian message [Alf, He, Lns, TG, TNTC, Vn]. It may refer to special people among them: those who can speak with eloquence [EBC, Herm, NCBC], those who preach [Alf, He, Lns], those who teach [Gdt, Ho, ICC, Lns], those who prophesy [Gdt, HNTC, Ho, NIC2], those who speak in tongues [Gdt, He, HNTC, Ho, NIC2], or all those with the gifts of spiritual utterance in chapters 12–14 [NIC2].

QUESTION—What does the word γνῶσις 'knowledge' refer to in this context?

It means religious knowledge [Ho] about God and Christ [AB, EBC], about Christian truth [BAGD, Ed, Gdt, HNTC, TG, TH, TNTC, Vn], knowledge and insight about all spiritual realities [NIC, TH], understanding what is uttered by those who have the ability to speak and teach [Alf, ICC]. It includes the wisdom to apply one's understanding to Christian life [Gdt, HNTC]. Some think it is the gift of special knowledge, probably like prophetic revelation [NIC2].

1:6 even-as/because[a] the testimony[b] of Christ was-confirmed[c] in[d] you,

LEXICON—a. καθώς (LN 78.53; 89.34) (BAGD 3. p. 391): 'even as' [Lns, NIC2; KJV, NASB], 'as' [AB, HNTC], 'just as' [LN (78.53), NIC2; NRSV], 'in exact proportion to' [ICC], 'in accordance with' [He], 'so' [NJB], 'because' [LN (89.34); NIV, REB, TNT], 'since, in so far as' [BAGD], not explicit [LB]. It is also translated in conjunction with the word ὥστε 'that', which begins the following verse: 'likewise...so...(that)' [NAB], 'so...(that)' [TEV].

b. μαρτύριον (LN 33.262; **33.264**) (BAGD 1.b. p. 494): 'testimony' [AB, BAGD, He, HNTC, ICC, LN, Lns; KJV, NASB, NIV, NRSV, TNT], 'witness' [**LN**; NAB, NJB], 'message' [TEV], 'what we testified' [REB], 'proof, that which serves as testimony or proof' [BAGD]. Testimony is the provision of information about a person which the speaker has direct knowledge [LN (33.262)]. The content of what is said is testimony or witness [LN (33.264)].

c. aorist pass. indic. of βεβαιόω (LN 28.44) (BAGD 1. p. 138): 'to be confirmed' [BAGD, HNTC, LN, Lns; KJV, NAB, NASB, NIV, REB, TNT], 'to be strengthened' [NRSV], 'to become firmly established' [TEV], 'to be effectively presented' [He], 'to be brought home' [ICC], 'to be made firm, to be established' [BAGD], 'to be verified, to be proven to be true and certain' [LN]. The passive voice is also translated actively: 'to take root' [Alf], 'to take root firmly' [NJB], 'to happen' [LB]. It is also translated actively with God as the actor: 'to confirm' [AB].

d. ἐν (LN 83.13; 83.9): 'in' [HNTC, LN, Lns; KJV, NASB, NIV, NJB, REB, TEV, TNT], 'among' [AB, LN, NIC2, TH; NAB, NRSV], 'in (your) midst' [He], 'to' [ICC].

QUESTION—What relationship is indicated by καθώς 'even as, because'?

1. It indicates the extent of their enrichment [AB, HNTC, ICC, NIC, Rb; NJB]: you were enriched to the degree that the testimony of Christ was confirmed among you.
2. It indicates the reason they were enriched [Alf, BAGD, Ed, Herm, Ho, My, TH; NIV, REB, TNT]: you were enriched because the testimony of Christ was confirmed in you.
3. It indicates that their enrichment was evidence or proof that the testimony of Christ was confirmed among them [Gdt, NIC2]: You were enriched which proves that the testimony of Christ was confirmed among you. If God is the actor of the passive 'was confirmed', then he is giving proof of this confirmation by his gifts of enrichment [NIC2].

QUESTION—How are the nouns related in the genitive construction τὸ μαρτύριον τοῦ Χριστοῦ 'the testimony of Christ'?

1. It means the testimony which Christ gave as he proclaimed the Good News [Ho, Lns]: the testimony which Christ gave.
2. It means the testimony which others gave as they proclaimed the Good News about Christ [AB, Alf, BAGD, EBC, Ed, EGT, Gdt, Herm, HNTC, ICC, LN, My, NIC, NIC2, Rb, TG, TH, TNTC, Vn; LB, NAB, NASB, NIV, NJB, TEV, TNT]: the testimony others gave about Christ. The testimony of Christ refers to the preaching of the gospel [AB, BAGD, Ho, My, NIC, NIC2].

QUESTION—In what sense was the testimony of Christ confirmed among them?

1. The testimony was established in or among them, that is, they came to firmly believe the testimony [Alf, EBC, He, Ho, Lns, My, TG]: you have firmly believed the message about Christ.
2. The testimony was confirmed in their minds by God/the Holy Spirit [HNTC, ICC, NIC2, TH]: the Holy Spirit convinced you that the testimony of Christ is true.
3. The testimony of Christ was shown to be true by its effect in their lives [EGT, NCBC, TNTC, Vn]: your lives confirmed the truth of the testimony of Christ.

QUESTION—What is meant by ἐν ὑμᾶς 'in you'?

1. It refers to an internal effect within individuals [EBC, Ed, Lns, My]: the testimony of Christ was confirmed in your hearts.
2. It refers to an internal effect among a group [AB, Alf, Gdt, Herm, NIC2, TH; NAB, NRSV]: the testimony of Christ was confirmed among you/in your midst.

1:7 so-that[a] you are not lacking[b] in any spiritual-gift,[c]

LEXICON—a. ὥστε (LN 89.52) (BAGD 2.a.β. p. 900): 'so that' [BAGD, HNTC, ICC, LN, Lns, NIC2; KJV, NASB, NRSV], 'that' [NAB, TEV], 'therefore' [AB, LN, TNTC; NIV], 'so' [LN; TNT], 'and so' [NJB], 'there is indeed' [REB], 'as a result' [LN, TG, TH], 'now' [LB], 'this is why' [He].

b. pres. pass. infin. of ὑστερέω: (LN **13.21**; 57.37; 65.51) (BAGD 2. p. 849): 'to be lacking' [BAGD, He, LN (57.37, 65.51); NASB, NJB, NRSV, TNT]. The passive voice is also translated actively: 'to lack' [AB, BAGD; NAB, NIV, REB], 'to come short of' [BAGD, HNTC], 'to fail to receive' [TEV], 'to fail to attain' [**LN**], 'to go without' [BAGD], 'to come behind' [Herm, LN, Lns; KJV], 'to find oneself to be behind' [ICC]. It is also translated positively: 'to have' [LB].

c. χάρισμα (LN 57.103) (BAGD 1. p. 879): 'spiritual gift' [LB, NAB, NIV, NRSV, TNT], 'gift' [AB, BAGD, LN, Lns; KJV, NASB, NJB, REB], 'gift of grace' [HNTC, ICC], 'blessing' [TEV], 'endowment' [He]. It means that which is given freely and graciously [LN] and refers to the spiritual possession of a believer [BAGD].

QUESTION—What relationship is indicated by ὥστε 'so that'?

1. It indicates the result of 1:6 [AB, Ed, EGT, Ho, My, NIC2, TG; NAB, TEV]: the testimony was confirmed among you with the result that you are not lacking in any spiritual gift.
2. It indicates the result of 1:5 [Gdt, HNTC; NRSV]: you were enriched in him with the result that you are not lacking in any spiritual gift.
3. It indicates the result of both 5 and 6 [Lns, NIC, TNTC]: you were enriched in him and the testimony of Christ was confirmed among you, with the result that you are not lacking in any spiritual gift.

4. It indicates the result of 1:4 [Herm, ICC]: God's grace was given to you with the result that you are not lacking in any spiritual gift.

QUESTION—What is meant by μὴ ὑστερεῖσθαι 'not lacking'?

It is a figure called litotes (an emphatic affirmation of a fact by denying its opposite) and may be expressed positively as 'you have every gift' [TG; LB].

1. This means 'not lacking', referring to their possession of the gifts [AB, EBC, Gdt, He, Herm, HNTC, LN, NIC, NIC2, TG, TH, TNTC; all versions except KJV]. Their trouble was not a lack of spiritual gifts but a wrong estimation and use of them [HNTC]. They have all that could be expected for a church on earth to have [Gdt].
2. This means 'not behind', comparing them with other churches [Alf, Ho, ICC, Lns, My]. God has done as much for them as he has done for other churches [Ho].

QUESTION—To what does the term χάρισμα 'spiritual gift' refer?

It refers to the more extraordinary gifts of chapters 12–14 like knowledge, miracles, healings, speaking with tongues, and prophecy [NIC2]. It refers to the specific gifts of speech and knowledge of verse 5 [Gdt]. It refers to God's gifts in general, including salvation, speech and knowledge, and the special gifts of chapters 12–14 [Ho, ICC, TNTC, Vn]. It refers to the general gifts God gives to all believers and thus excludes the special charismatic gifts [Alf, EBC, Lns, My, NIC].

awaiting-eagerly[a] the revealing[b] of our Lord Jesus Christ;

LEXICON—a. pres. mid. participle of ἀπεκδέχομαι (LN 25.63) (BAGD p. 83): 'to await eagerly' [BAGD; NASB, NIV], 'to wait expectantly for' [LN; REB], 'to look forward eagerly' [LN], 'to loyally and patiently wait for' [ICC], 'to await' [He, HNTC], 'to wait for' [all other versions].

b. ἀποκάλυψις (LN 28.38) (BAGD 3. p. 92): 'revealing' [NRSV, TNT], 'revelation' [AB, BAGD, He, HNTC, LN, Lns; NAB, NASB], 'coming' [KJV], 'return' [LB]. This noun is also translated as a verb: 'to be revealed' [ICC; NIV, NJB, TEV], 'to reveal (himself)' [REB].

QUESTION—What relationship is indicated by the use of the present participle ἀπεκδεχομένους 'awaiting'?

1. It indicates an action which is going on concurrent with the action of the main verb 'you are not lacking' [AB, EBC, HNTC, ICC, NIC; NAB, NIV, NJB, NRSV, REB, TEV, TNT]: you are not lacking in any gift while you are awaiting the revelation of our Lord. This is indicated in translations by the use of certain time words such as: 'while' [AB, ICC; REB, TNT], 'as' [HNTC; NAB, NIV, NJB, NRSV, TEV].
2. It indicates the grounds for the preceding clause [Ed, Lns]: it is true that you are not lacking in any gift since you are waiting for the revelation of our Lord. Their expectation enabled Paul to know that they had not come behind or fallen short [Lns].

QUESTION—What attitude is implied in the verb ἀπεκδέχομαι ‘to await’?

1. It carries the component of meaning of ‘eagerly’ or ‘expectantly’ [BAGD, EBC, EGT, Ho, Lns, NCBC, NIC2, Rb, TH, Vn; NASB, NIV, REB].
2. It carries the component of ‘patiently’ [Ed, ICC, My]: patiently awaiting. It also carries the component of ‘loyally’ [ICC].

QUESTION—How are the two nouns related in the genitive construction ἀποκάλυψιν τοῦ κυρίου ἡμῶν Ἰησοῦ Χριστοῦ ‘the revelation of our Lord Jesus Christ’?

1. This means that Jesus Christ will reveal himself [Lns, NIC; KJV, REB]: while you wait for our Lord Jesus Christ to reveal himself.
2. This means that God will reveal Jesus Christ [NIC2]: while you wait for God to reveal our Lord Jesus Christ.

QUESTION—To what does this ἀποκάλυψις ‘revealing’ refer?

It refers to the second coming of Jesus Christ [BAGD, EBC, HNTC, Ho, Lns, NCBC, NIC2]. Christ will visibly appear in all his glory [Lns], and show his power and authority [TG].

1:8 who also will-confirm[a] you until[b] the-end[c]

LEXICON—a. fut. act. indic. of βεβαιόω (LN 31.91) (BAGD 2. p. 138): ‘to confirm’ [HNTC, Lns; KJV, NASB], ‘to strengthen’ [BAGD, He; NAB, NJB, NRSV], ‘to keep/make firm’ [BAGD; REB, TEV, TNT], ‘to keep strong’ [NIV], ‘to keep secure’ [ICC], ‘to guarantee that someone will be free from sin and guilt’ [LB], ‘to preserve’ [AB], ‘to establish’ [BAGD]. It means to cause one to be firm and established in his faith [LN]. This word had another meaning at 1:6.

b. ἕως (LN 67.119) (BAGD II.1.a. p. 334): ‘until’ [AB, BAGD, LN, Lns], ‘to’ [He, HNTC, LN; NAB, NASB, NIV, NRSV, REB, TEV, TNT], ‘up to’ [BAGD], ‘right up to’ [LB], ‘till’ [NJB], ‘unto’ [ICC; KJV].

c. τέλος (LN 67.66) (BAGD 1.d.β. p. 812): ‘the end’ [AB, BAGD, HNTC, LN, Lns; all versions except NJB], ‘the very end’ [He, ICC; NJB], ‘the last’ [BAGD].

QUESTION—What is the function of καί ‘also’?

1. It is coupled with the words ‘you were enriched’ of 1:5 [Ho]: he enriched you and he will also confirm you.
2. It is coupled with the words ‘testimony was confirmed’ of 1:6 [Gdt, NIC2]: the testimony of Christ was confirmed in you and he will also confirm you to the end. It means that the future work to be done in them will be a continuation of what has already been done [Gdt].
3. It has no meaning following a relative pronoun and is left untranslated [Herm, HNTC; NAB, NIV, NJB, REB]: who will confirm you.

QUESTION—To whom does ὅς ‘who’ refer?

1. It refers to the Lord Jesus Christ (1:7) [AB, Ed, EGT, Gdt, HNTC, ICC, Lns, My, NCBC, Rb, TH, TNTC]: Jesus Christ will confirm you to the end.

2. It refers to God (1:4) [Alf, EBC, Herm, Ho, NIC, NIC2]: God will confirm you to the end. God is the actor of the first occurrence of 'confirm' in verse 6, now he naturally continues as the actor of this occurrence as well [NIC2].

QUESTION—In what sense will they be confirmed?

They will be confirmed in faith, or kept from losing their faith [Ho, LN, Lns, TG, TH]; they will be confirmed in their present state of justification [AB, ICC]; they will not be blamed on the day of the Lord [AB].

QUESTION—To what does τέλος 'end' refer?

It refers to the end of the world [Herm]. It refers to Jesus' second coming [BAGD, Ed, Gdt, My, Rb, TH]. It refers to the day of the Lord [Lns]. It refers to the day when all people will be judged by Christ [TG]. It may also refer to the end of their lives if that happens before Jesus' coming [Gdt, Ho, Vn].

blameless[a] in the day[b] of our Lord Jesus Christ.

TEXT—The word Χριστοῦ 'Christ' does not occur in some manuscripts. It is included in brackets by GNT with a C rating, indicating difficulty in deciding whether or not to place it in the text. It is omitted by LB and REB. It is included in brackets by NAB.

LEXICON—a. ἀνέγκλητος (LN 33.433) (BAGD p. 64): 'blameless' [BAGD; KJV, NAB, NASB, NIV, NRSV], 'without blame' [AB], 'irreproachable' [BAGD, HNTC; NJB], 'without reproach' [He; REB], 'faultless' [TEV], 'with no accusation against (you)' [TNT], 'without accusation' [LN], 'against such accusations as would be fatal' [ICC], 'free from all sin and guilt' [LB]. This adjective is also translated as a verbal phrase: 'as not to be accused' [Lns]. It is a legal term meaning that no accusation or charge could be successfully brought against them [Ho, ICC, LN, Lns]. It means 'unimpeachable' [ICC, TNTC], 'unreprovable' [Vn]. Although not morally perfect, Christ's own righteousness is given to them so that they will be acquitted at the day of judgment [HNTC].

b. ἡμέρα (BAGD 3.b.β. p. 347): 'day' [AB, BAGD, HNTC, Lns; KJV, NAB, NASB, NIV, NRSV, REB], 'Day' [He, ICC; NJB, TEV, TNT]. This word is also joined with the words 'Jesus Christ' and translated 'day when he returns' [LB].

QUESTION—How are the words 'blameless in the day of our Lord' and the words 'who will confirm you' related?

1. The state of 'blamelessness' will be the result of 'being confirmed' [BAGD, My, Vn; NAB, NASB, NIV, NJB, TEV]: he will confirm you to the end so that no one can blame you.
2. The state of 'blamelessness' complements the meaning of 'being confirmed' [BAGD, ICC]: who will confirm you as being blameless [BAGD], or 'keep you secure against such accusations as would be fatal' [ICC].

QUESTION—To what specific time does the day of our Lord Jesus Christ refer?

It refers to the day of God's final judgment [BAGD, Lns, NIC2, TH]. It refers to the day of Christ's second coming [Ho, NIC; LB]. It refers to either God's final judgment or the day when Christ comes to glory [TH]. It is the same as the day of the Lord in Amos 5:18–20; Joel 2:31 [NIC2].

1:9 God (is) faithful[a]

LEXICON—a. πιστός (LN 31.87) (BAGD 1.a.β. p. 664): 'faithful' [AB, BAGD, He, HNTC, LN, Lns; all versions except LB, NJB, REB, TEV], 'dependable, inspiring trust or faith' [BAGD], 'trustworthy' [BAGD, LN], 'reliable' [LN]. This adjective is also translated by a passive verb: 'to be trusted' [TEV], or a verb with God as the actor: 'to keep faith' [REB], 'to always do just what one says' [LB]; or as a verb with others as actors: 'to be unable to prove false' [ICC], 'to rely on' [NJB]. Here it means that God will do what he promised [He, Ho, NIC2, Rb] and he will complete the work he has begun [EBC, Lns, NCBC, NIC].

QUESTION—What is the relationship of this verse to its context?

It stands as the reason or grounds for the preceding verse [Ed, EGT, HNTC, Ho, My, NIC, NIC2]: God will confirm you to the end because He is faithful. This verse is an emphasized restatement of 1:8: God's faithfulness guarantees the faithfulness of the believers [Gdt].

QUESTION: What is the significance of the fact that the word πιστός 'faithful' precedes the word θεός 'God' in the Greek order?

It serves to emphasize the word 'faithful' [Lns; LB]: 'God will surely do this for you' [LB].

through[a] whom you-were-called[b]

LEXICON—a. διά with genitive object (LN **90.4**) (BAGD A.III.2.b.β. p. 180): 'through' [BAGD, He, HNTC, **LN**, Lns; NASB], 'by' [LN; KJV, NRSV, TNT]. This word is also translated as indicating agency by making God the agent of the call: 'God called/invited you' [AB, ICC; LB, NAB, NIV, NJB, REB, TEV]. When used with persons and the genitive case this word denotes the agent or intermediary [BAGD].

b. aorist pass. indic. of καλέω (LN 33.312; 33.315) (BAGD 2. p. 399): 'to be called' [BAGD, He, HNTC, LN, Lns; KJV, NASB, NRSV, TNT], 'to be invited' [BAGD, LN], 'to be summoned' [BAGD, LN], 'to be called to a task' [LN]. This passive voice was also translated actively with God as the actor: 'to call' [AB, ICC; NAB, NIV, NJB, REB, TEV], 'to invite' [LB].

QUESTION—What relationship is indicated by the word διά 'through'?

It indicates that God is the agent of the calling [AB, BAGD, EGT, Herm, Ho, ICC, NIC, NIC2, Rb, TH; NAB, NIV, NJB, REB, TEV]: God called you into fellowship with his Son. God is the originator of the call [BAGD]. God is the author of the call, not the mediator of it [Herm]. The reason that God is the agent here is that the call to fellowship is given in relationship to his Son [NIC2]. The passive verb indicates that God is the agent of the call while this preposition indicates that he is also the medium through which the call was given [Lns, My]. The use of the unexpected 'through' perhaps means that God is the principal cause and also that the call took place indirectly, by God calling them through the preaching of the gospel [NIC].

into (the) fellowship[a] of his Son Jesus Christ our Lord.

LEXICON—a. κοινωνία (LN **34.5**) (BAGD 1.4. p. 439): 'fellowship' [BAGD, He, HNTC, ICC, LN, Lns; all versions except LB, NJB, REB], 'partnership' [AB], 'wonderful friendship' [LB], 'association, communion' [BAGD], 'close relationship' [BAGD, LN]. This noun is also translated by a verbal phrase: 'to share in the life' [REB], 'to be partners with' [NJB].

QUESTION—How are the nouns related in the genitive construction κοινωνίαν τοῦ υἱοῦ αὐτοῦ 'fellowship of his Son'?

1. It means that people will have fellowship with God's Son [EBC, ICC, LN, Lns, TNTC; LB, NAB, NASB, NIV, TEV, TNT]: you were called to have fellowship with his Son. It is a life of communion with the Son [Lns].
2. It means that people will be partners with the Son or share in the life of the Son [BAGD, Ed, EGT, Gdt, My, NIC, TG; NJB, REB]: you were called to be partners with his Son, or you were called to share in the life of the Son. This indicates a sharing in the sonship of Christ and a claim to privileges [Ed]. They will be unreproachable because they share in the Son's standing with the Father, and in the fruits of his work [NIC]. They share sonship to God with Christ [EGT].
3. It includes the meanings of both 1 and 2 [AB, HNTC, Ho, NIC2, Rb, TH, Vn]: You were called to have fellowship with and be partners with his Son. Believers are not only blameless by virtue of their standing in Christ, but also have fellowship with him through the Spirit [NIC2]. This can mean either the sharing of his friendship and love, or becoming a son as he is, or sharing in the life of the body of believers [AB]. It denotes primarily partnership, then fellowship or intimacy [Rb]. This is the same fellowship or communion that God has with his Son [TH]. It means sharing in his character, his sufferings, and his final glory [Ho].

DISCOURSE UNIT: 1:10–6:20 [HNTC, ICC, NIC2, TG]. The topic is urgent matters for censure [ICC], news from Corinth [HNTC], a response to reports [NIC2], disorders in the church [TG]. This is constituted as a unit in that it is a response to oral reports (1:11 and 5:1) before Paul responds to the Corinthian letter [NIC2].

DISCOURSE UNIT: 1:10–4:21 [AB, Alf, Ed, EGT, Gdt, Herm, HNTC, ICC, Lns, NCBC, NIC2, TG, TH, TNTC, Vn]. The topic is the threat of schism from party quarrels and class rivalry [AB], reproof of the party divisions among them [Alf], the report received from Chloe's household [NCBC], divisions in the church [Ed, Gdt, Herm, ICC, TG, TH, TNTC, Vn], the Corinthian parties and the gospel ministry [EGT], a church which is divided internally and is against

Paul [NIC2], wisdom and division at Corinth [HNTC], the preachers of the Corinthians [Lns].

DISCOURSE UNIT: 1:10–17 [AB, EBC, EGT, Gdt, GNT, Herm, HNTC, ICC, Lns, NCBC, NIC, NIC2, TG, TH, TNTC]. The topic is parties derived from leadership authorities [AB], the report about the parties and Paul's expostulation [EGT], the problem of division over leaders in the name of wisdom [NIC2], statement of the fact and its summary condemnation [Gdt], divisions in the church [EBC, GNT, Herm, HNTC], party strife [Lns, NCBC, NIC], the facts [ICC], the fact of division [TNTC].

DISCOURSE UNIT: 1:10–16 [Ho, My]. The topic is divisions in the church of Corinth.

DISCOURSE UNIT: 1:10–13 [AB]. The topic is the absurdity of the claims.

DISCOURSE UNIT: 1:10–12 [Ed, TNTC]. The topic is a statement of the case [Ed], the parties [TNTC].

1:10 Now/But[a] I-appeal-to[b] you, brothers,[c]

LEXICON—a. δέ: 'now' [Lns; KJV, NASB, NRSV], 'but' [He, ICC; LB], not explicit [AB, HNTC; all other versions].

b. pres. act. indic. of παρακαλέω (LN 33.168) (BAGD 2. p. 617): 'to appeal to' [BAGD, LN; NIV, NRSV, REB, TEV], 'to urge' [BAGD; NJB], 'to beg' [He, HNTC; LB, NAB, TNT], 'to beseech' [KJV], 'to entreat' [EBC, ICC], 'to ask for (earnestly), to request, to plead for' [LN], 'to exhort' [BAGD; NASB], 'to admonish' [Lns]. This verb is also translated with a vocative: 'Please' [AB]. It means 'to implore' or 'to entreat' [EBC]. It is an exhortation that is more than a request and slightly less than a command [AB]. It does not mean to beg, but to summon or admonish [Lns]. It is often used by Paul to mark the beginning of a new paragraph [TH].

c. ἀδελφός: 'brothers' [AB, BAGD, He, HNTC, ICC, LN, Lns; all versions except LB, NRSV, REB, TEV], 'brothers and sisters' [NRSV], 'dear brothers' [LB], 'my friends' [REB, TEV]. Women are included in this term [NIC2]. See this word at 1:1.

QUESTION—What relationship is indicated by δέ 'now'?

1. It indicates transition [Ed, Gdt, Lns, NIC2; probably KJV, NASB, NRSV]: now. Paul passes from thanksgiving to censure [Gdt]. It often indicates a new idea [TH].
2. It indicates contrast [Alf, EGT, He, ICC, TNTC, Vn; LB]: but. The contrast is between his greeting and thanksgiving and what follows [Alf, EGT, TNTC, Vn], between fellowship and their present division [TNTC].

QUESTION—What is the function of the word ἀδελφός 'brother'?

It serves to unite Paul with his readers in a loving relationship [Gdt]. It gives his approach a note of affection [TNTC]. Of the 21 times it occurs in 1 Corinthians, 17 are at the shift of an argument, and 4 are in conclusions.

Here a transition is indicated from thanksgiving to the body of the letter [NIC2]. In Paul's usage it usually indicates a new stage in an argument or a change in theme [TH].

by[a] the name[b] of our Lord Jesus Christ,

LEXICON—a. διά with genitive object (LN 89.76): 'by' [AB, He, ICC, LN; KJV, NASB, NRSV, TEV, TNT], 'in' [LB, NAB, NIV, NJB, REB], 'through' [EBC, LN, Lns], 'by means of' [LN, My], 'for the sake of' [HNTC].

b. ὄνομα (LN 33.126; 9:19) (BAGD I.4.c.α. p. 572): 'name' [AB, BAGD, He, ICC, LN, Lns; all versions except TEV], 'authority' [EBC, TG, TH; TEV]. It is also translated as standing for the person himself: '(for the sake of) our Lord Jesus Christ' [HNTC]. It implies authority [AB, EBC, NIC2, TG, TH; TEV]. It implies the person himself [Gdt, Herm, HNTC, Ho, TH]: I appeal to you on the behalf of our Lord Jesus Christ. It means all that Jesus is, and all that he is to the person [HNTC, Lns]. They should be so united that they share the same outlook and virtue system [AB]. The following clauses explain what this unity means [Vn].

QUESTION—What is the meaning of διά 'by' the name of our Lord Jesus Christ?

1. Paul makes his appeal with the authority he has from Christ as the ground of the appeal [AB, EBC, EGT, Gdt, NIC2, TG, TH; TEV]: I appeal to you with the authority given me by our Lord Jesus Christ. Paul was Christ's representative who spoke with authority from Christ [AB]. The appeal should be obeyed as if Christ himself addressed them [TH].
2. Paul makes his appeal based on who Christ is [Alf, BAGD, HNTC, Ho, ICC, My, Vn]: I appeal to you because of your regard for the name of our Lord Jesus Christ. The appeal should be obeyed because of their reverence and love of Christ and their regard for Christ's authority as Lord [Ho]. Christ's name is the one confession of all disciples and thus their motive to obey the exhortation [My]. They are united under Christ's authority [Vn]. They should obey for the sake of Christ, for all that Christ is and means to them [HNTC].

that[a] you-say all the same-thing,

LEXICON—a. ἵνα (LN 90.22; 89.59): 'that' [HNTC, LN, Lns; all versions except KJV, NASB, NIV, NRSV, REB], 'to' [NAB, NJB, TEV], not explicit [He]. It is also treated as though it were an introduction to a direct quote 'I appeal to you, agree ...' [REB], 'I beg you, let all of you say ...' [TNT], 'I beg you to stop arguing' [LB], 'I entreat you, do be unanimous' [ICC], 'Please all of you, be in agreement' [AB], 'I beg you all to be in accord' [He]. It controls the three verbs that follow making all the object of the appeal [NIC2]. It serves to mark the content of discourse [Alf, Ed, ICC, LN, Lns, My, Rb], especially when purpose is involved [LN]. This is explained in the following clauses [Vn].

QUESTION—What is the meaning of τὸ αὐτὸ λέγητε 'to say the same thing'? Commentaries agree that it means to agree together. Translations render it: 'to agree' [NASB], 'to be in agreement' [BAGD; NRSV], 'to agree in what you say' [HNTC; NAB, TEV], 'to agree among yourselves' [REB], 'to agree with one another' [NIV], 'to be in agreement in what you profess' [NJB], 'to be unanimous in professing your beliefs' [ICC], 'to be in agreement when you speak' [AB], 'to be in accord' [He]. This is needed because they were saying different things (1:12) [HNTC]. It is to have a united testimony [EBC].

and[a] there-be no divisions[b] among you,

LEXICON—a. καί: 'and' [AB, He, HNTC, ICC, Lns; KJV, NASB, NRSV, REB], 'so that' [LB, NIV, TEV], not explicit [NAB, NJB, TNT].

b. σχίσμα (LN 39.13) (BAGD 2. p. 797): 'divisions' [AB, BAGD, HNTC, ICC, LN; all versions except LB, NAB, NJB, NRSV], 'splits' [BAGD; LB], 'dissensions' [BAGD, Ed, TNTC], 'discord' [LN], 'schisms' [BAGD], 'factions' [Lns; NAB, NJB], 'cleavages' [He]. Others translate this noun with a verb: 'to be split up into parties' [ICC]. It means rent [HNTC, Ho, NIC, NIC2], tear [HNTC, LN, NIC2, TH], or fissure [NIC], and does not denote distinctly formed parties, but rather differences of opinion among them [He, Herm, Ho, ICC, NIC2, TH, TNTC]. This kind of division could exist together in the same group, and does not necessarily mean that they were divided into separate groups [He, Herm, Ho, NCBC, TH, TNTC].

QUESTION—What relationship is indicated by καί 'and'?

1. It indicates additional information [AB, HNTC, ICC; KJV, NASB, NRSV, REB]: that you all agree and that there be no divisions among you.
2. It indicates a negative restatement [EGT, Lns, NIC2]: that you all agree, that is, that there be no divisions among you.
3. It indicates result or purpose [LB, NIV, TEV]: that you all agree so that there be no divisions among you.

QUESTION—Did divisions already exist?

1. Divisions already existed and they must stop having them [Ed, He, Herm, Ho, ICC, NIC, NIC2, Rb, TNTC; LB]: that you all agree and that there no longer be divisions among you. The use of the present subjunctive 'there not be' indicates 'continue not to be' [Rb]. Paul is speaking of divided opinions over the different leaders which have developed into jealousy and quarrels [NIC2]. There were no groups separated from the church, but cliques within the congregation [He, TNTC]. These were the present divisions concerning preachers, immorality, law cases, marriages, meat sacrificed to idols, the place of women in church, the Lord's Supper, spiritual gifts, and the nature of the resurrection [Rb].
2. Divisions were not yet present and they must avoid them [HNTC, Lns, NCBC, TH]: that you all agree so that there will not be divisions among

you. The quarrels and party spirit might develop into outright divisions [NCBC].

but[a] (that) you-be united[b] in the-same[c] mind[d] and in the same opinion.[e]

LEXICON—a. δέ: 'but' [He, Lns; KJV, NASB, NRSV, TNT], 'but rather' [Alf, Ed, My], 'but on the contrary' [My], 'rather' [HNTC; NAB], 'so that' [NJB], 'and' [NIV], not explicit [AB, ICC; LB, REB, TEV].

b. perf. pass. participle of καταρτίζω (LN 75.5) (BAGD 1.b. p. 417): 'to be united' [LB, NAB, NRSV], 'to be perfectly united' [NIV, NJB], 'to be completely united' [TEV], 'to let complete unity be restored' [ICC], 'to let there be complete unity' [REB], 'to be perfectly joined together' [KJV], 'to be in harmony' [He], 'to be mended' [Ho, NIC2, TH], 'to be restored' [HNTC, NIC2; TNT], 'to be put into proper condition' [BAGD], 'to be made complete' [BAGD; NASB], 'to be fully adjusted, to be established in the right frame' [My], 'to be completely equipped' [AB], 'to cause to be fully qualified' [LN], 'to be perfected' [Lns]. It means 'to be knit together' [NIC2], 'to be united' [Alf, EGT], 'to be perfected together' [NIC].

c. ὁ αὐτός: 'the same' [BAGD, LN, Lns; KJV, NASB, NRSV], 'common' [AB; TNT], 'one' [He; LB], 'only one' [TEV], 'complete (unity)' [REB], not explicit [HNTC, ICC; NAB, NIV, NJB].

d. νοῦς (LN 26.14; 30.5) (BAGD 3.b. p. 545): 'mind' [AB, BAGD, HNTC, LN, Lns; all versions except LB, NJB, TEV], 'attitude' [BAGD], 'way of thinking' [BAGD, ICC], 'understanding' [My], 'thought' [LN; LB, TEV], 'belief' [NJB], 'spirit' [He]. It indicates the intellect in its judging faculty [NIC]. Here νοῦς refers specifically to the Christian attitude or way of thinking [BAGD]. It indicates the faculty of understanding, reasoning, thinking and deciding; or to the content of thinking and reasoning, 'thought, what is thought, opinion' [LN].

e. γνώμη (LN 30.67; 31.3) (BAGD 1. p. 163): 'opinion' [Gdt, HNTC, Ho, LN, My], 'judgment' [Gdt, He, Ho, ICC, Lns, Vn; KJV, NAB, NASB, NJB], 'purpose' [AB, BAGD, LN; LB, NRSV, TEV, TNT], 'intention' [BAGD, LN], 'mind' [BAGD], 'ultimate convictions' [ICC], 'thought' [NIV, REB]. It indicates expressed opinion or conviction [NIC]. Γνώμη signifies what is thought or considered to be the situation; or what is purposed or intended [LN].

QUESTION—What is meant by the perfect passive participle κατηρτίσμένοι 'you be united'?

1. It means to be restored to a correct condition, and in this context, to unity [He, HNTC, Ho, ICC, My, NIC2, TH, TNTC, Vn; TNT]: that you be restored to a perfect condition of unity. Their lack of unity was a matter of their minds and opinion, i.e., their doctrines [HNTC].
2. It means to be in a state of completeness [AB, Gdt, Lns, NIC]: that you be in a state of completeness. This interpretation focuses not on a broken condition to be restored, but on a state of wholeness and completeness to

be maintained [Gdt]. They need to be completely equipped with the same mind and purpose so as to overcome their pride and prejudice [AB]. When properly equipped with the same mind and judgment, they will not be differing among themselves [Lns].

3. It means both of the above [Ed]. The divisions needed repairing and they also needed to be fully equipped with grace so as to be reconciled with one another [Ed].

QUESTION—What is the difference between νοῦς 'mind' and γνώμη 'opinion'?

There is no significant difference [He, Herm, TH, TNTC]. Some describe the difference. 'Mind' is the Christian way of thinking in general and 'opinion' concerns deciding on a particular point [Ed, Gdt, ICC, Rb, TNTC]. Other contrasts are: mind and purpose [AB], feeling and opinion [Ho], intellect and expressed opinion [NIC], perception and judgment [TH], what one thinks and what one wants [TG], and the faculty of grasping the truth and the opinion formed concerning the truth [Vn].

1:11 For[a] it-was-reported[b] to-me concerning you, my brothers, by the-ones of-Chloe that there-are strifes[c] among you.

LEXICON—a. γάρ (LN 89.23): 'for' [AB, ICC, LN, Lns; KJV, LB, NASB, NRSV, TEV, TNT], 'because' [HNTC, LN], 'indeed' [He], not explicit [NAB, NIV, NJB, REB].

b. aorist pass. indic. of δηλόω (LN **28.42**) (BAGD p. 178): 'it has been reported' [He; NRSV], 'it has been declared' [KJV], 'it has been brought to notice' [REB], 'it was made plain' [**LN**], 'it has been signified' [Lns], 'it has been made known' [HNTC, LN], 'it was made clear' [BAGD], 'it was revealed' [BAGD, LN]. It is translated with Paul as subject: 'to be informed' [NAB, NASB], 'to be given information' [BAGD], 'to be told' [ICC]. It is also translated actively: 'to receive information' [TNT], '(Chloe's people) told/ reported/informed' [AB; LB, NIV, NJB, TEV].

c. ἔρις (LN 39.22; 33.447) (BAGD p. 309): 'strife' [BAGD, LN], 'contention' [BAGD, HNTC, Lns; KJV], 'contention and wrangling' [ICC], 'quarrels' [BAGD, LN; NASB, NIV, NRSV, REB, TEV, TNT], 'arguments and quarrels' [LB], 'serious differences' [NJB], 'squabbling' [AB], 'discord' [BAGD, LN], 'disputes' [He, LN]. This noun is also translated as a verb: 'to be quarreling' [NAB].

QUESTION—What relationship is indicated by γάρ 'for'?

It indicates the grounds for making his appeal to be united [EGT, Ho, My, NIC]: I appeal to you to be united since there are reports that you are not united. Some translations include an implied clause: 'I make this appeal because ...' [HNTC], 'I do not say this without good reason: for ...' [ICC].

QUESTION—What is implied in the verb ἐδηλώθη 'it was reported'?

The meaning component 'plainly' or the like is implied [Ed, ICC, TNTC; TEV]. It means that the facts have been made known [EGT]. Paul at first did not believe reports about conditions in Corinth, but on hearing from Chloe's people he came to believe them [Ed, NIC, TNTC].

QUESTION—Who are τῶν Χλόης 'the ones of Chloe'?

They are her household servants [NCBC], her dependents [HNTC], her slaves [EBC, ICC, NIC, NIC2, TH], her relatives [EBC, NIC2, TH], her friends [EBC], her former slaves [NIC2, TH]. Translations vary in how they render this phrase: 'Chloe's people' [AB, Lns; NASB, NJB, NRSV, REB], 'people from Chloe's family' [TEV], 'some from Chloe's household' [NIV, TNT], 'members of Chloe's household' [HNTC, ICC; NAB], 'them which are of the house of Chloe' [KJV].

1:12 Now[a] I-say[b] this, that/because[c] each[d] of-you says,

LEXICON—a. δέ: 'now' [He, Lns; KJV, NASB], not explicit [AB, Herm, HNTC, ICC; all versions except KJV, NASB].

b. pres. act. indic. of λέγω (LN 33.140) (BAGD I.2.β. p. 468): 'to say' [He; KJV], 'to mean' [BAGD, HNTC, ICC, LN, Lns; all versions except KJV, LB, TEV], not explicit [LB]. The phrase τοῦτο λέγω 'I say this' is translated 'what I mean is this' [Ed, HNTC, ICC, My, NIC2; all versions except NAB, TEV, TNT], 'this is what I mean' [BAGD, NIC, TG; NAB], 'I mean this' [Alf, Gdt, Lns; NASB, TNT], 'let me put it this way' [TEV], 'I am referring to this' [AB].

c. ὅτι: 'that' [AB, ICC, Lns; KJV, NASB, NRSV], 'because' [He], not explicit [LB].

d. ἕκαστος (LN 59.27) (BAGD 2. p. 236): 'each' [AB, BAGD, He, LN; NRSV, REB], 'each one' [BAGD, HNTC, Lns; NASB, TEV], 'every' [BAGD], 'every one' [BAGD; KJV, NJB], 'one' [NAB, NIV, TNT], 'there is hardly one ... who has (not got some party-cry)' [ICC], 'some' [LB]. It signifies each one of a group in a distributive sense [LN].

QUESTION—To what does τοῦτο 'this' refer?

1. It refers to what follows, with ὅτι, meaning 'that', giving the content of what Paul meant or said [AB, Alf, Ed, EGT, Gdt, Herm, HNTC, Ho, ICC, Lns, My, NIC, TNTC, Vn; all versions]: I say this, that, etc. Paul's charge is now made more precise [Lns, TNTC] and explains the nature of the quarrels [Herm, Ho]. When he speaks of strifes, Paul means this, that they claim loyalty to different preachers [Gdt].
2. It refers to what precedes, and the following ὅτι means 'because', indicating the grounds for saying that there were strifes among them [He]: I say this, since, etc.

QUESTION—What does ἕκαστος 'each' mean?

It should not be taken absolutely as though each person said all of the following statements [Gdt]. Nor should it be taken to mean that everyone in Corinth, without exception, was doing this [AB, Gdt, Herm, ICC, NIC2, TH, TNTC]. It shows that the problem was widespread [Herm, ICC, TNTC]. It means that 'some' said one thing, 'others' another [BAGD, Gdt]. Each is making only one of the claims and the claims are given by successive speakers who are challenging the others [EGT]. This is an exaggeration probably to show how absurd it was [AB].

I on-the-one-hand[a] am[b] of-Paul, I on-the-other-hand (am) of-Apollo, I on-the-other-hand (am) of-Cephas,[c] I on-the-other-hand (am) of-Christ.

LEXICON—a. μέν...δέ (LN 89.104; 89.136) (BAGD p. 502): 'on the one hand ... on the other hand' [BAGD, LN], 'to be sure ... but' [BAGD], 'some ... (others)' [LN]. Μέν . . . δέ are markers of two or more items which are conjunctively related 'some ... others, first ... then' or they are markers of items in contrast with each other [LN].

b. pres. act. indic. of εἰμί (BAGD IV.2. p. 225): 'to be' [He, Lns; KJV, NASB]. The phrase 'to be of' is translated 'to belong to' [AB, BAGD, HNTC; NAB, NJB, NRSV, TNT], 'to follow' [NIC2, TH; NIV, TEV], 'to be a follower of' [LB], 'to stand by' [ICC], 'to be someone's man' [EGT, NIC2], 'to be for someone'.[REB]. The combination of the verb εἰμί 'to be' and the genitive 'of', indicates attachment to someone [Lns].

c. Κηφᾶς: 'Cephas' [AB, BAGD, He, HNTC, LN, Lns; all versions except LB, TEV], 'Kephas' [ICC], 'Peter' [LB, TEV].

QUESTION—What does ἐγὼ εἰμι παύλου 'I am of Paul' mean?

It is a claim to be the person's disciple [NIC2, TH, TNTC; NIV, TEV], to belong to him [AB, BAGD, EGT, HNTC, Lns; NAB, NJB, NRSV, TNT], to support him [Herm, ICC]. Each group claimed special attachment to a prominent leader, probably having its own emphasis, and being antagonistic to the other three factions [EBC]. The reasons are all guesswork [TNTC]. This does not imply the leaders were responsible for the factions [NIC2].

QUESTION—Why would some say that they were of Paul?

They might major on Paul's emphasis on ministry to the Gentiles [EBC, Ho], possibly being Gentiles themselves. Some of the older members might have been converted by Paul himself [He, Lns]. They honored Paul as founder of the church in Corinth [HNTC, Lns].

QUESTION—Why would some say that they were of Apollos?

He was a Jew from Alexandria who was well educated and an eloquent speaker [Ho], and was a teacher who came to Corinth after Paul had left [NIC2]. Probably a group of the more well educated Corinthians were his followers [Ho, NIC2] because of his eloquence [EBC, He, Lns, NCBC].

QUESTION—Why would some say that they were of Cephas?

Cephas is Peter's Aramaic name [EBC, TG, TNTC, Vn]. Except for Gal. 2:7–8, Paul preferred to use the name "Cephas" [HNTC, NIC, NIC2, Vn]. This party might have been Jews from Jerusalem [He, Vn], perhaps even baptized by Peter [He]. They might be attracted by Peter's emphasis on the Jews [EBC].

QUESTION—Why would some say that they were of Christ?

They might have claimed some special relationship to Christ [EBC, Ho, Vn], or placed on him a special emphasis they felt the others lacked [EBC].

DISCOURSE UNIT: 1:13–2:5 [Ed]. The topic is the first argument against the factions.

DISCOURSE UNIT: 1:13–17 [TNTC]. The topic is the parties not being due to Paul.

1:13 Has-been-divided/assigned[a] Christ?

TEXT—Some manuscripts include μή 'not' before μεμέρισται 'has been divided'. It is omitted by GNT with an A rating, indicating certainty about omitting it. It is included by Lns and REB, either implying a negative answer to the question [Lns] or making a negative statement [REB].

LEXICON—a. perf. pass. indic. of μερίζω (LN **63.23**; 57.89) (BAGD 1.a. p. 504): 'to be divided' [AB, BAGD, He, **LN**, Lns; KJV, NASB, NIV, NRSV, REB, TNT], 'to be divided into parts' [NAB], 'to be divided into groups' [TEV], 'to be split up' [NJB], 'to be shared out' [HNTC], 'to be distributed' [LN (57.89)], 'to be given as a separate share' [ICC]. It is also translated actively with 'you' as agent: 'to break into many pieces' [LB].

QUESTION—What kind of sentence is this?

1. It is a rhetorical question [AB, Alf, EBC, EGT, Gdt, He, Herm, HNTC, Ho, ICC, Lns, NCBC, NIC, NIC2, Rb, TNTC, Vn; all versions except LB, TEV]: Has Christ been divided? A negative reply is implied [Herm, Vn; REB]. The function of the following two questions serve to show its impossibility [Gdt].
2. It is an exclamation [My; TEV] or a statement [LB]: Christ has been divided! The interrogative mood does not start until the following clause. The exclamation is emphasized by the absence of any connecting conjunction to begin the clause. It points out the actual appearance of their actions and shows the tragic result of the quarreling [My].

QUESTION—What is the function of such a rhetorical question?

1. It shows the impossibility of Christ being divided [Gdt, TNTC]: Has Christ been divided? How impossible! Since Christ cannot be divided and still be Christ, neither can the church be divided and still exist [TNTC].
2. It shows the absurdity of the divisions [AB, EBC, Ho, Lns, NIC2]: Since it is impossible that Christ be divided, it is also absurd that his body, the church, be divided.
3. It refutes the hypothesis that Christ was divided [ICC]: Has Christ been divided? I wish to show you he definitely has not!
4. It emphasizes the expected negative reply by omitting the negative particle μή 'not' [Herm]: Has Christ been divided? Definitely not!
5. It shows Paul's indignation [EGT, NCBC]: How dare anyone suggest that Christ is divided!

QUESTION—What is meant by μεμέρισται 'has been divided, assigned'?

1. It means that Christ is divided up among the four factions [AB, Alf, EBC, Ed, Gdt, He, HNTC, Ho, LN, Lns, My, NIC2, TG, TNTC, Vn; all versions]: Has Christ been divided up? The word is not simply 'to divide', but 'to divide up and distribute' [HNTC]. Christ is identified with his

followers, they are his body, so when they are divided, it seems that Christ is divided [TG, TH, Vn]. Christ cannot be divided, but, by their divisions, they act as though Christ himself was divided up among them [HNTC, NIC2]. Rather than thinking of Christ being divided in different parts, it is better to take it as different kinds of Christs: a Paul-Christ, an Apollo-Christ, a Cephas-Christ, and a Christ-Christ [Lns].

2. It means that Christ was allotted to one of the factions [EGT, ICC, NCBC, NIC, Rb]: Has Christ been assigned to a special group? The group claiming to be of Christ claimed an exclusive part of him [EGT]. They seemed to think that Christ had been given only to one faction [ICC]. When one group claimed Christ as the distinction for its party, it deprived the others of Christ [NIC].

Was-crucified[a] Paul not[b] for[c] you?

LEXICON—a. aorist pass. indic. of σταυρόω (LN 20.76) (BAGD 1. p. 765): 'to be crucified' [AB, BAGD, He, HNTC, ICC, LN, Lns; all versions except LB, TEV], 'to be nailed to the cross' [BAGD]. It is also translated actively: 'to die on the cross' [TEV], 'to die for sins' [LB]. It means to execute by nailing to a cross [LN].

b. μή (LN 69.15) (BAGD C.1. p. 517): 'not' [AB, BAGD; NASB], not explicit [BAGD, He, HNTC, ICC, LN, Lns; all versions except NASB]. This question with μή is translated 'Paul was not crucified for you, was he?' [NASB]. It is used in questions which expect a negative reply [AB, Alf, BAGD, Gdt, LN, Lns, My, NIC, TH; NASB].

c. ὑπέρ (LN 90.36; 89.28) (BAGD 1.a.ε. p. 838): 'for' [BAGD, He, HNTC, ICC, LN, Lns; all versions], 'in/on behalf of' [AB, BAGD, LN], 'for the sake of' [BAGD, LN]. It marks a participant who is benefited by an event [LN].

QUESTION—What is the function of the rhetorical question?

1. It emphasizes the fact that Paul was not crucified for them [AB, Alf, ICC, TG]: Paul was not crucified for you!, or, Was Paul crucified for you? Definitely not!
2. It reproves the Corinthians [EGT, Ho]: you should never even think that Paul was crucified for you! They were not purchased by Paul's blood so as to belong to him and therefore it was wrong to say that they were of Paul [Ho].
3. It, along with the following question, shows the impossibility of an affirmative answer to the first question [EBC, Gdt]: If Christ is divided, then it was Paul who was crucified for you and in whose name you were baptized.
4. It shows the absurdity of the claim 'I am of Paul', since the only way such a claim could be valid is for Paul to be crucified for them [NIC2]: Only if Paul were crucified for you (and he wasn't), could you say that you were of Paul.

or in the name[a] of-Paul were-you-baptized?[b]

LEXICON—a. ὄνομα (BAGD I.4.c.β. p. 572): 'name' [AB, BAGD, He, HNTC, Lns; all versions except TEV]. The phrase 'in the name of Paul' is translated 'as Paul's disciples' [TEV], 'was it allegiance to Paul that you pledged yourselves' [ICC]. See this word also at 1:10.

b. aorist pass. indic. of βαπτίζω (LN 53.41) (BAGD 2.b.β. p. 131): 'to be baptized' [AB, BAGD, He, HNTC, ICC, LN, Lns; all versions]. It signifies the use of water in a religious ceremony designed to symbolize purification and initiation on the basis of repentance [LN]. Here it is used with reference to Christian baptism [BAGD].

QUESTION—What is meant by being baptized in the name of someone?

It means to name that person's name when one is baptized [BAGD, Herm, TH]. It means to enter into fellowship with that person [ICC, NIC, Vn] or to give allegiance to that person [ICC, NIC2, Vn]. It means to be known by the name of that person [AB], to become the property of that person [BAGD, Gdt, HNTC, NIC2], to come under that person's control [BAGD]. It means that one is baptized by that person's authority [HNTC].

QUESTION—What is the function of this rhetorical question?

1. It shows the absurdity of the claim, 'I am of Paul', since only if they had been baptized in the name of Paul could they rightly say this [NIC2, TNTC]. They had been baptized in the name of Christ and therefore their allegiance must be to Christ alone [TNTC].
2. It functions along with the previous question to show the impossibility of an affirmative answer to the first question, 'Has Christ been divided?' [EBC, Gdt].
3. It emphasizes the fact that they were not baptized in the name of Paul [ICC, TG].

DISCOURSE UNIT: 1:14–16 [AB]. The topic is baptisms by Paul.

1:14 I-am-thankful[a] to God that I-baptized none of-you except Crispus and Gaius,

TEXT—Some manuscripts omit τῷ θεῷ 'to God'. GNT selects the reading 'to God' in brackets with a C rating, indicating difficulty in deciding whether or not to place it in the text. The words 'to God' are omitted by AB, HNTC; LB, NIV, NJB, TNT.

LEXICON—a. pres. act. indic. of εὐχαριστέω: 'to be thankful' [AB, HNTC; LB, NIV, NJB, REB, TNT], 'to thank' [He, ICC, LN, Lns; KJV, NAB, NASB, NRSV, TEV], 'to give thanks' [BAGD]. See 'I give thanks' at 1:4.

QUESTION—Who were Crispus and Gaius?

Crispus was the chief ruler of the synagogue in Corinth. He was converted when Paul visited the city (Acts 18:8). Gaius had been Paul's host in Rome (Romans 16:23) [Gdt, Ho]. They had been converted before Paul's assistants, Silas and Timothy, had arrived from Macedonia and so Paul baptized them himself [Gdt].

1:15 so-that[a] not anyone should-say that in my name you-were-baptized.

LEXICON—a. ἵνα: 'so that' [He, ICC; NJB, NRSV], 'then' [TEV], 'so' [AB; NAB, NIV], 'this means that' [HNTC], 'for now' [LB], 'that' [NASB, TNT], not explicit [REB]. This word is also joined with the following μή 'not' and translated 'lest' [Lns; KJV].

QUESTION—What relationship is indicated by ἵνα 'so that'?

1. It indicates the result from Paul's not baptizing [AB, Herm, HNTC, Ho, ICC, NIC, TH; NAB, NIV, NJB, TEV]: I baptized none of you, therefore no one can say that you were baptized in my name. The real purpose for not baptizing is given in 1:17 [HNTC].
2. It indicates the purpose for not baptizing [Alf, Gdt, Lns, My, Rb, Vn; KJV]: I baptized none of you, in order that no one might say that you were baptized in my name. It was Paul's purpose [Rb], or God's purpose [Alf, Gdt, My].
3. It indicates the reason why Paul was thankful [Ed]: I am thankful that I baptized none of you, because now no one can say that in my name you were baptized.

1:16 And[a] also I-baptized the household[b] of-Stephanas,

LEXICON—a. δέ: 'and' [KJV, TNT], 'now' [Lns; NASB], 'Yes' [ICC], 'Oh, yes' [LB, TEV], 'Yes' [NIV, NJB], 'Oh' [NAB], 'of course' [REB], not explicit [AB, He, HNTC; NRSV].

b. οἶκος (LN **10.8**) (BAGD 2. p. 560): 'household' [AB, BAGD, HNTC, ICC, LN, Lns; all versions except NJB, TEV], 'family' [BAGD, He, **LN**; NJB, TEV].

QUESTION—What relationship is indicated by δέ και 'and also'?

It serves to correct or limit what is said in 1:14–15 [AB, Ed, ICC, My, TG, TH]: I baptized none of you except Crispus and Gaius: *Oh yes*, *and* the household of Stephanas. Perhaps because of these particles, the following take this verse to be parenthetical: AB, NCBC; NIV, NRSV, TEV. A correction came to Paul's mind as he dictated this letter [ICC, NIC2, TH], or possibly his amanuensis reminded him [ICC].

QUESTION—How are the nouns related in the genitive construction τὸν Στεφανᾶ οἶκον, 'the household of Stephanas'?

Οἶκος 'house' can indicate all those related by blood and marriage and include slaves and servants living in the same house with Stephanas [EBC, LN, TG, TH], or it may refer specifically to Stephanas' family [He, Lns,; NJB, TEV]. The household of Stephanas is also mentioned in 16:15 and there it says that they were the first converts in Achaia.

beyond-that[a] I-know[b] not if any other I-baptized.

LEXICON—a. λοιπόν (LN **61.14**) (BAGD 3.b. p. 480): 'beyond that' [BAGD, **LN**; NAB, NASB, NIV, NRSV], 'besides' [Lns; KJV], 'besides that' [AB, HNTC; TNT], 'besides these' [ICC], 'but besides these' [NJB], 'apart from that' [He] 'finally' [BAGD, LN], 'as far as the rest is concerned, in addition' [BAGD], 'but' [TEV], not explicit [LB, REB].

Λοιπόν indicates an addition which serves as the last item in a series and marks a degree of finality or a conclusion and means ‘in summary, at last’ [LN].

b. perf. act. indic. of οἶδα (LN **29.6**) (BAGD 1.5. p. 556): ‘to know’ [He, HNTC, Lns; KJV, NASB, NRSV, TNT], ‘to remember’ [BAGD, **LN**; LB, NIV, TEV], ‘to recall, to recollect’ [LN], ‘to be aware of’ [AB; NAB], ‘to think’ [NJB], ‘to think of’ [REB]. This verb is also translated as a prepositional phrase: ‘to the best of my knowledge’ [ICC].

QUESTION—Why does he add this remark?

Having remembered Stephanas’ name, he covers himself lest he had left anyone else out [NIC2]. He did not consider it to be important [EGT, My, NIC2].

DISCOURSE UNIT: 1:17–31 [Ho, My]. The topic is Paul’s defense of his manner of preaching.

DISCOURSE UNIT: 1:17–25 [Ed]. The topic is the gospel being the proclamation of salvation through Christ as proven by the nature of the message.

DISCOURSE UNIT: 1:17b–25 [EGT]. The topic is the true power of the gospel.

DISCOURSE UNIT: 1:17 [AB]. The topic is Paul’s mission to evangelize.

1:17 For[a] Christ sent[b] me not to-baptize but to-preach-the-good-news,[c]

LEXICON—a. γάρ: ‘for’ [AB, He, HNTC, ICC, Lns; all versions except NJB, REB, TEV, TNT], ‘after all’ [NJB], not explicit [REB, TEV, TNT].

b. aorist act. indic. of ἀποστέλλω (LN **15.66**) (BAGD 1.b.γ. p. 98): ‘to send’ [AB, He, HNTC, **LN**, Lns; all versions], ‘to make (me his) apostle’ [ICC], ‘to send out or away’ [BAGD]. It means to send with a purpose [BAGD, LN].

c. pres. mid. infin. of εὐαγγελίζω (LN 33.215) (BAGD 2.a.δ. p. 317): ‘to preach the Good News’ [TNT], ‘to proclaim his Glad-tidings’ [ICC], ‘to preach the gospel’ [HNTC, Lns; KJV, LB, NAB, NASB, NIV, NJB, NRSV], ‘to tell the good news’ [LN; TEV], ‘to proclaim good news’ [AB], ‘to announce the gospel’ [LN], ‘to proclaim the gospel’ [He; REB], ‘to preach, bring or announce good news’ [BAGD]. It means to communicate good news about something. In the NT it has reference to the good news about Jesus [LN].

QUESTION—What is relationship is indicated by γάρ ‘for’?

1. It indicates the reason why Paul only baptized a few [Ed, EGT, Gdt, HNTC, Ho, Lns, NIC, TH]: I baptized none of you except Crispus and Gaius because Christ did not send me to baptize.
2. It indicates the reason why Paul did not remember baptizing any more [NIC2]: I don’t remember if I baptized anyone else because Christ did not sent me to baptize but to preach the gospel.

3. It serves as a transition to a new section [Alf, He, My, TH]. It summarizes this section and then leads into the next. It does this by beginning to talk about the themes: telling the Good News, wisdom, and the cross [TH]. His mission was not to baptize, but to preach [Alf].

QUESTION—Why did baptism not play an important part in Paul's role as an apostle?

Converts were to be baptized, but those who administered baptism did not require an apostolic call [Lns, My]. It was the practice of the apostles to leave the administration of baptism to their assistants or others [Ho, Lns, My].

QUESTION—What relationship is indicated by the use of the infinitive form εὐαγγελίζεσθαι 'to preach good news'?

The infinitive indicates the purpose of the verb 'to send' [BAGD, Ed]: Christ sent me in order that I preach the good news.

not with[a] wisdom[b] of-speech,[c]

LEXICON—a. ἐν with dative object (LN 90.10; 89.76): 'with' [ICC, LN; KJV, LB, NAB, NIV, NRSV], 'in' [AB, Alf, Lns; NASB, TNT], 'by means of' [LN; NJB], 'through, by' [LN]. This preposition is also combined with the word 'not' and translated 'without' [HNTC], 'without recourse to' [REB], 'without using' [He]. It is also translated as a verb: 'to use' [TEV].

b. σοφία (LN **28.8**) (BAGD 1. p. 759): 'wisdom' [AB, BAGD, Lns; KJV, NAB, NJB, NRSV], 'human wisdom' [Ho; NIV, TEV], 'cleverness' [BAGD; NASB], 'skill(s)' [HNTC, LN; REB], 'specialized knowledge' [LN], 'philosophy' [He]. This noun is also translated as an adjective: 'skillful' [**LN**], 'clever' [TH], 'studied' [ICC], 'profound' [LB]. It is combined with the preceding word 'not' and translated positively: 'plainest possible (language)' [TNT]. In this context, σοφία is used in a negative sense. It is clever, human, or worldly wisdom, as contrasted with God's wisdom [BAGD, EGT, Ho, Lns, NIC, TG, TH, TNTC; NIV, REB, TEV]. Σοφία signifies knowledge which makes possible skillful activity or performance and here it should be translated 'skillful (speech)' [**LN**].

c. λόγος (LN 33.98; 33.99) (BAGD 1.a.β. p. 477): 'speech' [AB, LN; NASB], 'words' [LN; KJV, NIV], 'words and high sounding ideas' [LB], 'language' [NJB, TEV], 'rhetoric' [ICC; REB], 'eloquence' [He], 'saying, statement' [LN], 'speaking' [BAGD, LN], 'message' [BAGD, LN], 'proclamation, instruction, teaching' [BAGD]. This noun is also translated as an adjective: 'word(-wisdom)' [Lns], 'eloquent' [NRSV], 'rhetorical' [HNTC], 'wordy' [NAB]. It is also joined with the words 'not' and 'wisdom' and translated 'in the plainest possible language' [TNT]. Λόγος refers in general to the act of speaking or to what has been said, with primary focus on its content [LN (33.98)] or to the act of speaking [LN (33.99)]. See this word at 1:5.

QUESTION—How are the nouns related in the genitive construction σωφίᾳ λόγου 'wisdom of speech'?

1. Wisdom is the main word, and speech modifies it [AB, Alf, Ed, EGT, Gdt, HNTC, Lns, My, NIC2; KJV, NAB, NRSV]: not with eloquent wisdom. This is wisdom characterized by rhetoric. There is a secondary emphasis on speech which entails Greek philosophical rhetorical tradition [NIC2]. It means philosophical knowledge presented by persuasive argument and rules of rhetoric [AB]. It means wisdom as a rhetorical device [HNTC]. 'Not in wisdom of speech' means not allowing the discourse to have a philosophical character [EGT, My]. Both terms are without the article, making them almost a compound word: word-wisdom [Lns]. This philosophical presentation then is contrasted with a simple presentation of the facts of Christ's death [Ed].
2. Speech is the main word, and wisdom modifies it [BAGD, EBC, Ho, ICC, LN, NIC, TG, TH, TNTC; NIV, NJB, REB, TEV, TNT]: not with wise speech. The fact that 'word' is the head of this phrase is seen in the next verse where Paul immediately begins to talk about the 'word of the cross'. Wisdom here focuses on a particularly persuasive form of argument [NIC]. It means 'studied rhetoric' [ICC]. Wisdom refers to Greek philosophical reasoning, such as inferences, deductions and conclusions [TG]. 'Wisdom of speech' means 'in cleverness of speaking', that is, in dependence on Greek philosophical form of reasoning [EBC].

so-that[a] not the cross[b] of Christ be-emptied-of-power.[c]

LEXICON—a. ἵνα: 'so that' [ICC; NRSV, TNT], 'in order that' [Lns], 'in order to make sure that' [TEV], 'that' [NASB]. Others combined ἵνα with μή 'not' and translated 'lest' [AB, HNTC; KJV, NAB, NIV, REB], 'for fear that/of' [He; LB], not explicit [NJB].

b. σταυρός (LN 6.27) (BAGD 3. p. 765): 'cross' [AB, BAGD, He, HNTC, ICC, LN, Lns; all versions except LB, TEV]. It was also translated as: 'death on the cross' [TEV], 'the simple message of the cross' [LB]. Σταυρός indicates the instrument by which capital punishment by crucifixion was carried out [BAGD].

c. aorist pass. subj. of κενόω (LN **76.27**) (BAGD 2. p. 428): 'to be emptied of power' [NIV, NRSV], 'to be emptied of significance' [HNTC], 'to be made empty' [Lns], 'to be robbed of meaning' [TNT], 'to be robbed of effect/power' [REB, TEV], 'to be rendered of no effect' [BAGD, NIC2], 'to be made of none effect' [KJV], 'to be rendered/made void' [BAGD; NASB], 'to be rendered void of meaning' [NAB], 'to be nullified' [AB], 'to be deprived of efficacy' [He], 'to be deprived of power' [**LN**]. It is also translated actively with 'wise words' as agent: 'to make pointless' [NJB]; with 'cross' as agent: 'to prevail by its own inherent power' [ICC]; and with Paul as agent: 'not to dilute the mighty power' [LB]. It could be translated 'to be rendered ineffective, to be invalidated' [NIC2], or 'rendered powerless and inoperative' [Ho]. This refers to the convincing power manifested when preaching about Christ crucified [HNTC].

QUESTION—What relationship is indicated by ἵνα 'so that'?

It indicates purpose [AB, HNTC, ICC, Lns, NIC2, Rb; KJV, NAB, NIV, NRSV, REB, TEV]: I did not use wisdom of speech in telling the good news so that the cross of Christ might not be made ineffective.

QUESTION—How are the two nouns related in the genitive construction ὁ σταυρός τοῦ Χριστοῦ 'the cross of Christ'?

It means the cross on which Christ was crucified. Paul is not referring to a literal cross, a wooden crossbeam, but, by metonymy, to Christ's crucifixion [Lns, TG, Vn; TEV], and to its atoning character [Vn]. It stands for Christ's death/crucifixion [Ed, Lns, My, TG, TH; TEV], the account of what happened when Jesus was put to death [AB] and all that was accomplished by his death: atonement and forgiveness [Lns].

DISCOURSE UNIT: 1:18–3:23 [Herm]. The topic is the gospel and the wisdom of the world. Its circular nature sets it off a self-contained unit. It begins with wisdom and foolishness and returns to them at the end [Herm].

DISCOURSE UNIT: 1:18–3:4 [Gdt, ICC]. The topic is the nature of the gospel [Gdt], the false wisdom and the true [ICC].

DISCOURSE UNIT: 1:18–2:16 [AB, EBC]. The topic is the wisdom of God: the preaching of Christ crucified [EBC], the message of the cross versus the wisdom of the world [AB].

DISCOURSE UNIT: 1:18–2:5 [Gdt, Herm, ICC, NCBC, NIC2, TNTC]. The topic is false wisdom [ICC], the gospel not being wisdom [Gdt], God's wisdom as foolishness [Herm], the gospel as a contradiction to wisdom [NIC2], the proclamation of Christ crucified [NCBC], the 'foolishness' of the gospel [TNTC], The whole unit serves to contrast the gospel and wisdom: 1:18–25 shows a crucified Savior as a contrast to wisdom; 1:26–31 shows the Corinthian believers as a contrast to wisdom; and 2:1–5 shows Paul's preaching as a contrast to wisdom [NIC2].

DISCOURSE UNIT: 1:18–31 [EBC, GNT, HNTC, Lns, NCBC, NIC, TG]. The topic is the word of the cross [HNTC], the foolishness of preaching the cross of Christ [Lns], divine and secular wisdom [NCBC, NIC], Christ, the power and wisdom of God [GNT].

DISCOURSE UNIT: 1:18–25 [EBC, Herm, NIC2, TH, TNTC]. The topic is Christ, the power and wisdom of God [EBC], God's folly: a crucified Messiah [NIC2], the message being 'foolish' [TNTC], the word of the cross as the judgment of the wisdom of the world [Herm]. The theme of this section is that Christ is the power and the wisdom of God [TH].

DISCOURSE UNIT: 1:18–21 [AB]. The topic is saving power and perishing folly.

1:18 For[a] the word[b] of the cross is foolishness[c] on-the-one-hand[d] to-the-ones perishing,[e]

LEXICON—a. γάρ (BAGD 1.e. p. 152): 'for' [AB, BAGD, He, HNTC, Lns; KJV, NASB, NIV, NRSV, TEV], not explicit [ICC; LB, NAB, NJB, REB, TNT].

b. λόγος (LN 33.98; 33.260) (BAGD 1.b.β. p. 478): 'word' [LN (33.98), Lns; NASB], 'message' [AB, HNTC, ICC, LN (33.98); NAB, NIV, NJB, NRSV, REB, TEV], 'preaching' [KJV, TNT], 'instruction' [He], 'what is preached, gospel' [LN (33.260)]. This word is also translated by its reciprocal in verbal form: '(they) hear that (Jesus died)' [LB]. Here it refers to God's revelation through Christ and his messengers [BAGD].

c. μωρία (LN **32.57**) (BAGD p. 531): 'foolishness' [AB, BAGD, He, HNTC, ICC, **LN**, Lns; KJV, NASB, NIV, NRSV, TNT], 'folly' [NJB], 'sheer folly' [REB], 'nonsense' [**LN**; TEV], 'complete absurdity' [NAB]. This noun is also translated as an adverbial phrase: 'how foolish' [LB]. It means 'stupid, silly, worthless' [Vn], 'an absurdity' [My].

d. μέν (LN 89.136) (BAGD 1.b. p. 502): 'on the one hand' [BAGD], not explicit [all versions]. This particle is sometimes used without any concessive force on the part of the μέν, but with adversative force in the δέ so that the μέν need not be translated at all [BAGD]. The δέ follows in the following phrase. See this combination at 1:12.

e. pres. mid./pass. participle of ἀπόλλυμι (LN **21.32**) (BAGD 2.a.α. p. 95): 'to be perishing' [AB, BAGD, **LN**, Lns; NASB, NIV, NRSV], 'to perish' [KJV], 'to be lost' [BAGD, LN; LB, TEV], 'to be on the way to destruction/perdition/ruin' [HNTC; NJB, REB, TNT], 'to be on the broad way that leads to destruction' [ICC], 'to be headed for ruin' [NAB], 'to be going towards destruction' [He], 'to die' [BAGD]. It means 'to experience eternal loss' [NIC2]. This word does not mean extinction, but ruin [Rb, Vn]. It means to be lost in the religious or spiritual sense [LN]. It is a loss of well-being, not a loss of being [Vn].

QUESTION—What relationship is indicated by γάρ 'for'?

1. It indicates the grounds for what he has just said in 1:17 [Alf, EGT, Gdt, Herm, Lns, NIC, TG]: Paul is not to announce the good news with wisdom of speech lest the cross of Christ be emptied of its power, because the word of the cross is the power of God.
2. It indicates an explanation of the final clause of 1:17 [NIC2]: not in the wisdom of words lest the cross of Christ be invalidated, for, you see, (the wisdom of words and the word of the cross do not go together and therefore) the word of the cross is foolishness to those perishing but power to those being saved.

QUESTION—How are the nouns related in the genitive construction ὁ λόγος ὁ τοῦ σταυροῦ 'the word of the cross'?

It means the message proclaimed about the cross of Christ (1:17) [AB, He, HNTC, ICC, NIC, TG, TH, Vn; LB, NRSV]. It means the teaching of salvation through the crucifixion of Christ on the cross for the sins of men [Ho]. It is the message about Christ's death on the cross [TEV].

QUESTION—What is the significance of the present participle ἀπολλυμένους 'the ones perishing'?

The present participle indicates that the action of the verb is in process of happening [AB, EBC, EGT, Gdt, HNTC, ICC, Lns, NIC, NIC2, Rb, TNTC; all versions except KJV, LB]. Both destruction and salvation are incomplete processes and are brought to consummation on the last day [HNTC]. The present tense indicates certainty [Ho, ICC, Vn], or is timeless [Rb]. The process is not yet complete [HNTC], and they may still be saved [Lns].

QUESTION—Why is the word of the cross foolishness to these people?

The Greeks had intricate philosophical arguments which showed that a god must not in any way be distressed or influenced by anything outside himself. He could not be defeated by weak human beings or suffer like men. Therefore Christ dying like a common criminal was unthinkable to them [AB].

QUESTION—What is implied by the verb ἐστίν 'is'?

It means 'seems like' or something similar [TH, Vn]: the word of the cross seems like folly to those who are perishing.

but[a] to-us the-ones being-saved[b] it-is (the) power[c] of-God.

LEXICON—a. δέ (BAGD 1.b. p. 502): 'but' [AB, BAGD, He, HNTC, ICC,; all versions], 'yet' [Lns]. It indicates a contrast between the two classes of people [TH, TNTC].

b. pres. pass. participle of σῴζω (LN 21.18; 21.27) (BAGD 2.b. p. 798): 'to be saved' [AB, BAGD, LN (21.27), Lns; KJV, LB, NASB, NIV, NRSV, TEV], 'to be on the way of salvation' [He], 'to be preserved from eternal death, to attain salvation' [BAGD], 'to be rescued, to be delivered, to be made safe' [LN (21.18)]. It was also translated actively: 'to experience salvation' [NAB], 'to be on the way to salvation' [HNTC, ICC; NJB, REB, TNT].

c. δύναμις (LN 76.1) (BAGD 1. p. 207): 'power' [AB, BAGD, HNTC, ICC, LN, Lns; all versions], 'the manifestation of the power' [He], 'strength, might, force' [BAGD].

QUESTION—Who is included in the word ἡμῖν 'to us'?

It includes both Paul and his readers [EGT, NIC, TG, TH] and all Christians as well [TH].

QUESTION—Who is the actor of the passive verb σῳζομένοις 'to the ones being saved'?

God is the actor [TG]: to the ones God is saving.

QUESTION—What is the significance of the present participle σῳζομένοις 'to the ones being saved'

The present participle indicates that the action is in process [AB, EBC, Gdt, He, HNTC, ICC, NIC2, TG, TNTC; all versions except KJV, LB]. It indicates certainty [Ho] or is timeless [Rb]. It indicates that they are in a saved condition and will remain in it [Lns]. Salvation can be considered from three aspects: past, present, and future [EBC, Rb, Vn]. Salvation is not yet totally gained; there is still a resurrection and a future age to come [He]. It means to be declared righteous by God and to be in the process of being made holy. This will be completed when Christ returns [EBC].

QUESTION—What is meant by the word of the phrase, 'the word of the cross is the power of God'?

It means that the word of the cross reveals God's power [ICC, TG, TH]. It means the word through which God's power becomes effective in lives and in history [TG]. Salvation is a result of God's power [NIC2]. God causes the message to speak to the heart and conscience [AB, Gdt, ICC], and reveal the nature of sin and give a basis for hope [AB].

1:19 For[a] it-has-been-written,[b]

LEXICON—a. γάρ: 'for' [AB, He, HNTC, ICC, Lns; all versions except NAB, NJB, REB, TEV], 'as' [NJB], not explicit [NAB, REB, TEV].

b. perf. pass. indic. of γράφω (LN 33.61) (BAGD 2.c. p. 166): 'to be written' [AB, BAGD, He, HNTC, LN, Lns; KJV, NASB, NIV, NRSV], 'to stand written' [ICC]. It is also translated actively: 'scripture says' [NAB, NJB, REB, TEV, TNT], 'God says' [LB]. The perfect tense indicates that what God promised in Isa. 29:14 continues to be true [EBC, TH]. Γέγραπται 'it is written' is a formula used to introduce OT quotations [BAGD].

QUESTION—What relationship is indicated by γάρ 'for'?

1. It indicates the grounds for what Paul stated in 1:18 [ICC, My, TG, TH]: the word of the cross is folly to those who are perishing. This is true because it is written, "I will destroy the wisdom of the wise ..."
2. It indicates a second grounds for the words 'not with eloquent wisdom' of 1:17, parallel with the word γάρ 'for' of 1:18 [Alf]: to announce the good news not with eloquent wisdom ... for the word of the cross ... for it is written, "I will destroy the wisdom of the wise .... "

QUESTION—What Old Testament reference is referred to?

1. It refers to Isa. 29:14 (in the Septuagint) [AB, Alf, EBC, Ed, Gdt, He, Herm, ICC, My, NIC2, Rb, TG, TH, TNTC].
2. No specific reference is intended. This rather refers to the teaching of the Old Testament as a whole that human wisdom could not lead man to the way of salvation. Although nearly the same words are used in Isa. 29:11, there the application is more limited [Ho].

I-will-destroy[a] the wisdom[b] of-the wise[c]

LEXICON—a. fut. act. indic. of ἀπόλλυμι (LN 20.31) (BAGD 1.a.β. p. 95): 'destroy' [AB, BAGD, He, HNTC, ICC, LN, Lns; all versions], 'ruin' [BAGD, LN].

b. σοφία: 'wisdom'. See this word at 1:17.

c. σοφός (LN 32.35) (BAGD 2. p. 760): 'wise' [AB, BAGD, He, HNTC, ICC, Lns; all versions except LB], 'philosophers' [He], 'learned'

[BAGD], 'wise man, one who is wise' [LN]. This word is joined with 'wisdom' and translated 'no matter how wise they seem to be' [LB]. It refers to a person who is regarded as especially capable in understanding the philosophical aspects of knowledge and experience [LN].

QUESTION—To whom does 'I' refer in this and the following clauses?

It refers to God [Lns, TH; LB].

QUESTION—What is meant by destroying wisdom?

The word 'wisdom' carries with it a negative sense of human or worldly wisdom, a wisdom that leaves God out of consideration [HNTC, Lns, TH]. 'Wisdom' is used ironically. God will prevent their plans from working out [TH]. God will show that their wisdom is useless, it means nothing [TG].

and the intelligence[a] of-the intelligent[b] I-will-bring-to-nothing.[c]

LEXICON—a. σύνεσις (LN 32.6; 32.26) (BAGD 1. p. 788): 'intelligence' [BAGD, HNTC, LN; NIV, TNT], 'cleverness' [NAB, NASB, REB], 'discernment' [ICC; NRSV], 'reason' [He], 'shrewdness' [AB, BAGD], 'understanding' [LN; KJV, NJB, TEV], 'the faculty of comprehension, acuteness' [BAGD], 'prudence' [Lns], 'best ideas' [LB].

b. συνετός (LN **32.27**) (BAGD p. 788): 'intelligent' [AB, HNTC, **LN**; NIV, TNT], 'clever' [NAB, NASB, REB], 'discerning' [ICC; NRSV], 'prudent' [Lns; KJV], 'scholars' [TEV], 'men of understanding' [He], 'any who understand' [NJB], 'intelligent, sagacious, wise, with good sense' [BAGD], 'insightful, understanding' [LN]. This word is also translated as an adjective: 'the most brilliant (ideas)' [LB].

c. fut. act. indic. of ἀθετέω (LN 31.100; 76.24) (BAGD 1.a. p. 21): 'to bring to nothing' [KJV, NJB, REB], 'to thwart' [BAGD; NAB, NRSV], 'to frustrate' [NIV], 'to set aside' [AB, BAGD, HNTC, LN, NIC2; NASB, TEV, TNT], 'to nullify' [BAGD, He], 'to declare/regard as invalid' [BAGD, LN], 'to confound' [BAGD], 'to reject' [LN, Lns], 'to set at naught' [ICC], 'to not rely on' [LN], 'ignore' [LB].

QUESTION—How is the clause 'I will bring to nothing the cleverness of the clever' related to the preceding clause, 'I will destroy the wisdom of the wise'?

It functions to restate the preceding clause in different words in keeping with Hebrew poetic style [He, Lns, TH]. This means that the words 'the wise' and 'the clever' are near synonyms [He, Ho, TNTC].

QUESTION—What area of meaning is intended by the word σύνεσις 'cleverness'?

The word 'cleverness' carries with it a negative sense of being merely human, a cleverness that leaves God out of consideration [TH]. It refers to quickness in apprehending something [Vn], tricky scheming [Lns].

1:20 Where[a] (is the) wise-man?[b] Where (is the) scribe?[c] Where (is the) debater[d] of this age?[e]

LEXICON—a. ποῦ: 'where' [AB, BAGD, He, HNTC, LN, Lns; all versions except LB, NAB, TEV]. It was also translated idiomatically: 'where does that leave' [TEV], 'where is to be found' [NAB], 'so what about' [LB], 'what, in God's sight' [ICC].

b. σοφός (LN **32.35**): 'wise man' [HNTC; NAB, NASB, NIV, TNT], 'wise' [Lns; KJV, TEV], 'man who is wise' [**LN**], 'one who is wise' [NRSV], 'a wise man' [AB], 'your wise man' [REB], 'wise men' [LB], 'philosopher' [He; NJB], 'Greek philosopher' [Gdt, ICC, NIC2]. See this word at 1:19.

c. γραμματεύς (LN 53.94; 27.22) (BAGD 2. p. 165): 'scribe' [BAGD, Lns; KJV, NAB, NASB, NRSV], 'expert in the law' [BAGD, LN], 'expert in the Jewish law' [EBC, LN], 'teacher of the Law' [NIC2; TNT], 'expert' [NJB], 'scripture expert' [AB], 'scholar' [HNTC, LN; LB, NIV, TEV], 'your man of learning' [REB], 'rabbi' [He], 'Jewish Rabbi' [ICC], 'scholar versed in the law' [BAGD], 'teacher' [LN]. Scribes were the teachers of the Jewish law [EBC, NIC2, TH]. They were skilled in the transcription, interpretation, and administration of the Jewish law [Ho].

d. συζητητής (LN **33.441**) (BAGD p. 775): 'debater' [AB, BAGD, **LN**; NASB, NJB, NRSV], 'skillful debater' [TEV], 'your subtle debater' [REB], 'brilliant debater' [LB], 'disputant' [BAGD, HNTC], 'disputer' [LN, Lns; KJV], 'skillful disputer' [ICC], 'arguer' [TNT], 'master of argument' [NAB], 'philosopher' [Ed; NIV], 'sophist' [He]. These were philosophers [Ho, NIC2]. This is a regular Greek term for disputants in Greek philosophical schools and in general discussions or debates [Lns].

e. αἰών (LN 67.143; 41.38) (BAGD 2.a. p. 27): 'age' [AB, BAGD, HNTC, LN, Lns; NASB, NIV, NJB, NRSV, TNT], 'evil age' [ICC], 'present age' [BAGD; REB], 'world' [BAGD, LN; KJV, TEV], 'present world' [He], 'world's great affairs' [LB], 'era', [LN], 'time' [BAGD], 'world system, world's standards' [LN]. This noun was also translated as an adjective: 'worldly (argument)' [NAB].

QUESTION—What is the function of these rhetorical questions?

They function to show that these men have been brought to nothing in accordance with Scripture [Alf, EGT, Gdt, ICC, My, NIC]. The implied answer is that such men have been overpowered by God and put to shame [NIC]. These people can have nothing worthwhile to say about God's power [TG]. Paul is reflecting the sarcasm of the Scripture passage and asking what is left of the wise people of this age in view of what God has done in the cross [NIC2]. They have turned out to be fools [Lns, NIC2]. Some take these questions to be the beginning of a debate with hypothetical disputants which presents a challenge to these classes of men to disprove his claims [Ho] or to do what has been done by the word of the cross [EBC].

QUESTION—How are the words σοφός 'wise man,' γραμματεύς 'scribe' and συζητητής 'debater' related?

1. 'Wise man' is the generic word to which 'scribe' and 'debater' are specifics [Ed, Gdt, Ho, My]: Where is the wise man, whether scribe or debater?
2. 'Debater' is the generic word to which 'wise' and 'scribe' are specifics [EGT]: Where is the debater, whether wise man or scribe? The wise man

is the Greek philosopher and the scribe is the Jewish rabbi or teacher of the Law [EGT].

3. This lists three groups without indicating generic-specific relationships [Alf, EBC, He, ICC, Lns, NIC2, Rb, TH, Vn]: Where is the wise man, scribe, or debater? The wise man is the Greek philosopher, the scribe is the Jewish expert in the Law, and the debater can be either Greek or Jew [EBC, He, NIC2, Rb]. Or the wise man is applicable to both Greek and Jew (especially to the people of Corinth who thought themselves to be such wise philosophers [Lns]), the scribe is the Jewish expert in the Law, and the debater is the Greek philosopher [Alf, Lns]

QUESTION—What is meant by αἰῶνος τούτου 'this age'?

It denotes the time before the Messianic age or the age to come, and has the negative sense of evil [ICC, NIC2, TH]. It carries with it a sense of temporality [ICC, TNTC]. The phrase 'of this age' is synonymous with 'of the world' [He, Herm, HNTC, Rb, Vn]. Αἰῶνος refers to a segment of time, an 'age'. Here the phrase means 'the present age (nearing its end)'. It indicates everything that is non-Christian and includes the striving after worldly wisdom [BAGD]. It refers to a unit of time as a particular period of history. It also refers to the system of practices and standards of secular society apart from God's requirements [LN].

QUESTION—With what is the genitive phrase τοῦ αἰῶνος τούτου 'of this age' connected?

1. It is connected with the last group, the debaters [AB, EGT, He, HNTC, ICC, Lns; all versions]: Where is the wise man? Where is the scribe? Where is the debater of this age?
2. The genitive phrase is to be taken with all three terms [Alf, Ed, Gdt, Herm, Ho, ICC, NIC2, TH]: Where is the wise man of this age? Where is the scribe of this age? Where is the debater of this age? Although grammatically connected to 'debater', it probably intends to describe all three groups as being of this age [Herm, NIC2, TH].

(Did) not[a] God show-to-be-foolish[b] the wisdom[c] of-the world?[d]

LEXICON—a. οὐχί (LN 69.12) (BAGD 3. p. 598): 'not' [AB, BAGD, He, HNTC, ICC, Lns; all versions except LB, REB, TEV]. This word is also taken as expecting a positive reply and translated 'God has made the wisdom of this world look foolish' [LB, REB, TEV]. This word is used in questions which expect a positive reply [BAGD, EBC, LN TG, TH; all versions]. Οὐχι is a strengthened form of οὐ 'not' [BAGD, EBC, LN].

b. aorist act. indic. of μωραίνω (LN **32.59**) (BAGD 1. p. 531): 'to show to be foolish' [BAGD; TEV], 'to show up as folly' [NJB], 'to make to look foolish' [REB], 'to make to look foolish and show to be useless nonsense' [LB], 'to make foolish' [AB, BAGD, He, Lns; KJV, NASB, NIV, NRSV, TNT], 'to make foolish and futile' [ICC], 'to cause to become nonsense' [**LN**] 'to make folly' [HNTC], 'to turn into folly' [NAB]. The aorist tense indicates a single past event, the death of Christ [TH].

c. σοφία: 'wisdom'. See this word at 1:17.

d. κόσμος: 'world' [AB, He, HNTC, Lns; all versions except LB, NJB], 'non-Christian world' [ICC], 'them' [LB]. This noun is also translated as an adjective: 'human (wisdom)' [NJB].

QUESTION—How are the nouns related in the genitive construction σοφίαν τοῦ κόσμου 'wisdom of the world'?

Wisdom is the head word and the phrase 'of the world' modifies it. Some suggestions for its meaning are: secular wisdom [NCBC], human wisdom [Lns; NJB], profane wisdom of the non-Christian world [ICC], wisdom which belongs to this world [Lns], wisdom of human self-sufficiency [NIC2], wisdom of humanity apart from God [Gdt].

QUESTION—What is the difference of meaning between αἰῶνος 'age' and κόσμος 'world'?

They are either synonymous or nearly synonymous [AB, He, Herm, ICC, NIC2, Rb, TG, TH, Vn].

QUESTION—How did God show the world's wisdom to be foolish?

God showed this by saving believers through what the wise people of the world considered to be foolish, that is, by the preaching of the cross [My]. It is not self-evident that God has done so, thus the rest of the paragraph explains how this is true [NIC2].

1:21 For[a]

LEXICON—a. γάρ: 'for' [AB, He, HNTC, ICC, Lns; all versions except LB, NAB, NJB, REB], not explicit [LB, NAB, NJB, REB].

QUESTION—What relationship is indicated by this word?

1. It explains how the preceding statement was accomplished [Alf, EBC, Ed, EGT, ICC, My, NIC2, Rb]: God made foolish the wisdom of the world in that God saved the ones who believed through the folly of preaching.
2. It indicates the grounds for the preceding statement [Ho, Lns, NIC]: It is true that God made foolish the wisdom of the world since he saved the ones who believed through the folly of preaching.
3. It indicates the reason why God decided to treat wisdom so harshly [Gdt, Herm]: God has made foolish the wisdom of the world because the world did not know God through wisdom.

since[a] in[b] the wisdom[c] of God the world[d] knew[e] not God through[f] wisdom,[g]

LEXICON—a. ἐπειδή (LN 89.32) (BAGD 2. p. 284): 'since' [AB, BAGD, HNTC, Ho, LN, Lns; NAB, NASB, NIV, NJB, NRSV, TNT], 'because, for, inasmuch as' [LN], 'since then, (just) because' [BAGD], 'as' [REB], 'when' [ICC, LN], 'after that' [Gdt; KJV], not explicit [He; LB, TEV].

b. ἐν with dative object: 'in' [AB, ICC, Lns; all versions], 'by' [He, HNTC]. See this word at 1:17.

c. σοφία (BAGD 3.b p. 760): 'wisdom' [AB, BAGD, LN, Lns; all versions], 'wise plan' [HNTC], 'providence' [ICC], 'wisdom (displayed in creation)' [He].

d. κόσμος: 'world' [AB, He, HNTC, ICC, Lns; all versions except TEV], 'people' [TEV].

e. aorist act. indic. of γινώσκω (LN 28.1; 27.18): 'to know' [HNTC, LN, Lns; all versions except LB, REB], 'to come to know' [AB], 'to recognize' [He], 'to attain a real knowledge of' [ICC], 'to find' [LB, REB], 'to know about, to have knowledge of, to be acquainted with' [LN].

f. διά with genitive object (LN 90.8; 89.76) (BAGD A.III.1.d. p. 180): 'through' [AB, BAGD, LN, Lns; all versions except KJV, REB, TEV], 'through the instrumentality of' [He], 'by means of' [BAGD, LN; TEV], 'by' [LN; KJV, REB], 'with' [BAGD, LN], 'in spite of' [ICC]. This preposition was also translated as a verb: 'exercising (its own wisdom)' [HNTC].

g. σοφία: 'wisdom' [AB; KJV, LB, NAB, NJB, NRSV, TNT], 'its wisdom' [Lns; NASB, NIV, REB], 'their own wisdom' [TEV], 'human brilliance' [HNTC], 'philosophy' [He], 'all its boasted intellect and philosophy' [ICC]. It refers to philosophy [He, ICC], intellect [ICC], human/worldly wisdom [Ed, HNTC, NIC2, TG, TH; TEV]. See this word at 1:17.

QUESTION—What relationship is indicated by ἐπειδή 'since'?

It indicates the reason why God used the foolishness of preaching to save people [Alf, Ho, Lns, NIC]: because the world did not know God through wisdom, God saved believers through the folly of preaching.

QUESTION—What relationship is indicated by ἐν 'in'?

1. It indicates location, meaning 'in the midst of' [Ed, Gdt, He, Ho, Lns, My]: although in the midst of evidences of God's wisdom, the world did not know God by means of its wisdom. God's wisdom was apparent in his works of creation [He, Ho, Lns, My], the course of history [Lns], and in OT revelation [My].
2. It indicates reason: what happened was due to God's wise plan [Alf, EBC, EGT, ICC, NIC2, TG, TNTC, Vn; REB, TEV]: God, in his wisdom, planned that the world would not know him by means of its own wisdom. This refers to God's wise plan of salvation [HNTC]. It means God's wise dealing with mankind, especially in letting them be ignorant [ICC].

God decided[a] through[b] the foolishness[c] of preaching[d] to-save[e] the-ones believing;[f]

LEXICON—a. aorist act. indic. of εὐδοκέω (LN 30.97) (BAGD 1. p. 319): 'to decide' [TH; NRSV, TEV], 'to resolve' [BAGD, Ed, Herm], 'to determine' [BAGD, He], 'to choose' [HNTC; REB], 'to make it one's good pleasure' [Lns], 'to consider good, to consent' [BAGD], 'to choose as better, to prefer' [LN], 'it pleased (God)' [KJV, NAB, TNT], 'to be pleased' [AB, LN; NIV], 'to be well-pleased' [NASB], 'to be one's own pleasure' [NJB], 'to be one's good pleasure' [ICC], 'to step in' [LB].

b. διά with genitive object: 'through' [AB, BAGD, He, LN, Lns; all versions except KJV, REB, TEV], 'by' [HNTC; KJV, REB], 'by means of' [ICC; TEV].
c. μωρία: 'foolishness' [AB, He, ICC, Lns; KJV, NASB, NIV, NRSV, TNT], 'folly' [HNTC; NJB, REB], 'absurdity' [NAB]. This noun was also translated as an adjective: 'the so-called "foolish" (message)' [TEV], 'foolish and silly (message)' [LB]. See this word at 1:18.
d. κήρυγμα (LN 33.258) (BAGD 2. p. 431): 'preaching' [BAGD, LN, Lns; KJV], 'preaching (about the cross)' [He], 'preaching of the gospel' [NAB], 'what is preached' [LN; NIV], 'Christian preaching' [HNTC], 'the message preached' [NASB], 'the message we preach' [TEV], 'proclamation' [AB, BAGD; NRSV], 'the message we proclaimed' [TNT], 'his message' [LB], 'the proclaimed Glad-tidings' [ICC], 'the gospel' [NJB, REB]. Here it is used to indicate apostolic preaching [BAGD]. It is derived from κηρύσσω which means to publicly announce religious truths while urging acceptance [LN].
e. aorist act. infin. of σῴζω (LN **21.27**) (BAGD 2.a.α. p. 798): 'to save' [AB, BAGD, He, HNTC, ICC, LN, Lns; all versions]. See this word at 1:18.
f. pres. act. participle of πιστεύω (LN 31.85; 31.102) (BAGD 2.b. p. 661): 'to believe' [AB, BAGD, LN (31.85), Lns; KJV, NAB, NASB, NIV, NRSV, TEV, TNT], 'to believe in' [BAGD, LN (31.85)], 'to have faith' [HNTC; REB], 'to have faith in' [ICC, LN (31.85)], 'to trust' [BAGD, LN (31.85)], 'to have confidence in' [LN (31.85)], 'to become a believer' [He], 'to believe (his) message' [LB], 'to be a believer, to be a Christian' [LN (31.102)]. This verb is also translated as a noun: 'believers' [NJB]. The present tense indicates a continuing faith [ICC, Lns, TNTC] or it refers to believers as a class of people who exercise the initial act of faith [Vn].

QUESTION—What is implied by the word μωρία 'folly'?

Paul uses this word ironically, saying one thing but meaning its opposite [TH; TEV]. It means foolish by the standards of secular human wisdom, not by God's standards [HNTC, ICC, NCBC, TG].

QUESTION—What is meant by κήρυγμα 'preaching'?

1. It focuses attention on the content of the message rather than on the act of preaching [EBC, Ed, EGT, HNTC, ICC, Lns, My, NCBC, NIC, NIC2, Rb, TH, TNTC; NASB, TEV, TNT]: through the folly of the message we preach. The folly of what is preached means practically the same thing as 'the word of the Cross' which seems to be folly to those perishing (1:18) [EBC, Ed, Herm, ICC, My, NIC2, TNTC].
2. Both the content of what is preached and the act of preaching are in focus [Ho, ICC, Vn]: through the preaching of the message of folly. There is a slight emphasis on presentation, but the content of the message is also indicated [ICC, Vn]. 'Preaching' denotes the action, not as a process, but as completed or viewed as a whole [ICC].

QUESTION—What is the implied object of πιστεύω 'to believe'?

1. The implied object is 'preaching/message' [Lns, NIC]: to save those who believe the message.
2. The implied object is 'God' [ICC, NIC2, TH]: to save those who believe in God. They must wholly trust God to save them in this way [NIC2].

DISCOURSE UNIT: 1:22–25 [AB]. The topic is Jews, Greeks, and God.

1:22 for[a] both/indeed[b] (the) Jews ask-for[c] signs[d] and Greeks[e] look-for[f] wisdom,[g]

TEXT—Instead of σημεῖα 'signs', some manuscripts have σημεῖον 'a sign'. GNT selects the reading 'signs' with no textual notation. The singular reading is taken by KJV and LB.

LEXICON—a. ἐπειδή: 'for' [He; KJV, NASB, NRSV], 'since' [AB, BAGD, HNTC, Lns], 'seeing that' [Rb], 'the truth of this is evident' [ICC], 'Yes' [NAB], 'while' [NJB], not explicit [all other versions except LB]. It is also translated with implied information: 'it seems foolish to the Jews because' [LB]. See this word at 1:21.

b. καί (LN 89.102) (BAGD I.6 p. 393): 'both' [BAGD, LN, Lns], 'and' [AB], 'on the one hand' [He], 'indeed' [EGT, Gdt; NASB], not explicit [all other versions]. When two καί's are linked together they mark two closely related items: 'both ... and' [BAGD, LN].

c. pres. act. indic. of αἰτέω (LN 33.163) (BAGD p. 25): 'to ask for' [AB, BAGD, HNTC, ICC, LN, Lns; NASB, TNT], 'to demand' [BAGD, He, Herm, LN; NAB, NIV, NJB, NRSV, REB], 'to require' [KJV], 'to want' [LB, TEV], 'to expect' [TH]. It means to ask for something with urgency, even to the point of demanding [LN]. The present tense implies a continued asking [EGT, ICC].

d. σημεῖον (LN 33.477) (BAGD 2.a. p. 748): 'sign' [AB, BAGD, He, HNTC, Lns; KJV, NAB, NASB, NRSV, REB, TNT], 'miracle' [BAGD, He, ICC, TH; NJB], 'miraculous sign' [NIC2, TNTC; NIV], 'a sign from heaven as proof' [LB], 'miracle for proof' [TEV], 'wonder' [BAGD]. Σημεῖον is 'a sign' consisting of a miracle or wonder that is contrary to the usual course of nature and is performed by God, by Christ, or by men of God [BAGD]. It is an event or miracle which is thought of as having some special meaning [LN]. It is not only a miracle or wonder, but its purpose is to validate a person's claims as true [Alf, HNTC, Ho, NIC2, TG, TNTC].

e. Ἕλλην (LN 11.40; 11.90) (BAGD 2.a. p. 252): 'Greek' [AB, He, HNTC, ICC, LN, Lns; all versions except LB], 'Gentile' [BAGD, LN; LB], 'non-Jews' [LN], 'pagan, heathen' [BAGD]. It indicates a man of Greek language and culture or all people who came under the influence of this culture [BAGD].

f. pres. act. indic. of ζητέω (LN **27.34**) (BAGD 2.c. p. 339): 'to look for' [NAB, NIV, NJB, REB, TEV, TNT], 'to seek' [He, HNTC; TNT], 'to seek for/after' [AB, Lns; KJV], 'to search for' [**LN**; NASB], 'to ask for'

[BAGD, ICC], 'to desire' [Herm; NRSV], 'to request, to demand' [BAGD], 'to try to learn, to try to find out, to seek information' [LN], not explicit [LB].

g. σοφία: 'wisdom' [AB, BAGD, HNTC, Lns; all versions except LB], 'philosophy' [He], 'a philosophy of religion' [ICC], 'what seems wise' [LB]. Here it means philosophy [NIC, NIC2], and perhaps rhetoric [NIC]. This refers to gnosticism [HNTC]. They demanded rational evidence [Gdt]. See this word at 1:17, 21.

QUESTION—What relationship is indicated by ἐπειδή 'for'?

1. It indicates the reason for the preceding clause [Alf, EBC, Ed, Gdt, ICC, NIC, Rb]: God saves men through the folly of preaching because the Jews demand signs and the Greeks seek wisdom. It explains the preaching of foolishness [Alf], the world seeking God through wisdom [EBC], God's decision to respond to the yearning for a revelation from God [Ed].
2. It indicates the reason for 1:20 [EGT, HNTC]: God has made foolish the wisdom of the world because the Jews demand signs and Greeks seek wisdom, but we proclaim Christ crucified, a stumbling block to Jews and folly to Gentiles.
3. It indicates the reason for 1:23 [AB, Ho, Lns, My]: Because Jews require signs and Greeks seek wisdom, we preach Christ crucified. Since Jews and Greeks were wrong, Paul proclaims Christ crucified [Ho, Lns].
4. It indicates a temporal relationship, meaning that 1:22 happens at the time of 1:23 [Herm; NJB]: while the Jews are requiring signs and the Greeks are seeking wisdom, we are preaching Christ crucified.

QUESTION—What is indicated by the construction καὶ ... καί 'both ... and'?

1. It indicates that both the Jews and Greeks are combined into one group and contrasted with the following 'we' [Lns]. It unites the two groups together [Alf, ICC] with the meaning, 'Both Jews and Greeks are in error, Jews, because they seek signs, and the Greeks, because they seek wisdom' [HNTC]. It unites not simply the two groups, but also the statements about them [My].
2. The two καίs should not be taken together. The first καί goes with ἐπειδή 'since' and means 'indeed' [EGT, Gdt; NASB]: Since indeed the Jews ask for signs and the Greeks . . . .

QUESTION—What does the lack of definite articles with the words Ἰουδαῖοι 'Jews' and Ἕλληνες 'Greeks' indicate?

It indicates Jews as a class and Greeks as a class [Lns], or it indicates the characteristic features of these peoples, rather than referring to individuals [ICC, Vn]. There were many exceptions [ICC, TH].

QUESTION—What is meant by the word Ἕλληνες 'Greeks'?

1. It primarily means 'the Greek people' [EBC, ICC, NIC2, TNTC]. The Greeks valued philosophy and looked down on barbarians [TNTC]. Here Paul refers to the native Greeks of Corinth, although in a broader sense the word refers to the whole non-Jewish world as seen in the next verse [EBC]. The Greeks were the ones who especially sought after wisdom

while not only the Greeks but also the Romans would think that a crucified messiah to be nonsense [NIC2].

2. It implies the non-Jewish world—the Gentiles [Gdt, HNTC, Lns, NCBC, TG, TH]. This is seen from the synonymous use of the term 'Gentiles' in the same sentence [HNTC]. Paul uses 'Greeks' as the chief representatives for all the Gentiles [Lns].

1:23 but[a] we proclaim[b] Christ crucified,[c]

LEXICON—a. δέ: 'but' [He, HNTC, ICC; all versions except LB, NJB, TEV], 'on the contrary, on the other hand' [My], 'as for us' [TEV], 'so' [LB], not explicit [AB, Lns; NJB].

b. pres. act. indic. of κηρύσσω (LN 33.206; 33.207; 33.256) (BAGD 2.b.β. p. 431): 'to proclaim' [ICC, LN; NRSV, REB, TEV, TNT], 'to proclaim aloud' [BAGD], 'to proclaim as heralds' [HNTC, Lns, TH, TNTC], 'to preach' [AB, He, HNTC, LN, Lns; all other versions], 'to announce, to tell' [LN]. It means to proclaim in a formal public manner and to publicly announce religious truths while urging acceptance [LN]. The present tense indicates a continuing action: 'to keep preaching' [AB; NJB].

c. perf. pass. participle of σταυρόω (LN 20.76) (BAGD 1. p. 765): 'to be crucified' [AB, BAGD, He, HNTC, ICC, Lns; all versions except LB, REB], 'nailed to the cross' [REB]. It is also translated in as an active verb: '(Christ) dying to save them' [LB]. See this word at 1:13.

QUESTION—What relationship is indicated by δέ 'but'?

It indicates a contrast between what the Jews and Greeks want and what Paul and others give them [EGT, Gdt, Herm, My, NIC2, Rb, TNTC]. Instead of giving them signs and wisdom, Paul and his companions gave them a message of offense and folly [NIC2]. The position of the pronoun ἥμεις 'we' at the beginning of the verse also emphatically contrasts the subjects of this verse with those of the preceding verse [Gdt, TG, TH, TNTC; TEV].

QUESTION—Who is included in the word 'we'?

1. Paul and his fellow evangelists are included [Gdt, Lns, TG, TH]. This would probably not include the Corinthians [TH].
2. It includes all who are being saved (1:18) [Herm].

QUESTION—What does it mean 'to proclaim Christ crucified'?

It means to proclaim to others that Christ was crucified [AB, EGT; TEV]. The perfect participle signifies that the effect of Christ's death is continuing into the present [EBC, Lns, TH, TNTC, Vn]. Not only was Christ once crucified, he continues in the character of the one who has been crucified and the crucifixion is permanently efficacious [TNTC].

(an) offense[a] to-Jews on-the-one-hand,[b]

LEXICON—a. σκάνδαλον (LN **25.181**) (BAGD 3. p. 753): 'offense' [AB, **LN**; TNT], 'what causes offense' [LN], 'a message that is offensive' [TEV], 'a revolting idea' [ICC], 'a scandal' [He, HNTC], 'an obstacle they cannot get over' [NJB], 'deathtrap' [Lns], 'stumbling block' [all other versions except LB], 'that which gives offense or causes revulsion, that which arouses opposition, an object of anger or disapproval, stain' [BAGD], This noun was also translated as a verb: 'to be offended' [LB].

b. μέν: 'on the one hand', not explicit [all versions]. See the combination μεν δέ at 1:12, the δέ being in the following clause.

QUESTION—What is meant by σκάνδαλον 'offense'?

1. It means something which annoys or offends to the point of creating opposition [AB, BAGD, EGT, ICC, LN, NIC2, TNTC; TEV, TNT].
2. It is the picture of a trap that kills its victim [Lns], or an obstacle over which one stumbles [Lns, NIC, TH, Vn; KJV, NAB, NASB, NIV, NJB, NRSV]. It hindered the Jews from believing since the claim that Jesus was the Christ was refuted by the crucifixion [Vn].

QUESTION—Why was the cross an offense to Jews?

The cross was an offense to Jews because they felt that God's highest blessing rested on the Messiah, but God's curse rested on anyone hanging on a cross. Therefore, a crucified Messiah was a contradiction in terms [NCBC, Vn]. A crucified Messiah contradicted their expectation of a political deliverer [EBC].

and[a] foolishness[b] to-Gentiles[c] on-the-other-hand,

LEXICON—a. δέ: 'and' [AB, ICC; KJV, LB, NAB, NASB, NIV, NRSV, REB, TEV], not explicit [all other versions].

b. μωρία: 'foolishness'. See this word at 1:18 and 21.

c. ἔθνος (LN 11:37): 'Gentiles' [AB, HNTC, Lns; all versions except KJV], 'Greeks' [ICC; KJV], 'pagans' [He, LN], 'heathen' [LN]. ἔθνος occurring in the plural (as it does here) refers to those who do not belong to the Jewish or Christian faith [LN].

QUESTION—What does 'foolishness' mean?

It means that in the opinion of the Gentiles it is foolishness [TH]. They thought that God could never act like that [TNTC]. They could not imagine God becoming incarnate and as a God-man provide atonement for sin [EBC].

1:24 but[a] to-them (who are) the called,[b] both to-Jews and to-Greeks,

LEXICON—a. δέ: 'but' [AB, He, HNTC, ICC, Lns; all versions except REB], 'yet' [REB].

b. κλητός (BAGD p. 436): 'called' [Lns], 'elect' [He], 'those called to salvation' [LB]. This pronominal adjective is also translated as a relative clause: 'who are the called' [NASB, REB], 'who are/have been called' [AB, BAGD, HNTC; KJV, NAB, NRSV, REB, TNT], 'who really accept God's call' [ICC], 'whom God has called' [NIV, TEV]. See this word at 1:2.

QUESTION—What relationship is indicated by δέ 'but'?

It indicates a contrast between 'the Jews and Gentiles' of 1:23, and 'the called ones' of 1:24 [Alf, Gdt, Herm, TH, TNTC].

QUESTION—What is implied in the phrase τοῖς κλητός 'the called'?

The actor is God [ICC, Lns, NIC, NIC2, TG; NIV, TEV]: to those whom God has called. 'The called' refers to the ones being saved of 1:18 [Alf, Lns, NIC2] or the believers of 1:21 [Gdt, ICC, Lns, NIC2]. They are called to faith and salvation [NIC], to God's kingdom [BAGD], to the blessings of redemption [Vn]. It implies that they have not only been called to God's kingdom, but that they have accepted the call [Gdt, Ho, ICC, Lns, NIC2, TNTC, Vn].

Christ (the) power[a] of-God and (the) wisdom[b] of-God;

LEXICON—a. δύναμις: 'power' [AB, He, HNTC, Lns; all versions except LB], 'mighty power' [LB], 'the supreme manifestation of (God's) power' [ICC]. See this word at 1:18.

b. σοφία: 'wisdom' [AB, He, HNTC, Lns; all versions except LB], 'God's wise plan' [LB], 'the supreme manifestation of (God's) wisdom' [ICC]. See this word at 1:17, 21.

QUESTION—What verb is implied before the word Χριστός 'Christ'?

1. The verb 'preach' is implied from verse 23 [EBC, EGT, Gdt, Lns, My, Rb]: we preach about Christ, the power of God and the wisdom of God. This is understood because 'Christ' is in the objective case and should be regarded as the direct object of 'preach' [Gdt].
2. The words 'he is' are implied [NJB, REB, TNT]: to them, he is Christ, the power of God and the wisdom of God.

QUESTION—In what way is Christ the power of God?

Christ is the supreme manifestation of God's power [Ed, ICC]. He demonstrates what God's power is [Ho, TG]. He has the power to save men from sin [EBC, Lns, NCBC, NIC2, TNTC, Vn]. He has the power to perform signs [Alf, EGT]. He is the power of God to defeat evil and set men free from its control [NCBC].

QUESTION—How is Christ the wisdom of God?

He shows how wise God is [Ed, TG]. Christ is the wisdom of God because through Him God solved the problem of deliverance from sin which their wisdom was unable to solve [NCBC]. Through Christ, God has revealed and carried out all that he has planned [Vn]. The doctrine of Christ crucified imparts true wisdom to people [Ho].

QUESTION—What is meant by the repetition of the words 'of God' in the phrases 'power of God' and 'wisdom of God'?

The repetition serves to emphasize that the source of power and wisdom was God [EGT, Lns, TH].

1:25 for[a] the foolishness[b] of God is wiser-than[c] men

LEXICON—a. ὅτι (LN 89.33) (BAGD 3.b. p. 589): 'for' [AB, BAGD, HNTC, ICC, LN; all versions except KJV, LB, NJB, REB], 'because' [Lns; KJV], 'since' [BAGD, LN], 'in view of the fact that' [LN], 'truly' [He], not explicit [LB, NJB, REB].

b. μωρός (LN 32.55; 32.58) (BAGD 2. p. 531): 'foolishness' [AB, BAGD, He, HNTC, Lns; all versions except LB, NAB, NJB, TEV], 'folly' [NAB, NJB, REB]. This word is also translated as a clause: 'what seems to be foolishness' [TEV], 'so-called "foolish" plan' [LB], 'what the Greek regards as the unwisdom (of God)' [ICC], 'the foolishness of God (in the judgment of unbelievers)' [BAGD]. See the noun form of this word at 1:18, 21.

c. σοφός (BAGD 4. p. 760): 'wiser than' [AB, He, HNTC, ICC, Lns; all versions]. See this word at 1:19. This is a condensed comparison meaning 'the foolishness of God is wiser than the wisdom of men' [ICC, NCBC, Rb; NIV, NJB, REB, TEV, TNT].

QUESTION—What relationship is indicated by ὅτι 'for'?

It indicates that this verse is the grounds for 1:24 [Alf, Ho, ICC, Lns, NIC, NIC2]: Christ is the power and wisdom of God since the foolishness of God is wiser than men and the weakness of God is stronger than men.

QUESTION—What is implied by μωρόν 'foolishness'?

The neuter of the adjective μωρός 'foolish' points to a particular act of foolishness [Alf, Ed, EGT, Gdt, HNTC, Ho, Lns, My, NIC, Rb, TNTC, Vn]. The particular thing pointed to is Christ crucified [Ed, EGT, Gdt, HNTC, Ho, Lns, My, NIC, TNTC, Vn]: God's foolishness of having Christ be crucified is wiser than men. This word therefore does not point to a character trait of God [Ed, Gdt, Lns, TH]. Further implied are the words 'in the opinion of men' [Alf, Ho, ICC, My, NIC, TG, TH, TNTC, Vn; TEV], or 'in the opinion of unbelievers' [BAGD]: 'foolishness in men's opinion'.

and the weakness[a] of God (is) stronger-than[b] men.[c]

LEXICON—a. ἀσθενής (LN 79.69) (BAGD 2.a. p. 115): 'weakness' [AB, BAGD, He, HNTC, Lns; all versions except TEV], 'what seems to be weakness' [TEV], 'what the Jew regards as the impotency (of God)' [ICC], 'weak' [BAGD, LN], 'feeble, miserable' [BAGD].

b. ἰσχυρός (LN 76.11) (BAGD 1.a. p. 383): 'stronger than' [AB, He, HNTC, ICC, Lns; all versions except LB, NAB], 'far stronger than' [LB], 'more powerful than' [NAB], 'strong, powerful' [BAGD, LN], 'mighty' [BAGD]. This is a condensed comparison meaning 'the weakness of God is stronger than the strength/power of men' [NCBC; NIV, NJB, REB, TEV, TNT].

c. ἄνθρωπος: 'men' [AB, He, HNTC, Lns; KJV, NAB, NASB, NIV, TNT], 'any man' [LB], 'human' [NJB, NRSV, REB, TEV], 'mankind' [ICC].

QUESTION—What is implied by ἀσθενής 'weakness'?

God's power at its very weakest is stronger than any power of men [ICC]. The neuter of the adjective ἀσθενής 'weak' is used and points to a particular act of weakness, Christ crucified [Alf, EGT, Gdt, Lns, My, TNTC]: God's weakness of having a crucified Messiah is wiser than men. This word therefore does not point to a character trait of God [Ed, Gdt, Lns, TH].

Further implied are the words: 'God's weakness in the opinion of men' [Alf, Ho, ICC, My, NIC, TG, TH; TEV].

DISCOURSE UNIT: 1:26–31 [AB, EGT, Herm, NIC2, TH, TNTC]. The topic is the shape of the community [Herm], the insignificance of the believers [TNTC], God's choice of the "nothings" [AB], the Corinthian believers [NIC2], the objects of the gospel call [EGT]. Now the theme changes to boasting and shows that the Corinthians themselves have nothing to boast about. The words 'for' and 'brothers' of 1:26 signal a turn in the argument [NIC2]. In this section the theme of weakness and folly is contrasted with strength and wisdom [TH].

1:26 For[a] consider[b] your calling[c], brothers,

LEXICON—a. γάρ: 'for' [He, ICC, Lns; KJV, NASB], 'indeed' [AB], 'in fact' [Gdt], 'now' [TEV], not explicit [LB, NAB, NIV, NJB, NRSV, REB, TNT]. This is also translated 'You can see what I mean' [HNTC].

b. pres. act. indic./impera. of βλέπω (LN **30.1**) (BAGD 4.b. p. 143): 'to consider' [BAGD, He, ICC, LN; NAB, NASB, NJB, NRSV, TNT], 'to note' [AB, BAGD], 'to notice' [LB], 'to think' [REB], 'to think of' [NIV], 'to remember' [TEV], 'to think about (what you were)' [**LN**], 'to see' [HNTC; KJV], 'to look at' [Lns], 'to direct one's attention to something, to take care' [BAGD].

c. κλῆσις (LN 33.312) (BAGD 1. p. 436): 'calling' [BAGD, Lns; KJV, NASB], 'calling as Christians' [He, HNTC], 'call' [BAGD, ICC; NRSV, TNT], 'invitation' [BAGD]. This noun is also translated as a clause: 'you are among those called' [NAB], 'whom God has called' [REB], 'when God called (you)' [TEV], 'when you were called' [AB], 'what you were when you were called' [NIV], 'how you were called' [NJB]. It is also translated from the perspective of the result of the call: 'you who follow Christ' [LB]. Here 'consider your call' implies, what happened when it occurred [BAGD]. Κλῆσις is derived from καλέω, meaning to urgently invite someone to accept responsibilities for a task resulting in a new relationship to the one doing the calling [LN].

QUESTION—What relationship is indicated by γάρ 'for'?

It indicates the grounds for the previous verse [Alf, HNTC, Ho, ICC, My, NIC, NIC2]: the foolishness of God is wiser than men and the weakness of God is stronger than men since not many of you were wise by men's standards, powerful, or nobly born, yet God chose you and not those who are wise, etc. It indicates that this paragraph and the next will give illustrations to support the point of 1:18–25 [NIC2].

QUESTION—Is the verb βλέπω 'consider' imperative or indicative?

1. The verb is imperative [AB, Alf, Ed, Gdt, ICC, My, NIC2, TNTC; all versions except KJV]: Consider your calling, brothers!
2. The verb is indicative [HNTC, NIC; KJV]: You see your calling, brothers.

QUESTION—What is the function of the word ἀδελφόι 'brothers'?

It functions to signal a turn in the argument as it does at 1:10 [NIC2].

QUESTION—Who is the implied actor of κλῆσις 'calling'?

God is the actor [EBC, HNTC, Ho, NIC2, TG, TH, TNTC; REB, TEV]: Consider your calling by God! This refers to their call to be saved [Ho, My, NIC, NIC2], to enter God's kingdom [BAGD]. God calls by means of his word and the Holy Spirit [Ho].

QUESTION—What were they to consider about their calling?

They were to consider the circumstances in which they were called [EBC, HNTC, ICC, TH], what took place when they were called [BAGD, HNTC, ICC, NIC], and what kind of people they were [HNTC, NIC2, TH, TNTC; REB].

that[a] not many[b] (of you were) wise[c]

LEXICON—a. ὅτι: 'that' [AB, Lns; LB, NASB], 'how that' [KJV], 'and you will see that' [He], 'for' [HNTC], not explicit [all other versions].

b. πολύς (LN 59.1) (BAGD 1.1.a.α. p. 687): 'many' [AB, BAGD, He, HNTC, LN, Lns; all versions except LB, REB, TEV], 'a great deal of, a great number of' [LN]. Some joined this word with the preceding οὐ 'not' and translated it positively: '(only) a few' [BAGD], 'few' [LB, REB, TEV], 'very few' [ICC], 'but few' [My].

c. σοφός: 'wise' [AB, He, HNTC, ICC, Lns; all versions except KJV, LB]. This adjective was also translated as a noun phrase: 'wise men' [KJV]; or as a clause: 'have big names' [LB]. See this word at 1:19.

QUESTION—What relationship is indicated by ὅτι 'that'?

It indicates that the following clause is to be treated as an apposition to the word 'calling' [ICC, Lns], and that this clause gives the specifics of the word 'calling' [ICC]: For consider your calling, specifically that not many of you were wise.

QUESTION—What verb is implied with the word σοφός 'wise'?

1. Some form of the verb 'to be' is implied [AB, Gdt, Herm, Lns, My, NIC2; all versions]: consider your calling, that not many (of you) were wise.
2. The verb 'to call' is implied [ICC]: consider your calling, that not many wise were called.

according-to[a] human-standards,[b]

LEXICON—a. κατά with accusative object (LN 89.4): 'according to' [He; NASB, TNT], 'with regard to' [LN], 'after' [Lns; KJV], 'by' [HNTC; NIV, NJB, NRSV, REB], 'from' [AB; TEV]. This preposition was also translated as a verb: 'as (men) count' [ICC], 'as (men) account' [NAB], not explicit [LB].

b. σάρξ (LN **26.7**) (BAGD 6. p. 744): 'human standards' [BAGD, EBC, HNTC, Ho; NIV, NJB, NRSV, TNT], 'any human standard' [REB], 'the human point of view' [**LN**; TEV], 'a human standpoint' [AB], 'flesh' [BAGD, He, Lns; KJV, NASB], 'men' [ICC; NAB], not explicit [LB]. What σάρξ indicates is the human nature with its reasoning and desires in contrast to the thoughts and behavior which relate to God and the spiritual life [LN].

QUESTION—With what is this phrase κατά σάρκα 'according to human standards' connected?

1. It is connected with all three adjectives: 'wise, mighty, and noble' [ICC, NIC2, Rb, Vn; TEV]: according to worldly standards, not many of you were wise, powerful, or of noble birth.
2. It is connected only with the adjective 'wise' [AB, Alf, EBC, Gdt, Herm, HNTC, Lns, My, TH; all versions except TEV]: not many of you were wise according to worldly standards, not many were powerful, not many were of noble birth. This is so because the word 'wise' is ambiguous and needs to be qualified but the other two do not [Alf, Herm]. It specifies the wisdom as being purely human and distinguishes it from Christian wisdom [My].

not many (were) powerful,[a] not many (were) well-born;[b]

LEXICON—a. δυνατός (LN 74.4) (BAGD 1.a.α. p. 208): 'powerful' [AB, BAGD, HNTC, Lns; NRSV, REB, TEV, TNT], 'mighty' [BAGD; KJV, NASB], 'strong, able' [BAGD], 'influential' [EBC; NAB, NIV, NJB], 'particularly capable, expert, competent' [LN]. This adjective is also translated as a prepositional phrase: 'of great influence' [ICC]. It is also translated as a verb phrase: '(you) have power' [LB]. It is also translated as a noun phrase: 'men of power' [He]. It here indicates powerful prominent people [BAGD]. It refers to those in high positions in government and religion [AB], in politics [EBC], or anyone having great influence [ICC, TNTC] or authority [Ho].

b. εὐγενής (LN **87.27**) (BAGD 1. p. 319): 'well-born' [AB, BAGD, Lns; NAB], 'high-born' [BAGD], 'nobly born' [HNTC], 'noble' [KJV, NASB], 'important' [LN]. This adjective is also translated as a prepositional phrase: 'of high status' [**LN**], 'of noble birth' [He; NIV, NRSV, REB, TNT], 'of high birth' [ICC], 'of high descent' [Ed, EGT, My], 'of high social standing' [TEV], 'from noble families' [NJB]. It was also translated as a verb phrase: 'to have wealth' [LB]. It has reference to high status, possibly implying special family relations [LN]. These would be free persons [AB, Ed, EGT], who were of the upper class [EBC, TNTC], descendants of ancient and noble ancestors [AB].

1:27 but[a] God chose[b] the foolish-(things)[c] of-the world,[d]

LEXICON—a. ἀλλά: 'but' [AB, He, HNTC; KJV, NASB, NIV, NRSV, TNT], 'on the contrary' [Lns], 'quite the contrary' [ICC], 'No' [My; NJB], 'No; but' [EGT], 'yet' [REB], 'instead' [LB], not explicit [NAB, TEV].

b. aorist mid. indic. of ἐκλέγομαι (LN 30.86; 30.92) (BAGD 3.b. p. 242): 'to choose' [AB, BAGD, He, HNTC, LN, Lns; all versions except LB, TEV], 'to deliberately choose' [LB], 'to choose for oneself' [BAGD, My], 'to select for oneself' [BAGD, EGT], 'to purposely choose' [TEV], 'to specially select' [ICC]. It means to make a special choice based on significant preference often implying a strongly favorable attitude toward what is chosen [LN]. The middle voice indicates that the action is done for one's own benefit [BAGD, EGT, Gdt, My, NIC].

c. μωρός (LN **32.58**) (BAGD 1. p. 531): 'foolish things' [AB, Lns; KJV, NASB, NIV], 'unwisdom' [ICC], 'those (whom the world considers) absurd' [NAB], 'those (who by human standards) are fools' [NJB], 'what (the world considers) nonsense' [**LN**; TEV], 'what (the world counts) foolish' [HNTC; LB, TNT], 'what (the world counts) folly' [REB], 'what is considered foolish' [BAGD], 'what is foolish' [He; NRSV]. See this word at 1:25.

d. κόσμος (BAGD 5.a. p. 446): 'world' [He; all versions except LB, NAB, NJB, REB, TEV], 'the world (as mankind)' [BAGD]. It is also translated as a prepositional phrase: 'by human standards' [NJB], a clause 'as the world considers' [LN; LB, NAB, REB, TEV].

QUESTION—What relationship is indicated by ἀλλά 'but'?

It indicates a positive restatement [EGT, Ho, My, NIC, TH]. Paul now states positively what he had just said negatively [Ho, My].

QUESTION—What words in these next two verses are emphasized?

The words 'God chose' are repeated three times and are emphasized [Ed, EGT, Gdt, Ho, Lns, My, TNTC]. The words 'of the world' are repeated three times and are emphasized [Ed]. The objects of the verb 'chose' plus phrases 'the foolish things', 'the weak things', 'the base things', and 'the despised things', are placed first in their propositions and are therefore emphasized [Gdt].

QUESTION—What does the neuter gender of the adjective μωρός 'foolish' indicate?

1. The neuter emphasizes the qualities and characteristics making up individuals rather than the individuals themselves [EBC, Ed, EGT, Gdt, Herm, Ho, My, NIC, Vn]. The context makes it evident that the persons included under this category are meant [Ho, My].
2. The neuter makes the reference indefinite [AB, Alf, NIC2, TNTC], to include both people and things such as the cross [AB, NIC2, TNTC]: God chose foolish things.

QUESTION—What do the words τοῦ κόσμου 'of the world' mean?

1. They mean 'belonging to the world/part of the world/pertaining to the world' [Alf, EBC, Ed, EGT, Gdt, Ho, ICC, My, TNTC; probably KJV, NIV]: God chose the weak things in the world.
2. They mean 'in the opinion of the world' [BAGD, He, HNTC, Lns, NIC, TG, TH, Vn; NAB, NJB, REB, TEV, TNT]: God chose the things that were foolish in the opinion of the world.

in-order-to[a] shame[b] the wise,[c]

LEXICON—a. ἵνα: 'in order to' [HNTC, ICC; LB, TEV], 'in order that' [Lns], 'to' [AB, He; all other versions].

b. pres. act. subj. of καταισχύνω (LN **25.194**) (BAGD 2. p. 410): 'to shame' [AB; all versions except KJV, TNT], 'to put someone to shame'

[BAGD, HNTC, ICC, **LN**, Lns; TNT], 'to confound' [He; KJV], 'to humiliate, to disgrace' [LN]. It means to cause someone to be greatly ashamed [LN].

c. σοφός: 'wise'. See this word at 1:19.

QUESTION—What relationship is indicated by ἵνα 'in order to'?

It indicates the purpose God had in choosing the foolish things [Herm, Lns, NIC2, TH, TNTC; probably all versions].

QUESTION—What is the meaning of καταισχύνω 'to shame'?

It means to shame or humiliate someone in the eyes of others [Herm, Lns, My, NIC2]. Their worthlessness will be made known whether or not they themselves are aware of it [My]. They will be discredited [TG, TH] and publicly humiliated [TH]. It is not primarily their mental condition, but the ignominy in which they are placed [Herm]. They will be shamed by the contrast between what they think of themselves and what is revealed by God's choice [NIC, TNTC]. They will be proved to be wrong [HNTC]. It includes their feeling ashamed of themselves [Ho, TH]. They will be convinced of the little value of the things on which they prided themselves [Ho].

QUESTION—Why is the word σοφός 'wise' in the masculine?

It brings attention to 'the men' who are wise [AB, HNTC, ICC, Lns; TNT].

and God chose the weak-things[a] of-the world, in-order-to[b] shame the strong,[c]

LEXICON—a. ἀσθενής (BAGD 2.a. p. 115): 'weak things' [Lns; KJV, NASB, NIV], 'feeble things' [AB], 'the weak' [NAB], 'uninfluential agencies' [ICC], 'those who (by human standards) are weak' [NJB]. '(ideas) of little worth' [LB]. This adjective is also translated as a clause: 'what (the world) considers weak' [HNTC; TEV, TNT], 'what is feeble/weak' [He; NRSV], 'what (the world) counts weakness' [REB], 'what is weak (in the eyes of the world)' [BAGD]. See this word at 1:25.

b. ἵνα: 'in order to' [HNTC, ICC; LB, TEV], 'in order that' [Lns], 'to' [all other versions]. This word indicates purpose [Lns, NIC2, TH].

c. ἰσχυρός (LN **76.11**) (BAGD 1.b. p. 383): 'strong' [NAB, NIV, NJB, NRSV], 'mighty' [AB], 'powerful' [**LN**; TEV], 'its strength' [ICC], 'things that are strong' [Lns; KJV, NASB], '(those) people considered by the world as great' [LB]. This adjective is also translated as a clause: 'what (it counts) strong' [HNTC], 'what is strong' [He; REB, TNT]. The emphasis is on physical strength [TNTC]. See this word at 1:25.

QUESTION—What does the neuter form of the adjective ἀσθενής 'weak' indicate?

1. The choice of the neuter emphasizes the meaning of the adjective rather than the individuals possessing these qualities [EBC, EGT, Gdt, Herm, My, NIC, Vn].
2. The neuter is chosen in order to make the reference indefinite [Alf, HNTC, Ho, Lns, NIC2], and include both people and things, including the

cross [NIC2]. Paul does this to keep from too direct a reference to the Corinthians themselves [HNTC].

1:28 and God chose the base-things[a] of-the world and the despised-things,[b]

LEXICON—a. ἀγενής (LN **87.59**) (BAGD p. 8): 'base things' [BAGD, Lns; KJV, NASB], 'insignificant things' [AB, BAGD], 'lowly things' [BAGD; NIV], 'things without rank' [REB], 'the low-born' [ICC, TH; NAB], 'those who (by human standards) are common' [NJB], 'what was inferior' [**LN**], 'what (the world counts) base' [HNTC], 'what is base/low' [He; NRSV], 'what (the world) looks down on' [TEV, TNT], not explicit [LB].

b. perf. pass. participle of ἐξουθενέω (LN 88.195) (BAGD 1. p. 277): 'to be despised' [BAGD, LN; NRSV], 'to be disdained' [BAGD], 'to be treated as of no account' [TNTC]. This participle is translated as a noun phrase: 'despised things' [NIV], 'despised agencies' [ICC], 'things which are despised' [KJV], 'the despised' [AB; NAB, NASB], 'things that are accounted as nothing' [Lns], 'things without standing' [REB], 'those who (by human standards) are contemptible' [NJB], 'what (the world) counts despised' [HNTC], 'what is despised' [He; NRSV], 'what (the world) despises' [TEV, TNT]. The perfect tense indicates an action that occurred in the past but is still in effect in the present [Lns].

QUESTION—What does the neuter form of the adjective ἀγενής 'base' indicate?

The word ἀγενής 'base things' literally means 'of low birth, not of noble birth' [BAGD, Ho, Lns, NIC, TG, TH, TNTC], and contrasts with the words εὐγενής 'of noble birth' of 1:26 [AB, HNTC, Lns, NIC, TG, TH, TNTC]. It refers to people of the slave class [EBC, NIC], to those who are not of noble families [EBC, TH], to inferior people [NIC], to those of low social standing [TG]. *Low-born* refers to their actual status while *despised* refers to how people regard them [Alf].

QUESTION—What does the neuter form of the adjective ἀσθενῆ 'weak' indicate?

1. The choice of the neuter emphasizes the meaning of the adjective rather than the individuals possessing these qualities [EBC, EGT, Gdt, Herm, My, NIC, Vn].
2. The neuter is chosen in order to make the reference indefinite [Alf, HNTC, Ho, NIC2], to include both people and things, including the cross [NIC2]. Paul does this to keep from too direct a reference to the Corinthians themselves [HNTC].

the-things not being,[a]

TEXT—Instead of τὰ μὴ ὄντα 'the things not being', some manuscripts have καὶ τὰ μὴ ὄντα 'and/even the things not being'. GNT selects the reading 'the things not being' with a B rating, indicating that the text is almost certain. The reading 'and/even the things not being' is taken by HNTC, ICC, Lns; KJV, NIV, NJB, TEV. If the καί is omitted, it may make the following phrase, 'the things not being', a summary of the preceding two classes 'low-born' and 'despised', rather than an additional class [AB, Alf, ICC, My, NIC2, TG]: God chose what is low-born and despised in the world, that is, things that are not. Or it may be a summary of all four preceding classes, the foolish, weak, low-born, and despised [Gdt, Lns; NJB].

LEXICON—a. pres. act. participle of μή εἰμί: 'to be'. The phrase is translated 'things that are not' [Lns; KJV, NASB, NIV, NRSV], 'the "nothings"' [AB], 'mere nothings' [REB], 'actual nonentities' [ICC], 'things that did not exist' [HNTC], 'those who count for nothing' [NAB, NJB], 'counted as nothing at all' [LB], 'what the world thinks is nothing' [TEV], 'what did not even exist' [TNT], 'what does not exist' [He].

QUESTION—Is the phrase 'things that are not' to be taken literally or figuratively?

1. It should be taken figuratively as the things that are so worthless are as though they did not exist in the world's opinion [Alf, EBC, Ed, EGT, Gdt, Herm, Ho, Lns, My, NIC, TG; NAB, NJB, TEV]: things that the world considers to be nothing. The negative word μή 'not', instead of οὐ 'not,' indicates a provisional kind of negative rather than an absolute negative [Alf, EGT, Gdt].
2. It should be taken literally since the things actually do not exist [HNTC]: things which have no real existence. When God made his plans, there was no church in Corinth [HNTC].

in-order-to[a] reduce-to-nothing[b] the-things being,[c]

LEXICON—a. ἵνα: 'in order to' [ICC; TEV], 'in order that' [AB, Lns], 'that' [HNTC; NASB], 'to' [all other versions except LB]. This conjunction is also translated as clause: 'used it to' [LB]. This word denotes purpose [Herm, Lns, TH]. See this word in the previous verse.

b. aorist act. subj. of καταργέω (LN **76.26**) (BAGD 1.b. p. 417): 'to reduce to nothing' [NAB, NJB, NRSV], 'to nullify' [AB, BAGD; NASB, NIV], 'to abolish' [BAGD, **LN**], 'to invalidate, to cause not to function' [LN], 'to make ineffective' [BAGD, TNTC], 'to bring down to nothing' [LB], 'to destroy' [TEV], 'to do away with' [HNTC], 'to make powerless, to make idle' [BAGD], 'to bring to nothing' [He, ICC, Lns; KJV], 'to overthrow' [REB, TNT].

c. pres. act. participle of εἰμί (BAGD I.1. p. 223): 'to be'. The phrase is translated 'things that are' [Lns; KJV, NASB, NIV, NRSV], 'things that are real enough' [ICC], 'existing things' [AB], 'existing order' [REB], 'those who were something' [NAB], 'those the world considers great' [LB], 'all those that do count for something' [NJB], 'what did exist' [HNTC], 'what does exist' [He; TNT], 'that which exists' [BAGD], 'what the world thinks is important' [TEV].

QUESTION—What are the things 'being' and how will they be reduced to nothing?

They are the persons who make their existence known [Ho], those who have authority in the world [NIC], the world powers [EGT], the wise and mighty

[Gdt], and everything that men count valuable and real [Lns]. Such people will be stripped of their power and glory [EGT], they will be made ineffective [ICC, TNTC], and they will have their influence nullified [EBC]. They will disappear from the scene [Gdt].

1:29 so-that[a] all flesh[b] might-boast[c] not before[d] God.

LEXICON—a. ὅπως (LN 89.59) (BAGD 2.a.α. p. 577): 'so that' [AB, He, LN; LB, NAB, NIV, NJB, NRSV], 'in order that' [BAGD], 'that' [HNTC, Lns; KJV, NASB, TNT], 'so' [REB]. This conjunction is also translated by a clause: 'he thus secured that' [ICC], 'this means that' [TEV].

b. σάρξ (LN 9.11) (BAGD 3. p. 743): 'flesh' [Lns; KJV], 'human being' [ICC, LN; NJB, TNT], 'human' [AB], 'person' [BAGD], 'man' [NASB], 'creature' [He], 'mankind' [NAB]. This word is also taken together with the word 'not' and translated as: 'no one' [HNTC; NIV, NRSV, TEV], 'no one anywhere' [LB], 'nobody' [BAGD]; or an adjective: 'any human (pride)' [REB].

c. aorist mid. subj. of καυχάομαι (LN 33.368) (BAGD 1. p. 425): 'to boast' [BAGD, He, LN; NAB, NASB, NIV, NRSV, TEV, TNT], 'to have anything to boast about' [ICC], 'to feel boastful' [NJB], 'to brag' [LB], 'to glory' [AB, BAGD, HNTC, Lns; KJV], 'to pride oneself in or about someone or something' [BAGD], 'to have place for pride' [REB]. It means to express a high degree of confidence in someone or something [LN]. In this context the meaning of 'boast' comes close to 'trust' or 'to put one's full confidence in': we tend to boast about the things we trust in this way [NIC2].

d. ἐνώπιον (LN 83.33) (BAGD 2.b. p. 270): 'before' [AB, He, ICC, LN; NAB, NASB, NIV, NJB, TNT], 'in the presence of' [BAGD, HNTC, Lns; KJV, LB, NRSV, REB, TEV], 'in the sight of' [BAGD].

QUESTION—What relationship is indicated by ὅπως 'so that'?

1. It indicates God's purpose [BAGD, Ed, EGT, Gdt, Herm, HNTC, Ho, Lns, My, NIC, NIC2, Rb, TNTC, Vn]: in order that no human being might boast in the presence of God. It indicates ultimate/final purpose in a series of subsidiary purposes indicated by ἵνα 'in order to' [Ed, EGT, Gdt, Herm, Ho, Lns, My, NIC2, Rb]: God chose the foolish in order to shame the wise; God chose the weak in order to shame the strong ... God chose the nothings in order to nullify the things that are, his ultimate purpose being that no flesh should boast in his presence.
2. It indicates the result of the process described in the previous context [ICC, TG, TH; TEV]: God chose the foolish to shame the wise; God chose the weak to shame the strong ... God chose the nothings to nullify the things that are, with the result that no one can boast in his presence.

QUESTION—Does the word μή 'not' negate 'flesh' or 'boast'?

It negates the verb 'to boast' [Alf, Gdt, ICC, My, NIC, NIC2, TH]: so that all flesh may not boast before God. This allows the phrase 'all flesh' to retain its inclusive meaning [Gdt].

QUESTION—What is the meaning of σάρξ 'flesh'?

It means people/man/mankind [AB, EBC, Ed, EGT, ICC, Lns, My, NIC, NIC2, TH, Vn; all versions except KJV]: all people. It means man in his fallen state [Lns], in his weakness [Ed, EGT, My] or imperfection [EGT, My], in his earthly existence [NIC], or in his human nature [Vn].

QUESTION—What is the implied topic about which one should not boast?

No one should boast that he is superior to someone else [TH], that he is wise, strong, or nobly born [My], that he has gained salvation by his own effort [EBC], that he has gained salvation by his own wisdom, birth, social standing, or anything else [Ho], that he has gained God's favor by his own ability [NIC2], that he has anything in himself worth boasting about [Herm].

1:30 But/Now[a] of[b] him you are in[c] Christ Jesus,

LEXICON—a. δέ: 'but' [HNTC; KJV, NASB, TEV], 'but on the other hand' [ICC], 'now' [Lns], 'for' [LB], not explicit [all other versions].

b. ἐκ (LN 89.25; 89.77; 90.16): 'of' [Lns; KJV], 'from' [LN], 'by means of' [LN], 'by' [ICC, LN; NJB], 'because of' [LN; NIV], 'thanks to' [He], 'related to' [HNTC]. The phrase 'of him' is translated 'from God/God's action' [AB; LB], 'it is by His will and bounty' [ICC], 'it is his doing' [NASB], 'God it is who has given (you life)' [NAB], 'by His doing' [NASB], 'by God's act' [REB, TNT], 'God has brought (you into union with)' [TEV], 'he is the source of (your life)' [NRSV].

c. ἐν (BAGD I.5.d. p. 259): 'in' [AB, BAGD, He, HNTC, Lns; all versions except LB, TEV], '(brought) into union with' [TEV], 'by adoption in' [ICC], 'through' [LB]. See this word at 1:2.

QUESTION—What relationship is indicated by δέ 'but/now'?

1. It indicates contrast [Alf, Ed, EGT, Gdt, He, ICC, My, NIC, NIC2, TNTC, Vn; KJV, NASB, TEV]: but. The contrast is between negative and positive [He]. The contrast is between the words ὑμεῖς 'you' and the 'worldly wise' of the preceding context [ICC, NIC2, TNTC, Vn], between their former low estate and their present union with Christ Jesus [Ed].
2. It indicates transition [Lns; LB]: now. Paul had begun addressing the Corinthians about their membership in the Kingdom of God in 1:26. In 1:27–29 he talks about the reasoning behind their membership. Now 1:30 again picks up the theme of membership [Lns].

QUESTION—What words are emphasized in this clause?

1. The words ἐξ ἀυτοῦ 'of him' should receive the main emphasis ('of him' comes first in the clause) [Ed, Lns, My, NIC2; LB, NAB, NIV, NJB]: It is of him that ...
2. The word ὑμεῖς 'you' is emphasized [HNTC, ICC, Lns, My, NIC2, TH, TNTC, Vn]: As for you ...

QUESTION—To whom does the word αὐτοῦ 'him' refer?

It refers to God [AB, EBC, Ed, EGT, Gdt, Herm, Ho, Lns, My, NIC2, TG, TH, TNTC; NAB, REB, TEV, TNT].

QUESTION—What is the meaning of this clause?

1. 'In Christ Jesus' is the predicate of 'you are': God is the source of their position in Christ [AB, EBC, Ed, Gdt, Ho, Lns, My, TG, TH; NASB, NIV, REB, TEV, TNT]: it comes from God that you are in Christ Jesus. God is the efficient cause that they are united to Christ [Ho]. It is God who has made them belong to Christ [TG]. It is God's work that they are Christians [My]. Because of God's plan they are in saving union with Christ [EBC].
2. 'In Christ Jesus' describes their existence: God is the source of their spiritual lives, such lives being in Christ [Alf, He, NCBC, TNTC; NAB, NJB, NRSV]: God brought it about that you exist, being in Christ Jesus. They derived their new life from God and this life is lived in close connection with Christ [TNTC]. God is the author of their spiritual life in union with Christ [Alf]. They have God to thank for their new form of existence, one which is in Christ by belonging to the body of Christ [He].
3. 'In Christ Jesus' indicates the means by which God gives them spiritual life [EGT, Gdt, HNTC, ICC, NIC, NIC2; LB]: God has given you life through Christ Jesus. They have received all their favors from God because of the work of Christ and the place they have is theirs only if they are closely united with Christ [NIC]. The new life God gave them is grounded in Christ [EGT]. Their Christian existence depends on God's call and the fact that the gospel is the message of the cross [HNTC]. They owed their existence to God's prior action which has been effected in history through Christ [NIC2].

who became[a] wisdom[b] to–us from[c] God,

LEXICON—a. aorist pass.-deponent indic. of γίνομαι (LN 13.48): 'to become' [AB, He, HNTC, ICC, LN, My; NASB, NIV, NRSV]. This is also translated as a true passive: 'to be made' [Lns; KJV, NJB]; as an active verb with God as the actor: 'to make' [NAB, REB, TNT], 'to make (Christ) to be' [TEV]. It is also translated actively with Christ as the actor: 'he showed (us God's plan of salvation)' [LB].

b. σοφία (BAGD 3.a. p. 760): 'wisdom' [AB, He, HNTC, ICC, Lns; all versions except LB], 'the true wisdom' [NIC2], 'God's plan of salvation' [LB], 'source of wisdom' [BAGD]. See this word at 1:17, 24.

c. ἀπό with genitive object (LN 90.7; 90.15) (BAGD V.4. p. 88): 'from' [AB, BAGD, He, LN, Lns; NASB, NIV, NJB, NRSV], 'manifested from' [ICC], 'of' [KJV], '(wisdom) that comes from (God)' [BAGD]. Some translated this word as indicating God as the agent: 'God's (gift)' [HNTC], 'God's (plan of salvation)' [LB], 'God (has made)' [TEV, TNT], 'by God's act' [REB], 'God it is who has given' [NAB].

QUESTION—What is the meaning of ἡμῖν 'us' in the dative case?

1. It means 'for us, in our behalf' [AB, EBC, Ed, He, HNTC, ICC, NIC2, TH; NIV, NJB]: Christ was made wisdom for our benefit. Through Christ we are made wise for salvation [EBC]. Christ manifests God's wisdom in

our behalf in that righteousness, sanctification, and redemption are the great necessities of man [Ed]. Christ crucified became the personal figure of Wisdom, God's means of restoring mankind to himself [HNTC].

2. It means 'to us' [Alf, Gdt, Ho, Lns, My, Vn; KJV, NASB]: Christ was made wisdom to us. For us, Christ takes the place of all earthly wisdom [Alf]. Christ revealed to us the knowledge of the divine plan of salvation [Gdt, Ho]. Union with Christ makes a person truly wise so as to know God, whose glory Christ revealed [Ho]. His manifestation and saving work revealed the plan of God [My]. He reveals to us the plans and effects of God's wisdom in the spiritual and practical application in what follows [Vn].
3. It indicates possession [TG, TH; NAB, NRSV, REB, TEV, TNT]: Christ was made our wisdom. Christ makes us wise, or Christ shows us how God is wise [TG]. Christ is the personification of God's wisdom so that God gives us his wisdom through Christ [TH].

QUESTION—With what are the words ἀπὸ θεοῦ 'from God' connected?

1. They are connected with the verb ἐγενήθη 'became'. This is then interpreted to mean 'made', with the phrase 'from God' meaning that God is the actor [Alf, Gdt, Herm, HNTC, Ho, NIC2; NAB, REB, TEV, TNT]: who was made by God to be wisdom for us. Or they are interpreted to mean 'came' [Ed]: who came from God and was seen to be wisdom for us.
2. They are connected with the word σοφία 'wisdom' [AB, EBC, EGT, NIC, Rb, Vn; NASB, NIV, NJB]: He became to us wisdom which is from God. This emphasizes the divine quality of wisdom that the Corinthians have in Christ in contrast to the wisdom of the world [EGT].

QUESTION—What is the relationship between the word 'wisdom' and the words 'righteousness', 'sanctification', and 'redemption'?

1. The last three explain the word 'wisdom' [EBC, Ed, EGT, Gdt, ICC, NCBC, NIC2, Rb, TH, TNTC, Vn; NIV]: wisdom, that is, righteousness and sanctification, and redemption. This is seen by use of the conjunctions τε καὶ…καὶ 'both…and…and' which unite the latter three nouns, but not the word wisdom [EBC, Ed, ICC]. Further reasons for accepting this interpretation are that the word σοφία 'wisdom' is separated from the word 'righteousness' by the words 'to us from God,' and that Paul has been showing that the gospel is the 'power' and 'wisdom' of God [Ed]. True wisdom did not involve intelligence, status, or rhetorical ability; it involved salvation through Jesus Christ [NIC2].
2. The last three qualities are additional qualities to 'wisdom' [AB, Alf, He, Herm, HNTC, Ho, Lns, My, NIC; probably KJV, NAB, NASB, NJB, NRSV, REB]: wisdom and righteousness and sanctification and redemption. The word τε 'both' connects 'wisdom' and 'righteousness,' and the two καίs 'and' add in 'sanctification' and 'redemption' [Lns].

righteousness[a] both-and[b] sanctification,[c]

LEXICON—a. δικαιοσύνη (LN 88.13; 34.46) (BAGD 3. p. 197): 'righteousness' [AB, BAGD, HNTC, ICC, LN (88.13), Lns; all versions except LB, NAB, NJB, TEV, TNT], 'justice' [NAB], 'saving justice' [NJB], 'justification' [He], 'uprightness' [BAGD]. This noun is also translated as a verb: 'to be put right with God' [TEV], 'to be restored in him' [TNT], 'acceptable to God' [LB]. It means the righteousness that is bestowed by God [BAGD]. It means doing what God requires [LN (88.13)], or to cause someone to be in right relationship with God [LN (34.46)].

b. τὲ καί (BAGD 3.a. p. 807): 'both ... and' [EGT, ICC], 'and also' [NAB], 'and ... and' [HNTC, Lns; KJV, NASB, NJB, NRSV], 'as well as ... and' [AB, He], 'and' [BAGD], not explicit [LB, REB, TEV, TNT]. This phrase indicates that 'righteousness' and 'sanctification' are to be grouped together as a unit [Alf, Gdt, Ho, My, TH]. See this combination at 1:24.

c. ἁγιασμός (LN 53.44) (BAGD p. 9): 'sanctification' [BAGD, He, HNTC, ICC, Lns; KJV, NAB, NASB, NRSV], 'holiness' [AB, BAGD; NIV, NJB, REB], 'consecration' [BAGD, LN], 'dedication' [LN]. This noun is also translated as an adjective phrase: 'pure and holy' [LB]; as a verb phrase: 'to become God's holy people' [TEV], 'to make (us) his people' [TNT]. Verbal nouns with the suffix -μος indicate primarily a process, then a resulting state [EGT]. Ἁγιασμός is derived from ἁγιάζω which means to dedicate to the service of and loyalty to God [LN]. See the verbal form of this word at 1:2.

QUESTION—What is meant by δικαιοσύνη 'righteousness'?

1. This is a legal term indicating acquittal from guilt by God [AB, Alf, EBC, Ed, EGT, Gdt, He, HNTC, Ho, Lns, My, NIC, NIC2, TH, TNTC; TEV, TNT]. This means the undeserved standing of innocence before God [NIC2]. Christ is our righteousness by putting us in right relationship with God [TG], by taking our sin upon himself [EBC].
2. It indicates a moral state of right living having to do with the good character of a man in day-to-day experience [ICC].
3. It includes both of the above [Herm, Vn]. It refers to the character of the justified person who is cleared of guilt before God and who expresses this effect in life [Vn].

QUESTION—What is meant by ἁγιασμός 'sanctification'?

1. It indicates a right relationship with God [HNTC, TG, TH; TNT]. This quality of 'holiness' is what is given to a believer by virtue of his relationship to Christ and enables him to approach God [HNTC]. This quality results from the action of God in making a person his own and setting him apart for his own purposes. Christ is our sanctification by making us God's people [TH].
2. It indicates the morally upright life of the believer [EBC, EGT, Gdt, Ho, ICC, Lns, My, NIC, NIC2]. This quality of holiness is seen in character revealed by good works. These are the natural outcome of Christ or His

Spirit being in us [Ho, Lns]. He becomes our sanctification by making possible our growth in the Christian life [EBC].

3. It includes both of the above [Vn]. It is both a matter of being set apart to God, and of bearing the character of God [Vn].

and redemption,[a]

LEXICON—a. ἀπολύτρωσις (LN 37.128) (BAGD 2.b. p. 96): 'redemption' [AB, He, HNTC, ICC, Lns; all versions except LB, REB, TEV, TNT], 'acquittal' [BAGD], 'liberation' [LN; REB], 'deliverance' [LN]. This noun is also translated as a verb: 'to be set free' [TEV, TNT], 'to give oneself to purchase something' [LB]. This originally referred to the 'buying back' of a slave or a captive, and 'making him free by the payment of a ransom price' [BAGD].

QUESTION—What is meant by ἀπολύτρωσις 'redemption'?

1. The emphasis is on the 'paying of a ransom' [TNTC]: whom God has made our ransom price. The ransom price was paid which was Christ's own body on Calvary [TNTC].
2. The emphasis here is on 'being set free' [EBC, Gdt, Ho, NIC2, TH, Vn; REB, TEV, TNT]: whom God has made our deliverance from sin.
3. Both are included [Ed, EGT, HNTC, My, NIC].

QUESTION—To what time does the word 'redemption' refer?

1. It refers primarily to a future event [Ed, Gdt, Ho, Lns, TNTC, Vn]. What is in view here is the final freedom from sin and death and entrance into glory [Lns]. Christ is our redemption in that he paid the ransom price [TNTC].
2. It refers primarily to a present condition [AB, Alf, EBC, He, HNTC, ICC, My, NIC, Rb]. Through Christ we are released from sin [AB, Alf, EBC, Ho], evil, [Ho], guilt, [AB, Ho], alienation, hostility [AB], the wrath of God [My], hell, the devil, and the grave [EBC, Ho]. Christ became our redemption by being the person who delivers us [EBC, Ho].
3. It includes both a present and a future reference [EGT].

1:31 in-order-that[a] as[b] it-has-been-written,[c] The-one boasting[d] let-him-boast in[e] (the) Lord.

LEXICON—a. ἵνα: 'in order that' [HNTC; NRSV], 'that' [Lns; KJV, NASB], 'so that' [AB, He, LN], 'therefore' [NIV, REB], 'so then' [TEV], 'so' [TNT], not explicit [LB, NAB, NJB]. This conjunction is also translated by a clause supplying implied information: 'God did all this in order that' [ICC].

b. καθώς: 'as' [AB, He; LB, NIV, NJB, NRSV, TEV, TNT], 'even as' [Lns], 'according as' [KJV], 'just as' [LN; NASB], '(each might take) as his guiding principle' [ICC], not explicit [HNTC; REB]. It is also translated with implied information added: 'this is just as you would find (it written)' [NAB]. 'As it is written' here has the meaning: 'in order to comply with what is written' [My].

c. perf. pass. indic. of γράφω: 'to be written' [AB, ICC, Lns; KJV, NAB, NASB, NIV, NRSV]. This verb is also translated as phrase: 'the written word' [HNTC], 'in the words of scripture' [REB]; or as a clause: 'as scripture says' [He; LB, NJB, TEV, TNT]. This is a condensed rendition of Jer. 9:23–24 [EBC, Ed, Ho, Lns, TG] which Paul adapts to the present context [NIC2]. It combines the LXX translation of Jer. 9:23–24 with 1 Sam. 2:10 [ICC]. See this word at 1:19.

d. pres. act. participle of καυχάομαι (LN **33.368**): 'to boast' [BAGD, He, **LN**; all versions except KJV], 'to glory' [AB, BAGD, HNTC, ICC, Lns; KJV]. See this word at 1:29.

e. ἐν: 'in' [AB, He, HNTC, ICC, LN, Lns; NAB, NASB, NIV, NRSV], 'about' [LN; TNT], 'of' [KJV, NJB, REB], 'of (what the Lord has done)' [LB, TEV].

QUESTION—What relationship is indicated by ἵνα 'in order that'?

1. It indicates purpose [EGT, HNTC, Ho, ICC, Lns, My, NIC, NIC2; NRSV]: God did this in order that, as it is written, "Let him who boasts, boast of the Lord." Since this purpose clause retains the imperative in the quotation, some supply a subjunctive "in order that *it may be* even as it is written ... " [NIC]. Others supply 'in order that the written word *might be fulfilled*' [HNTC], 'in order that *it might be confirmed* even as it is written' [NIC2]. Some think it should stand as a broken construction 'in order that, even as it is written, Let the one who boasts, boast in the Lord' [Lns, My; NRSV]. God's purpose in making wisdom, righteousness, sanctification, and redemption dependent on union with Christ, and that union dependent on God's own good pleasure is now given [Ho]. God's ultimate goal in choosing the foolish things of the world was to prevent human boasting (1:27) and here the final goal of the work of Christ was to make possible the one true ground for boasting [NIC2].
2. It indicates result or conclusion [AB, EBC, Ed, TH; NIV, REB, TEV, TNT]: therefore, as it is written, "Let him who boasts, boast of the Lord." Since God provided salvation in this way, all praise must go to the Lord [EBC]. Christ is the source of the spiritual privileges of justification, sanctification and redemption, therefore let the believer boast not in men but in Christ [Ed].

QUESTION—To whom does the word κύριος 'Lord' refer?

1. It refers to Jesus Christ [BAGD, Ed, EGT, Gdt, HNTC, Ho, ICC, NIC, NIC2, TG, TH, TNTC, Vn]: let him boast in the Lord Jesus Christ. This is supported by the fact that already Jesus has been referred to five times as 'Lord' in this chapter [EGT]. By applying the OT reference to Yahweh to Christ, no higher view could be taken of the person of Christ [TNTC].
2. It refers to God [Alf, EBC, Lns, My]: Let him boast in God. This is supported by the emphatic words 'of him' in 1:30, and the words 'in the presence of God' in 1:29 [My]. In Jeremiah the reference is to Yahweh and so it is here [Lns].

DISCOURSE UNIT: 2:1–16 [Ho, Lns, NIC]. The topic is a continuation of Paul's defense of his mode of preaching [Ho], the preachers of the wisdom of the cross [Lns], false and true wisdom [NIC].

DISCOURSE UNIT: 2:1–8 [AB]. The topic is Paul's personal demonstration of God's paradoxical wisdom.

DISCOURSE UNIT: 2:1–5 [Alf, EBC, Ed, EGT, GNT, Herm, HNTC, My, NCBC, NIC2, TG, TH, TNTC]. The topic is preaching Christ in the power of God [EBC], Paul's Corinthian mission [EGT], proclaiming Christ crucified [GNT], the figure of the preacher and the form of his preaching [Herm], a simple testimony [HNTC], Paul's reliance on spiritual power [NCBC], God's folly is Paul's preaching [NIC2], or Paul's preaching in divine power [TNTC]. This unit is tied together by Paul's two-part argument (2:1–2 and 3–5) both beginning with the words 'and I'. The first deals with the content of his preaching, the second with the form. The new unit is opened by the vocative 'Brothers!' as at 1:26 [NIC2].

2:1 And-I having-come to you, brothers, I-came not with[a] excellence[b] of-speech[c] or of-wisdom[d]

LEXICON—a. κατά with accusative object (LN 89.4; 89.113): 'with' [He, HNTC, LN (89.113), Lns; KJV, NAB, NASB, NIV, NJB, TNT], 'in' [NRSV], 'in relation to, in regard to' [LN (89.4)], not explicit [ICC]. This word is also translated with the preceding 'not': 'without' [AB; REB]. It is also translated as a verb: 'to use' [LB, TEV]. This refers to the form or manner of Paul's presentation [BAGD, EBC, Herm, Ho, My, NIC, NIC2]; he did not rely on rhetorical devices [EBC, Ho]. It means 'after the model of' or 'taking as my standard', saying that he did not follow the style of the orators and philosophers [Ed].

b. ὑπεροχή (LN **87.26**) (BAGD 1. p. 841): 'excellence' [AB], 'excellency' [Lns; KJV], 'superiority' [BAGD, TNTC, Vn; NASB, TNT], 'pre-eminence' [ICC, TNTC, Vn], 'brilliance' [NJB], 'prestige' [He], 'abundance' [BAGD]. This noun is also translated as an adjective: 'high sounding' [**LN**], 'preeminent' [HNTC], 'lofty' [LB, NRSV], 'big (words) ... great (learning)' [TEV], 'particular' [NAB], 'superior (wisdom)' [NIV], 'superior' [BAGD]. The phrase 'excellency of speech' is translated 'eloquence' [HNTC; NIV], 'particular eloquence' [NAB], 'pretensions to eloquence' [REB], 'oratory' [NJB]. This word implies a comparison, and here it must mean above the standard [NIC]. It indicates a state of high rank or position with the implication in some contexts of being too high or excessive 'high status, high sounding, pompous' [LN].

c. λόγος (LN 33.98): 'speech' [AB, ICC; KJV, NASB, TNT], 'statement' [LN, Lns], 'words' [LN; LB, NRSV, TEV], 'rhetoric' [He]. It means rational talk [HNTC]. Here the meaning focuses more on the form of speech than the content [NIC2]. See this word at 1:17.

d. σοφία (LN 28.8): 'wisdom' [AB, HNTC, ICC, Lns; all versions except LB, TEV], 'learning' [TEV], 'brilliant ideas' [LB], 'philosophy' [He], 'wise argument' [NJB], 'specialized knowledge, skill' [LN]. It means 'wordy cleverness' [HNTC]. This refers to the content of Paul's presentation [Ho, NIC], he did not rely on philosophical argument [EBC, Ho]. It refers to worldly wisdom and philosophy [Lns]. See this word at 1:17.

QUESTION—What is indicated by κἀγώ 'and I'?

It means 'and I, for my part' [NIC2], or 'and I also' [Gdt]. It is emphatic [EGT, HNTC, TH, TNTC]. It indicates that Paul's action now is in accordance with what he had just been talking about, having no reliance on human resources [Gdt, HNTC, Ho, ICC, My, NIC2, TNTC]. It serves to include Paul in the 'we' of 1:23 [Alf]. It includes Paul in the class of weak things with the Corinthians of 1:26 [EGT, TH, TNTC]. It joins Paul with the message of the Gospel, both being weak [Ed]. The word 'and' brings us back to the main thought, the word of the Cross (1:18) [NIC]. It indicates transition [Herm].

QUESTION—How are the nouns related in the genitive construction ὑπεροχὴν λόγου ἢ σοφίας 'excellence of speech or of wisdom'?

Because 'speech' and 'wisdom' are coordinate, 'excellence' applies to both [BAGD, EGT, Gdt, Herm, ICC, Lns, NIC, TNTC]. The words 'of speech' and 'of wisdom' define 'excellence' [Lns]. Speech and wisdom refer to the form and content of Paul's preaching [Ho, NIC]. Paul did not claim excellence in the way he presented his facts or in the way in which his mind arranged the facts [TNTC]. Effective use of language and skill of argumentation were not preeminent in Paul's evangelism [HNTC].

QUESTION—With what is the phrase 'with excellence' connected?

1. It is connected with the preceding verb 'having come' [AB, EBC, EGT, Herm, Ho; NASB, NIV, NJB, TNT]: I did not come with excellence of speech or wisdom to announce the mystery of God.
2. It is connected with the following verb 'announcing' [Ed, ICC, My; NRSV]: when I came, I did not announce the mystery of God with excellence of speech or wisdom.
3. It is connected with the combined verbal phrase 'come announcing' [Gdt, Lns, NIC; NAB]: I did not come announcing the mystery of God with excellence of speech or wisdom.

announcing[a] to-you the mystery[b] of God.

TEXT—Instead of μυστήριον 'mystery', some manuscripts have μαρτύριον 'testimony'. GNT selects 'mystery' with a B rating, indicating that the text is almost certain. AB, EBC, Ed, GNT, He, Rb, TH, Vn, NJB, NRSV, TEV, and TNT also accept 'mystery'. The reading 'testimony' is taken by EGT, Gdt, Herm, HNTC, Ho, ICC, Lns, My, NIC, NIC2, TNTC, KJV, LB, NAB, NASB, REB, and NIV.

LEXICON—a. pres. act. participle of καταγγέλλω (LN 33.204) (BAGD 1. p. 409): 'to announce' [He, LN; NJB], 'to proclaim' [AB, HNTC, ICC, Lns; NAB, NASB, NIV, NRSV, TNT], 'to proclaim solemnly' [BAGD], 'to tell' [LB], 'to declare' [KJV, REB], 'to preach' [TEV], 'to proclaim throughout, to speak out about' [LN]. The present tense indicates what he kept doing wherever he went [NIC] and the manner in which Paul occupied his time in Corinth [Ed, ICC]. This gives Paul's purpose in coming [NIC, TNTC]

b. μυστήριον (LN 28.77) (BAGD 2. p. 530): 'mystery' [AB, BAGD, He, LN; NJB], 'secret' [BAGD, LN], 'secret truth' [TEV], 'secret purpose' [TNT]. In the NT it refers to God's secret thoughts or plans which are kept secret from human reason but revealed to those whom God chooses [BAGD]. In Pauline usage it refers to a 'secret' or 'mystery' too profound for human ingenuity [BAGD, Vn]. Its content has not previously been known but now it has been revealed to a restricted group [LN, TG]. It means something not as fully understood at one time as it was at another [EBC]. The secret refers to justification by Christ's crucifixion and to victory over death by the resurrection [AB].

b. (alternate reading) μαρτύριον (LN 33.264) (BAGD 1.b. p. 494): 'testimony' [HNTC, ICC, LN, Lns; KJV, NAB, NASB, NIV], 'truth' [REB], 'message' [LB]. 'To proclaim a testimony' is to speak in plain and simple language [ICC]. See this word at 1:6.

QUESTION—How are the nouns related in the genitive construction τὸ μυστήριον/μαρτύριον τοῦ θεοῦ 'the mystery/testimony of God'?

1. 'Mystery of God' means the mystery or secret which belongs to God [TH], God's secret purpose [TNT], God's secret truth [TEV], or the mystery which God revealed [EBC, Ed].
2. 'Testimony of God' means the testimony about God [Alf, HNTC, ICC, My, NIC2; NIV]. The content of Paul's preaching was what God has done through Christ to bring salvation particularly through the crucifixion [NIC2], or the message of God's love for man as seen in Christ's saving work [ICC, My].
3. 'Testimony of God' means the testimony that God gave [EGT, Gdt, Ho, NIC]. It is what God revealed and affirmed to be true [Ho]. This includes the idea that God is the cause or initiator and that Paul is the actual speaker [EGT, Gdt].

2:2 For[a] I-decided[b] not to-know[c] anything among you except Jesus Christ and him crucified.[d]

LEXICON—a. γάρ (LN 89.23): 'for' [AB, He, HNTC, ICC, LN, Lns; KJV, LB, NASB, NIV, NRSV, TEV], not explicit [NAB, NJB, REB, TNT].

b. aorist act. indic. of κρίνω (LN **30.75**) (BAGD 3. p. 451): 'to decide' [AB, BAGD, He, LN, Lns; LB, NRSV, TNT], 'to make up one's mind' [**LN**; TEV], 'to determine' [KJV, NAB, NASB], 'to resolve' [HNTC; NIV,

REB], 'to think fit' [ICC], 'to reach a decision, to propose, to intend' [BAGD], 'to be resolved' [Herm; NJB].

c. perf. act. infin. of οἶδα (LN 28.1): 'to know' [AB, He, HNTC, ICC, LN, Lns; KJV, NASB, NIV, NRSV, TNT], 'to claim to know' [REB], 'to have knowledge' [LN; NJB], 'to speak of' [LB, NAB], 'to know about, to be acquainted with' [LN]. This word is also combined with the preceding 'not' and translated 'to forget (everything)' [TEV]. Οἶδα is the perfect form of γινώσκω and means to possess information about something [LN].

d. perf. pass. participle of σταυρόω (LN 20.76): 'to be crucified' [AB, He, HNTC, ICC, LN, Lns; all versions except LB, REB, TEV], 'to be nailed to a cross' [REB]. This word is also translated as a noun phrase: 'his death on the cross' [LB, TEV]. The force of the perfect participle is to state the reality of the event of the crucifixion [EBC, TH] and its present effects [AB, EBC, TH]. See this word at 1:13.

QUESTION—What relationship is indicated by γάρ 'for'?

1. It indicates the reason why Paul did not use excellency of speech or wisdom [EBC, Ed, Gdt, Ho, NIC, NIC2]: I did not use excellence of speech or wisdom because I decided only to know Christ.
2. It indicates that Paul will now explain in greater detail what he said in 2:1 [Herm, ICC, Lns, TH]. I did not use excellence of speech or wisdom; that is, I decided only to know Christ. He not only did not speak of anything else but Christ, he also had no thought of anything else [ICC].

QUESTION—With what is the word οὐ 'not' connected?

1. It is connected with 'I decided' [Alf, EBC, EGT, Gdt, Ho, ICC, My, Rb, Vn]: I did not judge it fit/good to know anything except Jesus Christ.
2. It is connected with 'to know' [Ed; KJV, LB, REB, TEV]: I decided not to know anything except Jesus Christ.
3. It is connected with 'anything' [AB, Herm, HNTC; NAB, NASB, NIV, NRSV, TNT]: I decided to know nothing except Jesus Christ.
4. It is connected with the whole clause and therefore negates either 'to know' or 'anything' [NIC2].

QUESTION—What is meant by 'knowing' nothing except Jesus Christ?

'Know' has an unusual meaning here. Paul meant that Jesus Christ was to be the only topic he preached about [AB]. His focus was on the gospel about the crucified Messiah [NIC2]. It means to pay attention to, or to emphasize, Christ and especially his crucifixion [HNTC, TG]. This refers not to general knowledge but to theological knowledge [Herm]. He did not care to know anything beyond Christ [ICC]. He did not present only a portion of the gospel, since Jesus Christ as the crucified one is a summary of the entire gospel. He omitted any addition of worldly wisdom to it [Ho, Lns]. Christ crucified refers to his death, sacrifice, atonement, substitution, and reconciliation [Lns].

QUESTION—Where is the emphasis in this clause?

The emphasis is on the words 'and him crucified' [Ed, Ho, ICC, Lns, NIC2, TG, TH; TEV]: to know nothing except Jesus Christ and especially his crucifixion. If the word Christ is taken as meaning 'Messiah', the object of 'to know' would then be, 'Jesus as Messiah', but (I would only know) him as a crucified Messiah [TH]. Paul thinks of the person and work of the Messiah as the essence of the whole gospel, and the crucifixion (and resurrection) as the real meaning of his work [ICC]. Christ as a propitiation was Paul's message [Ho].

2:3 And-I came/was[a] to/with[b] you in weakness[c] and in fear[d] and in much trembling,[e]

LEXICON—a. aorist mid. indic. of γίνομαι (LN 85.6) (BAGD II.4.a. p. 160): 'to come' [HNTC,; all versions except KJV, NASB, TNT], 'to be' [BAGD, My, NIC2; KJV, NASB, TNT], 'to be (in a place)' [LN], 'to appear' [AB], 'to get (face to face)' [Lns], 'to pay a visit' [ICC], 'to be present' [He].

b. πρός with accusative object (LN 89.112): 'to' [HNTC, ICC; LB, NIV, NRSV, TEV], 'with' [He, LN; KJV, NASB, TNT], 'face to face with' [Lns], 'among' [NAB, NJB], 'before' [AB, LN; REB]. The usual meaning of πρός is: 'to be in company with someone' [NIC2].

c. ἀσθένεια (LN **25.269**) (BAGD 2. p. 115): 'weakness' [AB, BAGD, HNTC, ICC, Lns; all versions except TEV, TNT], 'a condition of great weakness' [He], 'timidity' [BAGD, **LN**]. This noun is also translated as a verb: 'to be weak' [TEV, TNT].

d. φόβος (LN 25.251) (BAGD 2.a.α. p. 863): 'fear' [AB, BAGD, He, HNTC, LN, Lns; all versions except LB, TNT], 'timidity' [ICC], 'alarm, fright' [BAGD]. This noun is also translated as a verb: 'to be apprehensive' [TNT]; as an adjective: 'timid' [LB].

e. τρόμος (LN **16.6**) (BAGD p. 827): 'trembling' [AB, He, **LN**, Lns; KJV, LB, NASB, NIV, NJB, NRSV], 'trepidation' [HNTC; NAB, REB], 'painful nervousness' [ICC], 'quivering (from fear)' [BAGD]. This noun is also translated as a verbal phrase: 'to tremble all over' [TEV], 'to be afraid' [TNT].

QUESTION—What relationship is indicated by κἀγώ 'and I'?

It indicates additional information about Paul beyond that given in 2:1–2 [Lns]. It indicates a shift from Paul's preaching to his person [Gdt, NIC]. Paul, as well as his preaching, was marked by weakness [Ed, HNTC].

QUESTION—What is meant by ἐγενόμην πρὸς ὑμᾶς 'I came to you, I was with you'?

1. The focus is on his condition when he arrived [HNTC, ICC, Rb; LB, NAB, NIV, NJB, NRSV, REB, TEV]: when I came to you I was weak.
2. The focus is on his condition during the time he was with them [Ed, EGT, Gdt, He, Ho, My, NIC, NIC2, TH; KJV, NASB, TNT]: I was with you in weakness. He not only came to them, but was among them with weakness

[Ed]. He showed weakness in his ongoing relationship with them [NIC2]. This refers to both his public teaching and his private conversations [Gdt].

QUESTION—What is meant by ἀσθένεια 'weakness'?

1. It refers to Paul's poor physical condition or sickness [AB, Lns, NIC2, TH, Vn]: I was not well while I was with you. The word ἀσθένεια is the normal one for sickness, and probably refers to Paul's sufferings and hardships [NIC2]. This is the illness referred to as a thorn in the flesh in 2 Cor. 12:7 [Vn].
2. It refers to his mental attitude about his own abilities to do what he had to do [Alf, BAGD, EBC, Ed, Ho, My, NCBC]: I felt very inadequate when I was with you. This was because Paul was unable to rely on human wisdom and strength [My]. He had a work to do that he felt was beyond his ability [Ho]. He refers to this again in 2 Cor. 10:10 [Alf].
3. Both physical and mental weakness is indicated [EGT, ICC]: I was not well and I felt very inadequate while I was with you. It could include his shyness, anxiety, consciousness of the wickedness of Corinth and hostility of the Jews, as well as the illness mentioned in Gal. 4:13 [ICC].

QUESTION—What did he fear and tremble about?

He feared and trembled under the sense of the importance of the work and his responsibility in it [Alf, EBC, Ed, Gdt, HNTC, Ho, ICC]. Paul's fear was not of men, but of the possible failure to accomplish the great task God had called him to do [Lns, NIC, TNTC]. It grew from a sense of personal inadequacy [Ho, NCBC].

2:4 and[a] my speech[b] and my preaching[c] (were) not with[d] persuasive[e] words[f] of-wisdom

TEXT—Some manuscripts add the word ἀνθρωπίνης 'human' to 'wisdom'. GNT omits this word with a C rating indicating difficulty in deciding to omit it. Only Ho, KJV, and LB include it.

LEXICON—a. καί: 'and' [He, HNTC, ICC, Lns; KJV, LB, NASB, NJB, TEV], not explicit [AB; NAB, NIV, NRSV, REB, TNT].

b. λόγος (LN 33.98; 33.99): 'speech' [AB, ICC, LN (33.99); KJV, NRSV, TNT], 'message' [NAB, NASB, NIV], 'teaching' [TEV], 'argument' [HNTC], 'discussions' [He], 'statement' [LN (33.98), Lns], 'the word I spoke' [REB], 'what I spoke' [NJB], not explicit [LB]. Λόγος can refer to the content of communication, 'word, saying, message, statement' [LN (33.98)], or it can refer to the act of speaking [LN (33.99)]. See this word at 1:17, 2:1.

c. κηρύγμα (LN 33.258): 'preaching' [He, LN, Lns; KJV, LB, NAB, NASB, NIV], 'message' [ICC; TEV], 'proclamation' [AB, BAGD, HNTC; NRSV, TNT], 'what is preached' [LN], 'what is proclaimed' [NJB], 'the gospel that is proclaimed' [REB]. See this word at 1:21.

d. ἐν with dative object (LN 89.94): 'with' [LN; KJV, LB, NIV, NRSV, REB], 'in' [Lns; NASB], 'by' [NJB]. This preposition is also translated as a verb: 'to use' [TNT], 'to have' [NAB], 'to be expressed in' [AB], 'to be conveyed in' [ICC], 'to aim at' [He], 'to be enforced by' [HNTC], 'to be delivered with' [TEV]. It means 'to consist of' or 'to be set forth in' [Alf].

e. πειθός (LN **33.304, 33.306**) (BAGD p. 639): 'persuasive' [AB, BAGD, HNTC, ICC, **LN**, Lns; NASB, NIV, TNT], 'plausible' [NRSV], 'skillful' [TEV], 'convincing' [LN], 'enticing' [KJV]. This adjective is also translated as a noun phrase: 'persuasive force' [NAB]. It is also translated as a verb: 'to sway (with clever arguments)' [REB], 'to convince' [NJB]. If the alternate reading is chosen (one without the sigma, making the word 'persuasive' a noun), the meaning would be: 'with the persuasive power of (human) wisdom' [**LN**].

f. λόγος (LN 33.98): 'word' [AB, HNTC, ICC, LN, Lns; KJV, NASB, NRSV, TEV, TNT], 'words' [NIV], 'argument(s)' [NJB, REB], 'argumentation' [NAB], not explicit [He]. This word was also joined with πειθός 'persuasive' and translated 'oratory' [LB].

QUESTION—How do the words λόγος 'speech' and κήρυγμα 'preaching' differ in meaning?

There are a variety of explanations. 'Speech' means talk in general or private speech while 'preaching' means public discourse [Ho, Lns, My]. 'Speech' means the message of the Gospel, while 'preaching' means the act of proclaiming it [Ed, ICC, NIC2]. 'Speech' means the contents of what Paul said, while 'preaching' means the form or proclamation of it [Gdt, NIC, NIC2]. 'Speech' refers to the form or manner of his presentation, 'preaching' refers to the contents [Vn]. 'Speech' refers to Paul's reasoned argument, while 'preaching' refers to his proclamation of the life, death and resurrection [TH]. There is no difference in meaning, they are a rhetorical doublet [Herm; LB]. The repetition of two similar words is for emphasis [Lns, TH]. There is little difference between the terms. Probably together they stress the message he preached and the way he preached it [TNTC]. The repetition of the word 'my' (*my* speech and *my* preaching) is emphatic, contrasting Paul's message with the message of the philosophers [Ed].

QUESTION—How are the nouns related in the genitive construction σοφίας λόγοις 'words of wisdom'?

These are not words about wisdom, but words directed by worldly wisdom [HNTC]. This refers to persuasive words which are suggested by worldly wisdom [Ho]. False 'wisdom' was especially directed to the art of using persuasive words [ICC]. Paul did not object to the use of persuasive words, but he did object to those words being directed by worldly wisdom [NIC].

but[a] in demonstration[b] of-(the)-Spirit and of-power,[c]

LEXICON—a. ἀλλά (LN 89.125): 'but' [AB, He, HNTC, LN, Lns; all versions except REB], 'no' [ICC], not explicit [REB].

b. ἀπόδειξις (LN **28.52**) (BAGD p. 89): 'demonstration' [AB, He, Lns; KJV, NASB, NIV, NRSV, TNT], 'proof' [BAGD, EGT, Ho, LN, Lns, NIC2, TNTC, Vn], 'evidence' [**LN**], 'convincing proof' [TEV], 'conviction' [REB], 'cogency' [ICC], 'manifestation' [HNTC], 'verification, indication' [LN]. This noun is also translated as an adjective: 'convincing' [NAB]. It is also translated as a verb: 'to prove' [LB], 'to demonstrate' [NJB]. It means 'the most rigorous proof' [ICC, TNTC]. In Greek rhetoric it was a technical term for a compelling conclusion drawn from logical premises [NIC2]. This clause means proof consisting in possession of the Spirit and power [BAGD]. It is proof from facts or documents as opposed to theoretical reasoning [EGT]. This word indicates the clearness produced in the hearer's mind [Gdt].

c. δύναμις: 'power'. See this word at 1:18.

QUESTION—How are the nouns related in the genitive construction ἀποδείξει πνεύματος καὶ δυνάμεως 'demonstration of the Spirit and power'?

1. The Spirit is the subject of 'demonstrated' and 'power' adds the manner [AB, Ed, EGT, Gdt, Ho, My, NCBC, Vn]: the Spirit powerfully convinced the hearers that Paul's preaching was true. The Spirit did this in the minds of the hearers [AB, Alf, Ed, Gdt, Ho, NCBC]. He bore testimony to the truth of the gospel [Ho]. He brought clear understanding and conviction of the truth [Gdt] and applied the message to the conscience [NCBC]. He illuminated the mind and moved the will [Ed]. He won the people to belief and obedience [AB]. The Spirit acted in the minds of the preacher and the hearers to produce conviction [Gdt]. In addition, the Spirit also convinced them through his powerful actions in changing lives of others and by miracles [EGT].
2. The Spirit's power is the object of 'demonstrated' [Lns, TG, TH, TNTC; TEV]: Paul's preaching demonstrated the Spirit's power. It showed that the Spirit and his saving power were present [Lns]. In the light of Paul's weakness, the hearers' conviction brought about by his preaching demonstrated the power of the Spirit [TNTC]. His message was delivered in a way that proved how powerful the Spirit is [TG].
3. The Holy Spirit and God's power are the subjects of 'demonstrated' [Alf, ICC, My, NIC]: they demonstrated that Paul's preaching was true. They did not do this by miracles, but by the production of a strong conviction in the hearers and by the power to save [ICC]. They persuaded the hearers of the truth of Paul's preaching [Alf, My, NIC]. They manifested themselves in the preaching and so demonstrated the truth of the gospel [NIC].
4. The Spirit and his power are both subjects and objects of 'demonstrated' [HNTC, NIC2]: the Spirit powerfully worked in the hearers through the preaching and the results of the preaching was evidence that the Spirit was present in power. The Spirit's power was demonstrated in the hearers' conversion and their reception of the Spirit [NIC2].

2:5 so-that[a] your faith[b] may-be[c] not in the-wisdom of-men but[d] in the-power of-God.

LEXICON—a. ἵνα (LN 89.59; 89.49): 'so that' [He; NIV, NJB, NRSV, REB], 'in order that' [AB, Ho], 'that' [HNTC, Lns; KJV, NASB, TNT], 'as a consequence' [NAB], 'then' [TEV]. This conjunction is also translated as a clause expressing implied information: 'for God intended that' [ICC], 'I did this because' [LB].

b. πίστις (LN 31.102) (BAGD 2.d.α. p. 663): 'faith' [AB, BAGD, He, HNTC, ICC, Lns; all versions], 'Christian faith' [LN]. Faith is the act of believing [Ed, My, NIC, TG, TH, TNTC]. Another view is that it is the substance of what they believed, their Christian faith [EBC].

c. pres. act. subj. of εἰμί (BAGD III.4. p. 225): 'to be' [AB, Lns]. With ἐν 'in', this verb is translated 'to rest' [BAGD, He, ICC, NIC; NAB, NASB, NIV, NRSV, TEV], 'to depend' [HNTC; NJB, TNT], 'to stand' [KJV], 'to be built' [REB], 'to stand firmly' [LB], 'to arise from something' [BAGD]. It means 'to be rooted in', 'to depend on' [ICC], 'to be based on' [My]. Paul knew that a faith founded on logical argumentation could be refuted by logical argumentation [Gdt, ICC, TNTC, Vn].

d. ἀλλά (LN 89.125): 'but' [AB, He, HNTC, LN, Lns; all versions except LB]. Two translations reversed the clauses putting the positive clause first and carrying the contrast simply with the word 'not' [ICC; LB]: so that your faith might rest in God's power, *not* in the wisdom of men. This word serves to contrast the phrases 'in the wisdom of men' and 'in the power of God' [EBC, Herm].

QUESTION—What relationship is indicated by ἵνα 'so that'?

1. It indicates purpose [AB, EBC, Ed, EGT, Gdt, Herm, Ho, ICC, Lns, My, NIC, NIC2, Rb, TH, TNTC, Vn; LB, NIV, NJB, NRSV, REB]: my speech was in demonstration of the Spirit *in order that* your faith might not rest in men's wisdom. While the purpose refers primarily to 1:4, it refers to 1:1–4 as well [Lns].

1.1 It indicates God's purpose [Ed, Herm, ICC, Lns, My, NIC, Rb, TH, Vn]: my speech was in demonstration of the Spirit *for God intended* that your faith not rest in men's wisdom.

1.2 It indicates Paul's purpose [EBC, EGT, Gdt, Ho, TNTC; LB]: my speech was in demonstration of the Spirit *because I wanted* your faith not to rest in men's wisdom.

2. It indicates result [NAB, TEV]: my speech was in demonstration of the Spirit *and as a result* your faith rests not in men's wisdom.

QUESTION—What is the meaning of the phrase ᾖ ἐν 'may be in'?

It is causal in force [Alf, EBC, Ed, My, NIC, TG, TH]: so that men's wisdom *might not cause* your faith, but that God's power might cause it. It means 'to be in union with' [Lns]: that your faith might not be in union with men's wisdom, but in union with the power of God. Ἐν indicates the sphere in which faith had its roots [Vn]: that your faith *might not grow out of* men's wisdom but out of God's power. It means 'to be based on' [Gdt, ICC, My, TNTC, Vn; KJV, LB, REB]: so that your faith might not be based on men's wisdom but on God's power. Ἐν 'in' marks the object of one's faith, here (men's wisdom) [Ed]: that you might not believe in men's wisdom, but in God's power.

DISCOURSE UNIT: 2:6–3:4 [Ed, Gdt, ICC, Vn]. The topic is a second argument against the factions [Ed], the gospel containing a wisdom [Gdt], the true wisdom [ICC], the true wisdom, and a contrast in the Church at Corinth [Vn].

DISCOURSE UNIT: 2:6–16 [Alf, EBC, GNT, Herm, HNTC, My, NIC2, TG, TH, TNTC]. The topic is the wisdom of Christ revealed by the Holy Spirit [EBC], the revelation by God's Spirit [GNT], hidden wisdom [Herm], wisdom, false and true [HNTC], God's wisdom revealed by the Spirit [NIC2], a revealed message [TNTC]. This unit is an argument in three parts: 1:6–10a, the nature of God's wisdom; 1:10b–13, who this wisdom is for; 1:14–16, reaffirmation and conclusion [NIC2].

DISCOURSE UNIT: 2:6–13 [ICC, NCBC]. The topic is the true wisdom described [ICC], the hidden wisdom of God [NCBC].

DISCOURSE UNIT: 2:6–9 [EBC, Ed, EGT, TNTC]. The topic is Christianity as God's wisdom [Ed], the gospel considered as wisdom [EGT], the gospel not being human wisdom [TNTC].

2:6 Yet[a] among[b] the-mature[c] we-speak[d] wisdom,[e]

LEXICON—a. δέ (LN 89.124): 'yet' [LB, NASB, NRSV, TEV], 'but still' [NJB], 'however' [HNTC; NIV, TNT], 'not that' [ICC], 'howbeit' [KJV], 'nevertheless' [He, My], 'now' [AB, Lns], 'to be sure' [NAB], not explicit [REB].

b. ἐν with dative object (LN 83.9) (BAGD I.3. p. 258): 'among' [Ed, EGT, Gdt, Ho, LN, My; all versions except NJB, REB, TEV], 'to' [NJB, REB, TEV], 'in the presence of' [BAGD]. It means 'in the eyes of (those who are fully grown)' [NIC]. When Paul uses ἐν with λαλέω, he means 'to speak among' as though in a group with other speakers besides himself [HNTC].

c. τέλειος (LN 88.100) (BAGD 2.a.β. p 809): 'the mature' [BAGD; NIV, NRSV, REB, TNT], 'the spiritually mature' [NAB], 'spiritual adults' [BAGD], 'mature Christians' [He, HNTC; LB], 'those whose faith is ripe' [ICC], 'those who are mature' [AB; NASB], 'those who are spiritually mature' [TEV], 'those who have reached maturity' [NJB], 'the adult, the full-grown' [BAGD], 'mature, grown up' [LN], 'them that are perfect' [KJV], 'those perfected' [Lns].

d. pres. act. indic. of λαλέω (LN 33.70) (BAGD 2.b. p. 463): 'to speak' [AB, BAGD, HNTC, LN, Lns; KJV, LB, NASB, NRSV, REB], 'to speak a message of' [NIV], 'to impart' [ICC], 'to proclaim a message of' [TEV], 'to talk of' [NJB], 'to express' [NAB], 'to use the language of' [TNT], 'to teach' [He], 'to discourse of, to assert, to proclaim, to say' [BAGD].

e. σοφία (LN **32.37**): 'wisdom' [AB, HNTC, ICC, **LN**, Lns; KJV, NASB, NJB, NRSV], 'a wisdom' [AB, He; NJB], 'a certain wisdom' [NAB], 'a message of wisdom' [NIV, TEV], 'the language of wisdom' [TNT], 'words of wisdom' [REB], 'great wisdom' [LB], 'insight, understanding' [LN]. This word is in an emphatic position [Ho, Lns, TNTC].

QUESTION—What relationship is indicated by δέ 'yet'?

It indicates an contrastive relationship with the preceding [Alf, Gdt, Herm, HNTC, ICC, Lns, NIC2; KJV, LB, NASB, NIV, NRSV, TEV, TNT]: but. Only worldly wisdom is excluded from his preaching [TNTC]. It is both adversative and continuative [Lns]: yet further. In spite of all that he has written, he does speak wisdom, but of a different kind [Ho, NIC, NIC2, TH, TNTC]. It indicates a modification or limit on the previous idea that the cross is not wisdom [Gdt]: yet, we do speak wisdom, etc.

QUESTION—To whom does the word τέλειος 'mature' refer?

1. It refers to only some of the Christians, the mature ones, and contrasts them with immature Christians [Alf, Ed, EGT, Gdt, He, Herm, HNTC, ICC, My, NCBC, NIC, Rb, TH, Vn; probably NAB, TEV]: among mature Christians. The word 'mature' contrasts with the words 'infants' of 3:1 [ICC, NIC]. With the growth of Christian character comes a development of the capacity to discern spiritual things [Ed]. The 'mature' refers to all in the Corinthian church who valued Paul's preaching as true wisdom. This group contrasted with those who still valued highly the wisdom of the world and despised Paul's preaching [NIC].
2. It refers to all Christians and contrasts them with non-Christians [AB, EBC, Ho, Lns, NIC2, TNTC]: among Christians. If the 'mature' means advanced Christians, then the wisdom Paul preached is not the gospel, but its higher teachings. However, the wisdom of the following context does not refer to higher doctrines but to the gospel itself. Also the contrast here is between the wisdom of the world and the wisdom of God, not between lower and higher doctrines of the gospel. Further, those who despised Paul's doctrine were not babes in Christ, but the unbelievers [Ho]. It refers to the mature insight of the saved in contrast with the thinking of the unsaved [TNTC]. All those 'in Christ' are the mature, and thus includes all the Corinthian believers. However, in their behavior, they act as mere babes and Paul wants them to adopt the thinking that goes along with being mature in Christ [NIC2].

QUESTION—What is the meaning of λαλέω 'to speak'?

1. It refers to private communication or teaching as opposed to public proclamation [Gdt, He]: we talk among ourselves about wisdom.
2. It simply means 'to utter' and no distinction can be made for private as opposed to public speech [ICC, Vn]: we speak words about wisdom.

QUESTION—To whom does the pronoun 'we' refer?

1. It refers to Paul and other teachers [Alf, Ed, ICC, Lns, My, NIC, TNTC, Vn]. If it is taken with this meaning, it is the exclusive use of 'we' meaning Paul and other teachers (not the readers) [TG]. The others teachers are the Apostles [Alf, ICC, My] and all faithful preachers [NIC, Vn].

2. It is editorial and refers to Paul alone [Gdt, Herm, NIC2; LB, REB, TEV]. He is not speaking of preaching in general, but rather is justifying the manner in which he himself preached in Corinth [Gdt].

but[a] not a-wisdom of this age[b] nor of-the rulers[c] of this age the-ones doomed-to-perish;[d]

LEXICON—a. δέ (LN 89.124): 'but' [He, ICC; LB, NIV, TEV, TNT], 'however' [NAB, NASB], 'though' [NRSV, REB], 'yet' [Lns; KJV], 'that is' [AB]. This word is also translated as a clause: 'not, it is true' [NJB], 'only it is' [HNTC].

b. αἰών (LN 67.143): 'age' [AB, He, HNTC, ICC, LN; all versions except KJV, LB, REB, TEV], 'present age' [BAGD; REB], 'time' [BAGD], 'world' [KJV, TEV], 'world age' [Lns], '(that comes from) here on earth' [LB]. See this word at 1:20.

c. ἄρχων (LN 37.56) (BAGD 2./3. p. 113–14): 'ruler' [AB, He, HNTC, LN, Lns; all versions except KJV, LB, REB, TEV], 'power that rules' [TEV], 'governor' [LN], 'governing power' [REB], 'leader' [ICC], 'prince' [KJV], 'great man' [LB]. Ἄρχων refers generally to 'authorities' or 'officials'. It is possible in the 1 Cor. 2:6–8 passage that ἄρχων refers to evil spirits [BAGD].

d. pres. pass. participle of καταργέω (LN 13.100) (BAGD 2. p. 417): 'to be doomed to perish' [BAGD; NRSV], 'to pass away' [BAGD; NASB], 'to be headed for destruction' [NAB], 'to be on the way to destruction' [He], 'to come to nothing' [Lns; KJV, NIV], 'to be brought to nothing' [HNTC], 'to already be in decline' [REB], 'to be overthrown' [TNT], 'to be losing one's power' [TEV], 'to be about to pass away' [AB], 'to not last long' [NJB], 'to have one's influence be destined to decline' [ICC], 'to be doomed to fall' [LB]. Actively, καταργέω means 'to cause to come to an end, to cause to become nothing, to put an end to' [LN]. The present tense emphasizes the continual passing away of these rulers [EBC, NIC].

QUESTION—What relationship is indicated by δέ 'but/now'?

It indicates an explanation [AB, HNTC, ICC, Lns]: yet/now, by wisdom, I do not mean a wisdom of this age. It indicates resumption of the idea of 'wisdom' [Gdt]: now, as to wisdom, not a wisdom of this age.

QUESTION—How are the nouns related in the genitive construction σοφίαν τοῦ αἰῶνος 'wisdom of this age'?

It means a wisdom belonging to this age [AB, HNTC, Ho, ICC, TG; TEV]. It means a wisdom that is taught by this world [TG, TH]. It means a wisdom coming from the world [EBC]. The 'world-age' characterizes the quality of this type of wisdom [Lns]. Therefore it cannot be attained by men of this world [Ho].

QUESTION—What is meant by ἄρχων 'rulers'?

1. It refers to human rulers [AB, Alf, EBC, Ed, EGT, Gdt, Ho, ICC, Lns, My, NIC, NIC2, TNTC, Vn]. The context shows a contrast between God's wisdom and men's, not that of demons [TNTC, Vn]. Further, the

rulers of 2:8 who crucified Jesus are best understood as being the Jewish and Roman leaders. And the word ἄρχων 'rulers' is used repeatedly for Roman and Jewish leaders (Acts 3:17; 4:5, 8, 26; Rom. 3:13) [TNTC]. It refers to the leaders responsible for the crucifixion, and to leaders in general, including the 'wise ones' of 1:20, 26 [NIC2]. This term includes all those who have great influence due to their wisdom, birth, or power [Ho].

2. It refers to spiritual beings [Herm, HNTC, TG, TH]. Paul understood the present world-order to be controlled by supernatural beings. It is their wisdom which they perhaps communicated to men that Paul was referring to [HNTC]. It refers to evil spiritual powers who exercise their power through human beings [TG].

QUESTION—How are the nouns related in the genitive construction σοφίαν τῶν ἀρχόντων 'wisdom of the rulers'?

It means a wisdom possessed by the rulers [Lns, TG, TH], or taught by the rulers [TG]. Or it means a wisdom controlled by the rulers [NCBC].

2:7 but[a] we-speak[b] (the) wisdom of-God in a-mystery[c] (a wisdom which) has-been-hidden,[d]

LEXICON—a. ἀλλά (LN 89.125): 'but' [AB, LN; KJV, NASB, NRSV], 'no' [HNTC; NAB, NIV, TNT], 'on the contrary' [He, ICC, LN, Lns], not explicit [LB, NJB, REB, TEV].

b. pres. act. indic. of λαλέω: 'to speak'. See this word at 2:6.

c. μυστήριον: 'a mystery'. See this word at 2:1.

d. perf. pass. participle of ἀποκρύπτω (LN **28.80**) (BAGD p. 93): 'to be hidden' [AB, BAGD, He, Lns; all versions except KJV, NRSV], 'to be concealed' [BAGD, **LN**], 'to be kept secret' [BAGD, LN], 'to be kept hitherto secret' [ICC]. It is also translated as an adjective: 'hidden (wisdom)' [HNTC; KJV, NRSV]. The participle modifies wisdom: 'hidden wisdom' [HNTC, Lns, TNTC; KJV, NRSV]. The agent of the passive verb 'hidden' is God [Ed, Lns] and the force of the perfect indicates that it is still hidden, still mysterious [Lns]. Although now revealed to believers, it is still hidden to all others [TNTC].

QUESTION—What relationship is indicated by ἀλλά 'but'?

It indicates an adversative relationship [AB, EGT, Gdt, Herm, HNTC, ICC, Lns, NIC, NIC2, TH, TNTC; KJV, NAB, NASB, NIV, NRSV, TNT]. The contrast is between the wisdom of this verse and the wisdom of the previous verse [TNTC].

QUESTION—To what is the phrase ἐν μυστηρίῳ 'in mystery' connected?

1. It is to be connected with the word 'wisdom' [Gdt, HNTC, ICC, Lns, NIC, NIC2, Vn; NAB, NIV, NJB, NRSV, TEV, TNT]: we speak a mysterious or secret wisdom. The fact that this wisdom is also described as 'hidden' forces us to accept this interpretation [HNTC]. This mystery has been hidden in God until such a time as he was ready to reveal it [NIC2].

2. It is to be connected with the phrase 'we speak' [Alf, Ed, EGT, My]: we speak in a mystery the wisdom of God. He speaks as handling a mystery [Alf].

QUESTION—How are the nouns related in the genitive construction θεοῦ σοφίαν 'wisdom of God'?

It means wisdom that originates with God [Gdt, Ho, Lns, NIC2], or that God possesses [Alf, Gdt, My, NIC2]. It is wisdom derived from God, a wisdom he has revealed [Ho]. Because 'wisdom' lacks an article, the phrase means 'divine wisdom' [NIC]. 'Wisdom' here refers to the gospel [ICC, NCBC, Vn]. It refers to salvation through a crucified Messiah [NIC2].

QUESTION—What word is emphasized in this clause?

The word θεοῦ 'of God' is emphasized [Alf, ICC, My, NIC2, Rb, TNTC, Vn]: it is God's wisdom we speak about. In 2:6 the emphasis is on 'wisdom'; in this verse it is on 'we speak' [Ed].

which God predestined[a] before the ages[b] for[c] our glory,[d]

LEXICON—a. aorist act. indic. of προορίζω (LN 30.84) (BAGD p. 709): 'to predestine' [BAGD; NASB, NJB], 'to destine' [He; NIV], 'to predetermine' [AB], 'to determine ahead of time' [LN], 'to determine' [HNTC], 'to foreordain' [Lns, TNTC], 'to decide upon something beforehand' [BAGD, LN], 'to plan' [NAB, TNT], 'to decree' [NRSV], 'to ordain' [ICC; KJV], 'to chose' [TEV], 'to frame' [REB], 'to make for someone's benefit' [LB].

b. αἰών (LN 67.143): 'ages' [AB, He, LN; NASB, NRSV], 'world ages' [Lns], 'all ages' [NAB], '(from before) all time' [ICC], '(from) the very beginning' [REB], '(before) the world' [KJV]. This word is also translated as a clause: '(before) time began' [LB, NIV, TNT], '(before) the world was made' [TEV], '(before) the course of ages began' [HNTC], '(before) the ages began' [NJB]. It denotes an age and here it is in the plural, meaning that God's wisdom, the gospel, was planned by him before any spans of time began [Vn]. It denotes the world existing in time [NIC].

c. εἴς with accusative object (LN 90.41; 89.57): 'for' [HNTC, ICC, LN (90.41); NAB, NIV, NRSV, TEV, TNT], 'with a view to' [Herm], 'unto' [Lns; KJV], 'to' [He; NASB], 'for one's benefit' [LN (90.41); LB], 'for the purpose of, in order to' [LN (89.57)]. This preposition is also translated as a verbal phrase: 'to bring us to' [REB], 'to be for' [NJB], 'to contribute to' [AB]. It denotes 'in order to', and indicates the purpose of God's preordination [Alf, Herm, Lns].

d. δόξα (BAGD 1.b.β. p. 203): 'glory' [AB, He, HNTC, Lns; all versions except LB, REB], 'glories of heaven' [LB], 'our destined glory' [REB], 'eternal salvation' [ICC], 'brightness, splendor, radiance' [BAGD]. Here δόξα means the complete salvation of believers [ICC, Vn]. The disciples' participation in the radiance or glory describes the state of being in the next life [BAGD].

QUESTION—What is the antecedent of the relative pronoun ἥν 'which'?
The antecedent is God's wisdom [Ed, NIC2, Rb]. It refers to Christ crucified (1:18–24) [ICC], the scheme of redemption [Ho]. The mature believer sees God's wisdom in the plan of redemption [Ed]. What has been pre-planned is technically God's wisdom, but what Paul has in mind is God's loving activity in Christ to give eternal life to his people [NIC2].

QUESTION—What is meant by δόξα 'glory'?

1. It indicates a final state into which the believer is changed at the end of time [EBC, ICC, Lns, My, NCBC, NIC2, TNTC; LB]. It is the final goal of the Christian when he sees the Lord as he is and is made like him [Lns]. This glory begins at the Second Coming of Christ [My]. It is perfect conformity to the exalted Christ [NCBC].
2. It means a sharing in the glory of God at the present time [EGT, Ho, TH]. It means living close to God and sharing his own power and life [TH]. It means all the benefits of salvation [Ho]. This is not heavenly glory, it denotes the complete ministry of the Spirit changing the believer from glory to glory into the image of the Lord (2 Corinthians 3:8–18) [EGT].
3. It means both of the above [HNTC, Vn]. It signifies a state the believer enters at conversion, then a process in which the believer is changed by stages to resemble the character of Christ, then the consummation at the Rapture when he will be completely changed into the Lord's likeness [Vn].

2:8 which none of-the rulers[a] of this age has-understood;[b]

LEXICON—a. ἄρχων: 'rulers'. See this word at 2:6.

b. perf. act. indic. of γινώσκω (LN 32.16; 28.1) (BAGD 3.a. p. 161): 'to understand' [BAGD; LB, NASB, NIV, NRSV, TNT], 'to come to understand' [LN (32.16)], 'to comprehend' [BAGD, LN (32.16)], 'to know' [AB, He, HNTC, LN (28.1), Lns; KJV, NAB, REB, TEV], 'to recognize' [NJB], 'to acquire knowledge' [ICC], 'to know about, to have knowledge of' [LN (28.1)]. It denotes personal knowledge as opposed to merely a knowledge of facts [TH]. It denotes true understanding and realization [Lns]. 'Knowing' includes the sense of acknowledging [NIC].

QUESTION—To what does the relative pronoun 'which' refer?

1. It refers to the word 'wisdom' of 2:7 [AB, Alf, EBC, Ed, EGT, Gdt, He, Herm, HNTC, Ho, ICC, Lns, My, NIC, TH; KJV, NASB, NIV, NJB, REB, TEV, TNT]: none of the rulers of this age knew this wisdom. They did not understand God's plan of salvation nor did they recognize Christ as God's agent to save the world [HNTC].
2. It refers to the word mystery [NAB]: none of the rulers of this age knew this mystery.

for[a] if they-had-known, they-would-have-crucified not the Lord of glory.[b]

LEXICON—a. γάρ (LN 89.23): 'for' [AB, HNTC, ICC, LN, Lns; KJV, NASB, NIV, NJB, NRSV], not explicit [He; LB, NAB, REB, TEV, TNT].

b. δόξα (BAGD 1.a. p. 203): 'glory' [He, HNTC, Lns; all versions]. This noun is also translated as an adjective: 'glorious (Lord)' [AB]; or as a clause: 'whose essential attribute is glory' [ICC]. God's glory denotes God's saving power [TG]. Here δόξα is used literally meaning: 'brightness, splendor' or 'radiance', and refers to Christ [BAGD]. See this word at 2:7.

QUESTION—What relationship is indicated by γάρ 'for'?

It indicates the grounds for saying that they did not understand [Ho, ICC].

QUESTION—How are the nouns related in the genitive construction τὸν κύριον τῆς δόξης 'the Lord of glory'?

The word 'glory' modifies 'Lord' [Ed, EGT, HNTC, Ho, ICC, Lns, My, Rb, TH, TNTC]: glorious Lord. 'Glory' is his characteristic quality [EGT, Rb], his essential attribute [ICC]. Jesus is glorious because he shares in God's being and belongs to the heavenly realm [HNTC]. This phrase means the Son who possesses all the divine character traits which are summed up in the word 'glory' [Lns]. This phrase brings out the contrast between the indignity of crucifixion and the majesty of the Lord [Gdt, ICC, Lns, My, Vn]. The modifying phrase 'of glory' is emphatic [ICC, My].

DISCOURSE UNIT: 2:9–13 [AB]. The topic is the Spirit as revealer of God's wisdom.

2:9 But[a] as it-is-written,

LEXICON—a. ἀλλά (LN 89.125): 'but' [AB, HNTC, ICC, LN, Lns; all versions except LB, NAB, NIV, TEV], 'however' [NIV, TEV], 'on the contrary' [He, LN], not explicit [LB, NAB].

QUESTION—What relationship is indicated by ἀλλά 'but' ?

It indicates a contrast with the negatives of 2:8 [Alf, EGT, He, HNTC, ICC, Lns, My, NIC2, TH]: the rulers did *not* know ... but God has revealed it to those who love him.

QUESTION—Why is Scripture referred to?

The quotation from the Old Testament is given in support of the argument of 2:6–8 [NIC2]: the rulers did not understand because God's wisdom has not entered man's mind. Elliptical information is supplied: but 'it has happened' as it is written [Rb]; but 'it could not be otherwise for' as it is written [Gdt]; but 'in contrast with any of them knowing this wisdom' what is written 'is true about them' [ICC]; but 'this wisdom has been revealed' as it is written [HNTC]; but, 'in contrast with what the rulers did, the Scripture was fulfilled' as it is written [NIC], but 'it is' as scripture says [NJB], 'that is what is meant by' [LB].

QUESTION—What scripture is referred to?

Paul seems to have put together several passages [AB, NIC2]. It may be a reference to Isa. 64:4 [Alf, EBC, EGT, Gdt, He, ICC, Lns, NCBC, NIC, NIC2, Rb, TG, TH, TNTC, Vn] and Isa. 65:17 [Alf, EBC, EGT, Gdt, ICC, Lns, NIC, Rb, TNTC, Vn]; or Isa. 52:15 [Rb, TG, TH, TNTC]; or LXX Isa. 64:3 [NIC, NIC2]. The perfect tense indicates that the scripture still stands as authoritative [Ed]. Although 'it is written' is often used to quote specific Scripture, it might mean here 'to use the language of Scripture' or 'to speak generally from Scripture' [EBC]. Paul is not citing Scripture, but illustrating his argument with OT expressions [Alf].

"The-things-which eye saw not and ear heard not and into (the) heart[a] of-man entered[b] not, the-things-which God prepared[c] for-the-ones loving[d] him."

LEXICON—a. καρδία (LN 30.17) (BAGD 1.b.β. p. 403): 'heart' [ICC, Lns; KJV, NASB, NRSV], 'mind' [AB, BAGD, HNTC, TNTC; NIV, NJB, TNT], 'consciousness' [He], not explicit [LB, NAB, REB, TEV]. Καρδία was considered to be the center of physical, spiritual, and mental life. It was considered to be the center and source of the whole inner life: its thinking, feeling, and volition. It refers to the faculty of thought and understanding, and the organ of natural and spiritual enlightenment [BAGD]. The heart was considered to be the organ of thinking [He]. 'Heart' indicated the inner life, including thought, will, and emotions [TNTC].

b. aorist act. indic. of ἀναβαίνω (LN **30.17**) (BAGD 2. p. 50): 'to enter' [He, HNTC, ICC, Lns; KJV, NASB, TNT]. This word is also combined with 'into the heart' and translated 'to dawn on' [NAB], 'to occur (to mind)' [AB, Ho], 'to think could happen' [**LN**; TEV], 'to imagine' [LB, REB], '(heart/mind) to conceive' [NIV, NRSV], '(mind) to visualize' [NJB], 'to begin to think, to think, to have a thought occur to someone' [LN]. The phrase ἀναβαίνω ἐπὶ καρδίαν 'to enter the heart' is figurative for 'entering the mind' or 'conceiving in the mind' [BAGD, LN, Lns].

c. aorist act. indic. of ἑτοιμάζω (LN 77.3) (BAGD 3. p. 316): 'to prepare' [AB, BAGD, He, HNTC, ICC, LN; all versions except LB], 'to have ready' [LB], 'to make ready' [LN, Lns], 'to put or keep in readiness' [BAGD].

d. pres. act. participle of ἀγαπάω (LN 25.43) (BAGD 1.a.β. p. 4): 'to love' [AB, BAGD, He, HNTC, ICC, LN, Lns; all versions], 'to cherish' [BAGD], 'to regard with affection' [LN]. It means to love someone with sincere appreciation and high regard [LN].

QUESTION—To what is this scripture quotation connected?

1. It is the object of an implied 'we speak' from 2:7 [Ed, EGT, Lns, My]: we speak of the things which no eye has seen ...
2. It is the object of 'God revealed' of 2:10 [Alf, He, HNTC; NRSV]: God revealed the things which no eye has seen ...
3. It is not grammatically connected to anything and stands as a unit in itself.

3.1 The last clause is the main clause, the first three are the objects [NIC, NIC2, TG, TH; LB, NJB, TEV, TNT]: God prepared for those who love him what no eye has seen, ear heard, or mind conceived. This interpretation puts the emphasis on the last clause [NIC2, TH] which is the point of the argument beginning at 2:6, and requires that the second ἅ 'what things (God prepared)' function like a ταῦτα 'these things' [NIC2].

3.2 The last clause is the object of the first three clauses [KJV, NAB, NIV]: eye has not seen, ear has not heard, the mind has not imagined the things that God has prepared for those loving him.

3.3 The unit has no main verb [AB, EBC, Gdt, Herm, Ho, ICC; NASB]: what eye has not seen, nor ear heard, nor the mind of man thought of, what God has prepared for those loving him. That this is true is due to the Apostles' quoting of scripture without weaving them into the grammar of their own discourses [Ho].

QUESTION—What is the antecedent of the two occurrences of ἅ 'the things which' in the phrases '*the things which* eye has not seen', '*the things which* God has prepared'?

They refer back to the word 'wisdom' and its pronoun 'which' of 2:7, 8 [EBC, EGT, Gdt, HNTC, ICC, Lns, My].

DISCOURSE UNIT: 2:10–3:2 [EGT]. The topic is the revealing Spirit.

DISCOURSE UNIT: 2:10–13 [Ed, TNTC]. The topic is God's wisdom revealed inwardly by the Spirit [Ed], words 'taught by the Spirit' [TNTC].

2:10 But God revealed[a] to-us through[b] the Spirit;

TEXT—Instead of δέ 'but', some manuscripts have γάρ 'for'. GNT selects 'but' with a B rating indicating that the text is almost certain. The reading δέ 'but' is taken by EBC, Gdt, GNT, HNTC, Ho, Lns, TG, TH, Vn, KJV, LB, NAB, NIV, and TEV. The contrast is between the mysteriousness of what God prepared and what the Spirit revealed [Gdt, HNTC], and between the ignorance of the rulers and the revelation to the Corinthians [HNTC]. The contrast is between 'us' and the rulers who know not [Gdt]. The reading γάρ 'for' is taken by EGT, He, Herm, ICC, NIC, NIC2, Rb, and NASB. The 'for' gives the reason Paul could speak of things otherwise hidden [ICC, NIC2, Rb] and explains why they were no longer hidden [Rb].

LEXICON—a. aorist act. indic. of ἀποκαλύπτω (LN 28.38) (BAGD 2. p. 92): 'to reveal' [AB, BAGD, He, HNTC; all versions except LB, NJB, TEV], 'to make revelation' [Lns], 'to give revelation' [NJB], 'to unveil these mysteries' [ICC], 'to make known his secret' [TEV], 'to tell about' [LB], 'to disclose, to make fully known' [LN], 'to uncover' [BAGD]. The aorist indicates a definite time when this revelation took place [ICC, NIC], at the time when the Gospel entered the world [EGT, ICC], or at the times their individual lives of faith began [Vn].

b. διά with genitive object (LN 90.4): 'through' [AB, HNTC, LN, Lns; all versions except KJV, LB, NIV, TEV], 'by' [He; KJV, NIV], 'by means of' [TEV], 'through the operation of' [ICC]. This word is also translated by making 'the Spirit' the agent of 'reveal': '(God sent) his Spirit (to tell us)' [LB]. It denotes agent [Gdt].

QUESTION—Who is included in the phrase ἡμῖν 'to us'?

1. It refers to the apostles or other leaders [EBC, Gdt, Ho, Lns, My]: God revealed to us apostles and preachers. Paul is referring back to the words 'we speak' of 2:6–7 [Gdt, Lns]. It refers to the apostles and prophets [Ho].
2. It refers to all believers [Ed, ICC, NCBC, NIC, NIC2, TG, TNTC, Vn]: God revealed to all of us. The emphatic position of 'to us' places these words right next to the words 'those who love him' meaning, 'to those who love him, namely, to us' [ICC, NIC2]. Specifically, it refers to the 'mature' of 2:6 [Ed].

QUESTION—What words are emphasized in this clause?

The words ἡμῖν 'to us' are emphasized [Gdt, Herm, ICC, Lns, My, NIC2, TNTC; TEV]. These words are in emphatic contrast to the rulers of 2:8 [ICC].

QUESTION—What is it that God revealed?

It is the things that God prepared (2:9) [AB, HNTC, My, NIC2, Rb; KJV, NASB, TNT]. It is God's wisdom which was hidden (2:7) [Lns, NIC2, TH, Vn; NAB, NIV, TEV]. It is the fact that Christ is God's wisdom [NIC]. It is the significance of Christ, his death, and benefits for those who believe the good news [AB].

for the Spirit searches[a] all-things,[b] even[c] the deep-things[d] of God.

LEXICON—a. pres. act. indic. of ἐραυνάω (LN 27.34) (BAGD p. 306): 'to search' [BAGD, LN, Lns; KJV, NASB, NIV, NRSV, TEV], 'to search out' [He, HNTC; TNT], 'to scrutinize' [NAB], 'to explore' [TG; REB], 'to be able to explore' [ICC], 'to explore the depths of' [NJB], 'to fathom' [AB, BAGD], 'to examine, to investigate' [BAGD], 'to try to learn, to try to find out, to seek information' [LN]. It means 'to probe, to investigate, to know' [TG]. The word means to investigate, to accurately and thoroughly know. The results, rather than the process of the investigation is indicated, namely, profound knowledge [Ho]. The word does not mean 'search in order to know' [Ed, ICC, TNTC, Vn], but rather 'to light up the deep things of God' for the believer [ICC, Vn]. It means that there is nothing beyond his knowledge [TNTC]. The present tense indicates the continual and effective work of the Holy Spirit [EBC]. It is the timeless present [Lns].

b. πᾶς (BAGD 2.a.δ. p. 632): 'all things' [AB, BAGD, He, HNTC, ICC, Lns; KJV, NASB, NIV], 'everything' [BAGD; all other versions except LB, NAB], 'all matters' [NAB]. This pronoun is also translated as an adjective: 'all of (God's deepest secrets)' [LB].

c. καί (BAGD II.2. p. 393): 'even' [BAGD, He, HNTC, ICC, LN, Lns; all versions except KJV, LB], 'including' [AB], 'yea' [KJV], not explicit [LB].

d. βάθος (LN **28.76**) (BAGD 2. p. 130): 'deep things' [He, HNTC, Lns; KJV, NAB, NIV], 'deep secrets' [**LN**], 'deepest secrets' [LB], 'depths' [BAGD; NASB, NJB, NRSV, TNT], 'depths of (God's mind)' [AB], 'depths of (God's own nature)' [REB], 'hidden depth of (God's purposes)' [TEV], 'deep mysteries of (the Divine Nature and Will)' [ICC], 'secrets difficult to find out about' [LN]. These 'deep things' are the same as 'the things of God' of 2:11, and refer to the person of God himself in his infinitude. The context indicates that the work of salvation is indicated [NIC]. 'Deep things' refer to God's essence, attributes, thoughts, purpose, plans, etc. [Gdt, Lns, Vn], to God's eternal plan known only through revelation [AB].

QUESTION—What relationship is indicated by γάρ 'for'?

It indicates the reason the Spirit is able to make this revelation [EGT, Gdt, Ho, ICC, NIC, NIC2]: God revealed these things through the Spirit, for the Spirit searches all things.

QUESTION—Who is indicated by 'the Spirit'?

God's Holy Spirit is indicated [Alf, EBC, Gdt, Ho, My, NIC, NIC2, Vn].

2:11 For[a] who of-man[b] has-known[c] the-things[d] of-the man except the spirit[e] of-the man which (is) in him?

LEXICON—a. γάρ (LN 89.33): 'for' [AB, HNTC, LN, Lns; KJV, NASB, NIV, NRSV], 'for example' [NAB], 'we can understand this a little from our own experience' [ICC], 'indeed' [He], 'after all' [NJB], not explicit [LB, REB, TEV, TNT].

b. ἄνθρωπος (LN 9.1) (BAGD 3.a.ζ. p. 69): 'man' [KJV, NAB, NASB, NIV, TNT], 'men in general' [Lns], 'human being' [AB, ICC, LN; NRSV], 'human agency' [HNTC], 'us' [TEV], 'who' [He; REB], 'anyone' [BAGD; NJB], 'no one' [LB]. It is almost equivalent here to the indefinite pronoun with its basic meaning greatly weakened [BAGD]. The reference to man is inclusive of all men everywhere and of all times [NIC].

c. perf. act. indic. of οἶδα (LN 28.1; 32.4) (BAGD 4. p. 556): 'to know' [He, HNTC, ICC, LN (28.1), Lns; all versions], 'to understand' [AB, BAGD, LN (32.4)], 'to comprehend' [LN (32.4)], 'to recognize, to come to know, to experience' [BAGD].

d. τά (BAGD 7. p. 552): 'things' [BAGD, Lns; KJV], 'thoughts' [NASB, NIV], 'affairs' [AB, BAGD], 'nature' [TNT], 'qualities' [NJB], 'situation' [BAGD]. This article is also translated as a phrase: 'all about (him)' [TEV], 'innermost self' [NAB], 'inmost thoughts' [ICC], 'inward truths' [HNTC]. It is also translated as a clause: 'what (a human being) is' [REB], 'what is truly (human)' [NRSV], 'what is in (man)' [He], 'what anyone else is thinking, or is really like' [LB]. These things are a person's memories, thoughts, and motives [ICC].

e. πνεῦμα (LN **26.9**) (BAGD 3.b. p. 675): 'spirit' [BAGD, HNTC, ICC, **LN**, Lns; all versions except LB], 'human spirit' [AB, He], '(that) person (himself)' [LB] 'breath, life-spirit, soul' [BAGD], 'spiritual nature, inner being' [LN]. It refers to the spirit as a part of the human personality. It refers to the source and seat of insight, feeling, and will, all that is the representative part of man's inner life [BAGD]. It refers to the non-material, psychological faculty which is potentially sensitive and responsive to God [LN].

QUESTION—What relationship is indicated by γάρ 'for'?

It indicates that this verse is the grounds for the statement that the Spirit knows the depths of God [AB, EBC, HNTC, ICC, Lns, My, NIC, NIC2; probably KJV, NASB, NIV, NRSV]: the Spirit searches the depths of God for just as only a man's own spirit knows what a man is like, so also only God's Spirit knows what God is like.

QUESTION—What is the function of this rhetorical question?

It functions as a strong negative statement [TH]: absolutely no one knows the thoughts of a man aside from a man's own spirit. The question implies a negative answer [NIC].

QUESTION—What is indicated by 'the spirit of the man'?

It denotes an element in man's psychological make-up [ICC]. It is almost the same as 'mind' [Herm]. It denotes the person himself [NIC, NIC2; LB], or his ego [NIC], his self-awareness [AB, HNTC, NIC, Rb, TG], his intellectual and moral nature [Ed], or the human personality [EBC], the part of man by which he perceives, thinks, and desires [Vn].

in-the-same-way[a] also the-things[b] of God no-one has-known[c] except the Spirit of God.

LEXICON—a. οὕτως (LN 61.9): 'in the same way' [HNTC; NIV, NJB, REB, TEV], 'so' [NRSV, TNT], 'even so' [Lns; KJV, NASB], 'thus' [AB], 'just so' [ICC], 'similarly' [NAB], 'and' [LB], not explicit [He].

b. τά: 'things' [Lns; KJV], 'thoughts' [LB, NASB, NIV], 'affairs' [AB], 'nature' [TNT], 'qualities' [NJB], not explicit [He]. This article is also translated as a phrase: 'all about (God)' [TEV], 'inmost thoughts' [ICC], 'inward truths' [HNTC]. It is also translated as a clause: 'what is truly God's' [NRSV], 'what (God) is' [REB], 'what lies at the depths' [NAB]. See this word in the preceding clause.

c. perf. act. indic. of γινώσκω (BAGD 3.a. p. 161): 'to know' [HNTC, Lns; all versions except NRSV], 'to understand' [BAGD], 'to comprehend' [AB; NRSV], 'to attain to knowledge of' [ICC], not explicit [He]. The difference between these two perfects ('has known') may be that this one is a truer perfect and therefore means 'no one has ever known' [AB, HNTC, Lns, NIC2, TH].

QUESTION—What is meant by οὕτως καί 'in the same way also'?

Paul did not add 'which is in him' because that would suggest a closer comparison between the relation of a man's spirit to the man and that of God's Spirit to God than the argument requires [EBC, Ho, ICC, Lns, NIC]. There is a difference between the spirit of a man and the Spirit of God. Man's spirit is in him, put there by God. But there is no counterpart in God since the essence of the Spirit is identical with that of the Father and of the Son [Lns]. The comparison is that as the human spirit knows human wisdom, so the Spirit of God, who is God himself, knows the wisdom of God [EBC]. The point of the comparison is that a spirit can know something that anyone else cannot know [NIC]. As every person knows his own thoughts, so God's Spirit knows God's thoughts [Ho, Lns].

2:12 Now/But[a] we received[b] not the spirit of-the world[c]

LEXICON—a. δέ (LN 89.87; 89.124): 'now' [AB, Lns, NIC2; KJV, NASB, NJB, NRSV], 'and' [LB], 'and ... now' [REB], 'as for us' [He], 'but' [HNTC], 'yet' [ICC], not explicit [NAB, NIV, TEV, TNT].

b. aorist act. indic. of λαμβάνω (LN 57.125) (BAGD 2. p. 465): 'to receive' [AB, BAGD, He, HNTC, ICC, Lns; all versions except LB], 'to get, to obtain' [BAGD], 'to accept' [LN]. This word is also translated by its reciprocal with 'God' as agent: 'to give' [LB].

c. κόσμος (LN 41.38) (BAGD 7. p. 446): 'world' [AB, BAGD, He, HNTC, LN, Lns; all versions], 'non-Christian world' [ICC], 'world system, world's standards' [LN]. Κόσμος is 'the world' and everything that belongs to it as completely hostile to God, lost in sin, ruined and depraved [BAGD]. It indicates the system of practices and standards of secular society apart from any requirements of God [LN]. It refers to the ordered universe [TNTC].

QUESTION—What relationship is indicated by δέ 'now/but'?

1. It indicates a resumption of the argument [AB, Lns, NIC2; KJV, NASB, NJB, NRSV]. Paul now resumes the argument begun in 2:10 [Lns, NIC2]: God has revealed them through the Spirit and now we have received the Spirit.
2. It indicates contrast [HNTC, ICC, TNTC]: but. The contrast is with 2:11. No one comprehends the thoughts of God, but we are not in this position—we have received the Spirit of God [HNTC].

QUESTION—To whom does 'we' refer?

1. It refers to the apostles or other preachers [Gdt, Ho, Lns]: we apostles received the Spirit to understand. He explains how they get the wisdom to preach to God's people [Lns]. To receive the Spirit is to come under the Spirit's influence; here he is speaking of revelation and inspiration [Ho].
2. It refers to all Christians [AB, ICC, NCBC, NIC, Rb, TNTC]: we believers received the Spirit to understand. Paul is referring to 'our glory' of 2:7 and the 'to us who love him' in 2:9, 10, and is especially referring to Corinthian believers [NIC2]. The aorist indicates that this happened at one point in time [AB], when each believed the gospel [AB] and was regenerated [Vn].

QUESTION—Where is the emphasis in this clause?

The word ἡμεῖς 'we' is emphasized [Lns, NCBC, TNTC].

QUESTION—What is meant by τὸ πνεῦμα τοῦ κόσμου 'the spirit of the world'?

1. It refers to a personal spirit [Alf, HNTC, My]: This evil spirit is sent out by Satan who rules the world [My]. It is a spiritual force opposed to God

and connected with this world [HNTC]. This refers to the 'spirit now working in the sons of disobedience' Eph. 2:2 [Alf].

2. It refers to a principle or idea [EBC, Ed, EGT, Gdt, Ho, ICC, Lns, TNTC]. It could refer to Satan, but he is not referred to by this term elsewhere, and such a reference is not required by the context [ICC, TNTC]. It should rather be taken to mean 'the temper of this world' [TNTC], 'the spirit of human wisdom' [ICC, TNTC]. It means reason [Ho], the principle of knowledge in men [Gdt, Ho], a principle of invention, enthusiasm, and exaltation [Gdt], or the wisdom of this world [EBC]. It is the principle working in mankind that is alienated from God [EGT, ICC, Vn]. It means the spirit that animates and guides the world [ICC]. It is the principle of evil that ties the kingdom of darkness together and has as its goal the subversion of Christ's kingdom [Ed]. This spirit, which animates the world and gives it its distinctive character, is received at birth and by all kinds of contact [Lns].
3. A spirit of the world does not exist. God's Spirit is the topic and this simply states that God's Spirit is not of this world [NIC, NIC2]. He does not suggest that there is a "spirit" of the world that is an alternative to the Spirit from God [NIC2].

but the Spirit which (is) from[a] God,

LEXICON—a. ἐκ with genitive object (LN 90.16): 'from' [AB, Gdt, He, LN, Lns; NASB, NIV, NRSV, REB, TNT], 'of' [KJV]. This preposition is also translated as denoting possession: 'God's Spirit' [NAB], 'God's own Spirit' [LB, NJB]. It is also translated as a clause: 'who comes from' [HNTC], 'sent by' [TH; TEV], 'which proceeds from' [ICC].

QUESTION—To whom does τὸ πνεῦμα 'the Spirit' refer?

1. It refers to the Holy Spirit [all commentaries except Lns; probably all versions]: but the Holy Spirit which is from God. The reference here is to Pentecost when the Spirit came 'from' God to believers [NIC]. 'To receive the Spirit' is the usual NT language for the gift of the Spirit and in Paul's terminology refers to Christian conversion [NIC2].
2. It refers to a spirit possessed by people which is derived from God. This refers to a spirit of faith and trust toward God, a spirit of humility and love, a spirit which gives people a God-like character [Lns].

so-that[a] we-may-understand[b] the-things[c] (which) have-been-freely-given[d] to-us by[e] God;

LEXICON—a. ἵνα (LN 89.59): 'so that' [He, LN; NJB, NRSV, REB, TEV], 'in order that' [AB, Lns], 'that' [HNTC, ICC; KJV, NASB, NIV, TNT], 'helping us to' [NAB], 'to' [LB].

b. perf. act. subj. of οἶδα (LN **32.4**; 28.1): 'to understand' [**LN**; NIV, NJB, NRSV], 'to comprehend' [AB, LN (32.4)], 'to know' [He, HNTC, LN (28.1), Lns; KJV, NASB, REB, TEV, TNT], 'to recognize' [NAB], 'to appreciate' [ICC], not explicit [LB]. It means 'to experience' or 'to participate in' [TH]. See this word at 2:11.

c. τά: 'the things' [AB, HNTC, Lns; KJV, NASB], 'the blessings' [He], 'the gifts' [NAB, NRSV], 'the lavish gifts' [NJB], 'all' [REB, TEV], 'what' [NIV, TNT], 'the benefits' [ICC], 'the wonderful free gifts of grace and blessing' [LB]. See this word at 2:11.

d. aorist pass. participle of χαρίζομαι (LN 57.102) (BAGD 1. p. 876): 'to be freely given' [AB, BAGD; KJV, NASB], 'to be given graciously (as a favor)' [BAGD, Vn], 'to be graciously granted' [Lns], 'to be granted' [He, LN], 'to be bestowed on' [NRSV], 'to be given, to be bestowed generously' [LN]. This passive verb is also translated actively with God as agent: 'to give freely' [HNTC; NIV, TNT], 'to lavish upon' [ICC; REB], 'to give' [LB, NAB, NJB, TEV].

e. ὑπό with genitive object (LN 90.1): 'by' [AB, ICC, LN, Lns; NASB, NRSV], 'of' [KJV]. This preposition is also translated by making God the actor of the verb 'given': [He, HNTC; LB, NAB, NIV, NJB, REB, TEV, TNT]. With the genitive it indicates agent [Lns]. See this word at 1:11.

QUESTION—What relationship is indicated by ἵνα 'so that'?

It indicates purpose [AB, EBC, HNTC, Lns, My, TG; NAB, NJB, REB, TEV]: we received the Spirit from God in order that we may understand. It is God's purpose in giving the Spirit [My].

QUESTION—To what does 'things freely given by God' refer?

These things are the same as the wisdom given for our glory (2:7) [Ho, ICC, Lns], and the things God prepared (2:9) [ICC, Lns]. They refer to the gospel [AB, Ho, Lns, NIC2]. They refer to the contents of the mystery, namely, the facts of the Christ's death and resurrection [Ed]. They refer to the benefits acquired by Christ spoken of in 1:30: righteousness, sanctification, and redemption [Gdt, NIC]. They refer to salvation through the crucified Christ [AB, NIC2]. They refer to the benefits of the Messianic kingdom to be received in the future [My].

2:13 which-things[a] also[b] we-speak[c]

LEXICON—a. ἅ: 'which things' [Lns; KJV, NASB], 'these things' [He, HNTC; NRSV], 'these gifts' [LB], 'these gifts of God' [REB], 'these' [NAB], 'them' [AB], not explicit [TEV]. This pronoun is also translated as a clause: 'this is what' [NIV, TNT], 'these are what' [NJB], 'what He has revealed to us' [ICC]. These refer to the things revealed by the Spirit [Ho, ICC]. They refer to the things that God has freely given us in 2:12 [NIC2].

b. καί (LN 89.93): 'also' [LN, Lns, TH; KJV, NASB], 'further' [HNTC], 'and' [AB, ICC, LN; NJB, NRSV, REB], 'so then' [TEV], not explicit [He; LB, NAB, NIV, TNT].

c. pres. act. indic. of λαλέω (LN 33.70): 'to speak' [LN, Lns; KJV, NASB, NIV, TEV], 'to speak of' [AB, HNTC; NAB, NJB, NRSV, REB, TNT], 'to talk of' [He], 'to tell about' [LB], 'to teach' [ICC]. The present tense indicates what is usual or habitual for Christians who are once given the Spirit [NIC]. See this word at 2:6.

QUESTION—What is the relationship indicated by καί 'also'?

It indicates that Paul is saying something new [TH]: in addition to understanding God's gifts, we also speak about them. It emphasizes Paul's grounds for the claim that God revealed things through His Spirit (2:10b–12) by personally applying these grounds [ICC, Vn]: and these are the very things that we speak about. It simply adds to the action of knowing of 2:12: we also communicate these things [Alf, Ho]. It resumes the 'we speak' of 2:6 [NIC2]. It indicates additional information that not only does the Spirit reveal divine truths, he also provides the language to communicate these truths [Gdt, HNTC].

QUESTION—To whom does 'we' refer?

1. It refers to Paul and the other apostles [Ho, Lns]: we apostles speak.
2. It refers to Paul and his associates, not only the apostles [EBC, ICC]: we apostles/teachers speak.
3. It refers to all believers who proclaim the gospel [Ed, HNTC, NIC, TNTC, Vn]: we all speak. It probably refers to all mature Christians [Ed, HNTC].
4. It is an editorial 'we' and means 'I' [NIC2]: I speak. Since the verb 'we speak' is a repetition of λαλοῦμεν, 'we speak' of 2:6, 7, it is likely that the editorial 'we' is also used here [NIC2].

not in words[a] taught[b] of-human[c] wisdom but[d] in (words) taught of-the-Spirit,

LEXICON—a. λόγος (LN 33.99): 'words' [AB, HNTC, LN, Lns; all versions except NJB], 'terms' [NJB], 'choice words' [ICC], not explicit [He]. Λόγος means message or meaning as well as language [NIC2].

b. διδακτός: (LN **33.227**) (BAGD 2. p. 191): 'taught' [BAGD, HNTC, ICC, **LN**, Lns; all versions except KJV, NJB], 'instructed' [AB, He], 'learned' [NJB], 'imparted' [BAGD]. This word is also translated as a verb: '(man's wisdom) teacheth' [KJV].

c. ἀνθρώπινος: (LN **9.6**) (BAGD 3. p. 68): 'human' [AB, BAGD, He, HNTC, **LN**; all versions except KJV, LB], 'man's' [Lns; KJV], 'we as men' [LB], '(rhetoric) of the schools' [ICC].

d. ἀλλά: 'but' [AB, He, HNTC, ICC, Lns; all versions except LB]. This word is also translated by putting the positive statement first and expressing the contrast by the word 'not' [LB]: in words taught of the Spirit, *not* in words taught of human wisdom.

QUESTION—What is the meaning of the genitive phrase ἀνθρωπίνης 'of human wisdom'?

It means 'by human wisdom' and functions as the agent of 'taught' [AB, Alf, BAGD, EGT, Gdt, HNTC, ICC, NIC2; KJV, NASB, NIV, NRSV, REB, TEV, TNT]: we are not taught by human wisdom. The use of the genitive as agent is also seen in John 6:45 ('they shall all be taught of God') [NIC2]. It means 'from human philosophy' [NJB]: not in terms learned from human philosophy.

QUESTION—What relationship is indicated by ἀλλά 'but'?

It indicates a contrast with the preceding [AB, HNTC, ICC, Lns; all versions]: but.

combining/interpreting[a] spiritual-things[b] with-spiritual-things.[c]

LEXICON—a. pres. act. participle of συγκρίνω (LN **33.154**) (BAGD 1./2.b./3. p. 774): 'to combine' [BAGD, Lns; NASB], 'to bring together' [BAGD], 'to compare' [BAGD; KJV], 'to match' [ICC], 'to fit' [NJB], 'to interpret' [AB, BAGD, HNTC, TG, TH; NAB, NRSV, REB, TNT], 'to explain' [BAGD, He, **LN**; LB, TEV], 'to make clear' [LN], 'to express' [NIV]. It means to explain primarily by means of comparison [LN].

b. πνευματικός: (LN **12.21**) (BAGD 2.b.α. p. 679): 'spiritual things' [Lns; KJV, NAB, NRSV, TNT], 'spiritual truths' [He, HNTC, ICC, **LN**; NIV, REB, TEV], 'spiritual matters' [AB, BAGD], 'spiritual thoughts' [NASB], 'spiritual language' [NJB], 'the Holy Spirit's facts' [LB], 'spiritual, pertaining to the spirit' [BAGD].

c. πνευματικός: (LN **12.20**) (BAGD 2.b.β. p. 679): 'spiritual things' [BAGD; KJV, NJB], 'those who have the Spirit' [BAGD, **LN**; REB, TEV], 'those who are spiritual' [NRSV], 'spiritual men' [He; TNT], 'one who is spiritual' [LN], '(in) spiritual terms' [NAB], '(we use) the Holy Spirit's words' [LB], '(by/by means of/with/in) spiritual words' [AB, HNTC, Lns; NASB, NIV], '(with) spiritual language' [ICC]. It refers to one who has received God's Spirit and presumably lives in accordance with this relationship [LN].

QUESTION—What are the meanings of συγκρίνω 'interpreting/combining' and πνευματικός 'spiritual things'?

1. Συγκρίνω means 'to combine' or 'to match', and πνευματικός means 'spiritual truths' and 'spiritual words' respectively [EGT, ICC, Lns, My, TNTC; NASB, NJB]: 'combining spiritual thoughts with spiritual words' [NASB], 'combining with spiritual words spiritual things' [Lns, TNTC], 'matching spiritual truth with spiritual language' [ICC], 'fitting spiritual language to spiritual things' [NJB]. It means to join things revealed by the Spirit, with the words taught by the Spirit [My]. Because the meaning of 'interpreting' is found only in the LXX, and there only in the context of interpreting dreams, the meaning of 'combining' should be chosen [TNTC].
2. Συγκρίνω means 'to compare' and πνευματικός means 'spiritual truths' and 'spiritual truths' respectively [Ed, NIC; KJV]: comparing spiritual truths with spiritual truths. Spiritual truths are compared so as to discover more definite meaning and delve more deeply. This precedes speaking [NIC].
3. Συγκρίνω means 'to interpret' or 'to explain' and πνευματικός means spiritual truths and spiritual words respectively [AB, EBC, Herm, HNTC, Ho, NCBC, NIC2; LB, NAB, NIV]: 'interpreting spiritual things in spiritual terms' [Ho; NAB], 'expressing spiritual truths in spiritual words'

[EBC; NIV], 'interpreting spiritual truths by means of spiritual words' [AB, HNTC, NCBC], 'explaining the things of the Spirit by means of the words taught by the Spirit' [NIC2], explaining spiritual truths by means of spiritual matters [LN].

4. Συγκρίνω means 'to interpret' or 'to explain' and πνευματικός means spiritual truths and spiritual people respectively [Alf, Gdt, He, LN (12.20, 21), TH; NRSV, REB, TEV, TNT]: 'interpreting spiritual truths to those who have the Spirit' [REB], 'we explain spiritual truths to those who have the Spirit' [TEV], 'interpreting spiritual things to spiritual men' [Alf; NRSV, TNT]. In support of the second πνευματικός meaning 'spiritual people' Paul nowhere else talks of 'spiritual words' whereas he does use 'spiritual people' in 2:15 and 3:1 [TH].

QUESTION—What is the function of the participle συγκρίνοντες 'combining/ interpreting'?

The participle serves to further define the verb 'we speak' [NIC, NIC2].

DISCOURSE UNIT: 2:14–3:4 [Ed, ICC, NCBC]. The topic is God's wisdom understood only by the spiritual man [Ed], the spiritual and animal characters [ICC], spiritual, unspiritual and fleshly men [NCBC].

DISCOURSE UNIT: 2:14–16 [AB, Gdt, NCBC, TNTC]. The topic is the spiritual person and the mind of Christ [AB], the source of spiritual insight [NCBC], spiritual discernment [TNTC].

2:14 But/Now[a] (an) unspiritual[b] man accepts[c] not the-things[d] of-the Spirit of God;

LEXICON—a. δέ (LN 89.124; 89.87): 'but' [KJV, LB, NASB], 'now' [AB, ICC, Lns], not explicit [all other versions].

b. ψυχικός: (LN **41.41**) (BAGD 1. p. 894): 'unspiritual' [BAGD, **LN**; NRSV, REB], 'natural' [AB, He, HNTC, **LN**, Lns; KJV, NAB, NASB, NJB], 'merely natural' [TNT], 'worldly' [**LN**], 'human' [LN]. This adjective is also translated by a phrase: 'without the Spirit' [NIV]; as a clause: 'whoever does not have the Spirit' [TEV], 'who isn't a Christian' [LB], 'whose interests are purely material' [ICC].

c. pres. mid. indic. of δέχομαι (LN 57.125; 31.51) (BAGD 3.b. p. 177): 'to accept' [BAGD, LN, My; NAB, NASB, NIV, TNT], 'to be able to accept' [LB], 'to receive' [He, HNTC, LN, Lns; KJV, NRSV, TEV], 'to have a mind to receive' [ICC], 'to have capacity for' [AB], 'to have room for' [NJB], 'to put up with, to tolerate, to approve' [BAGD], 'to believe' [LN]. This word is joined with the word 'not' and translated 'to refuse' [REB], 'to refuse to accept' [Alf, Ed, NIC2, TNTC]. It indicates a complete inability to receive [Herm, Rb]. It does not indicate inability to receive but simple refusal to accept [ICC, NIC2].

d. τά: 'the things' [Lns; KJV, NASB, NIV, TNT], 'the gifts' [NJB, NRSV, TEV], 'these thoughts' [LB], 'the truths' [He, HNTC], 'the affairs' [AB]. This article is also translated as a clause: 'what is taught by' [NAB], 'what belongs to' [REB], 'what (the Spirit of God) has to impart (to him)' [ICC]. See this word at 2:11.

QUESTION—What relationship is indicated by δέ 'but/now'?

1. It indicates contrast [Gdt, Ho, NIC2, TH; KJV, LB, NASB]: but. We do not speak in such a way to unspiritual people because they are not able to understand [Gdt]. Although the truths are clearly revealed, yet unspiritual people reject them [Ho].
2. It indicates that the thought continues [AB, ICC, Lns]: now. Paul has spoken of the character and transmission of divine wisdom and now he speaks of its reception [Lns].

QUESTION—What are the things of the Spirit?

They are what the Spirit teaches [NAB], the truths revealed by the Spirit [EBC, HNTC], the truth of his word [Ho], the matter and form of the teaching [My], the insights about the meaning of the gospel [AB], enlightenment [EBC].

QUESTION—What is the meaning of ψυκικός 'unspiritual'?

This refers to an unconverted man [EBC, Ed, EGT, Herm, Ho, ICC, My, NIC, NIC2; LB]. It refers to animal life [Alf, ICC, TNTC], not intrinsically evil, but lacking spiritual discernment [TNTC]. Such a man is one who has not received the Spirit [HNTC, ICC, NCBC, NIC, NIC2; NIV, TEV]. This is probably the Greek equivalent of the Hebrew word *nepesh* designating mankind in its natural physical existence [NIC2]. Ψυχικός is a man who only has a ψυχή 'soul', and no πνεῦμα 'spirit' which is given birth by the Holy Spirit [NIC]. It means 'pertaining to the soul' or 'life' and denotes the life of the natural world and what belongs to it, in contrast to the supernatural world which is characterized by spirit. Here it means 'an unspiritual man' that is, one who lives on the purely material plane, without being touched by the Spirit of God [BAGD]. He is a 'soulish' man, controlled by his soul or natural self [EBC, NCBC].

for they-are foolishness[a] to-him and he-is-not-able to-understand[b] (them), because they-are-discerned[c] spiritually.[d]

LEXICON—a. μωρία (LN 32.57): 'foolishness' [AB, He, HNTC, ICC, LN, Lns; KJV, NASB, NIV, NRSV, TNT], 'folly' [NJB, REB], 'nonsense' [LN; TEV], 'absurdity' [NAB]. This noun is also translated as an adjective: '(they sound) foolish' [LB]. See this word at 1:18.

b. aorist act. infin. of γινώσκω (LN 32.16): 'to understand' [He, ICC, LN, Lns; LB, NASB, NIV, NRSV, TEV, TNT], 'to grasp' [REB], 'to comprehend' [AB, LN], 'to know' [HNTC; KJV], 'to come to know' [NAB], 'to recognize' [NJB], 'to be able to take in' [LB]. This word means 'to get to know' [Vn]. See this word at 2:8.

c. pres. pass. indic. of ἀνακρίνω (LN 27.44; 30.109) (BAGD 2. p. 56): 'to be discerned' [BAGD; KJV, NIV, NRSV], 'to be appraised' [NAB, NASB], 'to be judged' [BAGD, He, Lns; REB], '(one's value) to be judged' [TEV], 'to be examined' [TNT], 'to be investigated' [AB,

HNTC], '(one's value) to be assessed' [NJB], 'to be examined carefully, to be investigated, to be studied thoroughly; to be judged or evaluated carefully' [LN], 'to be called to account' [BAGD]. This passive verb is also translated actively: 'to see real value of' [ICC], 'to be able to understand' [LB]. It denotes the work of a judge sifting through evidence to discover the truth [Rb]. It means both examining and arriving at a decision [EBC, Ed, TH, Vn]. It is close to 'discern' in the sense of making appropriate judgments about God's activity in the world. The emphasis is on the process of examining rather than on the verdict itself [NIC2]. It means to make an examination, analyze, and arrive at a conclusion [Gdt].

d. πνευματικῶς (LN 12.21; 26.12) (BAGD 2. 679): 'spiritually' [BAGD, He, HNTC, Lns; KJV, NASB, NIV, NRSV, TNT]. This adverb is also translated with a phrase: 'in terms of the Spirit' [**LN**], 'in a spiritual way/manner' [AB, **LN**; NAB], 'only on a spiritual basis' [**LN**; TEV], 'in the light of the Spirit' [REB], 'only in the Spirit' [NJB], 'in a manner consistent with the Spirit' [BAGD]. It is also translated as a clause: 'it requires a spiritual eye' [ICC], 'only those who have the Holy Spirit within them (can understand)' [LB]. It means 'in a spiritual manner, in a manner caused by or filled with the Spirit' [BAGD]. It means to judge by one's renewed spirit [Alf, Rb]. It can refer to the Holy Spirit or to the spiritual nature or being of a person [LN].

QUESTION—What is meant by the things of the Spirit being 'discerned spiritually'?

It requires a spiritual eye to see their true value [ICC]. A person's inward state must be changed by the influence of the Spirit in order for him to apprehend the truth of the gospel [Ho]. It is only by the agency of the Spirit that they can be discerned [AB, Ed, Ho, My, NIC2, TG, TH; NJB]. They can be understood only with the guidance of the Spirit [EBC].

2:15 But[a] the spiritual-man[b] judges[c] all-things,

LEXICON—a. δέ (LN 89.124): 'but' [He, ICC, LN, Lns; KJV, LB, NASB], 'however' [HNTC; TEV], 'yet' [AB], 'on the other hand' [LN; NAB, NJB], not explicit [all other versions].

b. πνευματικός (LN 12.21): 'spiritual man' [AB, He, HNTC, ICC, Lns; LB, NAB, NIV, TNT], 'spiritual person' [LN, NIC2; NJB, REB] 'those who are spiritual' [NRSV], 'he who is spiritual' [KJV, NASB], 'whoever has the Spirit' [TEV].

c. pres. act. indic. of ἀνακρίνω (LN **30.109**): 'to judge' [He, Lns; KJV], 'to make judgments about' [NIV], 'to make careful judgments about' [**LN**], 'to be able to judge the worth of' [REB, TEV], 'to examine' [ICC; TNT], 'to investigate' [AB, HNTC], 'to appraise' [NASB], 'to be able to appraise' [NAB], 'to discern' [NRSV], 'to be able to assess the value of' [NJB], 'to have insight into' [LB], 'to see the true value of' [ICC], 'to judge or evaluate carefully' [LN]. It means to judge on the basis of careful and detailed information [LN]. See this word under 'discerned' at 2:14.

QUESTION—What relationship is indicated by δέ 'but'?

It indicates a contrast with 2:14 [AB, Alf, EBC, HNTC, ICC, Lns, NIC, NIC2; KJV, NAB, NASB, NJB, TEV].

QUESTION—What is the meaning of πνευματικός 'spiritual man'?

It means a 'person with the Spirit' [EBC, Gdt, Herm, ICC, My, NCBC, NIC, NIC2, TH; TEV]. To view it as meaning spiritually mature is to miss Paul's argument [NIC2]. This man's complete moral and intellectual nature have been made spiritual [Ed]. A spiritual man is one who is guided by the Holy Spirit [EBC, My], and who lives under his influence [My]. The spiritual man judges with the help of the Spirit within him [EGT]. This man's spiritual nature is empowered and set in motion by the Spirit [Vn].

QUESTION—What is the range of πάντα 'all things'?

1. It is limited by the context to all things pertaining to salvation or things of the Spirit [AB, EBC, Ho, NCBC, NIC2]: all things pertaining to the work of salvation. It refers specifically to the gifts bestowed on us by God (2:12) [NCBC]. For the spiritual man there is no barrier to his systematic search for truth. He is completely competent to correctly evaluate the things that come his way and to estimate their true value [AB].
2. It is not limited only to the things of the Spirit [Alf, Ed, EGT, Gdt, Lns, My, TNTC, Vn]. While the natural man cannot understand the things of the Spirit, the spiritual man can understand the things of his old life [Ed]. It means every circumstance, situation, and person he meets [Gdt]. In everything he encounters, he can assign the right estimate because the Holy Spirit has enlightened his power of judgment [My].

but he-himself is-judged[a] by no-one.

LEXICON—a. pres. pass. indic. of ἀνακρίνω: 'to be judged' [He, Lns; KJV], 'to be examined' [TNT], 'to be investigated' [AB], 'to be subject to judgment' [NIV, REB], 'to be subject to scrutiny' [NRSV], 'to be appraised' [NASB], 'to be able to be appraised' [NAB], 'one's own value to be assessed' [NJB], 'one's true value to be seen' [ICC]. This passive verb is also translated actively: 'to be able to judge' [TEV], 'to be open to comparable investigation' [HNTC], 'to be able to be understood at all' [LB]. This does not mean that the spiritual man is above criticism [ICC]. See this word at 2:14.

QUESTION—To whom does οὐδενός 'no one' refer?

1. It refers to the unbeliever, the natural man [Alf, EBC, Ho, ICC, Lns, My, Rb, TG, TNTC, Vn]: he himself is not judged by any natural or unspiritual man. Elsewhere Paul teaches that Christians judge the spiritual condition of other Christians [EBC, ICC, TNTC], as in 5:9–12; 12:3; Gal. 1:8 [EBC]. The person who does not know spiritual things (2:14) is unable to judge spiritual people [TNTC]. One who is not spiritual cannot see his true value [ICC] and he cannot be appreciated [Ho]. Although others might pass judgment on him, the spiritual man refuses to accept such decisions of ignorant judges [Rb].

2. It refers to absolutely anyone other than the Lord Himself [AB, HNTC, NCBC, NIC2, TH]. In 4:3 Paul argues that human condemnation or approval mean nothing to him and that only God is his judge [HNTC, NIC2]. He is answerable to God alone [NCBC]. No one can bring a valid charge against one who knows the wisdom of God and is saved by the power of God in Christ [AB].

2:16 For[a] who knew[b] (the) mind[c] of-(the)-Lord, who will-instruct[d] him?

LEXICON—a. γάρ (LN 89.23): 'for' [AB, He, HNTC, ICC, LN, Lns; KJV, NAB, NASB, NIV, NJB, NRSV], 'indeed' [TNT], not explicit [REB, TEV]. This conjunction is also translated with implied information: 'how could he, for' [LB].

b. aorist act. indic. of γινώσκω (LN 28.1; 32.16): 'to know' [He, HNTC, ICC, LN (28.1); all versions], 'to understand' [LN (32.16), Lns], 'to comprehend' [AB, LN (32.16)]. To know the Lord's mind as to its contents, thoughts, plans, and purposes [Lns].

c. νοῦς (LN 26.14) (BAGD 4. p. 545): 'mind' [AB, BAGD, He, HNTC, LN, Lns; all versions except LB], 'thought' [BAGD, ICC; LB], 'opinion, decree' [BAGD]. In the Greek text that Paul was quoting, 'mind' is used to translate the Hebrew word *ruah*, primarily meaning 'spirit' [HNTC, NCBC, NIC2]. Νοῦς denotes 'understanding', not 'spirit'. The Spirit communicates the 'mind' of God to the spiritual man [Gdt]. This is the faculty in which the thoughts and plans of God originate and develop [My]. See this word at 1:10.

d. pres. act. indic. of συμβιβάζω (LN **33.298**) (BAGD 4. p. 777): 'to instruct' [BAGD, He, HNTC, LN, Lns; KJV, NAB, NASB, NIV, NRSV], 'to be able to instruct' [TNT], 'to be able to instruct and guide' [ICC], 'to advise' [AB, BAGD, **LN**], 'to be able to give advice' [TEV], 'to be one's adviser' [NJB], 'to teach' [BAGD], 'to be one's counselor' [REB], 'to discuss with' [LB].

QUESTION—What relationship is indicated by γάρ 'for'?

1. It indicates the grounds of 2:15 [AB, Alf, EBC, Ed, Gdt, HNTC, Ho, ICC, Lns, My, NIC2, TG; KJV, LB, NAB, NASB, NIV, NJB, NRSV]. This supports the statement of 2:15 that the spiritual man judges all things [Ed, ICC]. This supports the statement of 2:15 that no one judges the spiritual man [Alf, EBC, Gdt, Ho, Lns, My, NIC2, TG]: just as the natural man cannot judge the Lord, so he cannot judge the spiritual man (who is in the same position as the Lord Himself) [Gdt].
2. It indicates emphasis [TNT]: Who, indeed, knows the mind of the Lord?

QUESTION—Is γάρ 'for' a part of the scripture quotation?

1. This word should be part of the scripture quotation [AB; NIV, NRSV].
2. This word should be outside of the scripture quotation [TH; NAB, NJB, REB, TNT].

QUESTION—What Scripture is quoted here?

The scripture quoted is Isa. 40:13 [AB, EBC, HNTC, ICC, My, NIC, TH, Vn], and is close to the LXX (Greek Version) [EBC, EGT, HNTC, My, NIC, Vn].

QUESTION—What is the implied answer to the rhetorical question?

The implied answer is 'No one'. [EBC, Gdt, HNTC, Ho, Lns, NIC, NIC2, TG]. The reply forms the major premise of a syllogism: (Major Premise): no one can instruct the Lord; (Minor Premise): we have the mind of the Lord; (Implied conclusion): therefore no one can instruct or judge us [Ho, Lns].

QUESTION—What relationship is indicated by the word ὅς 'who'?

1. It adds a second part to the question [LB, NJB, REB, TEV, TNT]: who knew the mind of the Lord *and who* will instruct him?
2. It indicates the result of the first question [AB, He, HNTC, ICC, Lns, NIC2, Rb; KJV, NAB, NASB, NIV, NRSV]: who knew the mind of the Lord *so that he* will instruct him? This relative finds a kind of antecedent in τίς 'who' in the first part of the question [ICC] and has a consecutive idea [HNTC, NIC2].

But[a] we have (the) mind of-Christ.

LEXICON—a. δέ: 'but' [He, ICC, Lns; all versions except LB, REB, TEV], 'yet' [AB; REB], 'however' [HNTC; TEV]. This conjunction is also translated with implied information: 'but, strange as it seems' [LB]. This word is adversative and contrasts 'we' with those who do not have the Spirit and who do not know the mind of the Lord [NIC2, TH].

QUESTION—To whom does 'we' refer?

1. It refers to Paul and other teachers [Gdt, Lns, TG]. The words 'but we' stand in sharp contrast to the 'you' of the following verses, 3:1–3 [Gdt].
2. It refers to all spiritual Christians [Alf, EBC, Herm, HNTC, ICC, My, NCBC, NIC, Rb]. The emphatic 'we' joins all spiritual people with the Apostle and includes all the ones being saved of 1:18 [ICC]. Paul includes himself with spiritual Christians [Alf, My].

QUESTION—Where is the emphasis in this verse?

'We' is emphatic [EGT, ICC, Lns, My, NCBC, NIC2, TH, TNTC], along with the verb 'have' [Lns].

QUESTION—What does it mean 'to have the mind of Christ'?

It does not mean to be able to understand all of Christ's thoughts; it means that the Spirit reveals Christ to the believer [TNTC]. We can understand spiritual truths and wisdom in a way similar to the way the Lord knows them [EBC]. 'Mind' means the thoughts of Christ as they are revealed by the Spirit [NIC2].

DISCOURSE UNIT: 3:1–4:21 [EBC]. The topic is servants of Christ.

DISCOURSE UNIT: 3:1–23 [AB, EBC, GNT, Ho, TG]. The topic is leadership and nurture in the church [AB], workers with God, a false estimate corrected [EBC], fellow workmen for God [GNT], reproof of the Corinthians for their dissensions about their religious teachers [Ho]. In 3:1–9 Paul speaks about the lack of spiritual discernment seen in the Corinthian misconceptions about God's co-laborers. He points out the remedy by showing the importance of working correctly for the Lord (3:10–17) and of not depending on mere human wisdom (3:18–23) [EBC].

DISCOURSE UNIT: 3:1–17 [Herm, NIC]. The topic is a concluding discussion of the party system: preacher and community [Herm], God, his servants and his congregation [NIC].

DISCOURSE UNIT: 3:1–9 [EBC, Lns, TNTC, Vn]. The topic is spiritual immaturity and divisiveness [EBC], the preachers as God's co-workers [Lns], a carnal misunderstanding [TNTC].

DISCOURSE UNIT: 3:1–4 [AB, Alf, Ed, HNTC, ICC, My, NCBC, NIC2, TH, TNTC]. The topic is strife and immaturity [AB], even true wisdom unsuitable for babes [HNTC], milk for spiritual infants [NCBC], on being spiritual and divided [NIC2], carnal Christians [TNTC]. This unit serves as a transition between the theory of hidden wisdom and its practical application [Herm].

3:1 And[a] I, brothers,[b]

LEXICON—a. καί (LN 89.83; 91.1; 91.12): 'and' [ICC, Lns; KJV, NASB], 'and so' [NJB, NRSV], 'yet' [AB], 'but' [REB], 'as a matter of fact' [TEV], 'accordingly' [TNT], not explicit [LB, NAB, NIV]. The combination κἀγώ 'and I' is translated 'as far as my own experience of you goes' [HNTC], 'for my part' [He].

b. ἀδελφός: 'brothers'. See this word at 1:10.

QUESTION—What relationship is indicated by καί 'and'?

It indicates a transition [Alf, Ed, EGT, Gdt, ICC, NIC2; KJV, NASB] from a general statement to its application [Ed]. Paul now applies the argument of 2:6–16 to the situation at Corinth [Ed, Gdt, ICC, NIC, NIC2]: we have the mind of Christ, and specifically I, as a spiritual man, etc. Or the transition is from 2:14 [Alf, EGT]: the natural man does not receive the things of the Spirit, and I similarly could not talk to you as to spiritual men. A contrast is also included [AB, NIC, TH; REB]. The word 'I' is emphatic [HNTC, Lns, TH], contrasting Paul and his readers [TH].

QUESTION—What is the function of the word ἀδελφοί 'brothers'?

This term functions to soften the rebuke [Gdt, TNTC]. It indicates that Paul is introducing a new subject and asks the special attention of his readers [NIC]. It indicates that Paul still included them in the family of God [HNTC]. Although all may not be guilty, Paul addresses the whole church since all are affected by the actions of the majority [NIC2].

was-unable to-speak[a] to-you as[b] to-spiritual-men[c]

LEXICON—a. aorist act. infin. of λαλέω (LN 33.70): 'to speak' [He, HNTC, LN, Lns; all versions except NAB, NIV, NJB, TEV], 'to talk' [LN; LB, NAB, NJB, TEV], 'to address' [AB; NIV], 'to treat (someone)' [ICC].

b. ὡς (LN 64.12) (BAGD III.a. p. 898): 'as' [AB, He, HNTC, ICC, LN, Lns; all versions except LB, TEV]. This conjunction is also translated with the implied information added: 'as I talk to' [LB, TEV]. This word introduces the distinctive characteristic of a person [BAGD].

c. πνευματικός (LN **41.40; 41 fn 4**) (BAGD 2.b.β. p. 679): 'spiritual men' [HNTC; NAB, NASB, TNT], 'spiritual people' [AB, He, ICC, **LN**; NJB, NRSV], 'people who have the Spirit' [REB, TEV], 'healthy Christians, who are filled with the Spirit' [LB], 'spirit-filled people' [BAGD]. It is also translated as an adjective: 'spiritual' [Lns; KJV, NIV]. See this word at 2:13.

QUESTION—To what specific time does the aorist οὐκ ἠδυνήθην λαλῆσαι 'was not able to speak' refer?

It apparently refers to Paul's visit to Corinth [Alf, Ed, NIC, NIC2, TNTC], and perhaps to a previous letter [Ed]. The historical aorist points back to the time when the Corinthians were just beginners in the Christian faith [Lns].

QUESTION—What is meant by πνευματικοῖς 'spiritual men'?

In 2:14–15 this word indicated those who had received the Spirit as contrasted with unbelievers, but here it indicates a maturity in spiritual things as contrasted with immaturity [EBC, HNTC, Ho]. In comparison with the world, all Christians are spiritual (2:14–15), but here, in a modified sense, the comparison is among Christians and spirituality means eminently spiritual [Ho] or mature [AB, EBC, HNTC]. Ideally and positionally, all Christians are spiritual, but in actual fact not all are [ICC]. It is not that the Corinthians did not have the Spirit, but that they were thinking and living as though they did not [Alf, NIC, NIC2]. The term denotes people who have received and obey the leading of the Spirit of God [HNTC]. Their immaturity was the result of lack of submission to the Spirit [AB]. The focus here seems to be more on behavior patterns rather than on the presence of the Holy Spirit in them, as in 2:13 [**LN**].

but[a] as to-men-of-flesh,[b]

LEXICON—a. ἀλλά (LN 89.125): 'but' [AB, Herm, LN; KJV, LB, NASB, NIV, REB, TNT], 'but only' [He, HNTC, Lns; NAB], 'but rather' [NRSV], not explicit [LB, NJB, REB, TEV].

b. σάρκινος (LN **41.42**; **79.4**; 79 fn 4) (BAGD 2. p. 743): 'men of flesh' [NAB, NASB], 'worldly people' [LN (79.4)], 'fleshly men' [HNTC], 'fleshly people' [He, Lns], 'people of the flesh' [NRSV], 'ordinary human beings' [LN (79.4); TNT], 'people of this world' [LN (79.4)], 'physical ones' [AB], 'mere creatures of flesh and blood' [ICC], 'people still living by their natural inclinations' [NJB]. This word is also translated as an adjective: 'carnal' [BAGD, Gdt; KJV], 'worldly' [NIV], 'natural, human' [LN]. It is also translated as a prepositional phrase: 'on the natural plane' [REB]. It is also translated as a clause: '(as though) you belonged to this world' [TEV], 'who are not following the Lord' [LB].

QUESTION—What words should be supplied before the phrase 'as to men of the flesh'?

In contrast with 'I was unable to speak to you', the implication is 'but I had to speak/talk to you' [Alf, EGT, My; NJB, TEV] or 'but I had to deal with you' [REB].

QUESTION—What is meant by σάρκινος 'men of flesh'?

The word σάρκινος means 'fleshly, belonging to the realm of the flesh' in that it is weak, sinful, and transitory [BAGD]. It refers primarily to their humanness and physical orientation as over against the spiritual [NIC2]. Σάρκινος is not synonymous with ψυχικός 'unspiritual' of 2:14, for the term in 2:14 describes one who is devoid of the Spirit and the Corinthians had received the Spirit [Gdt, Lns, NIC2]. It does not refer to the body, but to fallen mankind with all of its sinful tendencies inherited by natural birth [NCBC]. It means 'flesh and blood', which is what every man is, but what he needs to subordinate to the higher law of the Spirit [ICC]. Σάρκινος refers to their unspiritual nature, a nature ruled by the flesh [My]. It implies spiritual immaturity [EBC, TNTC]. It does not mean that they habitually practiced sensual sins, but that their existence was determined by ungodly human considerations rather than by God himself [HNTC]. It means 'fleshy, made of flesh' [TNTC]. Here Paul says 'as if they were only of the flesh', but in 3:3 he drops the comparison and asserts that they are still of the flesh [Alf].

as to-infants[a] in[b] Christ.

LEXICON—a. νήπιος (LN 9.43) (BAGD 1.b.α. p. 537): 'infant' [AB, BAGD; NAB, NJB, NRSV, REB, TNT], 'mere infant' [NIV], 'minor' [BAGD], 'babe' [He, HNTC, ICC, Lns; KJV, NASB], 'just babies' [LB], 'children' [TEV], 'immature Christian' [BAGD].

b. ἐν (LN 89.119; 90.23): 'in' [AB, HNTC, LN, Lns; all versions except LB, TEV], 'in union with' [LN (89.119)], 'with respect to' [LN (90.23)]. The phrase ἐν Χριστῷ 'in Christ' is translated 'Christian' [He], 'in the Christian life' [LB], 'in the Christian course' [ICC], 'in the Christian faith' [TEV]. 'In Christ' denotes the realm of their infancy [My], the sphere in which Christ rules [NIC]. They were in Christ because they were believers [NIC2]. Being in Christ shows that they were members of God's family [AB, ICC, Lns, NIC].

QUESTION—What is the point of comparison with 'infants'?

The point of comparison is immaturity [AB, BAGD, HNTC, Lns, NIC2, TG, Vn]; their behavior was inappropriate for mature adults [NIC2] or for mere beginners [My]. Νήπιος 'infant' is figurative of one who views spiritual things from the standpoint of a child [BAGD]. This word qualifies σάρκινος 'fleshly' and serves to keep the Corinthians in the Christian family [HNTC]. It is used most frequently with a negative sense referring to thinking and behavior which is not fitting for a mature person [NIC2]. They were children in Christian knowledge [Herm, Ho] and experience [Ho].

3:2 To-you I-gave-to-drink[a] milk,[b] not solid-food;[c]

LEXICON—a. aorist act. indic. of ποτίζω (LN 23.35) (BAGD 1. p. 695): 'to give to drink' [BAGD, Lns; NASB], 'to supply to drink' [AB], 'to feed' [HNTC; KJV, NAB, NJB, NRSV, TNT], 'to feed someone on' [REB], 'to have to feed' [LB, TEV], 'to give' [ICC; NIV], 'to offer' [He]. This figure is a zeugma, in which the verb 'give to drink', serves for 'food' as well as 'milk', while it strictly collocates only with 'milk' [Ed, Herm, HNTC, ICC, Lns, Rb].

b. γάλα (LN **5:19**) (BAGD 2. p. 149): 'milk' [AB, BAGD, He, HNTC, **LN**, Lns; all versions], 'quite elementary teaching' [ICC].

c. βρῶμα (LN **5.7**) (BAGD 1. p. 148): 'solid food' [AB, BAGD, He, HNTC, **LN**; all versions except KJV], 'food' [BAGD], 'meat' [Lns; KJV], 'the more solid truths of the Gospel' [ICC].

QUESTION—How is this statement related to 3:1?

It enlarges on the reference to 'infants' in 3:1 [EBC, Herm]: I treated you as infants, that is, I gave you milk to drink. It indicates the result of 3:1 [EGT, HNTC, Ho, NIC, TNTC]: you were infants, therefore I gave you milk to drink.

QUESTION—To what is 'milk' being compared?

This word is figurative of elementary Christian teaching [BAGD, EBC, EGT, ICC, TG, Vn]. 'Milk' refers to what Paul said in 2:2 [EGT, Gdt, Vn]: the preaching of Christ crucified, expiation, justification, and sanctification [Gdt]. It is preaching in order to convert unbelievers [EBC, NIC]. 'Milk' is the good news of salvation; 'solid food' is knowing that all of the Christian life is based on this mystery [NIC2]. 'Milk' is material such as in 1 Thess. and the Synoptic gospels as over against the 'solid food' of Romans and Colossians and the Gospel of John [EGT]. The subject matter of 'milk' and 'solid food' are the same [HNTC, Ho, Lns, NIC, NIC2], wisdom as the word of the cross [NIC2], but the form is somewhat different [Ho, Lns, NIC2]. The distinction between milk and solid food is in presentation, milk is truth simply presented, solid food is the same truth more fully treated and developed [Ho]. This word is intended critically, mere baby food, but the words 'not yet' give a opening for improvement [Herm].

QUESTION—To what is 'solid food' being compared?

'Solid food' is figurative for more complex matters which require greater understanding [EBC, TG]. It is what Paul said in 2:6–13 [Gdt, ICC, Vn]. It is the secret wisdom of 2:7, the deep meaning of Christ crucified [NCBC]. It is preaching to Christians the full magnificence of the Gospel [NIC]. There are not two sets of doctrines here, but a more perfect development of the doctrines that were first presented as 'milk' [Ho]. It differs in form, not in content [HNTC].

for not-yet[a] were-you-able.[b]

LEXICON—a. οὔπω (LN 67.129) (BAGD p. 593): 'not yet' [BAGD, He, ICC, LN, Lns; NASB, NIV, NJB, REB, TNT], 'not' [LB, NAB, NRSV, TEV], 'not...even now' [AB], 'hitherto...not' [KJV], 'still not' [HNTC, LN].

b. imperf. act. indic. of δύναμαι (LN 74.5) (BAGD 2. p. 207): 'to be able' [BAGD, He, LN, Lns; KJV], 'to be ready for' [NAB, NIV, NRSV, REB, TEV], 'to be strong enough' [BAGD]. This verb is also translated with implied information supplied: 'to be able to receive' [NASB], 'to be able to take' [AB, HNTC; NJB, TNT], 'to be able to bear' [He], 'to be able to digest anything stronger' [LB], 'to be strong enough to digest' [ICC]. The implied information is: '(not able) to eat solid food' [Alf]. The imperfect tense refers to a continuing state [EGT]. The weakness of body is figurative of weakness of mind and spirit [My], or spiritual understanding [EGT].

QUESTION—To what specific time does Paul refer by the imperfect tense ἐδύνασθε 'you were able'?

It refers to the time when Paul was first in Corinth [EGT, Gdt]. At that stage they were but babes and there is no blame implied regarding their immature condition [NIC, TNTC].

Indeed[a] not yet now are-you-able,

LEXICON—a. ἀλλά (LN 91.11) (BAGD 3. p. 38): 'indeed' [AB, TNTC; NASB, NIV, REB, TNT], 'and indeed even' [HNTC], 'even' [NRSV], 'and even' [LB, NJB, TEV], 'nay' [Lns], 'and not only this but' [BAGD], 'certainly, emphatically' [LN], not explicit [He; KJV, NAB]. It is used to introduce a strong addition [HNTC, NIC2, TNTC], possibly, 'yes, indeed' [NIC2]. It has its strongest intensifying force, 'Nay, but (not yet) even' [ICC]. The ἀλλά is emphatic [EBC, Herm, TH, TNTC].

QUESTION—To what specific time does Paul refer by the present tense δύνασθε 'you are able'?

It is now, when they should have made progress [ICC]. It is after a period of teaching by Paul, Apollos, and regular preaching of the gospel [NIC]. A rebuke is implied since by now they should have been able [HNTC, NIC, TNTC].

DISCOURSE UNIT: 3:3–9 [EGT]. The topic is God's rights in the church.

3:3 for[a] you-are still fleshly.[b]

LEXICON—a. γάρ (LN 89.23): 'for' [AB, He, HNTC, ICC, LN, Lns; all versions except NAB, NIV, REB, TEV], 'because' [LN; TEV], 'being' [NAB], not explicit [NIV, REB].

b. σαρκικός (LN **79.4**) (BAGD 3. p. 743): 'fleshly' [He, HNTC, Lns; NASB], 'physically oriented' [AB], 'carnal' [BAGD; KJV], 'worldly' [NIV], 'natural, human' [LN]. It is also translated as a noun phrase: 'people of this world, ordinary human beings' [**LN**], 'mere beginners' [ICC], 'only baby Christians controlled by your own desires not God's'

[LB]. It is also translated as a clause: 'belonging to the flesh' [BAGD], 'live as people of this world' [TEV], 'living by one's natural inclinations' [NJB]. It is also translated as a prepositional phrase: 'in the manner of the flesh' [BAGD], 'of the flesh' [NRSV], 'in a natural condition' [NAB], 'on the merely natural plane' [REB], 'on the ordinary human level' [TNT]. Here it means 'belonging to the realm of the flesh' in so far as it is weak, sinful, and transitory, and therefore opposite of the spirit. It is used in reference to immature Christians [BAGD]. It means 'conformable to and governed by the flesh' [ICC]. This word contrasts with the phrase 'of the Spirit' [TH], and means controlled by human impulses [NIC, TH]. It describes a life that is self-centered and self-directed [HNTC].

QUESTION—What relationship is indicated by γάρ 'for'?

It indicates the grounds for saying that they were unable to digest solid food (3:2) [Ho, Lns, NIC, NIC2] or that they were men of flesh (3:1) [Ed].

QUESTION—Is there a distinction in meaning between the words σάρκινος 'of the flesh' of 3:1 and σαρκικός 'of the flesh' of this verse?

1. There is a distinction between the meanings of the two words [AB, Alf, BAGD, EBC, EGT, ICC, Lns, My, NIC, NIC2, Rb, TNTC, Vn]. The suffix -ινος indicates 'made of', so σάρκινος would mean, 'made of flesh'. The -ικος suffix indicates 'characterized by', so σαρκικός means, 'characterized by flesh' [EGT, HNTC, TNTC]. The distinction can be described as (-ινος) fleshy and (-ικος) fleshly respectively: fleshy and it is not your fault, fleshly and it is your fault [Lns, My, TNTC]. Whereas σάρκινος emphasizes their humanness and the physical side of their life, in contrast to the spiritual, σαρκικός emphasizes their ethical moral behavior [ICC, NIC2]. Σάρκινος describes their existence as physical; σαρκικός indicates that physical orientation is their characteristic [AB].
2. There is no meaning distinction between these words [Herm, HNTC, LN (79.4 fn 4), TH]. Σάρκινος properly means 'made of flesh'; σαρκικός means 'having the character of flesh', but Paul apparently did not intend to make any distinctions in this paragraph [HNTC].

For[a] where[b] (there is) jealousy[c] and strife[d] among you,

TEXT—Some manuscripts add the words καὶ διχοστασίαι 'and divisions' after the word ἔρις 'strife'. GNT omits these words with a B rating, indicating that the text is almost certain. They are included by Ho, KJV, and LB.

LEXICON—a. γάρ (LN 89.23): 'for' [HNTC, ICC, LN, Lns; KJV, NAB, NASB, NIV, NRSV], 'indeed' [He], not explicit [AB; LB, NJB, REB, TEV, TNT].

b. ὅπου (LN **89.35**) (BAGD 2.b. p. 576): 'where' [Alf, BAGD, EGT, HNTC]; 'when' [LB, TEV, TNT], 'as long as' [NAB, NJB, NRSV, REB], 'so long as' [He, ICC], 'whereas' [AB, Ed, **LN**, Lns; KJV], 'since' [BAGD, Herm, LN; NASB, NIV], 'in so far as' [BAGD]. Here it has a causal sense: 'in so far as, since' [AB, BAGD, Ed, Gdt, Herm, HNTC,

LN, Lns, TH; KJV, NASB, NIV]. Although the causal sense is present, the locative is likewise present [ICC].

c. ζῆλος (LN 88.162) (BAGD 2. p. 337): 'jealousy' [AB, BAGD, ICC, LN, Lns; all versions except KJV, LB], 'envy' [BAGD, HNTC, LN; KJV], 'rivalry' [Ed], 'resentment' [LN]. This noun is also translated as a verb: 'to be jealous' [LB]. It is also joined with the following word and translated '(as long as) dissensions rage' [He].

d. ἔρις (LN **33.447; 39.22**): 'strife' [HNTC, **LN**; KJV, NASB, REB], 'contention' [AB, ICC], 'quarreling' [NAB, NIV, NRSV, TNT], 'quarreling groups' [LB], 'rivalry' [LN; NJB], 'wrangling' [Lns], 'discord' [BAGD, LN]. This noun is also translated as a verb: 'to quarrel' [**LN**; TEV]. See this word at 1:11.

QUESTION—What relationship is indicated by γάρ 'for'?

It indicates the grounds for saying that they are still fleshly [Ho, Lns, NIC, NIC2]. It makes the accusation that they are fleshly more specific [TNTC].

are-you not fleshly and behave[a] like[b] man?[c]

LEXICON—a. pres. act. indic. of περιπατέω (LN 41.11) (BAGD 2.a.δ. p. 649): 'to behave' [ICC, LN; NRSV, TNT], 'to live' [BAGD, He, LN; NJB, REB, TEV], 'to act' [LB, NIV], 'to conduct oneself' [AB, BAGD, HNTC], 'to go about doing' [LN], 'to walk' [BAGD, Lns; KJV, NASB]. It is also translated as a noun: '(your) behavior' [NAB]. It is used figuratively of 'the walk of life' [BAGD, NIC2].

b. κατά with accusative object (LN 89.8) (BAGD II.5.b.β. p. 407): 'like' [LB, NASB, NIV, TNT], 'as' [KJV], 'just as, similar to' [BAGD], 'according to' [NRSV], 'in accordance with' [BAGD, LN], 'after the manner of' [He]. See also under the next Greek word.

c. ἄνθρωπος (LN 9.1) (BAGD 1.c. p. 68): 'men' [BAGD, He; KJV], 'mere men' [NASB, NIV, TNT], 'ordinary men' [NAB], 'people who don't belong to the Lord at all' [LB], 'the manner of men' [Lns], 'human beings' [BAGD, LN], '(no better than) the mass of mankind' [ICC]. Κατὰ ἄνθρωπον 'according to man' is translated 'on the purely human level' [REB], 'by the world's standards' [TEV], 'in a human way' [BAGD, EBC], 'from a human standpoint' [BAGD], 'according to the practices of fallen humanity' [Vn], 'in accordance with human standards' [AB, HNTC], 'according to human inclinations' [NRSV], 'by your natural inclinations' [NJB]. This manner of living is not distinguishable from the natural man of 2:14 [ICC]. Ἄνθρωπος has practically the same meaning as 'flesh' and includes women as well [TH]. Paul does not say that they were natural men, but that they were behaving like them [NIC].

QUESTION—What relationship is indicated by καί 'and'?

It indicates an explanation of the previous statement [HNTC, Lns, NIC2, TH]: are you not fleshly, that is, do you not walk like men?

QUESTION—What reply is expected to this question with οὐχι 'not'?

It indicates that a positive reply is expected; they should admit their fleshly behavior [EBC, TG; NJB, REB].

3:4 For[a] whenever[b] anyone says, "I, on-the-one-hand am of-Paul," another on-the-other-hand, "I (am) of-Apollos,"

LEXICON—a. γάρ: 'for' [AB, He, HNTC, ICC, Lns, My; KJV, NASB, NIV, NRSV, TNT], not explicit [all other versions].

b. ὅταν (LN 67.31) (BAGD 3.a. p. 48): 'whenever' [AB, BAGD, LN, Lns, TNTC; TNT], 'when' [He, HNTC, ICC, LN; all versions except KJV, NJB], 'while' [KJV, NJB]. The word ὅταν is a contraction of ὅτε 'when' and ἄν the indefinite particle [BAGD], and is used with the subjunctive to indicate regularly recurring action [BAGD, EGT].

QUESTION—What relationship is indicated by γάρ 'for'?

It indicates the grounds for Paul's claim that there was envy and strife among them or that they are living according to the manner of men [Ho, Lns, My, NIC, NIC2, TNTC].

QUESTION—To whom does 'anyone' refer?

Although 'anyone' and 'another' are singular, they do not refer to only two individuals, but two groups [TG].

QUESTION—Why are only the names of Paul and Apollos mentioned, leaving out Cephas and Christ (1:12)?

These two names may have been the most prominent parties [Lns]. Two names are enough for an example [EGT, NIC2]. The main cause of the strife concerning the wisdom of words was best illustrated by these two extremes [EGT, NIC2]. Paul could speak most freely about Apollos because of their close relationship [EGT, Ho, TNTC].

are-you not[a] men?[b]

LEXICON—a. οὐκ (LN 69.11): 'not' [AB, BAGD, He, HNTC, ICC, LN, Lns; all versions]. This word is used in questions that expect a positive reply [TH; all versions].

b. ἄνθρωπος: 'men' [TNT], 'mere men' [Lns; NASB, NIV], 'men, that and nothing more' [HNTC], 'men who are still uninfluenced by the Spirit of God' [ICC], 'worldly people' [TEV]. This noun is also translated as an adjective phrase: 'merely human' [He; NRSV], 'carnal' [KJV], 'all too human' [REB], 'only too human' [NJB], 'still at the human level' [NAB]. This clause is translated 'are you not on the ordinary human level, behaving like mere men?' [TNT], 'is it not clear that you are still at the human level?' [NAB], 'are you not being only too human?' [NJB], 'are you not all too human?' [REB], 'aren't you acting like worldly people?' [TEV]. 'Are you not men?' is the equivalent of 'behave according to man' of 3:3 [Herm]. The word is used figuratively here and indicates a purely human life without the Holy Spirit [TH]. The word 'men' is emphasized and means persons taken up with the unspiritual natural ways of men

[My]. 'Men' here means 'unchanged men' and is the same as 'men' in 3:3 [NIC]. See this word at 3:3.

DISCOURSE UNIT: 3:5–4:21 [ICC]. The topic is the true conception of the Christian pastorate.

DISCOURSE UNIT: 3:5–4:5 [Gdt]. The topic is the true nature of the Christian ministry.

DISCOURSE UNIT: 3:5–20 [Ed, Gdt]. The topic is the argument against the factions [Ed], the place of preachers in relation to the Church [Gdt].

DISCOURSE UNIT: 3:5–17 [HNTC, NCBC, NIC2]. The topic is Paul and Apollos [HNTC], God's field and God's building [NCBC], correcting a false view of church and ministry [NIC2].

DISCOURSE UNIT: 3:5–15 [Alf, My]. The topic is discussion of the position occupied by the two teachers.

DISCOURSE UNIT: 3:5–9/9a [AB, Ed, ICC, NIC2, TH, TNTC]. The topic is cooperative roles of leadership [AB], the Apostles and teachers as servants of God [Ed], the true relation between Paul and Apollos [TNTC], leaders are servants with God as the Master over all [NIC2].

3:5 What then[a] is Apollos? And what is Paul?

TEXT—Instead of the neuter τί 'what', some manuscripts have the masculine τίς 'who'. GNT selects the neuter form without rating its selection. LN; KJV, LB, NAB, and TEV use the masculine form.

TEXT—Some manuscripts reverse the order from 'Apollos...Paul', to 'Paul...Apollos'. GNT selects the order 'Apollos...Paul' with an A rating indicating that the text is certain. KJV and LB use the reverse order.

LEXICON—a. οὖν (LN **91.7**; 89.50): 'then' [AB, HNTC, **LN**, Lns; KJV, NASB, NRSV], 'after all' [NAB, NIV, REB, TEV], 'really' [He, ICC], 'for' [NJB], not explicit [LB, TNT].

QUESTION—What relationship is indicated by οὖν 'then'?

1. It indicates a conclusion drawn from the party division about Paul and Apollos [Alf, EBC, EGT]: since such division is wrong, therefore consider their true value. Paul answers the question, How should Paul and Apollos be viewed? [EBC, EGT].
2. It indicates transition from the mention of Paul and Apollos to a discussion about their positions [Gdt, HNTC, ICC, My, NIC]. This conjunction is translated with implicit information included: 'I have mentioned the names of Apollos and myself. Well then...' [HNTC]. 'This situation being true, I am forced to ask the question...' [My]. 'If Paul and Apollos are not the heroes you make them out to be, what are they then?' [Gdt]

QUESTION—Why is the neuter τί 'what' used, rather than the masculine τίς 'who'?

The neuter serves to focus attention on the function or significance of these men [Gdt, ICC, My, NIC, TNTC] rather than on their persons [NIC, TNTC]. The neuter anticipates the word 'anything' in 3:7: neither he who plants nor he who waters is 'anything' [AB]. The word 'what' indicates disdain [EGT, Vn].

QUESTION—What is the function of these questions?

The questions are rhetorical and express disdain: 'Are Paul and Apollos some kind of lords to whom you may belong? Don't you know what Paul and Apollos really are?' [NIC2].

Servants[a] through[b] whom you-believed,[c]

LEXICON—a. διάκονος (LN 35.20) (BAGD 1.a. p. 184): 'servant' [AB, BAGD, HNTC, LN; NASB, NJB, NRSV, TEV, TNT], 'only servants' [NIV], 'just servants' [ICC], 'just God's servants' [LB], 'servants (of Christ)' [He], 'ministers' [Lns; KJV], 'simply ministers' [NAB], 'simply God's agents' [REB]. Διάκονος should not be understood in its technical sense of the office of 'deacon' in a church, but in the general sense of servants of a master [EBC, TNTC].

b. διά with genitive object (LN 89.76): 'through' [HNTC, LN, Lns; NAB, NASB, NIV, NJB, NRSV, TNT], 'through whose instrumentality' [Ho, ICC], 'by' [KJV, TEV], 'by whose efforts' [AB], 'with (our) help' [LB]. This word is also translated as a verb with 'who' as its agent: 'who led you (to the faith)' [He], 'in bringing (you to the faith)' [REB]. Apollos as well as Paul was one of those through whom the Corinthians became believers [EGT, Gdt]. See this word at 1:9.

c. aorist act. indic. of πιστεύω (LN 31.85; 31.102): 'to believe' [LN, Lns; KJV, LB, NASB], 'to come to believe' [NIV, NJB, NRSV, TNT], 'to become believers' [HNTC; NAB], 'to come to faith' [AB], 'to receive the faith' [ICC], 'to lead to the faith' [He] 'to be led to believe' [TEV], 'to bring to faith' [REB]. The aorist points to a specific time of conversion to Christ [AB, EGT, ICC, NIC, NIC2, TH, Vn]. The aorist not only points to conversion but to their continued believing since then [EBC, ICC], and even to the 'planting' and 'watering' and 'God-given increase' of 3:6 [EBC]. See this word at 1:21.

QUESTION—Why did Paul use the term 'servant'?

Servants are not masters and cannot therefore be the authors or objects of the Corinthians' faith [ICC]. They were servants of God [BAGD, EBC, Lns, NIC2, TG, TH, TNTC; LB, REB, TEV], of Christ [He, NCBC], or of both the Lord and the church [HNTC, Ho]. Paul has in mind the service they rendered to the Corinthians [Lns]. This word stresses the lowly character of the service [TNTC]. This role does not negate Paul's authority as an Apostle, but it does negate his human authority in favor of his delegated authority from God [Herm]. In calling himself a servant Paul was saying that the cross is not only the center of the Gospel, but that it also was a pattern for Christian ministry [NIC2].

even[a] to-each-one as[b] the Lord assigned.[c]

LEXICON—a. καί (LN 89.93) (BAGD I.3. p. 393): 'even' [LN; KJV, NASB], 'and' [AB, HNTC, Lns; NJB], not explicit [all other versions]. Καί here means 'and that, and moreover', indicating that in addition to being servants, even their service is directed by someone else [Gdt]. Here it indicates that the following serves to explain the foregoing: 'that is, namely, and so' [BAGD, Ed].

b. ὡς (LN 64.12) (BAGD I.2.c. p. 897): 'as' [AB, BAGD, LN, Lns; KJV, NASB, NIV, NRSV], 'according to' [BAGD, ICC], 'in accordance with' [He]. The phrase is translated 'each has what the Lord gave to him' [NJB, TNT], 'each one of us does the work which the Lord gave him to do' [HNTC; NAB, REB, TEV], 'each with his own special abilities' [LB].

c. aorist act. indic. of δίδωμι (LN 37.98): 'to assign' [LN; NRSV], 'to assign a task' [NAB, NIV, REB], 'to appoint' [LN], 'to give' [Lns; KJV, NJB, TNT], 'to give a task' [Ed, HNTC; TEV], 'to give opportunity' [NASB], 'to give ability' [AB], 'to give grace' [ICC], 'to grant gifts' [He], not explicit [LB].

QUESTION—Who is the antecedent of ἑκάστῳ 'each one'?

1. It refers to the Lord's servants [AB, Ed, EGT, Gdt, He, Herm, HNTC, Ho, Lns, NCBC, NIC, NIC2, TH, TNTC, Vn; LB, NAB, NIV, NJB, REB, TEV]: as the Lord assigned tasks to each of his servants. The Corinthians have no right to make the differences between the work of Paul and that of Apollos an occasion for quarreling, since God assigned each a special task [NIC, NIC2].
2. It refers to those who believed [Alf, ICC; probably KJV, NASB]: as the Lord gave faith to each of you who believe. They received faith according to the grace the Lord gave to each [ICC].

QUESTION—Where is the emphasis in this phrase?

The phrase 'to each one' is emphasized [EGT, My].

QUESTION—To whom does the phrase 'the Lord' refer?

1. It refers to Christ [Ed, EGT, Gdt, NCBC, NIC2, TH, Vn]: even as the Lord Jesus Christ gave to each one. As a rule when this phrase is used in the New Testament apart from an Old Testament quote, it refers to Jesus Christ [Gdt].
2. It refers to God [AB, Ho, ICC, Lns, My, NIC, TG]: even as God gave to each one.

3:6 I planted,[a] Apollos watered,[b]

LEXICON—a. aorist act. indic. of φυτεύω (LN 43.5) (BAGD p. 870): 'to plant' [AB, BAGD, He, HNTC, LN, Lns; KJV, NASB, NJB, NRSV], 'to plant seed' [LB, NAB, NIV, REB, TEV, TNT], 'to plant the faith (in you)' [ICC].

b. aorist act. indic. of ποτίζω (LN **43.9**) (BAGD 3. p. 695): 'to water' [BAGD, He, HNTC, **LN**, Lns; all versions], 'to irrigate' [AB, BAGD, LN], 'to nourish' [ICC]. The implied object for this verb is 'plants' [AB, HNTC, TH; TEV], or 'seeds' [LB, NAB, NIV, REB, TNT].

QUESTION—What relationship is indicated by the lack of a conjunction?

The lack of a conjunction indicates that 3:6 reaffirms and develops the last statement of 3:5 [Gdt, Herm, NIC]: as the Lord gave to each, I planted, Apollos watered, but God caused the growth.

QUESTION—With what does 'planting' compare?

It is figurative for proclaiming the gospel for the first time, winning converts [AB, HNTC, My], and for founding a church [AB, Gdt, My, NIC, NIC2]. 'Planting' is figurative for the apostle's work [BAGD]. What Paul planted was the faith of the Corinthians, using the figure of a tree [My]. Paul is not thinking of individuals here, but of the planting of the whole church (3:9 'you plural are God's field') [Herm, NIC2]. The plants are the Corinthians [Alf].

QUESTION—With what does 'watering' compare?

Apollos assisted in the growth of what Paul planted [Gdt, My, Vn]. It is figurative for instructing the church [AB, My, NIC2], directing its work and guiding its growth [AB, Gdt, My, NIC, Vn]. It, along with 'planting', is figurative for the founding of a church [BAGD].

but[a] God made-(it)-grow;[b]

LEXICON—a. ἀλλά (LN 89.125): 'but' [AB, He, ICC, Lns; all versions except LB], 'it was not we, however, but' [HNTC], 'but it was (God) not we' [LB].

b. imperf. act. indic. of αὐξάνω (LN 59.63) (BAGD 1. p. 121): 'to make grow' [AB, HNTC; LB, NAB, NIV, REB, TEV, TNT], 'to cause to grow' [BAGD, He, ICC, Lns; NASB], 'to give growth' [NJB, NRSV], 'to cause to increase' [BAGD, LN], 'to give increase' [KJV], 'to grow' [BAGD]. 'Αυξάνω must also include the spiritual germinating principle that only God can initiate (John 3:5), in addition to the sense of causing to grow [EBC]. The natural object of this verb is 'plants' [AB, HNTC; TEV], or 'seeds' [NAB, NIV, REB, TNT]. The imperfect tense serves to indicate that the action of causing growth is a continuing one [Lns, NIC, Rb, TNTC], or one that was going on all the time, even during planting and watering [Ed, EGT, Gdt, ICC, NIC2, Vn]. The aorists 'I planted' and 'Apollos watered' point to work completed in the past. The imperfect points to an act begun in the past but going on indefinitely [Lns].

QUESTION—What relationship is indicated by ἀλλά 'but'?

This strong adversative serves to emphasize the word 'God' [ICC, TH; LB, TEV, TNT]: it was not we, but God who made it grow. It does more than contrast God with the servants. It has the function of singling out God from all others as the one who makes the plants grow. [EGT]. It serves to negate the preceding subjects: it was not we however [HNTC].

QUESTION—With what is 'to make grow' compared?

It is compared with creating and nurturing faith [HNTC], or with causing the work to succeed or prosper [Gdt, My, TG].

QUESTION—What is the function of this figure?

It puts Paul and Apollos on an equal footing as servants and redirects the focus of the Corinthians to God [NIC2]. It shows the diversity of the service of Paul and Apollos and points out the subordinate nature of their service [Ho]. It shows that though the tasks are distinct, they are not separate, and both tasks together are yet incomplete apart from the work of God [NIC].

3:7 so[a] neither the-one planting is anything[b] nor the-one watering but[c] God the-one making-to-grow.

LEXICON—a. ὥστε (LN 89.52) (BAGD 1.a. p. 899): 'so' [AB, BAGD, LN; NIV, NRSV, TNT], 'so then' [ICC, LN, Lns; KJV, NASB], 'in this' [NJB], 'as a result' [LN], 'for this reason' [BAGD], 'therefore' [BAGD, LN], 'this is why' [He], 'this means that' [NAB], 'it is' [REB], 'it follows that' [HNTC], not explicit [LB, TEV]. Ὥστε means 'from the preceding we must conclude that...' [NIC, TH]. See this word at 1:7.

b. τίς (LN 92.12; 92.13) (BAGD 1.b.ε. p. 820): 'anything' [BAGD, He, LN (92.12), Lns; KJV, NASB, NIV, NRSV], 'anyone, someone, something' [LN (92.12)], 'someone or something important' [LN (92.13)]. This pronoun is also translated as an adjective phrase: '(isn't) very important' [LB]. It is also translated as a prepositional phrase: 'of any special account' [NAB], or as a clause: 'who count' [REB], 'counts for anything' [HNTC; NJB], 'counts for anything at all' [ICC], 'amounts to anything' [AB], 'matters' [TNT], 'really do (not) matter' [TEV]. 'Is anything' means 'is anything of importance, anything worth speaking of' [BAGD, EGT, My]. Paul had asked, 'What is Apollos and what is Paul?' (3:5) and now he answers [Rb]. They had no independent importance from the perspective of ultimate responsibility for the Corinthians being God's people [NIC2]. Compared to God, anything people do is unimportant [TG].

c. ἀλλά: 'but' [AB, He; KJV, LB, NASB, REB], 'but only' [HNTC, ICC, Lns; NIV, NRSV, TNT], 'only' [NAB, NJB], not explicit [TEV]. It is strongly adversative and indicates the opposite of the previous statement: but God is everything [ICC]. 'God' is in apposition to 'the one making things grow' [HNTC, NIC2]. The attention of the Corinthians should be on God who is behind all spiritual growth rather than on the instruments he uses [TNTC].

QUESTION—Where is the emphasis in this verse?

It is on the word 'God' [ICC, Lns, Vn; TEV] which is placed emphatically last [ICC, Lns, Vn].

QUESTION—What predicate is implied with 'God' in this clause?

'God is everything' [Alf, Ed, EGT, Gdt, He, Herm, ICC, Lns, My, Vn]. The contrast implies that God is not only something, he is everything [Lns]. 'It is

God who matters' [TEV], he is important [AB; LB]. In general, whatever is the opposite of 'anything' in the preceding clause is what is implied here [AB, TH; LB].

3:8 Now[a] the-one planting and the-one watering are one,[b]

LEXICON—a. δέ (LN 89.87): 'now' [ICC, Lns; KJV, NASB], 'and' [HNTC, LN], not explicit [all other versions].

b. εἷς, ἕν (BAGD 1.b. p. 230): 'one' [BAGD, HNTC, Lns; KJV, NASB]. This numeral is also translated 'equally important' [TNT], 'in one class, equals in aim and spirit' [ICC], 'serve one function' [AB], 'have one purpose' [NIV, NRSV], 'work as a team' [REB], 'work as a team with the same aim' [LB], 'it is all one (who does the planting)' [NJB], 'there is no difference between' [TEV], 'it's a matter of indifference' [He].

QUESTION—What relationship is indicated by δέ 'now'?

It indicates a relationship of addition [HNTC, Lns, TNTC]: and. It indicates a transition with just a bit of contrast. Although their work is distinct, these servants are one [Gdt]. The δέ is adversative: the servant by himself is nothing, yet together they accomplish one work [Ed].

QUESTION—What is meant by Paul and Apollos being ἕν 'one'?

It means that they are of the same class, they are fellow workers [Alf, Ho, ICC, My, TH], have the same interest [EGT, Vn], and the same motive power [HNTC]. 'One' indicates unity of aim or purpose [Ed, EGT, HNTC, ICC, NIC2, Vn; NAB, NIV, REB], which is the growth of the church. Their goal is singular, the growth of the crop to an abundant harvest [Gdt, NIC2]. Their roles are complementary not competitive [EGT]. With such unity, to think of rivalry between them is not permissible [Gdt, ICC]. How can there be rivalry when the work of one is dependent on that of the other? [Gdt]. This means that the work of each is equally important [TG]. They are on the same side, the subordinate side of the work [NIC].

and[a] each will-receive[b] his-own[c] wages[d] according-to[e] his-own labor;[f]

LEXICON—a. δέ (LN 89.87): 'and' [HNTC, LN, Lns; KJV, NIV, NJB, NRSV], 'but' [He; NASB], 'and yet' [ICC], 'though' [AB; LB, REB, TNT], not explicit [NAB, TEV]. They are one in the work, 'but' they are distinct in responsibility to God [EBC, Ed]. The δέ is adversative [EBC, Ed, EGT, Gdt]: but. The contrast is in the reward that each will receive dependent on their work [Gdt].

b. fut. mid. indic. of λαμβάνω (LN 57.125) (BAGD 2. p. 465): 'to receive' [AB, He, HNTC, ICC, LN, Lns; KJV, NAB, NASB, NRSV, TNT], 'to get' [REB], 'to have' [NJB]. It is also combined with 'wages' and translated 'to be rewarded' [LB, NIV], 'God will reward' [TEV]. See this word at 2:12.

c. ἴδιος (LN 57.4) (BAGD 1.a.β. p. 369): 'his own' [AB, BAGD, He, HNTC, LN, Lns; KJV, NASB, REB, TNT], 'his own special' [ICC], 'his' [NAB], 'the proper' [NJB], 'appropriate, specific' [EGT], 'belonging to an individual' [BAGD, LN], not explicit [LB, NIV, NRSV, TEV].

d. μισθός (LN **38.14**) (BAGD 2.a. p. 523): 'wages' [AB, He, ICC, Lns; NAB, NRSV, TNT], 'pay' [HNTC; NJB, REB], 'recompense' [LN], 'reward' [BAGD, **LN**, TH; KJV, NASB]. This noun is also combined with 'receive' and translated as a verb: 'will be rewarded' [LB, NIV], 'God will reward' [TEV]. This is figurative for reward by God for the moral quality of an act [BAGD].

e. κατά with accusative object (LN 89.8) (BAGD II.5.a.β. p. 407): 'according to' [AB, BAGD, He, HNTC, ICC, Lns; KJV, NASB, NIV, NRSV, TEV], 'in accordance with' [LN; TNT], 'for' [LB, NJB, REB], 'in proportion to' [NAB].

f. κόπος (LN 42.47) (BAGD 2. p. 443): 'labor' [AB, BAGD, HNTC, Lns; KJV, NASB, NIV, NRSV, REB], 'work' [BAGD, He; NJB, TEV], 'hard work' [LN; LB], 'toil' [BAGD, LN; NAB, TNT], 'responsibility and toil' [ICC]. It means not only the effort expended to do the work, but the exhaustion following [Ed]. The servants are rewarded according to their labor, not their success [Ho, TNTC]. This word indicates hard work implying difficulties and trouble [LN].

QUESTION—What is the function of this clause?

It again points out the servant nature of the workers in that they both work under one who determines their pay [HNTC, NIC, NIC2]. Although they are one, yet they are individually responsible to God [Alf, EBC, Ed, EGT]. It also prepares for the following argument that each worker should take care how he builds since fire will determine their wages [My, NIC2].

QUESTION—What are the wages?

'Wages' may here refer to the rewards given out at the last day [AB, Gdt, Herm, My, NCBC]. The wage may also be the reward of having a successfully established and well-working church as the result of one's labor [AB]. The wage is sharing in Christ's joy (Matthew 25:21). Paul mentions wages to emphasize the responsibility of the servant to his Master [HNTC, NIC, NIC2]. The reward of each will not be based on a comparison with the other, but on the true value of the work of each, and only God can judge that [Gdt].

3:9 for[a] we-are God's fellow-workers,[b]

LEXICON—a. γάρ (LN 89.23): 'for' [He, HNTC, ICC, LN, Lns; KJV, NASB, NIV, NRSV, TEV], 'after all' [NJB], 'you see' [AB], not explicit [LB, NAB, REB, TNT].

b. συνεργός (LN 42.44) (BAGD p. 788): 'fellow workers' [BAGD, He, HNTC, LN; NASB, NIV, REB, TNT], 'laborers together' [KJV], 'co-workers' [Lns; LB, NAB], 'partners in (God's) work' [AB], 'partners working together' [TEV], 'helpers' [BAGD], 'servants, working together' [NRSV]. This noun is also translated as a clause: '(we) do share in (God's) work' [NJB], '(who) allows (us) a share in (His) work' [ICC].

QUESTION—What relationship is indicated by γάρ 'for'?

1. It indicates the grounds for 3:8a [Ed, ICC, TH, Vn]: the workers are one, because they are fellow-workers of God.
2. It indicates the grounds for 3:8b [Alf, Gdt, Lns, My]: God determines the wages because God is involved with both workers and the field.
3. It indicates the grounds for all of 3:8. The planter and waterer are one because they are both co-workers with God in the same work, and they get paid according to their labor because that is the rule for workers [Ho].
4. It indicates the grounds for the whole paragraph 3:5–9 [EGT, NIC2].
5. It introduces a conclusion to this part of the argument [TH].

QUESTION—What is meant by συνεργός 'fellow worker'?

1. It means that they work together with God [Alf, Ed, Gdt, Herm, Ho, ICC, Lns, My, Rb, TH, TNTC; KJV, LB, NJB]. This is the meaning of 3:6 which includes God in a cooperative effort: I planted, Apollos watered, but God caused it to grow. Perhaps to the idea of co-worker needs to be added the idea of dependence [Gdt]. The preposition σύν 'with' connects the workers with God and not with each other [Lns].
2. It means that they work together with each other for God [EGT, HNTC, NCBC, NIC, NIC2, TG, Vn; NRSV, REB, TEV]. The context stresses that Paul and Apollos are co-workers, not in opposition to each other. They are God's paid laborers not his colleagues [HNTC]. The genitives 'of God', all being emphatic, are possessive: fellow workers who belong to God. The thrust of the paragraph stresses their unity in work under God not with Him. The three genitive constructions bring the whole paragraph to a climax emphasizing God's ownership not his collaboration [NIC2]. In the light of 3:5 this is the better interpretation [TG]. The preposition σύν 'with' refers back to the words 'they are one' of 3:8. The genitive shows possession [EGT].

QUESTION—To whom does the word 'we' refer?

It refers to Paul and Apollos [TG, TH]. It refers to Paul and Apollos and to their fellow ministers, but not to Christians in general [Lns].

you-are God's field,[a] God's building.[b]

LEXICON—a. γεώργιον (LN **1.96**) (BAGD p. 157): 'field' [BAGD, HNTC, ICC, **LN**; NASB, NIV, NRSV, TEV], 'farm' [AB; NJB], 'farm land' [TNT], 'garden' [He; LB, REB], 'cultivation' [NAB], 'husbandry' [Lns; KJV], 'cultivated land' [BAGD]. Γεώργιον includes the sense of cultivation, meaning 'cultivated field' [EBC, Gdt, LN, My].

b. οἰκοδομή (LN **42.34**) (BAGD 2.b. p. 559): 'building' [AB, BAGD, HNTC, ICC, Lns; all versions], 'house' [He], 'construction' [**LN**], 'that which God has made' [**LN**], 'edifice' [BAGD]. This word is used figuratively [BAGD, Lns], and acts as a transition to the next paragraph [EBC, Lns]. Some think it focuses on the result of building [LN, NIC2], the finished building [Ed, He]. Others take it to focus on the process which results in a building, not the finished product [Gdt, HNTC, ICC, Vn].

QUESTION—How are the nouns related in the genitive construction θεοῦ γεώργιον 'field of God'?

1. It means that the field belongs to God [AB, EGT, Lns, My, NIC2, Vn; all versions]: God's field.
2. It means that the field is where God works [Ed, HNTC, ICC]. It means that God is cultivating the field through his servants [HNTC].

QUESTION—How are the Corinthians similar to a field?

'Field' depicts the location of labor and the toil of the servants in their ministry and care for the church [Vn]. The meaning is that the Corinthians display God's operations in 'spiritual husbandry' [ICC]. This figure depicts the organic growth of the Church [EGT]. The church is God's field which he makes productive by giving it light (his truth) and water (his undeserved favor) [Ho]. The field represents the raw material God works with, or each Christian in his power of life and growth [Ed].

QUESTION—How are the nouns related in the genitive construction θεοῦ οἰκοδομή 'building of God'?

1. It means that the building belongs to God [AB, EGT, Lns, My, NIC2, Vn; all versions]: God's building.
2. It means that the building is the structure God is erecting [Ed, HNTC, ICC, LN]: a house God is building. It means the building that God through his servants is erecting [HNTC].

QUESTION—How are the Corinthians similar to a building?

The meaning is that the Corinthians display God's operations in spiritual architecture [ICC]. This figure depicts the working together of the various parts of the Church [EGT]. The building represents the Church in its unified design and beauty and strength of structure [Ed].

QUESTION—Where is the emphasis in this verse?

The emphasis is on the three-time repeated words 'of God' [Alf, Ed, Herm, ICC, Lns, My, NIC2, TNTC; LB]: 'We are *God's* fellow workers, you are *God's* field, you are *God's* building'.

DISCOURSE UNIT: 3:10–23 [Lns]. The topic is God's building.

DISCOURSE UNIT: 3:10–17 [AB, EBC, EGT, TH, TNTC, Vn]. The topic is the church as God's building [AB], building on Christ, the foundation [EBC], the responsibility of the human builders [EGT], the foundation and the building [TNTC].

DISCOURSE UNIT: 3:9b/10–15 [Ed, ICC, NIC2, TNTC]. The topic is the requirement for doctrine to be in character with God's plan [Ed], the builders [ICC], the necessity for the church being built with care [NIC2], the test of a good building [TNTC]. While still on the topic of leadership in the church, Paul now shifts his emphasis from the true nature of leadership in the church to sternly warn those who are building the church [NIC2].

3:10 According-to[a] the grace[b] of God given to-me

LEXICON—a. κατά with accusative object (LN 89.8): 'according to' [He, Lns; KJV, NASB, NRSV], 'in accordance with' [HNTC, LN], 'as to' [ICC], 'in cooperation with' [AB], 'by' [NIV, NJB, TNT], 'in (his kindness)' [LB], not explicit [REB]. This preposition is also translated 'thanks to' [NAB], 'using (the gift that God gave)' [TEV]. See this word at 3:8

b. χάρις (LN 57.103) (BAGD 4. p. 878): 'grace' [BAGD, He, HNTC, Lns; KJV, NASB, NIV, NJB, NRSV, TNT], 'favor' [NAB], 'kindly favor' [AB], 'privilege' [REB], 'gift' [LN; TEV], 'gracious gift' [LN], 'kindness' [LB], 'grace to found churches' [ICC]. See this word at 1:3, 4.

QUESTION—Who is the actor of the passive verb 'given', and what is the significance of the aorist tense?

God is the actor [AB, ICC, Lns, NIC2, TH; LB, NAB, NIV, TEV, TNT]: the grace God gave me. The aorist point to a specific time in the past when this gift was given [Lns].

QUESTION—What is the grace given to Paul?

Grace is not the gift of apostleship, but a special gift which disposed Paul to found new churches [Alf, ICC, My, NIC2]. 'According to the grace of God' means that God in his kindness gave Paul a special gift to enable him to found churches in non-Christian cities [AB]. 'Grace' does not refer to one specific gift, but to the all the gifts Paul had received for this work of founding the Church, and particularly the congregation in Corinth [Gdt]. These gifts not only qualified Paul for the work, but also made him so hard-working and faithful [Ho]. 'Grace' refers to skill, ability, capacity [TG], or to God's enabling power [TNTC]. 'According to the grace given to me' has the same force as 'God gave the increase' and serves to keep the Corinthians from being able to make Paul a party leader [NIC].

like (an) expert[a] master-builder[b] I-laid[c] (a) foundation,[d]

LEXICON—a. σοφός (LN **28.9**) (BAGD 1. p. 760): 'expert' [ICC, **LN**, TNTC; LB, NIV, TEV], 'skilled' [Alf, Ed, EGT, HNTC, Ho, TG, Vn; NRSV, REB], 'trained' [NJB], 'experienced' [AB, BAGD], 'clever, skillful' [BAGD, LN], 'wise' [He, HNTC, LN, Lns; KJV, NAB, NASB, TNT]. Paul calls himself a 'wise' master-builder in contrast to the other 'wise' builders of Corinth who are using faulty building material [NIC2]. Σοφός means 'one who understands the art' [My, NIC], 'competent' [Herm]. In its non-figurative sense it means 'skilled' [HNTC, Vn].

b. ἀρχιτέκτων (LN **45.10**) (BAGD p. 113): 'master builder' [AB, BAGD, ICC, **LN**; all versions except LB, NIV, TEV], 'expert builder' [LN], 'master of works' [HNTC], 'architect' [Ed, He, Ho, Lns, TG, TH], 'builder' [LB, NIV, TEV]. This means not just the work of a carpenter, but of an architect and chief engineer [NIC2]. The Greek ἀρχιτέκτων was not a designer who put his plans on paper, but one who developed his ideas though the materials [EGT]. This term is not used of one who oversees other workers, but of one who is engaged in the initial work

[Vn]. However, he did feel responsible for the total work of the church [EBC].

c. aorist act. indic. of τίθημι (LN 85.32) (BAGD I.1.a.α. p. 815): 'to lay' [AB, BAGD, He, HNTC, ICC, Lns; all versions], 'to put, to place' [BAGD, LN]. The aorist tense refers to the time of Paul's visit in Corinth [ICC, NIC].

d. θεμέλιος (LN 7.41) (BAGD 2.a. p. 356): 'foundation' [AB, BAGD, He, HNTC, LN, Lns; all versions], 'foundation for the edifice' [ICC]. 'Foundation' is used figuratively of the building's stability and overall design [Ed].

QUESTION—What is meant by laying a foundation?

The building that is being constructed is the body of believers, the church [AB, Alf, EBC, Ed, EGT, Gdt, HNTC, Ho, ICC, NIC, NIC2]. 'Foundation' is figurative for the elementary beginnings of a thing, that is, the founding of a body of believers [BAGD]. The 'foundation' must refer to Jesus Christ [AB, NIC], whom Paul, by his preaching, laid beneath the growing church [AB]. 'Foundation' is figurative for the doctrine of Jesus Christ crucified [EBC], the basic teachings of doctrine [Herm], for Jesus Christ, his redemption, and the reception of this by faith by the believer [Alf]. The foundation is Jesus Christ (3:11). Laying the foundation means preaching the Good News about Jesus Christ [AB, Alf, EBC, Ed, Gdt, ICC, NCBC, NIC], teaching about the person and work of Christ [Ho], making Christ the object of the church's faith [My], placing Christ and the gospel in their hearts [Lns], enabling the Corinthians to believe in Christ [My].

and another[a] is-building-on[b] (it). But[c] each-one should-be-careful[d] how[e] he-builds-on (it).

LEXICON—a. ἄλλος: 'another' [He, Lns; KJV, NASB], 'another man' [TEV], 'another person' [AB], 'someone else' [HNTC, ICC; NAB, NIV, NJB, NRSV, TNT], 'others' [REB], 'Apollos' [LB].

b. pres. act. indic. of ἐποικοδομέω (LN **45.5**) (BAGD p. 305): 'to build on' [BAGD, He, HNTC, ICC, **LN**, Lns; all versions except REB], 'to put up the building' [REB], 'to build the superstructure' [AB], 'to build on to' [BAGD]. The present tense indicates action which goes on indefinitely and was going on as Paul wrote [Lns].

c. δέ (LN 89.87; 89.124): 'but' [AB, He, ICC; KJV, LB, NASB, NIV, TEV], 'however' [NAB], 'well' [HNTC], 'and' [Lns], 'now' [NJB], not explicit [NRSV, REB, TNT].

d. pres. act. impera. of βλέπω (LN 27.58) (BAGD 4.c. p. 143): 'to be careful' [ICC; NAB, NASB, NIV, NJB, TEV], 'to be very careful' [LB], 'to take care' [AB, He, HNTC; REB, TNT], 'to take heed' [Lns; KJV], 'to choose with care' [NRSV], 'to pay attention to, to beware of' [LN].

e. πῶς: 'how' [AB, He, HNTC, Lns; all versions except LB], 'as to the materials with which' [ICC], not explicit [LB]. 'How' means 'with what materials' [Alf, Gdt, Ho, ICC, My], the kind of building he builds [TG], what doctrine he teaches [My]. This warning is addressed to ministers [Ho] and to all who teach [AB, EBC, Gdt, NIC, Vn]. Only truth can be used in the fostering of Christian character [Ho]. This warning is general and is addressed to all believers [TNTC].

QUESTION—To whom does the word 'another' refer?

1. It refers to Apollos [TH; LB], or possibly Peter [NCBC].
2. It refers to someone among the Corinthians themselves, not to Apollos or Peter [AB, NIC2]. That this refers to Apollos would contradict 3:5–9 where Paul and Apollos were 'one'; again, Apollos was not at that time in Corinth and he is not mentioned in this paragraph; the whole analogy focuses rather on Paul's confrontation with the church over their standing on 'wisdom' [NIC2].
3. It refers to all teachers who followed Paul [Alf, EBC, Ed, EGT, Gdt, ICC, Lns, My, NIC, Vn]. The present tense of 'build on' prohibits a reference to Apollos since he was not at that time in Corinth. Further, the reference to 'each' following, shows that Paul is referring rather to a general class [Gdt].

QUESTION—With what is the action of 'building on' compared?

It is compared with instructing and building up believers and making new converts [HNTC]. It may be compared to development in organization, teaching of scriptural doctrine, development of leadership in worship and witness and social service [AB]. It is figurative for teaching to develop the character of the believers [ICC, My], or increasing another's knowledge and faith [Alf]. It is compared to increasing the size of the congregation and strengthening its faith [Lns]. It can either refer to the teaching of sound doctrine, or to the edifying the body of believers, or to the building of Christian character [TNTC].

3:11 For[a] other[b] foundation no-one is-able to-lay than that-which is-laid,[c] which is Jesus Christ.

LEXICON—a. γάρ (LN 89.23; 91.1): 'for' [AB, HNTC, LN (89.23); all versions except LB, NAB, REB, TNT], 'for, as regards foundation' [Lns], 'for, as regards the foundation, there is no room for question' [ICC], 'and' [LN (91.1); LB], 'it is true that' [He], not explicit [NAB, REB, TNT].

b. ἄλλος (LN 58.36; 58.37) (BAGD 1.e.β. p. 40): 'other' [AB, BAGD, LN; all versions except LB, NJB], 'any other' [He, ICC; LB, NJB], 'any other real' [LB], 'another' [BAGD, LN, Lns], 'different' [BAGD, HNTC, LN, My], 'other than' [LN]. Paul possibly had in mind a particular other foundation that threatened the work in Corinth, that Peter was the foundation of the church [HNTC, NCBC]. Paul was not thinking of Peter, but of the Corinthians themselves and their involvement in 'wisdom' which threatened to destroy the church [NIC2]. 'Other than' may suggest: 'in competition with' or 'contrary to' [EGT].

c. pres. mid./pass. deponent participle of κεῖμαι (LN 85.3) (BAGD 1.b. p. 426): 'to be laid' [AB, BAGD, He, ICC, LN; all versions except LB,

NJB, TEV], 'to be there' [LN; NJB]. It is also translated as an active verb: 'to lie' [Lns], 'to lie there' [HNTC], 'to place' [TEV], '(that one we) already have' [LB]. The present participle requires the word 'already' with the verb [HNTC, ICC, Lns, My, NIC2, TH; LB, NIV, NJB, REB, TEV]: that which is *already* laid. Κεῖμαι means that the foundation has been laid and lies there permanent and immovable [Ed].

QUESTION—What relationship is indicated by γάρ 'for'?

1. It indicates that this verse is the grounds for 3:10 [Alf, EBC, HNTC, Lns, NIC]: let each man take care how he builds on it, because the foundation is Jesus Christ. Each man should be careful how he builds, because all true building needs to be in perfect alignment with the only true foundation [Lns]. Each man should be careful how he builds, because faulty building can result from tampering with the foundation [HNTC]. Each man should take care how he builds, because it is assumed that a building of God is being built and this can only be built on one foundation [Alf].
2. It indicates that 3:12–15 stands as the grounds for 3:10 [Gdt, ICC, My, NIC2]: let each man take care how he builds on it because each man's work will be shown for what it is.
3. It indicates a shift from figurative language about Christ to Christ himself [TH]: each man must be careful how he builds on the foundation of the building, and that foundation is Christ.

QUESTION—Where is the emphasis in this phrase?

The word 'foundation' is emphasized [ICC, Lns, Vn], standing first in the verse [ICC]. Paul did not write ἄλλον θεμέλιον 'other foundation' but θεμέλιον ἄλλον 'foundation other', fronting the word θεμέλιος and emphasizing it [Lns].

QUESTION—Who is the actor of the passive verb 'that which is laid'?

1. The actor is God [Alf, Ed, Gdt, My, TG, TH, Vn; TEV]: than that which God has laid. The τίθημι 'to lay' of the previous phrase has the preacher as its actor, but the κείμενον 'which is laid' of this phrase, has God as its actor. Paul takes the foundation God laid and puts it in their hearts by preaching [Gdt]. This is not talking about Paul's founding of the church in Corinth, but of God's establishing Jesus Christ as the once-for-all foundation of the universal church [Alf, TH].
2. The actor is Paul [EGT, He, Ho, ICC, NCBC]: than that which I laid. This is the foundation Paul laid in Corinth by preaching Christ crucified [NCBC]. If 'Jesus Christ' is taken to be the doctrine of Christ, then Paul laid the foundation in preaching of Christ and him crucified. The latter is in keeping with the context [Ho]. For Corinth, the founder is Paul; for the church universal, the founder is God [ICC].

3:12 Now/But[a] if anyone builds on the foundation (with) gold, silver, precious[b] stones,[c] wood,[d] hay,[e] straw,[f]

LEXICON—a. δέ (LN 89.94; 89.124): 'now' [Lns; KJV, NASB, NRSV], 'but' [He, ICC; LB, TNT], not explicit [AB, HNTC; all other versions].

b. τίμιος (LN **2.29**; **65.2**) (BAGD 1.a. p. 818): 'precious' [AB, BAGD, He, HNTC, LN (2.29); all versions except LB, NIV, NJB], 'costly' [BAGD, Lns; NIV], 'valuable' [LN (65.2)], 'sumptuous' [ICC], not explicit [LB, NJB].

c. λίθος (LN **2:29**) (BAGD 1.c. p. 474): 'stones' [AB, BAGD, He, HNTC, ICC, LN, Lns; all versions except LB, NJB]. This word is also combined with the word 'precious' and translated 'jewels' [LB, NJB].

d. ξύλον (LN 3.60) (BAGD 1. p. 549): 'wood' [AB, BAGD, He, HNTC, ICC, LN, Lns; all versions except LB], 'sticks' [LB]. Here the plural is used to indicate 'wood' as a building material [BAGD].

e. χόρτος (LN 3.15) (BAGD p. 884): 'hay' [BAGD, He, HNTC, ICC, Lns; all versions except TEV], 'grass' [AB, BAGD, LN; TEV], 'small plants' [LN]. Χόρτος refers to green grass standing in a meadow. Here 'grass' implies building material of inferior quality [BAGD].

f. καλάμη (LN 3.58) (BAGD p. 398): 'straw' [BAGD, He, HNTC, ICC, LN, Lns; all versions except KJV], 'thatch' [AB], 'stubble' [Lns; KJV], 'stalk' [BAGD].

QUESTION—What relationship is indicated by δέ: 'now/but'?

1. It indicates transition [EGT, Lns; KJV, NASB, NRSV]: now. It indicates a transition from the foundation to the superstructure [EGT].
2. It indicates contrast [Alf, Gdt, He, ICC, My, TNTC; LB, TNT]: but. The contrast is between Paul and those who build on the foundation [Gdt]. There is one foundation, but there are many ways to build on it [Alf].

QUESTION—What is implied by 'precious stones'?

1. The stones are good quality building material [Alf, EGT, Ho, LN, My, Rb]: gold, silver, and good quality stone. Material such as granite [Ho], marble [Alf, Ho], porphyry or jasper is meant [Alf]. In the figurative context of a foundation, 'valuable' may be a better choice here [LN].
2. The stones are jewels for ornamentation [ICC; LB, NJB]: gold, silver, and jewels. They are for interior decoration [ICC].

QUESTION—How were hay and straw used in building?

Hay was dried grass which might be mixed with mud or clay for building walls [EBC, Ho]. Straw could be used to thatch a roof [AB, EBC, Ho]. Either might be used for mixing in mud or for thatching [ICC].

QUESTION—What is the point of comparison?

The point of comparison is perishability [EGT, Herm, Ho, My, NCBC, NIC, NIC2, Rb], or the relative values of the materials [EGT, Herm, My, NIC, TNTC, Vn].

QUESTION—How many kinds of material are referred to here?

There are only two groups intended [EBC, Ed, EGT, Gdt, Ho, ICC, Lns, My, NCBC, NIC2, Rb, TNTC, Vn]. Although there are six materials listed in descending order of value, only two groups are indicated, the first three and the last three [NIC2]. There is good material (gold, silver, and precious stones) or there is inferior material (wood, hay, and straw) [ICC].

QUESTION—What are the six materials being compared with?

1. They are compared to various kinds of teaching or wisdom [Alf, EBC, Ed, Ho, Lns, My, NCBC, NIC, NIC2, Vn]. This concerns the substance of what the ministers teach [Lns]. Because the laying of the foundation refers to preaching, so does the work on the building. Just as Paul's preaching of Christ Jesus forms the foundation of the church, so building on that foundation with good or bad teaching has the church for a result [NIC]. It refers primarily to teachings, but by inference to people affected by the teaching who become living stones in the building [Alf]. The good materials are teachings compatible with the foundation of the gospel about Jesus Christ [NIC2]. The bad materials are false teachings [Ho] and human 'wisdom' [NIC2].
2. They are compared to the moral fruits produced in the people by preaching. The teacher in his presentation of the truth works such virtues in his hearers as faith, hope, and love which can endure trial by fire [Gdt].
3. They are compared both to the moral fruits produced in people, and to the people themselves. Since these two are meaningless as separate entities, both are intended [ICC].

3:13 each-man's work[a] will-become evident,[b] for the day[c] will-expose[d] (it),

LEXICON—a. ἔργον (LN 42.12; 42.42) (BAGD 3. p. 308): 'work' [AB, BAGD, He, HNTC, LN (42.42), Lns; all versions except NJB], 'handiwork' [NJB], 'good or bad work' [ICC], 'workmanship, result of what has been done' [LN (42.12)]. It refers to what has been produced by work [BAGD, NIC2].

b. φανερός (LN 28.58; 24.20) (BAGD 1. p. 852): 'evident' [BAGD, LN (24.20); NASB, TNT], 'visible' [BAGD; NRSV], 'clear' [BAGD, LN (24.20); NAB], 'manifest' [HNTC, ICC, Lns; KJV], 'clearly known, easily known' [LN (28.58)], 'known, plainly to be seen, open' [BAGD], 'plain' [BAGD, LN], 'seen' [TEV], 'brought to light' [REB], 'shown for what it is' [NIV, NJB], 'revealed' [He], 'exposed' [AB]. It is also translated as clause: 'to see what kind of material each builder has used' [LB].

c. ἡμέρα: 'day' [AB, BAGD, Lns; KJV, NASB], 'Day' [HNTC; NAB, NIV, NJB, NRSV, TNT], 'day of judgment' [REB], 'Day of Judgment' [He, ICC], 'Day of Christ' [TEV], 'Christ's Judgment Day' [LB]. See this word at 1:8.

d. fut. act. indic. of δηλόω (LN **28.42**): 'to expose' [REB], 'to make clearly known' [**LN**], 'to make clear' [NJB], 'to show' [NASB], 'to clearly show' [AB], 'to show up' [HNTC], 'bring to light' [NIV], 'to disclose' [He, ICC; NAB, NRSV], 'to declare' [Lns; KJV], not explicit [TEV, TNT]. It is also translated by its reciprocal: 'so that all can see' [LB]. The object of this verb is 'each man's work' [Lns]. The thing being exposed is the truth or falsehood of the doctrines taught [Ho].

QUESTION—To what does the word 'day' specifically refer?

It refers to the 'Day of Judgment' [AB, BAGD, HNTC, Ho, ICC, Lns, NCBC, NIC, Rb]. It is that day when Christ will return, the day of judgment (1 Thessalonians 5:4; Hebrews 10:25) [Alf, Ed, EGT, Gdt, He, My, TNTC, Vn]. It refers to the great day, the day of judgment, the day of the Lord [Ho, NIC2]. The definite article with day shows that Paul is referring to the time of judgment for Christians referred to in 2 Corinthians 5:10 when they give account for their Christian service [EBC]. It refers to a time of light when what had been hidden will be clearly seen [ICC].

because[a] it-is-revealed[b] with[c] fire;[d]

LEXICON—a. ὅτι (LN 89.33): 'because' [AB, He, HNTC, ICC, LN, Lns; KJV, NASB, NRSV], 'for' [REB, TEV], not explicit [LB, NAB, NIV, NJB, TNT].

b. pres. pass. indic. of ἀποκαλύπτω (LN 28.38) (BAGD 4. p. 92): 'to be revealed' [AB, HNTC, ICC, LN, Lns; KJV, NASB, NIV, NRSV], 'to be made fully known' [LN], not explicit [He]. This passive verb is also translated actively: '(that day will) make its appearance' [NAB], '(the day) dawns' [NJB, REB, TNT], '(fire) will reveal (everyone's work)' [TEV]. It is also translated with implicit information: '(so that) all can see whether or not it keeps its value and what was really accomplished' [LB]. The present tense implies certainty by indicating a future event as though it were already here [EGT, Ho, ICC, TNTC, Vn]. The present tense indicates the nature of the day, a day to be known by fire [Ed]. The agent of this passive verb is God [Lns]. This verb should be taken as a middle rather than a passive and thus means 'the Day manifests itself with fire' [NIC2]. See this word at 2:10.

c. ἐν with dative object (LN 89.80; 89.76): 'with' [NAB, NASB, NIV, NRSV, TNT], 'by' [AB, He; KJV], 'in' [HNTC, ICC, Lns; NJB, REB], 'through' [LB]. This preposition is also translated as indicating the actor of 'reveal': 'the fire will reveal it' [TEV]. It should be taken here as indicating accompanying circumstance [He, Herm]. It should be taken to indicate the element 'in which' the revelation occurs. In 2 Thess. 1:8 it is said that the Lord Jesus will be revealed 'in flaming fire' [Alf, Ed, Ho, ICC].

d. πύρ (LN 2.3) (BAGD 1.b. p. 730): 'fire' [AB, BAGD, He, HNTC, ICC, LN, Lns; all versions]. The fire is literal and means fire that originates in heaven and has a heavenly quality. Here the phrase means that the Judgment Day will make its appearance with fire [BAGD].

QUESTION—What is to be revealed?

1. It refers to the Day [Alf, BAGD, Ed, EGT, He, Herm, HNTC, Ho, ICC, My, NIC, NIC2, Rb, TH, TNTC; NAB, NJB, REB, TNT]: the Day will be revealed with fire. If 'it' refers to 'the work of each', then the next clause

is redundant [Alf, HNTC, NIC, NIC2, TH]. 'Day' is the closer of the two possible antecedents [HNTC, TH]. Fire is a figure for the cleansing judgment which will punish evil [NIC]. Fire is a symbol for trial and judgment [Ho].

2. It refers to the work [Lns, TG, Vn; LB, NRSV, TEV]: each man's work will be revealed with fire.
3. The word 'it' is impersonal and this states a principle that it is with fire that anything is revealed [Gdt].

and[a] the fire itself will-test[b] each-one's work of-what-sort[c] it-is.

TEXT—Some manuscripts omit αὐτό 'it/itself'. GNT encloses it within brackets to indicate that it is uncertain. Of those who include it, some take it to intensify the word fire: 'the fire *itself* will test the work' [AB, Alf, EBC, Ed, Lns, My, Rb; NASB, NJB, TNT]; others take it to be the object of the verb: 'the fire will test it (the work)' [EGT, Gdt, Herm, ICC].

LEXICON—a. καί: 'and' [AB, BAGD, He, HNTC, ICC, LN, Lns; all versions except LB], not explicit [LB]. It indicates that this is also part of the reason indicated by ὅτι 'because' [ICC]. If 'day' is the subject of 'is revealed' of the previous phrase, then this is an independent clause and is not part of the reason indicated by 'because' [NIC].

b. fut. act. indic. of δοκιμάζω (LN 27.45) (BAGD 2.a. p. 202): 'to test' [He, HNTC, LN, Lns; all versions except KJV, LB, TEV], 'to put to the test' [AB], 'to test something to show' [ICC; TEV], 'to try' [KJV], 'to prove by testing' [BAGD], 'to examine' [LN], 'to try to determine the genuineness of' [LN]. This word is also translated 'work will be put through (the fire) so that all can see' [LB]. 'To test' means to reveal the real quality of a thing [TG]. It is not the character of the person that will be tested, but his work [ICC, Vn]. The fire does not punish, it tests [HNTC, ICC].

c. ὁποῖος (LN 58.30) (BAGD p. 575): 'of what sort' [AB, BAGD, LN, Lns; KJV, NRSV], 'of what character' [ICC], 'what kind of' [LN], 'what (it is) like' [HNTC], '(so that all can see) whether or not it keeps its value, and what was really accomplished' [LB]. This pronoun is also translated as a noun which complements the verb 'to test': '(to test the) worth of' [REB], '(to test the) quality of' [He; NAB, NASB, NIV, NJB, TNT], '(test it and show) its real quality' [TEV]. This word refers to the quality of the material, that is, the kinds of doctrine taught and life lived [EBC].

QUESTION—What is the point of comparison indicated by 'fire'?

The point of comparison in 'fire' is its consuming power: worthless materials will be burned up [Ed, EGT, ICC, Lns, NIC, TNTC]. The focus is the testing quality of fire, not its purifying quality [EBC, HNTC, NIC2].

QUESTION—How will the fire test the material?

The building will be wrapped in fire and the wood, hay, and straw will burn up while the solid materials will remain standing [HNTC, Ho, ICC]. The fire does not purify the worker; it tests his workmanship as to its quality [NIC2].

3:14 If anyone's work which he-built-on survives,[a] he-will-receive[b] wages;[c]

LEXICON—a. fut. act. indic. of μένω (LN 13.89) (BAGD 1.c.β. p. 504): 'to survive' [BAGD, He; NIV, NRSV, REB, TEV], 'to remain' [BAGD, LN; NASB], 'to last' [BAGD; TNT], 'to persist, to stay' [BAGD], 'to still stand' [LB, NAB], 'to remain standing' [AB], 'to stand up to (it)' [NJB], 'to stand the ordeal' [ICC], 'to abide' [HNTC, Lns; KJV]. Μένω here means 'to remain unharmed' [Herm, HNTC, Lns, My, Vn]. The gold, silver and precious stones can endure the fire [NIC]. The future tense indicates that it will remain standing after the fire [TH].

b. fut. mid. indic. of λαμβάνω: 'to receive'. See this word at 3:8.

c. μισθός: 'wages'. See this word at 3:8.

QUESTION—To what is μισθόν 'wages' being compared?

The workman's wages for work on a building is compared with the teacher's reward from God [My]. Some translations have changed the translation of this word from 'wages' in 3:8 to 'reward' here [He, ICC; NRSV, TNT]. The reward consists of higher levels of glory and the privilege of meditating on the work they have been able to accomplish with God's help [Gdt, Lns]. It is compared with chances for higher service [ICC], or simply with God's approval [Gdt, HNTC], or with knowing that one's work endures [NIC].

3:15 if anyone's work will-be-burned-up,[a] he-will-suffer-loss,[b]

LEXICON—a. fut. pass. indic. of κατακαίω (LN 14.66) (BAGD p. 411): 'to be burned up' [BAGD, He, HNTC, LN, Lns; NASB, NIV, NRSV, TEV, TNT], 'to be burned' [KJV], 'to be burned down' [BAGD, LN; NJB], 'to be consumed' [BAGD], 'to be reduced to ashes' [LN], 'to be burnt to the ground' [ICC]. This passive is also translated actively: 'to burn' [NAB], 'to burn up' [LB], 'to burn down' [AB; REB]. The future tense refers to the Day of Judgment [TH].

b. fut. pass. indic. of ζημιόω (LN **38.7**) (BAGD 2. p. 338): 'to suffer loss' [Lns; KJV, NAB, NASB, NIV, NRSV], 'to suffer the loss of it' [NJB], 'to have to bear the loss' [REB], 'to sustain a loss' [AB], 'to have a great loss' [LB], 'to be deprived of a reward' [He], 'to lose one's reward' [ICC; TEV, TNT], 'to be mulcted of one's pay' [HNTC], 'to suffer punishment' [**LN**], 'to be punished' [BAGD, LN]. Ζημιόω usually means 'to deprive someone of something' [He]. It can mean, 'to be punished' but this does not match the words 'he himself' that follow [Ed, HNTC].

QUESTION—What is the relationship of this verse to 3:14?

Verses 14 and 15 are in a contrastive relationship [Lns, NIC, TH; LB, TEV]. The lack of a conjunction serves to heighten the contrast [Lns].

QUESTION—What loss does a man suffer?

The loss will be of his pay or reward [Alf, EBC, Ed, EGT, Gdt, He, HNTC, Ho, ICC, Lns, My, NIC2, TH, TNTC, Vn; TNT]. The words 'he himself' favor the interpretation that the man's loss is his pay: he will lose his pay but he himself will be saved [ICC]. The loss he bears is a lower position in the kingdom of heaven than otherwise [Ho]. His loss will be watching his work being destroyed by fire [AB, Gdt].

but he-himself will-be-saved,[a] but only/thus[b] as[c] through[d] fire.[e]

LEXICON—a. fut. pass. indic. of σῴζω (LN 21.27) (BAGD 3. p. 798): 'to be saved' [AB, BAGD, HNTC, LN, Lns; all versions except REB], 'to be saved from destruction' [ICC], 'to be kept from harm, to be preserved, to be rescued' [BAGD]. This passive is also translated actively: 'to escape with one's life' [REB], 'to escape' [He]. Here escape from a burning house is figurative for obtaining eternal salvation [BAGD]. This salvation refers to eternal salvation [Alf, BAGD, EGT, Herm, Ho, ICC, My, NCBC, NIC]. Also see this word at 1:18, 21.

b. οὕτως (LN 61.9) (BAGD 2. p. 598): 'only' [HNTC; NAB, NIV, NRSV], 'thus' [BAGD, LN, NIC2], 'so' [Lns; KJV, NASB], not explicit [He, ICC; LB, REB, TEV, TNT]. It refers to what follows: 'in this way' [BAGD, LN]. This word is also translated by repeating the previous clause indicating that οὕτως refers to what precedes: 'he will be saved' [NJB], 'being rescued' [AB].

c. ὥς (BAGD I.1. p. 897): 'as' [BAGD, HNTC, Lns; KJV, NAB, NASB, NIV, NJB, NRSV, TNT], 'as if' [TEV], 'as it were' [AB, NIC2], 'like' [BAGD, He, ICC], 'only by' [REB]. This particle is also translated as a clause: 'like a man escaping' [LB]. Combined with the preceding οὕτως 'so' it means 'so, in such a way'. Here the meaning of the passage is 'he will be saved, (but only) in such a way as (a man in an attempt to save himself, must go) through the fire (and therefore suffer from burns)' [BAGD]. It shows that this language is figurative: he will be saved, but 'as it were' through fire [NIC2]. 'So as through fire' is the figure of a person escaping from a house through a burning wall of fire [BAGD, EBC, HNTC, TNTC]. 'As through fire' is figurative for a narrow escape from grave danger [EGT, ICC, Lns, NIC], or being saved with difficulty [Ho]. It is implied that those who continue to teach about 'worldly wisdom' are in serious danger and will be snatched from danger in just the nick of time [NIC2]. 'But only as through fire' needs to be filled out to: 'as if he had escaped through fire' [TH].

d. διά with genitive object (BAGD A.I.2. p. 179): 'through' [AB, He, Lns; LB, NAB, NASB, NIV, NRSV, TEV, TNT], 'by', [KJV], 'from' [NJB]. Implied information is included: 'one who has passed through' [HNTC, ICC], 'passing through' [REB], 'as if he had come through' [BAGD]. Here it is used in its local rather than its instrumental sense [BAGD, EGT, Gdt, HNTC, ICC, Lns, TNTC, Vn; NAB, NIV, TEV, TNT]. The workman dashes through the flames, safe, but only just [HNTC].

e. πύρ (BAGD 1.a. p. 730): 'fire' [AB, BAGD, He, HNTC, ICC, Lns; all versions except LB, NIV], 'flames' [NIV], 'a wall of flames' [LB]. See this word at 3:13.

QUESTION—What relationship is indicated by δέ 'but'?

This indicates the contrast between between 'the reward' and 'he himself' [Ed, EGT, Gdt, ICC, My, TH]: the reward will be lost but the worker will be saved.

QUESTION—What is meant by οὕτως 'only/thus'?

1. It has an intensive meaning [HNTC; NAB, NIV, NRSV]: he himself will be saved but only as through fire.
2. It means 'thus' and refers to what follows [BAGD]: he himself will be saved, as follows, through fire.
3. It means 'thus' and refers to what precedes [AB; NJB]: he himself will be saved, saved that is, as through fire.

QUESTION—What is meant by 'as through fire'?

1. This continues the picture of the fire testing the construction and the person escapes through the flames of the burning house [Alf, EBC, Ed, EGT, HNTC, My, NCBC, Rb, TNTC, Vn]. It is through the fire of God's judgment [HNTC, Lns].
2. It is an idiom [Ho, ICC, NIC, NIC2], meaning to escape with difficulty [Ho], to have a narrow escape [ICC, NIC]. The idiom is occasioned by the reference to the fire that tests their work [ICC, NIC].

DISCOURSE UNIT: 3:16–23 [Alf, My]. The topic is a warning addressed to the readers [My].

DISCOURSE UNIT: 3:16–20 [Ed]. The topic is the worldly-wise teaching of party-leaders destroying God's temple and incurring his displeasure.

DISCOURSE UNIT: 3:16–17 [ICC, NIC2, TNTC]. The topic is the temple of God [ICC, TNTC], warnings to those who would destroy the church, God's temple in Corinth [NIC2].

3:16 Do-you-know[a] not that you-are (a) temple[b] of-God

LEXICON—a. perf. act. indic. of οἶδα (LN 28.1) (BAGD 1.e. p. 556): 'to know' [AB, BAGD, He, HNTC, ICC, LN, Lns; all versions except LB, NAB, NJB], 'to be aware' [NAB], 'to realize' [LB, NJB]. It means to know by perception or observation [Vn].

b. ναός (LN 7.15) (BAGD 2. p. 533): 'temple' [AB, BAGD, He, HNTC, ICC, LN; all versions except LB], 'sanctuary' [LN, Lns], 'house' [LB]. Ναός refers to a building in which a deity is worshipped [LN]. It means the sanctuary which contained the Holy of Holies. The οἰκοδομή 'building' of 3:9 is more specifically defined as a ναός, a sanctuary for God to live in [NCBC]. The idea changes from God's building to his dwelling [Herm]. There is emphasis on the word ναός here [Alf, My].

QUESTION—What is the relationship between this verse and the preceding context?

It provides the reason why unfaithful workers deserve to be punished, since they have the responsibility of building a very extraordinary building [Ho]. The lack of a conjunction shows that Paul is suddenly gripped with the seriousness of what the bad workers have done [Gdt]. The lack of conjunction forcefully introduces a new part of the argument. Paul had been talking about the relationship between the teachers and the church. Now he explains that the church is a 'temple' [My]. This verse does not connect with the preceding context, but with 3:9b where Paul spoke about the excellence of the church. He now talks about this, combining it with 3:10ff [NIC, NIC2].

QUESTION—How are the nouns related in the genitive construction ναὸς θεοῦ 'temple of God'?

The temple belongs to God or is owned by him [TG, TH], or it is the place where he is worshipped [TG].

QUESTION—What is the function of the rhetorical question?

The rhetorical question with οὐκ 'not' expects a positive reply [Lns, NIC, TG, TH; REB, TEV]. It functions as a rebuke [ICC, TNTC]: you should remember that you are God's temple. They had failed to remember that they were the temple of God's Spirit [ICC]. It functions to startle them [Lns, My], and to vividly remind the Corinthians that they were the temple of God's Spirit [Lns, NIC]. It functions as irony or sarcasm [NIC2]: 'Can it be that you who boast in 'knowledge' do not know that?' It functions to draw their attention to a fact that they should know by the very nature of things [NIC2]. It functions as a challenge addressed as it is to a church of superior knowledge [EGT].

QUESTION—What is indicated by the lack of the definite article with ναός 'temple'?

1. It indicates *the* temple of God [Alf, Ed, EGT, He, ICC, Lns, My]. Since only one temple of God exists, no article is needed [Lns]. There is only one temple of God and it is truly either the whole church, the local church, or the individual Christian. Here it is the local church [ICC]. There is only one temple of God, but there are many churches each one of which is the true spiritual temple of God [Alf, My].
2. It means that they had the characteristic or quality of being God's temple and not that they were *the* temple of God [Gdt, TNTC, Vn]. They were not the church universal, but the church of Corinth [Gdt].

and[a] God's spirit lives[b] in[c] you?

LEXICON—a. καί (LN 89.93): 'and' [He, HNTC; LB, TNT], 'and that' [AB, EGT, Herm, Lns; KJV, NAB, NASB, NIV, NRSV, TEV], not explicit [NJB, REB]. The καί serves to introduce the explanation of what it meant to be the temple of God [ICC, Lns, My].

b. pres. act. indic. of οἰκέω (LN 85.67; 85.73) (BAGD 1. p. 557): 'to live' [BAGD, LN; LB, NIV, NJB, TEV], 'to dwell' [AB, BAGD, He, HNTC, LN, Lns; KJV, NAB, NASB, NRSV, REB, TNT], 'to live in, to dwell in, to reside in' [LN], 'to have one's habitation' [BAGD]. Paul is thinking of God living among his people by means of the miraculous cloud

(Leviticus. 2:11f). Now he lives among his people by means of the Holy Spirit [NIC].

c. ἐν with dative object 'in' [He, HNTC, ICC, Lns; all versions except LB, REB], 'where' [REB], 'among' [AB; LB]. Here Paul probably means that God's Spirit 'lives in their midst' rather than in each of them [AB, Gdt, HNTC, Lns, My, NIC, NIC2, TH, TNTC]. God lives among believers only by living in them individually, so the one implies the other [Gdt].

QUESTION—What is the significance of using the plural ὑμῖν 'you'?

It shows that the focus is on the whole congregation as being God's temple [AB, HNTC, NCBC].

3:17 If anyone destroys[a] God's temple, God will-destroy[b] him;

LEXICON—a. pres. act. indic. of φθείρω (LN **20.39**) (BAGD 1.b. p. 857): 'to destroy' [AB, BAGD, He, HNTC, ICC, **LN**, Lns; all versions except KJV, LB], 'to defile' [EBC; KJV], 'to defile and spoil' [LB], 'to ruin, to corrupt, to spoil' [BAGD]. It means 'to destroy by corrupting' [ICC, Vn], 'to bring into a worse state' [EBC, Ho, NIC], 'to profane, to inflict evil on, to go against the character of the church as God's temple' [NIC]. The sense 'to corrupt morally' is probably the intended meaning [EGT, TG, TH]. The form of the condition is particular, meaning 'If anyone is destroying...' [AB, NIC2]. This was a greater error than building with faulty materials [HNTC, TNTC]. It could have been the attempt to import Jewish legalism which would have destroyed the church. If we think of God's temple as the local church, it is possible for it to be destroyed [HNTC]. This could be done by worthless teaching and thereby engendering party spirit [Vn].

b. fut. act. indic. of φθείρω (BAGD 2.c. p. 857): 'to destroy' [AB, BAGD, He, HNTC, ICC, Lns; all versions]. Here it means 'to punish with eternal destruction' [BAGD, Gdt]. The verb is repeated to show that the punishment mirrors the crime [ICC, My, TNTC].

QUESTION—How is a church destroyed?

It is destroyed by the teaching of false doctrine [EGT, HNTC, Ho, NIC, Vn], by divisive behavior [AB, EGT, HNTC, ICC, NCBC, NIC2, TNTC], by the immoral conduct discussed in chapters 5 and 6 [EGT], by disrupting the unity of the church [ICC], or by breaking a church's relationship with God [HNTC]. When a local church ceases to exist at a location, it is destroyed [HNTC].

QUESTION—How is a person destroyed?

It is not clear whether temporal or eternal death is indicated [Ed]. Terrible ruin and eternal loss of some kind are indicated [ICC]. The future tense refers to the last day, the verb refers to destruction in Hell [Lns]. Φθείρω denotes the punishment of death [My]. Spiritual death is probably intended here [Alf].

QUESTION—Which word is emphasized in this clause?

1. The word ‘him’ is emphasized [Gdt, TH]. ‘Him’ refers to the non-Christian party of the Corinthians [Gdt, ICC], or to the ones mainly involved in the activity of the divisions [NIC2].
2. The word ‘God’ is emphasized [EGT].

for[a] God’s temple is holy,[b] which you are.

LEXICON—a. γάρ (LN 89.23): ‘for’ [AB, He, HNTC, ICC, LN, Lns; all versions except NJB, REB], ‘because’ [NJB, REB]. This marks the following as the reason why God will destroy the one who destroys His temple [EBC, NIC2]. This clause constitutes the reason for God’s punishment: God cannot permit part of his holy work to be destroyed without penalty [EBC, Gdt, Ho].

b. ἅγιος (LN 88.24; 53.46) (BAGD 1.a.β. p. 9): ‘holy’ [AB, BAGD, He, HNTC, ICC, LN (88.24), Lns; all versions except LB, NIV], ‘holy and clean’ [LB], ‘sacred’ [NIV], ‘pure’ [BAGD, LN (88.24)], ‘perfect, worthy of God’ [BAGD], ‘devout, godly, dedicated’ [LN (53.46)]. It means to be in possession of high moral and godly qualities or to be dedicated to God’s service [LN]. It means ‘belonging to God alone’ [TH]. The root meaning of ἅγιος is ‘relation with God’. Therefore if a man destroys a church’s relation with God (by introducing legalism, for example), he also denies his own relation with God [HNTC]. It means ‘set apart for God’ [Lns, TNTC], and points to the character of the church as God’s own possession [TNTC]. It has a moral-ethical meaning as opposed to ritualistic holiness [NIC2]. Because the Corinthians were holy they shared in the very inviolability of God Himself [Gdt]. The church’s holiness was because of who lived in her [NCBC, NIC], not because of the action of her members [NIC].

QUESTION—To what does the word οἵτινες ‘which’ refer?

1. It refers back to the word temple [Ed, He, Herm, Ho, ICC, NCBC, NIC, NIC2, Rb, TH, Vn; all versions except NASB]: which temple you are. The relative pronoun, although referring to a singular ναός ‘temple’, is plural agreeing with the ὑμεῖς ‘you pl.’ [Gdt, Herm, HNTC, ICC, Lns, NIC2, Rb]. This relative has the sense of belonging to a category or class ‘and this is what you are’ [ICC].
2. It refers to the word ‘holy’ [Alf, EGT, Lns, My; possibly NASB]: God’s temple is holy, which you are as well. It means ‘of which character’ and therefore refers to the quality of being holy [My]. The word has the sense of ‘since’: ‘since of such kind are you’ [Lns].
3. It refers to both of the above [Gdt]: God’s temple is holy, and you are a holy temple.

QUESTION—Where is the emphasis in this clause?

The word ‘you’ is emphasized [Lns, TH, TNTC, Vn; TEV].

DISCOURSE UNIT: 3:18–4:13 [TNTC]. The topic is the preachers’ lowly place.

DISCOURSE UNIT: 3:18–4:5 [ICC, NCBC]. The topic is a warning against a merely 'human' estimate of the pastoral office [ICC], stewards of the mysteries of God [NCBC].

DISCOURSE UNIT: 3:18–23 [AB, EBC, EGT, Herm, HNTC, NCBC, NIC, NIC2, TH, TNTC, Vn]. The topic is belonging to God [AB], complete dependence on God, not men [EBC], the church and the world [EGT], critique of boasting [Herm], Paul, Apollos, Cephas, and Christ [HNTC], the foolishness of worldly wisdom [TNTC], warning and encouragement [NCBC], summary [NIC], the conclusion of the matter is that all are Christ's [NIC2]. This paragraph is in two parts: 3:18–20 and 3:21–23. Each is marked by the words, 'Let no one.' The first concludes the discussion of quarreling, the second one concludes the discussion of doing so under the guise of wisdom [NIC2]. He now concludes the discussion of wisdom and folly. At the same time he resolves the conflict of party strife by showing the absolute absurdity on which it is based [HNTC].

3:18 Let-deceive[a] no-one himself;

LEXICON—a. pres. act. impera. of ἐξαπατάω (LN 31.12) (BAGD p. 273): 'to deceive' [BAGD, He, HNTC, LN, Lns; KJV, NASB, NIV, NRSV, TNT], 'to delude' [AB; NAB], 'to fool' [LB, TEV], 'to mislead' [LN], 'to make a mistake' [REB]. This verb is also translated as a noun phrase: '(self)-delusion' [NJB], '(the danger of) a false estimate of oneself' [ICC].

QUESTION—What is the significance of the present tense imperative?

The present imperative indicates that this activity was already going on and that they should stop doing it [EBC, Rb, TNTC; LB].

QUESTION—To what should this warning be connected?

1. It should be connected with the following context [Alf, EBC, EGT, Gdt, HNTC, Ho, Lns, NCBC, NIC]: let no one deceive himself by thinking that he is wise when God thinks of him as a fool. A man may deceive himself about human wisdom and God's wisdom, but not about the certainty of God's punishment [EGT].
2. It should be connected with the previous context [My, Vn]: let no one deceive himself by thinking that he will not be punished.
3. Both connections are indicated [Ed, ICC, My, NIC2]. Some may erroneously think that God will not punish them but this is the result of self-deception concerning true wisdom [Ed]. Those seeking 'wisdom' are destroying the church and a fearful judgment awaits them [My, NIC2].

if anyone among[a] you thinks[b] (himself) to-be wise[c] in[d] this age,[e]

LEXICON—a. ἐν with dative object (LN 83.9): 'among' [Ed, EGT, He, HNTC, LN, Lns; KJV, NASB, REB, TEV, TNT], 'of' [NAB, NIV, NJB], 'in (your) company' [AB], 'in his intercourse with (you)' [ICC], not explicit [LB, NRSV]. Some think that the word ἐν 'among' indicates that this person referred to was not one of themselves [Ed, ICC]. Others think that ἐν 'among' does not prove that this man was not one of the Corinthians; it is a simply a general reference to anyone who may qualify [Gdt, HNTC]. See this word at 2:6.

b. pres. act. indic. of δοκέω (LN **31.29**) (BAGD 1.b. p. 201): 'to think' [AB, BAGD, He, **LN**, Lns; all versions except KJV, LB, REB], 'to fancy' [REB], 'to seem' [KJV], 'to count oneself' [LB], 'to imagine' [ICC, LN], 'to suppose' [BAGD, HNTC, LN], 'to believe' [BAGD, LN], 'to presume, to assume' [LN], 'to consider' [BAGD]. The condition using the indicative mood indicates that this kind of thinking was already happening among the Corinthians [EBC, NIC2, Rb, TH]. Because this was happening, Paul's seeming hypothesis serves as a kind of irony to deter them or to make them listen to his argument [NIC2]. Another view is that the 'if' clause does not indicate that the danger has become a reality [NIC].

c. σοφός (LN 32.33) (BAGD 3. p. 760): 'wise' [BAGD, He, HNTC, ICC, LN, Lns; all versions except LB], 'above average in intelligence' [LB]. This adjective is also translated as a verbal phrase: 'to have (superior worldly) wisdom' [AB]. Wisdom here is considered divine in nature and origin [BAGD]. See this word at 1:19, 20, 25-27.

d. ἐν with dative object (LN 89.5): 'in' [AB, He, LN, Lns; KJV, NAB, NASB, NRSV], 'in terms of' [TNT], 'by' [LN; NJB], 'by the standards of' [HNTC; NIV, REB, TEV], 'as judged by' [LB], 'with the wisdom of' [ICC].

e. αἰών (LN **41.38**) (BAGD 2.a. p. 27): 'age' [BAGD, HNTC; NASB, NIV, NRSV, REB, TNT], 'world' [He, LN; KJV, TEV], 'world system' [LN], 'world age' [Lns], 'the non-Christian world' [ICC], 'world's standards' [**LN**; LB, NJB], 'world-period' [EGT]. This noun is also translated as a phrase: '(in a) worldly way' [NAB], 'superior worldly (wisdom)' [AB]. It is the same as 'world' in the following verse. One can either think of a time span or of the space within which people spend their lives [HNTC]. See this word at 1:20.

QUESTION—With what should the phrase 'in this age' be connected?

1. It modifies the word 'wise' [AB, EBC, Ed, HNTC, Ho, ICC, NIC2, TG, TH, TNTC; LB, NAB, NIV, NJB, REB, TEV, TNT]: if any one thinks that he is wise by the standards of this age.
2. It should be connected with the preceding phrase as a whole [Alf, Herm, Lns, My, NIC]: if any one in this age thinks that he is wise.
3. It should be connected with the following phrase [BAGD, Gdt]: let him become a fool in this world. That is, in the eyes of the wise of the world [Gdt].

let-him-become[a] foolish,[b] in-order-that he-may-become wise.[c]

LEXICON—a. aorist mid. deponent impera. of γίνομαι (LN 13.48) (BAGD I.4.a. p. 159): 'to become' [AB, BAGD, He, HNTC, ICC, LN, Lns; all versions except NJB], 'to learn to be' [NJB]. Here γίνομαι implies a change in nature and an entrance into a new condition [BAGD].

b. μωρός (LN 32.55): 'foolish' [AB, BAGD, LN; NASB, TNT], 'stupid' [BAGD], 'foolish by the standards of this age' [HNTC], 'simple enough to accept Christ crucified' [ICC]. This adjective is also translated as a noun: 'a fool' [He, Lns; KJV, LB, NAB, NIV, NJB, NRSV, REB, TEV]. See this word at 1:25, 27.

c. σοφός (LN 32.33): 'wise' [AB, He, LN, Lns; KJV, NASB, NIV, NRSV, TNT], 'truly wise' [HNTC, My, NIC2; REB], 'really wise' [ICC, TH; NAB, NJB, TEV]. This adjective is also translated as a noun: 'true wisdom from above' [LB]. Σοφός infers 'in the true sense of the word' [Lns]. True wisdom involves renouncing the wisdom of this world [TNTC]. See this word in 1:19.

QUESTION—What sense of 'foolish' is intended?

1. It means 'foolish in the world's opinion' [AB, Alf, EGT, Gdt, He, HNTC, Ho, Lns, My, NIC2, Rb, TG, TH, TNTC, Vn]: let him become foolish in the world's opinion. This is done by receiving the simple gospel [Alf]. The word of the cross is the foolishness referred to [Herm].
2. It means 'foolish in God's opinion' [Ho, ICC, NIC]: let him become foolish in God's opinion. Recognizing one's self to be a fool and devoid of true wisdom is to be on the way to true wisdom [Ho, NIC].
3. It means both in the world's opinion and in God's [Ed].

3:19 For[a] the wisdom of this world is foolishness[b] in-the-sight-of[c] God;

LEXICON—a. γάρ (LN 89.23): 'for' [AB, BAGD, He, HNTC, ICC, LN, Lns; all versions]. This word signals the grounds of renouncing the world's wisdom, it is because it is folly in God's eyes [Alf, EGT, Ho, Lns, My, NIC, NIC2].

b. μωρία: 'foolishness' [AB, BAGD, He, HNTC, ICC, LN, Lns; all versions except NAB, NJB, REB, TEV], 'folly' [NJB, REB], 'nonsense' [TEV], 'absurdity' [NAB]. See this word at 1:18.

c. παρά with dative object (LN 90.20) (BAGD II.2.b. p. 610): 'in the sight of' [BAGD, EBC, ICC, LN, TNTC; NIV, REB, TEV, TNT], 'in the judgment of' [Alf, BAGD, LN], 'in the opinion of' [LN], 'with' [He, HNTC, Lns; KJV, NAB, NRSV], 'before' [NASB], 'to' [LB, NJB], 'from the viewpoint of' [AB]. Παρά means, 'before God as judge' [Ed, ICC].

QUESTION—How are the nouns related in the genitive construction ἡ σοφία τοῦ κόσμου 'the wisdom of this world'?

It means 'what this world's people consider to be wisdom' [TG, TH; TEV].

for it-is-written,[a] "The-one catching[b] the wise[c] in[d] their craftiness;"[e]

LEXICON—a. perf. pass. indic. of γράφω (LN 33.61): 'to be written' [AB, He, LN, Lns; all versions except LB, NAB, NJB, TNT]. Others include implied information: 'as it stands written in Scripture' [ICC], 'Scripture says' [NAB, NJB, REB, TEV, TNT], 'in Scripture (God) is described as' [HNTC], 'as it says in the book of Job' [LB]. The scripture quoted is from Job 5:13 [AB, Gdt, ICC, Lns, NIC, TH, TNTC]. The Scriptures are the grounds of the statement that the world's wisdom is folly with God [Lns, My]. See this word at 1:19.

b. pres. mid. deponent participle of δράσσομαι (LN **27.32**) (BAGD p. 206): 'to catch' [AB, BAGD, HNTC, LN; NAB, NASB, NIV, NRSV, TNT], 'to trap' [**LN**; LB, NJB, REB, TEV], 'to seize' [BAGD, He, LN], 'to take' [ICC, Lns; KJV]. It means 'to close the fist on' [Gdt]. It suggests a firm grasp on a slippery object [Vn]. The image is that of a hunter who uses the cunning of the animal as the means of capturing it [NIC2]. 'The one catching' refers to God [HNTC]. The cleverness of the wise becomes the trap in which God ensnares them [Gdt]. The fact that God does this plainly shows that his wisdom completely excels theirs [Lns]. God grasps them apparently for punishment but perhaps for salvation if they will become foolish [AB].

c. σοφός (LN 32.33): 'wise' [AB, He, HNTC, ICC, LN, Lns; all versions except NJB], 'crafty' [NJB]. The wise are like cunning animals for whom the hunter is too ingenious [HNTC]. The wise are those who use the wisdom of the world to gain their own objectives [Vn]. See this word at 1:19.

d. ἐν with dative object (LN 89.76): 'in' [He, HNTC, ICC, Lns; all versions except LB], 'by' [AB, LN]. This preposition is also translated as a verb: 'to use' [LB]. It means 'in' as in a net [Ed].

e. πανουργία (LN 88.270) (BAGD p. 608): 'craftiness' [AB, BAGD, HNTC, ICC, LN, Lns; all versions except LB, REB, TEV, TNT], 'cunning' [BAGD; REB, TNT], 'cleverness' [TEV], 'brilliance' [LB], 'treachery' [LN], 'knavery' [He], 'trickery' [BAGD], 'snare of their own cunning' [NJB]. It means 'readiness for anything' [BAGD, Gdt, ICC] in order to gain one's own ends [Gdt, ICC]. Πανουργία is capable of doing anything evil [Gdt, Lns]. It indicates trickery plus evil cunning [LN] or unscrupulous conduct [Vn]. Cleverness may be better here than craftiness [ICC]. The idea is that if God uses the wisdom of the wise to trap them, then his view of their wisdom is that it is folly because it trapped its authors [Alf]. The wise plan to escape from God by their cleverness [AB], but as it turns out, their cleverness is what is their downfall [AB, My].

QUESTION—What is meant by 'catching the wise in their craftiness'?

It refers to God's judgment on them [TG]. While the wise seem to accomplish many things by their craftiness, God comes and stops their work [NIC]. God keeps the wise from accomplishing their goals by using their own craftiness [My]. God has a strong grip on the slippery cleverness of evil men [ICC].

3:20 and again,[a]

LEXICON—a. πάλιν (LN 67.55) (BAGD 3. p. 607): 'again' [AB, He, HNTC, LN; all versions except LB, TEV], 'another Scripture says' [TEV], 'in another passage' [ICC], 'furthermore, thereupon' [BAGD], not explicit [Lns]. This word is also translated with implied information: 'again in the book of Psalms, we are told' [LB]. Πάλιν serves to connect things that are similar. Here it connects quotations [BAGD]. 'And again' is a standard formula in biblical Greek for introducing the next item in a series of quotations [NIC, TH]. The passage quoted is Psalms 94:11 and follows the Septuagint except that it substitutes the word 'wise' for 'men' [TH].

"(The) Lord knows[a] the thoughts[b] of-the wise that they-are futile."[c]

LEXICON—a. pres. act. indic. of γινώσκω (LN 28.1) (BAGD 6.c. p. 161): 'to know' [AB, BAGD, He, HNTC, ICC, LN, Lns; all versions except LB], 'to know full well' [LB], 'to know about, to have knowledge of, to be acquainted with' [LN]. When used of God, it indicates full knowledge [NIC]. 'Knows' means that God recognizes these thoughts for just what they are [Lns]. The verb 'to know' has two objects in Hebrew and Greek: what is known (the thoughts), and what is known about the thoughts, (they are vain) [Gdt].

b. διαλογισμός (LN 30.10; 30.16) (BAGD 1. p. 186): 'thoughts' [BAGD, He, HNTC, ICC; all versions except NASB, NJB, REB], 'reasonings' [BAGD, LN (30.16), Lns; NASB], 'arguments' [LN; REB], 'dialectics' [AB], 'plans' [NJB], 'opinions, designs' [BAGD]. It is also translated as a clause: 'how the human mind reasons' [LB]. It refers more to crafty plotting or machinations than it does to simple thoughts [NIC2]. The word often has a bad sense as it does here, indicating the questioning or opposing of God's ways [ICC]. It means 'a thought-out plan' or even 'plot', and can refer to philosophical thinking [HNTC]. It means 'idea' [Herm]. This term may include the process of reasoning of men's minds [EBC].

c. μάταιος (LN 65.37) (BAGD p. 495): 'futile' [He, LN; NIV, NRSV, REB, TNT], 'useless' [BAGD, Herm, LN, Lns, TH; NASB], 'empty' [BAGD, LN, My], 'how empty' [NAB], 'how insipid' [NJB], 'vain' [HNTC, ICC; KJV], 'worthless' [TEV], 'foolish and futile' [LB], 'idle, fruitless, powerless, lacking truth' [BAGD]. This adjective is also translated as a noun: 'nonsense' [AB]. Here it means 'ineffectual' [HNTC, Lns, Vn]. They are unable to accomplish anything of lasting value. Their wisdom is only involved in things that pass away [TNTC]. Human wisdom is empty both in its results and in its essence. Paul criticizes wisdom here only in regard to the discovery and attaining of salvation, and salvation is a thought of God that is superior to all that human wisdom has discovered [Gdt].

QUESTION—To whom does the word 'Lord' refer?

'Lord' here refers to 'God' [NIC, TG].

3:21 So[a] let-boast[b] no-one about[c] men;

LEXICON—a. ὥστε (LN 89.52): 'so' [He, HNTC, LN; LB, NJB, NRSV, REB, TNT], 'therefore' [AB, LN; KJV], 'so then' [EBC, Gdt, ICC, NIC2; NASB, NIV], 'then' [TEV], 'wherefore' [Lns, NIC], not explicit [NAB]. It indicates the consequence not merely of the preceding context, but of the whole argument [NIC]. It indicates the conclusion of the argument [EBC, Gdt, ICC, My, NIC2, TH]. Because God knows the world's wisdom and makes it ineffectual, the Christian should not boast about men [EBC]. Because human wisdom is folly before God, then...[My]. It indicates the transition in the argument where the explanation moves to the imperative [EGT, ICC]. Now the reference to divisions in 1:10–12 is addressed directly, though this command also flows out of the thought that God knows that the reasonings of the wise are futile [NIC2]. See this word at 3:7.

b. καυχάομαι (LN 33.368) (BAGD 1. p. 425): 'to boast' [BAGD, He, LN; NAB, NASB, NIV, NJB, NRSV, TEV, TNT], 'to make one's boast' [HNTC], 'to be proud' [LB], 'to plume oneself' [ICC], 'to glory' [AB, BAGD, Lns; KJV], 'to make someone a cause for boasting' [REB], 'to pride oneself' [BAGD]. See this word at 1:29.

c. ἐν with dative object (LN 90.23): 'about' [LN; NAB, NIV, NJB, NRSV, TEV, TNT], 'in' [HNTC, LN, Lns; KJV, NASB], 'of following' [LB], 'of' [He], 'on' [AB, ICC]. This preposition is also translated as marking the direct object of 'boasting': '(to make any human being) a cause for (boasting)' [REB].

QUESTION—What is meant by boasting in men?

'To boast in men' means to boast about them, their characters, teachings and wisdom [Lns], to brag about belonging to them [Gdt, Ho], or to trust in them [Ho]. Paul is referring to their erroneous thinking about himself, Apollos, and others as in 4:6 [ICC]. 'Men' is used to indicate the teachers upon whom the parties were founded [My].

for[a] all-things[b] are yours,

LEXICON—a. γάρ (LN 89.23): 'for' [AB, He, HNTC, ICC, LN, Lns; all versions except NAB, NIV, NJB, TEV], 'actually' [TEV], not explicit [NAB, NIV, NJB].

b. πᾶς (LN **59.23**) (BAGD 2.a.δ. p. 633): 'all things' [AB, BAGD, He, HNTC, Lns; KJV, NAB, NASB, NIV, NRSV], 'everything' [BAGD, **LN**; NJB, REB, TEV, TNT], 'everything you need' [LB], '(your heritage is) universal' [ICC].

QUESTION—What relationship is indicated by γάρ 'for'?

It indicates the grounds for the preceding command [EGT, Lns, NCBC, NIC, NIC2]: do not boast about men since all things are yours. They should not give allegiance to only certain men, since all are theirs [NIC]. By claiming only one leader, they are impoverishing themselves, since all of God's servants are equally theirs [NCBC].

QUESTION—What is meant by πάντα 'all things'?

'All things' should be understood in the broadest sense [Ho, My, NIC, TNTC], as seen in the following verse which states that the universe belongs to the church [Ho]. It is the world with its events and circumstances [Alf]. The contents of 'all things' are detailed in the following verses [Gdt]. 'All things are yours' means that all things are designed to serve the interests of the church, and that the church is the heir of the world (Romans 4:13). All things serve the best interests of Christians (Romans 8:28), and are therefore ethically theirs [My]. All things have been given to Christ as head of the church, and therefore to the church as well [Ho]. 'All things' means all the blessings of God in the entire universe [EBC]. Because all things belong to the church, it is wrong to choose certain teachers [NIC]. The Corinthian slogans, I belong to Paul, etc., actually reversed the truth that Paul belonged to the Corinthians [Ed, Gdt, HNTC, ICC, NIC2], with the significant change of pronoun from singular to plural ('yours') [NIC2]. They wanted to make Paul their chief, he was really their servant. The church did not belong to the Apostles, rather the Apostles were ministers of the church [ICC]. The word πάντα is emphasized [My].

DISCOURSE UNIT: 3:22–23 [Ed]. The topic is the fourth argument against the factions.

3:22 whether[a] Paul or Apollos or Cephas,

LEXICON—a. εἴτε (LN **89.69**) (BAGD VI.13.b. p. 220): 'whether' [AB, BAGD, He, **LN**, Lns; KJV, NASB, NIV, NRSV], 'whether it is' [NAB, NJB], not explicit [HNTC, ICC; LB, REB, TEV, TNT]. εἴτε…εἴτε means either, 'if…if' or, 'whether…or' [BAGD, LN].

QUESTION—How is this sentence related to the preceding?

It is an amplification of the preceding verse [Ho]. This verse is a detailed explanation of πάντα 'all things' [Alf, My], followed by an emphatic repetition of the words 'all things are yours' [My]. It is representative rather than a detailed list of the kinds of things belonging to 'all things'. It is divided into three pairs of opposites: the Apostles and the world, life and death, and the present and the future [Ed].

QUESTION—How are these men said to be theirs?

The three teachers are the property of the church because God appointed his servants to serve the church [NIC]. God puts all his servants at the disposal of the church [NIC]. They are theirs in the sense of 3:5, 'Servants through whom they became believers' [HNTC]. The ministry of the teachers are theirs [EBC, Gdt, Ho, My]. These leaders owe their allegiance to the church [TG]. These three men form one group [Gdt, ICC, Lns, TG]. 'Cephas' is the same as Peter [TH].

or (the) world[a] or life[b] or death,[c]

LEXICON—a. κόσμος (BAGD 2. p. 446): 'world' [AB, BAGD, He, HNTC, ICC, Lns; all versions]. Κόσμος refers to 'the world' as the sum total of everything here and now, 'the (orderly) universe'. In this context it refers to creation in its entirety [BAGD, Lns]. It refers to the world without ethical implications [ICC, TH, TNTC], the physical universe [ICC, TNTC]. The 'world' should be understood in its broadest reference [EGT, Ho], and refers to the existing system of material things [EGT]. It is the world with its events and circumstances [Alf]. The 'world' is the totality of beings and entities both animate and inanimate which obey Christ [Gdt]. A different view is that the 'world' refers to the kingdom of evil which is now subjected to the church [Ed].

b. ζωή (LN 23.88) (BAGD 1.a. p. 340): 'life' [AB, BAGD, He, HNTC, ICC, LN, Lns; all versions]. Physical life is indicated here [BAGD, ICC]. 'Life' refers to spiritual life in Christ Jesus [Lns]. To Paul the only real life was in Christ and death was gain (Phil. 1:21). This was also true for all believers [TNTC].

c. θάνατος (LN 23.99) (BAGD 1.a. p. 350): 'death' [AB, BAGD, He, HNTC, ICC, LN, Lns; all versions]. Physical death is indicated here [BAGD, ICC, Lns].

QUESTION—What is meant by the phrase 'the world is yours'?

It means that the world belongs to the Corinthians and that the present world order is directed to promote the work of redemption [Ho]. It means that the Christian will inherit the world (Rom. 4:13), and rule over it (Rom. 6:2) [NCBC]. The world is not theirs in the sense that the teachers are. Paul is now talking about the sovereignty of the church over the world, a lost authority recovered through union with Christ [HNTC]. The wisdom of the world is subdued by the church [Ed].

QUESTION— What is meant by the phrase 'death and life are yours'?

It means that the people of God live or die with reference to their own best interests and also that others, including the leaders of the world, live or die so as to best fulfill God's designs for the church [Ho]. It means that Christians are not slaves to the whims of chance or to the pressures of life and death, all being beneath their rule [NIC2]. It means that things like weakness, sickness, and decay may oppose the believer, but are under Christ's control [Gdt]. It means that life and death are now the servants of believers because they are co-rulers with Him who is 'Lord of the living and the dead' (Romans 14:9, Ephesians 4:9, Revelation 1:18) [EGT]. It is by life in the world that eternal life is gained; death is entry to eternal life [ICC].

or things-present[a] or things-to-come;[b] all-things (are) yours,

LEXICON—a. perf. act. participle of ἐνίστημι (LN 67.41) (BAGD 1. p. 266): 'things present' [AB, HNTC, Lns; KJV, NASB], 'present' [He, LN; all versions except KJV, LB, NASB], 'all of the present' [LB]. This participle is also translated a clause: 'whatever is' [ICC]. 'Ενίστημι means 'to be present' [BAGD, LN], or 'to have come' [BAGD]. The perfect participle denotes that which is in evidence, on the spot [EGT]. The present and the future should also be interpreted as referring to this life only [ICC]. While 'the present' refers to all that can happen in this life, 'the future' has reference to eternity [EBC, Ed, Gdt, Lns].

b. pres. act. participle of μέλλω (BAGD 2. p. 501): 'things to come' [HNTC, Lns; KJV, NASB], 'things to be' [AB], 'the future' [BAGD, He; all versions except KJV, LB, NASB], 'all of the future' [LB]. This participle is also translated as a clause: 'whatever is to be' [ICC]. This refers to the time of the second coming of Christ and after (Ephesians 1:21) [EBC].

QUESTION—What is indicated by the phrase 'all things are yours'?

It means that all things work together for your good [ICC, TNTC, Vn]. The world, life, death, the present, and the future are the final tyrants to which people are enslaved. Now that Christ has died and has risen from the dead, this enslavement is ended and all is under Christ's authority [NIC2].

QUESTION—Where is the emphasis in these verses?

The words 'all things are yours' are repeated and emphasized [Ed, My].

3:23 and/but[a] you (are) Christ's, and Christ (is) God's.

LEXICON—a. δέ (LN 89.96; 89.125): 'and' [AB, HNTC, Lns; all versions except NJB, TNT], 'but' [He, ICC; NJB, TNT].

QUESTION—What relationship is indicated by δέ 'and/but'?

1. It indicates a causal relationship [AB, Gdt, NIC]: All things belong to the believers because they belong to Christ [AB].
2. It indicates an additive relationship [NIC2; all other versions]: and you are Christ's.
3. It indicates a contrastive relationship [Alf, EBC, EGT, He, ICC, My, NIC, TNTC; NJB, TNT]: 'All things' are yours, but Christ is not yours, rather, you are Christ's [Alf]. Paul is not adding to the list of possessions, but by contrast he now turns to responsibility. Believers should live as though they belonged to Christ, not to themselves [TNTC]. All things belong to the Christian, but they are not centered in him, for all things ultimately belong to God [EBC].

QUESTION—How are the nouns related in the genitive construction ὑμεῖς Χριστοῦ 'you of Christ'?

1. The meaning is that they were the possession of Christ [AB, HNTC, ICC, Lns, NIC2, TG; all versions except NIV]: you belong to Christ. The fact that all things belonged to believers needed to be corrected with the fact that this ownership was dependent on their belonging to Christ [HNTC, NIC2]. This also indicates an intimate relationship [AB].
2. The meaning is that they were a part of Christ and were the possession of Christ [NIC]: you are members of Christ's body and you belong to him. The main thing is that those who belong to Christ share his power and glory [NIC].

QUESTION—What relationship is indicated by δέ 'and' in the last phrase 'and Christ is God's?

1. It indicates an additive relationship [My, NIC2; all versions]: and Christ is God's.
2. It indicates a causal relationship [Gdt]: because Christ is God's. The believers' possessed all things because they belonged to Christ; Christ in turn possesses all things because he belongs to God (11:3) [Gdt].
3. It indicates a contrastive relationship [Alf]: but Christ is God's. You belong to Christ, but Christ belongs to God.

QUESTION—How are the nouns related in the genitive construction Χριστὸς θεοῦ 'Christ of God'?

It means that Christ belongs to God [AB, EGT, Gdt, HNTC, ICC, Lns, My, NIC2, TG, TNTC; all versions except NIV]. It indicates subordination to God [Alf, Ed, EGT, Gdt, Herm, HNTC, Ho, My, NCBC, NIC, NIC2, TNTC, Vn]. 'Christ' denotes the office of 'The Anointed One'. It is in the areas of his office of redemption and his work that he belongs to God [Lns, NIC2]. This indicates functional subordination, not subordination arising out of inherent being [NIC2]. This does not deny the deity of Christ since subordination to the Father is only in reference to his work as a man [TNTC]. Christ's subordination to God does not pertain merely to his office or his role as a man, but is true eternally as is seen in 1 Cor. 15:28 [Ed, EGT, Gdt, Herm, HNTC, Ho, My]. Christ renders obedience, rising out of his perfect love, to the will of the Father which is born out of perfect love [HNTC].

QUESTION—What is the significance of the fact that 'Christ is God's'?

It shows that the church's authority is formed on the pattern of Christ's authority, and in both cases it is delegated and its final source is God [Ed]. By this statement Paul corrects the slogan of the fourth party that they belonged to Christ by showing that Christ Himself was subject to God and not the head of a party [My]. It shows that God's sovereignty is the cornerstone of the structure of authority in the universe (11:3, 15:28) [EGT].

DISCOURSE UNIT: 4:1–21 [AB, EBC, Ed, GNT, Ho, Lns, NIC2, TG]. The topic is the stewardship of apostolic ministry [AB], the ministry of the apostles [EBC, GNT], ministers, as stewards, being faithful, as Paul had proved himself to be [Ho], God's faithful stewards [Lns], the Corinthians and their apostle [NIC2].

DISCOURSE UNIT: 4:1–13 [Herm, NIC]. The topic is a demonstration with reference to Paul and Apollos [Herm], letting nobody judge in pride [NIC].

DISCOURSE UNIT: 4:1–5 [AB, Alf, EBC, Ed, EGT, Gdt, Herm, HNTC, My, NCBC, NIC2, TH, TNTC, Vn]. The topic is the Lord as judge [AB], faithful servants [EBC], a personal appeal from the judgment of men to that of Christ [Ed], Christ's servants answerable to himself [EGT], the application of the criterion [Herm], servants of Christ and their work [HNTC], the one valid judgment [NCBC], on being a servant and being judged [NIC2], God's commendation is what matters [TNTC]. Paul now addresses two items from the previous context: apostles as servants (3:5–9), and future judgment (3:13–15) [NIC2]. Paul defines the true nature of the office of a teacher and appeals to the judgment of Christ whose servant he is [Ed]. He speaks against a mere human appraisal of the servants of God and gives a real definition of the office and its accountability to the Lord [Vn].

4:1 In-this-manner[a] a-person[b] should-regard[c] us

LEXICON—a. οὕτως (LN 61.9) (BAGD p. 598): 'in this manner' [NASB], 'in this way' [LN; NRSV], 'so' [BAGD, LN; KJV], 'thus' [BAGD, LN, Lns], 'given such conditions' [AB], 'the right way (of regarding)' [ICC], 'so then' [NIV], 'because these things are so' [He], not explicit [LB, NAB, NJB, REB, TEV, TNT]. This clause is translated as a rhetorical question: 'how then should a man think of us?' [HNTC].

b. ἄνθρωπος (LN 9.1) (BAGD 3.γ. p. 69): 'person' [AB, LN], 'people' [NIC2; NJB], 'man' [HNTC, Lns, My; KJV, NASB], 'men' [NAB, NIV], 'one' [BAGD, My], 'you' [BAGD; TEV, TNT]. This word is made implicit by changing the verb to a passive: 'we are to be regarded' [He; REB], 'we should be looked upon' [LB]; or an imperative: 'think of us' [NRSV]. It occurs here in its indefinite and general sense: 'this is how one (i.e., you) should regard us' [Alf, BAGD, EBC, Gdt, Ho, NIC2]. See this word at 2:11.

c. pres. mid. impera. of λογίζομαι (LN 31.1) (BAGD 1.b. p. 476): 'to regard' [ICC, LN; NAB, NASB, NIV], 'to be regarded' [He; REB], 'to think of' [HNTC; NJB, NRSV, TEV, TNT], 'to account' [KJV], 'to look upon' [BAGD; LB], 'to consider' [AB, BAGD, LN, Lns], 'to reckon, to calculate' [BAGD], 'to have an opinion, to hold a view' [LN]. It indicates a reasonable conclusion drawn from admitted premises. The present imperative indicates habitual action [EGT].

QUESTION—To what does the word οὕτως 'in this manner' refer?

1. It refers forward to what follows [Alf, BAGD, EGT, Gdt, ICC, NIC2, Vn; LB, NAB, NASB, NJB, NRSV, REB, TEV, TNT]: a person should regard us as servants and administrators. The οὕτως 'thus', is correlative with the following ὡς 'as' and refers to what follows (3:15, 9:26) [NIC2].
2. It refers to what precedes [Ed, He, Herm, HNTC, Ho, Lns, My, NIC, Rb, TH]: all things belong to you and that is how a person should regard us as well. This is a conclusion to be drawn from the preceding discussion [Ho]. The apostles belong to and serve the church because the church belongs to Christ. From this perspective a man should so regard us [Ed].
3. It refers both to what precedes and to what follows [AB]: All things are yours and that is how a person should regard us, as servants of Christ. The οὕτως not only looks forward to the ὡς 'as', but it also refers back to what has just been said [AB].

as servants[a] of-Christ and administrators[b] of-(the)-mysteries[c] of-God.

LEXICON—a. ὑπηρέτης (LN 35.20) (BAGD p. 842): 'servant' [BAGD, HNTC, LN; all versions except KJV, REB], 'minister' [He; KJV], 'subordinate' [REB], 'assistant' [AB, BAGD], 'attendant' [Lns], 'officer' [ICC], 'helper' [BAGD]. Ὑπηρέτης originally meant one who rowed on the lower tier of a three-tiered boat, and then came to mean anyone who worked under another [ICC, NIC2], with emphasis on the relationship of a servant to a superior [NIC2]. It signifies directed service of a lowly kind

[TNTC]. Its general and normal use refers to menials, a lower class of servants [Ho]. It refers to someone who serves a person who is in an official position [AB, TH]. Here it refers to a servant who is a free man in contrast to a slave [EBC]. There is little distinction in meaning between this word for servant and διάκονος 'servant' which was used in 3:5 [HNTC, My, NCBC, TG]. The Corinthians should think of them as servants and refrain from honoring them [NIC]. 'Servants' brings out their humble or subordinate position to Christ [AB, Ed, Lns, NIC2; REB].

b. οἰκονόμος (LN **37.39**) (BAGD 2. p. 560): 'administrator' [BAGD, He, LN; NAB], 'steward' [HNTC, ICC, Lns; KJV, NASB, NRSV, REB], '(house)-steward' [BAGD], 'manager' [AB, BAGD, LN], 'stewards entrusted with' [NJB], 'one who is responsible for' [**LN**], 'one who is in charge of' [LN], 'one who has been entrusted with' [NIV, TNT], 'one who has been put in charge of' [TEV], 'one who distributes God's blessings by explaining (God's secrets)' [LB]. Οἰκονόμος originally referred to a servant who was assigned the task of giving out supplies, tools, and food to the workers on an estate [AB]. It refers to a person who is the overseer of an estate. A wealthy landowner had many servants so he needed someone to oversee their work, this being the οἰκονόμος. The overseer was a slave of his master, but he was an administrator of the master's slaves [TNTC]. This person was the responsible officer of an establishment. He assigned duties to slaves and administered the goods [Gdt, ICC]. The term denotes a person who has been entrusted with managing a household. The two notions that are in focus here are 'accountability', in focus in this paragraph, and 'delegated authority' the other matter of interest of this chapter [NIC2]. The ὑπηρέτας 'servants' and the οἰκονόμους 'stewards' are the same persons, and their belonging to Christ and God respectively simply indicates equality in the Godhead [Lns].

c. μυστήριον (LN 28.77) (BAGD 2. p. 530): 'mystery' [AB, BAGD, He, HNTC, LN, Lns; KJV, NAB, NASB, NJB, NRSV], 'secret' [BAGD, LN; LB, REB, TNT], 'secret truth' [TEV], 'the secret things' [NIV], 'truths which His Father has revealed to us' [ICC]. See this word at 2:1.

QUESTION—How are the nouns related in the genitive construction ὑπηρέτας Χριστοῦ 'servants of Christ'?

1. It indicates that the servants belong to Christ [EBC, NIC2; LB]: Christ's servants.
2. It indicates that the servants serve Christ [Gdt, TH]: men who serve Christ.

QUESTION—What word is emphasized?

The word 'us' is emphatic [ICC, Lns, Vn]: so far as we are concerned, people should regard us as servants of Christ.

QUESTION—To whom does the word ἡμᾶς 'us' refer?

It refers to Paul and Apollos [Alf, Gdt, HNTC] (see 3:5 and 4:6) and possibly to Cephas as well [HNTC]. It refers back to 3:22 to Paul, Apollos, and Cephas [NIC2]. It refers to Paul and his colleagues [My, TG], or to all who are entrusted with the ministry of the New Covenant [ICC]. Although here it refers only to a few, it may be applied generally to the role of ministers in the church [HNTC].

QUESTION—To what does μυστηρίων 'mysteries' refer?

The word is used here in the plural to denote Christian preaching by the apostles and teachers [BAGD]. It means the truths which God had revealed, but which could not be discovered by human reason [Ho]. It refers to the truths of the gospel [AB, HNTC, Lns, NCBC, NIC2, TG]. It is equivalent to the Christian message [TH]. 'Mysteries' include the good news of salvation by faith, the inclusion of the Gentiles in God's family, Christ's presence among the Gentiles, Israel's sure salvation, the unsurpassed significance of Christian marriage, and future events related to the last day [AB]. It means the revelation of the gospel by the Spirit [NIC2]. It means all that God has revealed in Jesus Christ with the work of Christ as central. The apostles proclaimed the message of the coming Messiah and the completion of his work [NIC].

QUESTION—What are the parts of the metaphor and to what do they refer?

The stewards are servants who administer the goods of their master. The goods which they administer are the mysteries of God [ICC]. The stewards administer the mysteries by proclaiming or teaching them to others [Alf, HNTC, ICC, My, NIC2, TG; LB]. Paul and Apollos are the stewards who are accountable to God who had given them this task [NIC2]. The grounds of comparison are: 'accountability' [AB, Gdt, Lns, NIC2, TG, TH; NIV, NJB, TEV, TNT], and 'delegated authority' [NIC2, TG, TH].

4:2 Here[a] moreover[b] it-is-required[c] in[d] administrators, that one be-found[e] faithful.[f]

LEXICON—a. ὧδε (LN **92.35**) (BAGD 2.b. p. 895): 'here' [BAGD, ICC], 'in this case' [BAGD, **LN**, Lns; NASB], 'in this connection' [AB, Vn], 'hence' [He], 'in this' [LN], 'at this point, on this occasion, under these circumstances' [BAGD], not explicit [NAB, TEV]. It refers to a particular state concerning its relevance to the discourse [LN]. This adverb is also joined with the following word λοιπόν, 'remaining', and translated 'moreover' [KJV, NRSV], 'now' [LB, NIV, REB, TNT], 'well now' [HNTC], 'in such a matter' [NJB]. Ὧδε means 'under the present circumstances' [He, NIC, Vn], or 'such being the case' [Ed, My]. It refers to 'on the earth and in human life', or perhaps 'in these circumstances' [Ho, ICC]. If the meaning of 'here in this place' is taken, Paul may be bringing out a contrast between human judgment and the divine judgment which he treats later on [Alf, TH].

b. λοιπόν (LN **89.98**) (BAGD 3.b. p. 480): 'moreover' [AB, BAGD, He; NASB, NRSV], 'then' [BAGD, Lns], 'furthermore' [BAGD, ICC, **LN**], not explicit [KJV, LB, NAB, NIV, NJB, REB, TEV, TNT], 'also' [LN]. Λοιπόν here means, 'there is only one more thing to do, namely' [He].

c. pres. pass. indic. of ζητέω (LN 33.167) (BAGD 2.c. p. 339): 'to be required' [BAGD, HNTC, ICC, Lns, Vn; KJV, NASB, NIV, NRSV, REB, TEV], 'to be expected' [NJB, TNT], 'to be demanded' [AB, BAGD, LN], 'to be asked for, to be requested' [BAGD], 'to be especially sought' [LN]. This verb is also translated as a noun phrase: 'the first requirement' [NAB], 'the most important thing' [LB]. It is also translated as an active verb: 'to seek nothing else' [He]. The ἵνα 'that' following 'required' serves to point out the object of the verb [Ed, NIC2]. It is required in daily life [TNTC].

d. ἐν with dative object (LN 89.5): 'in' [HNTC, LN, Lns; KJV], 'about' [LB], not explicit [ICC; NIV, REB], 'of' [AB, He; all versions except KJV, LB, NIV, REB]. This ἐν functions as a dative of reference, 'required in reference to stewards' [NIC2].

e. aorist pass. subj. of εὑρίσκω (LN 13.7) (BAGD 2. p. 325): 'to be found' [BAGD, HNTC, Lns; KJV, NASB, NJB, NRSV], 'to be found to be' [LN], 'to be discovered' [BAGD, LN]. It is also translated actively: 'to prove' [ICC; NAB, NIV], 'to show themselves' [REB], 'to be' [He; TEV, TNT], 'to turn out to be' [AB, LN], 'to do (just what his master tells him to)' [LB]. Here it is used figuratively to indicate intellectual discovery based on reflection, observation, examination, or investigation [BAGD]. The aorist tense indicates that the person's ministry will be looked at as a whole [EBC, Lns], when his master reviews his work [Lns].

f. πιστός (LN 31.87) (BAGD 1.a.α. p. 664): 'faithful' [BAGD, He, LN; KJV, NIV], 'faithful to his master' [TEV], 'dependable' [AB, BAGD, LN; TNT], 'trustworthy' [BAGD, HNTC, ICC, LN, Lns; NAB, NASB, NJB, NRSV, REB], 'inspiring trust or faith' [BAGD]. This word is also translated as a clause: 'to do just what his master tells him to' [LB]. 'Worthy of the trust that has been placed in one's care' is the sense of this word. Paul's intent is to establish the single criterion about which God alone could be his judge, and thus release him from the Corinthian criticism [NIC2]. Other qualities may be desired in a steward, but faithfulness is the most essential qualification [EBC, Ho, Lns, NIC, TNTC; TEV]. See this word at 1:9.

QUESTION—What is the function of this verse?

It is a parenthesis between 4:1 and 4:3, adding a comment that Paul and his colleagues are to be held accountable [NIC].

QUESTION—What is the meaning of ὧδε λοιπόν 'here moreover'?

The first word ὧδε 'here' summarizes 4:1 and λοιπόν 'moreover' attaches a supplement to it: in addition to being a steward, faithfulness is expected [EGT, Lns]. The words mean 'in this connection, then' [BAGD, NIC2], showing that Paul means to expand the figure and focus on the matter of prime concern, faithfulness [NIC2]. It is best to give the phrase a simple resumptive sense and translate: 'well now' [HNTC]. The phrase serves to further develop the idea [Herm]. It means that nothing else remains for stewards than that they be faithful, this is their whole duty [Ed; TEV]. These words mark a shift to another aspect of Paul's argument [TH].

QUESTION—In what sense should God's servant be faithful?

He must obey Christ's commands and carefully teach the truths which God has revealed, not mixing them with human wisdom or substituting other truths in their place [Ho]. He must reveal the mysteries of God at the right time to the right people and be completely loyal to Christ. The point of this is that the leaders have no personal importance and therefore should not be compared with each other [AB]. He must conscientiously give out what has been given to him and have only one interest, his master's work [Gdt].

4:3 But/Now[a] to-me it-is to[b] (a) very-small-thing,[c]

LEXICON—a. δέ: 'but' [HNTC; KJV, NASB, NRSV], 'for although' [He], 'now' [AB, Lns; TEV], not explicit [all other versions].

b. εἰς with accusative object (LN 78.51): 'to' [Ed], 'to the point of, to the extent of, to the degree that, up to' [LN], not explicit [AB, He, HNTC, ICC, Lns; all versions].

c. ἐλάχιστος (LN 79.125) (BAGD 2.a. p. 248): 'very small thing' [KJV, NASB, NRSV], 'very small, quite unimportant, insignificant' [BAGD]. This superlative form of the adjective is also translated with the verb 'it is' as follows: 'it matters little' [NAB], 'it counts for very little' [TNT], 'it matters not at all' [REB], 'it is of no importance' [NJB], 'it is a matter of very little importance' [AB], 'I care very little' [NIV], 'I am not at all concerned' [TEV], 'it is a matter of the smallest importance' [HNTC], 'it is a very small matter' [Lns], 'it is a matter of small moment' [ICC], 'it is of very little consequence' [He], 'I don't worry over' [LB]. Ἐλάχιστος is the superlative form of μικρός 'small' [BAGD]. Paul does not say that it does not matter but that it matters little [ICC, Vn]. Εἰς ἐλάχιστόν ἐστιν 'to a very small thing' means 'it amounts to very little'. Paul intends to say that it matters little when compared with God's judgment [Ed]. Paul did subjectively feel their judging, as is seen in 8:13 and 9:19. What he was stating here was the objective value of their judgment to his final acquittal or condemnation [NIC].

QUESTION—What relationship is indicated by δέ 'but/now'?

1. It indicates contrast [Alf, EGT, HNTC, Ho, ICC, My, NIC2, TH]: but. The contrast is between Paul and the stewards who will be judged ὧδε 'here on earth' [Alf, TH]. The contrast is to something implied: Paul admits to the need for inquiry into his faithfulness, but will submit only to God's judgment of him, not theirs [ICC, NIC2]. Faithfulness is required in stewards, but who will judge that faithfulness? Fidelity binds one only to one's particular master, the only one who can judge the steward [EGT, NIC2]. Christ, not a human court, was his judge [TH].
2. It indicates sequence [AB, Gdt, Lns; TEV]: now. Paul now uses himself as a specific example of the preceding verse [Lns].

QUESTION—Where is the emphasis in this phrase?

The words 'to me' are emphasized [Ed, Lns, TG, TNTC; LB]. Here Paul narrows the field emphatically to himself [Ed]. 'To me' is placed first in the Greek with emphasis. Paul contrasts himself with the Corinthians: they valued human judgments highly, he did not [TNTC].

that I-be-judged[a] by you or by a-human[b] court;[c]

LEXICON—a. aorist pass. subj. of ἀνακρίνω (LN 56.12; 33.412) (BAGD 1.b. p. 56): 'to be judged' [He; KJV, NIV, NRSV, TEV], 'to be scrutinized and judged' [ICC], 'to be examined' [BAGD, EBC, HNTC; NASB, TNT], 'to be investigated' [AB], 'to be investigated in court, to be interrogated' [LN (56.12)], 'to be called to account' [REB], 'to be subjected to judicial examination' [Lns], 'to be questioned' [BAGD, LN], 'to be criticized' [LN (33.412)]. This passive is also translated actively: 'to pass judgment' [NAB], 'to judge' [NJB], 'to think about something' [LB]. 'Ανακρίνω is used here of judging in judicial hearings [BAGD]. It means, 'to institute a juridical inquiry' [Lns]; to investigate with a view to passing sentence [Vn]. This word does not refer to the pronouncing of final judgment, but to the process of critical investigation which leads up to it [EGT, Gdt, TH, TNTC]. Although ἀνακρίνω denotes examination, it can also include the decision made following the examination as it does here [EBC]. Paul here implies judgment in regard to his fidelity [Alf]. Paul does not imply judgment in regard to his fidelity, but in regard to all his faults. He knew that in reference to fidelity he was blameless [Ed]. It is a real possibility that the criticism of Paul as a full-scale attack as seen in 2 Corinthians had already started [HNTC].

b. ἀνθρώπινος (LN 9.6) (BAGD 3. p. 68): 'human' [AB, BAGD, He, HNTC, ICC, LN, Lns; all versions except KJV, LB]. This word is also joined with 'court' and translated 'man's (judgment)' [KJV], 'anyone else' [LB].

c. ἡμέρα (LN **56.1**) (BAGD 3.b.α. p. 347): 'court' [BAGD, ICC, **LN**, Lns; all versions except KJV, LB, TEV], 'court of justice' [LN], 'judgment' [KJV], 'judiciary' [AB], 'tribunal' [Gdt, He], 'standard' [TEV], 'assize' [HNTC], 'day appointed by a human court' [BAGD, NCBC]. 'Human day' refers to man's judgment, either any man or all men together. Paul will wait for 'the day' of the Lord [EGT]. 'By human court' is not the same as 'by men', but rather referred to the judgment of the constituted authorities [Ed].

but[a] not myself I-judge.

LEXICON—a. ἀλλά (LN 89.125; 91.1) (BAGD 3. p. 591; 3. p. 39): 'but'. The phrase ἀλλ' οὐδέ 'but not' is translated 'but not even' [BAGD], 'nay, indeed...not even' [HNTC], 'yet...not' [ICC], 'indeed...not even' [NIV], 'Why...not even' [AB], 'in fact...not even' [NASB], 'yea...not even' [Lns, My], 'not even' [He; LB, NAB, NJB, NRSV, TEV, TNT], 'nor' [REB], 'yea...not' [KJV]. 'Αλλ' οὐδέ means 'but not even' and serves to call out another suggestion that will also be rejected [EGT]. The 'but' here indicates while he rejects them or any human court, he does not thereby set himself up as his own judge [Gdt, ICC]. The ἀλλά is not contrastive, but connective and means 'yea' [Lns, Rb].

QUESTION—Why does Paul say this?

Paul takes his previous statement to its logical conclusion [TNTC]. He knows more about himself than anyone else does, but it is still a human judgment that is incompetent [ICC]. This is not because he is irresponsible, but because he is in the service of God [NIC2].

4:4 For[a] I-am-aware-of[b] nothing (against) myself,

LEXICON—a. γάρ (LN 89.23; 91.1): 'for' [AB, He, HNTC, LN (89.23), Lns, TNTC; KJV, REB], 'it is true that' [NJB], 'mind you' [NAB], not explicit [all other versions].

b. perf. act. indic. of σύνοιδα (LN **28.4**) (BAGD 2. p. 791): 'to be aware of' [**LN**; NRSV], 'to be conscious of' [AB, BAGD, LN, Lns; NASB, TNT], 'to have consciousness of' [ICC], 'to know with' [BAGD], 'to know' [LN; KJV]. This word is also joined with 'not' and translated 'to be unaware (of any fault)' [He]. It is also joined with the word 'myself' and translated 'I have nothing on my conscience' [HNTC; NAB, REB], 'my conscience does not reproach me' [NJB], 'my conscience is clear' [LB, NIV, TEV]. It means, 'to know with' in the sense of sharing a guilty secret [HNTC]. It means to be aware of information about something [LN]. Σύνοιδα with a reflexive pronoun connotes a guilty conscience [EGT]. It here means, 'to know about oneself' that which is unknown to others [ICC, Vn]. Σύνοιδα is the root from which the noun συνείδησις 'conscience' is derived [HNTC, NCBC, NIC2].

QUESTION—What relationship is indicated by γάρ 'for'?

1. It indicates grounds [Ed, EGT, Ho, Lns, My, NIC, TH, TNTC]: because. It indicates the grounds of why Paul does not judge himself (4:3) [Ed, Ho, Lns, My, NIC, TH]; or as the grounds of all of 4:3 [EGT]. The grounds indicated by 'for' is the last clause in this verse, 'I do not judge myself because...the Lord is my judge' [Ho]. The grounds is in the first two clauses of this verse: I do not judge myself because, although I am not aware of anything against myself, I am not thereby acquitted [Ed, EGT, My, TH].
2. It indicates additional information [NIC2]: and. Here the γάρ has the force of δέ 'and'. Having stated that he does not judge himself regarding his stewardship, he adds: 'and' regarding my faithfulness in carrying out my duties as a steward, my conscience is clear. Paul adds this qualifier lest they think he has hidden motives [NIC2].

QUESTION—What is the function of the dative case of ἐμαυτῷ 'myself'?

1. It indicates 'against' [AB, Alf, EGT, ICC, Lns, NIC, Vn; LB, NASB, NRSV, TNT]: against myself.
2. It indicates 'by' [KJV]: by myself.

QUESTION—What does Paul imply by the statement 'I am not aware of anything against myself'?

1. He is making a statement of fact about himself [AB, Alf, Ed, Ho, Lns, NIC, NIC2, TG, TH; all versions]: I am not aware of anything against myself, but this does not serve to acquit me. Note that he says a similar thing about himself in 7:25, 'I give my judgment as one who by the Lord's mercy is trustworthy' [NIC2].
2. He is making a hypothetical statement about himself [ICC, Rb]: even if I were not aware of anything against myself, I would not thereby be acquitted. Paul was actually conscious of many faults [ICC].

but[a] not by this[b] have-I-been-acquitted,[c]

LEXICON—a. ἀλλά (LN 89.125): 'but' [He, LN; all versions except KJV, NASB], 'yet' [AB, Lns, Rb; KJV, NASB], 'nevertheless' [ICC], not explicit [HNTC].

b. οὗτος: 'this' [NASB], 'this fact' [AB], 'that' [He, HNTC; LB, NIV, REB, TEV, TNT]. This pronoun is also joined with 'by' and translated 'hereby' [ICC, Lns; KJV], 'thereby' [NRSV]. 'By this' is then conflated with 'not' and translated 'that does not mean that' [NAB], 'that is not enough' [NJB]. 'In this' means, 'under these circumstances' [NIC].

c. perf. pass. indic. of δικαιόω (LN 56.34) (BAGD 3.a. p. 197): 'to be acquitted' [BAGD, LN; NASB, NRSV, TNT], 'to have one's guilt removed' [LN], 'to be set free' [LN], 'to be justified' [AB, BAGD, HNTC, Lns; KJV], 'to be proved guiltless' [ICC], 'to be pronounced and treated as righteous' [BAGD]. This passive is also translated actively: 'to prove that one is innocent' [REB, TEV], 'to be the final proof of one's innocence' [LB], 'to make one innocent' [NIV], 'to declare oneself innocent' [NAB], 'to justify someone' [He; NJB]. It always has a forensic meaning: 'to pronounce a verdict of acquittal' and never means 'to make just' [Lns]. The force of the perfect tense is that Paul does not stand in a perfect state of innocence just because his conscience is clear [EBC].

QUESTION—What is meant by δεδικαίωμαι 'I have been acquitted'?

1. It refers to Paul's acquittal in regard to his faithfulness as a steward [AB, Alf, EBC, Ed, Gdt, Ho, ICC, Lns, NIC, NIC2, TG, TH, TNTC, Vn]: but I am not thereby acquitted of being unfaithful. To think of this as indicating justification by faith is to miss the meaning of the context which deals with the question of who is competent to judge a man's work [ICC]. Justification by faith is foreign to the theme of this passage [Ed]. The emphasis here is on the final judgment and not on a judgment previously pronounced through Christ's death [NIC2]. All he means to say is that whether he was faithful or not was not for his conscience to decide, but for the Lord [Ho].
2. It refers to Paul's justification by faith [EGT, My]: but I do not thereby have a righteous standing before God.

but[a] the-one judging[b] me is (the) Lord.

LEXICON—a. δέ: 'but' [He, Lns; KJV, NASB], not explicit [AB, HNTC, ICC; all other versions]. This δέ 'but' refers back to the words 'I do not even judge myself', the material that intervenes being parenthetical [ICC]: I do not even judge myself (...), but the one who judges me is the Lord. The δέ is adversative and contrasts the Lord with the Corinthians or with Paul himself [Lns].

b. pres. act. participle ἀνακρίνω: 'to judge'. See this word in 4:3.

QUESTION—To whom does the word 'Lord' refer?

1. It refers to Jesus Christ [Alf, Ed, EGT, He, HNTC, Ho, ICC, My, NIC, NIC2, TG, TNTC, Vn]. In normal Pauline usage the term 'Lord', used absolutely, usually refers to Christ [NIC2] and 4:5 confirms that this indeed is Christ [Ed, HNTC, ICC, NIC2].
2. It refers to God [EBC, TH].

4:5 So[a] judge[b] not anything before (the) time[c]

LEXICON—a. ὥστε (LN 89.52): 'so' [HNTC; LB, NAB, REB, TEV, TNT], 'therefore' [Gdt, LN, Lns, NIC2; KJV, NASB, NIV, NRSV], 'for that reason' [NJB], 'so then' [EGT, ICC, LN], 'consequently' [AB, He]. This is Paul's third emphatic ὥστε (see 3:7 and 3:21) and means 'therefore' [NIC2]. It introduces a logical conclusion 'wherefore' [NIC, NIC2]. 'So then' is based on the fact that the Lord is the sole infallible judge [Alf]. The thought is that in view of the fact that I do not even judge myself, but Christ judges me, I 'therefore' advise you not to pass judgment on me prematurely [My].

b. pres. act. impera. of κρίνω (LN 56.20; 56.30) (BAGD 6.b. p. 452): 'to judge' [He, HNTC, Lns; KJV, NIV, NJB], 'to pass judgment' [ICC; NAB, NASB, REB, TEV, TNT], 'pronounce judgment (on)' [BAGD; NRSV], 'to make judgment' [AB], 'to decide a legal question, to act as a judge, to arrive at a verdict, to try a case' [LN (56.20)], 'to pass an unfavorable judgment on, criticize, find fault with' [BAGD], 'condemn' [BAGD, LN (56.30)], 'to judge as guilty' [LN (56.30)]. This word is also joined with the words 'before the time' and translated 'to jump to conclusions' [LB]. It refers to the pronouncing of the verdict at the end of a trial [EBC, HNTC, Lns, My, TH]. The present tense indicates that they stop doing something that they have already begun to do [EBC, ICC, NIC2, Vn; NAB, NASB]: stop passing judgment. The use of μή 'not' with the present imperative may indicate that the Corinthians had been doing this [Rb, TNTC]. They are to stop making judgments about Paul and his ministry [Alf, NIC2]. The τί 'anything' should not be taken as the object of 'judging' ('do not judge anything'), but as modifier of the verb itself ('do not pass any judgment') [AB, Gdt; REB, TNT].

c. καιρός (LN 67.1) (BAGD 3. p. 395): 'time' [HNTC, LN, Lns; KJV, NAB, NASB, NRSV], 'appointed time' [EBC, Ed, Ho, ICC; NIV, TNT], 'right time' [My, TH; TEV], 'due time' [NJB], 'proper time' [AB], 'fitting time' [EGT, ICC], 'occasion' [LN], 'the time of crisis, the last times, the end time, and the judgment' [BAGD], not explicit [LB]. This word is also joined with 'before' and translated 'premature (judgment)' [REB], 'prematurely' [EGT, He]. Καίρος indicates the right time or opportunity for something to happen. 'The right time' is when the Lord comes [TH]. 'Before the time' means, 'out of season' or 'untimely', the kind of judging the Corinthians were doing [Lns].

QUESTION—What is implied by the phrase 'before the time'?

1. It implies that when the time comes, people will have the right to judge [AB, Ed, ICC; NASB, NIV, REB]: Do not judge anything before the right time to judge comes. On Judgment Day they will judge (6:2–3) with all the facts known [Ed, ICC]. There is a proper time for judging and that is when the Lord comes. Before that time, no one is able to assess the value and meaning of a person's life [AB].
2. It implies that people will never have the right to judge. The context indicates that only the Lord can judge and he will do that when he returns [NIC].

until[a] the Lord comes,

LEXICON—a. ἕως (LN 67.119) (BAGD I.1.b. p. 334): 'until' [AB, BAGD, He, HNTC, ICC, LN, Lns; all versions except NAB, NRSV], 'till' [BAGD], 'before' [He; NRSV], not explicit [NAB]. The words ἕως ἄν means that the beginning of an event depends on circumstances. Here the circumstance, the coming of the Lord, defines 'the appointed time' [NIC2]. Ἕως ἄν with the subjunctive 'come', indicates that the Lord's coming is sure, but the time is unknown [EGT, ICC, TNTC], 'until the Advent, whenever that may be' [ICC]. 'Until the Lord comes' refers to the second coming of Christ [EBC, Ho, Vn].

QUESTION—To whom does the word 'Lord' refer?

It refers to Christ as is usual in Paul's writings [EBC, Ho, TH, Vn].

QUESTION—What is the relationship between the phrases 'before the time' and 'until the Lord comes'?

The phrase 'until the Lord comes' explains the meaning of 'before the time' [Alf, Gdt, Ho, Lns, My, NIC2, TH]: do not pronounce judgment before the time, that is, before the Lord comes.

who both/also[a] will-light-up[b] the hidden-things[c] of-the darkness[d]

LEXICON—a. καί (LN 89.93): 'both' [ICC; KJV, NASB, TNT], 'also' [Lns], 'then' [AB], not explicit [He, HNTC; all other versions].

b. fut. act. indic. of φωτίζω (LN 28.36; 14.39) (BAGD 2.c. p. 873): 'to light up' [Lns], 'to illumine' [ICC, LN (14.39)], 'to reveal' [BAGD, LN (28.36)], 'to throw light on' [Alf, HNTC], 'to shed light upon' [Ho], 'to turn on the light so that everyone can see exactly' [LB], 'to bring to light' [AB, BAGD, He; all versions except LB], 'to make known, to make plain, to bring to the light, to disclose' [LN (28.36)]. The truth about men's conduct is hidden in darkness, but the Lord shines a beam of light on it [HNTC].

c. κρυπτός (LN 28.69) (BAGD 2.a. p. 454): 'hidden things' [BAGD, Lns], 'things hidden' [HNTC; KJV, NASB, TNT], 'things now hidden' [NRSV], 'everything that is hidden' [NJB], 'facts that are now hidden' [ICC], 'secret' [BAGD], 'hidden, not able to be made known' [LN]. This adjective is also translated as a clause: 'what is hidden' [BAGD, He; NAB, NIV], 'what darkness hides' [REB], 'what people are really like, deep down in their hearts' [LB]. This word is also joined with the words 'of darkness' and is translated 'dark secrets' [AB; TEV]. The word 'now' is not in the Greek, but is implied from the word 'then' of the final sentence of this verse [TH]. The 'hidden things' are the object of the verb, not the darkness that hides them [HNTC].

d. σκότος (LN 14.53; 88.125) (BAGD 2.a. p. 757): 'darkness' [BAGD, He, HNTC, ICC, LN, Lns; all versions except TEV], 'gloom' [BAGD] 'evil world, realm of evil' [LN]. This noun is also translated as an adjective: 'dark (secrets)' [AB; TEV]. Σκότος is figurative for the state of being unknown [BAGD]. 'Darkness' signifies evil power as it does elsewhere in the NT [Lns]. 'Darkness' usually has an ethical sense in the NT and therefore here 'things' would refer to evil deeds, but it is best in this context to take it to mean all deeds which are now hidden in darkness [EGT, Gdt, ICC, TNTC].

QUESTION—What is the function of this relative clause?

Paul is giving the reason why judgment should be delayed until Christ comes. It is because Christ alone can reveal the hidden motives of men's hearts as a basis for true judgment [Ho].

QUESTION—What meaning is intended by καί 'both/also'?

1. It means 'both' in keeping with the following 'and' [ICC; KJV, NASB, TNT]: who will both bring to light the things hidden in darkness and expose the purposes of the heart.
2. It means 'also' [Ed, EGT, Lns, My]: who also will bring to light the things hidden in darkness. The 'also' in the ὅς καί 'who also' serves to highlight some element in reference to the antecedent 'who'. Here it refers to the Lord as judge who will come and will also light up the hidden things [My].
3. It means 'even' [Gdt]: who will even bring to light the things hidden in darkness and will expose the purposes of the heart. The 'even' serves to stress the two following verbs and contrast the activity of the Lord with that of other men [Gdt].

QUESTION—How are the nouns related in the genitive construction τὰ κρυπτὰ τοῦ σκότους 'hidden things of darkness'?

1. 'Darkness' is the place where things are hidden from view [Alf, EBC, HNTC, Ho, ICC, NIC, NIC2, TNTC; all versions except KJV, TEV, TNT]: things which are hidden in the darkness.

2. 'Darkness' describes the nature of the hidden things [AB; TEV]: dark secrets.
3. Both senses 1 and 2 are true here [Lns]: the wrong things hidden in the evil darkness.

and will-reveal[a] the purposes[b] of-the hearts;[c]

LEXICON—a. fut. act. indic. of φανερόω (LN 24.19; 28.36) (BAGD 1.a. p. 852): 'to reveal' [BAGD, He, LN; NJB, TNT], 'to expose' [NIV, TEV], 'to disclose' [AB, LN; NASB, NRSV, REB], 'to make known' [BAGD, HNTC, LN (28.36)], 'to manifest' [NAB], 'to make manifest' [ICC, Lns; KJV], 'to show' [BAGD], 'to make appear, to make visible, to cause to be seen' [LN (24.19)], 'to make plain, to bring to the light' [LN (28.36)]. This word is also translated by its reciprocal: 'everyone will know' [LB].

b. βουλή (LN 30.57) (BAGD 1. p. 145): 'purposes' [BAGD, LN; NRSV, TNT], 'hidden purposes' [TEV], 'motives' [BAGD, Ho; NASB, NIV], 'real motives' [ICC], 'plans' [HNTC, LN], 'designs' [NJB], 'intentions' [LN; NAB], 'thoughts' [He], 'counsels' [BAGD, Lns; KJV]. This word is also translated by a specific purpose: '(everyone will know) why we have been doing the Lord's work' [LB]. This word is also joined with the following word 'heart' and translated 'our inward motives' [REB], 'innermost purposes' [AB]. These secret purposes can include good and bad desires and drives [Lns, TNTC]. The 'counsels' of the heart which only God knows perfectly dictate action and are the essence of character [EGT].

c. καρδία (LN 26.3) (BAGD 1.b.γ. p. 404): 'hearts' [BAGD, He, LN, Lns; KJV, NAB, NRSV], 'men's hearts' [HNTC; NASB, NIV], 'all hearts' [NJB], 'men's minds' [TNT], 'people's minds' [TEV], 'deep down in our hearts' [LB], 'human conduct' [ICC], 'inner self, mind' [LN]. This noun is also translated as an adjective modifying 'purposes': 'innermost (purposes)' [AB], '(our) inward (motives)' [REB]. Καρδία indicates the center and source of the inner life, its thinking, feeling, and volition. Here the will and decisions made out of the will is indicated [BAGD]. It indicates the source of the intellect and will, more than of the emotions. Here it stresses a person's power of thought [TH]. It means the real self, the hidden inward man [EGT], the spring of a person's psychological life with special emphasis on thoughts [LN].

QUESTION—What relationship is indicated by καί 'and'?

1. It indicates the second result of the Lord's coming [ICC, Lns; KJV, NASB, TNT]: who will both reveal the things hidden in darkness and expose the purposes of the hearts.
2. It indicates a specific example of the previous general statement [EGT, Ho, My]: in general he will reveal the hidden things of darkness, and specifically he will expose the purposes of the heart. The 'purposes of the heart' are included in 'the hidden things of darkness' [Ho].

3. It indicates that what follows is a restatement of the previous clause [EBC, HNTC, NIC2]: who will reveal the things of darkness, that is, he will expose the purposes of the heart. This is an example of Semitic poetry where only one thought is intended even though it is said in two slightly different ways [NIC2]. The second clause explains the first [EBC].

and then praise[a] will-be to-each-one from God.

LEXICON—a. ἔπαινος (LN 33.354) (BAGD 1.a.β. p. 281): 'praise' [BAGD, He, ICC, LN, My; KJV, NAB, NASB, NIV, TNT], 'due praise' [Lns], 'such praise as he deserves' [LB, TEV], 'need of praise' [HNTC], 'commendation' [My; NRSV, REB], 'appropriate commendation' [NJB], 'approval, recognition' [BAGD]. This noun is also translated as a verb: '(God) will praise' [AB]. It means 'gives a favorable verdict' [TH]. It indicates 'much praise, applause, loud and clear acclaim of commendation' [Ho].

QUESTION—Does this imply that every person will deserve praise?

It may be what Paul means by 'reward' in 3:14 [NIC2, TH]. The definite article with ἔπαινος indicates the praise that is due to each steward [Lns, My], and this then excludes those to whom no praise is due [ICC, My]. Only the faithful will be praised [Ho]. The correct translation requires the word 'his' before 'praise' to indicate that the praise rightly belongs to him [Vn].

QUESTION—Where is the emphasis in this clause?

The emphasis is on the phrase 'from God' [Herm, ICC, My, TH], and implies 'not from men' [My, TH]. The emphasis is on the word 'then' [Ed, HNTC, Ho], meaning, 'at the judgment', not now.

DISCOURSE UNIT: 4:6–21 [Gdt, ICC, NCBC]. The topic is the apostles and their converts [NCBC], pride, the first cause of evil [Gdt], personal application and conclusion of the subject of the dissensions [ICC].

DISCOURSE UNIT: 4:6–13 [AB, Alf, EBC, Ed, EGT, Herm, HNTC, My, NIC2, TH, Vn]. The topic is standards of Christian living [AB], the proud Corinthians and the despised servants [HNTC], a sharp rebuke [Ed], disciples above their Master [EGT], application to the community [Herm], the Corinthians and their apostles [HNTC], the marks of true apostleship [NIC2]. Paul treats two themes in this section: the pride of the Corinthians (4:6–8, 10), and his weaknesses (4:9, 11–13) [NIC2]. Paul had stated the principles which should give the Corinthians a correct estimate of Apollos and himself. He now reminds them to apply the principles to others [Vn].

DISCOURSE UNIT: 4:6–7 [TNTC]. The topic is learning from Paul and Apollos.

4:6 Now,[a] brothers, I-applied[b] these-things to myself and Apollos for-the-sake-of[c] you,

LEXICON—a. δέ (LN 89.87): 'now' [HNTC, Lns; NASB, NIV], 'and' [KJV], not explicit [all other versions].

b. aorist act. indic. of μετασχηματίζω (LN **89.11**) (BAGD p. 513): 'to apply' [BAGD, **LN**; NIV, NJB, NRSV, REB, TEV], 'to figuratively apply' [NASB], 'to make something seem to apply' [HNTC], 'to modify in form so as to apply' [ICC], 'to apply as an illustration' [TNT], 'to apply by way of example' [NAB], 'to transfer' [AB], 'to transfer to someone in a figure' [Lns; KJV], 'to use someone as an example to illustrate' [LB], 'to represent in a figurative form the truth which applies' [He], 'to change the form of, transform, change' [BAGD], 'to regard as applicable to' [LN]. 'To apply something to someone' means, 'to give a teaching the form of an exposition concerning that person' [BAGD].

c. διά with accusative object (LN 90.38): 'for the sake of' [He, HNTC, ICC, LN, Lns; KJV, NASB, NJB, TEV], 'for the benefit of' [LN; NAB, NIV, NRSV, REB], 'for the enlightenment of' [AB], 'on behalf of, for' [LN], not explicit [LB]. This preposition is also translated as a verb: 'to help (you)' [TNT]. 'For the sake of' indicates 'the more easily to gain your acceptance of the truth thus presented' [Gdt], or 'for your better instruction' [EGT].

QUESTION—What relationship is indicated by δέ 'now'?

It indicates transition [EGT, NIC2]. Paul is pursuing his subject, but now turns to the final admonitions concerning party-spirit among them [My]. It introduces the conclusion and practical application of all of that Paul has been saying [Herm, ICC]. There are three factors that indicate that Paul's argument has reached a critical point: (1) the phrase 'these things' is placed forward in emphatic position; (2) this is followed by transitional δέ 'now'; (3) this is followed by the vocative 'brothers' which occurs 21 times in 1 Corinthians, 17 of which are at a shift in argument [NIC2, TH].

QUESTION—What specific meaning is intended by the word μετασχηματίζω 'to apply'?

1. It means to use a figure of speech in which one thing is named and another thing is meant [Ed, Gdt, HNTC, ICC, Lns, NCBC, NIC, Vn]. Μετασχηματίζω primarily means, 'to change the figure or shape' but it came to indicate, 'to use a figure of speech in which one thing is named and another thing is meant'. Paul teaches a lesson to certain teachers in the Church under the guise of applying the lesson to himself and Apollos. This word cannot mean, 'to teach a general truth by means of an example' [Ed]. The rhetorical sense of σχῆμα 'form' is used here to indicate a 'veiled allusion' [ICC]. If the Corinthians can see that it is wrong to judge Paul and Apollos, they will more easily admit that all judging is wrong [NIC].
2. It means that Paul had changed the form of the figure from gardener to builder, and to steward, and applied them all to Apollos and himself [NIC2]. The context and the emphatic position of the words 'these things' indicate that Paul was changing the form of the figures, not the persons to whom the figures applied. He had applied the figures to himself and

Apollos so that they might apply them to themselves and learn not to have pride in persons [NIC2].

3. It means that Paul had given a specific example to illustrate a general truth [Alf, EGT, TG; LB]. He had used the names of Apollos and himself as examples, so that the Corinthians would learn how to think of all leaders [Alf].
4. It means to express abstract truths in figurative language [EBC, He, Ho, TNTC]: I have spoken figuratively of Apollos and myself. Paul is teaching by personal illustration rather than abstract principles [EBC].

QUESTION—To what does ταῦτα 'these things' refer?

1. It refers to what Paul has said in the previous chapter, especially from 3:5 onwards [Ed, Gdt, HNTC, Ho, ICC, My], except for 3:22. The section 3:5–17 is especially in focus [HNTC].
2. It refers to the figures of speech of 3:5–4:5 [NIC2]. This interpretation agrees with the verb μετασχηματίζω which indicates 'to change form'. Paul is saying that he has gone from figure to figure changing images as he went, and applying it to Apollos and himself [NIC2].
3. It refers to 4:1–5 with greatest stress on the command not to judge [NIC].

so-that[a] you-may-learn[b] through[c] us

LEXICON—a. ἵνα (LN 89.59): 'so that' [NIV, NJB, NRSV, REB, TEV], 'that' [He; KJV, NASB], 'in order that' [AB, HNTC, ICC, LN, Lns], not explicit [LB]. This preposition is also translated as a clause: 'I want you to' [TNT]. It is also translated as a verbal aspect: 'may you (learn)' [NAB]. This word indicates Paul's purpose [AB, HNTC, ICC, Lns, TNTC; NAB, TNT].

b. aorist act. subj. of μανθάνω (LN **32.14**; 27.12) (BAGD 1. p. 490): 'to learn' [BAGD, He, LN (27.12), Lns; all versions except LB, NJB, REB, TNT], 'to understand' [**LN**], 'to learn how' [NJB], 'to be instructed, to be taught' [LN (27.12)], 'to learn the meaning of' [AB, HNTC, ICC; TNT], 'to learn the true meaning of' [REB], not explicit [LB].

c. ἐν with dative object (LN **90.6**) (BAGD I.2. p. 258): 'through' [NRSV], 'from' [He, **LN**; NAB, NIV], 'of' [NJB], 'by reference to' [AB], 'by means of' [TNT], 'by (our) example' [HNTC], 'by (us) as examples' [ICC], 'by' [BAGD, LN], 'in' [Lns; KJV, NASB]. This preposition is also translated as a verb: 'using (the two of us as) an example' [TEV], 'take (our case as) an example' [REB]. It can indicate agent and often agent used as instrument [LN]. 'Eν joins the two senses of instrument (by means of), and of sphere (in) [Ed]. 'Eν ἡμῖν 'by us' includes the notion of Paul and Apollos being examples to the Corinthians [Alf, BAGD, HNTC, ICC, My; REB, TEV].

the not (to go) beyond[a] that-which has-been-written,

LEXICON—a. ὑπέρ (LN **88.95**) (BAGD 2. p. 839): 'beyond' [AB, BAGD, HNTC, ICC, Lns; NAB, NIV, NJB, NRSV, REB], 'above' [KJV], 'more than' [BAGD], 'over and above' [BAGD], not explicit [He; LB]. This preposition is also translated as verb: 'to exceed' [NASB]. It is also joined with the word 'not' and translated positively: 'to keep close to' [TNT], 'to observe (the saying)' [TEV]. The words 'not above what is written' are an idiom meaning 'to act sensibly in keeping with rules, to observe rules properly' [LN]. Here it could be translated 'so that you may learn from us what it means to live according to the rules' or 'what the saying means, Observe the rules' [LN].

QUESTION—What is indicated by the Greek word τό 'the' at the beginning of this phrase?

It indicates that the following is a quotation from a well-known saying [Gdt, HNTC, ICC, NIC, NIC2, TH, TNTC]. It could therefore be translated 'that you learn the principle or the maxim' [Gdt, ICC]. It indicates that the following phrase should be taken as a unit: 'the not-above-what-is-written' [My]. It serves to make the following phrase the object of 'that you might learn' [EGT].

QUESTION—What is implied between the words 'not' and 'beyond'?

The verb 'to go' is implied [AB, BAGD, EGT, ICC, Lns, NIC; NAB, NASB, NIV]: not to go beyond. The words 'to think of men' is implied [KJV]: not to think of men above that which is written.

QUESTION—What is meant by the phrase 'what is written'?

1. It refers to what has been written in the Scriptures [AB, Alf, EBC, Ed, EGT, Gdt, HNTC, Ho, ICC, Lns, My, NIC, NIC2, TNTC; TNT]. The neuter article τό (1:19, 29, 31) is the standard way to introduce quoted material. The verb γέγραπται 'has been written' is Paul's usual way of citing scripture [NIC2]. Paul probably had in mind that they not go beyond the scriptures he had cited in chapters 1 and 3. Particularly that they not boast in men (1:19, 29, 31), and that they not be deceived by the 'wise' (3:19, 20) [Alf, ICC, NIC2]. Paul probably has in mind the OT scriptures in general [EBC, Ed, HNTC, Ho, Lns, My]. It may refer to the OT, which reference is then explained in the following 'that-clause', 'that you be not puffed up' [AB]. In particular, the OT scriptures teach that men should not be proud or quarrelsome [Lns]. The Corinthians were to value their ministers according to biblical standard and not higher [Alf, Ho]. Paul is thinking of the biblical standard of humility and modesty [My]. It probably refers to a maxim used in the Rabbinical schools concerning not going beyond what is written in Scripture [Gdt]. Paul intended that they learn the scriptural principle of the subordination of man and the exaltation of God [TNTC].
2. It refers to an unspecified rule [TH; TEV]: not to go beyond what is written in the rules. The article in the Greek before the phrase 'not beyond what is written' suggests that this is a quotation of a current saying [TH].
3. It refers to the terms of a contract [Vn]: not to go beyond the terms of the contract. The phrase seems to be a technical reference to the terms of an agreement. Here it would indicate that they not go beyond the terms of a contract with a teacher [Vn].

4. It refers to a saying [NJB, REB]: you can learn how the saying, 'Nothing beyond what is written', is true of us.

so that/that[a] not one (of) you-be-puffed-up[b] in-favor-of[c] the one against[d] the other.

LEXICON—a. ἵνα (LN 89.49; 90.22; 91.15): 'so that' [HNTC, LN (89.49); NAB, NRSV], 'in order that' [AB, LN (89.59); NASB], 'that' [LN (90.22); KJV], 'namely that' [LN (91.15), Lns], 'then' [NIV], not explicit [He, ICC; LB, NJB, REB, TEV]. It is also translated as a verb with the repetition of 'learn': 'I want you to learn' [TNT].

b. pres. pass. indic. of φυσιόω (LN **88.216**) (BAGD p. 869): 'to be puffed up' [BAGD, He, HNTC, LN; KJV, NRSV], 'to be puffed up with pride' [AB], 'to be inflated with pride' [REB], 'to be made proud, arrogant, to become puffed up, conceited' [BAGD]. This passive is also translated actively: 'to puff oneself up' [Lns], 'to grow self-important' [NAB], 'to become arrogant' [NASB, TNT], 'to become filled with one's own importance' [NJB], 'to take pride' [NIV], 'to be proud' [LN; LB, TEV], 'to speak boastfully (in favor of one)' [ICC], 'to be haughty' [LN], 'to be proud of (one person and despise another)' [**LN**]. The present tense indicates that they are never at any time to act in this manner [Lns]. The present tense indicates that they were to stop an action already begun. They were to stop boasting about one so as to oppose the other [NIC2]. 'Puffed up' primarily indicates pride, here linked with self-deception (see 3:18). The prohibition here is against praising one leader with the purpose of attacking another [TH].

c. ὑπέρ with genitive object (LN 90.36) (BAGD 1.a.δ. p. 838): 'in favor of' [ICC, Lns; NRSV], 'in behalf of' [AB, BAGD, HNTC, LN; NASB], 'for' [BAGD, He, LN; KJV], 'for the sake of' [BAGD, LN], 'in (your) support of' [REB, TNT], 'in' [NIV], 'of' [LB, TEV], 'by reason of one's association with' [NAB]. This preposition is also translated as a verb: 'to make comparisons' [NJB]. It means 'to be for someone, to be one someone's side' [BAGD].

d. κατά with genitive object (LN 90.31) (BAGD I.2.b. p. 405): 'against' [AB, BAGD, He, HNTC, LN, Lns; KJV, NASB, NRSV, REB, TNT], 'over against' [NIV], 'rather than' [NAB], 'more than' [LB], 'to (another's) detriment' [NJB], 'to the disparagement of (the other)' [ICC], 'in opposition to, in conflict with' [LN]. This preposition is also translated as a verb: 'to despise (another)' [TEV].

QUESTION—What relationship is indicated by ἵνα 'so that'?

1. It indicates the purpose of their learning not to go beyond what is written [AB, Gdt, Ho, NIC2; NASB]: that you may learn not to go beyond what is written in order that none of you will be puffed up.
2. It indicates Paul's purpose for applying all this to himself and Apollos [Ed, ICC, TH; REB, TNT]: I applied these things to myself and

Apollos...so that none of you may be puffed up. Both occurrences of ἵνα depend on the verb 'I have applied' [Ed; REB, TNT].

3. It indicates the result of learning not to go beyond what is written [EBC, HNTC; NAB, NIV]: that you may learn not to go beyond what is written with the result that you will not be puffed up.
4. It indicates the content or explanation of learning what is written [EGT, Lns; KJV]: not to go beyond what is written, namely that none of you may be puffed up.

QUESTION—To whom does 'one' and 'the other' refer?

1. The reference is general applying to whichever teachers were concerned [Gdt, HNTC, Ho, TH]. The reference is to the leaders that the Corinthians have chosen [HNTC].
2. The reference may be to Apollos and Paul [NIC2]. Two factors support this view: (1) The word 'puffed up' occurs again in 4:18 in a definite reference to Paul; (2) the combination of 'the one' and 'the other' when they follow the mention of two people would usually refer back to them. The remaining argument of the chapter implies that there were some who were definitely opposed to Paul, whose pride he now addresses [NIC2].

4:7 For[a] who regards-as-superior[b] you?

LEXICON—a. γάρ (LN 89.23): 'for' [He, HNTC, ICC, LN; KJV, NASB, NIV, NRSV], not explicit [AB, Lns; all other versions].

b. pres. act. indic. of διακρίνω (LN **30.99**; 30.113) (BAGD 1.b. p. 185): 'to regard someone as superior' [**LN**; NASB], 'to concede distinction to' [He], 'to concede superiority to' [BAGD, NCBC], 'to confer any distinction on someone' [NAB], 'to single someone out for distinction' [AB], 'to make someone important' [NJB, REB], 'to make someone superior to someone' [TEV], 'to give a special position to someone' [TNT], 'to make someone differ' [Lns], 'to make someone different from someone' [HNTC; KJV, NIV], 'to see something different in someone' [NRSV], 'to be puffed up about something' [LB], 'to give someone the right to prefer one man to another' [ICC], 'to prefer, to regard as more valuable' [LN (30.99)], 'to make a distinction' [BAGD, LN (30.113)], 'to judge that there is a difference' [LN (30.113)], 'to differentiate' [BAGD]. 'To differ' implies 'so as to have advantage over another'. The verb refers specifically to the idea of inflating one's own idea of one's self by boasting about one's leader and thereby diminishing other leaders [Lns]. Here διακρίνω means 'to distinguish favorably from others' [ICC].

QUESTION—What relationship is indicated by γάρ 'for'?

It indicates the grounds for saying that they should not be puffed up [Alf, EBC, Ed, HNTC, ICC, Lns, NIC, NIC2]: that you not be puffed up since all that you have comes from God. This justifies the use of the saying [Ed].

QUESTION—To whom does σε 'you' refer and why is it singular?

Paul changes from addressing the one who is puffed up about someone else to addressing the person who thinks himself superior to others [TG]. He now addresses a hypothetical Corinthian who is puffed up. The 'you' is emphatic by its position in the clause [TNTC]. 'You' refers to the ones who are puffed up against Paul. The singular probably reflects the word 'one' of 4:6, and shows Paul's Semitic background in which OT legal materials use the singular for greater force ('Thou shalt') [NIC2]. 'You' refers to anyone showing a spirit of partisanship [Vn]. 'You' refers to those who declared loyalty to a leader even though he was not willing to be a leader [AB]. 'You' refers to each individual of the preceding 'you (pl.)' [My]. The singular indicates that 'you' is a reference to all Christians in general [Herm].

QUESTION—What is meant by the verb διακρίνω 'to regard as superior' and what answer is expected to the rhetorical question?

1. It means, Who made you to be superior to others? No one [AB, Alf, Herm, HNTC, Lns, My, NIC, NIC2, Rb, TG, TH, TNTC]. God surely did not do this [TH]. This question is directly related to 4:6 and their pride in regard to Paul. This question is ironical in that Paul denies that this person is superior [TG]. It implies that this boasting about wisdom to examine Paul is only self-proclaimed [NIC2]. Paul asks why they take pride in some teacher over others, since 'who really makes you different from others' [EBC].
2. It means, Who gives you the right to consider one teacher to be superior to another teacher? No one [ICC, Vn]. The verb here means 'to distinguish favorably from others', and should thus be translated 'who gave you the right to set one up and put another down?' The answer is, 'no one' [ICC]. The question implies that this attitude arises out of self-conceit [Vn].
3. It means, Who has made you different from the apostles? No one [Ed]. Paul is asking who made them different than the apostles so that while the apostles must prepare for the judgment of Christ, the Corinthians can exalt one leader in favor of the other and thus create factions in the church [Ed].
4. It means, Who made you superior to others? Not yourself [Gdt].

And[a] what do-you-have that you-received not?

LEXICON—a. δέ: 'and' [He, HNTC, ICC, Lns; KJV, NASB], not explicit [all other versions]. The δέ serves to add another probing question, the point of which is that they had nothing other than that which had been given to them [ICC].

QUESTION—Who is the source of 'you received'?

The source is God [Alf, EBC, EGT, HNTC, ICC, NIC2, TG, TH, TNTC, Vn; TEV]: what do you have that you did not receive from God?

QUESTION—What is the implied answer to this question?

The answer is: 'nothing' [Gdt, Herm, HNTC, NIC2, TNTC]. Absolutely everything a man has is a gift [NIC2].

Now if indeed[a] you-received (it), why do-you-boast[b] as-if[c] not receiving (it)?

LEXICON—a. καί (LN 91.12): 'indeed' [ICC, LN], 'it is true' [He], 'also' [Lns], 'and' [NJB], not explicit [all other versions]. Καί can mark emphasis involving the element of surprise [LN]. The καί 'indeed' serves to emphasize the verb 'receive' [HNTC, ICC, Lns], and not to indicate that Paul conceded that they had received it [Lns]. Eἰ καί 'if indeed' indicates 'which I concede' [Alf, Ed, Gdt, My, NIC2], it reinforces the fact that they had received it [ICC, NIC2]. The καί with the εἰ forms the singular meaning of 'though'. 'How, though having received, do you boast as if you had not received?' [Gdt]. The εἰ 'if' introduces a condition assumed to be true [EBC]. Καί stresses the contrast to οὐκ ἔλαβες 'you did not receive' [Herm].

b. pres. mid. indic. of καυχάομαι (LN 33.368): 'to boast' [He, HNTC, ICC, LN; all versions except KJV, LB, REB], 'to glory' [AB, Lns; KJV], 'to take credit to oneself' [REB], 'to act as though one is so great' [LB]. 'To boast' is to say that one is better than someone else [TH]. See this word at 1:29, 31; 3:21.

c. ὡς (LN 64.12): (BAGD III.2. p. 898): 'as if' [HNTC, ICC, Lns; all versions except LB, NIV, NJB, REB], 'as though' [AB, BAGD, He; LB, NIV, NJB], not explicit [REB]. In this context it could be rendered 'why do you boast, as though you (as you think) had not received?' [BAGD]. Ὡς μή 'as if not' indicates 'as if thinking you had not received' [Ed]. Ὡς indicates 'from the point of view of having received' [EGT].

QUESTION—What is the implied answer to this question?

The implied answer was that they had no right to boast [EBC, EGT, TG, TNTC]. 'Boasting' implied forgetfulness of the fact that all that any minister had was a gift from God [ICC].

QUESTION—What is meant by the word 'it'?

'It' indicates whatever gift a man may have [HNTC, NCBC]. 'It' refers to their Christian insight, wisdom, and eloquence [My]. 'It' refers to the powers of the Spirit [He].

DISCOURSE UNIT: 4:8–13 [TNTC]. The topic is the trials endured by the apostles. Paul changes from an exposition of principles to a contrast of the miserable lot of the apostles as compared with the untroubled lot of the Corinthians. His irony is biting.

4:8 Already[a] you-have-all-you-want,[b]

LEXICON—a. ἤδη (LN 67.20): 'already' [AB, He, HNTC, ICC, LN, Lns; all versions except KJV, LB, NAB], 'now' [KJV], 'at the moment' [NAB]. This word is also translated to show the irony: 'you seem to think you already have all you need' [LB]. It indicates that they had reached the goal of perfection prematurely [NIC]. It serves to intensify the sarcasm of this address: you 'already' have that which was only expected to come in the coming age [My]. This word is emphatic by its position [Alf, My, NIC2, Vn], and brings out that the Corinthians thought they had already arrived in full realization of the Messianic kingdom [HNTC, NIC2]. It is emphatic in both occurrences and adds to the irony of the exclamations [Vn]. Paul holds 'already' and 'not yet' in opposing tension; the Corinthians majored largely on the 'already' to the neglect of the 'not yet' [NIC2]. The two 'already's give a certain force to their statements: 'Think of it, already you are filled!' [Lns].

b. perf. pass. participle of κορέννυμι (LN **25.80**; 57.22) (BAGD 2. p. 444): 'to have all one wants' [NRSV], 'to have everything one wants' [NIV, TNT], 'to have everything' [NJB], 'to have everything one could desire' [REB], 'to have everything one needs' [TEV], 'to have all the spiritual food one needs' [LB], 'to have enough' [BAGD, LN (57.22)], 'to be filled' [NASB], 'to be filled full' [Lns], 'to be full' [KJV], 'to be satisfied' [**LN**], 'to be completely satisfied' [NAB], 'to be in perfect felicity' [ICC], 'to be stuffed full' [AB], 'to be surfeited' [He], 'to be satiated' [BAGD, LN (57.22)], 'to reach satiety' [HNTC], 'to be content' [LN (25.80)]. Κορέννυμι is used here figuratively and ironically meaning 'you think you already have all the spiritual food you need' [BAGD]. It primarily refers to food and denotes satiation or satisfaction [Ed, TNTC]. It means 'to glut, to feed full' [EGT]. The perfect tense stresses the continuance of a state which has been reached: you are already living in a state of having all the spiritual food you need [EBC]. They feel they have enough talent [EGT], righteousness [Alf, Gdt], and all of the God-given gifts [HNTC].

QUESTION—Are the propositions of this verse statements or questions?

1. They are statements [EGT, GNT, HNTC, Ho, ICC, Lns, My, NCBC, NIC, TNTC, Vn; KJV, NAB, NASB, NIV, NJB, NRSV, REB, TNT]. Six consecutive questions would not be good style, and questions would spoil the irony [ICC]. The statements are ironical, stating one thing but meaning its opposite [Alf, BAGD, EBC, Ed, EGT, Herm, HNTC, Ho, ICC, LN, Lns, My, NCBC, NIC, Rb, TH, TNTC, Vn]. They are even sarcastic [Ho, Lns, My, NIC]. The irony is biting [NIC2, TNTC]. Paul now contrasts himself and the Corinthians in a series of antithetical statements to which the only fitting response is shame [NIC2]. The irony is derisive, intended to show the foolishness and sinfulness of pride [EBC, Ed].
2. They are questions [AB, He; TEV]. The question punctuation is that of Westcott and Hort. Paul continues his series of questions by asking them to think about a few absurdities. The questions imply that the Corinthians had unwarranted feelings of self importance and were trying to perform things reserved for God. If taken as statements, the last wish cancels them out. If irony is assumed, it seems a bit too harsh. The rhetorical questions function to bring out their own absurdity [AB].

QUESTION—What is the significance of the plural 'you'?

Now Paul changes back to the plural of you, referring to all who shared this attitude and especially the leaders of the parties [TG].

already you-became-rich,[a]

LEXICON—a. aorist act. indic. of πλουτέω (LN 57.28) (BAGD 2. p. 674): 'to become rich' [AB, BAGD, He, HNTC, LN; NASB, NIV, NRSV, TNT], 'to be rich' [KJV, NJB, TEV], 'to be quite rich' [ICC], 'to grow rich' [Lns; NAB], 'to come into one's fortune' [REB], 'to become wealthy, to prosper' [LN]. This verb is also translated as an adjective: 'rich (kings)' [LB]. Πλουτέω is used here figuratively [BAGD, TH]. The aorist is ingressive, denoting entrance into a condition [Lns, Rb, TNTC]. The richness refers primarily to spiritual gifts (1:5, 7) [EGT, Gdt, NIC, TH]. Paul's rebuke did not apply to their possession of spiritual gifts but to the pride that went with them [Gdt]. The notion 'by their own efforts' is implied and contrasts with 1:5 'you were enriched in him' [NIC].

without us you-became-kings;[a]

LEXICON—a. aorist act. indic. of βασιλεύω (LN 37.64) (BAGD 2. p. 136): 'to be/become king' [AB, BAGD, LN; LB, NASB, NIV, NRSV, TEV, TNT], 'to obtain royal power' [BAGD], 'to reign' [LN, Lns], 'to reign as kings' [KJV], 'to launch upon one's reign' [NAB], 'to come into one's kingdom' [HNTC, ICC; NJB, REB], 'to enter into the possession of the kingdom' [He], 'to rule' [LN]. There may be a reference here to the Kingdom of God [Alf, Ed, EGT, Gdt, Herm, HNTC, Ho, ICC, My, NCBC, NIC2, Vn] meaning that they were acting as though the Kingdom of God had already arrived [HNTC]. Paul claims that the Corinthians had already entered the full realization of the Messiah's reign [Ho]. Paul taught that suffering preceded glory as it did with Christ (Col. 3:4). The Corinthians had attained glory without the suffering [NCBC]. The force of the aorist in verbs of state is inceptive, meaning entrance into a state: 'became kings' [EGT, Lns, Rb, TNTC].

QUESTION—What is the significance of these three verbs?

The three verbs 'to be filled, to become rich, to become kings' represent the fulfillment of all the desires of the Messianic Kingdom (Luke 22:29, 30; 1 Thess. 2:12; 2 Tim. 2:12) [ICC].

QUESTION—What is intended by the phrase χωρὶς ἡμῶν 'without us'?

1. It means 'without our company' [Ed, Gdt, Ho, ICC, Lns, NIC, NIC2, TH, TNTC, Vn; TEV]. This agrees with the last part of the verse, 'so that we also might be kings with you' [NIC2, TH]. The Corinthians believed that they had reached a position that neither Paul nor the other apostles had [TNTC]. The phrase 'without us' is in the emphatic position in the clause [Alf, Lns, NIC2], they had left behind the very people to whom they owed everything [Lns].
2. It means 'without our help' [EBC, EGT, HNTC, My; NAB, NJB, TNT]. They felt that they had outgrown Paul's teaching [EGT] and did not need assistance from such an insignificant teacher [HNTC].

QUESTION—To whom does the word ἡμῶν 'us' refer?

It refers to Paul, the apostles, and all their teachers [NIC2]. It refers to Paul and Apollos (4:6) [EBC, HNTC, My], to Paul and his colleagues [TG].

and would-that[a] really[b] you-became-kings,[c] so-that[d] we also[e] might-be-kings-with[f] you.

LEXICON—a. ὄφελον (LN **71.28**) (BAGD p. 599): 'would that' [BAGD, Ho, LN, Lns; NAB, NASB], 'O that' [BAGD, Ho], 'I wish that' [AB, HNTC;

LB, NJB, NRSV, TEV], 'How I wish' [NIV, REB, TNT], 'I would to God' [ICC; KJV], 'I could wish that' [He]. It is a fixed form functioning to introduce unattainable wishes [BAGD, NIC2]. It implies that the wish had not been fulfilled [BAGD, Ed, EGT, Lns, Rb, TNTC] and was impossible of being attained [Gdt]. Some think that this wish is ironical [AB, ICC], stating that if by chance the Corinthians had become spiritual rulers, this might somehow, by association, give their leaders power as well, to whom they owed their conversion [AB]. Others think that here Paul stops his irony with a sincere wish for future peace [Alf, Ed, EGT, HNTC, Lns, NIC2, Vn].

b. γέ (LN 91.6) (BAGD 3.h. p. 153): 'really' [LB, NAB, NIV, TEV, TNT], 'indeed' [BAGD, LN, Lns; NASB, NRSV, REB], 'yes' [HNTC], 'at least' [My], 'then' [LN], 'in truth' [He], not explicit [AB, ICC; KJV, NJB]. This enclitic particle is attached to the word it refers to and functions to emphasize the word [BAGD]. Γέ emphasizes the wish [Alf, ICC, Lns, My]. It means 'to be sure' and emphasizes Paul's personal feeling [EGT]. Καί...γε 'and... certainly' introduces with emphasis an unexpected addition [Ed].

c. aorist act. indic. of βασιλεύω: 'to become king' [AB; NASB, NIV, NRSV, TNT], 'to be king' [NJB, TEV], 'to reign' [Lns; KJV, NAB], 'to enter into one's kingdom' [HNTC; REB], 'to be on one's throne' [LB]. This word is also carried implicitly: '(I could wish that) it were so' [He]. See this word in this verse above.

d. ἵνα (LN 89.59; 89.49): 'so that' [He, LN (89.59); NASB, NIV, NRSV, TNT], 'in order that' [Lns], 'that' [HNTC, ICC; KJV, NAB], 'and' [NJB], 'then' [TEV], 'so as a result' [LN (89.49)], 'so' [AB], 'for' [LB].

e. καί (LN 89.93): 'also' [AB, He, ICC, LN; KJV, NASB, TNT], 'too' [HNTC, Lns], 'even' [NIC2], 'together' [TEV], 'too' [LB], not explicit [all other versions]. It serves to emphasize 'we' [NIC2]: even we ourselves.

f. aorist act. subj. of συμβασιλεύω (LN **37.66**) (BAGD p. 777): 'to be king with someone' [**LN**; NIV, NJB, NRSV, TEV, TNT], 'to rule (as king) with' [BAGD], 'to share one's kingdom with someone' [REB], 'to reign with someone' [AB, LN; KJV, LB, NAB, NASB], 'to reign with someone's help' [Lns], 'to be in the kingdom with someone' [ICC], 'to be crowned with someone' [HNTC], 'to be able to reign with' [He]. 'We' refers to Paul and his colleagues [TG].

QUESTION—What relationship is indicated by ἵνα 'so that'?

1. It indicates Paul's purpose for wishing that they would become kings [He, HNTC, ICC, Lns; KJV, NAB, NASB, NIV, NJB, NRSV, TNT].
2. It indicates the result of their becoming kings [AB; TEV].

QUESTION—What is meant by this wish?

Actually, Paul was leading a miserable life, showing that they hadn't really become kings [BAGD]. This ironical wish is that by their coming into power, the teacher who had founded the church would be carried into power along with them [AB]. Paul could at least expect them to give him a humble part in their kingly glory [Alf, Lns, My]. They would only become kings when Christ returned and when that happened, Paul would also reign with them [Ed, EGT, Ho, ICC, NIC2]. This is Paul's true longing for that time when there will be no more divisions [Vn].

4:9 For[a] I-think,[b] God exhibited[c] us apostles last[d]

LEXICON—a. γάρ (LN 89.23): 'for' [AB, He, HNTC, ICC, LN, Lns; all versions except NAB, TNT], not explicit [NAB, TNT].

b. pres. act. indic. of δοκέω (LN 31.29) (BAGD 1.e. p. 202): 'to think' [AB, BAGD, He, HNTC, LN; KJV, LB, NASB, NRSV], 'to believe, to suppose, to consider' [BAGD, LN]. This word is also translated idiomatically: 'it seems to me' [ICC, Lns; NIV, NJB, REB, TEV, TNT], 'as I see it' [NAB]. It is here used of a person's subjective opinion [BAGD, NIC]. This expresses Paul's true feelings [Ed]. See this word at 3:18.

c. aorist act. indic. of ἀποδείκνυμι (LN **28.65**) (BAGD 1. p. 89): 'to exhibit' [BAGD, ICC; NASB, NRSV, TNT], 'to show publicly' [**LN**], 'to demonstrate publicly' [LN], 'to put on display' [NIV], 'to put on show' [NJB], 'to set forth' [He, Lns; KJV], 'to appoint' [AB, BAGD, NIC2, TH, TNTC], 'to put' [NAB], 'to put on someone' [HNTC], 'to make' [BAGD; REB], 'to give (the very last place)' [TEV], 'to put at (the end)' [LB], 'to render, to proclaim' [BAGD]. Here the reference may be to a triumphal procession [BAGD]. It indicates a public presentation [Gdt, Ho], either to honor or ridicule [Gdt]. It means, 'to show off' [EGT]. It is used in the technical sense of displaying gladiators in an arena as a grand finale, to provide exciting entertainment [Vn]. Those also mentioning the figure of an arena in connection with these words are: Alf, Ed, Gdt, He, HNTC, ICC, Lns, NCBC, TG, TH, TNTC, and Vn. The reference to 'spectacle' in the following clause requires that ἀποδείκνυμι be taken in the sense of 'to exhibit' [Ed]. It means more than 'to show to be' or 'to exhibit'. It means 'to make to be, to appoint'. God had appointed them to the last place [AB, NIC2, TH, TNTC].

d. ἔσχατος (LN 61.13) (BAGD 2. p. 313): 'last' [BAGD, LN; KJV], 'last of all' [He, ICC; NASB, NRSV, TNT], 'last (act) in the show' [HNTC; REB], 'the very last place' [TEV], 'right at the end' [NJB], 'at the end of the procession' [NIV], 'at the end of the line' [LB, NAB], 'final, finally' [LN], 'the least (of men)' [AB], 'the lowest' [Lns]. It refers to rank [AB, BAGD, TH] and succession and indicates 'last, least, most insignificant', and refers especially to the apostles who were exhibited as the 'least' among men by the misfortunes they had suffered [BAGD]. The metaphor is one of a triumphant parade in which the conquering general displayed his armies and his booty. At the end of the parade were the captives who were condemned to die in the arena [ICC, NIC2, TH].

QUESTION—What relationship is indicated by γάρ 'for'?

It indicates the reason why Paul wished he did share the rule with the hypothetically reigning Corinthians [Alf, EGT, HNTC, Ho, Lns, My, NIC]. Paul wished to reign with the Corinthians because his present situation was a sad one [NIC].

QUESTION—To whom does the word 'apostles' refer?

1. It is not limited to the original twelve, but refers to Paul and others who have been sent to proclaim the good news [Alf, EBC, Gdt, NIC, NIC2, TG, Vn]. Paul must have meant Apollos as well as Peter [EBC, NIC2]. He perhaps includes Barnabas (Acts 14:4), Andronicus and Junius (Rom. 16:7), and James, the Lord's brother (Gal. 1:19), as well [EBC].
2. It refers to the twelve apostles [Lns]. Paul questions the validity of the reign of the Corinthians when the twelve apostles, who expect to sit on twelve thrones, are in such a low position [Lns].

as[a] condemned-to-death,[b]

LEXICON—a. ὡς (LN 64.12): 'as' [AB, HNTC, ICC, LN, Lns; NASB], 'as though' [NRSV], 'as it were' [KJV], 'like' [NAB, NIV, NJB, REB, TEV, TNT]. This word is also translated with implied information: 'and exhibited us like' [He], 'like prisoners' [LB]. This word indicates the explanation of what it means to be last [Gdt, Ho].

b. ἐπιθανάτιος (LN **23.116**) (BAGD p. 292): 'condemned to death' [BAGD; NASB, NJB], 'sentenced to death' [LN, Lns; NRSV], 'doomed to death' [AB, **LN**; TNT], 'appointed to death' [KJV], 'condemned to death in the arena' [NAB, NIV, REB], 'condemned to die in public' [TEV], 'under sentence of death' [HNTC], 'sentenced to die' [Lns], 'soon to be killed' [LB]. This adjective is also translated as a phrase: '(as) men doomed to death are the last spectacle in a triumphal procession' [ICC], 'those condemned to death' [He]. Ἐπιθανάτιος is used of condemned criminals who were thrown to the lions, two daily [ICC, NIC2]. This word referred to the gladiators who were part of the spectacle of the amphitheater [Gdt, He].

QUESTION—What is the point of comparison in this metaphor?

It is the utter humiliation that the apostles were subjected to in their service [NIC2]: as a man who is put in last position and is condemned to die is utterly humiliated, so we apostles have been placed last in God's service and are only good enough to be killed as a show to the world.

because/so-that[a] we-became (a) spectacle[b] to-the world[c] and to-angels[d] and to-men.[e]

LEXICON—a. ὅτι 'because' [NASB, NRSV, TNT], 'for' [HNTC, ICC; KJV], 'since' [AB, Lns], 'so that' [He], not explicit [LB, NAB, NIV, NJB, REB, TEV].

b. θέατρον (LN **24.15**) (BAGD 2. p. 353): 'spectacle' [AB, BAGD, He, HNTC, ICC, **LN**; all versions except LB, NJB], 'theatrical spectacle' [Ed, Lns], 'unusual sight' [LN]. This noun is also translated as a verb: 'to be exhibited as a spectacle' [NJB], 'put on display at the end of a victor's parade to be stared at' [LB]. Here θέατρον 'theater' refers to what one sees at a theater, 'a play' or 'a spectacle' [BAGD, HNTC, Ho, ICC, TNTC].

c. κόσμος (BAGD 3. p. 446): 'world' [AB, BAGD, He, Lns; KJV, NASB, NRSV, TNT], 'the whole world' [HNTC; TEV], 'the universe' [EBC, Ed, Ho, ICC, TNTC; NAB], 'the whole universe' [NIV, NJB, REB], not explicit [LB]. It refers to the sum total of all beings above the level of the animals, meaning 'the universe of intelligent beings' [Gdt, ICC, TNTC, Vn]. The concept of 'universe' includes the universe where angels live, and the earth where men live [EBC].

d. ἄγγελος (LN 12.28) (BAGD 2.b. p. 8): 'angels' [AB, BAGD, He, HNTC, ICC, LN, Lns; all versions except NJB]. This noun is also translated as an adjective: 'angelic (universe)' [NJB]. This is talking about intermediary beings in general with no reference to their relationship to God [BAGD]. Some think that both good and bad angels are indicated [Ed, EGT, Gdt]. Others think that this refers only to good angels [Alf, Ho, ICC, My, NIC2], for Paul refers to evil angels, not as angels, but as 'principalities and powers' [NIC2]. Ἄγγελοι 'angels' when used alone without any qualifiers in the NT always refers to good angels [Alf, Ho, My].

e. ἄνθρωπος (BAGD 1.a.β. p. 68): 'men' [AB, BAGD, He, HNTC, ICC, Lns; all versions except NJB, TEV], 'mankind' [TEV]. This noun is also translated as an adjective: 'human (universe)' [NJB]. This term includes all mankind, both hostile and sympathetic [Gdt, NIC]. 'Men' includes women as well [TH].

QUESTION—What relationship is indicated by ὅτι 'because/that'?

1. It indicates the grounds for Paul's statement that the apostles were like men condemned to death [AB, Ed, ICC, Lns, My, NIC; KJV, NASB, NRSV, TNT]: God has placed us last of all as men condemned to death since we have become a spectacle to the world. Paul has in mind flogging, stoning, and killing that the apostles had gone through as the world looked on [Lns].
2. It indicates an explanation of the statement that the apostles were like men condemned to death [Ed, EGT]: I think (that) God has placed us last of all as men condemned to death, that is, we have become a spectacle to the world. In the first clause the ὅτι 'that' was left implicit; here it is explicit. Both clauses depend on 'I think', and serve as its object, the second is in apposition to the first [EGT]. The words 'we have become a spectacle' serve to explain more fully the words 'condemned to death' [Ed].
3. It indicates result [He]: God has exhibited us last of all, with the result that we became a spectacle.

QUESTION—What is the relationship between the phrases 'to the world', 'to angels', and 'to men'?

1. The last two define the first [Alf, BAGD, EBC, Ed, Gdt, HNTC, Ho, ICC, Lns, My, NIC, NIC2, Rb, TG, TH, TNTC, Vn; NAB, NASB, NIV, NJB,

REB, TEV]: to the world, that is, both to angels and men. This is supported by the fact that only the word 'world' has the definite article in the Greek [Ed, HNTC, NIC]. The construction καί...καί means 'both...and', showing the two realms into which the universe is subdivided [Gdt].

2. They are coordinate and refer to three separate entities [AB; KJV, NRSV, TNT]: to the world, and to angels, and to men.

4:10 We (are) foolish[a] for-the-sake-of[b] Christ, but you (are) wise[c] in[d] Christ;

LEXICON—a. μώρος (LN **32.55**) (BAGD 1. p. 531): 'foolish' [BAGD, LN; LB]. This adjective is also translated as a noun phrase: 'fools' [AB, He, HNTC, **LN**, Lns; all versions except LB]; as a clause: '(we) poor simpletons go on with the foolishness (of preaching Christ)' [ICC]. Foolish here must be by worldly standards [HNTC, Ho, ICC, NIC]. They were fools in the eyes of the Corinthians [EBC, Ho, LN]. The apostles were 'fools' in their own estimation [EGT]. It is important to understand that Paul is using rhetorical exaggeration, he is not saying that they actually acted foolishly [LN]. See this word at 1:25, 27; 3:18.

b. διά with accusative object: 'for the sake of' [NIC2; all versions except NIV], 'for' [NIV], 'on account of' [NAB], not explicit [ICC]. They were fools for their devotion to the cause of Christ [Ho], or for preaching Christ [ICC]. See this word at 4:6.

c. φρόνιμος (LN 32.31) (BAGD p. 866): 'wise' [AB, BAGD, He, LN; all versions except LB, NASB, NJB, REB], 'prudent' [BAGD, Vn; NASB], 'sensible' [BAGD, HNTC; REB], 'smart' [Lns], 'wise and sensible' [LB], 'thoughtful' [BAGD]. This adjective is also translated as a noun phrase: 'the clever ones' [NJB], 'men of sagacity' [ICC]. Φρονίμως means 'wise', but with stress on the notion of 'sensible' [EGT, NIC2]. Here it has a negative connotation as it usually does in Paul's usage. Most of the Corinthians were not in this class (1:26), but they were acting as if they were [NIC2]. Paul uses φρονίμως in place of the σοφός 'wise' of 1:26 with no essential meaning difference [Herm, TNTC]. They regarded themselves as wise [EBC, EGT, Ho, ICC, NCBC, NIC, TNTC, Vn], and others did too [Ho]. Paul does not mean that they were actually wise, but that they thought they had wisdom which Paul could not claim [TNTC]. They claimed, as Christians, to have great powers of discernment and to possess the true wisdom [ICC]. 'Wise' is too good a word. They were 'smart', smart enough to know how to use Christ for their own advantage [Lns]. Paul's use of 'wise' here is very close to worldly wisdom [HNTC].

d. ἐν with dative object: 'in' [AB, He, HNTC; all versions except LB, REB, TEV], 'in union with' [Ho, Vn; TEV], 'in relation to' [ICC], 'in connection with' [Lns]. This preposition is also joined with the word 'Christ' and translated 'Christians' [LB, REB]. Here it means 'in communion with Christ' or 'in the sphere of Christ', that is, through

Christ and where He is ruling. The Corinthian error was not in claiming to be wise in Christ, but in boasting in it as though they had not received it [NIC]. Paul writes ἐν 'in' Christ, not διά 'for the sake of' Christ, because the Corinthian wisdom had 'other' motives [My]. The structure of the sentence indicates that there is not much difference in meaning between 'for Christ's sake' and 'in Christ' [TH]. 'In Christ' means 'as Christians' [Ed]. See this word at 1:2.

QUESTION—What is the relationship between this verse and the preceding verses?

It explains the preceding verses [Ed]. It explains Paul's right to say that they were a spectacle [NIC]: we have become a spectacle to the world because we are fools for Christ's sake while you are wise in Christ. This verse and the following serve to amplify what he has just said [Ho].

QUESTION—Is the verse ironical or sincere?

The verse is ironical [Alf, Ed, HNTC, ICC, My, NIC, NIC2, Rb, TG, TNTC, Vn]. The purpose of the irony is pedagogical. The Corinthians must learn the theology of the cross and they must learn to respect his apostleship [NIC2]. The threefold contrast alludes to 1:23–28 which makes the irony more biting [Ed].

we (are) weak,[a] but you (are) strong;[b]

LEXICON—a. ἀσθενής: 'weak' [He, HNTC, Lns; all versions], 'feeble' [AB]. This adjective is also translated as a noun: 'weakness' [ICC]. They were weak in their own feeling [Ho, ICC], and were so considered by others [Ho]. 'Weak' is not used of physical strength but of outward show. They were unimpressive because they would not use cheap means to impress people [Lns]. It is in the opinion of the world that the apostles are weak [NIC]. It is in the apostles' own estimation that they are weak [EGT, TNTC]. It is in the opinion of the Corinthians that the apostles were weak [EBC]. See this word at 1:25.

b. ἰσχυρός (LN 79.63): 'strong' [He, HNTC, LN, Lns; all versions except LB, REB], 'so strong as to stand alone' [ICC], 'powerful' [REB], 'mighty' [AB], 'not weak' [LB], 'vigorous' [LN]. They were strong in their own eyes [EBC, EGT, Ho, NCBC, NIC, TNTC], and in the eyes of others [Ho]. Their strength lay in the area of wisdom as a spiritual gift [NIC]. In keeping with 1:26–28, this is the ultimate irony, that the Christians were not among the powerful and prominent Corinthians, but when they judged Paul, they assumed themselves to be [NIC2]. See this word at 1:27.

you (are) honored,[a] but we (are) dishonored.[b]

LEXICON—a. ἔνδοξος (LN **87.6**) (BAGD 1. p. 263): 'honored' [BAGD, He, **LN**; NIV, NJB, REB, TEV], 'respected' [LN], 'honorable' [KJV], 'held in honor' [HNTC; NRSV], 'highly honored' [TNT], 'distinguished' [BAGD; NASB], 'eminent' [AB, BAGD], 'refulgent' [Lns], 'well thought of' [LB]. This adjective is also translated as a clause: 'they honor you'

[NAB], 'you have the glory' [ICC]. In this context, ἔνδοξος means not merely 'honored', but 'glorious' [Ed, Vn]. It carries with it the senses of 'glitter' and 'show' [Ed]. It is in their own estimation that the Corinthians are 'honored' [EBC, EGT, NCBC, TNTC]. Paul says 'honor', but he intends 'self-honor' [EGT, NIC2]. The world spoke well of them [NIC].

b. ἄτιμος (LN **87.72**) (BAGD 1. p. 120): 'dishonored' [BAGD, **LN**; NIV], 'held in dishonor' [HNTC], 'without honor' [AB; NASB], 'lacking in honor' [LN], 'held in disrepute' [NRSV], 'despised' [He; KJV, TEV, TNT], 'disgraced' [Lns; NJB], 'in disgrace' [REB], 'laughed at' [LB]. This adjective is also translated as a clause: 'they sneer at us' [NAB], 'we have the contempt' [ICC]. Paul's dishonor was in the world's opinion only [NIC2]. The apostles were 'dishonored' in their own estimation [EGT, TNTC]. It was in the opinion of the Corinthians that the apostles were 'dishonored' [EBC].

QUESTION—What is the significance of the chiastic structure A-B-A-B-B-A (we-you-we-you-you-we)?

The chiastic order serves to place the emphasis on the outer segments, the apostles, rather than on the readers [TH]. It serves to place the phrase 'we are dishonored' at the end where it can more easily be expanded on by the following clauses [Gdt, Herm, ICC, Lns, My, NIC2]. It serves to strengthen the stress on the pronouns and to give prominence to the word 'dishonor' [Vn].

4:11 Until the present hour[a] both we-hunger and we-thirst and are-poorly-clothed[b]

LEXICON—a. ὥρα: (LN **67.42**) (BAGD 2.b. p. 896): 'hour' [AB, BAGD, He, Lns; all versions except NJB, REB, TEV, TNT], 'day' [NJB, REB], 'moment' [BAGD, HNTC, ICC; TEV, TNT]. The phrase ἡ ἄρτι ὥρα 'the present hour' is an idiom which is an emphatic reference to the coincidence of the present with their state of existence and means 'until this very time' [LN]. 'Until this present hour' contrasts with the word 'already' of 4:8 [HNTC, Lns, NIC, NIC2].

b. pres. act. indic. of γυμνιτεύω (LN **49.24**) (BAGD p. 167): 'to be poorly clothed' [AB, BAGD, EBC, LN; NAB, NASB, NRSV, TNT], 'to wear ragged clothing' [**LN**], 'to wear rags' [LN], 'to be clothed in rags' [NIV, TEV], 'to go in rags' [REB], 'to go short of clothes' [NJB], 'to go scantily clothed' [ICC, Vn], 'to go naked' [HNTC], 'to be naked' [Lns; KJV], 'to go without even enough clothes to keep warm' [LB], 'to suffer destitution' [He]. Γυμνιτεύω primarily means 'to go lightly armed'. Here it means 'to go scantily clad' (see James 2:15) [ICC].

QUESTION—To what particular time was Paul referring?

The present tenses of these verbs in 4:11–13 emphasize that these are daily experiences of Paul and his companions [EBC, EGT, Lns]. These events are not necessarily the situation of Paul at the time of writing, but rather describe in general the type of life to which the apostles were exposed [Alf, HNTC].

Paul was referring to his present sufferings in Ephesus [Ed]. The verbs in this verse should not be taken in an absolute sense, since no one could live without food and drink [NIC]. In their travels, they often went hungry and their clothing wore out [Lns] and might have met up with robbers or simply run out of supplies [HNTC].

and are-roughly-treated[a] and are-homeless[b]

LEXICON—a. pres. pass. indic. of κολαφίζω (LN 19.7; 20.27) (BAGD 1. p. 441): 'to be roughly treated' [BAGD; NAB, NASB], 'to be cuffed' [BAGD, HNTC, Lns], 'to be beaten' [BAGD, He; NRSV, TEV], 'to be beaten with the fist' [LN], 'to be beaten up' [NJB, REB], 'to be kicked around' [LB], 'to be brutally treated' [NIV], 'to be knocked about' [TNT], 'to get plenty of hard blows' [ICC], 'to be buffeted' [KJV], 'to be struck with the fist' [BAGD, LN]. This passive is also translated actively: 'to endure a rough life' [AB]. It does not mean simply to strike, but to strike in an insulting manner [HNTC, TH]. There is nothing inherent in the meaning of the word or in the context to indicate that the added sense of insult is present [NIC2]. The word means to hit with the fist on the body or face as was often done to slaves and criminals. It does not refer to official scourgings, but to unprovoked, vulgar, physical mistreatment [Lns]. It means to hit with the back of the hand [TH], to hit with the fist [EGT, Gdt, Lns, My, Vn], or the palm of the hand [Gdt]. It refers in general to physical violence [EGT, My]. This is the word used of the treatment given to the Lord (Matt. 26:67) [TNTC, Vn], and to slaves (1 Pet. 2:20) [Vn]. Paul refers to times in which he was assaulted (Acts 14:19; 17:5) [NIC], and gives a detailed account of such abuse in 2 Cor. 11:26 [Lns]. Paul uses this word figuratively here to highlight the contrast between the life of the Corinthians and himself. By comparison, his was a life of abject slavery [Vn]. See 2 Cor. 12:7 where Paul says he was given a messenger of Satan to buffet him [ICC].

b. pres. act. indic. of ἀστατέω (LN **15.25**; **85.80**) (BAGD p. 117): 'to be homeless' [BAGD, He, HNTC, LN (15.25, 85.80), Lns, Vn; NASB, NIV, NRSV, TNT], 'to have no place of residence' [**LN** (85.80)], 'to wander about homeless' [NAB], 'to have no home' [NJB], 'to have no proper home' [ICC], 'to have no home of one's own' [LB], 'to have no certain dwelling place' [KJV], 'to wander from place to place' [**LN** (15.25); REB, TEV], 'to be unsettled, to be a vagabond' [BAGD], 'to be constantly going from place to place' [LN (15.25)]. This adjective is also translated as a verb: 'to endure a homeless life' [AB]. The primary meaning of ἀστατέω is 'to live an unsettled life moving from place to place' [TH]. Since he had begun his missionary activity, Paul had no settled residence [HNTC]. 'To hunger and thirst', 'to be ill-clad', and 'to be roughly treated and homeless' contrast directly with the words 'filled, rich, and reigning' of 4:8 [NIC2].

4:12 and we-work-hard[a] working[b] with our-own hands;

LEXICON—a. pres. act. indic. of κοπιάω (LN 42.47) (BAGD 2. p. 443): 'to work hard' [BAGD, LN; NAB, NIV], 'to become/grow weary' [AB; NRSV], 'to toil' [BAGD, HNTC, LN; NASB], 'to labor' [LN, Lns; KJV], 'to wear oneself out' [REB, TEV], 'to weary oneself' [TNT], 'to work wearily' [LB], 'to earn one's living' [NJB], 'to strive, to struggle' [BAGD]. The two words 'work hard' and 'working' are joined and translated 'to work hard to earn one's daily bread' [ICC], 'to toil at work' [He]. Κοπιάω includes both mental and physical exertion [BAGD]. It indicates really hard work to the point of weariness [TNTC, Vn]. 'Working with one's own hands' indicated dishonor [Lns], or that Paul had not yet begun to reign [NIC2]. Difficulties and troubles are implied in this verb [LN].

b. pres. mid. participle of ἐργάζομαι (LN 42.41) (BAGD 1. p. 307): 'to work' [AB, BAGD, HNTC, LN, Lns; KJV, NASB, TNT], 'to be active' [BAGD], 'to labor' [LN; NJB], 'to earn a living' [LB, REB], not explicit [NIV]. This verb is also translated by a noun: 'work' [NRSV]. It is also joined with the phrase 'with our own hands' and translated 'with hard work' [TEV], 'at manual work' [NAB]. The Greeks despised manual labor [EGT, ICC, NIC, TNTC, Vn]. It was folly in the world's opinion that a learned teacher should work with his hands [Ed].

being-cursed[a] we-bless,[b] being-persecuted[c] we-endure,[d]

LEXICON—a. pres. pass. participle of λοιδορέω (LN **33.393**) (BAGD p. 479): 'to be cursed' [LB, NIV, NJB, TEV], 'to be insulted' [AB, He; NAB], 'to be strongly insulted' [LN], 'to be slandered' [**LN**], 'to be reviled' [BAGD, Lns; KJV, NASB, NRSV], 'to be abused' [BAGD, HNTC; TNT]. It is also translated actively: 'people curse us' [REB], 'men revile us' [ICC]. It means 'insults with sneering' [Gdt], or 'reviling to one's face' [Ed, EGT]. It implies insulting abuse [EGT]. The present tense in these participles indicates habitual treatment [EGT].

b. pres. act. indic. of εὐλογέω (LN 33.470) (BAGD 2.a. p. 322): 'to bless' [BAGD, He, HNTC, ICC, LN, Lns; all versions except NAB, NJB], 'to return a blessing' [AB], 'to answer with a blessing' [NJB], 'to respond with a blessing' [NAB]. It means to call down God's gracious power on someone [BAGD], to ask God to favor someone [LN], to speak well of or to implore good upon someone [Ho], to wish someone well [Gdt, My] by prayer [Gdt].

c. pres. pass. participle of διώκω (LN 39.45) (BAGD 2. p. 201): 'to be persecuted' [AB, BAGD, He, HNTC, LN, Lns; all versions except LB, NAB, NJB, REB], 'to be hounded' [NJB], 'to be injured' [LB], 'to be harassed' [LN]. This passive is also translated actively: 'persecution comes our way' [NAB], 'they persecute us' [ICC; REB]. It means 'injurious acts' [Ho].

d. pres. mid. indic. of ἀνέχω (LN 25.171) (BAGD 1.c. p. 66): 'to endure' [BAGD, He, LN; NASB, NIV, NRSV, TEV], 'to endure something passively' [NJB], 'to put up with something' [AB, BAGD, EGT], 'to bear with' [BAGD], 'to bear something patiently' [Ed; NAB], 'to be patient (with)' [ICC, LN; LB, TNT], 'to submit' [REB], 'to suffer something' [Ho; KJV], 'to forbear' [BAGD], 'to be forbearing' [HNTC], 'to hold out' [Lns], 'to have patience' [LN]. It means 'to exercise self-control' [Gdt]. We remain quiet and patient when persecuted [My]. In spite of persecution, they continue to bring the gospel to their persecutors [NIC].

4:13 being-slandered[a] we-speak-kindly;[b]

LEXICON—a. pres. pass. participle of δυσφημέω (LN **33.398**) (BAGD p. 209): 'to be slandered' [AB, BAGD, HNTC, ICC, LN; NAB, NASB, NIV, NRSV], 'to be defamed' [BAGD, **LN**, Lns; KJV], 'to be reviled' [TNT], 'to be insulted' [NJB, TEV], 'to have evil things said about one' [LB], 'to be calumniated' [He]. This passive is also translated actively: 'they slander us' [REB]. It means to have evil acts or motives ascribed to one [Ho], to speak so as to damage one's reputation [TH].

b. pres. act. indic. of παρακαλέω (LN 33.168) (BAGD 5. p. 617): 'to speak kindly' [HNTC, Lns; NRSV, TNT], 'to give a courteous answer' [NJB], 'to answer kindly' [EBC; NIV], 'to reply quietly' [LB], 'to answer back with kind words' [TEV], 'to try to be conciliatory' [AB, BAGD; NAB, NASB, REB], 'to humbly make one's appeal' [NIC2], 'to entreat' [KJV], 'to appeal to' [LN], 'to merely deprecate' [ICC], 'to comfort' [He], 'to try to console, to speak to in a friendly manner, apologize to' [BAGD]. It means 'to give a soft reply' [EBC, HNTC, Lns; LB, NIV, NJB, NRSV, TEV, TNT].

we-became like (the) garbage[a] of-the world, (the) scum[b] of-all-things, until now.

LEXICON—a. περικάθαρμα (LN **79.53**) (BAGD p. 647): 'garbage' [**LN**; TEV], 'refuse' [BAGD; NAB], 'dirt under foot' [LB], 'scum' [He, ICC, LN; NASB, NIV, REB], 'filth' [KJV, TNT], 'dirt scoured (from the world)' [AB], 'dregs' [NJB], 'rubbish' [LN; NRSV], 'rubbish heap' [Lns], 'offscouring' [BAGD, LN], 'dirt, that which is removed as a result of a thorough cleansing' [BAGD], 'scapegoats' [BAGD, HNTC]. The apostles were regarded as the vilest of men [TNTC], or the filthiest of mankind [Ho], or the most completely worthless of existing things [My]. These terms refer to the very worst possible degradation, a filth that is gotten rid of through the gutter and sink [EGT]. The two words 'garbage' and 'scum' have the emphatic positions in the sentence [Lns].

b. περίψημα (LN 79.53) (BAGD p. 653): 'scum' [HNTC, LN; NAB, TEV], 'the very lowest scum' [NJB], 'off-scouring' [BAGD, LN, Lns; KJV, NRSV], 'dregs' [NASB, NRSV, REB], 'refuse' [He; NIV], 'the refuse of society' [ICC], 'rubbish-heap' [TNT], 'rubbish' [LN], 'garbage' [LN; LB], 'dirt' [BAGD]. This noun is also translated as a clause: 'that which cleanses all' [AB]. It means 'that which is removed by wiping' [BAGD, My, TNTC, Vn]. Περίψημα and περικάθαρμα are nearly synonymous [Alf, Ed, My, NIC2, Vn] meaning 'that which is scoured or scraped off while cleaning a pan' [Ed, Ho]. Paul knows that they are thought of as the most despicable thing in the world, in fact that the world does not even recognize them as belonging to it [NIC]. This term is more contemptuous while meaning about the same as περικάθαρμα [Alf]. Περικάθαρματα refers to sweepings from the floor and περίψημα to dirt washed from the body [NIC2]. Both words referred figuratively to anything that is contemptible [NIC2, TG, TNTC].

QUESTION—What is meant by περικάθαρμα 'refuse'?

1. It simply means 'refuse' or 'off-scouring' [Herm, Ho, ICC, Lns, My, NIC2, Vn]. It was the basic form κάθαρμα that had the reference to expiatory offering, not the full form περικάθαρμα [My].
2. It has an additional sense of being a sacrifice or scapegoat [AB, BAGD, EBC, Ed, EGT, He, HNTC, NCBC, TNTC]. A simple form of this word κάθαρμα was used to designate the means by which a community could be ritually cleansed, here by means of a human sacrifice. The custom was, however, to use the most worthless of men for this purpose. The word came therefore to be used as a term of abuse. 'Scapegoat' might have the double reference to despised persons who perform a ritual cleansing role for the community by self-sacrifice [HNTC]. Both terms were used of condemned criminals who were sacrificed as scapegoats [EGT].

QUESTION—What is meant by τοῦ κόσμου 'the world'?

It refers to the people of the world [Ho, My, TH].

QUESTION—How are the nouns related in the genitive constructions 'refuse of the world' and 'scum of all things'?

The first construction means 'refuse in the opinion of the world' [EBC, EGT, Lns, TH], or 'dirt scoured from the world' [AB], and the second means 'scum in the opinion of all men' [Lns, TH], or 'everybody's rubbish-heap' [TNT].

QUESTION—To what does πάντων 'of all things' refer?

Because 'of all things' is synonymous with 'of the world', it should be taken to be masculine with the meaning: 'of all men' [Ho, ICC, Lns, My, TH; REB, TNT]. It should be taken as neuter [HNTC; KJV, NASB, NRSV]: of all things. It can be either neuter or masculine. He may mean both [AB].

QUESTION—What words are emphasized in this verse?

The words 'until now' are repeated with emphasis from 4:11 [EGT, My, Vn].

DISCOURSE UNIT: 4:14–21 [AB, Alf, EBC, Ed, EGT, Gdt, Herm, HNTC, My, NIC, NIC2, TH, TNTC]. The topic is Paul's authority in Corinth [AB], the challenge to be God's humble servants also [EBC], what has been said is a father's admonition [Ed], Paul's fatherly discipline [EGT], conclusion and correspondence [Herm], the Corinthians and their apostle; Paul's plans [HNTC], matter of fact communications [NIC], appeal and exhortation [NIC2], a personal appeal [TNTC]. This section is the conclusion of all that Paul has written from 2:12 [Gdt]. Using the metaphor of a father and his children, Paul is able to 'admonish' the Corinthians (4:14), to 'urge' a change in their behavior (4:16–17), and to threaten to discipline them (4:18–21) [NIC2]. Paul concludes this section by making reference to the pride of the Corinthians, which was their chief sin. This lays the foundation for the next section [NIC].

4:14 Not shaming[a] you do-I-write these-things but as my dear[b] children[c] instructing[d] (you).

LEXICON—a. pres. act. participle of ἐντρέπω (LN **25.196**) (BAGD 1.a. p. 269): 'to shame' [He, HNTC, LN, Lns; all versions except LB, NJB, NRSV, TEV], 'to embarrass' [**LN**], 'to make ashamed' [BAGD; LB, NJB, NRSV], 'to put someone to shame' [AB, ICC], 'to make someone feel ashamed' [TEV].

b. ἀγαπητός (LN 25.45) (BAGD 2. p. 6): 'dear' [BAGD, HNTC, LN; NIV, NJB, REB, TEV], 'dearly loved' [ICC], 'beloved' [BAGD, LN; all other versions]. This word is also translated as a clause: 'whom I love' [He].

c. τέκνον (LN 9.46) (BAGD 2.b. p. 808): 'children' [AB, BAGD, He, HNTC, ICC, LN, Lns; all versions except KJV], 'sons' [KJV]. Τέκνον is used here figuratively of a spiritual child in relation to a master, apostle, or teacher [BAGD]. It can refer to a person of any age for whom there is a relationship of endearment and association [LN]. By establishing the church in Corinth, Paul became the spiritual father of the believers there [AB, Gdt]. Paul does not use the word 'disciple'. His converts are to him his children [NIC2]. Pride is difficult to rebuke because the proud person looks down on others. Paul therefore addresses them as his 'beloved children' [NIC].

d. pres. act. participle of νουθετέω (LN 33.231; 33.418) (BAGD p. 544): 'to instruct' [BAGD, LN (33.231); TEV], 'to teach' [LN (33.231)], 'to counsel' [TNT], 'to show someone where they were wrong' [ICC], 'to warn and counsel' [LB], 'to remind' [NJB], 'to admonish' [AB, BAGD, He, HNTC, LN (33.418), Lns; NAB, NASB, NRSV], 'to warn' [BAGD, EBC; KJV, NIV], 'to rebuke' [LN (33.418)], 'to bring someone to reason' [REB]. It means to put in mind and carries the sense of sternness and possibly blame [ICC]. It has a primary sense of attempting to have a corrective influence on someone while not provoking or embittering them [NIC2]. It means to teach a lesson to someone or to make someone understand [TG]. It generally indicates parental instruction or admonition [HNTC, Ho]. It means to admonish or warn [Lns], to lead one back to a calm and settled frame of mind [Gdt]. It refers to positive and creative correction given in love [HNTC]. Although it includes blame for wrongdoing, it is criticism given in love [TNTC]. It is a warning appealing to the mind rather than a direct censure [EGT].

QUESTION—To what does ταῦτα 'these things' refer?

They refer to the preceding words of irony spoken in reference to the Corinthians [Ed, Lns, NIC, TH], and to what Paul had said about factions in the church [Ed]. It refers at least to 4:6–13, if not to all of what precedes [NIC, NIC2].

QUESTION—What relationship do the participles 'not shaming' and 'instructing' suggest?

1. They indicate Paul's purpose in writing [Gdt, HNTC, Ho, ICC, NIC2, Vn; all versions]: I write these things to you, not with the purpose of shaming you, but of instructing you. The present tense is connative: 'I am not trying to shame you' [HNTC].
2. They merely give accompanying circumstances to his writing [Lns]: not as shaming you do I write, but as admonishing you. Paul uses the negative particle οὔ instead of μή indicating that he is simply stating a fact that he is not shaming them but admonishing them. Usually future, not present, participles are used to express purpose [Lns].

4:15 For[a] if[b] you-have countless[c] guardians[d] in Christ

LEXICON—a. γάρ (LN 89.23): 'for' [AB, He, HNTC, ICC, LN, Lns; all versions except NAB, NIV, REB, TNT], not explicit [NAB, NIV, REB, TNT].

b. ἐὰν: 'if' [AB, HNTC; NASB], 'even if' [TEV], 'even though' [EBC; NIV, NJB], 'though' [He, Lns; KJV, NRSV, TNT], 'although' [LB], 'granted' [NAB], '(you) may (have)' [ICC; REB].

c. μυρίος (LN **60.7**; 60.45) (BAGD p. 529): 'countless' [BAGD, **LN**; NASB], 'innumerable' [BAGD, LN (60.7)], 'any number of' [ICC], 'thousands of' [AB, HNTC; REB, TNT], 'very very many' [LN], 'ten thousand' [He, LN (60.45), Lns; all other versions]. Literally it means 'tens of thousands', but Paul is speaking figuratively [HNTC, NIC2]. In this context, it means 'innumerable, countless' [LN, NIC2], and is hyperbolic (rhetorical exaggeration) [Herm, Lns, NIC2]. Paul's intention in using μυρίος is to indicate that the guides were more in number than he wished [Alf, Ed, Lns].

d. παιδαγωγός (LN 36.5) (BAGD p. 603): 'guardians' [AB, He, LN; NAB, NIV, NRSV, TEV, TNT], 'slave guardians' [Lns], 'guides' [BAGD, LN], 'leaders' [LN], 'slave-guides' [EBC], 'tutors' [Alf, HNTC; NASB, REB], 'slaves to look after you' [NJB], 'instructors' [ICC; KJV], 'attendant (slave), custodian' [BAGD], 'others to teach you' [LB]. The παιδαγωγός, which literally means 'boy-leader', was usually a male slave. It was his duty to escort the child to and from school and monitor his conduct generally. He was not a teacher [BAGD, Lns]. Παιδαγωγός referred in a general sense to an instructor or teacher [Ho, TG]. He was usually a slave and was the boy's constant attendant, not his teacher. But since he had charge of the boy's education, the term came in NT times to mean instructor [Ho]. The term is applied figuratively to the later workers in the church who continued to foster Christian development after Paul had given it spiritual birth [My]. The term has reference not to the role of teachers, but to the role of pastors, who are to care for the believers [Vn]. The term has a slight negative connotation and Paul probably has this in mind in using it [Ed].

QUESTION—What relationship is indicated by γάρ 'for'?

It indicates that this verse is the grounds for Paul's admonishing the Corinthians [EGT, ICC, My, NIC]. It indicates that this verse is the grounds for Paul's calling the Corinthians his beloved children [Alf, My, NIC, TG]. It indicates that Paul is going to develop the theme of a father-children relationship with the Corinthians [TH].

QUESTION—With what is the phrase ἐν Χριστῷ 'in Christ' connected?

1. It modifies the word 'guardians' [He, HNTC, Lns, NIC]: you may have countless Christian guardians.
2. It modifies the verb 'you have' [Ho, TG, TH; TEV]: you as Christians may have countless guardians. In the Greek, the words 'in Christ' follow the verb 'you have' showing that that is what they modify: 'you have in Christ, that is, in reference to Christ, or as Christians, countless guardians' [Ho].

yet[a] (you have) not many fathers;[b]

LEXICON—a. ἀλλά (LN 89.125) (BAGD 4. p. 38): 'yet' [AB, BAGD, HNTC, ICC, Lns; KJV, NASB], 'but' [LN; REB], 'nevertheless' [He], 'at least' [BAGD, NIC2], 'certainly' [BAGD], not explicit [LB, NIV, NJB, NRSV, TEV, TNT]. The ἀλλα after a condition indicates emphatic contrast [Ed, EGT, My]. There is strong contrast between 'many fathers' and 'I became your father' [EBC].

b. πατήρ (LN **36.8**) (BAGD 2.a. p. 635): 'fathers' [AB, He, HNTC, ICC, **LN**, Lns; all versions], 'spiritual father' [BAGD, LN], 'leader in the faith' [LN]. 'Father' here is used to mean one who has guided another into faith [HNTC, LN].

QUESTION—What is meant by saying that they do not have 'many fathers'?

It is figurative and means that they have only one father [EGT, ICC, Lns, NIC2; NJB, REB]. Paul was their only father [NIC2]. Being responsible for the first conversions among them, Paul was the spiritual father of the congregation even though later conversions were made by others [Lns].

for I-became-father[a] (to) you in[b] Christ Jesus

LEXICON—a. aorist act. indic. of γεννάω (LN 23.58) (BAGD 1.b. p. 155): 'to become one's father' [NASB, NIV, NRSV, TEV, TNT], 'to beget' [AB, BAGD, HNTC, ICC, Lns; KJV, NAB], 'to father someone' [NJB], 'to bring to birth' [He], 'to bring someone to Christ' [LB]. This verb is also translated by its reciprocal: 'you are my offspring' [REB]. It is used figuratively here of the influence of one person on another like a teacher on his pupils: 'I became your father as Christians through the gospel' [BAGD]. Γεννάω is the regular verb for begetting a child either for the father or mother [NIC2]. This word refers to spiritual fatherhood [Herm]. This fatherly relationship shows us two things: Paul's great love for them; and no matter how much they may have been helped by others, they were in greater debt to Paul and therefore should heed his instructions [TNTC]. Some of the Corinthians were converted by others. Paul became the father of the church by making the first conversions and laying the foundation (3:10) [Lns].

b. ἐν: 'in' [AB, He, HNTC, ICC, Lns; all versions except LB, TEV], 'in your life in union with (Christ Jesus)' [TEV], '(who brought you) to (Christ)' [LB].

QUESTION—What is the phrase 'in Christ Jesus' connected with?

1. It is connected with 'you' [NIC2; TEV]: I became your father to bring you into union with Christ Jesus. 'In Christ' indicates the believers' relationship with Christ resulting from their spiritual birth: now they are 'in Christ' [NIC2].
2. It is connected with 'Paul' [EBC, HNTC, Ho, Lns, Vn]: I became your father by virtue of my union with Christ Jesus. 'In Christ' means by virtue of Paul's union with Christ [Ho, Lns]. Paul was only Christ's instrument in bringing them to believe [Ho]. Ἐν indicates that Christ is the agent by whom men receive new life [EBC, HNTC]
3. It is connected with neither of the above, but indicates the element in which the birth took place [Alf, My]. The spiritual birth of the Corinthians takes place 'in Christ' as the element of its being [Alf, My].

QUESTION—What words are emphasized in the final clause?

The word 'I' is emphasized [AB, Alf, EGT, HNTC, ICC, Lns, My, NIC; NAB, NJB, REB]: I, myself. The word 'you' is also emphasized [Alf, ICC, Lns, NIC]: It is you whom I myself fathered. 'I' is emphasized because it is included as a separate pronoun in the Greek and because it is joined with 'you' [Lns].

through[a] the good-news.[b]

LEXICON—a. διά with genitive object (LN 89.76): 'through' [HNTC, ICC, LN, Lns; KJV, NASB, NIV, NRSV], 'by means of' [AB, LN], 'by' [He, LN; NJB]. This preposition is also translated with a verb: 'by bringing' [TEV], 'by preaching' [TNT], 'through my/the preaching of' [NAB, REB], 'when I preached' [LB]. It means 'by means of' [AB, Gdt, HNTC, Ho, ICC, My, NIC]. It indicates that the gospel is the instrument of their conversion [Ed]. It was the power of the gospel that gave birth to the Corinthian believers [Lns]. See this word at 1:21.

b. εὐαγγέλιον (LN 33.217) (BAGD 1.a. p. 318): 'good news' [BAGD, LN; TEV, TNT], 'gospel' [BAGD, LN; all other versions], 'the Glad-tidings which I brought you' [ICC]. This term refers to the contents of the good news about Jesus [LN].

4:16 I-urge[a] you therefore[b] be[c] imitators[d] of me.

LEXICON—a. pres. act. indic. of παρακαλέω (LN 33.168) (BAGD 2. p. 617): 'to urge' [AB, BAGD; NIV, NJB], 'to beg' [He, HNTC; NAB, TEV, TNT], 'to appeal to' [BAGD, LN; NRSV, REB], 'to beseech' [ICC; KJV], 'to exhort' [BAGD; NASB], 'to beg' [LB], 'to admonish' [Lns, NIC], 'to encourage' [BAGD], 'to ask for (earnestly), to request, to plead for' [LN].

b. οὖν (LN 89.50) (BAGD 1.a. p. 593): 'therefore' [BAGD, He, ICC, LN, Lns; NASB, NIV, REB], 'that is why' [NJB], 'wherefore' [KJV], 'then' [BAGD, HNTC; NAB, NRSV, TEV], 'thus' [AB], 'so' [BAGD, LN; LB, TNT], 'so then' [LN], 'consequently, accordingly' [BAGD, LN]. It introduces the logical consequence of what precedes [BAGD].

c. pres. mid. impera. of γίνομαι: 'to be' [HNTC, Lns; KJV, NAB, NASB, NRSV, TNT], 'to become' [He, My], 'to go on' [AB], not explicit [ICC; LB, NIV, NJB, REB, TEV]. The present imperative of this verb in moral admonitions indicates 'to be in effect' [EGT], or 'to show yourselves' [EGT, ICC]. The present tense indicates 'continue to become in practice (imitators)' [EBC], or 'be and continue to be' [Lns, Rb], or 'go on imitating me' [AB].

d. μιμητής (LN 41.45) (BAGD 1. p. 522): 'imitators' [BAGD, He, HNTC, LN, Lns; NAB, NASB, NRSV, TNT], 'one who does what others do' [LN], 'followers' [KJV]. This noun is also joined with 'to be' and translated 'to imitate (me)' [AB; NIV], 'follow (my) example' [REB, TEV], 'to follow (my) example and do as I do' [LB], 'follow (my) footsteps' [ICC], 'take (me) as your pattern' [NJB], 'use me as your model' [BAGD]. Paul is urging them to follow his example of humility, and self-sacrifice [Gdt, Ho, ICC, My]. Μιμητής does not mean 'to mimic', or 'to follow as a disciple', but 'to internalize and practice in life the model of another' [NIC2]. The character to imitate is that described in 4:9 and following [EGT]. Paul has verses 4:9–13 [NIC], or 4:11–13 in mind [NIC2].

QUESTION—What relationship is indicated by οὖν 'therefore'?

It indicates that the grounds of Paul's present appeal is that he is their father [Alf, EBC, EGT, Gdt, HNTC, Ho, ICC, Lns, My, NIC, NIC2, TG, TH, TNTC]: I became your father, therefore imitate me. Children should normally pattern their lives after their father [Lns, TG]. 'Be imitators of me' infers 'by your conduct, prove your parentage' [ICC].

4:17 Because-of[a] this I-sent Timothy to you,

LEXICON—a. διά with accusative object (LN 89.26): 'because of' [LN], 'this/that is why' [NAB, NJB, REB, TNT], 'that is the very reason' [LB], 'for this reason' [AB, He, HNTC, Lns; NASB, NIV, NRSV], 'for this cause' [KJV], 'for this purpose' [TEV], 'because I wish you to follow my example' [ICC], 'on account of' [LN].

QUESTION—To what does the word 'this' refer?

It refers back to the previous verse [Alf, Ed, EGT, HNTC, Ho, My, NIC, NIC2, TG, TH; LB]. I sent Timothy in order to help you follow my example.

QUESTION—What relationship is indicated by διά 'because'?

1. It indicates reason [AB, EGT, He, HNTC, ICC, Lns, NIC2; all versions except KJV, TEV]: because I wish you to be imitators of me, I sent Timothy to remind you of my ways.
2. It indicates purpose [Alf, Ed, Ho; KJV, TEV]: in order to help you be imitators of me, I sent Timothy to remind you of my ways.

QUESTION—What is indicated by the aorist tense, ἔπεμψα 'I sent'?

1. It is an ordinary aorist indicating that Paul had already sent Timothy before he wrote this letter [EBC, Ed, EGT, Gdt, HNTC, Lns, My, NCBC, NIC, NIC2, Rb, TNTC]: I have sent Timothy. Two factors support this interpretation: (1) Timothy is not mentioned in the opening of the letter inferring that he had already left; and (2) the conditional reference to Timothy's coming in 16:10 make it unlikely that he was the bearer of this letter [NIC2]. Probably Timothy had already departed from Ephesus [Ed, EGT, ICC, My], (Acts 19:22), was currently in Macedonia, and would arrive in Corinth after this letter [Ed, ICC]. Paul had apparently sent Timothy when he received the unfavorable news from Corinth. It later became necessary to write the letter which then was sent by sea and would arrive before Timothy, who went by land [NIC]. 'I sent' may mean that Paul had sent word to Timothy who was then on his way to Macedonia, that he should go on from there to Corinth [HNTC].
2. It is an 'epistolary' aorist indicating that although Timothy had not yet departed, he will have been sent by the time the letter was read [He; NIV, TEV, TNT]: I am sending Timothy. In using the epistolary aorist, the writer writes from the point of view of the recipient, so that 'I am sending' at the time of writing, becomes 'I sent' when the letter is finally received [He].

who is my beloved and faithful[a] child[b] in (the) Lord,

LEXICON—a. πιστός (LN 31.87): 'faithful' [AB, He, HNTC, Lns; all versions except LB, REB], 'trustworthy' [LN; LB, REB], 'loyal and trusty' [ICC]. Here the sense of one who may be trusted is in focus rather than one who believes [Gdt]. Paul probably meant that Timothy was faithful to Paul [My, NIC2, TG, TH], faithful in his service to the Lord [Ho], faithful to the faith [HNTC], or perhaps trustworthy or dependable in general [TG]. See this word at 4:2.

b. τέκνον: 'child' [AB, He, HNTC, ICC, Lns; LB, NASB, NRSV, TNT], 'son' [KJV, NAB, NIV, NJB, REB, TEV]. This means that Paul had converted Timothy [Alf, BAGD, Ed, Gdt, He, HNTC, Ho, ICC, Lns, My, NCBC, TG, TH]. In 1 Tim. 1:2 Paul refers to Timothy as 'his own son in the faith' [Ho]. See this word at 4:14.

QUESTION—With what is the phrase ἐν κυρίῳ 'in the Lord' connected?

1. It is connected with the word 'child' [Alf, He, My, NIC, TH; LB]: I sent Timothy to you who is my beloved and faithful child in the Lord. 'In the Lord' indicates that Timothy is Paul's son by means of and on the basis of the work of Christ (see 4:10 and 4:15) [NIC]. 'In the Lord' indicates the spiritual nature of the relationship [Alf, My, TH].
2. It is connected with the word 'faithful' [AB, EGT, Gdt, Ho, ICC; NIV]: I sent Timothy to you who is my beloved child and is faithful in his service for the Lord. 'In the Lord' indicates 'in the sphere of Christian responsibility' [EGT], or 'in the service of Christ' [Ho].

who will-remind[a] you (of) my ways[b] in Christ Jesus,

TEXT—Some manuscripts omit Ἰησοῦς 'Jesus' after Χριστός 'Christ'. GNT includes this word in brackets and with a C rating indicating uncertainty about its inclusion. It is also included by AB, HNTC, NIV, NRSV, TEV, and TNT.

LEXICON—a. fut. act. indic. of ἀναμιμνήσκω (LN 29.10) (BAGD p. 57): 'to remind' [AB, BAGD, He, HNTC, LN, Lns; all versions except KJV], 'to bring someone (back) into remembrance' [ICC; KJV], 'to cause to remember' [LN].

b. ὁδός (LN 41.16) (BAGD 2.c. p. 555): 'ways' [AB, BAGD, HNTC, Lns; KJV, NAB, NASB, NRSV, TNT], 'principles of conduct' [NJB], 'principles which I follow in the new life' [TEV], '(Christian) principles' [He], 'the simple and lowly ways which I have' [ICC], 'way of life' [LN; NIV, REB], 'what I teach' [LB], 'my (Christian) teachings' [BAGD].

QUESTION—What is meant by ὁδούς 'ways'?

1. It refers to Paul's conduct [AB, EGT, Ho, ICC, My, NIC; NJB, REB]. 'My ways' is a Semitic expression indicating a person's conduct (Ps. 37:23; Is. 57:18; Jer. 17:10; Ezek. 33:8) [NIC]. Ὁδός was commonly used to refer to the pattern of life of a religious group. Here the plural seems to refer to Paul's Christian practices in general [AB]. It is his character and conduct as a teacher [Ho, ICC].
2. It refers to the doctrine Paul taught [BAGD, Ed, Gdt, Herm, Lns, TH]. This interpretation is more in keeping with the context which is more concerned with Paul's teaching than his conduct [TH].
3. It refers to both his conduct and doctrine [He, NCBC, NIC2; TEV]. For Paul, teaching and conduct were one and the same [NIC2]. It is his moral principles expressed in a pattern of living [HNTC].

QUESTION—What is meant by the words 'in Christ Jesus'?

It means in Christ's service [Ho, My], as a Christian teacher [ICC], in union with Christ [TEV], or that his conduct was ruled by Christ, and only as such can it be an example for others [NIC].

as[a] I-teach everywhere[b] in every church.[c]

LEXICON—a. καθώς (LN 64.14): 'as' [HNTC, ICC; KJV, NJB, NRSV, TNT], 'just as' [AB, LN; NAB, NASB], 'even as' [Lns], 'such as' [He], 'which agrees with' [NIV], 'which' [TEV], 'something (I teach)' [REB], not explicit [LB]. Paul compares his way of teaching with his life and claims perfect consistency between them [Ed].

b. πανταχοῦ (LN 83.8) (BAGD 1. p. 608): 'everywhere' [AB, BAGD, He, HNTC, ICC, LN, Lns; all versions except LB, NAB], 'wherever' [LB], 'anywhere, all over' [LN], not explicit [NAB]. Paul taught the same Christian principles everywhere; he did not have different standards for different churches [Lns, TG, TNTC, Vn].

c. ἐκκλησία 'church' [AB, He, HNTC, ICC, Lns; all versions]. The doubling of the concepts 'everywhere' and 'every church' in Greek give greater emphasis [My, TH]. See this word at 1:2.

4:18 Now/But[a] as-though[b] I were-coming not to you some (of you) became-arrogant;[c]

LEXICON—a. δέ (LN 89.94; 89.124): 'now' [He, Lns, My; KJV, NASB], 'but' [HNTC], not explicit [AB, ICC; all other versions].

b. ὡς (LN 64.12) (BAGD III.2. p. 898): 'as though' [AB, BAGD, He, Lns; KJV, NASB], 'as if' [HNTC; NIV], 'on the assumption that' [EBC, My; NJB]. This conjunction is also translated as a clause: 'because they think...' [NAB, REB, TEV, TNT], 'thinking...' [LB, NRSV], '(my sending Timothy) meant' [ICC]. This clause, introduced by 'as', serves as the grounds of their being puffed up [My]. It questions the fact that was assumed, that Paul was not coming [NIC]. See this word at 4:9.

c. aorist pass. indic. of φυσιόω (LN 88.217): 'to become arrogant' [LN; NASB, NIV, NRSV], 'to be filled with self-importance' [REB], 'to grow full of self-importance' [NAB], 'to become filled with one's own self-importance' [NJB], 'to be puffed up' [HNTC, LN, Lns; KJV], 'to become puffed (up) with pride' [AB, He], 'to become proud' [LN; LB, TEV], 'to behave arrogantly' [TNT], 'to boastfully declare' [ICC]. The notion of pride is present in this verb [AB, NIC, TG, TH, TNTC; NAB, NASB, NIV, NJB, NRSV, REB, TEV, TNT]. Paul uses the aorist tense to state a fact that had been reported to him [ICC, NIC2, Vn]. Paul could not use the present as he did not know if it was still true [ICC]. The aorist tense indicates the moment when they heard of Timothy's coming [EGT]. The opinion of the Corinthians was that Paul was not coming and so they made themselves appear important as though Paul was afraid to face them [Lns]. These people believed that Paul was afraid to come again to Corinth (2 Cor. 10:1) [EBC, Ed, He, Ho, My, TNTC, Vn].

QUESTION—What relationship is indicated by δέ 'now'?

1. It indicates that Paul is simply continuing his writing [Lns, My; KJV, NASB]: now. Paul's sending of Timothy and this letter were only temporary measures, so Paul now continues by informing them of his own coming [Lns].

2. It indicates contrast [EGT, Gdt, HNTC, ICC]: but. It indicates the contrast between the true purpose of Timothy's visit, and the false report that Paul was not coming [ICC].

QUESTION—What is indicated by the use of the present tense participle μὴ ἐρχομένου 'not coming'?

The Greek retains the original tense when it employs indirect discourse [Lns]. The direct discourse was, 'Paul is not coming' [Lns, My]. That this refers to the original quote of the Corinthians is claiming too much [Gdt].

QUESTION—To whom does the word τινες 'some' refer?

It refers to an indefinite group in the Corinthian community who were definitely anti-Paul [EGT, NIC2], and were not just showing favoritism of one leader over another. The recognition of this tension is important to the correct understanding of chapters 5 and 6 and the rest of the letter [NIC2]. The Corinthians knew who they were, since they were some from among the group that boasted about their wisdom [Lns]. We can assume that it refers to some persons from the other three parties [NIC]. These were false teachers who were trying to weaken Paul's authority [EBC].

4:19 but[a] I-will-come to you soon[b] if the Lord wills,[c]

LEXICON—a. δέ (LN 89.124): 'but' [AB, He, HNTC, ICC, LN, Lns; all versions except REB, TEV], 'however' [TEV], not explicit [REB].

b. ταχέως (LN 67.56; 67.110) (BAGD 1.a. p. 806): 'soon' [BAGD, ICC, LN (67.56); LB, NAB, NASB, NJB, NRSV, TEV], 'very soon' [LN (67.56); NIV, REB], 'quickly' [AB, BAGD, HNTC, LN (67.110); TNT], 'shortly' [Lns; KJV], 'swiftly' [He], 'without delay, at once' [BAGD]. Paul says he will come after the following Pentecost (16:8) [Ed, ICC, Lns, My], that is, he will start in a few weeks [Lns]. Sending Timothy could be taken as a point of weakness on Paul's part, so he immediately tells them of his plans to come himself [NIC2].

c. aorist act. subj. of θέλω (LN 30.58) (BAGD 2. p. 355): 'to will' [AB, BAGD, HNTC, Lns; KJV, NASB, NRSV, REB], 'to be willing' [NAB, NIV, NJB, TEV, TNT], 'to wish, to want, to be ready' [BAGD], 'to please' [ICC], 'to let someone do something' [LB], 'to permit' [He], 'to purpose' [LN]. This is the 'will' of purpose or resolve [BAGD]. It indicates purpose, usually based on preference and desire [LN]. The aorist subjunctive refers the 'willing' to the unspecified time of Paul's visit [EGT]. God's will was the only possible restraint to Paul's coming [TNTC].

QUESTION—What relationship is indicated by δέ 'but'?

It indicates contrast [AB, EGT, Gdt, HNTC, Ho, ICC, Lns, My; all versions except REB]: but. In contrast to the mistaken assumption of the Corinthians, Paul was coming soon [EGT, HNTC].

QUESTION—To whom does the word 'Lord' refer?

1. It refers to Christ [Ed, EGT, Ho, Lns, Vn]: if Christ is willing. Christ directs the movements of his servants (1 Thess. 3:2; Acts 16:7, 18:9) [EGT].
2. It refers to God [My, TG]: if God is willing.

QUESTION—Where is the emphasis in this verse?

The emphasis is on the verb 'I will come' [Alf, Herm, Lns, TH].

and I-will-find-out[a] not the talk[b] of-the-ones having-become-arrogant but the power;[c]

LEXICON—a. fut. mid. deponent indic. of γινώσκω (LN 27.2): 'to find out' [AB, ICC, LN; all versions except KJV, REB, TNT], 'to discover' [TNT], 'to take cognizance of' [ICC, NIC], 'to take the measure of' [REB], 'to know' [He, HNTC, Lns; KJV], 'to learn (of)' [LN], 'to ascertain' [EBC]. Paul talks like a judge conducting a trial [Gdt, ICC, Vn].

b. λόγος (LN 33.99) (BAGD 1.a.α. p. 477): 'talk' [AB; NRSV], 'words' [NASB], 'speech' [LN; KJV], 'word' [BAGD, Lns], 'speaking' [BAGD, LN], 'what they say' [ICC; NAB, NJB, REB, TEV, TNT], 'how they are talking' [NIV], 'eloquence' [He], 'just big talkers' [LB]. This noun is also translated as an adjective: '(how) eloquent' [HNTC]. 'Word' here refers to logically reasoned discourses, eloquently delivered [Gdt]. Paul has reason to believe that his opposition is only talk, without power [NCBC].

c. δύναμις (BAGD 1. p. 207): 'power' [AB, BAGD, He, Lns; all versions except LB, NAB]. This noun is also translated as a clause: 'what they can do' [ICC; NAB], 'to really have God's power' [LB]. It is also translated as an adjective: '(how) powerful' [HNTC]. See this word at 1:18.

QUESTION—What is indicated by the perfect tense of πεφυσιωμένων 'having become arrogant'?

It indicates a present condition of arrogance: they have become arrogant and that is their present state [EBC, EGT, Lns].

QUESTION—What is meant by δύναμιν 'power'?

It refers to the power to win men to Christ [Ed, Gdt, ICC, NIC2]. It refers to spiritual power [He, TG], not physical or that of rank [TG]. It refers to the amount of energy spent in trying to produce results for God's Kingdom [My]. It refers to the power to live a genuine Christian life [Ho, NIC]. 1 Corinthians 2:4 indicates that 'power' is the power of the Holy Spirit. Paul will find out if these Corinthians have the Holy Spirit's power [Alf, Gdt, TG, TH]. Do they have the presence of the Spirit among them to save and sanctify the lost [Ed, NIC2]? It is the power of God's Kingdom (1:18, 24; 2:4) [EGT]. It refers to the ability to produce genuine spiritual effects [Vn].

4:20 for[a] the kingdom[b] of God (consists) not in talk[c] but in power.[d]

LEXICON—a. γάρ: 'for' [AB, He, HNTC, ICC, Lns; all versions except NAB, TNT], not explicit [NAB, TNT].

b. βασιλεία (LN 1.82; 37.64) (BAGD 3.b. p. 135): 'kingdom' [AB, BAGD, He, HNTC, ICC, LN, Lns; all versions except TNT], 'rule' [LN; TNT], 'royal reign' [BAGD], 'reign' [LN]. 'Kingdom' here indicates: 'sovereignty' or 'kingship' [AB]. The kingdom of God refers to the unseen reality behind the outward activities of the Church. It is through the outward forms that the kingdom of God is expressed and realized [ICC].

c. λόγος: 'talk' [AB; NAB, NIV, NRSV], 'mere talk' [Lns], 'just talking' [LB], 'words' [ICC; KJV, NASB, REB, TEV, TNT], 'spoken words' [NJB], 'eloquence' [He, HNTC]. See this word at 4:19.

d. δύναμις: 'power' [AB, He, HNTC, Lns; all versions except LB], 'living by God's power' [LB], 'spiritual power' [Ed, ICC]. Δύναμις has the same sense as in 4:19, reality as opposed to mere profession [Ho]. God's rule is carried out through the work of the Holy Spirit [AB]. 'Power' refers to what people do in their Christian lives rather than what they say [TG, TH, TNTC]. 'Power' is the power of the Holy Spirit [HNTC, NCBC, NIC2, Vn], producing the fruit of the Spirit in a person's life (Gal. 5:22) [Vn]. By 'power' Paul means the life that Christ gives (2 Cor. 5:17), the power of the new birth (John 3:3–8) [EBC].

QUESTION—What is indicated by γάρ 'for'?

It indicates that this verse is the grounds for Paul's purpose to discover the power of the Corinthians [Alf, Gdt, Herm, My, NIC, NIC2]: I will find out the power of these arrogant people, because the kingdom of God consists of power.

QUESTION—What is the meaning of the phrase 'kingdom of God'?

1. It means God's rule in people's lives [EBC, Gdt, Ho, Rb, TG, TH; TNT], God's reign or dominion in men's hearts [Ho], God's reigning over people and showing his power in them [EBC]. God's kingdom exists in the souls of believers where the will of God is the guiding principle [Gdt].
2. It means the final Messianic kingdom (6:9; 15:24, 50) [EGT, My].
3. It means both 1 and 2 [Ed, NIC2]. It refers to both a present and future event, both to 'right now' as well as 'not yet'. It was begun at the resurrection of Jesus, and its power is the power of the Spirit. To the Corinthians, the Kingdom had already come in its future realization, to Paul it was still mixed with weakness [NIC2].
4. It means the realm or dominion of God [NIC, Vn]. The kingdom of God is the sphere where God's rule is acknowledged, either in the individual believer, or the body of believers [Vn].

QUESTION—What verb is implied between 'kingdom of God' and 'not in talk'?

The kingdom of God does not consist of mere talk [Alf, Ho, Vn; NAB, NASB, NJB], is not a matter of talk [ICC; NIV, REB, TEV, TNT], is not in talk [AB; KJV, LB], does not operate in eloquence [HNTC], is not established on words [Ed], is not caused by talk [My], depends not on talk [NRSV], is not accompanied with mere words [Lns].

4:21 What do-you-want?[a] Should-I-come to you with[b] (a) stick,[c]

LEXICON—a. pres. act. indic. of θέλω (LN 25.1) (BAGD 1. p. 354): 'to want' [AB, BAGD, LN, Lns; NJB, TNT], 'to desire' [BAGD, LN; NASB], 'to wish' [BAGD, LN], 'to wish to have' [BAGD], 'to prefer' [He; NAB, NIV, NRSV, TEV], 'to will' [KJV], 'to choose' [LB, REB], 'to like' [HNTC]. It is also translated idiomatically: '(which) is it to be then?' [ICC].

b. ἐν with dative object (LN 90.10): 'with' [AB, He, HNTC, LN, Lns; all versions] '(rod) in hand' [ICC]. It indicates accompanying circumstance in general and means 'furnished with' or 'attended by' both here and in the following occurrence [Ho]. It indicates 'accompanied by' [ICC], or 'provided with' [ICC, My], and refers to equipment when used with the word 'stick' [ICC]. The contrast between 'with a stick' and 'in love' refers to the manner of Paul's coming, not to his motive. His motive was love in either case [NIC, NIC2].

c. ῥάβδος (LN 6.218) (BAGD p. 733): 'stick' [BAGD, LN; NJB], 'whip' [NIV, TEV], 'staff' [BAGD], 'rod' [AB, BAGD, He, HNTC, ICC, LN, Lns; all versions except LB, NIV, NJB, TEV], 'punishment and scolding' [LB]. Here it is used as a means of punishment [Alf, BAGD, EBC, EGT, Ho, Lns, My, NIC, NIC2, TNTC; LB].

QUESTION—With what is figure of 'stick' compared?

It is compared with harsh action whose purpose is discipline [Lns, NIC, NIC2; TNT]. 'Stick' is used figuratively [Gdt, ICC, Lns, My, NIC2, TH, Vn], indicating spiritual reprimand and discipline [Gdt, Ho, ICC, NCBC, NIC2, TNTC, Vn]. It indicates harsh authority [AB].

or in love[a] and in-a-spirit[b] of-gentleness?[c]

LEXICON—a. ἀγάπη (LN 25.43) (BAGD I.1.a. p. 5): 'love' [AB, BAGD, He, HNTC, ICC, LN, Lns; all versions], 'loving concern' [LN]. This is love which is based on a sincere appreciation and high regard [LN]. 'Love' must be understood here in terms of words. In either case Paul would come in love, only the expression of love might not seem loving to them if he had to punish them [NIC].

b. πνεῦμα (LN 30.6) (BAGD 3.c. p. 675): 'spirit' [AB, BAGD, He, HNTC, ICC, Lns; all versions], 'disposition' [BAGD, LN], 'attitude, way of thinking' [LN], 'spiritual state, state of mind' [BAGD].

c. πραΰτης (LN 88.59) (BAGD p. 699): 'gentleness' [BAGD, HNTC, ICC, LN; LB, NASB, NJB, NRSV, TEV, TNT], 'meekness' [BAGD, He, LN; KJV], 'mildness' [LN, Lns], 'humility, courtesy, considerateness' [BAGD]. This noun is also translated as an adjective: 'gentle' [AB; NAB, NIV, REB]. It is the opposite of harshness or rudeness [ICC]. 'In a spirit of gentleness' serves to define the specific expression of love in which Paul would come [EGT]. It means kindness or meekness [NIC]. It refers to behavior, not attitude [Herm]. 'Meekness' is not helplessness in facing problems with others, but a composure of spirit arising from power which overcomes adversity rather than intensifying it [Vn].

QUESTION—How are the nouns related in the genitive expression πνεύματι πραΰτητος 'spirit of gentleness' and to what does 'spirit' refer?

1. 'Gentleness' modifies 'spirit', and 'spirit' refers to Paul's spirit or disposition [AB, Alf, BAGD, EBC, EGT, Herm, ICC, Lns, NIC2, TH, TNTC, Vn; NAB, NIV, REB, and probably all other versions]: with a gentle spirit. Joined as it is with the phrase 'in love', 'in a spirit of gentleness' indicates that Paul may come in a manner expressing gentleness [EBC, Ed]. The absence of the article with 'spirit' favors this interpretation [ICC, Lns]. It refers to the spirit or disposition of a man here, but a reference to the Holy Spirit is in the background providing Paul with strength [Ed, NIC2]. Paul is talking about treating the Corinthians in a loving, gentle manner [TH].
2. 'Gentleness' modifies 'spirit', and 'spirit' refers to the Holy Spirit [Gdt, Ho, My]: with the gentleness inspired by the Holy Spirit. Paul knows that the gentleness does not come from him, but comes as the fruit of the Spirit [Gdt]. It means 'with the Spirit of gentleness'. In all cases in the NT where πνεῦμα 'spirit' is joined in a genitive construction with an abstract noun, it indicates the Holy Spirit, and the noun indicates his effect, as in the Spirit of truth, adoption, love, glory, wisdom, and power [Ho, My].

DISCOURSE UNIT: 5:1–7:40 [EGT]. The topic is questions about social morals.

DISCOURSE UNIT: 5:1–6:20 [AB, EBC, Ed, Herm, Lns, NCBC, NIC2, TNTC]. The topic is scandals reported in the church [AB], Paul's response to further reports [EBC, NCBC], church discipline [Ed], moral delinquencies in the congregation [Lns, TNTC], immorality and litigation: test cases of the crisis of authority and gospel [NIC2]. Paul now turns from the general problem of division to specific problems he had learned about [AB].

DISCOURSE UNIT: 5:1–6:11 [Ed]. The topic is union with Christ determining the nature of church discipline.

DISCOURSE UNIT: 5:1–13 [Alf, EBC, Ed, Gdt, GNT, Herm, HNTC, Ho, ICC, Lns, NCBC, NIC, NIC2, TG, TH, TNTC, Vn]. The topic is Paul's condemnation of sexual immorality—incest [EBC, GNT], the case of incest [Ed, Herm, Lns, NIC2, TNTC], church discipline [Gdt, NCBC], fornication inside and outside the church [HNTC], reproof for retaining an unworthy member in the church [Ho], absence of moral discipline [ICC], outrageous fornication [NIC], immorality countenanced by the church [Vn]. This section is linked to the previous section by the spiritual problem of arrogance. This underlies the two errors of the Corinthians: undue importance placed on external differences, and insensitivity to essential questions of morality [ICC].

DISCOURSE UNIT: 5:1–8 [AB, Alf, EBC, EGT, My]. The topic is a case of incest [AB, Alf, EGT], reproof and apostolic judgment respecting an incestuous person in the church [My].

DISCOURSE UNIT: 5:1–5 [Gdt, Ho, NIC2]. The topic is the case of the incestuous member of the church [Ho], Paul's judgment: expulsion [NIC2].

DISCOURSE UNIT: 5:1–2 [AB, TNTC]. The topic is the sin of toleration of one having his 'father's wife' [AB], the fact [TNTC].

5:1 Actually/Commonly[a] it-is-reported[b] (that there is) sexual-immorality[c] among you,

LEXICON—a. ὅλως (LN **70.1**) (BAGD p. 565): 'actually' [AB, BAGD, HNTC, ICC, **LN**; all versions except KJV, LB, NJB], 'really' [LN], 'commonly' [KJV], 'widely' [NJB], 'in general' [Herm, Lns], 'generally speaking' [BAGD], 'everyone (is talking)' [LB], 'everywhere' [BAGD, He]. It ordinarily means 'totally' or 'completely', and therefore can mean: 'universally, in general' or 'in a word' [NIC2].

b. pres. pass. indic. of ἀκούω (LN 33.212) (BAGD 3.b. p. 32): 'to be reported' [AB, BAGD, HNTC; KJV, NAB, NASB, NIV, NJB, NRSV], 'to be said' [TEV], 'to be talked about' [He], 'to be informed about' [BAGD], 'to be heard' [LN], 'to be notorious' [ICC]. This passive is also translated actively: 'to hear' [Lns], 'to hear reports' [REB], 'to receive news' [LN]. It is also translated by its reciprocal with 'everyone' as actors: 'to talk' [LB]. It is also translated as a noun: 'a report' [TNT]. The present tense indicates that this report was being circulated up to the day of the writing of this letter [NIC], or was continually spreading [EBC]. The impersonal, 'it is heard', indicates a common report among the believers [EGT].

c. πορνεία (LN 88.271) (BAGD 1. p. 693): 'sexual immorality' [AB, LN; NIV, NJB, NRSV, REB, TEV], 'sexual vice' [TNT], 'immorality' [NASB], 'fornication' [BAGD, HNTC, LN, Lns, NCBC; KJV], 'lewd conduct' [NAB], 'unchastity' [BAGD], 'a case of unchastity of a revolting character' [ICC], 'the terrible thing' [LB], 'a case of misconduct' [He]. Πορνεία primarily refers to using a harlot [TNTC], but then has come to refer to any kind of sexual evil [EGT, HNTC, NIC, NIC2, Rb, TNTC]. It refers to all kinds of unlawful sexual intercourse [BAGD, EBC, ICC, LN].

QUESTION—What is meant by ὅλως 'actually/commonly'?

1. It means 'actually' and modifies 'reported' [AB, BAGD, EBC, Ed, HNTC, ICC, NIC2, TG, TH, TNTC; all versions except KJV, NJB]: it is actually reported. It means 'most assuredly, incontrovertibly, actually' [ICC]. It means 'absolutely, without any qualification or doubt' [Ed]. Judging from Paul's use of the word in 6:7 and 15:29, it is better to translate, 'altogether' or 'actually' than 'universally' [NIC2].

2. It means 'commonly' [Herm, NIC; KJV], 'in general' [Herm, My], or 'everywhere' [He; NJB] and modifies 'reported': it is commonly reported that there is sexual immorality among you.
3. It means 'in general' and modifies 'immorality' [Gdt]: it is heard that fornication in general exists among you, and specifically, it is of such a kind that is not found even among pagans. The following correlative adjective 'of such a kind that' shows that the meaning of ὅλως is 'in general'. The correlative (of such a kind) then specifies the particular kind of immorality [Gdt].

QUESTION—To what is the phrase ἐν ὑμῖν 'among you' to be connected?

1. It should be connected with the word 'sexual immorality' [AB, Gdt, Herm, HNTC, NIC2; KJV, LB, NAB, NASB, NIV, NJB, NRSV, TEV]: it is reported that there is sexual immorality among you. It was reported to Paul [NIC2].
2. It should be connected with the word 'reported' [Alf, Ed, EGT, ICC, Lns, My, NIC]: it is reported among you that there is sexual immorality. The case was well known in all of Corinth [NIC]. This does not mean that people outside the church were talking about this case, but that it was commonly talked about among 'you Christians', in the midst of the church of Corinth itself, it was no longer a secret [Lns].

and[a] such-a-kind[b] (of) sexual-immorality which (is) not-even[c] (found) among pagans,[d]

TEXT—Some manuscripts supply ὀνομάζεται 'is named' after 'not even'. GNT does not mention this addition. Only KJV includes it.

LEXICON—a. καί: 'and' [He, Lns; KJV, NASB, NIV, NRSV, TNT], 'and even' [AB, EGT], not explicit [HNTC, ICC; LB, NAB, NJB, REB, TEV].

b. τοιοῦτος (LN 92.31) (BAGD 2.g. p. 821): 'of such a kind' [BAGD, LN; NASB], 'of a kind that' [NIV, NJB, NRSV], 'of a kind' [NAB], 'such as this' [BAGD], 'of a kind such as this' [LN], 'of such a sort' [He], 'such' [AB, HNTC; KJV, TNT], 'of such' [Lns], 'such as' [REB], 'so (terrible)' [TEV], 'something so (terrible)' [LB], 'so (revolting)' [ICC]. This word is also joined with the words 'sexual immorality' and translated 'a character so revolting' [ICC]. Even after the father had died, Roman law prohibited such a relationship [He]. Not that this kind of thing did not occur among pagans, but it was not common and was not condoned [HNTC, TNTC].

c. οὐδε (LN 69.7; 69.8) (BAGD 3. p. 591): 'not even' [AB, BAGD, He, HNTC, LN; all versions except KJV], 'not so much as' [KJV], 'not' [ICC, Lns].

d. ἔθνος (LN 11.37; 11.55): 'pagans' [He, LN; NAB, NIV, NRSV, REB], 'heathen' [AB, ICC, LN; LB, TEV], 'Gentiles' [HNTC, Lns; KJV, NASB, NJB, TNT]. The word means 'nation' or a group of people who constitute a distinct socio-political community. In the plural, (as here) it refers to all those who do not belong to the Jewish or Christian faith [LN].

Because the term seems to be used here to contrast with the Corinthian Christians, it is best to use a term like 'heathen' [AB].

QUESTION—What relationship is indicated by καί 'and'?

1. It indicates the specific kind of immorality [Alf, EGT, Lns]: there is immorality among you, *and specifically* it is of a kind that is not even found among pagans. The καί is explanatory, specifying the particular sin found among the Corinthians [Lns]. The καί is climactic [Alf, EGT], and has an ellipsis of 'not only...but' before it [Alf]: there is 'not only' immorality among you 'but' it is of such a kind that is not found even among pagans.
2. It indicates one example of immorality in general [Herm]: there is immorality among you, *for example,* there is a kind not even found among pagans.

QUESTION—What verb is implied between 'which' and 'not among the nations'?

Some verbs that have been supplied are 'to be found' [NAB, NJB, NRSV], 'to be practiced' [HNTC; LB], 'to exist' [EGT; NASB, TNT], 'to occur' [ICC; NIV], 'to be reported' [AB], 'to be heard of' [Herm], 'to be guilty of' [TEV], 'to tolerate' [REB], 'to be named' [KJV]. Some later manuscripts use the verb 'to be permitted', borrowing from Eph. 5:3 [HNTC]. The meaning probably is that pagan laws do not allow such a thing [TH].

that[a] someone has[b] (his) father's wife.[c]

LEXICON—a. ὥστε (LN 89.52) (BAGD 2.b. p. 900): 'that' [BAGD, ICC, Lns; KJV, NASB, NJB], 'of such a kind that' [AB, BAGD], 'so that' [BAGD, HNTC, LN], 'for' [NRSV], not explicit [all other versions].

b. pres. act. infin. of ἔχω (BAGD I.2.b.α. p. 332): 'to have' [AB, BAGD, Lns; KJV, NASB, NIV, TNT], 'to possess, to take (as wife)' [BAGD], 'to have as his concubine' [ICC] 'to live with' [HNTC; NAB, NJB, NRSV], 'to actually live with' [He], 'to live in sin with' [LB], 'to sleep with' [TEV]. This verb is also translated as a noun: 'the union (of a man with his stepmother)' [REB]. Ἔχω indicates a permanent relationship of some kind [EBC, EGT, ICC, NIC, NIC2, Rb, Vn], but possibly not formal marriage. In the lowest classes of Roman culture, the line between wife and concubine was not too sharply specified [ICC]. It may indicate 'to have as a wife' [Alf, Ed, Herm, Ho, My, TNTC], or 'to have as a concubine' [Ed, Gdt, Herm, TNTC]. The present tense indicates that this was either a case of marriage or concubinage and not a single offense [HNTC, TH]. When used in the context of sexual relations, 'to have' is a euphemism for an continuing relationship [NIC2]. It means to physically possess a woman, either by marriage or otherwise [AB]. Ἔχω, in relation to a woman, is used in the NT to indicate marriage (Matt. 14:4; 22:28; 1 Cor. 7:2, 29) [EBC, My]. Here it does not indicate marriage since it was forbidden by Roman law [Lns].

c. γυνή (LN 10.54) (BAGD 2. p. 168): 'wife' [AB, BAGD, He, HNTC, LN, Lns; all versions except NJB, TEV]. This word is also joined with the word 'father' and translated 'stepmother' [ICC; NJB, TEV]. It is used here of a stepmother [Alf, BAGD, EBC, Herm, HNTC, Lns, My, NCBC, NIC, TH], who may not have been married to the man in question [BAGD]. This refers most likely to a woman who was not the mother of the man in question [AB, ICC, NIC2, TG, TNTC]. She was either another wife in a polygamous relationship, or a stepmother in a case where the man's mother had died [AB]. In Lev. 18:7, 8, verse 7 forbids sexual intercourse with one's mother, while verse 8 forbids sexual intercourse with one's father's wife. This supports the interpretation that 'father's wife' does not refer to the man's mother, otherwise Paul would have specified that [NIC2]. The woman was probably not at that time the wife of the guilty man's father. She may have been divorced or her husband may have died [ICC]. She was probably a pagan as Paul does not accuse her (5:12) [EGT, Gdt, ICC, My, NIC2]. Since Paul does not call the sin adultery, we may assume either that the man's father had died, or he had divorced his wife. He does not call the sin incest, so we may assume that the woman was the man's stepmother [HNTC]. It is possible that the woman was still married to the man's father [AB]. Probably the father was still alive (2 Cor. 7:12, 'the one who was wronged') [Alf, Ed, Ho, My], and was a Christian [My]. We assume that the man's father had died [Gdt, Herm, TG].

QUESTION—Where is the emphasis in this clause?

Both the words 'father's' and 'wife' are emphasized by the position of the word τινα 'someone' [Gdt, Herm, ICC]. The arrangement of the words puts emphasis on the word 'wife' [My].

5:2 And[a] are you puffed-up[b] and not rather[c] have-mourned,[d]

LEXICON—a. καί (LN 91.12) (BAGD I.2.g. p. 392): 'and' [AB, ICC; all versions except NAB, TEV], 'and...in these circumstances' [HNTC], 'and...still' [Lns], 'still' [NAB], 'yet' [He, LN], 'then' [TEV], 'and yet, and in spite of that, nevertheless' [BAGD]. It serves to connect sentences and emphasizes a fact as surprising, unexpected, or noteworthy [BAGD].

b. perf. pass. participle of φυσιόω (LN 88.216): 'to be puffed up' [HNTC, LN, Lns; KJV], 'to be puffed (up) with pride' [AB, He], 'to be proud' [NIV, TEV], 'to be proud of oneself' [REB], 'to be/become arrogant' [NASB, NRSV], 'to be self-satisfied' [NAB], 'to be conceited' [LB], 'to be filled with one's own self-importance' [NJB]. This passive is also translated actively: 'to remain arrogant' [TNT], 'to go on in one's inflated self-complacency' [ICC]. The perfect tense serves to emphasize the attitude of arrogant pride Paul referred to in 4:18, 19 [EBC], or it refers to a permanent condition [Vn]. See this word at 4:6.

c. μᾶλλον (LN **89.126**) (BAGD 3.b. p. 489): 'rather' [AB, BAGD, He, HNTC, ICC, Lns; KJV, NIV, NRSV, TNT], 'instead of' [BAGD; NAB,

NASB], 'but on the contrary' [**LN**], 'on the contrary' [LN; TEV], 'instead, but rather' [LN], not explicit [LB, REB]. This word is also translated with a clause: 'it would have been better if' [NJB].

d. aorist act. indic. of πενθέω (LN 25.142) (BAGD 1. p. 642): 'to mourn' [AB, BAGD, Lns; KJV, NASB, NRSV, TNT], 'to mourn in sorrow and shame' [LB], 'to go into mourning' [He, HNTC; REB], 'to grieve' [BAGD; NAB], 'to be filled with grief' [NIV], 'to grieve bitterly' [NJB], 'to be overwhelmed with grief' [ICC], 'to grieve for, to weep for' [LN], 'to be filled with sadness' [TEV], 'to be sad' [BAGD, LN]. 'Mourned' is used for sorrow for one who had died [Ed, EGT, ICC, TNTC], and may hint that the Corinthian church has lost a member as in death [TNTC]. 'Mourned' indicates genuine agony of spirit related to true repentance. The Corinthians lacked a sense of sin or ethical responsibility in their life in the Spirit. This contrasted with the Good News of Christ crucified [NIC2]. 'Mourning', in Jewish custom, included with sorrow an expression of horror and condemnation [TH]. The aorist tense refers to the time when the sin first became known among them [Alf, EGT, Herm, Vn], indicating what their immediate reaction should have been [Herm, Vn].

QUESTION—What relationship is indicated by καί 'and'?

1. It introduces the whole verse as a statement [He, ICC, Lns, Vn; KJV, NAB, NASB, NJB, REB].
2. It introduces the whole verse as a question [Alf, Ed, EGT, GNT, Herm, HNTC, My; LB]. This verse should be taken as a question in view of the οὐχί 'not' in the second clause and in consideration of Paul's reasoning style [EGT].
3. It introduces the first clause as an exclamation and the rest of the verse as a question [AB, NIC2; NIV, NRSV, TNT]: You are arrogant! Should you not rather have mourned in order that the one who has done this deed might be removed from among you?
4. It introduces the first clause as a question and the rest of the verse as a statement [TEV]: How, then, can you be proud? On the contrary, you should to be filled with sadness in order that he who has done this deed might be removed from among you.
5. It indicates a contrast between the immorality of 5:1 and the pride of 5:2 [TH]: but you are arrogant.

QUESTION—Why would they be puffed up in this circumstance?

1. They were puffed up in spite of this immorality in their midst [Gdt, Ho, ICC, Lns, My, NIC, Vn; LB, NAB, NJB]. Paul does not mean that the Corinthians were puffed up because of the sin, but in spite of it [ICC]. They were so proud that they did not recognize the actual condition of their fellowship [NIC, Vn]. They continued to be proud of their wisdom and perfection in general [Alf, My]. They are still self-satisfied [NAB], self-important [NJB], and proud of being spiritual [LB].

2. They were puffed up because they allowed this immorality in their midst [AB, NCBC, NIC2, TNTC]. Such earthly matters were of no consequence to truly “spiritual” persons as they felt themselves to be [NIC2]. It may be implied that the Corinthians were proud that their Christian freedom was enhanced by their acceptance of this unusual sexual relationship [AB, NCBC, NIC2].

QUESTION—What words are emphasized in the first clause?

The word ‘you’ is emphatic [Ed, HNTC, ICC, Lns, My, Rb, TH, Vn], pointing to the atrociousness of their condition [Vn]. Οὐχὶ μᾶλλον ‘not rather’, strongly emphasizes the contrast between the arrogance and the absent grief [EBC].

that[a] the-one-who did this deed[b] might-be-removed[c] from your midst?[d]

LEXICON—a. ἵνα (LN 89.49; 89.59; 91.15): ‘that’ [HNTC; KJV], ‘in order that’ [Ed, Ho, Lns, My; NASB], ‘so that’ [AB, He; NJB, NRSV, TNT], ‘and’ [NAB, NIV]. This conjunction is also translated as a clause: ‘and seeing to it that’ [LB], ‘that it should have become necessary that’ [ICC], not explicit [REB, TEV].

b. ἔργον (LN 42.11) (BAGD 1.c.β. p. 308): ‘deed’ [AB, BAGD, HNTC, LN, Lns; KJV, NASB], ‘thing’ [NJB, TEV, TNT], ‘crime’ [He], ‘dreadful offense’ [ICC], ‘act’ [LN], ‘action, accomplishment, evil or disgraceful deed’ [BAGD], not explicit [LB, NIV, NRSV]. The phrase ‘the one who did this deed’ is translated ‘the offender’ [NAB], ‘anyone who behaves like that’ [REB].

c. aorist pass. subj. of αἴρω (LN 15.203) (BAGD 4. p. 24): ‘to be removed’ [AB, BAGD, ICC, LN, Lns; LB, NASB, NRSV], ‘to be taken away’ [BAGD, HNTC, LN; KJV], ‘to be turned out of’ [NJB, REB], ‘to be expelled’ [BAGD; TEV, TNT], ‘to be separated’ [He], ‘to be carried off, to be carried away’ [LN]. This word is also translated actively: ‘to put out of’ [NIV]. It is also joined with the words ‘from your midst’ and translated actively: ‘to get rid of’ [NAB]. Removal of sinful objects in Israel always accompanies national repentance [NIC2].

d. μέσος (LN 83.9; 83.10) (BAGD 2. p. 507): ‘midst’ [AB, ICC, Lns; NASB, TNT], ‘fellowship’ [NIV, TEV], ‘community’ [He; NJB, REB], ‘membership’ [LB], ‘in the midst’ [LN (83.10)], ‘among’ [BAGD, LN (83.9); KJV, NRSV], not explicit [NAB]. It is also joined with the word ‘you’ and translated ‘from you’ [HNTC]. When used with the genitive plural of the words which modify it, as here, it means ‘(from) among’ [BAGD].

QUESTION—What relationship is indicated by ἵνα ‘in order that’?

1. It indicates the result of their mourning [EGT, Gdt, ICC, NIC, Rb]: you should have mourned so that he would be removed. This would be the normal effect of their mourning [ICC].
2. It indicates the purpose of their mourning [Alf, Ed, HNTC, Ho, Lns, My; NASB]: you should have mourned in order to remove this person. They

would mourn because of this evil and with a view to removing it [Alf]. They would show their sincerity in mourning by acting in order to remove him [HNTC]. They have not mourned with the desire to remove this person [Ho].

3. It indicates an explanation of the nature of the mourning [AB, Herm]: you should have mourned in the sense of removing this person.
4. It indicates a command [NIC2]: mourn and remove this person.

QUESTION—Who is the implied actor of the verb 'to be taken away'?

1. The implied actor is God [Gdt, He]: you rather mourned in order that God might take away from your midst the man who has done this deed. God would have responded to the grief of the church members by removing the offender as he had Ananias and Sapphira [Gdt].
2. The implied actors are the members of the church [Alf, EBC, Ed, Ho, ICC, NIC, Rb, TG, TH; NJB]: you should have mourned so that you would remove the man who has done this from your midst.

DISCOURSE UNIT: 5:3–5 [AB, Ho, TNTC]. The topic is the judgment pronounced by Paul [AB], the punishment of the offender [TNTC]. This section is one sentence in the Greek and in brief means 'I have decided to deliver this man to Satan'. All other clauses are subordinate and circumstantial [Ho].

5:3 For[a] I for-my-part,[b] being-absent[c] in body[d]

LEXICON—a. γάρ (LN 89.23): 'for' [HNTC, Lns; KJV, NASB, NRSV], 'indeed' [AB], not explicit [He, ICC; all other versions].

b. pres. act. participle of ἀπείμι (LN 85.27) (BAGD p. 83): 'to be absent' [AB, BAGD, He, HNTC, ICC, LN, Lns; all versions except LB, NJB, TEV], 'to be far away' [TEV], 'to be away' [BAGD], 'to be distant' [NJB], 'to not be there' [LB]. Paul was in Ephesus and the Corinthians were in Corinth [Lns]. The word 'far' is implicit in the Greek [TH; TEV].

c. μέν (LN 89.139, 91.6): 'for my part' [AB; NJB, REB, TNT], 'on my part' [NASB], 'as for me' [He; NAB], 'on the other hand' [LN (89.139)], 'as for my view of it' [ICC], 'as far as I am concerned' [HNTC], 'verily' [KJV], 'indeed' [LN (91.6)]. The μέν 'on the one hand' signals a contrast with 'you' of 5:2 [ICC]. Although μέν does not have a corresponding δέ 'but' in 5:2, it contrasts with the ὑμεῖς 'you' in that verse [NIC2]. The μέν isolates Paul, strengthening the force of ἔγω 'I', and contrasting him with the preceding 'you' [Gdt, NIC2]. The μέν strengthens the emphasis on 'I' [Ed]. Ἔγω μέν means 'I, at least' [Ed, EGT, Ho, My].

d. σῶμα (LN 8.1) (BAGD 1.b. p. 799): 'body' [AB, BAGD, He, HNTC, ICC, LN, Lns; all versions except LB, NIV, NJB], 'the living body' [BAGD], not explicit [LB]. This noun is also translated as an adverb: 'physically' [NIV, NJB]. He was not personally present [TG].

QUESTION—What relationship is indicated by γάρ 'for'?

1. It indicates the grounds on which Paul is demanding that this man be removed from their midst [Gdt, HNTC, Ho, ICC, Lns, My, Rb]: he must be removed since I have already pronounced judgment on him.

2. It indicates a continuation of the argument [Herm]: and I have already pronounced judgment. It approaches the sense of δέ 'and' [Herm].

but being-present[a] in spirit,[b]

LEXICON—a. pres. act. participle of πάρειμι (LN 85.23) (BAGD 1.a. p. 624): 'to be present' [AB, BAGD, He, HNTC, ICC, LN, Lns; all versions except LB, NIV, TEV], 'to be with someone' [NIV, TEV]. 'To be present in spirit' is taken as an idiom and translated 'to be thinking about the matter' [LB].

b. πνεῦμα (LN 26.9) (BAGD 3.a. p. 675): 'spirit' [AB, BAGD, He, HNTC, ICC, LN, Lns; all versions except LB], not explicit [LB]. Πνεῦμα refers to spirit as the immaterial part of the human personality [BAGD]. Here it refers to Paul's thoughts and concern (Col. 2:5) [HNTC, Lns, TG, TH], his spirit has not left his body and gone to them [TG]. This does not mean simply that Paul was thinking about them, but that his knowledge, authority, and power were present with them [Ho]. It means that he was actually present with them in spirit/Spirit as 5:4 indicates. The Spirit is present with them and Paul is present with them by that same Spirit [NIC2]. Paul's spirit must have been given extraordinary insight into the state of the Church in far away Corinth, by the Holy Spirit [EGT]. See this word at 2:11.

QUESTION—What word is emphasized in this clause?

The pronoun 'I' is emphatic [AB, Alf, Ed, EGT, Gdt, HNTC, Ho, ICC, Lns, NIC2, Rb, TH, TNTC, Vn; KJV, NAB, NASB, NJB, REB, TNT]: I, for my part. This emphatic 'I' corresponds to the 'you' of 5:2: 'you' may be arrogant, but 'I' see this from another perspective [HNTC, ICC, NIC2, Rb, TH, Vn].

as-though[a] being-present already I-have-judged[b] the-one-who so[c] has-done[d] this;

LEXICON—a. ὡς (LN 64.12): 'as though' [AB, He; KJV, NASB, TEV, TNT], 'just as though' [LB, NJB], 'as if' [HNTC; NRSV], 'just as if' [NIV], 'as' [Lns, NIC2], not explicit [NAB, REB]. This conjunction is also translated as a verbal phrase: 'had I been (present)' [ICC]. Ὡς παρών does not mean, 'as if present', as though Paul were not actually there, for this would weaken the previous παρὼν δὲ τῷ πνεύματι 'but being present in spirit'. It should rather be translated 'as one who is present' [EGT, NIC2]. 'As though I were present' when taken with the preceding 'being present in spirit' means rather 'because I am present' [NIC]. It does not mean 'as being present' but 'as if really present' [Alf]. See this word at 4:18.

b. perf. act. indic. of κρίνω: 'to judge' [KJV, NASB, TNT], 'to pass judgment on' [Lns; NIV, TEV], 'to reach one's judgment on' [REB], 'to pronounce judgment on' [NRSV], 'to decide' [He], 'to reach a decision in regard to' [HNTC], 'to come to a decision' [AB], 'to make up one's mind' [My], 'to decide what to do' [LB], 'to condemn' [NJB], 'to pronounce the sentence on' [ICC], 'to pass sentence on' [NAB]. The perfect tense indicates a sense of finality to the sentence [TNTC], or that what Paul has done now stands as done [Lns, TH]. The word ἤδη 'already' adds emphasis indicating either that Paul had acted while they remained inactive or that he had acted even before arriving there [Gdt].

c. οὕτως (BAGD 1.b. p. 597): 'so' [He, NIC; KJV, NASB], 'in this way' [NJB], 'thus' [AB, HNTC, Lns], 'after such fashion, in such a way' [My], 'so basely' [BAGD], not explicit [all other versions except NRSV]. This adverb is also translated as an adjective: 'such (a thing)' [NRSV]. 'Thus' refers to the circumstances just described [HNTC]. It means 'in this abominable way' [Lns, Vn]. This word probably has reference to the man's being a Christian [Ed, EGT], and means 'under these circumstances' [EGT].

d. aorist mid. participle of κατεργάζομαι (LN 90.47; 42.17) (BAGD 1. p. 421): 'to do' [AB, BAGD, HNTC, LN; all versions except LB, NASB, NJB], 'to commit' [NASB], 'to behave (in this way)' [NJB], 'to act (thus)' [AB], 'to perpetrate something' [ICC, Lns, My, Vn], not explicit [He; LB]. The participle is equivalent to the 'perpetrator' [Lns].

QUESTION—What is 'the man who has done this' the object of?

1. It is the object of the verb 'to judge' [AB, Ed, ICC, Lns, NIC, NIC2; NAB, NASB, NIV, NJB, NRSV, REB, TEV, TNT]: I have already pronounced judgment on the man who has done this. The accusative 'the man who has done this' is the direct object because of its position, and cannot be the object of the remote verb (of 5:5) 'to deliver' [Lns].
2. It is the object of the verb 'to hand over' of 5:5 [Gdt, HNTC, Ho, My]: I have already decided to hand over the man who has done this thing to Satan. Because so much intervenes between the object and the verb, the object is again repeated in 5:5 [Ho]. If we take 'the man who had done this' as the object of 'to judge', it leaves the verb 'to deliver' without any connection in the sentence [HNTC].

5:4 in the name[a] of our Lord Jesus you being-assembled[b] and my spirit

TEXT—Some manuscripts omit ἡμῶν 'our'. GNT includes it in brackets with a C rating indicating difficulty in deciding to include it. Others including this word are TH and all versions except LB and NRSV.

TEXT—Some manuscripts include the word Χριστοῦ 'Christ'. GNT does not include this word. It is included by LB and KJV.

LEXICON—a. ὄνομα (LN 33.126) (BAGD I.4.c.γ. p. 573): 'name' [AB, BAGD, He, HNTC, ICC, LN, Lns; all versions]. In most cases when this word is used with God or Jesus, it means 'with mention of the name, while naming or calling on the name'. Here it could be translated 'meet and call on the name of the Lord Jesus', that is, as a Christian church [BAGD]. To do anything in another's name is to act with that person's authority [Ho, NIC2, TG, TNTC], or as his representative [Ho]. 'In the name of' means 'in union with, or in accord with the revelation of, our Lord' [Lns].

b. aorist pass. participle of συνάγω (LN 15.125) (BAGD 2. p. 782): 'to be assembled' [BAGD; NASB, NIV, NRSV, REB, TNT], 'to be assembled in solemn congregation' [ICC], 'to be duly assembled together' [Lns], 'to be gathered together' [BAGD, HNTC, LN; KJV], 'to be brought together' [BAGD], 'to be called together' [LN]. This passive is also used as a reflexive and is translated actively: 'to gather, to assemble' [BAGD], 'to gather together' [NJB], 'to come together' [AB, BAGD], 'to meet together' [TEV], 'to call a meeting of the church' [LB]. This verb is also translated with 'my spirit' or 'I' being actor: 'united in spirit (with you...I)' [NAB], '(my spirit and yours) are united together' [He]. Συνάγω was used as a technical term for the assembling of the Christian believers [HNTC].

QUESTION—With what is the phrase 'in the name of our Lord Jesus' to be connected?

1. It is connected with the phrase 'I have already pronounced judgment' [AB, Ho, NCBC, NIC2; LB, NAB, NASB, NRSV, TEV]: I have already pronounced judgment in the name of our Lord Jesus. This is a crisis of authority and Paul is declaring the authority on which he is pronouncing his judgment. The distance of this phrase from the verb it modifies is explained by the rather long direct object which intervenes [NIC2]. He is acting as the Lord's representative [Ho].
2. It is connected with the phrase 'you are assembled' [BAGD, Gdt, He, HNTC; NIV, NJB, REB, TNT]: you are assembled in the name of our Lord Jesus. To meet in the name of the Lord Jesus means to meet under his authority, ready to obey him [HNTC]. The words 'In the name of our Lord Jesus' gives competence to the assembly [Gdt].
3. It is connected with the verb 'to deliver' [Alf, Ed, EGT, ICC, Lns, My, NIC, TNTC]: to deliver this man to Satan in the name of our Lord Jesus. On the authority of the Lord they are to deliver him [NIC].
4. It is connected with 'you are assembled' and 'to deliver' [Vn]: in the name of our Lord Jesus you must assemble and hand deliver this man to Satan.

QUESTION—What relationship is indicated by the present participle 'being assembled'?

1. A temporal relationship is indicated [AB; KJV, NASB, NIV, NJB, TEV]: when you are assembled.
2. An imperative relationship is indicated [LB, TNT]: Hold a meeting!

QUESTION—What is the function and meaning of the words 'and my spirit'?

The phrase 'my spirit' is the other member of a compound subject of 'assembled' [Gdt, He, Lns, NIC2; TEV]: you and my spirit being assembled. Paul's spirit was present with them when they were assembled [LB, NAB, NASB, NIV, NJB, NRSV, REB, TEV, TNT]: you being assembled and my spirit being present with you. In 1 Cor. 14:14–15 Paul says that his own spirit prays as the Holy Spirit gives him the words. We could then translate, 'my S/spirit prays'. Something very much like this is meant here where Paul says, 'you and my S/spirit are assembled' [NIC2]. Because Jesus is the spiritual Head of the Church, Paul can be present with the Corinthians in the spiritual presence of Christ [Gdt]. Paul means that the Corinthians are to ask themselves what the Apostle would have done under these circumstances, they are to remember the spirit of Paul [NIC].

QUESTION—Where is the emphasis in this phrase?

The emphatic ἔμου 'my', a possessive adjective, replaces the possessive pronoun μου 'my', and is in the emphatic position [My, NIC2]: my own spirit.

with the power[a] of our Lord Jesus,

LEXICON—a. δύναμις (LN 76.1): 'power' [AB, He, HNTC, LN, Lns; all versions except NAB], 'effectual power' [ICC], 'authority' [TH]. This noun is also translated as a verb: 'empowered (by our Lord Jesus)' [NAB]. 'With the power' and 'in the name' probably mean essentially the same thing [TH]. 'With the power' is not simply a repetition of 'in the name', but refers to God's power given to his obedient people [HNTC].

QUESTION—With what is the phrase 'with the power of our Lord Jesus' to be connected?

1. It is connected with 'being assembled' [AB, Ed, EGT, He, ICC, NIC, NIC2, TH, TNTC; LB, NIV]: being assembled...with the power of our Lord Jesus. The σύν 'with' duplicates the σύν of συνάγω 'to assemble'. Σύν is seldom used with an instrumental sense, and Paul never uses it that way. Therefore this phrase should not be taken with the verb 'to deliver' [NIC2]. The assembly is to be a very solemn one in which the Lord Jesus is there in power [TNTC]. Paul anticipated that his judgment would be carried out when the Corinthians and his spirit unitedly became the channel for the power of the Lord Jesus [AB]. The power of Christ lives in the assembled believers [Ed].
2. It is connected with 'to deliver' [Gdt, HNTC, Lns; REB, TEV, TNT]: to deliver this man to Satan with the help of the power of the Lord Jesus. Σύν has an instrumental sense and means that they are to act 'with the help of' the power of the Lord Jesus [HNTC, Lns].
3. It is connected with 'and my spirit' [Alf, My]: and my spirit equipped with the power of the Lord Jesus. Σύν indicates 'in efficient connection with'. Paul's spirit is present in the assembly endowed with the authority of Christ. This means that Christ's power is not to be thought of as a third party in the assembly [My].

5:5 to-hand-over[a] such-a-person[b] to Satan for (the) destruction[c] of-the flesh,[d]

LEXICON—a. aorist act. infin. of παραδίδωμι (LN 57.77) (BAGD 1.b. p. 615): 'to hand over' [AB, BAGD, HNTC, ICC, LN; NAB, NIV, NJB, NRSV, TEV], 'to deliver' [BAGD, He; KJV, NASB, TNT], 'to deliver over' [Lns], 'to give over' [BAGD, LN], 'to turn over, to give up' [BAGD], 'to consign to' [REB], 'to cast out from the fellowship of the church and into (Satan's hands)' [LB]. Παραδίδωμι is the verb often used to describe people being handed over to evil powers (Romans 1:24, 26, 28) [TH]. This verb is also seen in 1 Tim. 1:20, where Paul delivered Hymenaeus and Alexander to Satan so that they might learn not to blaspheme [Gdt]. 'To deliver over to Satan' is a declaratory pronouncement expelling one from the sphere of Christian fellowship into the power of the ruler of the world [My]. This is the same verb used in the Septuagint translation where God spoke to Satan about Job, "Behold I hand him over to you" [ICC].

b. τοιοῦτος (LN 64.2) (BAGD 3.a.α. p. 821): 'such a person' [AB, BAGD], 'such a man' [Lns; NJB, TNT], 'such a man as this' [HNTC], 'such a one' [KJV, NASB], 'such an offender' [ICC], 'this man' [LB, NIV, NRSV, REB, TEV], 'this malefactor' [He], 'him' [NAB].

c. ὄλεθρος (LN **20.34**) (BAGD p. 563): 'destruction' [AB, BAGD, He, HNTC, **LN**, Lns; all versions except LB, NIV, NJB, TEV], 'ruin' [BAGD, Vn], 'destruction by suffering' [ICC], 'death' [BAGD]. This word is also translated as a verb: 'to punish' [LB]. Here it means death and indicates that handing the man over to Satan would result in his death [BAGD]. This noun is also translated by a passive verb: 'to be destroyed' [NIV, NJB, TEV]. This word refers to complete destruction [LN]. It signifies the ruin of the man's physical condition. It is used elsewhere in the NT only in 1 Thess. 4:3; 2 Thess. 1:9; and 1 Tim. 6:9 [Vn].

d. σάρξ (LN **8.63**; 8.4) (BAGD 2. p. 743): 'flesh' [AB, He, HNTC, LN, Lns; KJV, NAB, NASB, NRSV], 'body' [BAGD LN; REB, TEV, TNT], 'physical body' [LN], 'natural life' [NJB], 'sensual body' [NJB], 'sinful nature' [NIV], 'the flesh in which he has sinned' [ICC], 'him' [LB]. Here it refers to the body [BAGD, EBC, Ho, TG] or the bodily nature [EGT]. It should be understood here in the sense of 'sinful flesh' [My, NIC]. It must be taken not as 'fleshly life', but as an integral part of the man, his 'outward man'. Of this, Paul says that the 'outward man' will perish (2 Cor. 4:16) [Gdt].

QUESTION—What is meant by handing the man over to Satan?

1. It means to excommunicate the man from the church [He, HNTC, ICC, Lns, My, NIC, NIC2, TH, TNTC; LB]. It means to expel the man from the Church to the realm where Satan rules [HNTC, ICC, NIC2, TNTC]. This assumes that Satan was used as an instrument of the church. It does not mean that Satan would have his way with him, but rather that ultimately the man might be saved [HNTC]. It probably means that the man be excluded from gatherings of the believers for worship, meals, and the Lord's Supper. The language should probably not be taken literally as indicating a personal surrendering of the man to Satan for physical harm [NIC2]. Negatively the man is to be expelled from Christ's kingdom, positively he is to be assigned to Satan's kingdom [Lns]. As an apostle, Paul is able to deliver to Satan, but the church can go no further than to

expel him from their midst [My, NIC]. The phrase indicates the loss of all Christian privileges [TNTC].

2. It means to put the person under the power of Satan to harm him [AB, Alf, BAGD, EBC, Ed, EGT, Gdt, Ho, NCBC, NIC, Vn; NJB]. In favor of this interpretation are the following: (1) that in Scripture Satan is seen as inflicting bodily harm; (2) that the apostles were able to supernaturally inflict such evils (Acts 5:1–11; 13:9–11; 2 Cor. 10:8; 13:10); (3) that Paul does the same thing in 1 Tim. 1:20; (4) that this phrase is never used by the Jews when referring to excommunication; and (5) that excommunication would not destroy the flesh [Ed, Ho]. Paul delegated to the church a special power to inflict bodily death or disease as a punishment for sin [Alf].

QUESTION—Who is the implied actor of 'to hand over to Satan'?

1. The implied actor is the Christian community [NIC2; LB, NIV, NJB, NRSV, TEV, TNT]: that you hand over such a person to Satan.
2. The implied actors are the Christian community and Paul's spirit [AB, HNTC, Lns]: that we hand over such a person to Satan.
3. The implied actor is Paul [Herm, My, NIC; NAB, NASB]: I have decided to hand over such a person to Satan.

QUESTION—What is meant by 'the destruction of the flesh'?

1. It means that the man's body would be destroyed or that he would at least suffer [AB, BAGD, EBC, EGT, Gdt, He, Herm, HNTC, Ho, NCBC, TG, TH, TNTC, Vn; LB, NJB, REB, TEV, TNT]: to hand him over to Satan that he may die, or to hand him over to Satan that he may be afflicted. Σάρξ here means 'body' [BAGD, EBC, HNTC, Ho; NJB, REB, TEV, TNT]. At least suffering is indicated [HNTC, Ho], probably death [AB, BAGD, Herm, HNTC]. What is indicated by σάρξ is the earthly existence of the man. 'Destruction of the flesh' indicates a death similar to that of Ananias and Sapphira, but a slow death, leaving time for repentance [EGT, Gdt]. Σάρξ refers to physical flesh, an area in which Paul had personal experience with a messenger of Satan (2 Cor. 12:7) [HNTC].
2. It means that the man's evil nature would be destroyed [Ed, Lns, My, NIC, NIC2]: to hand him over to Satan that his evil nature may be destroyed. Σάρξ here should be taken to mean 'sinful flesh', so that the destruction of his sinful nature is indicated [NIC]. The real purpose of 'the handing over to Satan' is 'that his spirit may be saved'. Paul nowhere else uses the phrase 'destruction of the flesh' to refer to death. In 5:11, Paul commands them not to associate or eat with this man, indicating that immediate death is not in view. Rather, destruction refers the abolition of his carnal nature (Gal. 5:24; Rom. 7:5–6) [NIC2].
3. It means both of the above [ICC]. The punishment was remedial, intended to destroy the man's sinful lusts (Rom. 8:13; Col. 3:5), and to inflict physical suffering as a judgment on sin (1 Cor. 11:30; Acts 5:1f, 13:11) [ICC].

in-order-that the spirit[a] may-be-saved[b] in the day of-the Lord.

TEXT—Instead of κυρίου 'Lord', some manuscripts have κυρίου Ἰησοῦ 'Lord Jesus', others have κυρίου ἡμῶν Ἰησοῦ Χριστοῦour Lord Jesus Christ'. GNT selects the reading 'Lord' with a B rating indicating that the text is almost certain. The reading 'Lord Jesus' is selected by He, KJV, NASB and Lns. The reading 'our Lord Jesus Christ' is selected by LB.

LEXICON—a. πνεῦμα (LN **26.9**): 'spirit' [AB, HNTC, ICC, **LN**, Lns; all versions except LB], 'soul' [LB], 'he' [He]. By using πνεῦμα instead of 'he', the reference is to the center of the personality, the chief and distinctive feature in man's makeup [ICC]. It indicates the whole person as oriented towards God [NIC2]. It does not denote 'spiritual life', but an integral part of his existence, his spirit itself. It is the part of man which can contact and understand God [Gdt]. See this word at 2:11.

b. aorist pass. subj. of σῴζω (BAGD 2.b. p. 798): 'to be saved' [AB, BAGD, HNTC, ICC, Lns; all versions], 'to be saved spiritually' [He], 'to be preserved from eternal death, to attain salvation' [BAGD]. The punishment, although destructive, was remedial [ICC]. Σῴζω is used of being rescued in the last day [NIC2]. This does not mean that only part of the man will be saved, rather all of him, body, soul, and spirit, will be saved, but the spirit is mentioned as representing the whole [Vn]. See this at 1:18 and 3:15.

QUESTION—How are the nouns related in the genitive construction τῇ ἡμέρᾳ τοῦ κυρίου 'the day of the Lord'?

It means the day when the Lord returns [EBC, Gdt, Ho, TH, Vn; LB], or the day when the Lord will judge [NIC, TH, TNTC, Vn].

DISCOURSE UNIT: 5:6–13 [Ho]. The topic is exhortation to purity and to fidelity in discipline [Ho].

DISCOURSE UNIT: 5:6–8 [AB, Gdt, NIC2, TNTC]. The topic is an argument by analogy: the Passover [NIC2], analogue: leaven and the Christ-passover [AB], exhortation to clean out all evil [TNTC]. Paul, using a metaphor, now bases the action of 5:1–5 in theology [NIC2]. He moves from the specific to the general, showing that the whole congregation as well must be involved [AB].

5:6 Your boasting[a] (is) not good.[b]

LEXICON—a. καύχημα (LN **33.368**) (BAGD 1. p. 426): 'boasting' [He, HNTC, **LN**; NAB, NASB, NIV, NRSV, TNT], 'boast, object of boasting' [BAGD], 'glorying' [ICC; KJV], 'self-satisfaction' [NJB, REB], 'arrogant pride' [AB], 'reason for glory' [Ho, Lns], 'what you are so proud of' [BAGD]. This noun is also translated as a verb: 'to be proud' [TEV], 'to boast' [LB].

b. κάλος (LN 88.4; 65.22; 66.2) (BAGD 2.b. p. 400): 'good' [AB, BAGD, LN, Lns; KJV, NASB, NIV, TNT], 'a good thing' [HNTC; NRSV], 'right' [TEV], 'honorable' [NCBC], '(to one's) credit' [ICC], 'morally good, useful, noble, contributing to salvation' [BAGD], 'praiseworthy'

[BAGD, LN, NIC2], 'fine, fitting' [LN]. This adjective is also joined with 'not' and translated as a phrase: 'an ugly thing' [NAB], 'a terrible time' [LB]; as verb: 'to ill become (you)' [REB], 'to be ill founded' [NJB], 'to certainly have no grounds for (boasting)' [He]. Κάλος means 'excellent' in a moral sense [Lns], or 'seemly, of fine quality' [EGT]. 'Boasting' was not good for two reasons: the church had a rotten spot in its structure, giving it no reason to boast [HNTC, Lns, TG], and its gifts had been freely given and therefore there was nothing to boast about [HNTC]. Paul is showing them how absurd their boasting is when they are in real danger of corruption by evil [NIC2].

QUESTION—What is meant by καύχημα 'boasting'?

1. It refers to the act of boasting [Herm, ICC]: it is not good that you are boasting. Paul does not mean that the thing they are boasting about, their understanding or their freedom, is not good, but that their boasting itself is not good in such circumstances [ICC].
2. It refers to the thing about which they are boasting [Alf, BAGD, Ed, Gdt, He, Ho, Lns, My, NCBC, TNTC, Vn]: what you are boasting about is not good. Καύχημα indicates the thing about which one boasts, while καύχησις refers to the act of boasting. That the reason for their boasting is wrong is seen in this case of open immorality [Lns].

2.1 The thing about which they were boasting was evil [Ed, NCBC, TNTC]. This evil situation was the kind of thing they were proud of [Ed].

2.2 The thing about which they were boasting was good in itself but they could not really claim to have it [Gdt, Ho, Lns]. They were proud of their abundance of spiritual gifts, but the purpose of these was to increase spiritual life in the church. Because this was not happening, Paul tells them they do not really have a ground for boasting [Gdt]. They do not have a valid reason for boasting of their good state [Lns].

Know-you not that (a) little[a] yeast[b] ferments[c] the whole batch-of-dough?[d]

LEXICON—a. μικρός (LN 59.15) (BAGD 2.a. p. 521): 'little' [AB, He, HNTC, LN, Lns; all versions except LB, TEV], 'little bit of' [BAGD; TEV], 'very little' [ICC], 'limited amount of' [LN]. This word is also translated by dropping the figure: '(even if) one person (is allowed to go on sinning)' [LB]. Μικρός comes first and is emphatic indicating that if such a small thing can have such a large effect, how much more can a scandal as bad as this, affect the whole church [ICC, Vn].

b. ζύμη (LN **5.11**) (BAGD 1. p. 340): 'yeast' [BAGD, LN; NAB, NIV, NJB, TEV], 'leaven' [BAGD; all other versions except LB]. This word is also translated by its topic: 'sinning' [LB]. Ζύμη pictures the influence of seemingly insignificant factors in the moral sphere [BAGD]. 'Leaven' came to be a symbol of bad behavior or false teaching [AB].

c. pres. act. indic. of ζυμόω (BAGD p. 340): 'to ferment' [BAGD], 'to leaven' [AB, BAGD, He, HNTC, Lns; all versions except LB, NAB, NIV,

TEV], 'to make rise' [TEV], 'to have its effect' [ICC; NAB], 'to work through' [NIV], 'to be affected' [LB].

d. φύραμα (LN **63.12**) (BAGD p. 869): 'batch of dough' [AB, BAGD, **LN**; NIV, NJB, NRSV, TEV], 'lump of dough' [BAGD, HNTC, ICC; NASB], 'lump' [He, Lns; KJV], 'dough' [NAB, REB, TNT], 'that which is mixed or kneaded' [BAGD], 'mixture' [LN], 'all (people)' [LB].

QUESTION—What are the parts of the metaphor and with what are they compared?

The image is that of a small amount of yeast or leaven permeating a whole batch of dough [HNTC, Lns, NIC2, TNTC]. The topic is that of a small amount of evil spreading to spoil a whole community [AB, EGT, HNTC, Ho, ICC, My, NIC2, TNTC]. The point of comparison is the nature of a thing to spread itself throughout its host [Gdt, Ho, TG]; or that a small thing can affect its 'entire' host [BAGD, Gdt, Herm, Lns, TH, TNTC]. Specifically, the leaven (the evil) is: the presence of the offender among them [Alf, TNTC; LB]; or his sin [EGT, My, NCBC]; or the moral influence of his evil example [Ed]; or the implied concurrence of the church, a weakened standard of moral judgment [ICC]; or the glorying of the church which simultaneously tolerates immorality [NIC]; or all evil, however small, willingly tolerated by an individual or group [Gdt, Ho].

QUESTION—What is the function of the rhetorical question?

It has the effect of saying that they should know this [Herm, HNTC, NIC, NIC2, TG, TH]: you surely must know that a little yeast ferments the whole batch of dough! This is said with emphasis [TH].

5:7 Clean-out[a] the old yeast,[b] in-order-that you-may-be (a) fresh[c] batch-of-dough,

LEXICON—a. aorist act. impera. of ἐκκαθαίρω (LN **79.50**) (BAGD 1. p. 240): 'to clean out' [AB, BAGD, **LN**, Lns; NASB, NRSV, TNT], 'to clean away' [LN], 'to cleanse' [BAGD], 'to cleanse away' [ICC], 'to purge out' [HNTC; KJV], 'to get rid of' [NAB, NIV, REB], 'to remove' [LB, TEV], 'to purge out thoroughly' [EBC, Ed], 'to throw out' [NJB], 'to sweep out' [He]. The aorist imperative tense indicates urgency [EGT, Lns, Rb], that is, that the action be carried out at once lest the whole church be affected [Rb]. It also indicates a very thorough cleaning [Lns], as does the prefix ἐκ 'out' [EGT, Lns]. The imperative is 2nd person plural as are other references to 'you' in the verse [AB].

b. ζυμή (LN **88.237**): 'yeast' [**LN**; NAB, NIV, NJB, NRSV], 'yeast of sin' [TEV], 'leaven' [AB, He, HNTC, ICC, Lns; KJV, NASB, REB, TNT]. This word is also translated as what it stands for: 'evil cancer—this wicked person' [LB]. Ζυμή is figurative for hypocritical behavior. It involves hidden attitudes and motivations [LN]. See this word at 5:6.

c. νέος (LN 57.71) (BAGD 1.a. p. 536): 'fresh' [AB, BAGD, He, HNTC; NAB, NJB], 'as free from leaven as a new (lump)' [ICC], 'new' [BAGD, LN, Lns; all other versions except LB]. This word is also joined with 'unleavened' and translated '(you can stay) pure' [LB]. It means fresh dough with no yeast in it and is symbolical of Christians [BAGD]. It is νέος 'new' in the sense of not having existed before, whereas καίνος indicates 'new' as contrasted with 'old' [Lns]. Νέος refers to new as to time [EGT, Gdt] rather than as to quality [Gdt]. 'Fresh batch of dough' refers to 'a morally new church' [My].

QUESTION—What is the basis for this metaphor?

The figure is taken from the custom of ridding the Jewish household of all leaven in preparation for the Passover (Exodus 12:15f; 13:7) [Ed, ICC, NCBC]. Cleaning out the old leaven was a picture of moral purification [ICC].

QUESTION—To what does the word 'yeast' refer in this clause?

It refers to evil in general as shown in 5:8 [Ed, Gdt, Ho]. It refers to the sins which were left over from their former lives before they became Christians [AB, ICC, Lns, My, NIC]. In the context, the old yeast refers to the offending man [NIC2; LB].

QUESTION—To what does the phrase 'fresh batch of dough' refer?

It refers to the people themselves [Herm; LB]. It refers to the morally new church after the separation from it of all immoral elements [My]. It refers to the Christian life and character of the church which has just had a completely new beginning [Lns].

as[a] you-are unleavened;[b]

LEXICON—a. καθώς (LN 89.34; 64.14) (BAGD 3. p. 391): 'as' [KJV, LB, NIV, NJB, NRSV], 'as indeed' [HNTC; TEV], 'indeed' [REB], 'just as' [LN (64.14); NASB], 'even as' [Lns], 'of course, as' [ICC], 'inasmuch as' [AB, LN (89.34)], 'as it were' [NAB], 'in fact' [TNT].

b. ἄζυμος (LN **5.13**) (BAGD 2. p. 20): 'unleavened' [AB, BAGD, He, HNTC, **LN**, Lns; all versions except NAB, NIV, TEV, TNT], 'without yeast' [LN; NIV, TEV], 'free from leaven' [ICC; TNT], 'without fermentation, made without yeast' [BAGD], 'not having yeast' [LN]. This adjective is also translated as a noun phrase: 'unleavened loaves' [NAB]. Here it is figurative of a pure and true life [LN]. In principle they were unleavened because they were part of the Christian society [AB, BAGD]. The use of ἄζυμος 'unleavened', corresponds to the word 'sanctified' in 1:2 [EGT].

QUESTION—What relationship is indicated by καθώς 'as'?

It indicates the grounds for the preceding exhortation [AB, Alf, BAGD, Ed, EGT, He, HNTC, Ho, ICC, Lns, My, NIC, Rb]: clean out the old leaven since you are unleavened. They are exhorted to be in practice what they are in principle [AB, Ed, ICC], in their ideal state [ICC, NCBC, Rb], in their normal state as Christians [Ho, ICC, Rb]. This is their Christian characteristic [Lns, My]. Christ removed the leaven when he redeemed them [NIC].

For[a] indeed/also[b] Christ our Passover-lamb[c] was-sacrificed.[d]

LEXICON—a. γάρ: 'for' [AB, He, HNTC, Lns; all versions except LB, NAB, REB], 'because' [ICC; REB], not explicit [LB, NAB].

b. καί: 'indeed' [NIC2], 'also' [Ed, Gdt, Lns, My; NASB], 'even' [KJV], 'besides' [HNTC], 'already' [AB], not explicit [all other versions]. 'Also' serves to connect two statements of a similar nature, here the second is the grounds of the first [Gdt].

c. πάσχα (LN 4.27) (BAGD 2. p. 633): 'Passover lamb' [AB, HNTC, LN; NIV, REB, TEV], 'Paschal lamb' [BAGD, He; NRSV], 'spotless Paschal Lamb' [ICC], 'God's Lamb' [LB], 'Passover' [Lns; KJV, NAB, NASB, NJB, TNT]. Πάσχα simply means 'Passover', the word 'lamb' is only implied [NCBC]. Πάσχα refers to 'lamb' when terms like 'kill' or 'sacrifice' are in the context [LN].

d. aorist pass. indic. of θύω (LN 53.19; 20.72) (BAGD 2. p. 367): 'to be sacrificed' [He, HNTC, ICC, LN, Lns; all versions except LB]; 'to be slaughtered' [AB, BAGD, LN], 'to be slain' [LB], 'to be killed' [BAGD, LN]. It can mean to kill an animal in a ritual manner as in sacrifice to a deity or simply to kill a person or animal in a violent and merciless way [LN]. The aorist points to a single event in the past [NIC2, TH].

QUESTION—What relationship is indicated by γάρ 'for'?

1. It indicates the grounds for saying that they are unleavened [Gdt, ICC, NIC2, TNTC]: you are unleavened because Christ has been sacrificed. This is the primary reason for saying they are unleavened: it was by the death of their Savior that they had been purified from the leaven of their old self. Secondarily, it is the grounds for the command to clean out the old leaven [ICC].
2. It indicates the grounds for the action of cleaning out the old yeast [HNTC, Ho, Lns, My, NCBC, NIC]: clean out the old yeast, because Christ has been sacrificed. When the paschal lamb was sacrificed, the Israelis were commanded to clean all leaven from their homes (Exod. 12:15). There is a similar obligation to Christians to clean sin out of their lives because Christ, our Passover lamb has been sacrificed [Ho]. Paul implies that the time is past for the removal of the leaven because the Passover lamb has already been sacrificed. They are to hurry therefore and remove it [Lns, NCBC].

QUESTION—Where is the emphasis in this clause?

The word Christ comes last for emphasis: 'even Christ!' [Alf, Ed, ICC, TH, Vn]. The word 'Passover' is emphatic [Ed, Lns, My].

5:8 Therefore[a] let-us-celebrate-the-feast[b]

LEXICON—a. ὥστε (LN **89.52**) (BAGD 1.b. p. 900): 'therefore' [AB, BAGD, He, LN; KJV, NASB, NIV, NRSV, TNT], 'then' [NJB, TEV], 'so' [HNTC, LN; LB, REB], 'and so' [**LN**, Lns], 'consequently' [ICC], not explicit [NAB]. It is strongly inferential: 'so then' [NIC2].

b. pres. act. subj. of ἑορτάζω (LN **51.1**) (BAGD p. 280): 'to celebrate the feast' [HNTC; NAB, NASB, NJB], 'to celebrate the festival' [AB, BAGD; NRSV], 'to celebrate our Passover' [TEV], 'to keep the Festival' [NIV, TNT], 'to keep the feast' [He, ICC; KJV, NJB], 'to observe the festival' [LN; REB], 'to participate in a festival' [LN], 'to celebrate' [**LN**, Lns]. This word is also translated with part of the figure explicit: 'feast upon him and grow strong in the Christian life' [LB]. Here it refers to celebrating the Passover as a figure of the Christian life [BAGD]. The force of the present subjunctive is that this is to be done continually [AB, EGT, Gdt, NIC2, Rb, TNTC, Vn]: let us keep on celebrating the festival. The celebration was to be for a lifetime [Gdt, ICC, Lns, NCBC]. The Passover was followed by the Feast of Unleavened Bread which lasted for seven days (Exod. 23:15; 34:18; Deut. 16:3f) [NCBC].

QUESTION—What relationship is indicated by ὥστε 'therefore'?

It indicates an exhortation based on the words 'Christ our Passover lamb has been sacrificed' [Ho, NIC]: because Christ was sacrificed, therefore, let us celebrate the feast. It is the logical conclusion to Paul's argument [NIC2, TH].

QUESTION—To what does 'celebrating the feast' refer?

It refers to holy living by which believers celebrate God's forgiveness [NIC2]. It refers to living a life of purity and truth, separated from evil [AB, My, Vn]. A feast was a period of time dedicated to God, therefore 'celebrating the feast' refers to living a life consecrated to God as a sacred festival [EBC, Ho]. The figure of 'keeping the Passover' pictures the whole conduct of a Christian's life [Ed, EGT, My, TNTC; LB], and specifically it refers to joy and thanksgiving for salvation [Ed].

not with[a] (the) old yeast nor[b] with (the) yeast of-evil[c] and of-wickedness[d]

LEXICON—a. ἐν (LN 90.10): 'with' [AB, He, HNTC, ICC, LN, Lns; all versions except REB, TEV], 'with bread having' [TEV]. This preposition is also translated as a verb: 'to use' [REB].

b. μηδέ (LN 69.7) (BAGD 1.a. p. 517): 'nor' [BAGD, He, LN; NASB], 'nor yet' [ICC], 'or' [AB], 'neither' [LN, Lns; KJV], 'not' [HNTC], 'and not' [BAGD, LN], 'but not' [BAGD]. All other translations leave this word untranslated, taking it as introducing an apposition to the phrase 'old leaven'.

c. κακία (LN **88.105**) (BAGD 1.a. p. 397): 'evil' [AB, **LN**; NJB], 'malice' [He, HNTC; KJV, NASB, NIV, NRSV], 'badness' [LN, Lns], 'depravity' [BAGD; REB], 'wickedness' [BAGD, LN; TNT], 'corruption' [NAB], 'sin' [TEV], 'hatreds' [LB], 'vice' [BAGD, ICC]. It is used here with πονηρία 'wickedness', as having the same general meaning [BAGD, Herm, ICC]. In the Septuagint translation, both words are used interchangeably to translate the same Hebrew words [ICC]. The two words combine one idea because they are synonyms. Κακία denotes 'badness' in the sense of inferior or imperfect, while πονηρία denotes 'active evil'

[Lns]. Κακία is weaker than πονηρία, meaning 'badness', whereas πονηρία carries the sense of doing something bad with delight and persistence [Ho]. Κακία refers to a perverted state, while πονηρία refers to deliberate willful wrongdoing [EGT, Gdt]. The two words are synonymous and together denote all forms of evil [NIC2]. The 'yeast of evil and wickedness' refers to lives characterized by evil and wickedness [TH].

d. πονηρία (LN 88.108) (BAGD p. 690): 'wickedness' [AB, BAGD, HNTC, ICC, LN, Lns; all versions except NRSV, TNT], 'evil' [He; NRSV, TNT], 'baseness, maliciousness, sinfulness' [BAGD].

QUESTION—To what does the 'old yeast' refer?

The old yeast stands for sin and evil [TG]. It refers to the old way of life before becoming Christian [TNTC; LB], their former lives [Alf, ICC].

QUESTION—How is the phrase 'nor with the yeast of evil and wickedness' related to the phrase, 'not with the old yeast'?

1. It serves to define it [Ed, Ho, TG, TNTC; LB, NAB, NIV, NJB, NRSV, REB, TEV, TNT]: not with the old yeast, that is, with the yeast of evil and wickedness.
2. It serves to give an example of it [Alf, EGT, Gdt, Lns, My, NIC, Vn]: not with the old yeast, for example, the yeast of evil and wickedness. The old leaven is the unconverted state and evil and wickedness are particulars of it [Alf].
3. It serves to give a completely different type of leaven [ICC]: not with the old yeast of our old lives, nor yet with the yeast of evil and wickedness.

QUESTION—How are the nouns related in the genitive construction 'yeast of evil and of wickedness'?

It functions to define yeast [Alf, Ed, Herm, ICC, Lns, My]: yeast, that is, evil and wickedness. The genitive indicates 'which represents' [TG]: the yeast which represents evil and wickedness.

but with (the) unleavened-(bread) of-purity[a] and of-truth.[b]

LEXICON—a. εἰλικρίνεια (LN **88.42**) (BAGD p. 222): 'purity' [AB; TEV, TNT], 'sincerity' [BAGD, **LN**; all other versions except LB], 'unsullied innocence' [ICC], 'purity of motive' [BAGD, LN, TNTC], 'honor and sincerity' [LB]. It indicates: 'unalloyed' or 'pure' and was used of unmixed substances [Vn]. It means 'transparency, limpid purity, ingenuousness' [ICC]. It refers to purity, that is, harmony between one's thoughts and actions [Ed, NIC, Vn]. It means 'proven transparency'. It has the force of being perfectly sincere before God, and unsympathetic towards evil [Gdt]. Εἰλικρίνεια has to do with purity of motives, while ἀλήθεια 'truth' has to do with purity of action [TNTC].

b. ἀλήθεια (LN 72.2) (BAGD 1. p. 35): 'truth' [AB, He, HNTC, ICC, LN, Lns; all versions], 'truthfulness, dependability, uprightness' [BAGD]. It means 'integrity, rectitude' [ICC]. It is the harmony of thoughts, words, and actions with reality [Ed]. 'Truth' here probably refers to what people speak. 'Unleavened bread of sincerity and truth' refers to lives characterized by these qualities [TH]. Εἰλικρίνεια denotes: 'moral purity', while ἀλήθεια denotes: 'moral truth' [My]. Ἀλήθεια denotes active righteousness, an inflexibility in maintaining goodness and in combating evil [Gdt].

QUESTION—How are the nouns related in the genitive construction 'unleavened bread of sincerity and of truth'?

The genitive here means the unleavened bread which consists of sincerity and truth [Gdt], the unleavened bread which represents sincerity and truth [LN, TG], the unleavened bread which stands for sincerity and truth [LN].

DISCOURSE UNIT: 5:9–13 [AB, Alf, EBC, Ed, EGT, Gdt, Herm, My, NIC2, TNTC]. The topic is clarification of Paul's instruction regarding association with immoral persons [AB], a previous letter misread [EGT], correcting a misunderstanding [NIC2, TNTC]. This new section may seem unconnected with the flow of thought, but, the command in 5:13 is grounded on the thought developed in verses 5:1–8, and on that of 5:9–12 [NIC].

5:9 I-wrote to-you in the letter[a] not to-associate-with[b] sexually-immoral-people,[c]

LEXICON—a. ἐπιστολή (LN 6.63; 33.48) (BAGD p. 300): 'letter' [AB, BAGD, He, HNTC, ICC, LN, Lns; all versions except KJV, LB], 'epistle' [BAGD; KJV]. This word is left implicit with the verb 'to write' [LB].

b. pres. mid. infin. of συναναμίγνυμι (LN **34.1**) (BAGD p. 784): 'to associate with' [BAGD, **LN**, Lns; all versions except KJV, LB, NJB, REB], 'to mingle with' [BAGD], 'to mix with' [AB, HNTC; LB], 'to (keep) company with' [ICC; KJV], 'to have to do with' [NJB, REB], 'to have relations with' [He], 'to be in the company of, to be involved with' [LN]. Συναναμίγνυμι is a reciprocal middle meaning: 'not to mingle yourselves with' [Lns], literally, 'mix yourselves up with' [Lns, My, TNTC]. It refers to any kind of intercourse, eating together or meeting with people [AB]. It indicates living in an intimate and continuous relationship with someone [Gdt].

c. πόρνος (LN **88.274**) (BAGD p. 693): 'sexually immoral people' [AB, **LN**, NIC2; NIV, NRSV], 'those who are sexually immoral' [REB], 'one who practices sexual immorality' [BAGD], 'fornicators' [BAGD, ICC, Lns, My; KJV], 'people guilty of fornication' [HNTC], 'immoral people' [He; NAB, NASB, TEV, TNT], 'people living immoral lives' [NJB], 'evil people' [LB]. Its extended meaning is male persons who are publicly involved in sexual sin [AB]. It includes all kinds of fornication [EBC, NIC], including incest [EBC].

QUESTION—Does the aorist aspect 'I wrote' refer to a previous letter, or is Paul using it rhetorically to refer to the present letter from the readers' time perspective?

The context seems to indicate that Paul refers to a previous letter, not the present one [AB, Alf, EBC, Ed, EGT, Gdt, He, Herm, HNTC, Ho, ICC, Lns,

My, NCBC, NIC, NIC2, Rb, TG, TH, TNTC]. The phrase 'in the letter' is not appropriate to use with the epistolary aorist (one taken from the reader's perspective and referring to the present letter) [AB, Alf, Ed, EGT, HNTC, Ho, ICC, My, NCBC, NIC, NIC2] since it refers to another letter [ICC]. One reason that this reference is to a letter other than the present one is that there is no general prohibition against companying with fornicators in this letter [Ho, TNTC]. Another reason is that 5:11 begins with νῦν 'now' and refers to the present letter [NIC2].

5:10 not at-all[a] with-the sexually-immoral-people of this world[b]

LEXICON—a. πάντως (LN 91.10) (BAGD 5.a.β. p. 609): 'at all' [AB, LN]. 'altogether' [KJV], 'entirely' [Lns], 'the absolute sense' [HNTC]. It is also joined with 'not' and translated 'by no means' [BAGD], 'I did not at all mean' [NASB], 'not at all meaning' [AB; NIV, NRSV], 'I certainly did not mean' [TNT], 'I did not exactly mean' [ICC], 'I was not including everybody' [NJB], 'not in general' [He; REB], not explicit [LB, NAB, TEV]. It is a marker of strong emphasis completely validating what has been said: 'indeed, certainly, at all, at least, in any event' [LN].

b. κόσμος: 'world' [AB, HNTC, Lns; all versions except LB, REB, TEV], 'non-Christian world' [ICC], 'age' [He], 'people in general' [REB], not explicit [LB]. This word is also joined with 'immoral-people' and translated 'pagans who are immoral' [TEV]. See this word at 2:12.

QUESTION—What concept is limited by the phrase 'not altogether'?

1. It modifies the prohibition of 5:9 'not to associate with sexually immoral people' [Ed, EGT, Gdt, He, Herm, HNTC, Ho, ICC, Lns, My, NIC, Rb, TNTC, Vn; KJV, NJB, REB]: I did not mean to forbid association with all of the immoral people of the world without exception. He did not forbid association 'altogether' [Ed, EGT], 'absolutely' [ICC], 'in all circumstances' [ICC, NIC, TNTC]. He did not mean all the fornicators of this world in general [Gdt]. This limits the prohibition to the immoral in the church and does not apply to those outside [ICC]. He meant Christians given to fornication [My]. Another view is that circumstances might arrive when they must meet with them [NIC, TNTC]. It means 'not entirely', since some business matters might require it [Lns]. It was not without exceptions [NIC].
2. It modifies the implied orienter 'I mean' [AB, Alf, EBC, NCBC, NIC2; LB, NAB, NASB, NIV, NRSV, TEV, TNT]: I did not at all mean to forbid association with the immoral people of this world, only those within the church. He clarifies by first telling what he did not intend. His prohibition concerned the immoral people in the church, not the pagans outside the church [NIC2].

or with-the greedy[a] and thieves[b] or idolaters,[c]

LEXICON—a. πλεονέκτης (LN **25.23**) (BAGD p. 667): 'greedy' [AB, BAGD, **LN**; NIV, NRSV], 'everybody who is greedy' [NJB], 'pagans who are greedy' [TEV], 'cheat' [ICC], 'greedy cheat' [LB], 'rogue' [He], 'covetous' [BAGD, LN, Lns; KJV, NAB, NASB], 'avaricious' [TNT], 'extortioner' [REB], 'rapacious' [HNTC]. They are people who desire to have more [TNTC], especially those who will defraud in order to gain more [Ho].

b. ἅρπαξ (LN 57.239) (BAGD 2. p. 109): 'thief' [HNTC; LB, NAB, TEV], 'robber' [BAGD, LN; NRSV], 'swindler' [AB, BAGD; NASB, NIV, REB, TNT], 'dishonest' [NJB], 'extortioner' [ICC, Lns; KJV], 'rogue' [BAGD], 'brigand' [He], 'plunderer' [LN]. It is derived from the verb meaning 'to carry off by force' [LN]. It refers to one who seizes something, i.e., a robber [TNTC]. This is not confined to seizing by force, but to all undue extractions [Ho].

c. εἰδωλολάτρης (LN 53.64) (BAGD p. 221): 'idolater' [AB, BAGD, He, HNTC, ICC, LN, Lns; all versions except LB, NJB, TEV], 'idol worshiper' [LN; LB]. This word is also translated as a clause: 'who worship idols/false gods' [NJB, TEV]. This word should be taken literally [ICC, Vn]. It should be taken either literally or as including those who do anything that amounts to idol worship apart from an actual idol [Ho].

QUESTION—What sense is intended of the Greek word ἤ 'or' before 'greedy'?

It means 'any more than' [ICC, Vn; NJB]; not to associate with the immoral, any more than with the greedy and robbers or idolaters. A principle is involved which applies to all flagrant sinners [EGT, Lns].

QUESTION—What is the significance of the word καί 'and' joining 'greedy' and 'robbers'?

It signifies that these two words form a single class [Alf, Gdt, Ho, ICC, My, TNTC]. It may signify that these two form a single problem [NIC2]. The greedy want more for themselves while the robbers seize what is not theirs either by force or by any other means [Ho].

for[a] then[b] you-would-have[c] to-go-out[d] of the world.[e]

LEXICON—a. ἐπεί (LN 89.32) (BAGD 2. p. 284): 'for' [BAGD, He, LN; KJV, LB, NASB], 'since' [AB, BAGD, HNTC, LN, Lns; NRSV, TNT], 'because' [BAGD, LN], 'inasmuch as' [LN], not explicit [NAB, NIV, REB, TEV]. This word is also joined with ἄρα 'then', and translated 'for otherwise, you see' [BAGD], 'that would mean (that)' [ICC; NJB]. This is the reason he did not prohibit all association with wicked people [Ho].

b. ἄρα (LN 89.46) (BAGD 1. p. 103): 'then' [AB, BAGD, HNTC, LN, Lns; KJV, NASB, NRSV, TNT], 'so, consequently' [BAGD, LN], 'as a result' [LN], 'in that case' [He; NIV], 'you see' [BAGD], not explicit [ICC; LB, NJB]. It is also rendered as a verb: 'to avoid them' [NAB, REB, TEV]. It is a marker of result inferred from what has preceded [LN]. It implies 'if that were true, then…' [Rb]. 'were it not so, then…' [ICC].

c. ὀφείλω (LN **71.35**) (BAGD 2.a.β. p. 599): 'to have to' [BAGD, He, HNTC, ICC, **LN**; all versions except KJV, LB, NRSV], 'to need to' [AB; KJV, NRSV], 'to be obligated to' [BAGD, Lns]. This word is also translated as a reciprocal: 'to be unable to (stay)' [LB].

d. aorist act. inf. of ἐξέρχομαι (LN 15.40) (BAGD 1.b.δ. p. 275): 'to go out of' [LN; KJV, NASB, NRSV, TNT], 'to go out of altogether' [ICC], 'to leave' [BAGD, He; NAB, NIV], 'to come out of' [HNTC], 'to withdraw from altogether' [REB], 'to get out completely' [TEV], 'to cut oneself off completely from' [NJB], 'to depart out of', [AB, LN, Lns], 'to be unable to live in' [LB]. Ἐξέρχομαι 'to leave' used euphemistically with 'the world' means 'to die' [BAGD].

e. κόσμος (BAGD 4.b. p. 446): 'world' [AB, He, HNTC, ICC, Lns; all versions except REB], 'society' [REB]. Κόσμος as used here refers to the world as the habitation of mankind [BAGD], or to the universe [TH].

5:11 But now[a] I-wrote to-you not to-associate-with if anyone is-called[b] brother[c]

LEXICON—a. νῦν (LN 67.38; 67.39) (BAGD 2. p. 546): 'now' [AB, He, HNTC, Lns; KJV, NIV, NRSV], 'in fact' [NJB], 'actually' [NASB, TNT], 'what I meant was' [ICC], 'as a matter of fact, as things stand now' [BAGD], not explicit [LB, NAB, REB, TEV].

b. pres. pass. participle of ὀνομάζω (LN 33.127) (BAGD 1. p. 574): 'to be called' [BAGD, LN, Lns; KJV], 'to be given a name' [BAGD, LN], 'to go by the name of' [NJB], 'to be known as' [HNTC], 'to be named' [BAGD], 'to be given a title' [LN]. This word is also translated as an adjective: 'so-called' [AB, BAGD, He; NASB, REB, TNT]. It is also translated actively: 'to claim to be' [LB], 'to call oneself' [NIV, TEV], 'to bear the title' [NAB], 'to bear the name' [ICC, LN; NRSV].

c. ἀδελφός: 'brother' [AB, Lns; KJV, NAB, NASB, NIV, NJB, TNT], 'Christian' [He, ICC; REB], 'Christian brother' [HNTC], 'a brother Christian' [LB], 'a believer' [TEV], 'brother or sister' [NRSV]. See this word at 1:1.

QUESTION—Does the word νῦν 'now' have a temporal or a logical reference?

1. It has a logical reference and the aorist verb form refers to a previous letter [Alf, BAGD, Ed, Gdt, Herm, Ho, ICC, Lns, My, NCBC, TNTC; LB, NAB, NASB, NJB, REB, TEV, TNT]: but I wrote you. After stating what the former letter did not mean, he now states what it did mean [ICC].
2. It has a temporal reference and the verb is an epistolary aorist referring to this present letter [AB, EBC, EGT, He, HNTC, NIC, NIC2, Rb; NIV, NRSV]: but I am now writing to you. He repeats what he wrote in the former letter and now gives an explanation [NIC]. If anyone wondered what was meant in the former letter, Paul now clearly states his meaning [EGT].

(if) he-be sexually-immoral or greedy or (an) idolater, or (a) slanderer[a] or (a) drunkard[b] or (a) thief,[c] not-even[d] to-eat-with[e] such-a-one.

LEXICON—a. λοίδορος (LN 33.395) (BAGD p. 479): 'slanderer' [He, LN; NIV, NJB, REB, TEV], 'reviler' [AB, BAGD, Lns; NASB, NRSV], 'abusive person' [BAGD, HNTC; TNT], 'railer' [KJV]. It is also translated as an adjective: 'abusive' [LB, TNT]. It is also translated as a verb: 'to be given to abusive language' [ICC]. This kind of person says evil things which are not true about others or falsely accuses others of sinning [TG]. He speaks in a highly insulting manner [LN].

b. μέθυσος (LN 88.288) (BAGD p. 499): 'drunkard' [AB, BAGD, He, HNTC, LN, Lns; all versions except TNT], 'heavy drinker' [LN]. This word is also translated as a verb: 'to be given to hard drinking' [ICC]. It is also translated as an adjective: 'drunken' [TNT].

c. ἅρπαξ: 'thief'. See this word at 5:10.

d. μηδέ (LN 69.8) (BAGD 2. p. 518): 'not even' [BAGD, HNTC, LN, Lns; all versions except KJV, NAB, NJB], 'never even' [NJB], 'no not' [KJV], 'and not' [He]. It is also translated to bring out emphasis: 'it is clear that (you must) not (eat with)' [NAB].

e. συνεσθίω (LN 23.12) (BAGD p. 788): 'to eat with' [AB, BAGD, He, HNTC, Lns; all versions except LB, NJB, TEV], 'to share/ have a meal with' [ICC; NJB], 'to eat lunch with' [LB], 'to sit down to eat with' [TEV], 'to eat together' [LN].

QUESTION—How inclusive is the prohibition 'not even eat with such a person'?

It refers to meals of any type [EBC, Ed, EGT, HNTC, ICC, Lns, My, NIC, Rb, TH, Vn]. They are not to invite such a person to their homes nor are they to accept invitations to the person's home [ICC, My, Vn]. This underscores the idea of avoiding them entirely [Lns]. The purpose of this is to prevent the spread of evil and to cause the offender to see the error of his ways [ICC]. There is to be no close fellowship that might seem to countenance sin [TNTC]. Some think that this refers specifically to Christian communal meals [NCBC, NIC2]. Perhaps private fellowship may not have been included in this prohibition [NIC2].

5:12 For[a] what (is it) to-me to-judge[b] outsiders?[c]

LEXICON—a. γάρ: 'for' [AB, He, HNTC, Lns; KJV, NASB, NRSV], 'after all' [TEV], 'of course' [ICC], not explicit [LB, NAB, NIV, NJB, REB, TNT].

b. pres. act. inf. of κρίνω (LN 56.30) (BAGD 4.a.α. p. 451): 'to judge' [BAGD, He, HNTC, Lns; all versions], 'to pass judgment on' [AB], 'to sit in judgment on' [ICC], 'to condemn' [BAGD, LN], 'to judge, decide, hale before a court' [BAGD]. 'To judge' here is to bring before a Christian court and pronounce either a favorable or an unfavorable verdict [Lns]. See this word at 4:5.

c. ὁ ἔξω (LN **11.10**) (BAGD 1.a.b. p. 279): 'outsiders' [AB, He, ICC, **LN**, Lns; all versions except KJV, NIV, NRSV, TNT], 'them that are without' [KJV], 'those outside the church' [NIV], 'those (who are) outside' [HNTC; NRSV, TNT], 'those without' [Lns], 'those who are not Christians' [ICC]. This means a person who is not a member of a particular in-group [LN] and refers to non-Christians [BAGD, ICC]. The reference is to those outside the church [Ho; NIV].

QUESTION—What relationship is indicated by γάρ 'for'?

It indicates the grounds for 5:11, and that what Paul wrote in 5:11 was the true meaning of his earlier letter [NIC]. It indicates the grounds of why the Corinthians should never have thought that he meant that they should not associate with non-Christians who were sexually immoral [ICC]. It indicates that the first question is the grounds for 5:10 (we do not judge unbelievers), while the second is the grounds for 5:11(we do judge believers) [Gdt].

QUESTION—What is meant by the phrase τί μοι 'what to me'?

The phrase means 'what business is that of mine?' [ICC, Lns; NAB, NIV, REB, TEV, TNT]. It means 'why should it be my job?' [He].

QUESTION—What answer is expected to this question?

The expected answer is: 'It is none of your business' [Alf, Lns, My, NIC2, TNTC; LB, NJB, REB, TEV, TNT]. The clause, 'God will judge them', is placed immediately after this question to supply the answer [REB, TEV, TNT].

QUESTION—What significance is there in the unemphatic μοι 'to me'?

It implies that Paul is not referring to himself personally, but to himself as representing the Christian community, so as to indicate none of them should judge outsiders [Gdt, NIC2; LB]. 'It isn't our job to judge outsiders' [LB].

(Is-it) not[a] insiders[b] (whom) you-judge?

LEXICON—a. οὔχι: 'not' [AB, He, HNTC, ICC, Lns; all versions except LB, REB], not explicit [LB, REB]. See this word at 1:20.

b. ὁ ἔσω (LN **11.11**) (BAGD 2. p. 314): 'insiders' [AB, LN], 'those (who are) inside' [He, HNTC; NIV, NJB, NRSV, TNT], 'those within' [Lns], 'those who are in the church' [ICC; NASB], 'those who are members of the church' [LB], 'them that are within' [KJV], 'those inside the community' [NAB], 'the members of your own fellowship' [TEV]. This word is also translated as a prepositional phrase: 'within the fellowship' [REB]. Ὁ ἔσω refers in general to those who are members of an in-group [LN]. Here it refers to those within the church, that is, to Christians [BAGD].

QUESTION—What answer is expected to this question?

The word οὔχι 'not' is used in questions which expect a positive reply [BAGD, EBC, LN, Lns, NIC, TG, TH]. Because of this, two versions translated this question as a positive statement: it is the insiders whom you are to judge [LB, REB]. NJB and TNT translate it as a tag question: 'It is...is it not?'

QUESTION—In what sense is the word 'judge' used here?

It is used in the sense of church discipline [HNTC, Ho, My, NIC]. Another view is that it refers to Christians judging each other as to whether or not they really belong to the fellowship [Lns].

QUESTION—What is the function of this question.

1. It functions as the second grounds introduced by the 'for' at the beginning of the verse. [EGT, Gdt, Herm, Ho, ICC, Lns, My, TNTC]: For (1) what

have I to do…for (2) is it not the insiders…? There are two grounds for judging an offending man within the church: (1) Paul does not judge outsiders; (2) the church does judge insiders. To the Corinthians these were taken as facts and therefore stood as reasonable grounds [Lns].

2. This does not relate back to the 'for', but simply reminds them of their duty to judge [Ed, NIC, TG, TNTC]: Remember you must judge those inside the church.

QUESTION—What word is emphasized in this clause?

The word 'you' is emphasized [Gdt, NIC2] in contrast to 'God' of the following sentence [Gdt, Herm; TNT]: Is it not the insiders whom you are to judge? But God judges the outsiders?

5:13 But[a] God judges the-outsiders.

LEXICON—a. δέ (LN 89.124): 'but' [AB, LN; KJV, NASB, NJB], 'whereas' [Lns], 'while' [He], 'and' [HNTC], not explicit [ICC; all versions except KJV, NASB, NJB].

QUESTION—What relationship is indicated by δέ 'but'?

It indicates a contrast between the judgment of Paul and the Corinthians concerning insiders, and God concerning outsiders [EGT, My]. It indicates a contrast between Paul and God which is interrupted by Paul's word to the Corinthians [He].

QUESTION—Should the verb be κρινεῖ 'he will judge' or κρίνει 'he judges'?

1. This is the future tense [AB, EBC, GNT, He, Herm, HNTC, NIC; NAB, NIV, NRSV, TEV, TNT]. It makes little difference which is chosen since the present can be interpreted as a future. However, the meaning intended is that: 'God will judge' [EBC].
2. This is the present tense [Alf, Ed, EGT, Ho, ICC, Lns, My; KJV, LB, NASB, NJB, REB]. It should be taken as a present stating a norm: It is God's responsibility to judge those outside [ICC].

"Expel[a] the evil-person[b] from you yourselves."

LEXICON—a. aorist act. impera. of ἐξαίρω (LN **34.36**) (BAGD p. 272): 'to expel' [NAB, NIV, TNT], 'to exclude' [HNTC, **LN**], 'to drive out' [BAGD; NRSV], 'to drive away' [BAGD], 'to put away' [KJV], 'to put out' [LB], 'to remove' [BAGD, ICC, Lns; NASB, TEV], 'to banish' [NJB], 'to root out' [REB], 'to clear away' [He], 'to clean out' [AB], 'to get rid of, to separate' [LN].

b. πονήρος (LN 88.110; 65.27) (BAGD 2.a. p. 691): 'evil person' [TEV], 'evil man' [TNT], 'evildoer' [BAGD; NJB], 'evil one' [AB], 'evil' [He], 'wicked person/man' [BAGD, HNTC, ICC, Lns; KJV, NAB, NASB, NIV, NRSV], 'wrong-doer' [REB], 'evil-intentioned person' [BAGD], 'this man' [LB], 'immoral, evil, wicked; bad, worthless' [LN]. The reference is at least to the immoral person of 2:1 [EBC, EGT, HNTC, My, NIC2, Rb], possibly a general reference to the wicked [Gdt, HNTC], and probably not to Satan [Ed, HNTC].

QUESTION—What Scripture is Paul referring to as he says this?

He is referring to Deut. 17:7 [AB, Herm, ICC, NIC2]. This quotation brings a conclusion to the treatment of the sexual immorality present in the church [ICC]. This is a specific application concerning the incestuous person of 5:1 [EBC, EGT, HNTC, My, Rb], or a general application church disciple as treated from 5:6 [Gdt].

DISCOURSE UNIT: 6:1–20 [EBC]. The topic is the application of Christian morality to legal and sexual matters.

DISCOURSE UNIT: 6:1–11 [Alf, EBC, Ed, Gdt, GNT, Herm, HNTC, Ho, ICC, Lns, My, NCBC, NIC, NIC2, TG, TH, TNTC]. The topic is the church and the world [Herm], lawsuits [Ed, Gdt, Ho, Lns, NIC, TNTC], Christian morality in respect to legal matters [EBC], prohibition of lawsuits [NIC], a prohibition to settle quarrels in civil courts and advice to avoid all types of quarrels [Ed, HNTC], a case of litigation [NIC2].

DISCOURSE UNIT: 6:1–9a [AB]. The topic is lawsuits between Christians.

DISCOURSE UNIT: 6:1–8 [ICC]. The topic is lawsuits before the heathen.

DISCOURSE UNIT: 6:1–6 [AB, EGT, NIC, NIC2]. The topic is lawsuits before the heathen [EGT, NIC], the scandal of having such lawsuits [AB], shame of the church [AB].

6:1 Dare[a] anyone of-you having (a) case[b] against[c] another[d]

LEXICON—a. pres. act. indic. of τολμάω (LN 25.161) (BAGD 1.b. p. 822): 'to dare' [AB, Herm, HNTC, LN, Lns; KJV, NAB, NASB, NIV, NRSV, TEV, TNT], 'to take it upon oneself' [ICC], 'to be so brazen' [NJB], 'to have the face' [REB], 'to have the audacity' [He], 'to bring oneself, to presume' [BAGD]. This word is also translated idiomatically: 'How is it that?' [LB]. It means to be so bold as to defy possible danger or opposition [LN]. This word does not refer to courage, but to lack of shame [Lns]. It means to be so bold as to shock the Christian sense of what is right [Ho].

b. πρᾶγμα (LN **56.2**) (BAGD 5. p. 697): 'case' [AB, He, Herm, **LN**; NAB, NASB, TNT], 'lawsuit' [BAGD, LN], 'suit' [HNTC], 'dispute' [BAGD, ICC; NIV, REB, TEV], 'complaint' [NJB], 'grievance' [NRSV], 'difference' [He], 'legal action' [LN], 'something' [LB], 'matter' [Lns; KJV].

c. πρός with accusative object (LN 90.33) (BAGD III.4.a. p. 710): 'against' [AB, BAGD, Herm, HNTC, LN, Lns; KJV, LB, NAB, NASB, NJB, NRSV, TNT], 'with' [BAGD, He, ICC; NIV, REB, TEV].

d. ἕτερος (LN 58.37) (BAGD 1.b.ε. p. 315): 'another' [AB, LN, Lns; all versions except LB, NASB, TEV], 'his neighbor' [BAGD; NASB], 'his fellow' [HNTC], 'fellow Christian' [ICC; TEV], 'another Christian' [LB], 'brother' [He], 'other' [LN].

QUESTION—How is this section related to the preceding chapter?

Paul is not through with instructions about sexual life, but he spoke of judging those inside the church (5:12) and this brings up the matter of judging disputes among Christians [HNTC, ICC, NIC, TNTC]. There is no connection with what precedes except that it is another item to be censured [My].

QUESTION—What is the function of this rhetorical question?

It indicates that Christians should not go to law against fellow Christians before unbelievers; instead they should go before fellow Christians [AB, HNTC, NIC, TG, TH; NAB, NJB, TEV]. It shows how indignant Paul is [EGT]. It shows Paul's horror at what he has heard [NIC2]. It serves to condemn the action [TG].

QUESTION—What is the significance of the verb 'to dare' being placed first in the sentence?

Its position at the beginning of the sentence makes this word emphatic [TH]. It show that Paul is horrified by what he has heard [NIC2].

QUESTION—What relationship is indicated by the participial form ἔχων 'having'?

1. It indicates a condition [NIV, REB, TEV], or circumstance [AB, Herm, HNTC, ICC; NASB, NRSV, TNT]: dare anyone, if/when he has a matter against another, go to law before the unjust?
2. It modifies τις 'anyone' [He; NAB, NJB]: dare anyone who has a matter against another, go to law before the unjust?

QUESTION—Who is τὸν ἕτερον 'another'?

The dispute is with a fellow Christian [all commentaries; LB, TEV], or one's neighbor [BAGD, ICC; NASB].

QUESTION—What is meant by πρᾶγμα 'matter'?

The word is a generic term for any act or dispute [AB], but here it has specific reference to a legal matter [AB, BAGD, Herm, HNTC, Ho, ICC, LN, My, NIC, TH, TNTC, Vn; NAB, NASB, TNT]. It was a legal term meaning a cause for having a trial [AB, ICC, NIC, Vn]. The term includes property disputes [EBC]. Criminal cases are not referred to here, since Paul teaches in Rom. 13:3–4 that civil courts must handle these [EBC].

to-go-to-law[a] before[b] the unrighteous[c]

LEXICON—a. pres. pass. infin. of κρίνω (LN 56.20) (BAGD 4.a.β. p. 451): 'to go to law' [AB, BAGD, Herm, HNTC, Lns; KJV, LB, NASB, REB, TNT], 'to stand trial' [LN], 'to seek judgment' [NJB], 'to bring a matter for judgment' [NAB], 'to take a matter to a tribunal' [ICC], 'to take for judgment' [NIV], 'to take to court' [NRSV], 'to go before a judge' [TEV], 'to have a case tried' [He], 'to dispute, to quarrel, to debate' [BAGD], 'to stand trial' [LN]. Some commentaries take this to be the middle voice [Ed, EGT, ICC, Lns] meaning to go to law on one's own behalf [Lns].

b. ἐπί with genitive object (LN 83.35): 'before' [AB, Herm, HNTC, LN, Lns; KJV, NASB, NIV, NRSV, REB, TEV, TNT], '(to bring) to/before'

[ICC; NAB], '(to seek) from' [NJB], '(to have a case tried) by' [He]. It has the implication of being before an authority [LN, Rb]. This word is also translated as a verb: 'to ask (a heathen court to decide)' [LB].

c. ἄδικος (LN **11.20**) (BAGD 1. p. 18): 'unrighteous' [Herm, HNTC, Lns; NASB, NRSV], 'unjust' [BAGD; KJV], 'heathen judges' [TEV], 'heathen tribunal' [ICC], 'pagan/heathen court' [LB, REB], 'wicked' [NAB], 'ungodly' [NIV], 'unrighteous judges' [AB], 'sinners' [NJB], 'pagan courts' [TNT], 'unbelievers' [He, **LN**]. It refers to doing what is contrary to what is right, an antonym of 'righteous' [BAGD]. This term is now used for the 'outsiders' and is interchanged with ἄπιστος 'unbelieving' [Herm].

QUESTION—Why are the civil judges called by the term τῶν ἀδίκων 'the unrighteous'?

The term is not used in a moral sense of referring to a lack of personal integrity on the part of the judges, but is used in a religious sense as a technical term to designate the heathen in contrast with God's people (τῶν ἁγίων 'the holy ones, the saints') [AB, Ed, He, Herm, Ho, Lns, My, NCBC, NIC, TNTC, Vn]. The complaint is not that the civil judges were corrupt, but that they were unbelievers [Ho, TNTC]. This does not imply that there would be little chance of obtaining justice [Ed, He, ICC, NCBC, TNTC, Vn]. The term 'unjust' is one applied to the whole world and the courts were a part of the non-Christian world [AB, Lns, Vn]. 'Unjust' means that they are not justified in God's sight [AB, TH] and the word is equivalent to ἀπίστων 'unbelievers' in an identical phrase in 6:6 [Herm, NIC2].

and not before the saints?[a]

LEXICON—a. ἅγιος: 'saints' [AB, Herm, HNTC, Lns; KJV, NASB, NIV, NRSV], 'God's people' [LN; REB, TEV, TNT], 'God's holy people' [NAB, NJB], 'believers' [ICC], 'Christians' [He], 'other Christians' [LB]. This term refers to their standing as God's holy people and not necessarily to their moral behavior [HNTC]. See this word at 1:2.

6:2 Or know-you not that the saints will-judge[a] **the world?**[b]

LEXICON—a. fut. act. indic. of κρίνω: 'to judge' [AB, He, HNTC, Lns; all versions], 'to sit with Christ to judge' [ICC].

b. κόσμος (LN **9.23**): 'world' [AB, He, HNTC, ICC, Lns; all versions], 'the people of the world' [LN]. Κόσμος here refers to people associated with a world system alienated from God [LN, NIC]. It refers to the whole universe of intelligent beings including angels as seen in 6:3 [TNTC]. It refers only to angelic powers since unconverted people are already judged [He]. It refers to those who have rejected the gospel [Gdt]. It refers to the whole anti-God system of things [NIC2]. See this word at 4:9.

QUESTION—What is the function and meaning of ἤ 'or'?

It introduces an alternative explanation of why they had acted in error [HNTC, ICC]. It means 'Or if you can explain how you dare, do you know that, etc.' [Gdt].

QUESTION—What is the function of the rhetorical questions in this verse?

They give the grounds for not taking their cases before the unrighteous. It is because they themselves will finally judge the world [NIC2]. The first question functions to show the church how great its fault was. The question form of the second sentence functions to lessen the effect of the negative statement which it replaces, 'you are not unworthy then'. Paul expected a negative reply to this question [NIC]. The rhetorical questions are equivalent to strong positive statements such as: 'Surely you know, etc.' and 'If you will judge the world, then you are certainly qualified to judge trivial cases' [TH]. REB translates the first question as a statement: 'It is God's people who are to judge the world; surely you know that, etc.' [REB].

QUESTION—In what sense will the saints judge the world?

The context is talking about lawsuits, not about ruling [TNTC]. It should be understood in the sense of future and final judgment [Ho, NIC2]. This is the final judgment of the world when it comes under God's judgment. In some way God's people are involved in this judgment [HNTC, NIC2]. This refers to their association with Christ: at the final judgment Christ will be judge and he is the head and representative of his people [Ho] who will share in his reign [EBC, Ho, ICC]. The saints will assist in the final judgment [TNTC]. They will sit with Christ at that judgment [Ho].

And if the world is-judged by[a] you, are-you incompetent[b] of-trivial[c] cases?[d]

LEXICON—a. ἐν with dative object (LN **90.6**) (BAGD III.b. p. 260): 'by' [AB, He, HNTC, **LN**; KJV, NASB, NJB, NRSV, TNT], 'at (your bar)' [ICC], 'with the help of' [BAGD]. This word is also taken as indicating agent: 'you are to judge' [NIV, TEV], 'we Christians are to judge' [LB], '(you) sitting as a court' [Lns]. It is also translated as a genitive: 'your (judgment)' [NAB, REB].

b. ἀνάξιος (LN **65.19**) (BAGD p. 58): 'incompetent' [BAGD, ICC; NASB, NIV, NJB, NRSV, REB], 'not capable' [LB, TEV], 'unworthy' [AB, BAGD, HNTC, **LN**, Lns; KJV, NAB, TNT], 'unworthy of settling' [He], 'not meriting' [LN], 'not good enough' [BAGD].

c. ἐλάχιστος (LN 65.57) (BAGD 2.a. p. 248): 'trivial' [BAGD; NIV, NRSV], 'most trivial' [AB], 'small' [TEV], 'smallest' [KJV, NASB], 'lowest' [HNTC, Lns], 'minor' [NAB], 'trifling' [REB], 'petty' [NJB], 'pettiest' [ICC; TNT], 'even these little (things)' [LB], 'such little' [He], 'of least importance, of very little importance' [LN]. Its meaning here is 'totally insignificant' [NIC2].

d. κριτήριον (LN **56.2**) (BAGD 1. p. 453): 'case' [AB, **LN**; NIV, NJB, NRSV, REB, TNT], 'matter' [KJV, NAB, TEV], 'thing' [LB], 'difference' [He], 'lawsuit, legal action' [BAGD, LN]; 'law court' [NASB], 'court' [HNTC], 'tribunal' [ICC, Lns].

QUESTION—What is indicated by the present tense κρίνεται 'is judged'?

The present is used to express a principle [Gdt].

QUESTION—How are the nouns related in the phrase 'incompetent of trivial cases'?

In the matter of trivial cases, are they incompetent in the matter of judging [KJV, NAB, NIV, TEV, TNT], trying [NRSV], hearing [AB], deciding [LB], dealing with [REB], or settling [He] trivial cases? Another translation asks if they are incompetent of constituting the smallest law courts [NASB].

QUESTION—What is meant by κριτήριον 'case'?

1. It refers to 'the case or legal action itself and the judging of it' [Alf, BAGD, EBC, Ed, Herm, LN, NIC2; probably all versions except NASB]: are you incompetent of judging trivial cases?
2. It refers to 'the court that tries the case' [HNTC, ICC, Lns, NCBC, Rb, TNTC; NASB]: are you incompetent to judge in the trivial courts?
3. It refers to giving the verdict [Gdt]: are you incompetent to deliver such trivial sentences?

6:3 Know-you not that we-will-judge angels,[a]

LEXICON—a. ἄγγελος: 'angel'. See this word at 4:9.

QUESTION—Who are the angels?

1. This refers to good angels [Alf, My, NIC]. Paul always refers to good angels when he uses the term ἄγγελος without a modifier [NIC].
2. This refers to fallen angels [BAGD, Ed, Gdt, Herm, NIC2]. That fallen angels is intended see Jude 6 and 2 Pet. 2:4 [Herm]. In 15:24 of this letter Paul can only be referring to higher powers of evil [Gdt].
3. This refers to all angels, good and bad [HNTC]. Paul uses the term ἄγγελος to refer to both good and bad angels. See 2 Cor. 12:7, 'an angel of Satan' [HNTC].
4. This refers to good angels and the verb 'to judge' should rather be taken to mean 'govern' or 'rule over' [Ho].

QUESTION—What is the function of this rhetorical question?

It is the equivalent of a strong statement and could be rendered: 'Surely you know...' [TH]. By asserting that we will judge angels (who form a part of the world), this serves to intensify the point of 6:2 that we will judge the world [Gdt, NIC2].

how-much-more[a] **things-of-this-life?**[b]

LEXICON—a. μήτιγε (LN **91.9**) (BAGD p. 520): 'how much more' [**LN**; KJV, NASB, NIV, NRSV, REB], 'how much more, then' [TEV], 'not to mention' [AB, BAGD, HNTC, NIC2], 'one need hardly mention' [ICC], 'to say nothing of' [Lns; TNT], 'it follows then' [NJB], 'surely, then' [NAB], 'with how much greater reason' [He], 'let alone' [BAGD].

b. βιωτικός (LN **41.19**) (BAGD p. 142): 'things of this life' [**LN**; NIV, TEV], 'matters pertaining to this life' [NRSV], 'matters of this life' [NASB], 'matters of everyday life' [NJB], 'everyday matters' [AB], 'ordinary matters' [BAGD], 'everyday affairs' [NAB, TNT], 'things that pertain to this life' [KJV], 'mere matters of business' [REB], 'earthly matters' [He].

QUESTION—Is this part of the rhetorical question or does it begin a statement?

1. It continues the rhetorical question [AB, GNT, He, HNTC, NIC, NIC2; KJV, NASB, NRSV, REB, TNT]: Do you not know that we shall judge angels, not to speak of the things of this life?
2. It begins a statement [EGT, Gdt, Herm, ICC, Lns, My, TG; LB, NAB, NIV, NJB, TEV]: Do you know that we shall judge angels? It gives the conclusion in the form of an exclamation [ICC]. How much more are we able to judge the things of this life! The argument is from a stronger to a weaker assertion and the weaker here is an assertion with an elliptical μήτιγε which could be rendered: Not to speak of the fact that we shall judge (the things of this life) [Lns].

6:4 If then[a] you-have cases[b] (concerning) things-of-this-life,

LEXICON—a. μὲν οὖν (LN 89.50; 91.8) (BAGD 2.e. p. 503): 'then' [BAGD, ICC, LN, Lns; KJV, LB, NASB, NRSV], 'therefore' [LN; NIV, REB], 'so' [Alf, BAGD, HNTC, LN], 'but' [NJB], 'yet' [He], 'but then' [AB], not explicit [NAB, TEV, TNT]. Μὲν οὖν here means: 'accordingly, thus' [My]. It means 'nay but' or 'nay rather' and serves to emphasize the shame of having such cases at all [ICC]. This introduces the conclusion to the preceding argument [Gdt].

b. κριτήριον: 'cases' [NRSV, TNT], 'matter' [NJB, TEV], 'matter to decide' [NAB], 'dispute' [NIV], 'such disputes' [REB], 'differences' [He], 'question to be decided' [ICC], 'judgment' [KJV], 'law court' [NASB], 'court' [HNTC], not explicit [LB]. This noun is also translated as a verb: 'to hold court' [AB]. See this word at 6:2.

QUESTION—What word is emphasized in this clause?

The word βιωτικά 'things of this life' is emphasized by being repeated immediately from 6:3 [ICC, My, Rb], and by being placed first in the verse [ICC].

(how could) you-appoint-as-judges[a] those who-are-of-no-account[b] in the church?

LEXICON—a. pres. act. indic. of καθίζω (LN **37.104**) (BAGD 1.b. p. 390): 'to appoint as judges' [HNTC; NASB, NIV, NRSV, TNT], 'to set up as judges' [He], 'to set to judge' [ICC], 'to install as judges' [BAGD], 'to take to be settled' [TEV], 'to entrust jurisdiction to' [REB], 'to seat as judges' [AB, Lns], 'to bring before' [NJB], 'to set to judge' [ICC; KJV], 'to accept as judges' [NAB], 'to go to someone as a judge' [LB], 'to put in charge of, to appoint, to designate' [LN], but in this question, 'will you designate those who have no standing in church' means 'are you going to take these matters to be settled by people who have no standing in the church?' [**LN**].

b. perf. pass. participle of ἐξουθενέω (LN 88.195) (BAGD 1. p. 277): 'to be of no account' [BAGD, ICC; NASB, NJB, TNT], 'to be least esteemed' [KJV], 'to be of little account' [NIV], 'to be accounted nothing' [Lns], 'to be of no repute' [AB], 'to have no standing' [HNTC; NAB, NRSV, TEV], 'to not even be a Christian' [LB], 'to be despised' [BAGD, LN]. This verb is also rendered as a noun phrase: 'outsiders with no standing' [REB], 'people despised by' [He]. The verb is especially negative here meaning 'to despise, to reject with contempt' [NIC2]. See this word at 1:28.

QUESTION—Is this verse a question, an exclamation, or a command?

1. It is a question [AB, GNT, Herm, HNTC, Ho, Lns, My, NIC2, TG, TNTC, Vn; LB, NAB, NASB, NRSV, REB, TEV, TNT]: If then you have cases concerning things of this life, how could you appoint as judges those who are of no account in the church?

1.1 The words 'those of no account' refer to heathen judges [HNTC, Ho, LN, Lns, My, NIC2, TG, Vn; LB, REB]. It is unlikely that Paul would use such negative language to speak of fellow believers [NIC2]. This serves to trivialize the heathen courts with the other two previous questions: If you have everyday cases, you should not take them to outsiders who are held of no account by the church [NIC2]. Any heathen judge is nothing as far as spiritual qualifications are concerned [Lns, TG]. It serves to express surprise that they should act so out of keeping with their high calling [Ho].

1.2 The words 'those of no account' refer to members of the church [AB; NRSV]. But then if you hold court for everyday matters, do you appoint as judges those who are of no account in the church? The church has failed to provide the best qualified members to judge the cases that have come up in the church [AB].

2. It is an exclamation [He; NJB]: 'But when you have matters of this life to be judged, you bring them before those who are of no account in the church!' The church was proud of its wisdom, yet there was a lack of men who were competent to judge in cases brought before the church [He].

3. This is a command and refers to members of the church [Alf, EBC, Ed, EGT, Gdt, NIC; KJV, NIV]: If then you have cases concerning things of this life, appoint as judges those who are least esteemed in the church! Taken as an imperative it would have a sarcastic tone such as: If you have to settle minor things when you will one day judge angels, then go ahead and appoint as judges the least esteemed men of your congregation to judge them [EBC, Gdt]. The least qualified Christians is capable of judging such a case [Alf].

6:5 I-say (this) to[a] your shame.[b]

LEXICON—a. πρός with accusative object (LN 89.60) (BAGD III.3.a. p. 710): 'to' [HNTC; KJV, NASB, NIV, NRSV, REB, TEV, TNT], 'in an attempt to' [NAB], 'to make (you ashamed)' [He; LB, NJB], 'to move (you) to' [ICC, Lns], 'for the purpose of' [BAGD, LN], 'for' [AB, BAGD]. It indicates intention [Ho, Lns].

b. ἐντροπή (LN 25.195) (BAGD 1. p. 269): 'shame' [BAGD, HNTC, ICC, LN, Lns; KJV, NAB, NASB, NIV, NRSV, REB, TEV, TNT], 'ashamed'

[LB, NJB], 'humiliation' [BAGD], 'embarrassment' [LN], '(For) shame!' [AB]. This word is also translated as a verb: 'to make ashamed' [He].

QUESTION—Is Paul referring here to the preceding, or to the following statement?

1. He is referring to the preceding [Alf, BAGD, Ed, EGT, My]: Do you appoint as judges those who are of no account? I say this to shame you.
2. He is referring to the following [Gdt, TH]: I say this to shame you that among you there is not one wise enough to judge.
3. He is referring to the preceding but also to the following [NIC2]. His previous two sets of questions were asked to shame them. However, the word of shame also points to the following question [NIC2].

So[a] is-there no-one[b] among you wise, who will-be-able to-decide[c] between[d] his brother?

LEXICON—a. οὕτως (BAGD 1.b. p. 597): 'so' [BAGD, He; KJV], 'so then' [Lns], 'is it so' [NASB], 'can it really be' [NJB], 'has it come to this?' [HNTC], 'have things come to such a pass that' [ICC], '(is there) really' [TNT], not explicit [AB; LB, NAB, NIV, NRSV, REB, TEV]. This word occurs first in the sentence and is therefore emphatic. It means 'is it *so* with you that, etc.' and points to the condition in what follows [NIC2].

b. οὐδείς (LN 92.23): 'no one' [AB, He, LN; NAB, NRSV], 'anyone' [LB], 'not one' [HNTC; NASB, NJB], 'nobody' [NIV], 'not a single person' [ICC; REB], 'even a single man' [Lns], 'no man' [TNT], 'at least one' [TEV], not explicit [KJV].

c. aorist act. inf. of διακρίνω (LN 30.109) (BAGD 1.d. p. 185): 'to decide' [NASB, NRSV, TNT], 'to decide an argument' [LB], 'to decide questions' [NJB], 'to judge' [KJV], 'to judge a dispute' [NIV], 'to settle a case' [NAB], 'to settle a dispute' [TEV], 'to render a decision' [AB, BAGD; REB], 'to give a decision' [REB], 'to judge carefully, to evaluate carefully' [LN]. It has the meaning of making a judgment on the basis of careful and detailed information [LN]. The aorist aspect indicates a single decision to settle a case [Gdt, TNTC].

d. ἀνά μέσον (LN **89.143**) (BAGD 1.b. p. 49): 'between' [AB, BAGD, He, HNTC, ICC, **LN**, Lns; all versions except LB, REB], 'among' [LN], 'in (a fellow Christian's cause)' [REB], not explicit [LB].

QUESTION—What is the meaning of the phrase 'between his brother'?

It either means: 'between his brothers' or 'between one's brother and another' [Gdt, He, HNTC, Ho, ICC, LN, Lns, NIC2, Rb, TH, TNTC; all versions except LB, REB]. It means to arbitrate between one fellow Christian and another [ICC].

QUESTION—What is the function of this rhetorical question?

It functions as a strong assertion [Rb; TEV]: surely there is at least one wise person, etc. This question and the next serve to shame them by sarcasm [NIC2]. Paul's answer would be that there is no such person among them [AB].

6:6 But[a] brother goes-to-law[b] against[c] brother and this[d] before unbelievers?[e]

LEXICON—a. ἀλλά: 'but' [He, HNTC, Lns; KJV, NASB, NRSV], 'but instead' [LB, NIV], 'but that, on the contrary' [ICC], 'instead' [TEV], 'as it is' [AB], 'and that this is why' [NJB], not explicit [NAB, REB, TNT].

b. pres. pass. indic. of κρίνω: 'to go to law'. See this word at 6:1.

c. μετά with genitive object (LN 90.32) (BAGD II.3.a p. 509): 'against' [BAGD, He, LN; NIV, NJB, NRSV, TEV, TNT], 'with' [AB, BAGD, HNTC, ICC, LN, Lns; KJV, NASB, REB]. This preposition is also taken as marking the direct object: 'one Christian sues another' [LB], '(must) brother drag brother' [NAB].

d. οὗτος: 'this' [NIV], 'that' [KJV, NASB, NJB, TNT], 'at that' [NAB, NRSV, REB], not explicit [LB, TEV]. Καὶ τοῦτο 'and this' here indicates stress on what is referred to [Ho, ICC, TH, TNTC]. 'And this' could be translated 'and even more than that' [TH]. This word marks a climax going from bad to worse. From lawsuits about everyday affairs, to such lawsuits between Christians, to all this before non-Christians [ICC, Rb].

e. ἄπιστος (LN 31.106; 11.19) (BAGD 2. p. 85): 'unbeliever' [AB, BAGD, HNTC, ICC, LN, Lns; all versions], 'pagan' [He], 'one who is not a believer; non-Christian' [LN], 'faithless, heathen' [BAGD]. It refers to someone who does not believe the good news about Jesus Christ or belongs to such a group [LN].

QUESTION—Is this verse a separate question or part of the previous question, or is it a statement?

1. It continues the question from the previous verse [GNT, Herm, HNTC, ICC, Lns, TNTC; NASB, NJB, NRSV]: Can it be that there is not one wise among you who will be able to judge between brothers, but brother goes to law against brother and this before unbelievers?
2. It is a separate question [NIC2; NAB, REB, TNT]: But does brother go to law against brother and this before unbelievers?
3. It is a statement [Alf, Ed, EGT, Ho, My, NIC; KJV, LB]: But brother goes to law against brother and this before unbelievers. It makes more sense to take this as a contrastive statement beginning with 'but' and telling what, in practice, the Corinthians did do [NIC]. The verse serves as an answer to the question of 6:5, there was no man competent to judge [EGT, My].
4. It is an exclamation [AB, Gdt, He; NIV, TEV]: Brother goes to law against brother! It is gives a conclusion to the preceding [Gdt].

DISCOURSE UNIT: 6:7–11 [EGT, Gdt, NIC2]. The topic is a warning to immoral Christians [EGT], shame on the plaintiff and warning against the wrongdoer [NIC2].

DISCOURSE UNIT: 6:7–9a [AB]. The topic is the incongruity of injustice among brothers.

6:7 Already[a] then it-is completely[b] (a) defeat[c] for-you that you-have lawsuits[d] with[e] each-other

TEXT—GNT includes οὖν 'then' in brackets, indicating uncertainty about its inclusion. NIC2 and Gdt do not include it. Since it occurs with μέν which can have a similar meaning, it is difficult to determine which versions include this word and which omit it.

LEXICON—a. ἤδη (BAGD 2. p. 344): 'already' [AB, BAGD, Lns; NASB, NIV, NRSV, REB], 'now' [BAGD; KJV], 'it is already' [HNTC], 'actually' [TNT], 'at the very outset' [ICC], 'why' [NAB], 'no...by itself' [NJB], not explicit [LB, TEV]. This word is also joined with 'then' and is translated 'to begin with' [He]. It means 'before the results of the lawsuit itself are known (you are defeated)' [EGT, NIC, NIC2]. It means 'at once' and has a logical connotation here rather than temporal. If going to law before unbelievers is a shame, that 'at once' implies that a spirit that wants to take matters to court is unchristian [Ed]. See this word at 4:8.

b. ὅλως (LN **78.44**) (BAGD p. 565): 'completely' [**LN**; NIV, TEV], 'at all' [NJB, NRSV, REB], 'utterly' [KJV], 'actually' [AB, BAGD; NASB, TNT], 'totally' [LN], 'the very fact that' [NAB], 'in general' [Lns], not explicit [He]. This adverb is also translated as an adjective modifying 'defeat': 'complete' [LN; TNT], 'real' [LB], 'terrible' [ICC], 'nothing but' [HNTC]. It can mean 'by themselves'. That is, the lawsuits, no matter where they are tried, were a defeat [Alf, Ho].

c. ἥττημα (LN **13.22**) (BAGD p. 349): 'defeat' [AB, BAGD; LB, NASB, NRSV], 'mark of defect' [He], 'defect in your Christianity' [ICC], 'failure' [HNTC, **LN**; TNT], 'loss' [Lns], 'disastrous' [NAB], 'bad enough' [NJB], 'fault' [KJV, NJB]. This noun is also translated as a verb: 'to suffer defeat' [REB], 'to fail' [TEV]. It indicates defeat in the sense of suffering great loss [NIC2].

d. κρίμα (LN **56.2**) (BAGD 1. p. 450): 'lawsuit' [AB, He, HNTC, ICC, **LN**, Lns; LB, NAB, NASB, NIV, NRSV, TNT], 'dispute' [BAGD], 'legal dispute' [TEV], 'case, legal action' [LN]. This noun is also translated as a verb: 'to go to law' [KJV, NJB, REB].

e. μετά with genitive object (LN **90.32**): 'against' [**LN**]. See this word at 6:6.

QUESTION—What does ὅλως 'completely' modify?

1. It modifies the word 'defeat' [BAGD, HNTC, ICC, LN, NIC2, TH; LB, NIV, TEV]: to have lawsuits is a complete defeat for you.
2. It modifies the clause 'it is a defeat' [BAGD, Gdt, Lns, Rb; KJV, NJB]: it is actually/completely a defeat for you to have lawsuits.
3. It modifies the verb phrase 'to have lawsuits' [Alf, Ho; NAB, NASB, NJB, NRSV, REB]: to have lawsuits at all is a defeat for you.
4. It modifies both [TNT]: to have lawsuits at all is a complete defeat for you.

Why not rather be-wronged?[a] Why not rather be-defrauded?[b]

LEXICON—a. pres. pass. indic. of ἀδικέω (LN 88.22) (BAGD 2.a. p. 17): 'to be wronged' [BAGD, LN; NASB, NIV, NRSV, TEV], 'to allow oneself to be wronged' [HNTC, Lns], 'to submit to wrong' [REB], 'to take wrong' [KJV], 'to suffer injustice' [AB, He; TNT], 'to put up with injustice' [NAB], 'to accept injury' [ICC], 'to prefer to suffer injustice' [NJB], 'to be unjustly treated' [BAGD]. This verb is also joined with the following verb and translated actively: 'to accept mistreatment' [LB]. Both this and the following verb are probably middle voice [Alf, Ed, Gdt, ICC, Lns, Rb], and could be translated 'let yourselves be wronged' [Lns].

b. pres. pass. indic. of ἀποστερέω (LN 57.248; 57.47) (BAGD p. 99): 'to be defrauded' [AB, He, LN (57.248); NASB, NRSV, TNT], 'to prefer to be defrauded' [NJB], 'to let oneself be defrauded' [Lns; KJV, REB], 'to be cheated' [NIV], 'to let oneself be robbed/cheated' [BAGD, HNTC; LB, NAB]. 'to be robbed' [TEV], 'to submit to being deprived' [ICC], 'to be deprived by deception' [LN (57.47)]. It means to take something by means of deception or trickery [LN]. It refers to 'robbing, cheating, defrauding' and suggests that some kind of business or property dispute is the problem [NIC2]. It refers to wrongdoing in reference to property [Ed, Gdt, HNTC].

QUESTION—What is the function of these rhetorical questions?

They give Paul's evaluation of what should be done [NIC, NIC2, TG, TH, TNTC; LB]: 'it would be far more honoring to the Lord to let yourselves be cheated' [LB]. By choosing rhetorical questions Paul meant these as commands [NIC].

6:8 But[a] you wrong[b] and defraud,[c] and this[d] (your) brothers.

LEXICON—a. ἀλλά: 'but' [AB, He, HNTC, ICC; NRSV], 'but instead' [LB, REB], 'instead' [NAB, NIV, TEV, TNT], 'on the contrary' [NASB], 'nay' [Lns; KJV], 'and here you are' [NJB]. Coming after a question, ἀλλά has the meaning: 'nay but' [Ed].

b. pres. act. indic. of ἀδικέω: 'to (do) wrong' [HNTC, ICC, Lns; KJV, LB, NASB, NIV, NRSV, REB, TEV], 'to do injustice' [NJB], 'to practice injustice' [He], 'to commit injustice' [AB], 'to act unjustly' [TNT], 'to injure' [NAB]. See this word at 6:7.

c. pres. act. indic. of ἀποστερέω: 'to defraud' [Lns; KJV, NASB, NJB, NRSV, REB, TNT], 'to commit fraud' [AB], 'to rob' [TEV], 'to practice theft' [He], 'to cheat' [LB, NAB, NIV], 'to deprive others' [ICC]. See this word at 6:7.

d. οὗτος: 'this' [AB, ICC, Lns], 'that' [He; KJV, NASB], 'at that' [HNTC; NRSV, REB], 'even' [LB, TEV], 'very own (brothers)' [NAB], not explicit [NJB]. This word is also translated with implied information: 'you do this/it' [NIV, TNT]. Καὶ τοῦτο indicates a greater degree of wrong [Gdt]: you wrong and defraud your brothers! They were not only doing wrong and defrauding, they were not loving their brothers as well [TNTC]. See this word at 6:6.

QUESTION—Is this verse a rhetorical question or a statement of fact?

1. It is a statement [AB, Alf, Ed, GNT, He, Herm, HNTC, ICC, Lns, Rb; all versions]. The emphatic word 'you' shows that this is an assertion [Alf, Ed]. The words 'be defrauded' of 6:7 are elliptical requiring the words 'as our Lord commanded'. This is then followed by the emphatic 'you, on the contrary' [Alf].
2. This verse continues the questions of 6:7, otherwise the words 'or do you not know?' beginning 6:9 do not follow [My]: Why do you not let yourselves be wronged and defrauded, and, on your part, not do wrong and defraud?.

QUESTION—What word is emphasized in this verse?

The word 'you' is emphasized [Ed, Gdt, ICC, NIC2, Rb; LB, NAB, NASB, NIV, NRSV, REB, TEV]: it is you who wrong. Coming first it indicates indignation [Gdt].

DISCOURSE UNIT: 6:9–11 [ICC]. The topic is unrighteousness, a survival of a bad past which ought not to survive.

6:9a Or[a] know-you not that (the) unrighteous[b] will-inherit[c] not (the) kingdom[d] of-God?

LEXICON—a. ἤ (LN 89.139) (BAGD 1.d.α. p. 342): 'or' [AB, BAGD, HNTC, Lns; NASB], 'then' [He], not explicit [all versions except NASB]. This word indicates contrast: 'is this willfulness on your part, or is it that you do not know the consequences?' [ICC]. Here ἤ means 'or if you think you can act thus without danger' [Gdt]. Paul's thought process here is, 'I can't understand why you do not let yourselves be wronged unless it is that you do not know ...' [Lns].

b. ἄδικος (LN 88.20): 'unrighteous' [KJV, NASB], 'unrighteous person' [AB, HNTC, LN, Lns], 'wrongdoer' [ICC; NRSV, REB], 'unjust' [TNT], 'the unholy' [NAB], 'the wicked' [He; NIV, TEV], 'people who do evil' [NJB], 'those doing such things' [LB]. The fact that this word occurs here without an article focuses attention on the character of such people rather than grouping them in a class [Ed, Lns, TNTC]. Ἄδικος corresponds to the ἀδικέω 'to do wrong' of 6:7 and 6:8 [ICC, NIC2, Rb], and means 'wrongdoing' of any kind [ICC]. Paul uses the word 'unrighteous' in a purely moral sense and then follows it with specific examples [EGT, HNTC, ICC, My, NIC]. See this word at 6:1.

c. fut. act. indic. of κληρονομέω (LN 57.131; 57.138) (BAGD 2. p. 434): 'inherit' [AB, He, HNTC, LN (57.138), Lns; KJV, NASB, NIV, NJB, NRSV] 'to fall heir to' [NAB], 'to possess' [REB, TEV, TNT], 'to have a share in' [ICC; LB], 'to receive' [LN (57.131)], 'to acquire, obtain' [BAGD], 'come into possession of' [BAGD, LN (57.131)].

d. βασιλεία: 'kingdom' [AB, He, HNTC, ICC, Lns; all versions]. Here the word refers to the kingdom which will occur in the future [Ed, HNTC, ICC, Lns, NIC, NIC2, TG, Vn]. See this word at 4:20.

QUESTION—What is meant by κληρονομέω 'to inherit'?

It means 'to take possession of' as Israel took possession of Canaan. There is no thought of inheriting something from someone who has died [TH]. It means: 'to enter into full possession of' [TNTC]. It means 'to acquire, obtain, come into possession of something' especially in reference to participation in Messianic salvation [BAGD].

QUESTION—What answer is expected to this rhetorical question?

A positive answer is expected [Lns, TH; REB, TEV]: Surely you know that the unrighteous will not inherit the Kingdom of God.

DISCOURSE UNIT: 6:9b–20 [AB]. The topic is prostitution, a particular instance of immorality.

DISCOURSE UNIT: 6:9b–11 [AB]. The topic is the kingdom of God and immorality.

6:9b (Do) not be-deceived;[a]

LEXICON—a. pres. pass. indic. of πλανάω (LN 31.8) (BAGD 2.c.γ. p. 665): 'to be deceived' [LN, Lns; KJV, NASB, NIV, NRSV], 'to be misled' [HNTC, LN], 'to be led astray by false teachers' [ICC]. It is also translated actively: 'to fool oneself' [LB, TEV], 'to deceive oneself' [AB, BAGD, He; NAB], 'to make no mistake' [BAGD; NJB, REB, TNT]. The significance of the imperative in the present tense is that it means to stop doing something one is already doing: 'Stop deceiving yourselves!' [AB, EBC, NIC, NIC2]. They could be deceived by a wrong application of doctrine, by extending the idea of freedom to license, or by taking note of evil in others but not in themselves [AB].

neither (the) sexually-immoral[a] nor idolaters[b] nor adulterers[c] nor effeminate[d] nor homosexuals[e]

LEXICON—a. πόρνος: 'sexually immoral'. See this word at 5:9.

b. εἰδωλολάτρης: 'idolater'. See this word at 5:10.

c. μοιχός (LN **88.277**) (BAGD 1. p. 526): 'adulterer' [AB, BAGD, He, HNTC, ICC, **LN**, Lns; all versions], 'adulteress' [LN]. The word adultery refers specifically to married people having sexual relations outside of the marriage relationship [NIC2, TNTC].

d. μαλακός (LN **88.281**) (BAGD 2. p. 488): 'the effeminate' [He; KJV, NASB], 'effeminate man' [AB], 'homosexual' [**LN**], 'man who submits to homosexuality' [TNT], 'male prostitute' [NIV, NRSV], 'the self-indulgent' [NJB], 'sensualist' [ICC], 'catamite' [HNTC], 'voluptuary' [Lns]. This word is also joined with the following word and translated 'homosexual perverts' [TEV], 'sodomites' [NAB], 'sexual pervert' [REB], 'homosexuals' [LB]. It refers to the passive male member in homosexual intercourse [BAGD, Herm, HNTC, LN, Lns, NCBC, NIC, NIC2, TG, TH].

e. ἀρσενοκοίτης (LN **88.280**) (BAGD p. 109): 'homosexual' [He, **LN**; NASB], 'male homosexual' [AB], 'homosexual offender' [NIV], 'man who practice homosexuality' [BAGD; TNT], 'abuser of oneselves with mankind' [KJV], 'sodomite' [BAGD, HNTC, ICC; NJB, NRSV], 'pederast' [BAGD, Lns]. It refers to the active member of a homosexual relationship [Herm, HNTC, Lns, NCBC, NIC, NIC2, TG, TH].

6:10 nor thieves[a] nor (the) greedy,[b] nor drunkards, nor slanderers,[c] nor robbers[d] will-inherit (the) kingdom of-God.

LEXICON—a. κλέπτης (LN 57.233) (BAGD p. 434): 'thief' [AB, BAGD, He, HNTC, ICC, LN, Lns; all versions except TEV], 'people who steal' [TEV]. A κλέπτης 'thief' may differ from a ἅρπαξ 'robber' by the absence of violence from his crime [HNTC].

b. πλεονέκτης: 'greedy'. See this word at 5:10.

c. λοίδορος (LN **33.395**): 'slanderer'. See this word at 5:11.

d. ἅρπαξ (LN **57.239**): 'robber'. See this word at 5:10.

6:11 And these-things[a] some (of) you-were;

LEXICON—a. οὗτος (BAGD 1.b.ζ. 597): 'these things' [AB], 'such' [He, Lns; KJV, NAB, NASB, REB], 'like that' [TEV], 'just like that' [LB], 'of that kind' [NJB], 'of such vile sort' [ICC]. This word is also translated by a clause: 'that/this is what' [HNTC; NIV, NRSV, TNT], 'that is the sort of people' [BAGD]. It is noteworthy that the neuter 'these things' is used to refer to people. It serves to dramatically express contempt [EBC, EGT, ICC, My, NIC2, Rb] or horror: 'these abominations' [NIC2]. Ταῦτα 'these things' is not used here with contempt [Alf].

but[a] you-were-purified,[b]

LEXICON—a. ἀλλά: 'but' [AB, He, HNTC, ICC, Lns; all versions except LB], 'but now' [LB]. It is a strong adversative [NIC2]. It means: 'but moreover' and serves to bring out, with each repetition, a little greater emphasis on the contrast between their past and their new state [Gdt, ICC, TNTC]. This word is repeated before all three of the following verbs with the effect of emphasizing the contrast [Ed, EGT, Gdt, ICC, Lns, NIC2, TNTC].

b. aorist mid. indic. of ἀπολούω (LN **88.30**) (BAGD p. 96): 'to be purified' [He, **LN**], 'to be washed' [HNTC; KJV, NAB, NASB, NIV, NRSV, TNT], 'to have oneself washed' [Lns], 'to be washed clean' [NJB, REB], 'to be purified from sin' [TEV]. It is also translated with 'sins' as the subject: 'your sins are washed away' [LB]. And it is translated actively: 'to wash oneself' [AB, BAGD], 'to wash one's sins/pollutions away' [BAGD, ICC]. Here ἀπολούω is used figuratively meaning to cause someone to be morally pure [LN].

QUESTION—Does the middle voice have a passive sense or does it refer to something a person does in his own interest?

1. It has a passive sense [Herm, HNTC, NIC2, TH]: you were washed. This is a middle that functions like a passive and means: 'to be washed' rather than 'to have yourselves washed'. The verb occurs almost entirely in this mood [NIC2]. God, through the work of Christ and the Holy Spirit, removed them from among the wicked [NIC2].
2. It refers to something someone does for himself or in his own interest [AB, Alf, Ed, EGT, ICC, Lns, NCBC, NIC, Rb, TNTC, Vn]: you had yourselves washed, or you allowed yourselves to be washed, or you washed yourselves. It is a reflexive middle indicating that while the washing was not their own act, it required their participation [Ed]. The sense is, 'you washed away your sins' as in Acts 22:16 [ICC]. The middle voice means, 'you washed yourselves' [EBC], or 'you got/had yourselves washed' [EBC, Lns].

QUESTION—Does 'washing' refer to baptism?

1. 'Washing' alludes to baptism while not denying that the metaphor refers to purifying from sin [AB, Alf, BAGD, EBC, EGT, Gdt, Herm, HNTC, ICC, Lns, My, NCBC, NIC, Rb]. Paul refers to baptism which, in turn, refers to the cleansing from all sin and guilt [Lns]. They were spiritually cleansed from sin by God and this was symbolized in baptism [EBC, NCBC]. Their faith took voluntary and formal expression in baptism [EGT].
2. It is primarily a metaphor for purifying from sin [Ho, NIC2]. This verb is not used elsewhere in the NT to refer to baptism, though it is used with the word baptism in Acts 22:16. Paul uses εἰς 'into' not ἐν 'in' (as here) when baptism is collated with 'name' or 'Christ'. There is no other place where Paul asserts that one is both baptized 'in the name of Jesus Christ and in the Spirit of God'. These commentaries argue that Paul's primary reference here is not to the rite of baptism, but to the spiritual transformation affected by the Spirit of God [NIC2]. They were washed or purified from guilt and from sin's pollution [He].

but you-were-made-holy,[a] but you-were-justified[b]

LEXICON—a. aorist. pass. indic. of ἁγιάζω (LN 88.26) (BAGD 2. p. 8): 'to be made holy' [ICC, LN; TNT], 'to be sanctified' [AB, He, HNTC, Lns; KJV, NASB, NIV, NJB, NRSV], 'to be consecrated' [BAGD; NAB], 'to be dedicated to God' [REB, TEV], 'to be set apart for God' [Vn; LB], 'to be included in the inner circle of what is holy' [BAGD]. This term does not refer to ethical development but to an act of God in which he claimed them as his own people [HNTC]. The aorist aspect specifies a single act rather than a process [Gdt]. The terms 'made holy' and 'justified' explain the term 'to be washed' [Gdt, ICC, Lns]. See this word at 1:2.

b. aorist pass. indic. of δικαιόω (LN 56.34) (BAGD 3.c. p. 197): 'to be justified' [AB, He, HNTC, Lns; KJV, NAB, NASB, NIV, NJB, NRSV,

REB], 'to be acquitted, to be set free' [LN], 'to be put/made right with God' [TEV, TNT], 'to be made righteous' [ICC], 'to become pure' [BAGD]. This is also translated actively and reciprocally: 'he has accepted (you)' [LB]. It can mean 'to be made free' or 'to be made pure'. The verb is a legal term which refers to acquitted suspects. In Christian usage it refers to the act of God in which he gives believers a righteous standing and accepts them as his own on the basis of Christ's death [TNTC]. It means to be forgiven of sins and to be accepted as righteous [AB]. The aorist denotes a single act pointing to the initial moment when they were considered righteous before God [AB, Alf, Ed, Herm, HNTC, Ho, ICC, Lns, TNTC, Vn]. See this word, translated 'acquitted', at 4:4.

in[a] the name[b] of-the Lord Jesus Christ and in[c] the Spirit of our God.

TEXT—Some manuscripts omit Χριστοῦ 'Christ' after Ἰησοῦ 'Jesus'. It is included by GNT with a C rating, indicating difficulty in deciding whether to include it or not. AB, KJV, and REB omit this word.

LEXICON—a. ἐν with dative object: 'in' [He, HNTC, Lns; KJV, NAB, NASB, NIV, NJB, NRSV], 'through' [REB, TNT], 'by' [AB], 'by sharing in' [ICC]. This word is also joined with the word 'name' and translated 'by (the Lord Jesus Christ)' [TEV], 'because of (what the Lord Jesus Christ and the Spirit...have done)' [LB]. This preposition applies to all three verbs, 'to be washed, to be sanctified, to be justified' [Alf, EGT, Ho, Lns, NIC2].

b. ὄνομα: 'name' [AB, He, HNTC, ICC, Lns; all versions except LB, TEV], 'the Lord Jesus Christ' [LB, TEV]. 'In the name of' should be translated 'by the power of' [TH]. His name refers to his character while his title (as here) highlights his dignity [TNTC]. 'Name' refers to the 'authority' of Christ's person [EBC, NIC2]. For action to be done 'in the name of Christ' simply means 'to be done by Christ' [Ho; TEV].

c. ἐν with dative object: 'in' [HNTC, Lns; NAB, NASB, NRSV], 'by' [AB, He; KJV, NIV, TEV, TNT], 'through' [NJB, REB], 'by sharing in' [ICC], 'because of what (the Spirit of our God) has done for you' [LB]. The Spirit here should be taken as the means by which God accomplishes the work of Christ in a believer [NIC2]. 'Our' is inclusive: 'the God we worship or serve' [TG].

QUESTION—What is meant by 'in the name of the Lord Jesus Christ'?

Purification, sanctification, and justification were effected by Christ [Ho, NIC2, TH; TEV], by the power of Christ [TG, TH], because of our union with Christ [NCBC], on the authority of Christ [EBC], in the domain where Christ rules [NIC].

QUESTION—What is meant by 'in the Spirit of God'?

These were effected by the agency of God's Spirit [Alf, EBC, HNTC, Ho, NCBC, TH]. The Spirit is the means by which God accomplishes the work of Christ in a believer [Lns, NIC2].

DISCOURSE UNIT: 6:12–20 [Alf, EBC, Ed, EGT, Gdt, GNT, Herm, HNTC, Ho, ICC, Lns, My, NCBC, NIC, NIC2, TG, TH, TNTC]. The topic is Christian morality in sexual matters [EBC], the sanctity of the body [EGT, Lns], impurity [Gdt], glorifying God in the body [GNT], freedom and sexuality [Herm], the root of the trouble [HNTC], abuse of the principle of Christian liberty [Ho], fornication in the light of first principles [ICC], liberty and license [NCBC], fornication [NIC, TNTC], on going to prostitutes [NIC2], Christian morality [TG], the use of the body [TH].

DISCOURSE UNIT: 6:12–14 [AB, My]. The topic is God and the limitations of legality.

6:12 All-things are-lawful[a] for-me

LEXICON—a. pres. act. indic. of ἔξεστι (LN 71.1) (BAGD 2. p. 275): 'to be lawful' [Lns; KJV, NAB, NASB, NRSV], 'to be permissible' [AB, BAGD, He, HNTC; NIV, NJB, TNT], 'to be free to do' [REB], 'to be allowed to do' [TEV], 'to be able to do as one wants' [ICC; LB], 'to be possible' [BAGD, LN], 'to be proper' [BAGD]. It denotes the 'right to determine', and from that, 'authority' [NIC2].

QUESTION—Is this a quotation or a statement?

1. It is a quotation [Alf, Ed, Gdt, He, HNTC, Ho, ICC, Lns, My, NIC, NIC2, Rb, TG, TNTC; NAB, NIV, NJB, NRSV, REB, TEV, TNT]. 'For me' exemplifies what is true for any and every Christian [Lns, My]. Paul responds to the quotation by limiting its application in the following clause [Ed, ICC].

1.1. He is quoting from what he himself taught [Alf, Ed, Gdt, Ho, ICC, Lns, NCBC, NIC, Rb, TNTC]: As I say, 'All things are lawful for me'. This clause is in the form of a maxim [Alf, Ed, EGT, Gdt, Lns, NIC, Rb, TNTC], as seen in the lack of a conjunction and the use of the words 'to me' [Ed]. These are probably Paul's own words which had been misused by those to whom he is writing [ICC].

1.2. He is quoting an argument or slogan used by the Corinthians [He, HNTC, NCBC, NIC2, TG, TH; REB, TEV]: 'All things are lawful for me', you say. Those who misused this saying probably thought that since the body did not matter, they could do as they liked with it [TH]. These words were probably those of the gnostic party which trivialized material things such as the body and thereby encouraged moral indifference in that one could do with one's body as one pleased [HNTC]. Their error was in making absolute what Paul would have qualified with 'in Christ' [NIC2].

2. It is Paul's statement, not intended to quote anyone [KJV, LB, NASB].

QUESTION—How inclusive is πάντα 'all things'?

It refers to non-essential matters of the Christian life and not to matters of Christian ethics [Gdt, ICC, Lns, My, NIC, NIC2]. It refers to things like ceremonial matters or to distinctions having to do with clean and unclean things [Gdt, Ho]. It certainly would not refer to things like sexual immorality or deceit, but to things that are not wrong in themselves [ICC]. ‘All things’ applies to things that are not specifically commanded or forbidden by God [Lns]. This does not mean that a Christian is free to sin [NIC].

but not all-things are-beneficial;[a]

LEXICON—a. pres. act. indic. of συμφέρω (LN 65.44) (BAGD 2.a. p. 780): ‘to be beneficial’ [BAGD, Lns; NIV, NRSV, TNT], ‘to be advantageous’ [AB, BAGD, LN], ‘to be profitable’ [BAGD, He; NASB], ‘to be expedient’ [HNTC; KJV], ‘to be good for one’ [BAGD; LB, NAB, TEV], ‘to be better off’ [LN], ‘to do good’ [NJB, REB], ‘to do good to one’ [ICC], ‘to be useful, helpful’ [BAGD]. Here reference is possibly to the effect a person’s actions have on others [ICC, NIC2]. The reference to benefit is general, including both others and oneself [Ed, Lns, My].

all-things are-lawful for-me but I will-be-dominated[a] not by anything.

LEXICON—a. fut. pass. indic. of ἐξουσιάζω (LN 37.48) (BAGD p. 279): ‘to be dominated’ [Lns; NJB, NRSV], ‘to be mastered’ [BAGD; NASB, NIV], ‘to be overpowered’ [AB, HNTC], ‘to be brought under the power (of)’ [KJV, TNT], ‘to be enslaved’ [He], ‘to let oneself be enslaved’ [NAB], ‘to let something make one its slave’ [TEV], ‘to let something make free with one’ [REB], ‘to let something do as it likes with one’ [ICC], ‘to get such a grip on one that…’ [LB], ‘to be ruled by’ [LN]. Paul felt it imperative that he maintain the freedom he found in Christ, and this entailed the voluntary acceptance of self-discipline [AB]. Paul is alluding specifically to being controlled by sexual desires and practices [TG]. He applies this to himself with the purpose of applying it to Christians in general [Alf]. By becoming slave to a habit, he would be dominated by it [ICC].

6:13 Foods[a] for-the stomach[b] and the stomach for foods, but[c] God will-destroy[d] both this and those.

LEXICON—a. βρῶμα (BAGD 1 p. 148): ‘foods’ [HNTC, Lns; NJB], ‘meats’ [KJV], ‘food’ [AB, BAGD, He, ICC; all versions except KJV, LB, NJB], ‘appetite for food’ [LB]. See this word at 3:2.

b. κοιλία (LN **8.67**) (BAGD 1. 437): ‘stomach’ [AB, BAGD, ICC; all versions except KJV, REB], ‘belly’ [He, HNTC, **LN**, Lns; KJV, REB], ‘internal organs’ [LN]. The meaning is that each of these is specifically designed for the other [Ho].

c. δέ: ‘but’ [AB, Lns; KJV, NASB, NIV, TNT], ‘yes, but’ [TEV], ‘yet’ [ICC], ‘and’ [He, HNTC, NIC2; NAB, NJB, NRSV], ‘true; and’ [REB], not explicit [LB].

d. fut. act. indic. of καταργέω (LN 13.100) (BAGD 2. p. 417): ‘to destroy’ [He; KJV, NIV, NJB, NRSV], ‘to put an end to’ [ICC, **LN**; REB, TEV], ‘to abolish’ [BAGD, Lns; TNT], ‘to do away with’ [BAGD, HNTC; LB, NAB, NASB], ‘to nullify’ [AB], ‘to cause to come to an end, to cause to become nothing' [LN], 'to wipe out, set aside' [BAGD]. See this word translated as 'to reduce to nothing' at 1:28.

QUESTION—What words are implied in the phrase 'food for the stomach'?

Food is for the stomach [AB; NAB, NASB, NJB, REB, TEV, TNT], is meant for the stomach [NRSV], is intended for the stomach [He], belongs to the stomach [My].

QUESTION—Is this another quotation that Paul is citing?

1. This is a quotation used by some of the Corinthians [EBC, He, HNTC, Ho, NIC2, Rb, TG, TH, TNTC; NAB, NIV, NRSV, REB, TEV, TNT]: It is said, 'Food for the stomach and the stomach for food'. Apparently some were using the reasoning that since such physical activities as eating and digestion had nothing to do with Christian morals, so the physical activity of sex, whether moral or immoral, did not either [EBC, Ho, NIC2, Rb, TG].

1.1 The quotation stops before the words 'and God will destroy' [EBC, Ho, TH, TNTC; NAB, NIV, NRSV, REB, TEV, TNT]. It is best to follow the pattern of 6:12 where the quotation is given first and Paul's comment on the quote follows the words 'but' or 'and' [TH].

1.2 The quotation continues through the words 'God will destroy both one and the other' [He, HNTC, NIC2]: it is said, 'Food for the stomach and the stomach for food and God will destroy both one and the other'. The chiastic structure of the first half of the verse parallels that of the second better if the words 'and God will destroy both one and the other' are included as part of the quotation [NIC2].

2. This is simply another statement [ICC, Lns; KJV, NASB, NJB]: Food for the stomach and the stomach for food.

QUESTION—In what way will God destroy both the stomach and food?

This will occur after the Second Coming of Christ [EBC, Lns], and refers to the new status of the resurrection body where there will be no need for food or digestive processes [EBC, Lns]. The time of the end is intended [TG]. This will happen when earthly life ceases [HNTC, ICC] because food is broken down in the stomach and at death the stomach will be dissolved into its constituents [HNTC].

But[a] the body[b] (is) not for sexual-immorality[c]

LEXICON—a. δέ: 'but' [HNTC, Lns, NIC2; LB, NAB, NJB, REB], 'but it is not true that' [ICC], 'yet' [NASB], 'now' [KJV], 'at the same time' [He], not explicit [AB; NIV, NRSV, TEV, TNT]. There is a contrast between 'the stomach' and 'the body' in that whereas the stomach will be destroyed, the body is eternal [NIC2, Vn]. The argument that a person could eat what he wanted without affecting his spiritual life did not carry over into sexual behavior [HNTC].

b. σῶμα (LN 8.1): 'body' [AB, He, HNTC, ICC, LN, Lns; all versions]. The body is not like the belly, but is part of the very nature of man. It is not meant for destruction, but for eternity [NIC]. Paul used the word 'body' and not any of its parts since the whole body is involved in sexual relations [Lns]. See this word at 5:3.

c. πορνεία (LN 88.271): 'sexual immorality' [AB, LN; NIV, NJB, TEV], 'immorality' [He; NAB, NASB], 'fornication' [HNTC, ICC, LN, Lns; KJV, NRSV, REB], 'sexual vice' [TNT], 'sexual sin' [LB]. See this word at 5:1.

QUESTION—What words are implied in 'the body not for sexual immorality'?

The body is not to be used for sexual immorality [TEV], is not intended for sexual immorality [He], is not meant for sexual immorality [NRSV], is not made for sexual immorality [ICC; LB].

but for-the Lord, and the Lord for-the body;

QUESTION—What words are implied in the phrase 'the body (is) for the Lord' and what does it mean?

The body is to serve the Lord [ICC, TG; TEV]. The body belongs to the Lord [He, HNTC]. The body belongs to him and serves him [Gdt]. The body is to obey and honor the Lord [Lns]. The body is made for the Lord [LB]. This implies that the Lord owns the body. This is seen in 6:19 and 6:20 where the body is the home of the Holy Spirit, and it has been purchased at a price [NIC2].

QUESTION—To whom do the words 'the Lord' refer?

They refer to Jesus Christ [Lns, TG, TH].

QUESTION—What words are implied in the phrase 'the Lord for the body'?

The Lord belongs to the body [He, NIC2]. The Lord provides for the body [TEV]. The Lord is for the body to bless and save it [Lns]. The Lord is for the body to inhabit and glorify it [Gdt, ICC]. The Lord fills the body with himself [LB]. Although the two statements verbally match, the senses differ: the body's purpose is to serve the Lord, and the Lord controls or rules the body [TG].

6:14 and[a] God raised[b] the Lord also he-will-raise[c] us by his power.

LEXICON—a. δέ: 'and' [HNTC, ICC, Lns, NIC2; KJV, NRSV], 'now' [He; NASB], 'but' [AB], not explicit [all other versions].

b. aorist act. indic. of ἐγείρω (LN **23.94**) (BAGD 1.a.β. p. 214): 'to raise' [AB, BAGD, He, HNTC, Lns; NASB, NRSV, TNT], 'to raise up' [KJV, NAB, NJB], 'to raise from the dead' [ICC; LB, NIV, REB, TEV], 'to cause to live again' [**LN**], 'to raise to life, to make live again' [LN].

c. fut. act. indic. of ἐξεγείρω (LN **23.94**) (BAGD 2. p. 273): 'to raise' [AB; NAB, NIV, NRSV, REB, TEV, TNT], 'to raise up' [He, HNTC, ICC, Lns; KJV, NASB, NJB], 'to cause to live again' [**LN**], 'to raise from the dead' [BAGD; LB]. This focuses attention on the resurrection of the body, contrasting it with the physical stomach which will be destroyed [TNTC]. The Lord's body did not decay in the grave but ours do. This is the significance of the choice of verb to describe our resurrection. We will be raised ἐξ 'out of' that corruption [EBC, Lns] There is no significant difference intended in the use of the two verbs ἐγείρω and ἐξεγείρω [Alf,

HNTC, ICC, My; KJV, NJB, NRSV, TNT]. As the Lord was raised bodily, so the bodies of Christians will be raised [EBC].

QUESTION—What is the point of this statement?

This indicates the importance of the body. Since it is to be raised, it cannot be included with things that will be destroyed [ICC, TNTC]. It serves as a grounds for saying that the body is for the Lord and the Lord is for the body [NIC2]. The Lord's care for the body is shown by his resurrecting it [Ho].

QUESTION—With what verb is διὰ τῆς δυνάμεως 'by his power' connected?

1. This is connected with the last verb [ICC, Lns; NAB, NJB, NRSV, REB, TEV]: he will raise us by his power. It was necessary to remind the Corinthians of God's power so as to enable them to believe in their future resurrection [ICC].
2. This is connected with both verbs [EBC; LB, NIV]. The same power used to raise the Lord will be used to raise us [EBC].

DISCOURSE UNIT: 6:15–20 [AB]. The topic is the Christian body.

DISCOURSE UNIT: 6:15–18 [AB]. The topic is reasons for not being joined to a prostitute.

6:15 Know-you not that your bodies are members[a] of-Christ?

LEXICON—a. μέλος (LN 63.17) (BAGD 3. p. 501): 'members' [BAGD, He, HNTC, ICC, LN, Lns; all versions except LB, REB, TEV, TNT], 'parts of the body' [AB; TEV, TNT], 'parts and members' [LB], 'limbs and organs' [REB], 'parts, limbs' [BAGD]. As the church is the body of Christ (Rom. 12:5; Eph. 5:30), so members of that body are members of Christ [Gdt, NIC]. The bodies of Christians are members of Christ and belong to him because he purchased them with his blood [Ho].

QUESTION—What is the function of this rhetorical question?

It functions as a positive statement [NIC, NIC2, TG, TH; TEV]: you know that your bodies are members of Christ. It points out something that they should already know [HNTC, Ho, Lns, NIC2, TNTC], but act as though they did not know [HNTC]. He now reinforces the principle that the body is for the Lord (6:13) [ICC].

QUESTION—In what way are their bodies members of Christ?

Since the church is considered the body of Christ, the individual members are members of that body [NIC, TH]. They belong to Christ and are united to him, partaking of his life [Ho].

Having-taken[a] therefore the members of Christ should-I-make[b] (them) members of-a-prostitute[c]?

LEXICON—a. aorist act. participle of αἴρω (LN 15.203) (BAGD 4. p. 24): 'to take' [AB, BAGD, HNTC; all versions except NASB, TNT], 'to take away' [HNTC, ICC; NASB, TNT], 'to remove' [Lns], not explicit [He]. It means 'to take away' [Alf, Ed, Gdt, ICC, NIC2, Rb, TNTC, Vn]. These members must first be removed from Christ before they can be joined to a harlot [EGT, Lns]. Paul intends that uniting with a prostitute takes members away from Christ who belong to him [ICC]. Paul's point in asking this is to show the impossibility of the two relationships coexisting [Ed, Ho]. Because such a sin affects a man's personality, it destroys his union with Christ [Ed].

b. aorist. act. subj. of ποιέω (LN 13.9) (BAGD I.b.ι. p. 682): 'to make' [AB, He, HNTC, ICC, LN, Lns; KJV, NAB, NASB, NRSV], 'to make someone or something into something' [BAGD], 'to cause to be, to make to be' [LN]. This word was also joined with the word 'members' and translated 'to join to' [LB, NJB], 'to unite with' [NIV], 'to make (them) over to' [REB], 'to make (it) a part of' [TEV, TNT].

c. πόρνη (LN 88.275) (BAGD 1. p. 693): 'prostitute' [BAGD, He, LN; LB, NAB, NIV, NRSV], 'the body of a prostitute' [AB; NJB, TEV, TNT], 'harlot' [BAGD, HNTC, ICC, Lns; KJV, NASB, REB].

Never[a]!

LEXICON—a. opt. aorist deponent of μή γίνομαι(BAGD I.3.a. p. 158): 'Never!' [He; LB, NIV, NRSV, REB, TNT], 'No!' [HNTC], 'God forbid!' [BAGD, Lns; KJV, NAB], 'May it never be!' [NASB], 'Impossible!' [TEV], 'Certainly not!' [AB], 'Out of the question!' [NJB], 'Away with so dreadful a thought!' [ICC], 'May it not happen!' [Rb], 'by no means, far from it' [BAGD]. Μή γένοιτο expresses horror [ICC, Rb]. It is a strong rejection of this suggestion [TNTC]. For a person joined to Christ through the resurrection, it is unthinkable that he should be taken away from the body of Christ and joined to the body of a prostitute [NIC2].

6:16 Or[a] know-you not that he-who joins-himself[b] to-the prostitute is one body (with her)?

TEXT—GNT includes ἤ 'or' in parentheses, indicating uncertainty about its validity as part of the text.

LEXICON—a. ἤ: 'or' [AB, He, HNTC, ICC, Lns; NASB, NJB, TEV], 'and' [LB], not explicit [all other versions].

b. pres. mid./pass. participle of κολλάω (LN 34.22) (BAGD 2.b.α. p. 441): 'to join oneself to' [AB, BAGD, LN, Lns; LB, NASB, REB, TNT], 'to join' [BAGD, LN], 'to be joined to' [KJV, NAB], 'to join one's body to' [TEV], 'to attach oneself to' [NJB], 'to be united with/to' [He; NRSV], 'to unite oneself to/with' [HNTC; NIV], 'become a part of' [LN], 'to cling to, to associate with' [BAGD]. This verb is also translated as a noun phrase: 'the union of (a man with his harlot)' [ICC]. A form of this verb is used in the Septuagint translation of Gen. 2:24 where it talks of a man cleaving to his wife [NCBC]. 'Joins' here refers to sexual relations [EGT, Lns, My, TG]. The present participle does not infer continual union, but the idea of 'as often as' he does this, he becomes one body with her [NIC].

QUESTION—What is implied by ἤ 'or'?

It implies the condition 'or if you deny the validity of what I have just said' [Gdt, Lns, My], 'or if you object to my saying it like this' [EGT]. This introduces a further explanation of how a person becomes a member of a prostitute [NIC]. It justifies the expression 'member of a prostitute' [EGT, NIC].

QUESTION—What is the significance of the article with the word 'prostitute'?

It refers to the particular prostitute to whom Paul is referring [Lns, My]. It means the prostitute presupposed in the condition [Alf]. It means 'his prostitute' [Ed, ICC]. It signifies a generic reference to prostitutes [Alf, NIC, NIC2].

QUESTION—From where do the words 'with her' come?

They are implied logically from the words 'joined to' [AB, Alf, EGT, Gdt, He, HNTC, Lns; NAB, NASB, NIV, NJB, NRSV, REB, TEV, TNT].

QUESTION—What is meant by this statement?

'Body' indicates more than simply a physical organism. It is a whole complex personality. The word 'flesh' must mean the same as 'body' here by the figure of synecdoche [Ed]. The two become partakers of a common life [Ho]. While 'becoming one flesh' entails more than physical union, Paul's focus here is limited to the physical joining of two bodies [NIC2, TNTC]. This is a sexual union with a person who is not a member of Christ and not destined for resurrection [NIC2].

QUESTION—What is the function of this rhetorical question?

It functions to reproach the Corinthians [ICC]: You should know that, etc. It functions to remind them of something they already knew [Herm, TG, TNTC; REB]: Surely you know, etc. It does not request information, but serves to emphasize Paul's argument [TH].

For[a] it-says,[b] the two will-become[c] one flesh.[d]

LEXICON—a. γάρ (LN 89.23): 'for' [AB, He, HNTC, LN, Lns; all versions except NAB, NJB, TEV], 'since' [NJB], 'I am not exaggerating, for' [ICC], not explicit [NAB, TEV].

b. pres. act. indic. of φημί (LN 33.69) (BAGD 1.c. p. 856): 'it says' [AB, BAGD], 'it is said' [NIV, NJB, NRSV], 'the Scripture says' [He, HNTC, ICC; NAB, REB, TNT], 'the scripture says quite plainly' [TEV], 'he says' [Lns; KJV, NASB], 'God tells (us)' [LB]. Φήμι used without a subject indicates a Scriptural quote [BAGD]. The Scripture quoted is Gen. 2:24 in the Septuagint [AB, EBC, NIC2, TH].

c. εἴμι εἰς (LN 13.51) (BAGD III.2. p. 225): 'to become' [AB, BAGD, He, HNTC, ICC, LN; all versions except KJV, NRSV], 'to be' [Lns; KJV, NRSV]. This word is also translated reciprocally: '(one)...shall be formed from (the two)' [He]. Εἴμι εἰς 'to be into' is an idiom meaning to change from one state to another [LN].

d. σάρξ: 'flesh' [AB, HNTC, ICC, Lns; all versions except LB, TEV, TNT], 'body' [TEV], 'person' [LB], 'fleshly creature' [He]. This word is also joined with 'one' and translated 'one' [TNT].

QUESTION—What relationship is indicated by γάρ 'for'?

It indicates that the following quote functions to explain what he has just said [NIC2]. It indicates the grounds for saying that such a person is one body with her [ICC, Lns, NIC2].

QUESTION—Who or what is the actor of the verb 'to say'?

The actor is God [Alf, Ed, EGT, ICC, My, NCBC, Rb, Vn; LB], the Scriptures [He, Herm, HNTC, ICC, NCBC, Rb, TH; NAB, REB, TEV, TNT]. It should be taken as an impersonal construction: 'it is said' [AB, NIC2; NIV, NJB, NRSV].

6:17 But he-who is-united[a] to-the Lord is one spirit (with him).

LEXICON—a. pres. pass. participle of κολλάω: 'to be united with/to' [He; NRSV], 'to be joined to' [KJV, NAB]. This word is also translated actively: 'to unite oneself to/with' [HNTC; NIV], 'to join oneself to' [AB, Lns; NASB, REB, TEV, TNT], 'attach oneself to' [NJB], 'to give oneself to' [LB]. This word is also translated as a noun phrase: 'the union with' [ICC]. In 6:16 Paul used this word to refer to physical union. Here he uses it to refer to spiritual union with the Lord [TNTC]. 'To be united to' refers to the act of believing in him [EGT]. See this word at 6:16.

QUESTION—What relationship is indicated by δέ 'but'?

It signals a contrastive relationship [Lns, NIC, NIC2; all versions]. The results of fornication are now contrasted with union with Christ [NIC, NIC2].

QUESTION—What is meant by πνεῦμα 'spirit'?

1. It refers to spiritual union with the Lord [AB, Alf, EBC, Ed, EGT, Gdt, ICC, Lns, My, NCBC, NIC, Rb, TG, TNTC, Vn; TEV]. While this union is accomplished by the Spirit, Paul is referring to the nature and realm of the union, using the word 'spirit' without the article [EGT]. The word 'spirit' contrasts with 'flesh' of 6:16. The believer is united to the Lord by the Spirit (see 6:19, 20) and thereby becomes one spirit with him [NIC2]. The idea is that they become spiritually one [TG; REB, TEV]. We become one spirit with Him, that is, mystically he is in us and we are in him, and it is his will which governs both. But both maintain their own identity [Lns]. They have the mind of Christ and so react as Christ would react [TNTC]. Πνεῦμα refers to a complex personality on a supernatural plane [Ed]. Physical union with a prostitute is logically impossible because the believer's body belongs to the Lord and that body has become a member of Christ [NIC2].
2. It refers to the Holy Spirit [Ho]. The meaning is that they all have the same principle of life, the Holy Spirit being that principle [Ho].

QUESTION—What further words are implied in the words ‘to the Lord is one spirit’?

The words ‘with him’ are implied [EGT, Gdt, He, HNTC, Lns; NAB, NASB, NIV, NRSV, REB, TEV]: to the Lord is one spirit with him. See a similar question at 6:16 regarding the phrase ‘with her’.

6:18 **Flee-from[a] sexual-immorality.[b]**

LEXICON—a. φεύγω (LN **13.161**; 15.61) (BAGD 3. p. 856): ‘to flee from’ [BAGD, He, HNTC; NIV], ‘to flee’ [LN, Lns; KJV, NASB], ‘to run away’ [LN], ‘to run from’ [LB], ‘to shun’ [AB, BAGD; NAB, NRSV, TNT], ‘to avoid’ [BAGD, **LN**; TEV], ‘to keep away from’ [NJB], ‘to have nothing to do with’ [REB], ‘to not stop to parley with, to turn and fly’ [ICC]. It means to avoid doing something which is dangerous [LN]. The present imperative indicates habitual action [EBC, ICC, NIC, Rb, TNTC] or continuous action [NIC2]: keep running from.

b. πορνεία (LN 88.271): ‘sexual immorality’. See this word at 5:1 and 6:13.

QUESTION—What is the significance of the absence of a connector to introduce this verse?

It gives the logical conclusion to all that Paul has to say about this subject [NIC; LB]: therefore, flee from sexual immorality. It functions to mark the urgency of Paul’s words [Alf, ICC, Lns, My].

Every[a] (other) sin[b] which a-man commits[c] is outside[d] the body;

LEXICON—a. πάς (LN **58.28**): ‘every’ [AB, HNTC, Lns; KJV, NRSV], ‘every kind of’ [LN]. This word is also joined with the following ‘but’ and translated ‘every other’ [He; NAB, NASB, TNT], ‘all other’ [NIV, NJB, REB], ‘any other’ [TEV], ‘no other’ [ICC; LB].

b. ἁμαρτήμα (LN 88.290) (BAGD p. 42): ‘sin’ [AB, BAGD, He, HNTC, ICC, LN; all versions], ‘sinful act’ [Lns], ‘wrongdoing’ [LN], ‘transgression’ [BAGD]. It means a violation of the law and will of God [LN].

c. ποιέω (LN 90.45; 42.7) (BAGD I.1.c.γ. p. 682): ‘to commit’ [AB, BAGD, He, HNTC; all versions except KJV, LB], ‘to do’ [BAGD, ICC, LN, Lns; KJV], ‘to carry out, to perform’ [LN], ‘to practice’ [BAGD, LN], ‘to be guilty of (sins and vices)’ [BAGD], not explicit [LB].

d. ἐκτός (LN **89.121**) (BAGD 2.a. p 246): ‘outside’ [AB, BAGD, He, HNTC, Lns; all versions except KJV, LB, TEV] ‘without’ [KJV], ‘independent of’ [**LN**], ‘apart from’ [LN]. This word is also translated as a verb: ‘to not affect (the body)’ [LB, TEV], ‘to not injure (the body)’ [ICC].

QUESTION—What is meant by ἐκτὸς τοῦ σώματος ‘outside the body’?

Other sins, such as drunkenness, involve things that come from outside, while the sexual appetite comes from inside the body [TNTC]. Sins like drunkenness and gluttony, unlike sexual sins, are introduced from outside the body and are sinful in their effect rather than in their act [Alf]. ‘Outside the body’ must mean: ‘their purpose is outside the body’ [NIC].

but the-one committing-sexual-immorality[a] sins[b] against[c] his-own body.

LEXICON—a. pres. act. participle of πορνεύω (LN **88.271**) (BAGD 1. p. 693): 'to commit sexual immorality' [AB], 'to be guilty of sexual immorality' [TEV], 'to commit immorality' [**LN**], 'to commit fornication' [HNTC, LN, Lns; KJV], 'to sin sexually' [NIV], 'to practice sexual vice' [TNT], 'to engage in illicit sex' [LN], 'to sin' [LB], 'to prostitute, to practice prostitution or sexual immorality' [BAGD]. This word is also translated as an agent noun: 'the fornicator' [He, ICC; NAB, NRSV, REB], 'the immoral man' [NASB], 'the sexually immoral person' [NJB]. It means to engage in sexual immorality of any kind, often implying prostitution [LN].

b. ἁμαρτάνω (LN 88.289) (BAGD 4.b. p. 42): 'to sin' [AB, BAGD, He, HNTC, ICC, LN, Lns; all versions], 'to do wrong' [BAGD], 'to engage in wrongdoing' [LN]. It refers to offenses against the moral law of God [BAGD].

c. εἰς with accusative object (LN 90.23): 'against' [He, HNTC, ICC, Lns; all versions], 'within' [AB], 'concerning, with respect to, with reference to' [LN]. Ἁμαρτάνω εἰς is the common idiom meaning 'to sin against' [ICC, NIC2]. It is possible, however, that the meaning of 'within' is intended to contrast with ἐκτός 'outside' of the previous clause [AB, NIC2].

QUESTION—What is the meaning of δέ 'but'?

The word δέ gives an exception to the word 'every' of the previous clause [He, ICC, NIC2; LB, NAB, NASB, NIV, NJB, REB, TEV, TNT].

QUESTION—What does it mean 'to sin against one's own body'?

Sinning against one's body needs to be seen in the light of the body being for the Lord and of what Paul says in 7:4, that the wife rules the husband's body. When a man unites with a prostitute, he breaks his union with the Lord and lets her have the mastery over his body. This is a sin against his body [NIC2]. Fornication is a sin against the body because 'the body is for the Lord'. Fornication destroys this relationship and divests the person of eternal life [EGT, ICC]. It means that a person's personality will be affected [Ed, Vn]. It means that fornication is unique in its effects on the body—more on the moral and spiritual aspects than on the physical [Ho]. Fornication makes one's body the instrument of sin, destroys his life, damages his personality, and ruins its function of fulfilling God's design for it [Vn].

DISCOURSE UNIT: 6:19–20 [AB]. The topic is glorifying God as a temple of the Spirit.

6:19 Or know-you not that your body is (a) temple[a] of-the Holy Spirit (who is) in[b] you

LEXICON—a. ναός (LN **7.15**) (BAGD 2. p. 533): 'temple' [AB, BAGD, He, HNTC, ICC, **LN**; all versions except LB], 'home' [LB], 'sanctuary' [LN, Lns]. Ναός refers to the temple sanctuary and not to the entire temple complex as the word ἱερόν does [TNTC]. It indicates the parts of the temple known as the holy and most holy places [NIC]. See this word at 3:16.

b. ἐν: 'in' [Lns], 'within' [He; NRSV], 'among' [AB]. This word is also translated as an adjective: 'indwelling' [REB]. It is also translated as a clause: 'who lives within/in' [LB, TEV], 'who is in/within' [HNTC; KJV, NAB, NASB, NIV, NJB, TNT], 'who makes his home in' [ICC].

QUESTION—What is the meaning of ἤ 'or'?

It means 'or in case you doubt that' [My], 'or if you do not realize how horrible fornication is' [EGT], 'or if you deny that fornication is against the body' [Gdt]. It gives the theological justification for the command 'Shun immorality!' (6:18) [NIC2].

QUESTION—Does the phrase τὸ σῶμα ὑμῶν'your (plural) body' refer to individual bodies of believers or to all of them forming the body of Christ?

1. It refers to the individual bodies of believers [Alf, EBC, Ed, He, Herm, HNTC, ICC, My, NCBC, NIC2, Rb, TH, TNTC]. 'Ev 'in' here is distributive and refers to the presence of the Holy Spirit in each believer [NIC2]. The word 'body' is singular indicating that each individual believer is a temple [Alf, HNTC, My, TNTC]. In 3:16 Paul was referring to the church as a whole [HNTC, TNTC].
2. It refers to all of the believers forming the one body of Christ [AB, BAGD, NIC]. It is important to realize that the pronoun 'you' in this and the following verse is plural meaning 'among you'. Paul's emphasis here is on the body of believers as being the sphere in which the Holy Spirit works in the world [AB]. The word 'body' is plural in 6:15 indicating that their bodies were members of Christ. Here 'body' is singular as is 'temple' indicating that the Holy Spirit lives in the church as a whole [NIC].

QUESTION—How are the nouns related in the genitive construction ναὸς τοῦ ἁγίου πνεύματος 'a temple of the Holy Spirit'?

It means a temple which the Holy Spirit possesses [Lns], temple where the Holy Spirit lives [EBC, Ho, NIC2, TH], a temple for the Holy Spirit [TG].

QUESTION—What is the function of the rhetorical question?

It serves to make a positive affirmation reminding them of something they already knew [TH; NAB]: you must know that, etc. The contents of the question serve to reinforce and further explain the theology of the body of 6:13–17 [NIC2]. The question serves to emphasize Paul's argument that they should know this [TNTC].

whom you-have from God,

QUESTION—What is the meaning of this phrase?

It means that the indwelling Spirit was a direct gift from God himself [ICC, Lns, NCBC, TH, TNTC; TEV]. The emphasis here is on source rather than possession—the Holy Spirit came from God [Gdt, ICC, NIC2].

and you-are not your-own?

QUESTION—What is the meaning and implication of this clause?

The clause means that a believer belongs to God, not to himself [TNTC]. It implies that they had no right to do anything which would negate the ownership of the Holy Spirit [Alf].

QUESTION—Is the phrase 'and you are not your own' connected with the question or is it a new affirmation?

1. The phrase is connected with the question [Ed, EGT, GNT, He, HNTC, My, NIC2, TH; KJV, NASB, NRSV, TNT]: ...whom you have from God and you are not your own? This phrase refers back to the ὅτι 'that' of the first part of the question and adds another question to it [Ed, EGT, My]: do you know that...and (that) you are not your own?
2. The phrase forms a new affirmation [AB, Gdt, ICC, Lns; LB, NAB, NIV, NJB, REB, TEV]: ...whom you have from God? You are not your own. And what is more, you are God's property [ICC].

6:20 For[a] you-were-bought[b] with-a-price;[c]

LEXICON—a. γάρ (LN 89.23): 'for' [AB, LN, Lns; KJV, LB, NASB, NRSV], 'no, for' [HNTC], 'then' [NJB], not explicit [He, ICC; all other versions].

b. aorist pass. indic. of ἀγοράζω (LN 37.131) (BAGD 2. p. 13): 'to be bought' [AB, BAGD, He, HNTC, ICC, LN, Lns; all versions except LB, TEV], 'to be purchased' [BAGD, LN; NAB], 'to be acquired as property' [BAGD]. This word is also translated actively: 'to buy' [LB, TEV], 'to pay' [ICC]. The aorist tense points to Christ's work on the cross [EBC], to our purchase by God with the blood of his Son [Lns].

c. τιμή (LN 57.161) (BAGD 1. 817): 'price' [AB, BAGD, HNTC, LN, Lns; all versions except LB], 'great price' [LB], 'high price' [ICC], 'ransom' [He], 'amount, cost' [LN], 'value' [BAGD]. The price was the death of God's son (See this word at 1 Pet. 1:18–19; Rev. 5:9) [TG]. The price was the blood of Christ [Alf, BAGD, Ho, NCBC].

QUESTION—What relationship is indicated by γάρ 'for'?

It indicates the grounds for saying that they were not their own [Alf, Gdt, Herm, Lns, My, NIC2, TNTC]. It was a legitimate action for the Holy Spirit to possess the believer because the purchase price had been paid [Gdt].

QUESTION—Who is the actor of this passive verb?

The actor is God [Lns, NIC2, TG, TNTC; TEV], or Christ [EBC, Ed, TH].

QUESTION—What figure is indicated by the words 'bought with a price'?

1. The figure is that of a ransom whereby a slave is set free by the payment of a price [BAGD, Ed, HNTC, Ho, TNTC]. We were held in bondage until a ransom was paid, the blood of Christ, which set us free from sin's power and condemnation [Ho]. The idea of ransom is seen in many places in the OT such as Exod. 6:6; 13:13; Ruth 4:4; Ps. 103:4; Isa. 43:1 [HNTC].
2. The figure is that of a slave market in which a slave is purchased to become the slave of another [Alf, EBC, Herm, ICC, NIC, NIC2, TG, Vn].

This refers to a change of ownership and is different from paying a ransom [ICC]. The slave of sin is purchased by God with the blood of Christ [EBC]. The point is belonging to a new master [Herm]. It is the right of possession of the new owner [Alf, NIC2], stressing the concept that the 'body is for the Lord' [NIC2]. It is the loss of rights of the person so purchased [NIC].

so[a] glorify[b] God in[c] your body.[d]

TEXT—Some manuscripts include καὶ ἐν τῷ πνεύματι ὑμῶν 'and in your spirit' or καὶ ἐν τῷ πνεύματι ὑμῶν ἅτινά ἐστιν τοῦ θεοῦ 'and in your spirit which are God's' after ἐντῷ σώματι ὑμών 'in your body'. Both are omitted by GNT with an A rating, indicating that the text is certain. Only KJV includes the words, 'and in your spirit which are God's'.

LEXICON—a. δή (LN 91:6) (BAGD 2. p. 178): 'so' [LB, NAB, NRSV, TEV], 'therefore' [AB, BAGD, He; KJV, NASB, NIV], 'then' [BAGD, LN; REB, TNT], 'very well, then' [HNTC], 'by all means, then' [Lns], 'indeed' [LN], 'that is why' [NJB], 'surely you are bound' [ICC], 'now' [BAGD]. Δή is used with commands to give them greater urgency [Alf, BAGD, Ed, ICC, My, NIC2, TNTC]. It is a marker of relatively weak emphasis [LN]. 'Therefore' is not an exact translation. Better would be: 'Be sure to (glorify)' or 'I urge you to (glorify)' [ICC]. Δή is a shortened form of ἤδη 'already' and has the implication of doing something so quickly that it is already done [TNTC].

b. aorist act. impera. of δοχάζω (LN 87.24; 87.8) (BAGD 1. 204): 'to glorify' [He, HNTC, LN (87.24), Lns; KJV, NAB, NASB, NRSV], 'to give glory back to' [LB], 'to honor' [BAGD, LN (87.8); NIV, REB], 'to praise' [AB, BAGD], 'to use (one's body) for the glory of' [ICC; TEV], 'to magnify' [BAGD]. 'Glorify God' means to honor him and to behave in such a way that others will honor him too [Ho].

c. ἐν with dative object: 'in' [AB, HNTC, Lns; KJV, NAB, NASB, NRSV, REB, TNT], 'with' [NIV], 'by' [He]. This word is translated as indicating instrument: 'to use (one's body for the glory of)' [ICC; LB, NJB, TEV]. Here it probably means 'in' [Ed, EGT, NIC2] as in the personal activities in which you engage [NIC2]. The body is the sphere within which He honors God [Ed]. It has here an instrumental sense indicating that we are to use our bodies so people will see that our bodies belong to God, they are to be used to obey him [Lns].

d. σῶμα (LN **8.1**): 'body' [AB, He, HNTC, ICC, **LN**, Lns; all versions]. It indicates the physical body [LN].

QUESTION—What is meant by glorifying God in the body?

We should use our bodies so that others may see that we belong to God. We do not use them for sinful acts, but only to do God's will [Lns]. It implies that we do not use them for sexual immorality [HNTC]. We should live a chaste life [EGT, My, NIC2].

DISCOURSE UNIT: 7:1–16:12 [NIC2]. The topic is a response to the Corinthian letter. Paul is now responding to a letter written by the Corinthians which was probably in response to his previous letter to him mentioned in 5:9. In the letter they were taking exception to his position on point after point. He addresses the questions one by one, usually introducing his replies with the formula περὶ δέ 'now concerning'. In each instance he takes exception to their position.

DISCOURSE UNIT: 7:1–16:4 [HNTC, NCBC]. The topic is a letter from Corinth [HNTC], Paul's answers to a letter from Corinth [NCBC].

DISCOURSE UNIT: 7:1–15:58 [Herm]. The topic is answers to questions.

DISCOURSE UNIT: 7:1–14:40 [EBC]. The topic is Paul's answers to questions raised by the church. This section comprises Paul's reply to questions raised in a letter the Corinthians had written to him.

DISCOURSE UNIT: 7:1–11:1 [ICC]. The topic is a reply to the Corinthian letter.

DISCOURSE UNIT: 7:1–40 [AB, Alf, EBC, Ed, Gdt, Herm, HNTC, ICC, Lns, NCBC, NIC2, TNTC]. The topic is the question from Corinth concerning marriage [AB], instruction concerning marriage [EBC], marriage and celibacy [Ed, Gdt], celibacy and marriage in the passing world [Herm], questions regarding marriage [HNTC, Lns, NCBC], marriage and its problems [ICC], marriage and related matters [NIC2]. It is best to see this section as comprised of two subsections 7:1–24, in which Paul addresses matters related to those who are already married, and 7:25–38 in which he takes up matters concerning those who are not yet married [NIC2].

DISCOURSE UNIT: 7:1–24 [Ho]. The topic is instruction concerning marriage and other social relations.

DISCOURSE UNIT: 7:1–16 [EBC, GNT, NIC2, TG, TH]. The topic is problems concerning marriage [GNT], Christian obligation in marriage [EBC], the married and formerly married staying as they are [NIC2], questions about marriage [TG].

DISCOURSE UNIT: 7:1–9 [EGT]. The topic is marriage or celibacy.

DISCOURSE UNIT: 7:1–7 [AB, Ed, Herm, HNTC, ICC, Lns, NIC2, TNTC]. The topic is sexual intercourse [AB], behavior within marriage [HNTC], celibacy is good, but marriage is natural [ICC], general instructions regarding marrying or remaining unmarried [Lns], concerning marriage [NIC], no abstinence within marriage [NIC2], the general principle [TNTC]. Paul does not have a low view of marriage. He is not discussing his view of an ideal marriage. He is answering the questions of believers who lived in the sinful city of Corinth [ICC].

DISCOURSE UNIT: 7:1–4 [AB]. The topic is the mutuality of marriage.

7:1 Now[a] concerning[b] the-matters-about-which you-wrote,

LEXICON—a. δέ: 'now' [Lns; all versions except TNT], 'and now' [TNT], 'but now' [ICC], 'with reference to' [AB], not explicit [He, HNTC].

b. περί with genitive object (LN 89.6) (BAGD 1.h. p. 645): 'concerning' [BAGD, LN, Lns; KJV, NASB, NRSV, TNT], 'with reference to' [AB, BAGD; NAB, NIV, REB], 'about' [HNTC; LB, NJB], 'to deal with' [TEV], 'for' [REB], 'to come to' [He], 'as to' [ICC], 'in relation to, with regard to' [LN].

QUESTION—What relationship is indicated by δέ 'now'?

It indicates transition to another subject [Alf, My; all versions]: now. It may also signal a contrastive relationship to what he has just written [Ed, ICC], that was unlawful, but this is, in general, lawful [ICC]. Περὶ δὲ 'now concerning' signals a new section in Paul's letter. From this point he uses this formula five more times (7:25; 8:1; 12:1; 16:1; 16:12) where they introduce other matters brought up in the Corinthian letter to him [NIC2].

(it is) good[a] for-a-man not to-touch[b] a-woman.

LEXICON—a. καλός (LN 88.4) (BAGD 3.b. p. 400): 'good' [AB, He, HNTC, LN; KJV, LB, NASB, NIV, TNT], 'morally good' [BAGD], 'a good thing' [NJB, REB], 'excellent' [Lns], 'laudable' [ICC], 'well' [NRSV], '(a man is) better off' [NAB], 'pleasing to God, contributing to salvation' [BAGD], 'fine, praiseworthy' [LN]. This word is also translated as a verb: 'to do well' [TEV]. It means 'good', but not necessary or morally better [TNTC]. It is an understatement meaning 'right' or 'necessary' [AB]. It means 'expedient' [Alf, Ho], 'profitable' [He, Ho], 'becoming' and 'worthy' [Gdt], 'better' [Herm], 'valuable' or 'fortunate for' [He], 'desirable' or 'to one's advantage' [NIC2].

b. pres. mid. infin. of ἅπτω (LN **34.70**) (BAGD 2.a. p. 102): 'to touch' [HNTC, Lns; KJV, NASB, NJB, NRSV], 'to take hold of, to hold' [BAGD], 'to approach' [He], 'to have intercourse with' [BAGD; REB, TNT], 'to have sexual relations with' [AB], 'to have relations with' [NAB], 'to marry' [**LN**; LB, NIV, TEV]. This word is also taken with 'woman' and translated positively: 'continence (is an excellent thing)' [ICC].

QUESTION—Is this a quote from the letter from the Corinthians or Paul's own statement?

1. This is a quote from the letter from the Corinthians [AB, HNTC, NCBC, NIC2, TNTC; NRSV, REB]: You say, "It is good for a man not to touch a woman" or: Now about the question, "Is it good for a man not to touch a woman?" It is better to see this as a quote from the Corinthian letter because in 1 Tim. 4:3 Paul opposed the prohibition to marry and in Eph. 5:25–33 he takes a very positive stance toward it. Further, the abruptness of the quote following his mention of the letter (similar to the form at 6:12 where there may be a quote) versus the more formal introduction of new topics elsewhere, points to these words being a quote [NIC2]. It is

probably a quote, but it has difficulties. Paul seems to approve of it but then goes on to not only approve marriage but to oppose abstinence within it [HNTC]. It could be a quote or a question [TNTC].

2. This is Paul's own statement [Alf, EBC, Ed, Gdt, He, Herm, Ho, ICC, Lns, My, TG; KJV, NAB, NASB, NIV, NJB, TEV, TNT]. Paul is stating that it is good to live in celibacy [Gdt, ICC]. Because elsewhere in Scripture marriage is portrayed as right and desirable, we must interpret Paul's meaning as being: 'Under the present circumstances it is good not to marry' [Ho]. Paul is replying to a question about this matter [Ed, ICC] and his answer naturally comes as a statement, not as a quotation [Ed].

QUESTION—What is meant by 'touch a woman'?

1. It means to have sexual intercourse with a woman [AB, BAGD, EBC, Herm, HNTC, Lns, My, NIC2, TG, TH; REB, TNT]. This idiom is used nine times in Greek writings over a period of six centuries and in each case refers to having sexual intercourse and not to marrying [NIC2]. Here it refers to sexual intercourse in legitimate marriage relations [EBC, Lns]. Paul's reference should be understood as referring to both within and outside marriage [AB].
2. It means to marry a woman [EGT, Gdt, Ho, ICC, LN, NIC, TNTC, Vn; LB, NIV, TEV]. It is an idiom meaning to marry a woman [LN].

QUESTION—If this is a query from the Corinthians, what are they asking?

1. Is it good to live a celibate life and not get married? [EBC, Ed, EGT, Gdt, He, Ho, ICC, Lns, My, NIC, Rb, TG, TH, TNTC, Vn]. The question is not about what should happen in marriage, but about whether one should marry or not [NIC].
2. Is it good to avoid sexual intercourse? [AB, Alf, NCBC, NIC2]. This question applies to celibacy within and outside of marriage [AB]. They wondered about marriage, whether to avoid it or to break it off if already contracted [Alf].

7:2 But[a] because-of[b] the sexual-immoralities[c]

LEXICON—a. δε: 'but' [all versions except KJV, NJB, REB], 'Yes, but' [HNTC], 'rather' [REB], 'yet' [He, Lns; NJB], 'nevertheless' [KJV], 'now' [AB]. This word is also translated with implied information: 'but this ideal state is not for everyone, and' [ICC].

b. διά with accusative object (LN 89.26): 'because of' [AB, LN; NASB, NRSV], 'because' [HNTC; LB, TEV, TNT], 'on account of' [LN, Lns], 'since' [NIV], 'as' [ICC], 'in the face of' [REB]. This preposition is also translated as a verb: 'to avoid' [He; KJV, NAB, NJB]. It means 'to prevent sexual immorality' [Ho, NIC].

c. πορνεία: 'sexual immorality' [AB; NASB], 'immorality' [NAB, NIV, NJB], 'case of sexual immorality' [NRSV], 'case of fornication' [HNTC, Lns; KJV], 'so much immorality' [REB, TEV], 'so much sexual vice' [TNT], 'the danger of misconduct' [He], 'temptation' [ICC]. This word is also translated as a verb: 'to fall back into sin' [LB]. See this word at 5:1; 6:13, 18.

QUESTION—What relationship is indicated by δέ 'but'?

It indicates contrast [Gdt, NIC2, TNTC; all versions]: but. Although celibacy is honorable it should not be the rule [Alf, EGT, Gdt]. The reason why the rule of 7:1 cannot be applied to all circumstances is given in 7:2 [NIC]. Celibacy is good as you say, but there are temptations. What Paul is saying is that marriage is the norm [Ho, TNTC].

QUESTION—What is the function of the plural word πορνείας 'immoralities'?

The plural refers to various cases of immorality [Alf, Ed, Gdt, HNTC, ICC, My, NIC, TNTC; NRSV, REB, TEV, TNT]. In the context Paul is talking about prostitution. The lack of control within marriage is mentioned in 7:5. It is possible that husbands, being deprived of sexual relations within marriage, were going to prostitutes. This accounts for the plural which, with the definite article, indicates immorality which was actually occurring [NIC2]. The plural plus the article refers to acts of immorality that would occur if marriage were forbidden or should stop [Lns].

each-man let-him-have[a] his-own wife and each-woman let-her-have her-own husband.

LEXICON—a. pres. act. impera. of ἔχω (BAGD 2.b.α. p. 332): 'to have' [AB, He, HNTC, ICC, Lns; all versions except LB], 'to be married' [BAGD], 'to be married...to have' [LB]. 'To have a wife' is an idiom meaning either to have her sexually (Deut. 28:30; Isa. 13:16), to be married, or to be in on-going sexual relations with a man or woman (5:1; 7:29; Mark 6:18; John 4:18). There is no known evidence that it means 'to take a wife'. In this context these two verbs (to have) imply full reciprocal sexual relations [NIC2]. The idiom means: 'to be in a married state' [TH]. See this word at 5:1.

QUESTION—What is implied by the words 'his own' and 'her own'?

These words imply monogamy [AB, NIC, NIC2, TNTC, Vn].

QUESTION—Is this statement intended as a command?

1. It is intended as a command [Alf, Ed, EGT, Gdt, ICC, Lns, NIC, NIC2, TNTC]: Each man must have his own wife. The pervasiveness of immorality made it imperative for all who did not have the gift of celibacy to marry [Ed]. While saying 'each man' and 'each woman', Paul has in mind the exceptions he will speak about in 7:7 and 7:25–38. Paul is not giving rules for marriage in general, but is answering the questions that have been asked him [Gdt].
2. It is intended as a recommendation [He]. If it were an imperative, it would invalidate 7:1b. Yet it is more of a recommendation than a simple concession and is intended for all who lack the gift of celibacy [He].
3. It is intended as a contra-expectation [Herm]. Although it is good for a man not to touch a woman, yet, to avoid immorality, a man may have his wife and a wife may have her husband [Herm].

QUESTION—Is there any difference in meaning between ἑαυτοῦ 'his own', and ἴδιον 'her own'?

They both have the same meaning, the difference is only stylistic [Lns]. Perhaps ἑαυτοῦ 'his own' indicates subjection [EGT, NIC], while ἴδιον 'her own' simply indicates oneness [NIC].

7:3 The husband let-him-fulfill[a] the duty[b] to-the wife, and likewise[c] also the wife to-(her) husband.

LEXICON—a. pres. act. impera. of ἀποδίδωμι (LN 57.153) (BAGD 1. p. 90): 'to fulfill' [BAGD, He, LN; NAB, NASB, NIV, TEV], 'to render' [HNTC, ICC, LN, Lns; KJV, TNT], 'to give' [LB, NJB, NRSV, REB], 'to pay (the debt)' [AB, LN].

b. ὀφειλή (LN **71.24**) (BAGD 2. p. 598): 'duty' [BAGD, LN; NASB], 'marital duty' [**LN**; NIV], 'duty as a husband' [TEV], 'conjugal obligations/rights/duties' [He; NAB, NRSV], 'due of conjugal duties' [BAGD], 'her due' [HNTC, Lns; TNT], 'what she has a right to expect' [NJB], 'what is due to her' [REB], 'what is due' [ICC; TNT], 'all that is her right as a married woman' [LB], 'the debt he owes' [AB], 'due benevolence' [KJV], 'what one should do' [LN], 'one's due, obligation' [BAGD]. The present imperative means habitual duty [AB, TNTC].

c. ὁμοίως (LN 64.1) (BAGD p. 567): 'likewise' [AB, BAGD, LN, Lns; KJV, NASB, NIV, NRSV], 'in the same way' [BAGD, HNTC], '(do) the same' [LB], 'similarly' [BAGD, He; TNT], 'equally' [REB], 'so' [BAGD; NJB], 'like, such as, similar' [LN], not explicit [ICC; NAB, TEV].

QUESTION—What is meant by 'fulfilling their duty' to each other?

It implies that couples are sexually indebted to each other [NIC2]. The idea is not the granting of a favor, but the discharging of an obligation [ICC, Vn]. It means that the continuing of intercourse in marriage is not optional but obligatory [AB]. Paul is countering the ascetic attitude and practices some of the Corinthians [NIC].

QUESTION—What is the significance of repeating this for the woman?

It shows that the obligation is equally applicable to the woman [AB]. The word 'likewise' as well as the parallel wording show that both are under the same obligation regarding this debt [Lns].

7:4 The wife does-not have-authority-over[a] her-own body but the husband (does), and similarly also the husband does-not have-authority-over his-own body but the wife (does).

LEXICON—a. pres. act. indic. of ἐξουσιάζω (BAGD p. 279): 'to have authority over' [HNTC, Lns; NASB, NJB, TNT], 'to have power over' [BAGD], 'to rule over' [NRSV], 'to have jurisdiction over' [AB], 'to have full right to' [LB], 'to be the master of' [TEV], 'to have power of' [KJV], 'to belong to someone' [NAB], 'to belong to someone alone' [NIV], 'to claim as one's own' [REB], 'to dispose of' [He], 'to do as one likes respecting (one's body)' [ICC]. It means 'to have authority over' to the extent that one does with that as he/she wills. But the emphasis in this context is not on the one in authority doing as he pleases, but on the fact that the person him/herself does not have authority over his/her own body [NIC2]. She is bound to respect the sexual needs of her partner [TG].

QUESTION—What relationship does this verse have to the context?

This verse supplies the reason why the husband and wife must fulfill their marital duties to each other [Alf, Gdt, Lns, NIC2]. This relationship is signaled by adding 'for' [LB, NRSV].

QUESTION—What is this verse teaching?

It teaches that both partners are to respect the sexual needs of the other [TG]. Because the wife has just been mentioned in the preceding clause, the order is changed here so that the wife is mentioned first [ICC, Vn]. If the problem addressed was one of 'spiritual women' who were depriving their husbands sexually, then the primary emphasis is to her to give herself sexually to her husband. But Paul is also teaching here the full reciprocity of sex relations in marriage [NIC2]. Traditional Jewish teaching only addressed the husband's authority over his wife's body. This goes beyond to fill in the other side of the picture [TG].

DISCOURSE UNIT: 7:5–7 [AB]. The topic is special instances of abstention.

7:5 Do-not deprive[a] each-other,

LEXICON—a. pres. act. impera. of ἀποστερέω (LN 57.47) (BAGD p. 99): 'to deprive' [AB, BAGD, LN, Lns; NAB, NASB, NIV, NJB, NRSV, TNT], 'to refuse' [He], 'to defraud' [KJV], 'to rob' [HNTC]. Because of delicacy, the object is left unexpressed [Ed]. This word is also translated with implied information: 'to refuse (these) rights to' [LB], 'to deny oneself to' [REB, TEV]. It is also translated positively: 'to abandon the attempt to combine celibacy with matrimony' [ICC]. It indicates the taking away something that rightfully belongs to someone else [NIC2]. The meaning of the present imperative is to stop doing something already in progress [EBC, ICC, NIC2; NASB]. See this word also at 6:7.

QUESTION—What does this clause refer to?

This is the positive counterpart of 7:3 [Lns]. Each belongs to the other, so withholding one's body is an act of fraud [TNTC]. The meaning is that they should not abstain from sexual intercourse [TG]. Marriage must be real and attempts on the part of one partner to spiritualize the meaning of the word is to rob the other [HNTC]. Some were attempting a kind of celibacy within their marriage [EBC].

unless-perhaps[a] by agreement[b] for (a) time,[c] in-order-that[d] you-may-devote-yourselves[e] to prayer[f]

TEXT—Some manuscripts include τῇ νηστείᾳ καί 'to fasting and' before 'to prayer'. They are omitted by GNT with an A rating, indicating that the text is certain. Only KJV includes the words.

LEXICON—a. εἰ μήτι (BAGD VI.9. p. 220): 'unless perhaps' [BAGD; NAB, TNT], 'except perhaps' [NRSV], 'except as may be' [Lns], 'except' [AB; KJV, NASB, NIV, NJB, REB], 'the only exception to this rule (would be)' [LB], 'unless' [TEV], 'unless it be' [He, HNTC], 'unless indeed' [BAGD]. Εἰ μήτι indicates that the following is a hypothetical concession to the command not to deprive each other [NIC2].

b. σύμφωνος (LN **31.15**) (BAGD 2. p. 781): 'agreement' [AB, BAGD, HNTC, LN, Lns; LB, NASB, NRSV], 'mutual consent' [He; NAB, NIV, NJB], 'consent' [KJV]. This word is also translated as a verb: 'to agree to' [ICC, **LN**; REB, TEV, TNT]. The first condition of this concession is that both agree to it [NIC2], in which case it is not robbery or deprivation [HNTC].

c. καιρός (LN 67.78) (BAGD 1. p. 394): 'time' [LN; KJV, NAB, NASB, NIV, REB, TNT], 'limited period/time' [AB, BAGD, He, HNTC, ICC; LB, NJB], 'set time' [NRSV], 'while' [TEV], 'term' [Lns], 'period of time' [BAGD, LN].

d. ἵνα (LN 89.59): 'in order that' [HNTC, LN], 'in order to' [LN; TEV, TNT], 'so that' [LN; LB, NIV], 'that' [He, Lns; KJV, NASB], 'to' [AB; NAB, NJB, NRSV, REB], 'to have the intention of' [ICC].

e. aorist act. subj. of σχολάζω (LN **67.81**) (BAGD 1. p. 797): 'to devote oneself to' [BAGD, LN; NAB, NASB, NIV, NRSV, REB], 'to devote oneself the better to' [ICC], 'to give time to' [BAGD, **LN**], 'to give oneself to' [KJV], 'to busy oneself with' [BAGD], 'to give oneself more completely to' [LB], 'to be free for' [HNTC; TNT], 'to have the leisure for' [Lns], 'to have time for' [AB], 'to leave oneself free for' [NJB], 'to spend one's time in' [TEV], 'to be occupied in' [He]. It means to do something actively and earnestly for a period of time [LN]. The aorist refers to a specific occasion [Ed, Rb] rather than a permanent practice [Rb]. Paul does not mean that at normal times the couple would not pray. This refers to special periods of concentrated prayer for a set time [AB, Ed, My, NIC2, Vn].

f. προσευχή (LN 33.178)(BAGD 1. p. 713): 'prayer' [AB, BAGD, He, HNTC, ICC, LN, Lns; all versions].

QUESTION—What relationship is indicated by ἵνα 'in order that'?

It indicates the purpose of depriving each other for a time [Alf, EBC, Ed, Gdt, HNTC, Ho, ICC, Lns, My, NIC, NIC2, TG, TH; LB, NAB, NASB, NIV, REB, TNT]. There are three conditions for which abstinence may be permitted: it is by mutual agreement, it is for a limited time, and its purpose is for prayer [Ed, Gdt, HNTC, Ho, ICC, Lns, NIC, TG].

and[a] again you-be-together,[b]

LEXICON—a. καί: 'and' [AB, Lns; KJV, NASB], 'and then' [HNTC, ICC; NRSV, TNT], 'then' [He; NAB, NIV], 'and afterwards' [NJB, REB], 'afterwards' [LB], 'but' [TEV].

b. pres. act. subj. of εἰμί (BAGD III.1.a.ζ. p. 288): ‘to be’. The phrase εἰμί ἐπὶ τὸ αὐτό ‘to be at the same’ is translated ‘to be together’ [BAGD, HNTC, Lns], ‘to come together’ [He, ICC; KJV, LB, NASB, NIV, NJB, NRSV, REB, TNT], ‘to return to one another’ [NAB], ‘to resume normal marital relations’ [TEV], ‘to resume the same marriage relations’ [AB]. This phrase is a euphemistic expression for sexual union [AB, BAGD, Lns; TEV].

QUESTION—To what is the clause ‘you be together again’ related?

This clause is still dependent on the ἵνα ‘in order that’ in the preceding clause [My]: you agree to abstain *in order that* you may devote yourselves to prayer and (after a limited time, object achieved) come together again. It is a second purpose [Alf, Ed, EGT, Ho, ICC, Lns, My, NIC, TH]. It is awkward to take it as a purpose for depriving each other and most English versions turn it into an imperative [He; KJV, LB, NAB, NIV, NRSV, TEV]. The purpose for the separation is for prayer, and the purpose for agreeing that the separation be for a limited time is for coming together again [HNTC, NIC2]. Paul’s emphasis in this verse is on this clause as is seen in the following purpose clause [NIC2].

lest Satan tempt[a] you because-of[b] your lack-of-self-control.[c]

LEXICON—a. pres. act. subj. of πειράζω (LN 88.308) (BAGD 2.d. p. 640): ‘to tempt’ [BAGD, HNTC, LN, Lns; all versions except NJB, TEV, TNT], ‘to put to the test’ [AB, BAGD], ‘to put temptation in one’s way’ [TNT], ‘to take advantage and put someone to the test’ [NJB], ‘to trap’ [LN], ‘to lead into temptation’ [He, LN], ‘to use something to someone’s ruin’ [ICC]. This verb is also translated as a noun: ‘temptation’ [TEV]. The present tense indicates ‘may not keep on tempting you’ [Rb]. Satan would stir up strife [Lns] and tempt them to break their marriage vow [My]. Paul was referring to something which was happening among the Corinthians, the sexual immorality to which he referred in 7:2 [NIC2].

b. διά with accusative object: ‘because of’ [LB, NASB, NIV, NRSV, TEV, TNT], ‘on account of’ [AB, HNTC, Lns], ‘for’ [KJV], ‘through’ [NAB, REB]. This word is also translated ‘(Satan) may take advantage of’ [NJB], ‘by counting on’ [He], ‘a permanent opportunity of using’. This word is also translated as a verb: ‘to use (one’s incontinence)’ [ICC]. Their lack of self-control would be the basis on which Satan could tempt them [My, NIC2].

c. ἀκρασία (LN **88.91**) (BAGD p. 33): ‘lack of self-control’ [AB, BAGD, **LN**; all versions except KJV], ‘self-indulgence’ [BAGD], ‘incontinence/incontinency’ [HNTC, ICC, Lns; KJV], ‘want of self-control’ [He]. Here it means ‘uncontrollable desire for sexual relations’. If they did not find satisfaction in marriage, Satan would use it to tempt them to express it in sexual immorality [HNTC].

QUESTION—What relationship is indicated by ἵνα μή 'lest, in order that not'?

1. It indicates the purpose of 'not depriving each other' [ICC, NIC2, TG; probably REB, TEV, TNT]: do not deprive each other lest Satan tempt you. This clause is the point of the whole verse. It connects back to the imperative 'do not deprive each other' by way of the purpose clause 'that you may come together again'. The reason they must not deprive each other is so that their spouse will not be vulnerable to the Tempter [NIC2].
2. It is the purpose of 'coming together again' [AB, Alf, EGT, HNTC, Lns, My, TNTC; NAB, NIV, NRSV]: come together again lest Satan tempt you. Paul is probably indicating that it is by the normal practice of sexual intercourse in marriage that the couple may escape the temptation to be unfaithful to each other or unfaithful in their prayer life [AB].

7:6 But[a] I-say this by-way-of[b] concession[c] not by-way-of command.[d]

LEXICON—a. δέ (LN 89.124): 'but' [He, HNTC, ICC, LN; KJV, NASB], 'now' [AB, Lns], not explicit [all other versions]. 'But' is clearly contrastive with the preceding concession 'unless perhaps by agreement for a time that you may devote yourselves to prayer' [NIC2].

b. κατά with accusative object (BAGD II.5. p. 407): 'by way of' [AB, He, HNTC, ICC, Lns; all versions except KJV, NIV, TEV, TNT], 'as (a)' [BAGD; NIV, TEV, TNT], 'by' [KJV].

c. συγγνώμη (LN **13.141**) (BAGD p. 773): 'concession' [AB, BAGD, He, HNTC, LN, Lns; all versions except KJV, LB, TEV], 'permission' [**LN**; KJV, TEV], 'permission and indulgence' [ICC], 'indulgence, pardon' [BAGD]. This word is also translated as a verb: '(you) certainly may (marry)' [LB]. When a command is given and an exception to it is specified, it is right to refer to the exception as a 'concession' [Lns].

d. ἐπιταγή (LN 33.326) (BAGD p. 302): 'command' [AB, BAGD, HNTC, LN, Lns; NAB, NASB, NIV, NRSV, REB], 'injunction and command' [ICC], 'injunction' [BAGD], 'commandment' [KJV], 'order' [BAGD, He, LN; NJB, TEV, TNT], 'instruction, decree, ordinance' [LN], not explicit [LB].

QUESTION—To what does the word τοῦτο 'this' refer?

1. It refers to the whole preceding paragraph, particularly to the advice to continue sexual relations or to be married of 7:2 [EBC, Ed, EGT, Herm, Ho, ICC, NIC, Rb, TG, TNTC, Vn]. 'This' refers to 7:2. Although marriage is desirable and compatible with God's creation plan, it is not obligatory. This interpretation is supported by 7:7 where he says he wishes all men were single like him, while he recognizes that each man has his own gift [EBC]. 'This' cannot refer to 7:5 which is clearly a command, 'do not deprive each other'. Because 7:4 is a statement of fact, 'this' does not refer to that verse. It must therefore refer to 7:2 and 7:3 [NIC]. 'This' refers to 7:1–5 [Ed, Herm, ICC, TNTC]. Paul has spelled out the duties of all who are married, but he does not command that all

should be married [TNTC]. Marriage is permitted, not commanded, since Paul would wish that all were as he was [Ho].

2. It refers only to the exception in 7:5 where they agree to abstain in order to pray [He, HNTC, Lns, NCBC, NIC2]: unless perhaps by agreement for a time that you may devote yourselves to prayer...but I say this by way of concession. If we say that 'this' refers to 7:2 or 7:2–5, it makes the reference jump over a clear concession, 'unless perhaps...to devote yourselves', to an antecedent that is not a clear concession. In the context Paul was arguing against their practice of abstinence from sexual relations in marriage because it led to immorality. He rather commands that they stop depriving each other except it be for times of prayer, but this exception was a conceding to their viewpoint, not a command from him [NIC2].
3. It refers to the imperative against depriving one another [Alf, My]. 'My direction to not deprive each other should be taken as an indulgence to your lack of self-control, not as a command' [My].

7:7 But[a] I-wish[b] (that) all men[c] were as even I-myself (am);

TEXT—Instead of δέ 'but', some manuscripts have γάρ 'for'. GNT selects 'but' with a B rating, indicating that the text is almost certain. The reading 'for' is taken only by KJV.

LEXICON—a. δέ (LN 89.124; 89.94): 'but' [NRSV], 'yet' [Lns; NASB], 'rather' [AB], 'actually' [TEV], 'still' [ICC; NJB], not explicit [all other versions].

b. θέλω (LN 25.1): 'to wish' [AB, He, LN; LB, NASB, NIV, NRSV, TNT], 'to prefer' [TEV], 'to like' [NJB, REB], 'to desire' [HNTC, LN], '(I) would (that)' [Lns; KJV]. It is also translated as a noun: 'preference' [ICC; NAB]. Θέλω δέ expresses an unfulfilled wish: 'I wish, but it is impossible' [Lns]. The present tense here indicates a wish that is capable of being realized, while an imperfect tense would express something unobtainable [HNTC].

c. ἄνθρωπος: 'men' [He, HNTC, Lns; KJV, NASB, NIV, TNT], 'people' [AB, ICC, NIC2], 'we' [LB], 'each (one)' [NAB, NRSV, TEV], 'each person' [REB], 'everyone' [NJB].

QUESTION—What relationship is indicated by δέ 'but'?

1. It indicates contrast [AB, EGT, Gdt, Lns; NASB, NRSV]. Paul advises marriage in general but, in spite of that, he wishes that they were like him [Gdt].
2. It indicates transition [Herm, NIC2]. It is sequential rather than adversative [NIC2].

QUESTION—To what personal state is Paul referring in this clause?

1. He is referring to his unmarried state [Alf, EBC, Ed, EGT, Gdt, Herm, ICC, My, NIC, NIC2, TG, TNTC, Vn]. Paul is probably referring to the power to remain celibate, freedom from sexual need, which he sees as his gift [NIC2]. Given the sexually immoral surroundings of Corinth and

Ephesus, Paul was referring more to the gift to remain celibate than to remain unmarried. Without this gift it was a serious mistake not to marry [ICC].

2. He is referring to self-control, which is a gift for both married and unmarried people [HNTC, Lns]. Paul is not referring to staying unmarried, or to the cessation of the sexual side of marriage, or to celibacy for everyone. None of these qualify as a charismatic gift from God. He is referring to self-control of the sexual life both outside of and within marriage [Lns].

but[a] each has his-own gift[b] from God, the-one this, the other that.

LEXICON—a. ἀλλά (LN 89.125) (BAGD 2. p. 38): 'but' [BAGD, He, HNTC, ICC, LN; all versions except NAB, NASB], 'still' [AB; NAB], 'however' [NASB], 'nevertheless' [Lns], 'yet' [BAGD]. This statement modifies Paul's wish, he could not use his own gift to dictate what God would give others [Vn].

b. χάρισμα (LN 57.103) (BAGD 2. p. 879): 'gift' [BAGD, HNTC, ICC; all versions except LB, REB, TNT], 'spiritual gift' [TNT], 'charismatic gift' [Lns], 'the gift God has granted him' [REB], 'endowment' [He], 'gracious gift' [NIC2], 'individual gift' [AB], 'gift of a husband or wife' [LB]. Here it indicates a special gift from God to an individual [ICC]. It refers to the power to be continent in sexual matters [BAGD]. See this word at 1:7.

QUESTION—What is the other gift?

The Corinthians were asking for celibacy in marriage and Paul was saying that celibacy was for the unmarried, and it was a gracious gift. In the light of this and of the present verse that each has his own gift, there is good reason to conclude that sexual life in marriage is the other gift [NIC2]. The gift is an inclination [EBC] or aptitude [Gdt] to either pursue marriage or to refrain from it [EBC, Ed, Gdt, ICC, NCBC, TNTC]. There is not the gift of the desire to marry since nature itself supplies that [Lns]. Some have the gift of celibacy, but others do not and are advised to marry, since they have some other compensating gift [HNTC]. It is any special gift for service in Christ's kingdom [EGT].

DISCOURSE UNIT: 7:8–40 [ICC]. The topic is advice to different classes.

DISCOURSE UNIT: 7:8–24 [HNTC, Lns]. The topic is Christian and mixed marriages, slavery and freedom [HNTC], special groups and the question regarding marriage [Lns]. This section forms a unit since it is all about special groups in the Corinthian congregation [Lns].

DISCOURSE UNIT: 7:8–16 [Herm]. The topic is advice concerning the unmarried, the widowed, and those living in mixed marriages.

DISCOURSE UNIT: 7:8–9 [AB, Ed, Lns, NCBC, NIC2, TNTC]. The topic is remarriage of widows and widowers [AB], the case of a Christian who has not been married or is in a state of widowhood [Ed], the unmarried and the widows

[Lns, TNTC], advice to the unmarried [NCBC], either singleness or marriage for the unmarried and widows [NIC2]. This section is the application of the principle expressed in 7:1 [Ho, TNTC]. Here at 7:8, again at 7:10, and once again at 7:12 is the formula: 'Now I say to…', indicating that these are a series of situations to which Paul will apply the same rule: 'Stay as you are' [NIC2].

7:8 Now[a] I-say to-the unmarried[b] and to-the widows,[c]

LEXICON—a. δέ (LN 89.94; 89.124): 'now' [AB, Lns; NIV, TEV], 'but' [NASB], 'so' [LB], 'therefore' [He; KJV], not explicit [NAB, NJB, NRSV, REB, TNT]. It is connective and parallels the δέ at 7:10 and 7:12 [Alf, Gdt, Lns, NIC2].

b. ἄγαμος (LN **34.76**) (BAGD p. 4): 'unmarried' [ICC, **LN**, Lns; all versions except LB, NAB], 'those who are unmarried' [HNTC; LB, NAB], 'widowers' [AB, NIC2], 'the celibate' [He]. Ἄγαμος 'unmarried' can refer to either sex [BAGD].

c. χήρα (LN 10.61) (BAGD 1. p. 881): 'widows' [AB, BAGD, He, HNTC, ICC, LN, Lns; all versions].

QUESTION—To whom does the word ἄγαμος 'unmarried' refer?

1. It refers to both unmarried men and women [Alf, BAGD, Ed, Gdt, HNTC, Ho, Lns, My, NIC, TG, TNTC, Vn]. The term refers to all unmarried people contrasted with the 'married' of 7:10. This also requires the words 'and widows' to mean, 'and especially widows' [Alf, Ed, Ho, Lns, My]. 'Widows' are probably added because 'the unmarried' would naturally be taken to refer to 'those who were never married' and therefore 'widows' needed to be specified [Alf]. Because the word 'married' in 7:10 refers to all classes, it is best to take a similar reference to all classes here [Ho].
2. It refers only to unmarried men [EGT, ICC, TH]. Ἄγαμος is masculine and therefore refers to unmarried men, whether bachelors or widowers. The case of maidens is discussed later beginning at 7:25.
3. It refers only to widowers [AB, NIC2]. Koiné Greek has a word for 'widower', but it is not used in the New Testament. Ἄγαμος serves in its place which Paul typically uses to denote those who were formerly married but are not at the present. In this passage Paul refers 12 times to husband and wife in mutual terms. If ἄγαμος refers to all unmarried people, why add the term 'widows'? It is best, therefore, to take his meaning here as being 'demarried' men, that is, widowers [NIC2].

(it is) good[a] for-them if they-remain[b] as I-also[c] (am);

LEXICON—a. καλός (LN 65.43; 88.4) (BAGD 3.c. p. 400): 'good' [AB, BAGD, He, LN (88.4); KJV, NASB, NIV, NJB, TNT], 'well' [NAB, NRSV], 'better' [LN (65.43); LB, TEV], 'excellent' [Lns], 'a good thing' [HNTC; REB], 'an excellent thing' [ICC]. He doesn't mean 'better', but 'good' [Rb]. See this word at 7:1.

b. aorist act. subj. of μένω (LN 68.11) (BAGD 1.b. p. 504): 'to remain' [AB, BAGD, Lns; NASB, TNT], 'to abide' [KJV], 'to remain in, to continue, to keep on' [LN]. This word is also translated with implied information: 'to stay/remain as one is' [BAGD, HNTC, LN; NAB, NJB, REB], 'to stay/remain unmarried' [LB, NIV, NRSV], 'to continue to live alone' [TEV], 'to remain in their condition' [He], 'to remain single' [ICC]. The aorist tense indicates a life-long, final decision [ICC].

c. κἀγώ (BAGD 3.c. p. 386): 'I also' [ICC], 'even as myself' [AB], 'even as I' [Lns; KJV, NASB], 'even as I do myself' [NAB], 'just as I am' [LB], 'I am' [BAGD; NIV, NRSV, TNT], 'I do' [TEV], 'I myself' [He, HNTC], 'indeed I am' [EGT], 'like me' [NJB, REB]. The καί 'and' is redundant in comparisons [BAGD].

QUESTION—To what state was Paul referring?

He was referring to the state of being unmarried [Alf, HNTC, My, NCBC, NIC, NIC2, TG, TH; LB, NIV, NRSV]. Paul may be associating himself either with the unmarried or with widowers [NCBC].

QUESTION—Had Paul been previously married?

1. Yes, he probably had been married [HNTC, NIC2]. There were few unmarried rabbis, and marriage was probably obligatory for a Jewish man [HNTC].
2. No, he probably had not been married [Alf, Ed, Gdt, ICC, My, Vn]. The rule that a member of the Sanhedrin had to be a married man and a father was not a strong one [ICC].

QUESTION—Did Paul intend this to apply to all people in general?

It would not be in keeping with Paul's stand on marriage in the rest of scripture to have this as a universal rule. It is best to think of this sentiment in relation to the particular situation in Corinth at the time and not to people in general [Ho]. This is the first application of staying in the condition that one finds himself (7:28, 35) [HNTC].

7:9 But[a] if they-control-themselves[b] not, let-them-marry,[c]

LEXICON—a. δέ (LN 89.124): 'but' [AB, He, HNTC; all versions], 'however' [ICC], 'yet' [Lns].

b. pres. mid. indic. of ἐγκρατεύομαι (LN 88.83) (BAGD p. 216): 'to control oneself' [BAGD, LN], 'to practice self-control' [NRSV], 'to exercise self-control' [LN], 'to have self-control' [AB; NASB, REB], 'to have the special gift of self-control' [ICC], 'to be able to control oneself' [LN; LB, NIV, TNT], 'to be able to exercise self-control' [He; NAB, NJB], 'to be able to restrain one's desires' [TEV], 'to be able to contain' [KJV], 'to be living continently' [HNTC], 'to have continency' [Lns], 'to abstain from something' [BAGD]. It is used especially of sexual continence [BAGD].

c. aorist act. impera. of γαμέω (LN 34.66) (BAGD 2. p. 150): 'to marry' [BAGD, He, HNTC, ICC, LN, Lns; all versions], 'to get married' [AB]. 'Let them marry' is a command, not permission [TNTC]. Γαμέω refers to both sexes [BAGD].

QUESTION—What is the meaning of this conditional clause?

This condition should be understood in the light of the context as meaning: if they do not have the gift of ἐγκράτεια 'self-control' [Herm, ICC, Lns, NIC,

TNTC]. Paul does not intend reproach, as can be seen in 7:7 [Herm]. This means that deprived of the physical relationships of marriage, they have severe emotional distress [AB]. A first class condition is assumed to be actually occurring [EBC, HNTC, Lns, NIC, NIC2, Rb]. The solution for this is to get married [NIC2].

for it-is better[a] to-marry than to-burn-with-sexual-desire.[b]

LEXICON—a. κρείττων (LN 65.21) (BAGD 2. p. 449): 'better' [AB, BAGD, He, HNTC, ICC, LN, Lns; all versions], 'superior' [LN], 'more useful, more advantageous' [BAGD].

b. pres. pass. infin. of πυρόω (LN **25.31**) (BAGD 1.b. p. 731): 'to burn with sexual desire' [BAGD], 'to burn with sexual passion' [**LN**], 'to be aflame/inflamed with passion' [AB; NRSV], 'to burn with passion' [NIV, TEV], 'to burn with lust' [LB], 'to burn with desire' [REB, TNT], 'to be consumed by desire' [He], 'to burn' [HNTC, Lns; KJV, NASB], 'to be on fire' [ICC; NAB], 'to be burnt up' [NJB], 'to be sexually aroused' [LN]. The present infinitive indicates a continuing condition [EGT, Lns] whereas the aorist infinitive 'to marry' indicates a specific single act [Lns].

QUESTION—What relationship is indicated by γάρ 'for'?

It indicates the grounds for Paul's advice [NIC, NIC2]. It is an appeal to common sense that all will agree with [NIC].

QUESTION—What meaning is intended by the word πυρόω 'to burn'?

'To burn' means to experience intense sexual desire [LN]. It means 'to burn with unsatisfied sexual desire' [TG]. It refers to the fire of internal lusts in opposition to one's conscience [Gdt]. It can refer either to judgment or to inner passion. Since the immediate context is not referring to judgment, it is best to take this as referring to those who were committing immoralities and their being devoured by the passions of these sins [NIC2]. 'To burn' in the present tense indicates a long and painful conflict which destroys peace and growth [ICC].

DISCOURSE UNIT: 7:10–16 [AB, EGT]. The topic is divorce [AB], prohibition of divorce [EGT].

DISCOURSE UNIT: 7:10–11 [AB, Alf, Ed, Lns, NCBC, NIC2, TNTC]. The topic is the Lord's charge against ultimate separation [AB], the case of a Christian married to a Christian [Ed], divorce prohibited [NCBC], no divorce for Christian partners [NIC2].

7:10 Now/But[a] to-the married[b] I-give-(this)-command,[c]

LEXICON—a. δέ (LN 89.94; 89.124): 'now' [AB, Lns, NIC2; LB], 'and' [KJV], 'but' [ICC; NASB, TNT], not explicit [all other versions].

b. perf. act. participle of γαμέω (LN 34.66): 'married' [HNTC, LN, Lns; all versions except LB, NAB, TEV], 'those who have been married' [AB], 'those now married' [LB, NAB], 'married people' [He; TEV], 'those who have married as Christians' [ICC]. The perfect tense points to the fact that they have married and are still in that state [Lns, Rb].

c. pres. act. indic. of παραγγέλλω (LN 33.327) (BAGD p. 613): 'to give command' [Lns; NAB, NIV, NRSV], 'to command' [AB, BAGD, LN; KJV, TNT], 'to order' [LN], 'to give orders, to instruct, to direct' [BAGD], 'to give a ruling' [NJB, REB], 'to give instructions' [NASB], 'to have a command' [LB, TEV], 'to charge' [He], 'to give a charge' [HNTC, ICC].

QUESTION—What relationship is indicated by δέ 'now/but'?

1. It indicates transition [AB, Lns, NIC2; LB]: now. The δέ indicates transition to a new group [Lns]. This is the second in the series of directives introduced by the formula 'Now I say to' in which Paul argues that they should stay as they are. This is the second prohibition to the married, not only must they not refuse sexual relations in marriage, they must not break the bonds of marriage through divorce [NIC2].
2. It indicates contrast [Gdt, ICC; NASB, TNT]: but. There is a contrast between the married and the unmarried [Gdt].

QUESTION—Who are people classified as 'married' here?

The marriage is between two Christians [Alf, Ed, EGT, Gdt, He, HNTC, ICC, Lns, My, NCBC, NIC2, TG, TNTC, Vn]. This is seen in 7:12–16, where he addresses 'the rest', referring to marriages between believers and unbelievers [NIC2].

not I but the Lord,

QUESTION—To what is Paul referring by this statement?

He is referring to a command given by Jesus himself during his life on earth [AB, Alf, EBC, Ed, EGT, Herm, HNTC, Ho, ICC, Lns, My, NIC, NIC2, Rb, Vn]. Such commands are found in Matt. 5:32, 19:9; Mark 10:11; Luke 16:18 [Gdt]. It refers both to the Jesus of history and to the exalted Lord [Herm].

QUESTION—Why is Paul contrasting himself with 'the Lord'?

Paul is not saying the Lord's command was more authoritative than his. He means that there was no need for him to rule on this subject since Jesus had already addressed this matter [Ho]. Paul is contrasting his own inspired commands (see 7:40) and those of the Lord, not between his private views and his inspired ones [ICC]. On some matters, Jesus had not given any commands. On those he now speaks through his apostle. But both his own commands, and those through Paul have equal binding power [Lns].

(that) the-wife should-separate[a] not from (her) husband,

LEXICON—a. aorist pass. infin. of χωρίζω (LN 34.78; 63.29; 15.49) (BAGD 2.a. p. 890): 'to separate' [He, HNTC, LN; NAB, NIV, NRSV, TNT], 'to separate oneself' [BAGD; REB], 'to be separated' [AB, BAGD, Lns; NJB], 'to leave' [LN; LB, NASB, TEV], 'to depart' [LN; KJV], 'to seek divorce' [ICC], 'to divorce' [LN]. In the passive it means 'to separate oneself, to be separated' [BAGD]. The passive of χωρίζω has the force of a middle: 'to separate oneself from' [My, NIC2]. The passive does not imply that the other partner initiated the action [NIC2]. The passive does not specify whether this is by her own doing or her husband's [Alf].

QUESTION—What is the significance of the wife being mentioned first?

It is remarkable that Paul should begin by addressing the wife, especially since such an action by a woman was not usually allowed by the Jews. Further, his command to the husband in 7:11 comes almost incidentally. However, in the Greco-Roman world, this was something that a woman could do. This indicates that Paul was not addressing a simple question about divorce, but one that particularly fit the Corinthian situation [NIC2]. It indicates that in their letter they intimated that such a thing had, in fact, occurred or was likely to occur. It may have been women who brought up the subject [ICC]. Possibly the wife is mentioned first because she is thought of as leaving on her own accord and thus dissolving the marriage [Lns].

QUESTION—What is the significance of the two different words for divorce, χωρίζω 'to be separated' of the wife, and ἀφίημι 'to divorce' of the husband (7:11)?

It may be because among the Jews only the husband had the right to divorce [HNTC]. In the case of the wife, her role is more passive; she 'is separated from' her husband by something, while the husband's role is active, he 'sends her away' [Lns]. There seems to be little significance since, in 7:15, χωρίζω 'to be separated' is used of the husband as well; and in 7:13 ἀφίημι 'to divorce' is used of the wife [NIC2].

QUESTION—Why does not Paul mention adultery as being an exception as was done in Matt. 5:32 and 19:9?

Paul was not giving a general treatment of divorce but was answering specific questions [TNTC]. It was not mentioned because it was taken for granted [Gdt].

7:11 but-even[a] if she-is-separated,

LEXICON—a. δὲ καί 'but even' [AB, Lns], 'but and' [KJV], 'but' [LB, NASB, NIV, NRSV, TEV], 'but (if) unhappily' [ICC], 'or' [NJB], 'and' [He, HNTC], not explicit [all other versions]. Some have said that the καί implies that this had already taken place. But the pattern ἐὰν δὲ καί 'but if also' occurs in other places as well (4:7; 7:28; 2 Cor. 4:3; 7:9) where a previous verb or idea is repeated and modified. In these places it functions to emphasize the repeated structure [NIC2]. The καί functions to emphasize the verb 'is separated' [Ed]: if she actually separates.

QUESTION—What is the relationship of this conditional sentence to 7:10 and the rest of 7:11?

It is parenthetical material between these two parts [AB, Alf, Gdt, HNTC, Lns, My, NCBC; NASB, NJB, NRSV]: To the married I command that the wife should not be separated from her husband (but even if she is separated, let her remain single or else be reconciled to her husband) and that the husband should not divorce his wife. That this is parenthetical is seen by the fact that it occurs between two coordinate infinitive clauses [Lns].

QUESTION—What is the meaning of the condition?

It implies that such a case could occur [Ed, Lns, My, NIC2]. The ideal is no divorce (7:10), while the condition allows a situation which is permissible but not ideal [NIC2]. But, if in spite of Christ's command, she separates herself, she has two alternatives [Ed, Ho, ICC].

let-her-remain unmarried[a] or let-her-be-reconciled[b] to-(her) husband,

LEXICON—a. ἄγαμος (LN **34.76**): 'unmarried' [AB, HNTC, LN, Lns; all versions except LB, NAB, NRSV, TEV], 'single' [ICC; LB, NAB, NRSV, TEV]. This word is also translated '(to live) without remarrying' [He]. The words 'to anyone else' are implied [NCBC]: let her remain unmarried to anyone else. Both Jesus and Paul forbid marriage to a divorced wife (Luke 16:18) [ICC]. See this word at 7:8.

b. aorist pass. impera. of καταλλάσσω (LN 40.1) (BAGD 2.b. p. 414): 'to be reconciled' [AB, BAGD, He, HNTC, ICC, LN, Lns; all versions except LB, NAB], 'to become reconciled' [BAGD; NAB], 'to go back to' [LB], 'to make things right with' [LN]. Καταλλάσσω has to do with reestablishing friendly relations with someone after they have been broken [LN]. The aorist indicates accomplished action [EBC]. The initiative should be with the wife who initiated the divorce [NIC].

and the-husband should-divorce[a] not (his) wife.

LEXICON—a. pres. act. inf. of ἀφίημι (LN **34.78**) (BAGD 1.b.β. p. 125): 'to divorce' [AB, BAGD, HNTC, ICC, **LN**; all versions except KJV, NASB, NJB], 'send away' [BAGD, Lns; NASB, NJB], 'to put away' [KJV], 'to repudiate' [He], 'to let go' [BAGD], 'to separate' [LN].

QUESTION—What relationship does καί 'and' indicate?

This resumes the command of 7:10 [Ed, Gdt, ICC]: that the wife should not be separate from the husband *and that* the husband should not divorce his wife.

QUESTION—What is the significance of the lack of an exception for the husband?

It may indicate that this was not where the Corinthian problem lay. Otherwise, the exception of the wife would apply to him as well [NIC2].

DISCOURSE UNIT: 7:12–16 [Lns, NCBC, NIC2]. The topic is mixed marriages [Lns, NCBC], no divorce for mixed marriages [NIC2]. The question Paul may be answering here is whether or not the believing partner should separate from an unbelieving partner rather than be mismatched [NCBC]. Here is the third in the series of directives signaled by the formula 'I say now to...' He continues to advise on divorce, this time in the context of a mixed marriage. The main point of this passage is that in mixed marriages the believing partners should consider their spouses to be set aside for the gospel. Believers should then live so as to bring their spouses to believe [NIC2].

DISCOURSE UNIT: 7:12–14 [AB, Ed, TNTC]. The topic is Paul's recommendation that believers not divorce unbelievers [AB], the Christian married to an unbeliever who is willing to live with that Christian [Ed, TNTC].

7:12 Now[a] to-the rest[b] I say, not the Lord;

LEXICON—a. δέ (LN 89.94; 89.124): 'now' [AB, Lns, NIC2], 'but' [KJV, NASB], 'here' [LB], not explicit [all other versions].

b. λοιπός (LN 63.21) (BAGD 2.b. p. 480): 'rest' [AB, HNTC, Lns; KJV, NASB, NIV, NRSV, REB], 'others' [BAGD, He; TEV, TNT], 'other matters' [NAB], 'other cases' [NJB], 'those whose cases are not covered by these directions' [ICC], not explicit [LB].

QUESTION—To whom does 'the rest' refer?

It refers to Christians who are living in a mixed marriage of believer with non-believer [EBC, Gdt, Herm, HNTC, Ho, ICC, My, NIC, NIC2, Rb, TG, TNTC, Vn]. This kind of relationship developed out of a marriage between non-believers in which one partner became a believer [EBC, Gdt, HNTC, ICC, My, NIC, Rb, TG, TNTC, Vn]. Paul is not referring to believers marrying unbelievers to form these mixed relationships (see 7:39) [EBC, NIC; TNT].

QUESTION—Why does Paul add 'not the Lord'?

The Lord had given no command concerning mixed marriages [EBC, ICC, Lns, My, NIC2, Rb, Vn]. These specific problems were non-existent when Jesus was on earth [Lns, NIC2].

QUESTION—Does this mean that Paul's word is not authoritative?

This does not mean that Paul is speaking merely as a private individual without Apostolic authority [Alf, HNTC, ICC, Rb]. All of his directions were given with the inspiration and authority of an Apostle [Alf, HNTC, ICC]. Paul uses the formula 'I say' at 7:6, 8, and 35 where he speaks as one who can be trusted (7:25), because he has God's Spirit [NIC2]. The words 'I say' are a virtual repetition of 'I command' (7:10). Where he had a definite word from Jesus, he appeals to that. Here it is necessary that he give his own judgment and he makes that clear [EGT]. Paul means only that he is not quoting a command of the Lord [Rb]. This is Paul's opinion and is not based on Jesus' command [AB, TG]. This is not intended as a binding command since Paul had not received it from the Lord [NIC].

(that) if any brother[a] has (an) unbelieving[b] wife

LEXICON—a. ἀδελφός: 'brother' [AB, Lns; KJV, NAB, NASB, NIV, NJB, TNT], 'believer' [NRSV], 'Christian' [He; LB, REB], 'Christian brother' [HNTC], 'Christian man' [TEV], 'any member of the church' [ICC]. 'Brother' here is practically another word for a Christian [TG]. See this word at 1:1.

b. ἄπιστος (LN 11.19; 31.106): 'unbelieving' [AB, HNTC, Lns], 'pagan' [He]. This adjective is also translated as a relative clause: 'who is an unbeliever' [NAB, NASB, NRSV, TEV], 'who is not a believer' [ICC, LN (31.106); KJV, NIV, NJB, REB, TNT], 'who is not a Christian' [LB], '(who is a) non-Christian' [LN (11.19)]. While it is true that this word can mean 'unfaithful', here it has the meaning 'unbeliever' [AB]. This is a case of a Christian with an unbelieving wife whom he married at a time when he himself was an unbeliever [ICC]. See this word at 6:6.

QUESTION—What is the significance of the present condition?

In both this verse and the next the factual condition assumes the reality of such marriages among the Christian community in Corinth [EBC, NIC2].

and she consents[a] to-live[b] with him, let-him-divorce[c] her not;

LEXICON—a. pres. act. indic. of συνευδοκέω (LN **31.17**) (BAGD p. 788): 'to consent' [AB, BAGD, ICC, LN, Lns; NASB, NRSV], 'to agree' [BAGD, He, **LN**; TEV, TNT], 'to be willing' [BAGD; NAB, NIV, NJB, REB], 'to be content' [HNTC], 'to want' [LB], 'to be pleased' [KJV]. It means more than 'to be willing': 'to agree with' or 'to consent to' [NIC2]. It means that the unbelieving spouse agrees with the believing spouse to continue the marriage [EGT].

b. pres. act. infin. of οἰκέω (LN **85.67**): 'to live' [HNTC, ICC; NAB, NASB, NIV, NRSV, REB], 'to keep on living' [AB], 'to go on living' [He LN; TEV], 'to continue living' [TNT], 'to dwell' [Lns; KJV]. The words 'to live with him' indicate the continuance of the marriage relation [Lns].

c. pres. act. impera. of ἀφίημι: 'to divorce' [AB, HNTC, ICC; all versions except KJV, LB, NASB], 'to put away' [KJV], 'to send away' [Lns; NASB], 'to leave or to divorce' [LB], 'to repudiate' [He]. The present tense indicates that he should not be attempting at any point to divorce her [EBC]. See this word at 7:11.

QUESTION—What is the intent of this command?

What Paul, by way of command in 7:10 and 11, has said concerning marriage between believers holds true for mixed marriages, the believer must not initiate divorce [NIC2]. Paul applies Christ's ruling, as much as possible, to a mixed marriage [ICC]. By this Paul is saying that such mixed marriages are lawful and that the believer should not try to dissolve them [Ho].

7:13 And if any wife[a] has (an) unbelieving husband and he consents to-live with her, let-her-divorce[b] not her husband.

LEXICON—a. γυνή: 'wife' [AB, ICC, Lns], 'woman' [KJV, NAB, NASB, NIV, NJB, NRSV, REB, TNT], 'Christian woman' [He, HNTC; LB, TEV]. The same rule applies if a believing wife has an unbelieving husband [TG]. See this word at 5:1.

b. ἀφίημι (LN **34.78**): 'to divorce' [AB, HNTC, ICC, **LN**; NAB, NIV, NJB, NRSV, REB, TEV, TNT], 'to leave' [KJV, LB], 'to send away' [Lns; NASB], 'to repudiate' [He]. In 7:11, ἀφίημι was used for the husband, in this verse it is used for both husband and wife [EGT]. That here the verbs are same for both husband and wife shows that Paul meant no difference in 7:11 [Lns]. Paul uses the same verb for both husband and wife because in the Greco-Roman world, both had the legal right to divorce [Ho]. See this word at 7:11.

7:14 For[a] the unbelieving husband has-been-sanctified[b] through[c] his wife and the unbelieving wife has-been-sanctified through the brother;

TEXT—Instead of ἀδελφῷ 'brother', some manuscripts have ἀνδρί 'husband'. GNT selects the reading 'brother' with an A rating, indicating that the text is certain. This word is translated 'the brother' [AB, Lns; NJB, TNT], 'the Christian brother' [HNTC], 'husband' [NRSV], 'Christian husband' [KJV, LB, REB, TEV], 'believing husband' [He; NAB, NASB, NIV], 'a believer' [ICC].

LEXICON—a. γάρ (LN 89.23): 'for' [AB, BAGD, He, HNTC, ICC, LN, Lns; all versions except NAB, NJB, TNT], 'you see' [NJB], 'in fact' [He], 'and for this reason' [ICC], not explicit [NAB, TNT].

b. perf. pass. indic. of ἁγιάζω (BAGD 2. p. 8): 'to be sanctified' [BAGD, He, HNTC, ICC, Lns; KJV, NASB, NIV, NJB], 'to be consecrated' [BAGD; NAB, NRSV], 'to be made holy' [AB], 'to be made acceptable to God' [TEV], 'to become a Christian' [LB]. This passive is also translated actively: 'to belong to God' [REB, TNT]. The perfect tense indicates that the unbeliever has become and will continue to be a part of the marriage unit on which God has his claim [EBC]. See this word at 1:2.

c. ἐν with dative object (BAGD III.3.a. p. 261): 'through' [HNTC; all versions except LB, NAB, NASB, TEV], 'through union with' [ICC], 'by' [AB, He; NAB, NASB], 'by being united to' [TEV], 'with the help of' [LB], 'in' [Lns], 'because of, on account of' [BAGD]. The more precise meaning of ἐν here is 'in the person of' [AB]. The idea is 'because he is married to a Christian woman' [TG]. Ἐν denotes 'through close tie with' [NIC], 'the sphere within which' the partner is sanctified [ICC]. It means that the holiness of the unbelieving partner is located in his wife [Alf]. Ἐν probably indicates 'in relationship to' his wife rather than in relationship to God 'through' his wife [NIC2].

QUESTION—What relationship is indicated by γάρ 'for'?

It indicates that this verse is the reason for the rules Paul has given [NIC2, TNTC]. Here is proof that mixed marriages should continue [Ho]. This verse answers the question as to whether the believer would be defiled by union with an unbeliever [EGT].

QUESTION—What sense of 'sanctify' is in focus here?

The answer must be sought in the context. The Corinthians were concerned about what defiled a person. If it were good for a man to 'not touch a woman', then surely sexual intercourse with an unbelieving partner would defile one. Paul corrects this assumption by stating rather that the believing partner sanctified the unbelieving partner in the sense of setting them apart for God and for possible future salvation. This is similar to Rom. 11:16 [NIC2]. It does not mean that they have acquired salvation or holiness [HNTC, Ho, NIC2]. As in Matt. 23:17, 19, the temple sanctifies the gold associated with it, so the unbelieving partner is set apart to God's service by virtue of his union with his believing wife [Ho]. It means that the unbelieving partner is now affiliated with a holy group of Christians [My]. 'Sanctified' here must refer to the marriage relation which is made holy by the believing partner so that there is no need for divorce [Rb]. 'To be sanctified' means 'to belong to God's people' [TG, TH]. Being in a Christian family, the unbeliever is part of a family unit upon which God has a claim [EBC].

for[a] then your children are unclean,[b]

LEXICON—a. ἐπεί: 'for'. See this word at 5:10.

b. ἀκάθαρτος (LN 53.39) (BAGD 1. p. 29): 'unclean' [AB, BAGD, HNTC, Lns; all versions except LB, REB, TEV, TNT], 'impure' [BAGD, He], 'pagans' [TNT], 'like pagan children' [TEV], 'defiled, ritually unclean' [LN]. This adjective is also translated as a noun phrase: '(left in) heathen uncleanness' [ICC]. It is also translated as a verb phrase: '(might) never come to know the Lord' [LB], '(would) not belong to God' [REB].

QUESTION—What is implied by ἐπεὶ ἄρα 'for then, otherwise'?

Paul seems to be arguing with the Corinthians. 'Otherwise' implies 'if we allow your position' (that is, that the unbeliever defiles the believer) [NIC2]. 'Otherwise' implies 'if it were not true that the unbelieving partner is sanctified through his wife' [HNTC], or 'if it were not true that the believing partner makes the marriage acceptable to God' [TG].

QUESTION—What is meant by ἀκάθαρτος 'unclean'?

'Unclean' implies 'born outside the bounds of the believing community' [Ho]. It means 'ceremonially impure' or 'not fit for God's service' [TG]. It means to be spiritually separated from God [EBC]. It means that they lie outside of God's covenant [NIC2].

QUESTION—Whose children are indicated by the words τὰ τέκνα ὑμῶν 'your children'?

1. They are the children of believers married to unbelievers [Herm, Ho, Lns, NIC2].
2. They are the children of the Christian community in general [Gdt, He, NIC]. Paul is talking to the Christian community in general. His argument is that if your children who are not yet believers are holy by virtue of their union with you their parents, why is it difficult to believe that an unbelieving partner is holy by virtue of his union with his believing wife? [Gdt].

but as-it-is[a] they-are holy.[b]

LEXICON—a. νῦν (BAGD 2. p. 546): 'as it is' [NAB, NIV, NRSV, TEV, TNT], 'now' [AB, Lns; KJV, NASB], 'in fact' [HNTC, ICC; NJB, REB], 'in reality' [He], 'as things now stand, as a matter of fact' [BAGD]. The phrase 'as it is' implies: 'allowing my position' (that is, that the believer sanctifies the unbeliever) [NIC2].

b. ἅγιος (BAGD 1.b.α. p. 9): 'holy' [AB, BAGD, HNTC, ICC, Lns; all versions except LB, REB, TEV, TNT], 'acceptable to God' [TEV], 'sanctified' [He], 'belong to God' [REB, TNT], 'consecrated to God' [BAGD]. This adjective is also translated '(result in the children's) salvation' [LB].

QUESTION—What sense of the word ἅγιος 'holy' is in focus here?

The children are holy in the same sense as the unbelieving father and mother have holiness conferred on them [Lns, NIC2, TG]. It is the Jewish concept of holiness meaning that they are within God's covenant [HNTC, NIC2]. They are holy in that they belong to the church, in the same sense as Jews are holy because they belong to Israel [Ho]. Until the child of a believer can take responsibility for himself, he is regarded as Christian since the holiness comes from the parent [HNTC].

QUESTION—What is the thread of Paul's argument here?

He argues back from the children to the marriage itself. They must admit that a Christian's child is holy, which means that the child came from a marriage that was holy, which meant that it was not necessary to dissolve such a marriage [ICC, NIC2]. He is appealing for proof to the fact that the children were thought of as holy, which they could not be if the marriage they came from were not holy [Ho].

DISCOURSE UNIT: 7:15–16 [AB, Ed, TNTC]. The topic is believers not being bound by broken marriages with unbelievers [AB], the Christian married to an unbeliever who is not willing to live with the believer [Ed, TNTC].

7:15 But[a] if the unbeliever[b] separates[c] let-him/her-separate;

LEXICON—a. δέ: 'but' [He, Lns; KJV, LB, NIV, NJB, NRSV], 'but on the other hand' [ICC], 'yet' [NASB], 'however' [NAB, REB, TEV, TNT], not explicit [AB, HNTC].

b. ἄπιστος (LN **11.19**): 'unbeliever' [AB, HNTC; NAB, NIV, NJB, TNT], 'unbelieving partner/one' [ICC, Lns; NASB, NRSV, REB], 'one who is not a Christian' [**LN**; LB], 'one who is not a believer' [TEV], 'non-Christian' [LN], 'pagan partner' [He], 'unbelieving' [KJV]. See this word at 6:6.

c. pres. mid. subj. of χωρίζω (LN **34.78**): 'to separate' [AB, He, HNTC, LN; NRSV], 'to wish to separate' [**LN**; NAB, TNT], 'to wish for a separation' [REB], 'to insist on a separation' [ICC], 'to keep oneself separate' [Lns], 'to depart' [KJV], 'to leave' [NASB, NIV], 'to choose to leave' [NJB], 'to wish to leave' [TEV], 'to be eager to leave' [LB], 'to divorce' [LN]. Χωρίζω is the verb used in the papyri where by mutual agreement a marriage can be dissolved [NIC2]. It probably does not indicate full legal divorce [HNTC]. The verb in the middle voice means: 'to take oneself off' [Lns, TNTC]. In both verbs meaning 'to separate', the present tense indicates continuous aspect, 'to keep oneself separate' [Lns]. The present tense indicates the intention of the unbeliever, 'if he is intending to depart' [Ed]. See this word at 7:10.

QUESTION—What relationship is indicated by δέ 'but'?

It indicates a contrast with the preceding case where the unbeliever consents to remain with the spouse [He, Ho, Lns; KJV, LB, NAB, NASB, NIV, NRSV, REB, TEV, TNT]. It serves to introduce an exception to the previous rule [He, NIC2].

QUESTION—Why is ἄπιστος 'the unbelieving one' masculine?

Grammatically, it is masculine, but it includes both sexes as seen in the following clause [ICC].

in such-cases[a] the brother or the sister[b] is-bound[c] not;

LEXICON—a. τοιοῦτος (BAGD 3.a.β. p. 821): 'such cases' [AB, BAGD, HNTC, ICC; all versions except NIV, NJB], 'such a case' [NRSV], 'these/such circumstances' [BAGD, He, Lns; NIV, NJB], 'such things, similar things, things like that' [BAGD]. See this word at 5:1.

b. ἀδελφή (LN 11.24) (BAGD 3. p. 15): 'sister' [AB, Lns; KJV, NAB, NJB, NRSV, TNT], 'Christian wife' [LB], 'believing wife' [NAB, REB, TEV], 'believing woman' [NASB], 'Christian woman' [He, ICC], 'Christian sister' [HNTC], 'sister in the faith' [BAGD, LN], 'sister in Christ, fellow believer' [LN].

c. perf. pass. indic. of δουλόω (LN **37.24**; 87.82) (BAGD 2. p. 206): 'to be bound' [AB, BAGD, He, **LN**; NAB, NIV, NRSV], 'to be bound by the marriage' [REB], 'to be under bondage' [KJV, NASB], 'to be placed in bondage' [Lns], 'to be no longer tied' [NJB], 'to be enslaved' [BAGD, HNTC], 'to be under obligation' [**LN**], 'to be subjected' [BAGD], 'to be made a slave' [BAGD]. This word is also translated as a noun phrase: 'servile bondage to a heathen yoke' [ICC]. It is also translated as a verb phrase: 'to have to insist that the other stay' [LB]. It is also joined with 'not' and translated positively: 'to be free' [TNT], 'to be free to act' [**LN**; TEV]. The perfect tense indicates that the believer is released from the time that the unbeliever left and continues in that state [Lns].

QUESTION—In what sense are believers 'not bound'?

It means that they are free from having to maintain the marriage [NIC2, TG], they are not bound by the marriage vows [Ho, Lns, My, TG]. It means that they are free to agree with the unbelieving partner's desire to leave [HNTC, TG]. They are not bound to the departing spouse [ICC, NIC]. It means that now no law binds the believing partner [Lns]. Willful desertion is the other legitimate reason for divorce besides sexual immorality [EBC].

QUESTION—Does this freedom allow the believer to remarry?

1. The believer is not free to remarry [NIC2]. Paul is not treating the subject of remarriage here, but the subject of divorce. The believer is bound to marriage until death, but in this case he or she is released only from the obligation to maintain the marriage. There is a similar statement in 7:11 where remarriage is not allowed. Finally, the theme of the chapter, 'stay as you are', argues against remarriage [NIC2].

2. The believer is now free to remarry [AB, He, TNTC]. The marriage is regarded as being nullified [He].

but[a] God has-called[b] you to[c] peace.[d]

TEXT—Instead of ὑμᾶς 'you', some manuscripts have ἡμᾶς 'us'. GNT selects 'you' with a B rating, indicating that the text is almost certain. The word ἡμᾶς 'us' is selected by He, ICC, Lns, NIC2, KJV, NASB, and NIV.

LEXICON—a. δέ: 'but' [He, Lns; KJV, NASB, REB, TNT], 'for' [LB], not explicit [AB, HNTC, ICC; NAB, NIV, NJB, NRSV, TEV].

b. perf. act. indic. of καλέω (LN 33.312): 'to call' [AB, BAGD, He, HNTC, LN, Lns; all versions except LB, REB], 'to want someone to' [LB]. This verb is also translated as a noun: 'call' [REB], 'calling' [ICC]. The perfect tense indicates a lasting result [EBC, Lns, NIC]. The perfect tense emphasizes the initial call of God plus its continuing effect in day-to-day life [EBC]. See this word at 1:9.

c. ἐν with dative object: 'to' [KJV, NASB, NRSV], 'to live in' [He; LB, NAB, NIV, NJB, REB, TEV, TNT], 'in' [AB, HNTC, ICC, Lns].

d. εἰρήνη (LN 22.42; 25.248) (BAGD 1.c. p. 227): 'peace' [AB, He, HNTC, Lns; all versions except LB], 'peace and harmony' [LB], 'peace of mind' [ICC], 'order' [BAGD]. See this word at 1:3.

QUESTION—What is the meaning of ἐν εἰρήνῃ 'to peace' here?

It means: 'to live in peace' [He; LB, NAB, NIV, NJB, REB, TEV, TNT], 'in the sphere of peace' [Rb], or 'in the state of peace' and indicates how believers should live [Gdt, Ho]. Separation should take place without anger or recrimination [Ho]. It means 'into the ways of peace' [NIC2]. It means 'into peace' where the believer is to live [HNTC]. It means 'in a peaceful manner' and indicates how the marriage separation should take place [AB].

QUESTION—What is the function of this clause?

1. It gives the reason why the separation should take place if the unbeliever wants to depart [Alf, EBC, Ed, Gdt, Herm, ICC, My, NIC, TG]: let him separate...because God has called you to peace. God has not called believers to live in tension trying to keep a marriage going with an unwilling partner [TG].
2. It gives the reason why the believer should continue to live with the unbeliever and why he or she should let them separate if they desire [NCBC, TNTC]. Peace should be maintained in mixed marriages. In some cases it will mean living with the unbelieving partner, in others it will mean allowing that spouse to separate.
3. It functions as a contrast with separation [EGT, HNTC, Ho, NIC2]: let him separate...but God has called you to peace (not separation). Δέ contrasts with the exception 'let him/her depart', and thus indicates further reason why they should not divorce (7:12, 13). This fits in with the theme 'remain as you are' [NIC2]. The δέ 'but' contrasts with the bondage [Gdt, ICC]: let them separate, the believer is not bound, rather God has called us to peace. Although the believer is free when deserted by an unbelieving

spouse, the separation should be avoided, if possible, by maintaining peace among the partners of the marriage [Ho].

7:16 For[a] how do-you-know, wife, whether you-will-save[b] your husband? Or how do-you-know, husband, whether you-will-save your wife?

LEXICON—a. γάρ: 'for' [AB, ICC, Lns; NASB], 'for, after all' [LB]. 'but remember' [REB], 'now' [He], not explicit [HNTC; all other versions].

b. fut. act. indic. of σῴζω (LN 21.27) (BAGD 2.a.β. p. 798): 'to save' [AB, He, HNTC, LN, Lns; all versions except LB, NJB], 'to be the salvation of' [NJB], 'to convert' [ICC], 'to save, to preserve from eternal death' [BAGD]. This word is also translated as a passive with 'husband' as subject: 'to be converted' [LB]. 'Save' is used here in the sense of converting a partner to the Christian faith [HNTC, TG]. See this word at 1:18.

QUESTION—What relationship is indicated by γάρ 'for'?

1. It indicates the reason for accepting the separation of the unbelieving spouse [AB, Ed, Gdt, He, ICC, Lns, My, NIC, TG, TNTC; LB]. The questions imply an uncertain or negative result [Alf, Ed, Gdt, He, ICC, Lns, My, NIC, TG, TNTC; LB]. It means 'you have no assurance that your spouse will be converted' [LB]. The strain of maintaining a marriage with an unwilling partner is too great a price to pay for the chance of converting one's unbelieving partner [ICC]. The uncertain result does not justify the inevitable loss of peace [TNTC]. The certainty of bondage and quarreling do not have to be accepted to obtain so uncertain a goal [NIC].
2. It indicates the reason for avoiding divorce if at all possible [EBC, EGT, HNTC, Ho, NCBC, NIC2]. The questions imply a possible positive result [EBC, EGT, HNTC, Ho, NCBC, NIC2, TH; NRSV, REB, TEV, TNT]: how do you know if you will not save your spouse? It means 'for all you know, you might save your husband or wife' [NRSV]. The possibility of the unbelieving partner converting justifies maintaining the marriage [HNTC]. The context points to a positive reply to the following questions especially considering the clause, 'God has called you to peace'. This verse then offers a final reason for maintaining the marriage [NIC2]. The positive statements of 7:14 and 15c point to an optimistic and hopeful understanding of these questions [TH]. 'Who knows if' expresses hope [Ho]. Paul has already said that the unbelieving partner is sanctified by the believing partner. This implies that there is hope that he or she may come to believe [HNTC].

DISCOURSE UNIT: 7:17–24 [AB, EBC, Ed, EGT, Gdt, GNT, Herm, NCBC, NIC2, TG, TH, TNTC]. The topic is an excursus about Christians remaining in their preconversion status [AB], the Christian obligation to live according to God's call [EBC], a digression in reference to circumcision and slavery [Ed], God's calling and one's earthly station [EGT], the life which the Lord has assigned [GNT], eschatological freedom [Herm], calling and status [NCBC], the guiding principle: staying as one was when called [NIC2], leading the life God assigns to you [TNTC]. The Corinthians were concerned about change of status. To this Paul directs that they remain as they were when called. The concept of calling is dominant in the section and is applied to all four social conditions treated: circumcision, uncircumcision, slave, and free [NIC2]. Continuing the principle that God has called his people to live in peace, Paul teaches that they should live contentedly in any God-appointed situation [EBC]. The principle taught is that, although Christianity makes a change in the moral and spiritual life, it does not necessarily make a change in one's social status. It is best therefore to stay in the status in which one was when called by God [ICC]. This passage is a digression [AB, Gdt], but it is intended to illustrate the theme more completely [Gdt].

7:17 Nevertheless[a] as the Lord has-assigned[b] to-each-one, as God has-called[c] each-one, so let-him/her-live-one's-life.[d]

TEXT—Some manuscripts reverse the positions of 'Lord' and 'God' in this verse. GNT does not mention this alternative. Only KJV reverses this order.

LEXICON—a. εἰ μή (LN 89.131): 'nevertheless' [EBC, NIC2; NIV], 'however' [LN; TNT], 'however that may be' [NRSV, REB], 'only' [HNTC, Lns, NIC; NASB], 'but' [AB, EBC, LN; KJV, LB], 'anyway' [NJB], 'very well' [He], 'still, the general principle is this' [ICC], 'except that, instead, but only' [LN], not explicit [NAB, TEV]. Εἰ μή marks contrast by signaling an exception [LN]. The closest example to this usage by Paul is in Gal. 1:7 where it means 'nevertheless' [NIC2].

b. perf. act. indic. of μερίζω (LN 37.100) (BAGD 2.b. p. 504): 'to assign' [AB, BAGD; NAB, NASB, NIV, NRSV], 'to assign a lot' [BAGD ICC; REB], 'to apportion' [BAGD, Lns], 'to apportion a lot' [HNTC], 'to allot a part' [NJB], 'to allot a state' [He], 'to deal out' [BAGD], 'to distribute' [KJV], 'to give a gift' [TNT], 'to put one into a situation' [LB], 'to assign a particular responsibility, to give a particular task to, to appoint a particular part to' [LN]. This word is also translated as a noun: '(the Lord's) gift' [TEV]. It means to decide how one's life should be [TG]. It can refer to the distribution of God's gift and could be translated 'according to the ability which the Lord has given' [TH].

c. perf. pass. indic. of καλέω (LN 33.312): 'to call' [AB, He, HNTC, LN, Lns; all versions except LB, NJB, TNT], '(God) intended' [LB]. This word is also translated as a noun: 'call/calling' [ICC; NJB, TNT]. The perfect tense indicates a continuing condition from the time of conversion to the present [NIC2]. It indicates the present standing of the believer as one who is called by God [Lns]. See this word at 7:15.

d. pres. act. impera. of περιπατέω (LN 41.11) (BAGD 2.a.γ. p. 649): 'to live one's life' [TNT], 'to lead a life' [NAB, NRSV], 'to live' [LN; LB], 'to go on living' [TEV], 'to live in conformity with a state' [He], 'to conduct one's life' [AB], 'to accept a lot' [REB], 'to retain the place in life' [NIV], 'to continue in a part' [NJB], 'to walk' [Lns; KJV, NASB], 'to walk according to a lot' [HNTC], 'to be content with a lot' [ICC]. The force of the present imperative is that one should go on or continue doing this [EBC]. 'Walking' is one of Paul's favorite metaphors for living out one's life. The point of comparison is steady progress [TNTC]. Paul's concern was that they see their present condition as a valid one for living their lives as God wants them to [NIC2]. See this word translated as 'behave' at 3:3.

QUESTION—What is the function of this verse introduced by εἰ μή 'nevertheless'?

1. It introduces an exception or correction to the statement in 7:15 that the believer is not bound in such cases [Alf, Ed, EGT, HNTC, ICC, My, NIC2, Rb, TH, TNTC]. A person is free to allow his/her partner to separate; nevertheless, that is not to be the rule. They are urged to live according to God's unique calling for their lives [NIC2]. When the unbeliever chooses to leave, a divorce is allowed, but the believer must not seek the separation [Alf, Vn]. The general principle determining all questions about marriage is given and illustrated in respect to other situations [ICC, Lns, Rb, Vn].
2. It functions as the beginning of a new subject [AB, EBC, TG]. Εἰ μή can be translated, 'however that may be' or 'but to change the subject' [TG]. Paul digresses in 7:17–24, perhaps to comment on 'in peace' (7:15), but the relation of this passage to what precedes is not clear [AB].
3. It is related to the questions of 7:16 which imply doubt (one does not know) [He, NIC]. Εἰ μή 'only' introduces an implied conditional clause: 'if you are uncertain of saving your spouse', live the life which the Lord has assigned to you [NIC].

QUESTION—What 'call' of God is being referred to?

'Call' here refers to the invitation to salvation [AB, EGT, Gdt, HNTC, Ho, NIC, NIC2, TNTC], not to the vocation to which God may assign a person [HNTC]. They are to accept their social situation (celibate or married, slave or free) in which they found themselves at the time God called them to salvation [He, HNTC].

QUESTION—To whom does the word 'Lord' refer?

1. It refers to Christ [Ed, He, ICC, NIC2, TG, TH]. This refers to Jesus, as is usual in Paul's writings [NIC2, TH].
2. It refers to God [My; LB].
3. No distinction is intended [AB, NIC].

QUESTION—What 'gift' is being referred to as being assigned by the Lord?

The particular gift here in focus is that of being married to this or that person. It is also later specified as being circumcised or uncircumcised, slave or free [My]. It is the various social situations which 'are assigned' by the Lord at the time of one's calling to salvation [NIC2].

And thus[a] I-command[b] in all the churches.[c]

LEXICON—a. οὕτως (LN 61.9): 'thus' [LN, Lns; NASB], 'this' [AB, He, HNTC, ICC; all versions except KJV, NASB], 'so' [KJV]. Οὕτως refers to what has just been said [HNTC]. See this word at 3:15.

b. pres. mid. indic. of διατάσσω (LN 33.325) (BAGD p. 189): 'to command' [BAGD, LN], 'to direct' [BAGD; NASB], 'to ordain' [Lns; KJV], 'to give a direction' [AB], 'to give a charge' [HNTC], 'to give a rule' [NAB, NJB, REB], 'to teach a rule' [TEV], 'to make a rule' [BAGD; TNT], 'to lay down a rule' [ICC; NIV], 'to tell, to instruct' [LN], 'to order' [BAGD, LN], 'to lay down' [He]. This word is also translated as a noun: '(this is my) rule' [LB, NRSV]. The present tense indicates that this command applies now and forever [NIC].

c. ἐκκλησία (LN 11.23): 'church' [AB, He, HNTC, ICC, LN, Lns; all versions], 'congregation' [LN]. See this word at 1:2.

QUESTION—What is the function of this statement?

Paul refers to all the churches in order to indicate that this concerns a principle, not just an arbitrary rule made for the Corinthians [Ed]. The phrase 'in all the churches' functions to bring out the importance of this command [ICC, My]. This phrase, absent from his other letters, indicates that Paul was telling them that it was their theology which was in error, not his [NIC2].

DISCOURSE UNIT: 7:18–24 [Alf, Ed, GNT]. The topic is examples of the precept just given [Alf], the life which the Lord has assigned [GNT]. Circumcision and slavery are now discussed as two specific applications of the principle that each person's unique position in life is merely the outward form of his calling to salvation [Ed].

7:18 (If) anyone was-called being-circumcised,[a] let-him-remove-the-marks-of-circumcision[b] not;

TEXT—GNT third edition punctuates this verse as two questions followed by an imperative. GNT fourth edition punctuates it as two statements, each followed by an imperative. It does not rate its choice.

LEXICON—a. perf. pass. participle of περιτέμνω (LN 53.51) (BAGD 1. p. 652): 'to be circumcised' [AB, BAGD, He, HNTC, ICC, LN, Lns; all versions except LB, REB], 'to be in a state of circumcision' [BAGD, HNTC], 'to have the marks of circumcision on one' [REB], 'to go through the Jewish ceremony of circumcision' [LB], 'to have had oneself circumcised' [BAGD]. Being circumcised means being a Jew [NIC]. Circumcision was the ceremony of cutting off the foreskin of a Jewish boy as a sign of God's covenant with Israel (Gen. 17:9–14) [TG].

b. pres. mid. impera. of ἐπισπάομαι (LN **53.52**) (BAGD 3. p. 299): 'to remove marks of circumcision' [REB], 'to seek to remove the marks of circumcision' [NRSV], 'to try to conceal the signs of circumcision' [TNT], 'to try to hide one's circumcision' [NAB], 'to attempt to disguise one's circumcision' [AB], 'to attempt to efface the circumcision' [ICC], 'to undo one's circumcision' [HNTC], 'to become uncircumcised' [Lns], 'to conceal the circumcision' [**LN**], 'to extend the foreskin' [LN], 'to pull over the foreskin to conceal one's circumcision' [BAGD]. This word is also translated idiomatically: 'to not worry about something' [LB]. It is also joined with 'not' and translated 'to stay circumcised' [He; NJB]. The verb ἐπισπάομαι indicated a surgical operation [EGT, Gdt, Lns, My, NIC2]. During the period of Hellenization, many Jewish men underwent an operation that would conceal their circumcision [NIC2]. Either because of abandoning their religion or from the shame of appearing before Gentiles in baths as circumcised, the Jews tried to conceal their circumcision [My]. The Hellenistic Jews did this. Otherwise, in the gymnasium others could see that they were Jews [NIC].

QUESTION—What is the purpose of this verse?

It functions as the first application of the principle just given [Ho, My]. Paul now illustrates his point of living out their calling in their own unique social settings, by bringing up another social setting. This one has religious implications that marriage did not [NIC2]. Paul addresses racial distinctions, Jews (circumcised) and Gentiles (uncircumcised) [TG]. One's social standing has no effect on one's salvation. To seek to change it would indicate that it did [Herm].

QUESTION—Are the introductory clauses to the imperatives questions or conditions/statements?

1. They are conditional clauses or statements [Ed, Gdt, GNT, Herm, Ho, My; LB, NJB, TEV]: If anyone was circumcised when called, let him not remove the marks of circumcision.
2. They are questions [AB, EGT, He, HNTC, ICC, Lns, NIC2, TG, TH; KJV, NAB, NASB, NIV, NRSV, REB, TNT]. Was anyone circumcised when he was called? It is probably interrogative, not conditional, but the meaning is about the same [ICC].

QUESTION—Who is the actor of the passive verb 'to be called'?

God is the actor [AB, TH]. God is the one who calls as stated in 7:17 [TH].

QUESTION—To what does 'called' refer?

It refers to conversion or becoming a Christian [Alf, HNTC, Ho].

(if) anyone was-called in uncircumcision,[a] let-him-be-circumcised not.

LEXICON—a. ἀκροβυστία (LN 11.52) (BAGD 1. p. 33): 'uncircumcision' [ICC, Lns]. This word is also translated as an adjective: 'uncircumcised' [BAGD, LN; all other versions except LB]. It is also translated as a verb phrase: 'to not be circumcised' [LB]. The Judaizers were apt to insist on Gentile converts being circumcised [Ho]. A Gentile Christian might see it as a definite advantage to look as if he were originally one of the chosen people of Israel [Lns].

7:19 Circumcision is nothing and uncircumcision is nothing,

QUESTION—What do the words οὐδέν ἐστιν 'is nothing' mean?

This means 'to have no effect on our relationship to God' [Ho], 'to count for nothing' [NAB, NRSV], 'to not matter' [TNT], 'to mean nothing' [TEV], 'to not make a difference' [TG; LB], 'to be of no importance' [NIC; NJB], 'to be neither here nor there' [REB], 'to be of no consequence' [ICC]. To the Gentiles in Corinth, this statement would not have been very earthshaking. To the Jew, it was horrifying. Circumcision, as the sign of the covenant, counted for everything. It was evidence of their standing with God. But to give it significance negated the Good News. Paul hoped that the Corinthians would see the principle and apply it to marriage and celibacy in equal force [NIC2]. It functions to give the reason for Paul's instructions in 7:18 [TG; LB, TEV]: let him not be circumcised because circumcision is nothing.

but[a] obeying[b] (the) commandments[c] of-God.

LEXICON—a. ἀλλά: 'but' [Lns; KJV]. This word is also translated with implied information: 'but...is everything' [He, ICC; NRSV], 'but...is the important thing' [LB], 'but what matters is' [AB; NASB], 'but...does matter' [TNT]. It is also left untranslated with only the implied information: 'what matters is' [HNTC; NAB, REB, TEV], 'what really matters is' [ICC], 'what is important is' [NJB], '...is what counts' [NIV]. This is strongly adversative and implies the opposite of the preceding negative statement [ICC].

b. τήρησις (LN **36.19**) (BAGD 3. p. 815): 'obeying' [NRSV], 'obedience' [**LN**], 'observance' [AB, BAGD], 'keeping' [BAGD, He, ICC; KJV, NAB, NASB, NIV, NJB, TNT], 'pleasing (God) and keeping' [LB], 'guarding' [Lns]. This word is also translated as a verb: 'to keep' [HNTC; REB], 'to obey' [TEV]. The keeping of God's commandments means obeying the will of God as Jesus revealed it [HNTC].

c. ἐντολή (LN 33.330) (BAGD 2.b. p. 269): 'commandments' [AB, BAGD, He, HNTC, ICC; all versions except REB], 'commands' [BAGD; REB]. 'behests' [Lns], 'orders' [BAGD].

QUESTION—What is involved in obeying God's commandments?

To the Jew, to be circumcised was to keep God's command. What Paul had in mind were the moral commandments of the Christian faith, obedience to the will of God, which were distinct from the works of the law [NIC2]. The plural ἐντολῶν 'commandments' contrasts with 'the Mosaic law'. What is meant is the moral law which applies to Jew and Gentile alike [NIC]. The commandments of God include the Jewish law in regards to its moral content, Jesus' teaching and example, and the instructions of his Spirit [Gdt]. The commandments refer to those of the gospel, the requirements of faith and love [Lns].

7:20 Each-one in the station-of-life/calling[a] in-which he-was-called, in this let-him/her-remain.[b]

LEXICON—a. κλῆσις (LN **87.2**) (BAGD 2. p. 436): 'station of life' [BAGD, **LN**], 'calling' [AB, HNTC, LN; KJV], 'state' [He; NJB, TNT]. 'condition' [ICC; NASB, NRSV, REB], 'situation' [NIV], 'the work he was doing' [LB], 'call' [Lns], 'position, vocation' [BAGD]. This word is also translated as a phrase: 'as one was' [NAB, TEV].

b. pres. act. impera. of μένω (LN 68.11): 'to remain' [AB, He, Lns; NASB, NIV, NRSV, TEV, TNT], 'to be content to remain' [ICC], 'to stay' [NJB], 'to continue' [HNTC, LN; NAB], 'to abide' [KJV], 'to keep on with' [LN; LB]. The present tense implies a continuing activity [TNTC]. See this word at 7:8.

QUESTION—To what does the word κλῆσις 'station of life/calling' refer?

1. It refers to the condition or state a person was in when God called him [AB, BAGD, EBC, HNTC, Ho, ICC, LN, NIC2, TG, TH, Vn; NAB, NASB, NJB, NRSV, REB, TEV, TNT]. 'Calling' here refers to what one was doing occupationally when they were called by God to become a Christian [AB]. It does not refer to occupation, but to the circumstances or condition one was in at that time [ICC, Vn]. 'Calling' here focuses on racial and social status [TG].
2 It refers to God's calling to become a Christian [Lns, NCBC, NIC]. One should remain a Christian and continue to emphasize this fact [NIC]. 'The calling' refers to God's call from darkness to light. It is to this call, not to a social standing, that one should remain faithful. If he is a slave, he should not remain faithful to slavery, but to the call that came to him while he was a slave [NCBC].
3. It refers to both 1 and 2 [Alf, Ed, EGT, Gdt, My]. 'Calling' refers to the summons to become a believer. But the conditions of life are also intended, otherwise the meaning is not relevant [Ed]. It is God's call to salvation along with all the external circumstances that comprise the occasion of it [Gdt].

7:21 (If) you-were-called (as a) slave,[a] let-it-concern[b] you not;

TEXT—GNT third edition punctuates the first clause as a question followed by an imperative. GNT fourth edition punctuates it as a statement followed by an imperative. It does not rate its choice. All versions except NJB select the question punctuation. NJB selects the statement punctuation which it translates as a condition.

LEXICON—a. δοῦλος (LN 87.76) (BAGD 1.b. p. 205): 'slave' [AB, BAGD, He, HNTC, ICC, LN, Lns; all versions except KJV], 'servant' [BAGD; KJV], 'bondservant' [LN]. Slavery was everywhere present in the early church with many members from this class of society [AB].

b. pres. act. impera. of μέλω (LN **25.223**) (BAGD 4. p. 500): 'to concern' [BAGD, **LN**], 'to bother' [AB], 'to trouble' [He, HNTC; NIV, REB], 'to worry' [LB], 'to be of concern, to be anxious about' [LN]. This word is also translated actively: 'to worry about something' [Lns; NASB], 'to give something thought' [NAB], 'to care for something' [KJV], 'to think something matters' [NJB], 'to be concerned about something' [NRSV], 'to mind' [BAGD; TEV, TNT], 'to be distressed at something' [ICC]. It is also joined with 'not' and translated 'never mind' [BAGD].

QUESTION—Why should a slave not be concerned?

Paul's point is that the slave should not let his condition concern him, but to see it as a place where he can live out his Christian calling [NIC2]. He should not let it bother him since he is the Lord's freeman and is ultimately accountable to God, not men [AB]. If he was a slave when God called him, God will give him the strength to live as a slave [TNTC].

but even-if[a] you-are-able to-become free,[b] rather use[c] (it).

LEXICON—a. εἰ καί (BAGD 4. p. 220): 'even if' [AB, BAGD, He; NJB, NRSV, TNT], 'even supposing' [NAB], 'even though' [BAGD, HNTC], 'if also' [Lns], 'of course, if' [LB], 'if' [KJV, NASB, TEV], 'though if' [REB], 'although' [BAGD; NIV]. Εἰ καί indicates a strong exception, 'if indeed' [NIC2]. Some separate the καί from εἰ 'if', taking it with the word δύνασαι 'you are able', meaning 'if you are *also* able to become free' [ICC, Lns, Rb].

b. ἐλεύθερος (LN 87.84; 37.134) (BAGD 1. p. 250): 'free' [AB, BAGD, He, HNTC, ICC, LN (37.134), Lns; all versions except NJB, NRSV, REB, TEV]. This adjective is also translated as a noun: 'free man' [LN (87.84); TEV], 'free person' [LN (87.84)], 'freedom' [NIV, NJB, NRSV, REB]. It refers to political and social freedom [BAGD]. Slaves could be set free by a master's generosity or by his death and will [Lns].

c. aorist act. impera. of χράομαι (LN 42.23) (BAGD 1.a. p. 884): 'to use' [LN, Lns; KJV, TEV], 'to make use of' [AB, BAGD, ICC, LN; NRSV, TNT], 'to make full use of' [NJB]. 'to do' [NASB, NIV], 'to make the most of' [BAGD; NAB], 'to take an opportunity' [LB, REB], 'to take advantage of' [BAGD], 'to remain (in slavery)' [He], 'to put up with (your present status)' [HNTC]. The aorist implies a single act [NIC2].

QUESTION—What is it that they should use?

1. This means that they should make use of their opportunity for freedom and become free [EGT, Gdt, ICC, Lns, NCBC, NIC2, Rb, TH, TNTC; LB, NASB, NIV, REB, TEV]. This interpretation fits the context: (1) the normal meaning of εἰ καί is 'if indeed' not 'even though'; (2) in an elliptical sentence the implied words would usually come from that sentence rather than from a more remote source and 'freedom' is part of this sentence; (3) the verb 'to use' is an aorist infinitive indicating a single action and the present tense would be more in keeping with the idea of continuing on in slavery; (4) the word begins with the strong adversative ἀλλά 'but' which signals an exception rather than an intensification of the negative imperative; (5) the regular meaning of 'rather' is 'by all means'; (6) the verb 'to make use of' does not lend itself to use with a negative while Paul's common use of the verb means 'to make use of' or 'to take advantage of' (7:31; 9:12, 15); (7) the predominant pattern of this chapter has been imperative followed by an exception [NIC2]. Paul makes a similar exception to a general principle in 7:28: 'but if you do marry' [TH].

2. It means that they should make use of their slavery by remaining in slavery instead of taking their freedom [AB, Alf, Ed, He, Herm, HNTC, My; NAB, NJB, NRSV, TNT]. This choice fits in with the theme of the whole passage which is to remain as one is [Alf, Ed]. The slave would use his status for witnessing [AB]. The slave should apply himself even more to serving the master who offered freedom [Ed].
3. It means that they are to use their calling in their free state [NIC]. In this passage, vocation is central and therefore it is the natural object of the verb 'to use'. They are to make a better use of their vocation when they have the opportunity to become free [NIC].

7:22 For[a] the-one-who was-called in[b] the-Lord (as a) slave is (a) freedman[c] of-the-Lord,

LEXICON—a. γάρ: 'for' [AB, He, HNTC, Lns; KJV, NASB, NIV, NRSV, TEV], 'so' [NJB], not explicit [all other versions].

b. ἐν with dative object: 'in' [AB, Lns; all versions except LB, NIV, NJB, TEV], 'by' [He; LB, NIV, TEV], not explicit [HNTC; NJB]. This word is also joined with 'called' and 'the Lord' and translated 'to be/become (a Christian)' [ICC; REB].

c. ἀπελεύθερος (LN **87.85**) (BAGD p. 83): 'freedman' [AB, BAGD, He, HNTC, ICC, **LN**, Lns; all versions except KJV, LB, NRSV, TEV], 'freed person' [NRSV], 'free man' [KJV, TEV], 'free person' [**LN**]. This word is also translated as a verb phrase: '(Christ) has set (you) free' [LB].

QUESTION—What relationship is indicated by γάρ 'for'?

1. When the previous sentence means that they should remain in slavery, this verse gives the grounds for saying that a slave should remain a slave and not accept his freedom [Alf, Ed, HNTC]. It is the reason why they could endure being a slave [HNTC]: a person should not be concerned about his slavery because, in Christ, a slave becomes free and a free man becomes a slave.
2. When the previous sentence means that they should obtain their freedom if possible, this verse gives the grounds for saying they should not be concerned if they were slaves [Gdt, Ho, Lns, NIC2]. This verse is the grounds of the whole of 7:21; neither slaves nor freemen should dread being in their condition [Gdt, Lns]. Slavery does not take away spiritual liberty and freedom does not result in license since one still serves Christ [Gdt].
3. Those who take the previous sentence to mean they should use their calling. Additional proof to the focal point of vocation is given in 7:22 and it does not matter what one's worldly position is [NIC].

QUESTION—Who is the 'Lord'?

It is Jesus Christ [Ho, TG, TH, Vn].

QUESTION—What is the meaning of the phrase ἐν κυρίῳ 'in (the) Lord'?

1. It indicates agent [He, TG; LB, NIV, TEV]: called by the Lord.

2. It has a locative sense [Alf, Herm, HNTC, ICC, My, TH, TNTC; REB]. 'Called in the Lord' means to be 'in Christ', that is, to be a Christian [HNTC, NIC2, TH, TNTC]. The instrumental sense would say that the Lord did the calling, whereas in the context, it is God who does the calling [NIC2]. It indicates the element in which the calling has taken place, it was in Christ, not out of him [My]. He is called to be one with Christ [TH, TNTC].
3. It means 'under the authority of the Lord' [Vn]. One who is 'in the Lord' is one who is under his authority. There is no article with 'Lord' indicating that stress is being laid on the meaning of the term 'Lord' [Vn].

QUESTION—How are the nouns related in the genitive construction ἀπελεύθερος κυρίου 'freedman of the Lord'?

1. It means that the freedman belongs to the Lord [Ed, NIC2, TG; NRSV].
2. It means that the Lord is the agent who releases the slave into freedom [Ho, ICC, Lns, TH].

QUESTION—In what way is a slave a freedman?

Paul uses paradoxical language, a slave is a freedman, to emphasize that one's freedom in Christ so far outshadows his slavery that he can consider himself Christ's free man [HNTC]. In one's secular condition he is still a slave, but in his spiritual condition he is now free [ICC]. The believer is the Lord's 'freedman' because the Lord has set him free from the powers of darkness, the slaveholders of this age [BAGD]. Freedom consists in being free from sin [Herm, HNTC, Ho], from slavery to Satan and from the curse of the Law [Ho]. Paul's point in using the metaphor of a slave was that the slave belonged to his master, not to himself [NIC2].

likewise[a] the-one-being-called (being) free[b] is a-slave of-Christ.

LEXICON—a. ὁμοίως (LN 64.1): 'likewise' [AB, LN, Lns; KJV, NASB], 'similarly' [He, HNTC; NIV, TNT], 'in the same way' [NJB, TEV], 'equally' [REB], 'just as' [NAB, NRSV], 'the converse is true' [ICC], not explicit [LB]. This introduces an exact reversal of relations [My]. This is a comparison of an actual slave who becomes spiritually free, and an actual free man who becomes a spiritual slave [Alf]. The cases are similar: in both cases there is slavery and freedom [Lns]. See this word at 7:3.

b. ἐλεύθερος (LN **87.84**): 'free' [ICC; KJV, LB, NASB, NRSV, TNT]. This word is also translated as a noun phrase: 'free person' [**LN**; TEV]. 'freedman' [NAB], 'free man' [AB, He, HNTC, LN, Lns; NIV, NJB, REB]. See this word at 7:21.

QUESTION—How are the nouns related in the genitive construction δοῦλος Χριστοῦ 'slave of Christ'?

1. The slave belongs to Christ [Ho, Lns, TH].
2. The slave serves Christ [ICC; REB].

QUESTION—What is meant by being Christ's slave?

This slave belongs to Christ who is his spiritual master [Lns, NIC2]. He now obeys the Lord [ICC]. He owes Christ both loyalty and service [HNTC].

Since the actual slave who is now spiritually free is also a slave of Christ, the distinction between earthly master and slave is removed and both have Christ as Master [Ho]. Both the slave and free man have the very same relations of spiritual freedom and service to Christ [HNTC].

7:23 You-were-bought[a] with-a-price;[b] do-not become slaves of-men.

LEXICON—a. aorist pass. indic. of ἀγοράζω: 'to be bought'. See this word at 6:20.

b. τιμή (LN **57.161**): 'price'. The price is Christ's precious blood [Ho, ICC, Lns, Rb, TNTC, Vn]. See this word at 6:20.

QUESTION—What is the function of this statement?

This applies to both the slave and free person dealt with in 7:22. The slave has been freed and the free man has been made a slave because both have been purchased by Christ [NIC2]. All should be content with their external condition because all are equally subjects of redemption [Ho]. It gives the reason why men should obey Christ [EBC, Ho, NIC].

QUESTION—Who is the implied actor of ἠγοράσθητε 'you were bought'?

1. Christ is the actor [ICC, Lns, NIC2, Rb, TG, TH, TNTC, Vn; LB], see Rev. 5:9 [TH].
2. God is the actor [TEV].

QUESTION—What is the significance of the present imperative μὴ γίνεσθε 'do not become'?

The present imperative indicates that they should stop doing something they were already doing [AB, EBC, ICC, Rb]: Stop being slaves of men!

QUESTION—What is meant by being slaves of men?

1. This is metaphorical [Ed, EGT, Gdt, Ho, ICC, Lns, My, NIC, NIC2, Rb, TG, TNTC]. It takes a special frame of mind and spirit to live as free men. They should not automatically accept what others say and thus have the mentality of slaves [TNTC]. It means they are not to come under bondage to mere human wisdom and thus be anxious about the need to be free from social settings such as marriage [NIC2]. Although slaves externally, they should not be slaves in spirit [Ed, Ho]. They must not be subservient to what men wish and demand, but should do what Christ wants [Gdt, ICC, My, NIC]. They must not adopt the principles and practices of non-Christians [TG]. They should not let worldly ideas rule them about slavery, circumcision, or marriage [Lns].
2. This is addressed to free men, telling them not to sell themselves into actual slavery [HNTC, Rb].

7:24 Brothers, each-one in-(the-state)-which he-was-called, in this let-him-remain[a] with[b] God.

LEXICON—a. pres. act. impera. of μένω: 'to remain'. The present imperative indicates continuous action [TNTC]. See this word at 7:20.

b. παρά with dative object (LN 89.111; 90.20) (BAGD II.2.e. p. 610): 'with' [AB, He, HNTC, LN (89.111), Lns; KJV, NAB, NRSV, TNT], 'in fellowship with' [TEV], 'in the sight of, in the opinion of' [LN (90.20)], 'before' [BAGD; NAB, NJB, REB], 'responsible to' [NIV], 'in (God's) presence' [He]. It is also translated 'for the Lord is there to help him' [LB], 'remembering God's presence and His protecting care' [ICC]. See this word at 3:19.

QUESTION—What words are implied with ᾧ 'in which'?

It means 'in whatever situation' [NIC2; LB, NIV], 'in whatever condition' [He; NAB, NASB, NRSV, REB, TEV], 'in whatever state' [AB, HNTC, ICC; NJB, TNT].

QUESTION—What is meant by παρά 'with'?

1. It means 'in the presence of' or 'in fellowship with' [Alf, BAGD, EBC, Ed, Gdt, Ho, ICC, Lns, My, NCBC, NIC, NIC2, Rb, TH, TNTC, Vn; TEV]. Paul's point is not simply that a person should remain in the situation he was in when called but that he should also remain with God [NIC2]. It could mean 'on God's side', and this fits well with the verb 'remain' and contrasts well with 'slaves of men' [ICC]. It means 'near God, constantly aware of his presence' that is, 'in communion with him' [Ho, NIC, TNTC]. It means 'to be beside' God [Lns, Vn].
2. It means 'in the sight of, in the estimation of' [AB, TG]. In 3:19 this word was translated, 'from God's viewpoint'. Here it could be translated, 'as far as God is concerned' [AB]. The meaning then would be that the person is ultimately responsible to God, not men.

DISCOURSE UNIT: 7:25–40 [EBC, Gdt, GNT, Herm, HNTC, Ho, NIC, NIC2, TG, TH, Vn]. The topic is instruction concerning virgins [EBC, HNTC, NIC, NIC2], the unmarried and widows [GNT, Herm], virgins and widows [Ho], counsels concerning the unmarried [Vn]. This section is in reply to a question from the Corinthians about whether people should marry [TG]. The same introduction πέρι δέ now concerning' is given at 7:25 and at 8:1 showing clearly that these verses should be taken as a single section [TH].

DISCOURSE UNIT: 7:25–38 [Ed, Lns, My, NCBC, TNTC]. The topic is the case of virgins [Ed, TNTC], regarding maidens [Lns], advice on virgins [My, NCBC].

DISCOURSE UNIT: 7:25–35 [AB, EGT, Lns]. The topic is Paul's opinion regarding the unmarried [AB], advantages of the single state [EGT], the preliminary considerations [Lns].

DISCOURSE UNIT: 7:25–31 [AB, Gdt]. The topic is marriage being permissible but inadvisable because of the "form of this world" [AB], the present state of things [Gdt].

DISCOURSE UNIT: 7:25–28 [NIC2]. The topic is singleness being preferable but not required. This section introduces the subject and gives Paul's opinion about it.

7:25 Now[a] concerning virgins[b]

LEXICON—a. δέ (LN 89.94): 'now' [AB, Lns; all versions except NAB, NJB, REB, TNT], not explicit [He, HNTC, ICC; NAB, NJB, REB, TNT].

b. παρθένος (LN **34.77**) (BAGD 1. p. 627): 'virgin' [AB, BAGD, He, HNTC; KJV, NAB, NASB, NIV, NRSV], 'the unmarried' [**LN**; REB, TNT], 'unmarried person' [LN; TEV], 'unmarried daughter' [ICC], 'maiden' [Lns], 'girl who is not yet married' [LB], 'people remaining virgin' [NJB]. Παρθένος 'unmarried' may also imply virginity [LN].

QUESTION—What relationship is indicated by δέ 'now'?

It indicates a transition to a new topic [Ho, My, NIC2]. Paul now resumes his instructions about marriage [AB, Ho]. The words 'now about' occur at 7:1, 7:25, 8:1, 12:1, 16:1, and 16:12 and signal that Paul is addressing different topics in the Corinthian letter to Paul [NIC2].

QUESTION—To whom does the word παρθένων 'virgins' refer?

1. It refers only to women [Alf, Ed, EGT, Gdt, He, ICC, Lns, My, NCBC, NIC, NIC2, Rb, TH, TNTC; KJV, LB, NAB, NASB, NIV, NRSV]. The word in this context refers to young engaged women who were being pressured by the "spiritual" people of Corinth not to marry and who were therefore wondering whether to go through with their marriages or not [NIC2]. In five out of six occurrences of the word from 7:25–38, it is clearly feminine as shown by the form of the article. In 7:34 the term is contrasted with ἄγαμος 'unmarried woman' which may indicate that παρθένος here refers to a girl engaged but not yet married. The Corinthians were asking whether such should marry or remain unmarried [NCBC]. Verses that apply to women only are 7:28, 34, 36, 37 and 38 Contrast its reference to men in Rev. 14:4 [ICC]. Παρθένος can refer to a 'virgin' or to a woman who has never been married, or to a divorced woman or a widow [TH].
2. It refers to both men and women [AB, TG; TEV]. Παρθένος can refer to both men and women [TG]. After considering married people, Paul now turns to those who have not been married. The discussion about the advisability of marriage in 7:26–36 includes both men and women [AB].

I-have no command[a] of-the-Lord, but I-give (my) opinion[b]

LEXICON—a. ἐπιταγή: 'command'. See this word at 7:6.

b. γνώμη (LN 31.3) (BAGD 2. p. 163): 'opinion' [AB, BAGD, He, HNTC, ICC, LN; all versions except KJV, LB, NIV, REB], 'judgment' [BAGD, Lns; KJV, NIV, REB], 'wisdom' [LB], 'what is considered' [LN].

QUESTION—To whom does the word 'Lord' refer?

It refers to Jesus Christ [Gdt, ICC, NIC, TG].

QUESTION—What did Paul mean by this statement?

He meant that the Lord did not teach on this subject [ICC, NIC2]. Jesus neither taught on this subject, nor had he given any revelation to Paul on it [Gdt, NIC]. See 7:6, 10, and 12.

QUESTION—What is meant by γνώμη 'opinion'?

This is not a mere personal preference but a weighty judgment from a qualified source [Lns]. It indicates a carefully formed decision based on knowledge (see 2 Cor. 8:10) [NIC, Rb]. This is a word that he did not receive by revelation, but one that he deduced from Christian principles by the guidance of the Holy Spirit [Gdt, Ho]. This is not a question between grades of inspiration, but between command and conditional advice which required the concurrence of those whom he advised [EGT].

as (one who) is trustworthy[a] having-been-shown-mercy[b] by[c] (the) Lord.

LEXICON—a. πιστός (LN 31.87) (BAGD 1.a.α. p. 664): 'trustworthy' [AB, HNTC, LN, Lns; NAB, NASB, NIV, NRSV, TNT], 'worthy of trust' [TEV], 'fit to be trusted' [REB], 'faithful' [LN; KJV, NJB], 'dependable, reliable' [LN]. This word is also translated as a clause modifying 'wisdom': '(wisdom) that can be trusted' [LB]. It is also translated as a phrase modifying 'give my opinion': 'in my capacity as a believer' [He]. It is also translated as a clause: 'not unworthy of (your) confidence' [ICC]. Here it does not mean 'believing' since Paul uses this as a basis for his claim that he be heard with respect. He rather feels that in a special sense he has been called and commissioned because of the confidence God has in him. Πιστός is almost like the title 'trusted man, commissioner' [BAGD]. See this word at 1:9.

b. perf. pass. participle of ἐλεέω (LN 88.76) (BAGD p. 249): 'to be shown mercy' [LN], 'to be granted mercy' [AB, He; NJB], 'to have mercy conferred on one' [Lns], 'to obtain mercy' [KJV], 'to receive as a gracious gift, to be favored with' [BAGD], 'to be merciful toward' [LN]. This word is also translated actively: 'to give kindness' [LB]. The words 'having-been-shown-mercy by the Lord' is translated 'by the Lord's mercy' [HNTC; NASB, NIV, NRSV, REB, TEV], 'thanks to the Lord's mercy' [NAB], 'through the Lord's mercy' [ICC]. It means to show kindness or concern for someone in serious need [LN], or to have mercy on someone [BAGD, LN]. The perfect tense indicates that Lord's mercies are permanent [Lns, TNTC].

c. ὑπό with genitive object (LN 90.1): 'by' [AB, LN, Lns], 'of' [KJV]. Also see how the phrase is translated above.

QUESTION—Who is 'the Lord'?

1. It refers to Jesus Christ [EGT, Ho, NIC].
2. It refers to God [HNTC, TG].

QUESTION—How does ἠλεημένος 'having been shown mercy' relate to being πιστός 'trustworthy'?

1. 'Having been shown mercy' refers to Paul being given the quality of being 'worthy of trust' by people [AB, Ho]: You can trust my opinion because the Lord in his mercy has made me trustworthy. Christ has brought about the inward graces and qualities which entitled Paul to be trusted by his readers [Ho].

2. 'Having been shown mercy' refers to Paul's salvation and/or call to be an apostle.

2.1 As a result Paul is worthy of being trusted by people [Gdt, ICC, Lns, NIC2]: because God saved and called me to be an apostle, you can trust my opinion. His conversion and call to become an apostle are evidence that the opinion of one so favored is worthy of trust [ICC].

2.2 As a result Paul is now faithful to God or Christ [Ed, EGT, NIC]: because God saved and called me to be an apostle, I am faithful to Christ and my opinion is therefore trustworthy. This advice is given by one who is faithful to Christ and thus the advice must be pleasing to the Lord [NIC]. He had been entrusted by Christ with the responsibility of being an apostle. It was to this trust that he was faithful and therefore worthy of being trusted [EGT].

3. 'Having been shown mercy' refers to Paul's salvation which gave him the status of being a believer [He]. 'I give my own opinion in my capacity as a believer, which the mercy of the Lord has granted me'. The faithful transmission of a message is not in question here [He].

7:26 Therefore[a] I-think[b] this is[c] good[d] because-of[e] the present[f] distress,[g]

LEXICON—a. οὖν: 'therefore' [Lns; KJV], 'then' [NASB, REB, TNT], 'well then' [ICC; NJB], 'so' [AB], not explicit [He, HNTC; LB, NAB, NIV, NRSV, TEV]. It indicates that the present distress is the grounds for saying that in his opinion it was not best to marry [Ho]. This now states the opinion to which he referred in 7:25 [My].

b. pres. act. indic. of νομίζω (LN 31.29) (BAGD 2. p. 541): 'to think' [BAGD, He, ICC, LN; LB, NASB, NIV, NRSV, REB, TEV, TNT], 'to consider' [BAGD, HNTC], 'to deem' [AB], 'to suppose' [LN; KJV], 'to hold' [BAGD, Lns], 'to believe' [BAGD, LN], 'to presume, to assume, to imagine' [LN], 'it seems' [NAB, NJB]. It means to presume something to be true, but without certainty [LN]. 'To think' has the same sense as 'opinion' in 7:25. It does not imply a supposition, but rather a definite opinion [ICC, Lns, NIC].

c. pres. act. infin. of ὑπάρχω (LN 13.5) (BAGD 2. p. 838): 'to be' [AB, BAGD, He, HNTC, ICC, LN, Lns; all versions except NAB, NJB, REB], 'to seem (to someone)' [NAB], 'to seem to be' [NJB], not explicit [REB].

d. καλός (LN 88.4) (BAGD 3.a. p. 400): 'good' [AB, BAGD, LN; KJV, NASB], 'excellent' [Lns], 'desirable, advantageous' [BAGD]. This word is also translated as a noun phrase: 'a good thing' [HNTC], 'the right thing' [NJB]. It is also joined with the next occurrence of the same word in this verse and translated 'good' [NAB, NIV, TNT], 'better' [TEV], 'best' [LB], 'well' [NRSV], 'advisable' [He], 'the best way' [REB], 'an excellent thing' [ICC].

e. διά with accusative object (LN 89.26): 'because of' [AB, He, LN, Lns; NIV, NJB], 'in view of' [NASB, NRSV], 'on account of' [HNTC, LN; TNT], 'for' [KJV], 'in' [NAB, REB]. This word is also translated as a verb phrase: 'considering' [TEV], 'owing to' [ICC]. It is also translated as a clause: 'here is the problem:' [LB].

f. perf. act. participle of ἐνίστημι (LN **67.63**) (BAGD 2. p. 266): 'present' [AB, HNTC, Lns; all versions except LB, NJB, NRSV, REB], 'impending' [BAGD, **LN**; NRSV], 'imminent' [LN], 'approaching' [He]. This adjective is also translated as a verb phrase: '(which) is weighing upon us' [NJB], '(that) are upon us' [ICC]. It is also translated as a noun: '(the) present' [LB, REB]. See this word at 3:22.

g. ἀνάγκη (LN **22.1**) (BAGD p. 52): 'distress' [BAGD, LN, Lns; KJV, NASB, NRSV, TEV, TNT], 'distressful times' [ICC], 'stress' [NJB], 'time of stress' [NAB, REB], 'troublous times' [**LN**], 'crisis' [NIV, NRSV], 'pressure' [AB], 'calamity' [BAGD, He], 'necessity' [HNTC], 'great dangers' [LB], 'trouble' [LN].

QUESTION—To what does τοῦτο 'this' refer?

It refers to the ὅτι 'that' clause which follows [AB, Alf, Ed, EGT, He, Herm, ICC, Lns, My, NIC2, Vn].

QUESTION—What is the function of δία 'because of'?

It indicates the reason why Paul considers this advice to be good [ICC, Lns, TG].

QUESTION—Does ἐνίστημι refer to a 'present' or 'impending' distress?

1. It refers to a present distress [Alf, EGT, Gdt, HNTC, Lns, NIC, NIC2, TH, TNTC; all versions except NRSV]. Paul is thinking of the troubles preceding the last days referred to in 7:29 and already experienced in the sufferings of Christians [Gdt, HNTC]. Paul has in mind general suffering which is always the lot of the Christian [NIC, NIC2]. Some especially difficult crisis was troubling the Corinthians at the time [TNTC]. It refers to the persecution of the church [EGT].
2. It refers to an impending distress [BAGD, Ed, Herm, Ho, LN, My, TG; NRSV]. The reference is to the end of the age expected to happen soon [TG]. Specifically, it was the distress that would precede the Second Coming that is indicated [Ed]. Paul has in mind the troubles that will happen to Christians as they proclaim the Good News [Ho].

that (it is) good[a] for-a-person/man[b] so[c] to-be.

LEXICON—a. καλός (LN 88.4) (BAGD 3.c. p. 400): 'good' [AB, LN; KJV, NASB, NJB], 'excellent' [Lns]. This word is also translated as a noun phrase: 'a good thing' [HNTC]. 'Good' is used here in the sense of expedient [Ho]; or 'good in principle' or 'in nature' [EGT]. See this word at καλός above in this verse where some versions have joined the two words in a single translation.

b. ἄνθρωπος (LN 9.1): 'person' [AB, LN, Lns; LB, NAB, NRSV, TNT], 'people' [ICC; NJB], 'one' [BAGD, He], 'you' [NIV, NRSV], 'man' [HNTC; all other versions]. See this word at 4:1.

c. οὕτως (BAGD 1.b. p. 597): 'so' [Lns; KJV], 'as follows' [AB]. The phrase οὕτως εἶναι 'so to be' is translated 'to continue/remain/stay as he is' [HNTC, ICC; NAB, NASB, NIV, NJB, NRSV, REB, TEV, TNT], 'not to change the state in which one finds oneself' [He]. It is also translated as the state to which it refers: 'unmarried' [BAGD; LB].

QUESTION—What relationship is indicated by ὅτι 'that/because'?

1. It explains the word τοῦτο 'this' of the preceding clause [AB, Alf, Ed, EGT, Herm, ICC, Lns, My, NIC2, Vn]: I think this is good, namely that it is good for a person so to be.
2. It indicates the reason why celibacy is good [Gdt]: I think this (celibacy) is best (for virgins), because it is best for people so to be.

QUESTION—What is meant by ἀνθτρώπῳ 'a person/man'?

1. It means 'person', making this apply to both men and women [AB, Alf, EBC, EGT, Gdt, ICC, Lns, My, Rb; LB, NAB, NRSV, TNT].
2. It means 'man' [TG, TH]. Because the next verse addresses men, it is best to take that sense in this verse as well [TH].

QUESTION—To what does οὕτως 'so/thus' refer?

1. It refers to what follows [AB, Vn]: it is good for a person to be as I am about to relate.
2. It refers to what precedes, that is, being 'unmarried' (7:25) [BAGD, Gdt, Ho, My, NIC; LB]: it is good for a person to be unmarried.
3. It refers to the state in which a person may find him/herself [EBC, EGT, He, HNTC, ICC, My, NIC, TG, TH, TNTC, Vn]: it is good for a person to remain in the condition he is in.

7:27 (If) you-have-been-bound[a] to-a-wife, seek[b] not release;[c]

TEXT—GNT third edition punctuates this verse as two questions followed by two imperatives. GNT fourth edition punctuates it as two statements followed by two imperatives. It does not rate its choice. All versions except LB and NJB select the question punctuation. LB and NJB translate as statements giving conditions.

LEXICON—a. perf. pass. indic. of δέω (LN 18.13) (BAGD 3. p. 178): 'to be bound' [AB, BAGD, He, HNTC, Lns; all versions except LB, NIV, NJB, TEV], 'to be joined' [NJB], 'to be united' [ICC], 'to be tied, to be tied together' [LN]. This word is also translated actively: 'to have (a wife)' [TEV]. It is also conflated with the word 'wife' and translated 'to be married' [LB, NIV], 'to be bound in marriage' [REB]. Δέω here is figurative of binding by law and duty [BAGD]. The perfect aspect indicates a settled state [TNTC], or a permanent state [EBC]. 'Bound' here has the sense of being under obligation to a contract and so covers both engaged and married couples [NIC2].

b. pres. act. impera. of ζητέω (LN 57.59) (BAGD 2.b.α. p. 339): 'to seek' [AB, He, HNTC, ICC, LN, Lns; all versions except LB, NJB, TEV], 'to look for' [NJB], 'to try to get (rid of)' [TEV], 'to try to obtain' [LN], 'to attempt to get' [LN], 'to strive for, to aim at, to desire, to wish' [BAGD]. This word is also conflated with the word 'separation' and translated 'to separate' [LB]. The present tense indicates that never at any time should they seek freedom [ICC]. The present tense indicates an on-going action: 'do not be seeking' [EGT, Rb].

c. λύσις (LN **34.78**) (BAGD p. 482): 'release' [AB, BAGD, HNTC, Lns], 'divorce' [BAGD, **LN**; NIV], 'separation' [BAGD, He], 'freedom' [NAB], 'dissolution' [REB]. This word is also translated as a verb phrase: 'to be free' [NRSV, TNT], 'to be loosed' [KJV], 'to be released' [NASB, NJB], 'to be freed from the tie' [ICC], 'to get rid of' [TEV], 'to separate' [LB].

QUESTION—Why does Paul use the term λύσις 'release'?

This word is attested in the papyri as a technical term for releasing a person from the constraints of a contract. It is not used elsewhere to denote divorce. Paul uses this term so that it can apply both to married couples where the term would mean 'to divorce', and to engaged couples where it would have the meaning 'to break a contract' [NIC2].

(if) you-have-been-released[a] from a-wife, seek[b] not a-wife.

LEXICON—a. perf. pass. indic. of λύω (LN 37.127) (BAGD 2.b. p. 483): 'to be released' [AB, BAGD, LN, Lns; NASB], 'to be free/freed' [BAGD, He, HNTC, ICC; NAB, NJB, NRSV, TNT] 'to be set free' [BAGD, LN], 'to be loosed' [KJV]. This word is also conflated with the phrase 'from a wife' and translated 'to not be married' [LB], 'to dissolve a marriage' [REB], 'to be unmarried' [NIV, TEV]. A previous state of being 'bound' in this case need not be assumed [BAGD]. The perfect aspect indicates a settled state [TNTC], or a permanent state [EBC].

b. pres. act. impera. of ζητέω (LN 57.59) (BAGD 2.a. p. 339): 'to seek' [AB, He, HNTC, LN, Lns; KJV, NASB, NRSV, REB, TNT], 'to look for' [NIV, NJB, TEV], 'to go in search of' [NAB], 'to seek to be bound' [ICC], 'to try to obtain' [BAGD, Lns], 'desire to possess' [BAGD]. This word is also joined with the word 'wife' and translated 'to rush into (it)' [LB].

QUESTION—Does λέλυσαι 'you-have-been-released' mean that the person was married before?

1. It does not mean that the person must have been previously married [Alf, BAGD, Ed, EGT, Gdt, He, HNTC, ICC, My, NCBC, NIC, NIC2, Rb, TG, TH, TNTC]. The perfect tense indicates: 'Are you free from matrimonial ties?' [ICC]. It means freedom from the marriage bonds [Ed, Gdt, NCBC, TH] and applies to bachelors and widowers [EGT, He, HNTC, ICC, Rb, TNTC]. 'To be free from' means 'to be unentangled with' a wife, that is, to be single [My]. It can mean discharged from engagement obligations [NIC2].

2 It means that the person had been previously married [AB, Lns]. The perfect aspect of the verb λύω 'to set free' is 'have you been set free from a wife?'. This is not addressing those who have never been married. Paul has already spoken to the divorced in 7:10–16. Here he is talking to those

released from marriage by the death of a wife [AB]. The term is general and can apply to any form of release from a marriage [Lns].

7:28 But[a] even[b] if you-marry,[c] you-sin[d] not,

LEXICON—a. δέ (LN 89.124): 'but' [HNTC, ICC, LN; all versions except NAB, NJB, TNT], 'yet' [AB], 'however' [NJB], 'nevertheless' [Lns], 'nonetheless' [He], not explicit [NAB, TNT].

b. καί: 'even' [AB, Lns], not explicit [NAB, NRSV]. This word is also translated as a verbal auxiliary: '(if you) do (marry)' [He, HNTC, ICC; NIV, NJB, REB, TEV, TNT], '(if you) should (marry)' [NASB]. The combination ἐάν καί means 'if nevertheless' and not 'though' [Ed].

c. aorist act. subj. of γαμέω (LN 34.66): 'to marry' [He, HNTC, ICC, LN, Lns; all versions except LB, NJB], 'to get married' [AB; LB, NJB]. The aorist points to a single act, the subjunctive to the future [Lns]. See this word at 7:9.

d. aorist act. indic. of ἁμαρτάνω (LN 88.289) (BAGD 4.b. p. 42) (BAGD 1. p. 42): 'to sin' [Lns; KJV, NASB, NIV, NRSV, TNT], 'to commit (a) sin' [AB, He, HNTC, ICC; NAB, TEV], 'to be a sin' [LB, NJB], 'to do wrong' [REB]. See this word at 6:18.

QUESTION—What relationship is indicated by δέ 'but'?

It qualifies 7:27 by permitting its opposite [NIC2]. It functions to keep the advice of 7:27 from being too strict [EGT] and assures the Corinthians that if they go against his advice, it is not wrong [ICC]. He may be foolish, but he is not sinning [HNTC].

QUESTION—To whom does the 'you (singular)' refer in γαμήσῃς 'you marry'?

It refers to the man addressed in 7:26–27 [NIC2]. It refers to any male member of the Corinthian congregation [HNTC].

QUESTION—Why does Paul even suggest that marriage may be a sin?

For a Jew, marriage was normal if not almost obligatory. This makes it remarkable for Paul to speak like this. It must be that he is addressing a question put to him by the Corinthians suggesting that marriage was sinful [NIC2].

and if the virgin[a] marries, she-sinned not;

TEXT—Instead of ἡ παρθένος 'the (feminine) virgin', some manuscripts omit the article, which then allows for a reference to virgins of both sexes. GNT includes the feminine article without any indication of doubt.

LEXICON—a. παρθένος: 'virgin' [AB, He, HNTC; KJV, NAB, NASB, NIV, TNT], 'maiden' [ICC, Lns], 'girl' [LB, NRSV, REB], 'young girl' [NJB], 'unmarried woman' [TEV]. The definite article before this word indicates a general reference to virgins [AB, Alf, Herm, ICC]. Paul is merely addressing one virgin out of the group [Lns]. Another view is that the definite article refers back to the virgin mentioned in verse 7:25 [EGT]. See this word at 7:25.

but[a] such-ones will-have trouble[b] in-the flesh,[c]

LEXICON—a. δέ: 'but' [He, HNTC; NAB, NIV, NJB, TEV, TNT], 'yet' [ICC, Lns; NASB, NRSV], 'nevertheless' [KJV], 'however' [LB], 'it is only that' [REB], not explicit [AB].

b. θλῖψις (LN 22.2) (BAGD 1. p. 362): 'trouble' [KJV, NASB], 'everyday troubles' [TEV], 'many troubles' [NIV], 'trials' [NAB], 'affliction' [BAGD, He, HNTC; TNT], 'increased affliction' [ICC], 'distress' [AB, BAGD; NRSV], 'extra problems' [LB], 'hardships' [NJB], 'hardships to endure' [REB], 'tribulation' [BAGD, Lns], 'trouble and suffering, suffering, persecution' [LN], 'oppression' [BAGD]. 'Trouble' refers back to 'the present distress' of 7:26 [Ed].

c. σάρξ (LN 58.10) (BAGD 5. p. 744): 'flesh' [He, HNTC, Lns; KJV], 'this life' [NAB, NASB, NIV, NRSV], 'world' [TNT], 'human nature' [LN; NJB], 'outward life' [He], 'affairs of this life' [ICC], 'corporeality, physical limitation(s), life here on earth' [BAGD], 'physical nature of people' [LN], not explicit [LB, REB]. This word is also joined with 'in' and translated 'physical (distress)' [AB]. It is also translated as a clause: '(troubles) that married people will have' [TEV].

QUESTION—What word is emphasized in this clause?

The word θλίψις 'trouble' is fronted in its clause and emphatic [Rb].

QUESTION—To what troubles does the word θλίψις refer?

'Such ones' is masculine and includes both sexes [TNTC]. It refers to problems that accompany married life in general [TG, Vn]. The troubles are the result of 'the present difficulties' (7:26) [Ed, NIC2]. It could refer to the persecutions that will precede the Second Coming of Christ [ICC]. An example is Matt. 24:19 where pregnant and nursing mothers have physical difficulties during persecution [NIC]. Wars, earthquakes, pestilence, famine, and persecutions are at hand (Mark 13:7–13) [HNTC]. It will be easier on an unmarried person to suffer persecution than for a man who must consider what effect his actions will have on his dependents [NCBC].

and I would-spare[a] you (that).

LEXICON—a. pres. mid. indic. of φείδομαι (LN 22.28) (BAGD 1. p. 854): 'to spare' [BAGD, He, ICC, LN, Lns; KJV, NIV, NRSV, TEV], 'to like to spare' [NAB], 'to try/wish to spare' [AB, HNTC; NASB, TNT], 'to aim to spare' [REB], 'to wish that someone would not have to face something' [LB], 'to like someone to be without something' [NJB]. It means to prevent trouble from happening to someone [LN]. The present tense indicates that Paul is trying to spare them [AB, EGT, Rb, TNTC] by persuading them not to marry [ICC].

QUESTION—What word is emphasized in this clause?

The word ἔγω 'I' is emphasized: 'I for my part' [Lns, TNTC].

DISCOURSE UNIT: 7:29–35 [NIC2]. The topic is Paul's reason for singleness. This section functions as an explanation of what has preceded. It has two parts: 7:29–31, and 7:32–35. The first part gives a perspective of the last days intended to help the Corinthians' relationship to the world which is passing away. The second treats the theme of anxiety and Paul's desire that they be free from it.

7:29 But I-mean[a] this, brothers,[b]

LEXICON—a. pres. act. indic. of φημί (LN **33.140**) (BAGD 2. p. 856): 'to mean' [BAGD, **LN**, NIC2; NIV, NJB, NRSV, REB, TEV], 'to say' [AB, He, HNTC, Lns; KJV, NASB], 'to tell' [NAB, TNT], 'to affirm' [ICC], 'to imply' [LN]. This is also translated as a noun phrase: 'the important thing to remember' [LB]. It explains more fully the intent of what has been said [LN]. Paul's change from λέγω 'I say' to φημί 'I mean' probably lends seriousness to his words [Gdt, ICC]. This introduction indicates that Paul is giving a new revelation [He]. See a similar construction with λέγω at 1:12.

b. ἀδελφός (LN 11.23): 'brothers' [AB, He, HNTC, ICC, Lns; all versions except LB, NRSV, REB, TEV], 'brothers and sisters' [NRSV], 'fellow believers' [LN], 'my friends' [REB, TEV], not explicit [LB].

QUESTION—What is the function of the vocative ἀδελφοί 'brothers'?

The use of the vocative indicates a slight change in his argument and he now addresses everyone [NIC2]. The vocative shows that Paul is addressing the whole congregation with an important and tender message [NIC].

QUESTION—To what does the word τοῦτο 'this' refer?

It refers to the following words [AB, ICC, My, NIC, NIC2, Vn].

QUESTION—Does the phrase τοῦτο δέ φημι 'but this I say' function to introduce an explanation or a new topic?

1. It introduces an explanation [Alf, LN, NIC2, TG; NIV, NJB, NRSV, REB, TEV]. He has just said that marrying is not a sin. Some may therefore think that what he has advised is a matter of little concern. He therefore adds this serious consideration [Alf]. Paul is probably explaining what he meant by 'the present distress' and 'trouble in this life' [NIC2]. He explains why he advises them not to change their marital status [TG].
2. It introduces a new topic [TH]. Several reasons indicate that this is true: (1) the term 'brothers' usually occurs at a new paragraph; (2) the exact expression occurs at 15:50 where a new paragraph begins; (3) both here and at 15:50 there is reason to believe that Paul is dealing with a common Christian teaching, not with something new. Paul is then using this formula much like Jesus' words 'Truly, truly I tell you' [TH].

the time[a] has-been-shortened;[b]

LEXICON—a. καιρός (LN 67.78; 67.145): 'time' [He, HNTC, LN; all versions except LB, NRSV, REB], 'appointed time' [NRSV], 'time we live in' [REB], 'our remaining time' [LB], 'time allowed before the Advent' [ICC], 'period' [Lns], 'season' [AB]. Χρόνος refers to a time period, whereas καιρός refers to a specific or appointed time [NIC2]. See this word at 4:5.

b. perf. pass. participle of συστέλλω (LN **67.118**) (BAGD 1. p. 795): 'to be shortened' [BAGD, He, Lns; NASB], 'to become limited' [NJB], 'to be drawn together' [BAGD], 'to be drawn near, to be drawn to a close' [LN]. This word is also translated actively: 'to come to an end' [**LN**], 'to be short' [HNTC; KJV, NAB, NIV, TNT], 'to be very short' [LB], 'to become short' [AB], 'to grow short' [NRSV], 'to not last long' [REB], 'to not have much left' [TEV], 'to be very narrow' [ICC].

QUESTION—To what specific 'time' is Paul referring?

1. Paul is referring to the time before Christ's Second Coming [Alf, EGT, Gdt, He, Herm, HNTC, ICC, Lns, My, NCBC, NIC, TH, Vn]. In Rom. 13:11 ὁ καιρός is used to refer to the period before the Second Coming and is so used here [ICC].
2. Paul is referring to the time before an impending crisis at Corinth, the time of distress (7:26) [TNTC].
3. Other views [EBC, Herm, NIC2]. 'Time' here refers to the span beginning with Christ's death and resurrection and the gift of the Holy Spirit and proceeding to the last days. It is as though these have been compressed to enable the Corinthians to view the end of history and to order their lives accordingly [NIC2]. The time referred to is the time for doing the Lord's work which is coming to an end. The time will not be ended necessarily by the coming of the Lord, but by persecutions and their curtailing effect on Christian work and witness [EBC]. The time referred to is the world's time [Herm].

QUESTION—Is Paul referring to a time that was shortened or is he stating that there is not much time left or some other idea?

1. Paul is referring to a set period of time shortened from its original duration [Alf, He, Lns, Vn]. Mark 13:20 refers to the time of the end that God shortened. This is what is in view here [He]. Matt. 24:22 refers to the time of tribulation that God will shorten for the sake of His chosen. This what Paul has in mind here [Lns].
2. Paul is simply saying that now the time is short [Gdt, Herm, HNTC, ICC, TG]. The context does not suggest a shortening of the time as in Mark 13:20, but that time is running out as in Rom. 13:11 [HNTC]. In view of 7:31 the idea is that there is little time left [Herm].
3. Paul is talking about a compressing of time [NIC, NIC2]. Συστέλλω in reference to time means 'to compress'. What this means needs to be thought of in terms of the future. For most Greeks the future either did not exist or it was vague and far away. Paul is saying that, in Christ, the distant future has been brought up close where it is in clear view [NIC2].

from-now-on,[a]

LEXICON—a. τὸ λοιπόν (LN **67.134**) (BAGD 3.a.α. p. 480): 'from now on' [AB, BAGD, **LN**; all versions except KJV, LB, REB], 'henceforth' [BAGD, He, HNTC, LN, Lns], 'this means that henceforth' [ICC], 'henceforward' [He], 'in the future' [BAGD], 'while it lasts' [REB], 'for that reason' [LB], 'it remaineth' [KJV].

QUESTION—Does this phrase belong with the preceding or the following clause?

1. It belongs with the following clause [AB, He, HNTC, ICC, Lns, NIC, Vn; KJV, NAB, NASB, NIV, NRSV, REB, TEV, TNT]: From now on let those live, etc. 'From now on' goes with the ἵνα 'that' clause. It is placed before the ἵνα for emphasis [ICC, Lns]. It is very emphatic [Vn].
2. It belongs with the preceding clause [Alf, Gdt, Ho; LB]: the time from now on is short. Ἵνα 'that' does not go with 'this I say', but with 'the time is shortened' [Ho]: the time from now on is shortened in order that, etc.

that[a] even[b] those having wives may-be[c] as not having (them)

LEXICON—a. ἵνα (BAGD III.2. p. 378): 'that' [KJV], 'so that' [NASB], 'this means that' [ICC], not explicit [AB, He, HNTC; all versions except KJV, NASB, NIV]. With the subjunctive it is used to indicate a command [BAGD].

b. καί: 'even' [Lns; NRSV], 'both' [KJV], not explicit [AB, He, HNTC, ICC; all versions except KJV, NRSV].

c. pres. act. subj. of εἰμί: 'to be' [AB, HNTC, Lns; KJV, NASB, NRSV, REB, TNT], 'to live' [He; NAB, NIV, NJB, TEV], 'to stay as free (as)' [LB], 'to serve as strictly (as)' [ICC].

QUESTION—What relationship is indicated by ἵνα 'that/in order that'?

1. It indicates a command [AB, BAGD, EBC, He, Herm, HNTC, ICC, Lns, NIC; LB, NAB, NASB, NIV, NJB, NRSV, REB, TEV, TNT]: let those who have wives be as though they had none.
2. It indicates purpose [Alf, EGT, Gdt, My]: the time is shortened so that those having wives may be as though they had none. It is God's purpose for shortening the time [Alf, EGT].
3. It introduces the object of the verb φημί 'I say' [Ed]: I say this ...that those having wives should be as though they had none.

QUESTION—What is the meaning of this list of paradoxes?

This and the following five 'as-not' clauses are rhetorical and should not be taken literally. Paul expects that the Corinthians will continue to do all of the things he prohibits, but they will do them in a detached kind of way, free of their control. None of these things must determine one's life. Paul is emphasizing that the Christian should not live as though any of these things are his primary concern [NIC2]. Paul means that in the present distress a Christian should be free from and not become engrossed in temporal things [TNTC]. It means that Christians should not be preoccupied with earthly matters [TNTC].

QUESTION—What does 'being as not having a wife' mean?

He is not saying that a Christian should neglect his marriage, but that he should keep in mind that marriage is a temporary institution, not part of his eternal life [HNTC, NIC, TG]. Paul also means that the married man should give his undivided devotion and attention to the Lord as much as if he were single [HNTC].

7:30 and those-who weep[a] as not weeping

LEXICON—a. pres. act. participle of κλαίω (LN 25.138) (BAGD 1. p. 433): 'to weep' [AB, BAGD, He, HNTC, ICC, LN, Lns; all versions except LB, NIV, NJB, NRSV, REB] 'to cry' [BAGD], 'to mourn' [NIV, NJB, NRSV, REB], 'to wail, to lament' [LN]. This word is also translated as a noun: 'sadness' [LB]. Κλαίω is here an expression of sadness, care, or anxiety [BAGD].

QUESTION—What is the meaning of this clause?

The one who weeps should not be engrossed in his weeping. As a Christian, he should be detached from it [TNTC]. He will not be swayed by pain because he realizes that it is worth the trouble [Gdt].

and those-who rejoice[a] as not rejoicing

LEXICON—a. pres. act. participle of χαίρω (LN 25.125) (BAGD 1. p. 873): 'to rejoice' [AB, BAGD, He, HNTC, LN, Lns; KJV, NAB, NASB, NRSV, TNT], 'to be glad' [BAGD, LN], 'to be happy' [NIV], 'to laugh' [TEV], 'to enjoy life' [ICC; NJB]. This word is also translated as a noun phrase: 'happiness' [LB], 'the joyful' [REB].

QUESTION—What is the meaning of this clause?

It means that the one who rejoices should not be engrossed in his happiness. As a Christian, he should be detached from it [TNTC]. He will realize that it is temporary [Gdt].

and those-who buy[a] as not possessing[b] (goods),

LEXICON—a. pres. act. participle of ἀγοράζω (LN 57.188) (BAGD 1. p. 12): 'to buy' [BAGD, He, HNTC, ICC, LN, Lns; all versions except LB, NAB, NJB], 'to buy property' [NJB]. This word is also translated as a noun: 'buyers' [NAB]. It is joined with the next word and translated as: 'wealth' [LB]. See this word at 6:20.

b. pres. act. participle of κατέχω (LN 57.1) (BAGD 1.b.γ. p. 423): 'to possess' [AB, BAGD, He, HNTC, LN, Lns; KJV, NASB, REB, TNT], 'to take full possession' [ICC], 'to keep' [BAGD; NIV], 'to own' [LN; NAB, TEV], 'to have, to belong to' [LN], 'to hold fast' [BAGD], not explicit [LB]. This word is also translated as a noun: 'possessions' [NJB, NRSV].

QUESTION—What is the meaning of this clause?

It means that the one who purchases things should not be engrossed in his possessions. As a Christian, he should be detached from them [TNTC]. Paul is not saying that they should not buy, but that they should not buy just to possess things. The idea is that they should not be engrossed or absorbed in these things. This is because the person who has his vision of the end times correct "has nothing, and yet possesses all things" (2 Cor. 6:10; 1 Cor. 3:22) [NIC2].

7:31 and those dealing-with[a] the world[b] as not having-dealings-with[c] (it);

LEXICON—a. pres. mid. participle of χράομαι (LN **41.5**) (BAGD 1.b. p. 884): 'to deal with' [**LN**; NRSV], 'to have dealings with' [**LN**], 'to deal in' [TEV], 'to use' [He, HNTC, ICC, LN, Lns; NASB, NIV, REB], 'to make use of' [AB, BAGD, LN; KJV, NAB], 'to have business with' [TNT], 'to be involved with' [NJB], 'to be in frequent contact with' [LB], 'to employ' [BAGD]. It means to conduct oneself with respect to certain means [LN]. See this word at 7:21.

b. κόσμος (BAGD 6. p. 446): 'world' [AB, BAGD, HNTC, ICC, Lns; all versions except LB, NIV, REB, TEV], 'material goods' [TEV], 'the world's wealth' [REB], 'this world's goods' [He], 'the things of the world' [NIV], 'the affairs of the world' [BAGD], 'the exciting things the world offers' [LB]. The phrase 'using the world' includes marriage, commerce [Gdt, HNTC], politics, science, and art [Gdt].

c. pres. mid. participle of καταχράομαι (LN **41.6**) (BAGD p. 420): 'to have dealings with' [NRSV], 'to have business with' [TNT] 'to make/have full use of' [HNTC; NASB, REB], 'to use' [BAGD, He; NAB], 'to be eager to use to the full' [ICC], 'to make good use of one's opportunities without stopping to enjoy them' [LB], 'to use up' [AB], 'to overuse' [Lns], 'to be fully occupied with' [**LN**; TEV], 'to be engrossed in' [NIV, NJB], 'to abuse' [KJV]. The translations 'to abuse' or 'to misuse' are incorrect [Gdt, ICC, NIC2, Rb, TH, Vn]. It means to conduct oneself in such a way as to become completely occupied by certain means [LN].

QUESTION—Do the verbs χράομαι 'to deal with' and καταχράομαι 'to have dealings with' differ in meaning in this context?

1. There is little difference in meaning between these verbs [BAGD, He, TG; NAB, NRSV, TNT]. Καταχράομαι means 'to make full use of, misuse, use up'. However, in 1 Corinthians the meaning differs very little from the simple verb χράομαι 'to use' without the preposition [BAGD].
2. The second verb definitely adds meaning to the first [AB, Gdt, HNTC, ICC, LN, Lns, NCBC, NIC2, Rb, TH, TNTC, Vn; KJV, LB, NASB, NIV, NJB, REB, TEV]. The preposition κατά intensifies the meaning of the verb, though its intensification may not be very strong [TNTC]. Κατά adds a touch of possessiveness, of worldly security, of false independence [Gdt]. These two verbs were translated as follows: 'To make use of'...'to use up' [AB], 'to use'...'to have/make full use of' [HNTC; NASB], 'to use'...'to have full use of' [REB], 'to use'...'to be eager to use something to the full' [ICC], 'to use'...'to overuse' [Lns], 'to use'...'to abuse' [KJV], 'to be in frequent contact with'...'to make good use of' [LB], 'to be involved with'...'to be engrossed in' [NJB], 'to use'...'to be engrossed in' [NIV], 'to deal in'...'to be fully occupied with' [TEV].

QUESTION—What does this clause mean?

It means that the Christian is not to use the world as if it were all that mattered [NIC]. Paul is advocating an attitude of detachment from the world while focusing on Christ, one in which the Christian is in control rather than one in which he is controlled [Gdt]. Those who used their wealth should act as though they had no use for it [TG]. Or this could be considered a summary of the previous instructions [NIC, TH, TNTC]. Using the world includes marriage, property, commerce, politics, and other activities [Gdt]. It covers both social relations and commerce [HNTC].

for[a] the present-form[b] of this world is-passing-away.[c]

LEXICON—a. γάρ (LN 89.23): 'for' [AB, He, HNTC, ICC, Lns; all versions except NJB], 'because' [NJB]. This word indicates the grounds for having an attitude of detachment from the world [Gdt, Ho, ICC, NIC2].

b. σχῆμα (LN **58.7**) (BAGD 2. p. 797): 'present form' [BAGD; LB, NIV, NRSV], 'form' [AB, He, LN, Lns; NASB], 'fashion' [KJV], 'outward show' [HNTC], 'outward fashion' [ICC], 'way of life' [**LN**], '(this world and) all its affairs' [TNT], 'nature, structure' [LN]. This word is also translated as a clause; 'as we know it' [NAB, NJB, REB], 'as it is now' [TEV]. Σχῆμα refers to the culture, that is, the way of life of the world [LN].

c. pres. act. indic. of παράγω (LN 13.93) (BAGD 2.a.β. p. 613): 'to pass away' [AB, BAGD, He, HNTC, LN, Lns; all versions except LB, TEV], 'to not last much longer' [TEV], 'to soon be gone' [LB], 'to be transitory' [ICC], 'to cease to exist, to cease' [LN]. 'Passing away' indicates that the world is transitory, especially in reference to its attitude and behavior [NIC]. The present tense indicates that the world is in the process of passing away [Ho, NIC2]. This brings out Paul's perspective on the age to come, it is already here, but it is not yet fully come [NIC2].

QUESTION—What is the meaning of τὸ σχῆμα τοῦ κόσμου τούτου 'the form of this world'?

The form of the world refers to the condition the world is in [AB]. It means the world as it appears or the present state of things [Ho]. It signifies 'the outward appearance' [ICC]. Paul's point here is that the external pattern of the world in regard to social and commercial systems is impermanent [HNTC]. 'Form' indicates not only the external character, but also the attitude and behavior of the world [NIC]. 'Form' refers to the essence of a thing, to the world itself [Herm]. It is not merely the outward form that is indicated, but the entire system of things as they exist [NIC2]. Marriage, weeping, etc., are a part of this form [Lns]. Since the present condition of the world will not last long, we should not depend on earthly things [Ho].

DISCOURSE UNIT: 7:32–35 [AB]. The topic is marriage as a potential distraction from devotion to the Lord.

7:32 Now/But[a] I-want[b] you to-be free-from-concern.[c]

LEXICON—a. δέ: 'now' [AB, He, Lns], 'but' [Herm; KJV, NASB], 'yet' [ICC], not explicit [all other versions].

b. pres. act. indic. of θέλω: 'to want'. See this word at 4:21.

c. ἀμέριμνος (LN **25.226**) (BAGD 1. p. 45): 'free from concern' [AB, **LN**; NASB, NIV], 'free from anxiety' [HNTC; NRSV, TNT], 'free from the anxieties which the world produces' [ICC], 'free from (all) care' [BAGD, He, Lns], 'free from anxious care' [REB], 'free from (all) worry' [LB, NAB, TEV], 'to have one's mind free from all worry' [NJB], 'without worry, unworried' [LN], 'without carefulness' [KJV]. Ἀμέριμνος 'free from concern' and μεριμνάω 'to be concerned' (following verb) indicate less than anxiety but more than attention [AB].

QUESTION—What relationship is indicated by δέ 'now/but'?

1. It indicates a contrast [Alf, Herm; KJV, NASB]: but. This conjunction contains implied information: but because the time is short, and so that the Christian may be detached from the world, I wish you to be free from concern [Alf].
2. It indicates a transition [AB, Gdt, He, Ho, Lns, NIC2]: now. It indicates an addition of something else [NIC2]. This is another reason to remain unmarried [Ed, Ho].

QUESTION—How is Paul using the word ἀμέριμνος 'free from concern' and the following verb μεριμνάω 'to be concerned about'?

He wants them to be 'free from concern' about the things of the world, but he wants them 'to be concerned about' the things of the Lord [AB, Ed, EGT, Ho, ICC, Lns, NCBC, NIC, TNTC, Vn]. Paul wants them to be free from cares that interfere with the one legitimate care a man may have, and be concerned with how he may please the Lord [Lns]. Paul shows that there is the right kind of concern and a wrong kind [ICC]. This is a paradox. Freedom from care consists in caring about the Lord's work [Ed]. Married people would have anxious thoughts for the welfare of their partners in difficult times and this would distract from their service to the Lord. The unmarried could concentrate on the things of the Lord [TNTC]. Perhaps it is better to see Paul as saying that he wants them 'to care for' both the Lord and their wives but that, in both cases, he wants them, while caring, to be free from anxiety. He states that the married man is concerned about the affairs of this world, how he may please his wife. This is true, but he must do so without anxiety so as to live his life within the perspective of the last days. If this is true, Paul is using the following verb 'to be concerned about' as a kind of play on the sense of the adjective 'free from concern'. That is, they should live their lives in a kind of paradox, to be concerned, yet free from concern [NIC2].

The unmarried-man is-concerned-about[a] the-things[b] of-the Lord, how he-may-please[c] the Lord;

LEXICON—a. pres. act. indic. of μεριμνάω (LN 25.225) (BAGD 2. p. 505): 'to be concerned about/with' [AB, BAGD; NASB, NIV, REB, TNT], 'to concern oneself with' [TEV], 'to be anxious about' [HNTC, ICC, LN; NRSV], 'to be busy with' [NAB], 'to give one's mind to' [NJB], 'to care for/about' [BAGD, He, Lns; KJV], 'to be worried about' [LN], 'to spend one's time doing' [LB].

b. τά: 'the things' [He, HNTC, Lns; NASB], 'the affairs' [AB; NAB, NIV, NJB, NRSV, TNT], 'the work' [LB, TEV], 'the business' [REB], 'the interests' [ICC], 'the things that belong to' [KJV]. See this word at 2:11.

c. aorist act. subj. of ἀρέσκω (LN 25.90) (BAGD 2.a. p. 105): 'to please' [AB, BAGD, HNTC, ICC, LN, Lns; all versions except REB, TEV, TNT], 'to be pleasing to' [BAGD]. This word is also conflated with 'how' and translated 'to seek to please' [He], 'to try to please' [TEV], 'to want to please' [TNT], 'one's aim is to please' [REB]. Because the unmarried man has no family to provide and care for, he is more free to devote his time to the service of the Lord [Ho].

QUESTION—How are the statements of 7:32 and 33 to be taken?

These statements are not intended to mean that neither the unmarried nor the married man are concerned about absolutely nothing else. They rather point out the characteristic behavior of each [NIC].

7:33 but the married-man is-concerned-about the-things of-the world, how he-may-please his wife,

QUESTION—What is meant by κόσμος 'world'?

The term does not imply 'worldliness', as is typically understood by Christians. It rather denotes legitimate obligations and cares which the married man must attend to [He, TNTC]. The married man is more likely to be concerned than the unmarried one [NIC].

7:34 and he-is-divided.[a]

TEXT—Instead of connecting this clause to the previous one, some manuscripts connect it with the following, changing the meaning to something like, 'The married and unmarried woman are also divided', or 'And there is a difference between a wife and a virgin'. GNT connects it with the preceding clause with a D rating, indicating a very high degree of doubt about this matter. Only Alf, Gdt, Ho, ICC, My, and KJV connect it with the following clause.

LEXICON—a. perf. pass. indic. of μερίζω (LN 63.23) (BAGD 1.a. p. 504): 'to be divided' [BAGD, He, HNTC, Lns; NAB], 'to be divided in mind' [NJB, TNT], 'to be distracted' [AB], 'to be pulled in two directions' [REB, TEV], 'to be parted by a division of interests' [ICC], 'to be different' [KJV]. This word is also translated with 'one's interests' as subject: '(one's interests) are divided' [LB, NASB, NIV, NRSV]. Here it is the man's attention which is divided [BAGD]. This is the real difference between the unmarried and the married man. The latter has two areas of responsibility. But Paul is not implying that one is superior to the other [NIC2].

And the unmarried woman and the virgin is-concerned-about[a] the-things of-the Lord,

LEXICON—a. pres. act. indic. of μεριμνάω: 'to be concerned about'. See this word at 7:32.

QUESTION—Does this refer to one or two groups of women?

1. It refers to two groups of women [AB, Lns, My, NCBC, NIC, NIC2, TG; NAB, NIV, NJB, NRSV, REB, TEV, TNT]: the unmarried women and the virgins. It is common to use a singular verb with compound subject if each member is individually under focus [Lns]. The verb is singular because the two terms, the wife and the virgin, include the whole of the female sex [My]. The unmarried women are those whose marriages had been terminated by separations other than divorce, such as widows [AB, NIC, TG]. When Paul begins to address 'unmarried women', he is reminded that the subject under consideration is 'virgins' (see 7:25) by which he means young girls who were betrothed to be married [NIC2].
2. It refers to one group of women [Ed, Gdt]. They are the virgins who remain unmarried [Gdt]. 'The unmarried woman' refers to virgins, to widows, and to wives whose husbands have deserted them, while 'virgin' specifies which are in view [Ed].

that she-be holy[a] both in-her body[b] and in-her spirit;[c] but the-married-woman is-concerned-about the-things of-the world, how she-may-please her husband.

LEXICON—a. ἅγιος (LN 88.24; 53.46): 'holy' [AB, HNTC, ICC, LN (88.24), Lns; KJV, NASB, NJB, NRSV], 'devout' [LN (53.46)]. This word is also translated as a verb phrase: 'to please the Lord' [LB], 'to be devoted to the Lord' [NIV], 'to be dedicated' [TEV], 'to be dedicated to him' [REB], 'to belong to him' [TNT], 'to be consecrated' [He], 'in pursuit of holiness' [NAB].

b. σῶμα (LN 8.1): 'body' [AB, He, HNTC, ICC, LN, Lns; all versions except LB]. This word is also translated as a clause: '(to please the Lord) in all she does' [LB]. An unmarried woman can devote her body to the Lord because unlike the married woman, she has authority over her body (see 7:4) [Gdt, He].

c. πνεῦμα (LN 26.9): 'spirit' [AB, He, HNTC, ICC, LN, Lns; all versions except LB]. This word is also translated as a clause: '(to please the Lord) in all she is' [LB]. An unmarried woman can devote her spirit to the Lord because unlike the married woman, she is free from distracting responsibilities for her husband and family [Gdt]. See this word at 5:3.

QUESTION—What relationship is indicated by ἵνα 'that'?

It indicates purpose [Lns, NIC]: she is concerned about the things of the Lord, her purpose being to be holy in body and spirit. This clause functions to explain the meaning of 'to be concerned about the things of the Lord' [Lns].

QUESTION—What sense of ἅγιος 'holy' is in focus here?

'Holy' is used in the sense of total commitment [TG]. 'Holy' means 'dedicated' [TH]. 'Holy in body and spirit' means to be completely devoted to God's service [Gdt]. 'Consecration' and not ethical accomplishment is indicated. The unmarried woman's consecration is unmodified by worldly responsibilities [Ho, TNTC]. It is freedom from distracting cares [Ho]. This word is used here from the Corinthian viewpoint in which they meant purity by refraining from sexual relations. Although Paul approves, his position is that both unmarried and married should be holy [HNTC].

7:35 Now I-say this for your own benefit,[a]

LEXICON—a. σύμφορος (LN **65.45**) (BAGD p. 780): 'benefit' [AB, BAGD, He, **LN**; NASB, NRSV, TNT], 'help' [LB, NJB, TEV], 'advantage' [BAGD, HNTC, Lns, NIC2], 'profit' [KJV], 'spiritual profit' [ICC], 'good' [NAB, NIV, REB].

QUESTION—What is the function of this verse?

It concludes the 7:29–35 section by stating its purpose, and it also introduces the 7:36–38 section by referring to what is 'seemly' since the problem there is 'unseemly' behavior [NIC2].

QUESTION—To what does τοῦτο 'this' refer?

It refers to the immediately preceding words [NIC]. It refers to the 7:29–35 section. Paul is referring to their existence within the perspective of the last days and how it should determine their life now, particularly as it concerns marriage. His point is that either marriage or celibacy is acceptable but one should not be anxious about or coerced by either [NIC2]. It refers to section 7:26–34 which talks about the single life [My].

not in-order-to put-restrictions-on[a] **you**

LEXICON—a. βρόχον ἐπιβάλλω (LN **37.2**) (BAGD p. 147; 1.a. p. 289): 'to put restrictions on' [**LN**; NAB, TEV], 'to restrict' [LN; NIV, TNT], 'to put a restraint on' [NASB, NRSV], 'to put a bridle on' [NJB], 'to keep on a tight reign' [REB], 'to put a halter round one's neck' [HNTC], 'to throw a halter over and check Christian liberty' [ICC], 'to try to keep someone from marrying' [LB], 'to control, to impose restrictions' [LN], 'to put a noose on' [AB], 'to cast a noose upon' [Lns]; 'to set a trap for' [He], 'to cast a snare upon' [KJV]. 'To throw a bridle on' is an idiom meaning to impose restrictions on one's behavior [LN]. 'To put or throw a noose on someone' means to catch or restrain him [BAGD].

QUESTION—What is the figure and point of comparison in this metaphor?

The figure is throwing a halter or lasso over an animal or person to catch and restrain them [ICC]. The points of comparison are restriction, restraint, hindrance, or loss of freedom [Alf, Ed, Ho, ICC, Lns, My, NIC2, Rb, TG]. Paul intended that his words liberate them, not bind them. Whether married or celibate, they should be free from anxiety [NIC2]. They were free to do as they pleased. They were not obligated to remain single, nor was celibacy superior or more holy. His words were meant to be for their advantage under the circumstances [Ho].

but for-the-sake-of[a] what (is) proper[b] and devoted-service[c] to-the Lord without-distraction.[d]

LEXICON—a. πρός with accusative object (LN 89.60): 'for the sake of' [LN; TNT], 'for' [KJV], 'to' [TEV], 'so that' [NJB], 'as an aid to' [Lns]. This word is also translated as a verb phrase or clause: 'to (want to) promote' [NAB, NASB, NRSV], 'that you may' [HNTC], 'that you may be in' [AB], 'my desire is that' [He], 'to want someone to be' [REB], 'to want someone to do' [TEV], 'to desire that someone live' [He; NIV], 'I want you to choose' [ICC]. Πρός occurs twice in this verse and in both places it indicates purpose or reason. First, 'I say this (πρός) for your benefit'. Second, 'not to restrict you, but (πρός) for the sake of what is seemly' [Lns, NIC2]. See this word at 6:5.

b. εὐσχήμων (LN 79.15; 87.33) (BAGD 1. p. 327): 'seemly' [ICC, NIC2; NASB], 'seemliness' [HNTC, Lns], 'comely' [KJV], 'becomingly' [He], 'presentable' [BAGD, LN], 'good' [NAB], 'proper' [BAGD, NIC2], 'right and proper' [TEV], 'in a right way' [NIV], 'as it should be' [NJB], 'good order' [AB, BAGD; NRSV], 'due order' [TNT], 'beyond criticism' [REB], 'attractive; esteemed, honored' [LN]. This is also translated 'whatever will help you (serve the Lord) best' [LB]. It also means 'appropriate'. Paul wants what would be 'appropriate' in each case whether married or celibate [NIC2]. This word indicates 'propriety' especially in relation to observed conduct [Lns].

c. εὐπάρεδρος (LN **53.68**) (BAGD p. 324): 'devoted service' [**LN**], 'devotion' [LN, Lns; NASB, NIV, NRSV, REB, TNT], 'devoted' [AB, BAGD, LN], 'attachment' [He], 'constant' [BAGD]. This word is also translated as a verb: 'to give oneself completely to (the Lord's) service' [TEV], 'to give one's attention' [NJB], 'to wait upon' [HNTC, ICC; REB], 'to attend upon' [KJV], 'to serve (the Lord) best' [LB], 'to be devoted' [BAGD]. This word is also joined with the words 'without distraction' and translated 'to devote oneself entirely to' [NAB]. Εὐπάρεδρος is derived from the verb παρεδρεύειν 'to wait' and used in 'waiting on the altar'. Here it means: 'to give due attention to' the Lord [HNTC].

d. ἀπερισπάστως (LN **30.33**) (BAGD p. 84): 'without distraction' [AB, BAGD, **LN**, Lns; KJV], 'free from distraction' [REB], 'without Martha's distractions' [ICC], 'entirely' [NAB], 'without any reservation' [TEV], 'without hindrance' [HNTC]. This adverb is also translated as an adjective 'undistracted' [NASB], 'single-minded' [TNT], 'undivided' [NIV, NJB], 'unhindered' [NRSV], 'unwavering' [He], 'not distracting' [LN]. It is also translated as a verb: 'to distract one's attention from' [LB].

QUESTION—What kind of distractions does Paul have in mind here?

The betrothed were hindered or distracted in their devotion to the Lord by the demands of Corinthian ascetics who promoted celibacy [NIC2]. The cares and responsibilities of marriage distract a person from the Lord's work [HNTC].

QUESTION—What words does the preposition πρός 'for the sake of' govern?

It governs both τὸ εὔσχήμων 'what is seemly' and εὐπάρεδρος 'devotion', for there is only one article governing both. This says that Paul's major purpose was to foster full devotion to the Lord [Lns].

DISCOURSE UNIT: 7:36–40 [EGT, NIC2]. The topic is freedom to marry [EGT], marriage not being sin [NIC2]. This section is made up of two paragraphs (7:36–38 and 7:39–40) which function to conclude the argument running from 7:25–35 rather than present a new topic [NIC2].

DISCOURSE UNIT: 7:36–38 [AB, Lns]. The topic is the marriage of virgins [AB], the answer in regard to maidens [Lns].

7:36 But[a] if anyone thinks[b] he-behaves-indecently[c] towards his virgin,[d]

LEXICON—a. δέ: 'but' [He, NIC2; KJV, NASB, REB], 'now' [AB, Lns], 'still' [NJB], 'but there are limitations' [ICC], not explicit [HNTC; all other versions].

b. νομίζω (LN 31.29): 'to think' [AB, He, ICC, LN; all versions except LB, NJB, REB, TEV], 'to consider' [HNTC], 'to hold' [Lns], 'to feel' [LB, NJB, REB, TEV]. See this word at 7:26.

c. pres. act. infin. of ἀσχημονέω (LN 88.194) (BAGD 1. p. 119): 'to behave indecently' [BAGD, LN], 'to behave/act improperly' [NIV, NRSV, REB, TEV, TNT], 'to act unseemly' [ICC, Lns], 'to not behave in a seemly way' [HNTC], 'to behave dishonorably' [BAGD; NAB], 'to behave badly' [NJB], 'to act unbecomingly' [NASB], 'to not act in good order' [AB], 'to behave uncomely' [KJV], 'behave disgracefully' [BAGD]. This word is also translated '(one ought to marry because of) trouble controlling passions' [LB], '(the integrity of one's virgin is endangered) because he overflows with vitality' [He].

d. παρθένος: 'virgin' [AB, He, HNTC; KJV, NAB], 'virgin he is engaged to' [NIV], 'betrothed' [NRSV], 'the girl to whom he is betrothed' [REB], 'fiancée' [NJB], 'virgin companion' [TNT]; 'virgin daughter' [NASB], 'unmarried daughter' [ICC], 'maiden daughter' [Lns], 'young woman' [TEV], not explicit [LB]. See this word at 7:25.

QUESTION—To whom is this addressed?

1. It is addressed to a man who is engaged to a woman [EBC, HNTC, NCBC, NIC2, TH; LB, NIV, NJB, NRSV, REB, TEV]. The man is engaged to a girl and their marriage is now questionable because of pressure from the Corinthian ascetics [HNTC]. This verse begins with a contrastive 'but', and the point of contrast is 'acting seemly' (7:35) versus 'acting improperly' here. Improper behavior may mean either desiring to

get married (improper from the ascetics' viewpoint) or keeping the engagement without marrying (difficult for the girl) [NIC2].

2. It is addressed to a man who has determined to live with a woman without having sexual relations [He; TNT]. In this kind of arrangement the couple would promise to love each other and take mutual vows of virginity. Following this they would live together from time to time, but not break their vows [He].
3. It is addressed to a father who has an unmarried daughter [Alf, Ed, EGT, Gdt, ICC, Lns, My, NIC, Rb, TNTC, Vn; NASB]. This verse shows that the Corinthians had asked him about this. It was the father's wishes that were important, not the girl's and this was in keeping with the values of that time [ICC]. It was the father who was responsible for his daughter's marriage both among Jews and Greeks. 'Behave improperly' probably meant to cause his daughter disgrace by not arranging her marriage [Ho]. 'Anyone' here refers to a father or a guardian. 'Behave improperly' means to neglect seeing that his daughter gets married. This could have had very bad consequences in Corinth in those days [TNTC]. 'Behave unseemly' may mean to fail to consent to her marriage and thus open up the potential for fornication with her lover [Alf, Lns, My], or cause himself the disgrace of having an unmarried daughter at home [Alf, Gdt].

if he-be with-strong-passions/she-be past-her-prime[a]

LEXICON—a. ὑπέρακμος (LN **67.158**) (BAGD p. 839): 'with strong passions' [BAGD; NJB], 'of strong passion' [AB], 'over-sexed' [HNTC], '(his) passions are strong' [NRSV, REB], '(his) passions are too strong' [TEV, TNT], '(he has) trouble controlling his passions' [LB], '(he) overflows with vitality' [He], 'past one's prime' [LN], '(she) be past the flower of her age' [Lns; KJV], '(she) should be of full age' [NASB], 'she is getting along in years' [NIV], '(she) has long since reached a marriageable age' [ICC], 'she is past marriageable age, passed the right age to marry' [**LN**], 'a critical moment has come' [NAB], '(she is) past her prime, past marriageable age, past the bloom of youth' [BAGD].

QUESTION—What is the meaning of ὑπέρακμος 'with strong passions' or 'past one's prime'?

1. When taken as being addressed to a man who is engaged to a virgin.

1.1 It describes the man [AB, HNTC; LB, NJB, NRSV, REB, TEV]. It means '(he is) over-sexed' [HNTC], '(his) passions are (too) strong' [NJB, NRSV, REB, TEV], '(he has) trouble controlling his passions' [LB].

1.2 It describes the girl [EBC, NCBC; NIV]. It means 'she is getting along in years' [NIV], 'the bloom of her youth is past' [NCBC], '(she is) passing her prime marriageable years' [EBC].

2. When taken as being addressed to a man who is involved in a spiritual marriage [He; TNT]. Describing the man, it means '(he) overflows with vitality' [He], 'his passions are too strong' [TNT].

3. When taken as being addressed to a father of an unmarried daughter [NASB]. It always refers to the girl and means 'to be of full age' [NASB], 'to be past the flower of her age' [Gdt, Lns]. It means that she is sexually mature [Lns], that she has long since been of marriageable age [ICC].

and it-has[a] to-be so,

LEXICON—a. pres. act. indic. of ὀφείλω (LN 71.35): 'it has' [LN; NRSV], 'it ought' [Lns], 'it must' [HNTC, LN; NASB, TNT], 'something must/should (be done)' [NAB, REB], '(he/they) ought' [AB, He; NIV, TEV], '(she) ought' [ICC], 'things should take their course' [NJB], '(if) need require' [KJV], not explicit [LB]. See this word at 5:10.

QUESTION—What particular obligation is this referring to?

1. When taken as addressed to a man who is engaged to a virgin. The obligation may be family or social pressure [NCBC]. The obligation refers to the judgment of the man: 'when he feels he ought to marry' [NIC2; LB, NIV, NJB, TEV]. The obligation refers to the inevitable outcome of strong passions: 'and it has to be so' [HNTC; NRSV, REB].
2. When taken as addressed to a man who is involved in a spiritual marriage. The obligation refers to the inevitable outcome of strong passions: 'and it must to be so' [TNT]. The obligation refers to the judgment of the man: 'he feels that he ought to let things take their course' [He].
3. When taken as addressed to a father of an unmarried daughter. The obligation probably refers to the daughter's lack of the gift of celibacy [TNTC]. It is the moral obligation of the father not to prevent the marriage of his daughter [NIC]. The obligation refers to both the daughter's condition and the father's judgment [Lns]. The obligation refers to the unchangeable attitude of the couple in their determination to marry [Alf].

let-him-do what he-wishes,[a]

LEXICON—a. pres. act. indic. of θέλω: 'to wish' [AB, HNTC; NAB, NASB, NRSV, TNT], 'to want' [NIV, TEV], 'to desire' [He], 'to will' [BAGD; KJV], 'to think best' [ICC], 'to be minded' [Lns]. This word is also translated as a noun phrase: '(to follow) one's desires' [NJB], '(to carry out) one's intentions' [REB]. It is also translated as: 'it is all right' [LB].

he-sins not,

QUESTION—To whom does this refer?

1. When taken as being addressed to a man engaged to a virgin, it refers either to the man, 'he does not sin' [HNTC, NIC2, TH; NIV]; or to the act, 'it is not a sin' [EBC; LB, NJB, NRSV, REB, TEV].
2. When taken as being addressed to a man involved in a spiritual marriage, it refers to the man [He; TNT]: 'he does not sin'.
3. When taken as being addressed to the father of an unmarried daughter, it refers either to the father, 'the father does not sin' [Gdt, Ho, NIC]; or to the act, 'it is not a sin' [ICC].

let-them-marry.

QUESTION—To whom does 'them' refer?

When taken as being addressed to the father of an unmarried daughter, it refers to the daughter and her suitor [Alf, Ed, EGT, Gdt, Ho, ICC, Lns, My, NIC, Vn]. In the other two cases, it refers to the engaged couple [He, NIC2].

7:37 But[a] whoever stands[b] firm[c] in his heart[d]

LEXICON—a. δέ (LN 89.124): 'but' [AB, He, ICC, LN, Lns; all versions except KJV, NAB, NJB], 'however' [NAB], 'nevertheless' [KJV], 'on the other hand' [HNTC; NJB]. It indicates the opposite case, the decision is against marriage [Lns].

b. pres. act. indic. of ἵστημι (LN **31.7**) (BAGD II.2.c.α. p. 382): 'to stand' [AB, BAGD, HNTC, Lns; KJV, NAB, NASB, NJB, TNT], 'to be established' [NRSV]. This word is also joined with the words 'firm in his heart' and translated 'to be firmly convinced of one's views' [**LN**], 'to have the will power' [LB], 'to have settled convictions' [ICC], 'to not allow one's self to be moved' [He]. It is also joined with 'firm' and translated 'to settle the matter' [NIV], 'to be steadfast' [REB]. It is also joined with 'in his heart' and translated 'to make up one's mind' [TEV]. The idiom 'to stand in one's heart' means: 'to continue in one's views, to keep on being of an opinion, to remain with an opinion' [LN].

c. ἑδραῖος (LN 31.92) (BAGD p. 217): 'firm' [AB, BAGD, HNTC, LN; NAB, NASB, NJB, NRSV, TNT], 'steadfast' [BAGD, LN, Lns; KJV], 'unwavering' [LN]. This word is also translated as an adverb: 'firmly' [TEV]. This word indicates certainty or lack of wavering [Ed].

d. καρδία (LN 26.3): 'heart' [AB, LN, Lns; KJV, NASB], 'mind' [HNTC, NIC2; NIV, TNT], 'resolve' [NAB, NRSV], 'resolution' [NJB], 'purpose' [REB]. See this word at 4:5.

QUESTION—What is the meaning of 'whoever stands firm in his heart'?

1. When taken as being addressed to a man who is engaged to a virgin, it means that the man has come to a firm conclusion in his mind that he will not marry [NIC2].
2. When taken as being addressed to a man who is involved in a spiritual marriage, it means that the man does not allow himself to be shaken from his decision not to marry [He].
3. When taken as being addressed to a father of an unmarried daughter, it means that the father has reached a firm decision that a single life is best for his daughter [Gdt, Ho, ICC].

not having obligation,[a]

LEXICON—a. ἀνάγκη (LN 71.30) (BAGD 1. p. 52): 'obligation' [REB], 'necessity' [BAGD, HNTC, Lns; KJV, NRSV], 'constraint' [NAB, NASB], 'compulsion' [BAGD; NIV, NJB], 'pressure' [AB], 'strain' [TNT], 'complete or necessary obligation' [LN], 'need to surrender one's convictions' [ICC]. This word is also translated as a verb: 'to be forced (to marry)' [TEV], 'to (not) need to (marry)' [LB]. It is also joined with 'not' and translated 'to be free to make one's own decisions' [He].

QUESTION—What is the meaning of 'having no obligation'?

1. When taken as being addressed to a man who is engaged to a virgin, it probably means that he is under no external pressure [NCBC]. It means external pressure to marry, such as an engagement or the influence of a master on a slave [EBC]. It means that the man is able to overcome his natural desire [HNTC]. It means no compulsion either from the ascetics or from Paul's preference [NIC2].
2. When taken as being addressed to a man who is involved in a spiritual marriage, it means that the man has his desire under control [He], or that he is not under any strain [TNT].
3. When taken as being addressed to a father of an unmarried daughter, it means that the father is not being required to act against his own judgment [Ho]. It may point to an obligation to keep a marriage contract [TNTC]. It may refer pressure due to his daughter's incontinence [Ed, Lns, NIC]. It could be financial constraints, making it impossible to support his daughter [NIC].

but having control[a] over his-own desire[b]

LEXICON—a. ἐξουσία (LN 37.13) (BAGD 1. p. 278): 'control' [AB, He, LN; NIV, NRSV, TEV, TNT], 'full control' [NJB], 'authority' [HNTC; NASB], 'power' [Lns; KJV], 'full right (to carry out one's own will/wishes)' [ICC; NAB], 'freedom of choice, right to act or decide' [BAGD], not explicit [LB]. This word is also joined with 'having' and translated 'to be free to act' [REB], 'to be at liberty (with regard to something)' [BAGD].

b. θέλημα (LN 25.2) (BAGD 2. p. 354): 'desire' [BAGD, He, LN; NRSV], 'will' [AB, BAGD, HNTC, Lns; all versions except LB, NRSV, REB], 'wish(es)' [ICC, LN], 'discretion' [REB], not explicit [LB]. Many take 'desire' here to mean 'sexual desire' [BAGD].

QUESTION—What is the meaning of ἐξουσίαν ἔχει περὶ τοῦ θελήματος'he has authority over his own will'?

1. When taken as being addressed to a man who is engaged to a virgin, it means that he has authority over his sex drive [NCBC], no one is forcing him to do this [NIC2], he has control over his own will [NIV, NJB, TEV], his own desire is under control [NRSV], he is free to act at his own discretion [REB].
2. When taken as being addressed to a man who is involved in a spiritual marriage, it means that he is free to make his own decisions [He].
3. When taken as being addressed to a father of an unmarried daughter, it means that he has control over the situation [EGT], he is free to act as he pleases [Ho, ICC, NIC, Vn].

and this he-has-decided[a] in his-own heart,

LEXICON—a. perf. act. indic. of κρίνω (LN **30.75**) (BAGD 3. p. 451): 'to decide' [AB, BAGD, He, ICC, **LN**; NASB, REB, TEV], 'to reach/make a decision' [BAGD, Lns], 'to determine' [BAGD; NRSV], 'to decree' [KJV], 'to come to a conclusion, to make up one's mind' [LN]. This word is also joined with 'in his own heart' and translated 'to make up one's mind' [HNTC; NAB, NIV], 'to decide' [LB, NJB, TNT]. The perfect tense indicates that once the action is done, it stands [Lns]. See this word at 2:2.

QUESTION—What is the significance of these four prerequisites?

They serve to strongly emphasize that the person should be under no compulsion [NIC, NIC2], and are probably said to counter the influence of the Corinthian ascetics [NIC2].

to keep[a] his-own virgin,[b]

LEXICON—a. pres. act. inf. of τηρέω (LN **13.32**) (BAGD 2.b. p. 815): 'to keep' [AB, BAGD, LN, Lns; KJV, NAB, NIV, NJB], 'to keep someone as (one's virgin)' [He], 'to keep (a virgin) as she is' [HNTC], 'to keep someone unmarried' [**LN**; TNT] 'to keep one's daughter free' [ICC], 'to keep (a virgin) inviolate' [BAGD], 'to hold, reserve, preserve' [BAGD], 'to retain, to cause to continue' [LN]. This word is also joined with 'virgin' and translated 'to not marry' [LB, TEV], 'to let a girl remain as one's fiancée' [NJB], 'to keep a girl as one's fiancée' [NRSV], 'to respect a girl's virginity' [REB].

b. παρθένος (LN 89.94): 'virgin' [AB, He, HNTC; KJV, NAB, NIV], 'maiden/virgin daughter' [Lns; NASB], 'daughter' [ICC], 'fiancée' [NJB, NRSV], 'young woman' [TEV], 'virginity' [REB], 'virgin companion' [TNT], not explicit [LB]. See this word at 7:25.

QUESTION—What is the meaning of τηρεῖν τὴν ἑαυτοῦ παρθένον 'to keep his own virgin'?

1. When taken as being addressed to a man who is engaged to a virgin, it means to keep his virgin a virgin [HNTC, NIC2], that is, not to marry her [NIC2; LB, NIV, TEV]. It means 'to let her remain as his fiancée' [NJB, NRSV], 'to respect her virginity' [REB].
2. When taken as being addressed to a man who is involved in a spiritual marriage, it means 'to keep his virgin companion unmarried' [TNT], 'to keep her as his virgin' [He].
3. When taken as being addressed to a father of an unmarried daughter, it means to keep his virgin daughter unmarried [Ho, ICC]. It means to care for her at home as long as she is a virgin [Lns].

he-will-do well.[a]

LEXICON—a. κάλως (BAGD 4.a. p. 401): 'well' [AB, BAGD, He, HNTC; all versions except LB, NAB, NIV], 'rightly' [BAGD, ICC; NAB], 'the right thing' [NIV], 'what is right' [BAGD], 'excellently' [Lns], 'morally right'

[My]. This word is also joined with 'do' and translated 'to make a wise decision' [LB].

7:38 So-that[a] both the-one marrying[b] his-own virgin does well

LEXICON—a. ὥστε (LN 89.52): 'so that' [HNTC, LN; NRSV], 'so then' [LN, Lns, NIC2; KJV, NASB, NIV, NRSV], 'it comes to this therefore' [ICC] 'so' [AB; LB, TEV, TNT], 'thus' [He; REB], 'to sum up' [NAB], 'in other words' [NJB]. See this word at 3:7.

b. pres. act. participle of γαμίζω (LN **34.66**) (BAGD 1. p. 151): 'to marry' [He, HNTC, ICC, **LN**, Lns; all versions except KJV, NASB], 'to give (a woman) in marriage' [BAGD, ICC, Lns; KJV, NASB], 'to marry off' [AB].

QUESTION—What relationship is indicated by ὥστε 'so that'?

It functions to conclude the whole argument and the two previous verses [NIC2]. This indicates that this verse is a result clause [AB, My]. It is strongly inferential [NIC2].

QUESTION—Is there a distinction between γαμέω 'to marry' and γαμίζω 'to give in marriage' here?

1. There should be no distinction made, both mean 'to marry' [EBC, He, Herm, HNTC, Ho, LN, NIC2; all versions except KJV, NASB]. Evidence shows that the classical distinction between -εω (non-causative) and -ιζω (causative) verbs was no longer valid in the Koiné period. It may be that Paul used this verb for variety or that he was using it to bring out a more transitive sense [NIC2]. The distinction was breaking down in the Hellenistic period [HNTC].
2. There should be a distinction made: γαμίζω means 'to give someone in marriage', describing the act of the father [AB, Alf, BAGD, Ed, EGT, Gdt, ICC, Lns, NIC, Rb, TNTC, Vn; KJV, NASB]. No one has shown that this nuance was not valid in the New Testament period. Elsewhere this verb always indicates 'to give in marriage' [TNTC].

and the-one not marrying will-do better.[a]

LEXICON—a. κρείττων (LN **65.21**) (BAGD 3. p. 450): 'better' [AB, BAGD, HNTC, **LN**; all versions except LB, NIV, NJB, TEV], 'even better' [He; LB, NIV, TEV], 'better still' [ICC; NJB], 'more excellently' [Lns], 'superior' [LN].

QUESTION—What is meant by κρείττων 'better'?

'Better' here does not indicate that one action is in itself better than the other, but better only because of the present crisis [NIC2]. 'Better' is used here in the sense of 'wiser' in view of coming troubles [Ho]. Both actions are 'excellent', but the circumstances determine this action to be 'more excellent' [Lns]. Both the present crisis and the shortened time make this action better [Rb].

DISCOURSE UNIT: 7:39–40 [AB, Alf, Lns, NCBC, TNTC]. The topic is remarriage of widows [AB], concerning second marriages of women [Alf], appendix on remarriage [Lns], advice about widows [NCBC], widows [TNTC].

7:39 (A) wife is-bound[a] (to her husband) for (a) time as-long-as[b] her husband lives; but if her husband die,[c] she-is free to-marry whom she-wishes,

TEXT—After δέδεται 'is bound', some manuscripts have νόμῳ 'by law'. GNT does not note the possibility of this addition. Only KJV includes it.

LEXICON—a. perf. pass. indic. of δέω: 'to be bound' [AB, He, HNTC, ICC, Lns; all versions except NJB, TEV], 'to be tied' [NJB], 'to be not free' [TEV]. The perfect tense indicates that, once the bond is made, it continues as long as the husband lives [Lns]. See this word at 7:27.

b. ὅσος (LN **67.139**) (BAGD 1. p. 586): 'as long as' [AB, BAGD, He, HNTC, ICC, **LN**, Lns; all versions], 'while' [LN].

c. aorist act. subj. of κοιμάω (LN 23.104) (BAGD 2.a. p. 437): 'to die' [AB, BAGD, He, LN; all versions except KJV, NASB], 'to pass away' [BAGD], 'to be dead' [ICC, LN; KJV, NASB], 'to have died' [LN], 'to fall asleep' [BAGD, HNTC], 'to be fallen asleep' [Lns]. This word is used euphemistically to mean 'to die' [AB, BAGD, Lns].

QUESTION—What is the purpose of this verse?

Paul wants to curtail any desire of women to leave their husbands to devote themselves to the Lord's work [Ed]. It serves to conclude both section 7:1–24 (where marriage was under focus), and section 7:25–38 [NIC2].

only[a] in[b] (the) Lord.

LEXICON—a. μόνος: 'only' [Lns; KJV, NASB, NJB, NRSV], 'but only' [LB, TEV], 'though only' [TNT], 'remembering only' [HNTC], 'but on one condition' [NAB], 'but' [NIV], 'except that' [AB], 'providing' [He, ICC; REB].

b. ἐν with dative object (BAGD I.5.d. p. 260): 'in' [AB, BAGD, Lns; KJV, NAB, NASB, NJB, NRSV]. This word is also joined with 'Lord' and translated 'according to the Lord's will' [TNT], '(if he is) a Christian' [LB, TEV], '(she is) a Christian' [HNTC], '(it is) a Christian marriage' [He], '(he must) belong to the Lord' [NIV], 'within the Lord's fellowship' [REB], 'in holy matrimony with a Christian' [ICC].

QUESTION—What is the meaning of marrying ἐν κυρίῳ 'in the Lord'?

'To marry in the Lord' means 'to marry a Christian' [Alf, BAGD, EBC, Gdt, He, HNTC, ICC, My, NCBC, NIC, NIC2, TG, TH; LB, NIV, REB, TEV]. She must marry a man who is in the Lord [Ho]. It means that she must remember that she is a member of Christ's body and act accordingly [HNTC, ICC, NCBC, TH]. It means that her motive to marry must be to please the Lord [Ed].

7:40 But[a] in my opinion[b] she-is happier[c] if she-remain as-she-is;[d]

LEXICON—a. δέ (LN 89.12): 'but' [AB, HNTC, ICC, LN; all versions except NAB, NIV, NJB, TEV], 'however' [TEV], 'nevertheless' [He], 'yet' [Lns], not explicit [NAB, NIV, NJB].

b. γνώμη (LN **31.3**): 'opinion' [AB, He, HNTC, **LN**; all versions except KJV, NIV, NJB, NRSV], 'judgment' [ICC, Lns; KJV, NIV, NRSV], 'way of thinking' [NJB]. This means a 'judgment' which has been carefully thought out, not a quick opinion [Lns]. See this word at 7:25.

c. μακάριος (LN 25.119) (BAGD 1.a. p. 486): 'happier' [AB, BAGD, He, HNTC, ICC, LN; all versions except NRSV, REB], 'better off' [REB], 'more blessed' [BAGD, Lns; NRSV], 'more fortunate' [BAGD].

d. οὕτως: 'as she is' [AB, He, HNTC, ICC, Lns; all versions except KJV, LB, NAB], 'so' [KJV]. This word is also joined with 'remain' and translated 'to not marry again' [LB], 'to stay unmarried' [NAB]. See this word at 3:15.

QUESTION—What sense of μακάριος 'happy' is intended here?

It means 'more blessed' in the sense of richer in spirit [EGT, Lns]. It refers to the joy of knowing a close relationship to Christ which results from surrender to him alone [My]. It means more free from the troubles of married life and the cares of the world [Ho]. She will be happier on earth and can better serve the Lord [Lns, NIC].

and I-think[a] I-too[b] have (the) Spirit of-God.

LEXICON—a. δοκέω (LN 31.29) (BAGD 1.a. p. 201): 'to think' [AB, BAGD, He, HNTC, LN, Lns; all versions except NAB, NJB, REB], 'to be persuaded' [NAB], 'to believe' [ICC, LN; NJB, REB]. See this word at 3:18.

b. κἀγώ (BAGD 3.a. p. 386): 'I too' [BAGD, HNTC, TH; NIV, NJB, NRSV, REB, TEV], 'I also' [AB, BAGD; NASB], 'I, too, for my part' [Lns], 'I, no less than others' [ICC], 'moreover I' [TNT], 'also I' [KJV], 'I' [He; LB, NAB]. This means here: 'I, as well as others' [BAGD, Ed, HNTC, Ho, ICC, NIC]. 'I too' probably means that Paul was not alone in his judgment but that the Spirit of God also agreed with it [NIC2].

QUESTION—Who are the others Paul may have in mind when he says 'I too'?

He may be referring to those in Corinth who claimed to possess the Spirit of God [Gdt, HNTC, Ho, NCBC, NIC, NIC2]. These people were not sure that Paul possessed God's Spirit [NIC2]. He may be thinking of the spiritual guides noted in 4:15 [Gdt].

QUESTION—What does πνεῦμα θεοῦ ἔχειν 'to have the Spirit of God' mean?

It means to have the guidance of the Spirit of God in his judgment [Ho, ICC, My, NIC2, TH, TNTC; LB]. It means to be controlled or guided by the Spirit [TG].

DISCOURSE UNIT: 8:1–11:1 [AB, Alf, EBC, Ed, Herm, HNTC, Lns, NIC2, TNTC]. The topic is a second quandary: concerning idol-offerings [AB], instructions concerning Christian freedom [EBC], eating meat offered to idols

[Ed], freedom and idol sacrifices [Herm], food sacrificed to idols [HNTC, Lns, NIC2, TNTC]. This section is Paul's reply to the Corinthian question about eating food offered to idols. The reply expands to cover Christian liberty in general [EBC].

DISCOURSE UNIT: 8:1–10:33 [EGT, Gdt]. The topic is contact with idolatry [EGT], the use of meat offered to idols, and participation in the sacrificial feasts [Gdt].

DISCOURSE UNIT: 8:1–9:22 [Gdt]. The topic is the question considered from the viewpoint of our neighbor's salvation.

DISCOURSE UNIT: 8:1–9:1 [ICC]. The topic is food offered to idols.

DISCOURSE UNIT: 8:1–13 [EBC, Ed, GNT, HNTC, Ho, ICC, Lns, My, NCBC, NIC, NIC2, TG, TH]. The topic is the eating of meat offered to idols [EBC, Ho, NIC], a statement of the two opposite Christian conceptions of liberty and love [Ed], food offered to idols [GNT], source of the trouble, their exaltation of knowledge over love [HNTC], general principles [ICC], love for the weak [Lns], the question of idol meat [NCBC], the basis of Christian conduct: love, not knowledge [NIC2].

DISCOURSE UNIT: 8:1–6 [EGT, Gdt, Herm, TNTC]. The topic is knowledge of the one God and one Lord [EGT], the knowledge common to all [Gdt], the criterion of conduct: love and knowledge [Herm], knowledge about idols [TNTC].

DISCOURSE UNIT: 8:1–3 [AB, EBC, NIC2]. The topic is love, not knowledge, the guiding principle [AB], knowledge and love contrasted [EBC], the way of love and the way of knowledge [NIC2].

8:1 Now[a] concerning[b] food-offered-to-idols,[c]

LEXICON—a. δέ (LN 89.94): 'now' [AB, He, HNTC, ICC; all versions except LB], 'next' [LB], not explicit [He, HNTC, Lns].

b. περί with genitive object (LN 90.24; 89.6): 'concerning' [He, LN (90.24), Lns; NASB, NRSV, TEV, TNT], 'about' [HNTC, LN (90.24); NAB, NIV, NJB, REB], 'with reference to' [AB], 'as touching' [KJV], '(next) is your question about' [LB], 'as to the subject of' [ICC], 'with regard to' [LN (89.6)]. See this word at 7:1.

c. εἰδωλόθυτος (LN **5.15**) (BAGD p. 221): 'food offered to idols' [TEV, TNT], 'meat offered to idols' [AB, BAGD, He; NAB], 'food sacrificed to idols' [LB, NIV, NRSV], 'food that has been offered in sacrifice to idols' [ICC], 'food which has been dedicated to false gods' [NJB], 'meat consecrated to heathen deities' [REB], 'things offered/sacrificed to idols' [HNTC; KJV, NASB], 'offerings to idols' [Lns], 'sacrificial meat' [**LN**], 'meat of animals sacrificed to an idol' [LN]. The word means simply 'idol offering', but refers to meat [AB, ICC]. This word refers to sacrificial meat, a part of which was burned on the altar, another part was eaten at a solemn meal in the temple, and a third part was sold in the market for home use. For the Jews it was unclean and forbidden [BAGD].

QUESTION—What relationship is indicated by περὶ δέ 'now concerning'?

It indicates a transition to a new question raised by the Corinthians [AB, Alf, EBC, Ed, EGT, Ho, My, NIC, NIC2, TNTC].

QUESTION—What is the function of this phrase?

1. It functions as an introductory caption and is punctuated with a period or colon [AB, HNTC, Lns; all versions except KJV, NASB]: concerning food offered to idols. Some treat the text after this caption to the end of 8:3 as parenthetical [Lns; REB, TEV, TNT].
2. It functions as a clause in a sentence [Gdt, He, ICC; KJV, NASB]: Now, concerning food offered to idols, we know that we all have knowledge. Some treat the text beginning with 'knowledge puffs up' to the end of 8:3 as parenthetical [Alf, Gdt, He, My]. After mentioning 'knowledge', Paul digresses to talk about the uselessness of a certain kind of knowledge and to give the true nature of knowledge [Gdt].

QUESTION—What was the question concerning meat?

The question was whether or not Christians should eat anything that was offered in the temple to pagan gods [AB, Ho, ICC, Lns]. There was a question about whether the meat became a special sort of meat after part of it had been sacrificed. Another question was whether everybody may eat it when it was established that meat does not change when sacrificed to idols [NIC].

we-know that/because we all have knowledge.[a]

LEXICON—a. γνῶσις (LN **28.17**) (BAGD 1. p. 163): 'knowledge' [AB, He, HNTC, ICC, Lns; all versions except LB]. This word is also joined with 'we all have' and translated as a clause: '(everyone feels that) only his answer is the right one' [LB]. It means 'to be acquainted with the facts and understand them' [ICC]. This is a thematic word in Corinthians. Note its use elsewhere at 1:5, 12:8, and 13:1–3 [NIC2].

QUESTION—What is Paul quoting?

The phrase 'We all have knowledge' is a quotation of what the Corinthians had said [EGT, Gdt, Herm, HNTC, ICC, NIC, NIC2, TG; NRSV, REB, TEV, TNT]. This is seen in the use of the repeated words οἴδαμεν ὅτι 'we know that' in 8:1 and 8:4, plus the formula καὶ ὅτι 'and that' in the middle of 8:4. Paul never uses a repeated ὅτι 'that' when giving his own ideas. The formula οἴδαμεν ὅτι 'we know that' is often used to introduce a generally accepted fact [NIC2].

QUESTION—What relationship is indicated by ὅτι 'that/because'?

1. It indicates the content of what they knew [AB, Alf, Gdt, Herm, HNTC, Ho, ICC, NIC2, TNTC; NASB, NIV, NJB, NRSV, TEV, TNT]: we know that we all have knowledge.
2. It indicates the reason they knew [Ed, EGT]: we know because we all have knowledge. We know what to say about the question of eating

sacrificial meat because we all have knowledge about this matter from the Council of Jerusalem (Acts 15) [Ed]. 'We know', you say, because 'we all have knowledge' [EGT].

QUESTION—What is meant by γνῶσις 'knowledge'?

It refers to the Corinthians' Christian knowledge which they were using to justify their eating meat offered to idols [AB]. The lack of the article with 'knowledge' indicates that it refers to all knowledge including knowledge concerning idols [AB, NIC]. It refers specifically to knowledge concerning idols [Ho, Lns, My]. It refers to the knowledge that 'God is one' along with its corollary that gods do not exist [Herm]. It refers to a superior knowledge which permitted them to behave as they pleased [TG]. Paul is referring to a theoretical rather than a practical knowledge [Ho]. Knowledge to the Corinthians probably meant special knowledge which the Spirit had given and which, in their thinking, should function as the basis of Christian conduct [NIC2].

Knowledge puffs-up,[a]

LEXICON—a. pres. act. indic. of φυσιόω (LN **88.217**) (BAGD p. 869): 'to puff up' [BAGD, He, HNTC, Lns; KJV, NIV, NJB, NRSV], 'to puff (up) with pride' [AB; TEV], 'to make arrogant' [BAGD, LN; NASB, TNT], 'to make haughty' [**LN**], 'to make proud' [BAGD, LN], 'to inflate' [NAB, REB], 'to breed conceit' [ICC], 'to make someone feel important' [LB]. See this word at 4:6.

QUESTION—What does Paul mean by 'knowledge' here?

He has in mind the kind of knowledge the Corinthians were pursuing [Herm]. He refers to a head-knowledge only [Gdt]. The definite article with 'knowledge' refers back to the knowledge that all possess. This knowledge was knowing that there was nothing wrong with the meat. But Paul is saying that such knowledge makes men proud and indifferent [EBC]. He refers to knowledge by itself or knowledge that is emphasized out of proportion [Lns]. He means theoretical knowledge [Ho].

QUESTION—To what characteristic does being 'puffed up' refer?

It refers to pride [AB, BAGD, ICC, LN, Lns, NIC2, TG, TH, TNTC; NASB, TEV, TNT]. Those who are confident in their knowledge can become arrogant and be contemptuous of other people [AB].

but love[a] builds-up;[b]

LEXICON—a. ἀγάπη: 'love'. See this word at 4:21.

b. pres. act. indic. of οἰκοδομέω (LN 45.1) (BAGD 3. p. 558): 'to build up' [AB, BAGD, He, HNTC, Lns; all versions except KJV, LB, NAB, NASB], 'to upbuild' [NAB], 'to build up character' [ICC], 'to edify' [BAGD; KJV, NASB], 'to build' [LN; LB], 'to strengthen, benefit, establish' [BAGD].

QUESTION—What is meant by ἀγάπη 'love' here?

It means love for fellow Christians [Ho, Lns, My, NIC, TG], which is what drives them to do things to help them [Lns]. Love does good for others, improves relationships and produces good results [NIC]. Love is centered in others where it seeks its happiness [Ho]. Love for others is derived from love for God [Lns, My, NIC, TG].

QUESTION—To what characteristics does the verb οἰκοδομεῖ 'builds up' refer?

It refers to giving strength [AB, TH], or permanence [AB]. It refers to improving relationships and producing good results [NIC]. It refers to producing progress in moral behavior [Gdt]. It refers to doing things for the benefit and advantage of others [NIC2]. It is not the individual who is primarily in focus here, but the community that is built up [EGT, Herm, HNTC]. Knowledge without love can destroy others (8:11) [NIC2].

8:2 if anyone thinks[a] to-have-known something,

LEXICON—a. pres. act. indic. of δοκέω (LN 31.29): 'to think' [AB, HNTC, LN, Lns; all versions except NASB, NRSV, REB], 'to imagine' [ICC, LN], 'to suppose' [LN; NASB], 'to claim' [He; NRSV], 'to fancy' [REB]. See this word at 3:18.

QUESTION—What is the function of this verse?

It explains the disparaging remark about knowledge [Herm, My], by distinguishing two kinds of knowledge [Herm]. The lack of a connector indicates that this is an emphatic restatement of the previous statement [Gdt]. It further defines the clause 'We all possess knowledge' [NIC2]. Paul warns against depending on simply knowing something about a subject [EBC].

QUESTION—What is the significance of the perfect infinitive ἐγνωκέναι 'to have known'?

It indicates full and complete knowledge [Herm, NIC2, TNTC]. It indicates that the Corinthians felt they had reached perfection in knowledge [ICC, NIC2].

QUESTION—What is meant by τι 'something'?

It means 'something significant' [Herm]. It gives a specific content to what is known. The lack of knowledge here indicates a lack of true knowledge (γνῶσις) which has to do with love [NIC2]. It means 'some' knowledge and expresses an assumed modesty [Ed]. The Corinthians thought that they had acquired a complete knowledge [ICC].

he-knows not-yet as he-ought[a] to-know;

LEXICON—a. pres. act. indic. of δεῖ (LN 71.21; 71.34): 'he ought' [AB, He, HNTC, ICC, LN, Lns; all versions except LB, NRSV, REB]. 'he should' [LN; NJB] 'to have to do, to be necessary, must' [LN]. This word is also translated as an adjective: 'necessary (knowledge)' [NRSV]. It is also translated as a phrase: 'in the true sense (of knowing)' [REB]. It is also joined with the rest of the clause and translated as: 'he is just showing his ignorance' [LB].

QUESTION—What is the significance of the aorist of 'to know' in οὔπω ἔγνω 'he does not yet know'?

It means that he has not yet 'come to know' [AB]. The aorist is inceptive: he is not yet at the beginning of knowledge [He]. It is a timeless aorist giving a summary statement [Rb]. He does not understand the true nature of the things he pretends to know [Ho]. His knowledge is but partial and there is nothing in that to be proud about [TNTC]. He cannot yet know something as he ought until he adds love to such knowledge [Ed].

8:3 But[a] if anyone loves[b] God,

TEXT—Some manuscripts omit the words τὸν θεόν 'God'. GNT includes these words with an A rating indicating that the text is certain.

LEXICON—a. δέ: 'but' [AB, He, HNTC, ICC, Lns; all versions]. This verse is the antithesis of 8:2 [Gdt].

b. pres. act. indic. of ἀγαπάω: 'to love'. See this word at 2:9.

QUESTION—Why does Paul bring in 'love' when the subject is knowledge?

It is because love for God is essential to knowledge [Ho]. Paul's position is that true love is true knowledge [NIC2]. To base one's behavior on knowledge as the Corinthians wanted to do was wrong. Behavior should rather be based on love [HNTC, NIC2]. Paul goes from love for others to love for God because love for the brethren is one of the forms in which one's love for God manifests itself [Ho].

this-one is-known by him.

TEXT—Some manuscripts omit the words ὑπ' αὐτοῦ 'by him'. GNT includes them with an A rating indicating that the text is certain.

QUESTION—What is the significance of the perfect tense in ἔγνωσται 'is known'?

It refers to a knowledge which has become perfect and cannot be increased [NIC].

QUESTION—What does it mean that 'someone is known by God'?

It means that he is approved by God as having true knowledge [Ho]. It means that God has chosen him and allowed him to know him [NCBC]. It means that God acknowledges that a person belongs to him [ICC, Lns]. It means that God is personally intimate with him. Many more people may say that they know a king, than can say that the king knows them [Gdt]. When God acknowledges a person to be his, it may be assumed that person possesses a true knowledge [Ho, ICC].

QUESTION—Why does Paul substitute the clause 'is known by God' for the more logical 'knows God'?

It is because the words 'is known by God' also include the concept 'knows God' and includes intimacy with God [Gdt]. It is because Paul does not want to credit anything to human ability. Both man's love for and knowledge of God are the reflections of God's love for and knowledge of man [EGT].

DISCOURSE UNIT: 8:4–13 [AB, Ed]. The topic is the question of eating food offered to idols [AB]. This section is composed of two parts: (1) 4–8 talks about Christian knowledge; (2) 9–13 talks about Christian love [Ed].

DISCOURSE UNIT: 8:4–6 [AB, EBC, NIC2]. The topic is idols being nothing and God in Christ being everything [AB], the meaning of eating meat sacrificed to idols [EBC], the content of the way of knowledge [NIC2].

8:4 So-then[a] concerning the eating[b] of food-offered-to-idols,[c]

LEXICON—a. οὖν (BAGD 2.a. p. 593): 'so then' [NAB, NIV, TEV], 'then' [AB], 'let us return then from these thoughts' [ICC], 'well then' [REB], 'now' [He], 'so now, what about it?' [LB], 'hence' [NRSV], 'therefore' [KJV, NASB, TNT], 'so, as has been said' [BAGD], not explicit [HNTC, Lns; NJB]. Οὖν indicates the resuming of the topic of 8:1 [Alf, BAGD, Gdt, He, Ho, ICC, Lns, My, NIC2] after the parenthetical interruption [Ho]. The repetition of the words 'food offered to idols' supports the interpretation that οὖν is resumptive [NIC2].

b. βρῶσις (LN **23.3**) (BAGD 1. p. 148): 'eating' [AB, BAGD, He, HNTC, ICC, **LN**, Lns; all versions except LB]. This word is also translated as a verb: 'to eat' [LB].

c. εἰδωλόθυτος: 'food offered to idols'. See this word at 8:1.

we-know that (there is) no[a] idol[b] in (the) world

LEXICON—a. οὐδείς (BAGD 1. p. 591): 'no' [BAGD, He, HNTC, Lns; NRSV], '(has) no real existence' [BAGD; REB], 'nothing' [AB; KJV, NAB, TNT], '(is) nothing at all' [NIV], '(there is) no such thing as' [NASB], 'none exists in reality' [NJB], 'does not really exist' [TEV], '(there is) no such thing as the being that an idol stands for' [ICC], '(an idol) is not really (a god)' [LB].

b. εἴδωλον (LN 6.97) (BAGD 2. p. 221): 'idol' [AB, BAGD, He, HNTC, ICC, LN, Lns; all versions except NJB, REB], 'false god' [BAGD; NJB, REB]. Εἴδωλον refers to an object of worship which resembles a person, animal, or god [LN]. Here it means the actual pagan god rather than image, for there were images in the world [NIC].

QUESTION—To whom does 'we' refer to?

It refers to Paul and his readers [TH]. It is inclusive, meaning 'all of us Christians' [TG].

QUESTION—What do the words οἴδαμεν ὅτι 'we know that' indicate?

They indicate that the words 'there is no idol in the world' and 'there is no God but one' are quotes from the Corinthians [HNTC, NIC, NIC2, TH, TNTC; NRSV, REB, TNT]. Paul is not giving his full thoughts on the matter here since later he says that meat sacrificed to idols is really sacrificed to devils (10:20). But he agrees that what the heathen worship are no gods [TNTC].

QUESTION—Is οὐδείς 'no one, nothing' used as a modifier of 'idol' or the predicate complement of an implied verb 'to be'?

1. Οὐδείς modifies 'idol' [Alf, BAGD, Ed, EGT, He, HNTC, Ho, ICC, Lns, My, NIC, TG; probably NASB, NJB, NRSV, REB, TEV]: there is *no* idol in the world. It is better to take these two statements as parallel—there is *no* idol in the world and there is *no* God except one [Ho, ICC]. 'Idol' is a metonymy for a god the idol represents and there are no such beings as the heathen thought their gods to be [Ho]. The world contains many idols, but there are no beings that correspond to these images. Later Paul will say that there are demons connected with the idols [Lns].
2. Οὐδείς is the predicate complement [AB, EBC, Gdt, NIC2, Rb, TH; KJV, NAB, NIV, TNT]: an idol *is nothing* in the world. The heathen thought that behind the statues were beings who lived in the statue. Paul was saying that if they looked for their god there, they would find nothing [Gdt]. The meaning is that they have no actual existence in the real world [TH]. The Corinthian position was that there was no reality behind an idol. And because this was true, they should not be blamed for eating food offered to them [NIC2].

and that (there is) no God but[a] one.

LEXICON—a. εἰ μή 'but' [AB, He, HNTC, ICC; all versions except LB, NJB, TEV], 'other than' [NJB], 'save' [Lns]. This word is also joined with 'not' and translated 'only (one) and no other' [LB], 'only the (one)' [TEV].

8:5 For[a] even-if[b] there-are so-called[c] gods[d] either in heaven or on earth,

LEXICON—a. γάρ: 'for' [AB, He, HNTC, ICC, Lns; KJV, NASB, NIV], not explicit [all other versions].

b. καὶ εἴπερ (LN 89.66) (BAGD VI.11. p. 220): 'even if' [AB, He, ICC, Lns; NASB, NIV, TEV, TNT], 'if indeed' [BAGD, LN], 'even if indeed' [Rb], 'if after all' [BAGD, LN], 'though' [KJV, NJB], 'even though' [NAB, NRSV, REB], 'indeed though' [HNTC], 'since' [BAGD], not explicit [LB]. Εἴπερ is an emphatic conditional marker [LN]. The -περ of εἴπερ intensifies the condition supposing the extreme possibility [EGT].

c. pres. pass. participle of λέγω (LN 33.131) (BAGD II.3. p. 470): 'so-called' [AB, BAGD, He, HNTC, ICC, Lns; all versions except KJV, LB], 'to be called' [BAGD; KJV], 'to be named' [BAGD, LN]. This word is also translated as a phrase: 'according to some people' [LB]. That they are 'called' gods shows that they are not really gods [Ed, TNTC].

d. θεός (LN **12.1**)(BAGD 1. p. 357): 'god' [AB, BAGD, He, HNTC, ICC, **LN**, Lns; all versions]. In those days it was commonly thought that there were many divine beings both in heaven and on earth [HNTC, My]. They gave such gods names like Jupiter and Apollo. They believed that there were river gods, wood gods, and the like [Lns, My].

QUESTION—What relationship is indicated by γάρ 'for'?

It introduces an explanation for 8:4 [Lns, My, NIC2]. It supplies more information on idols [Lns, TNTC]. It indicates the grounds for the statement in 8:4 [NIC].

QUESTION—What is the function of εἴπερ 'even if'?

It serves to introduce a concessive clause [Lns, NIC2, Rb, TG]: although there are so-called gods. For the sake of argument, Paul concedes the existence of these gods [Lns, Rb, TG].

as-indeed[a] there-are many gods and many lords,[b]

LEXICON—a. ὥσπερ (LN 64.13) (BAGD 2. p. 899): 'as indeed' [AB; NASB, NIV, TNT], 'just as indeed' [BAGD], 'as in fact' [HNTC, ICC; NRSV], 'and indeed' [REB], 'and really' [He], 'even as' [Lns], 'just as' [BAGD, LN], 'as' [BAGD, LN; KJV], 'to be sure' [NAB], 'and' [NJB], 'even though' [TEV], not explicit [LB].

b. κύριος (LN 12.9) (BAGD 2.e.β. p. 460): 'lord' [AB, He, HNTC, ICC, LN, Lns; all versions except LB], not explicit [LB]. The Greeks believed that these non-human beings ruled between heaven and earth [TH]. 'Lords' are the deities of the mystery cults, while gods were the traditional deities [NIC2]. They are the heroes and demi-gods of Greek mythology, while 'gods' referred to idols [NIC]. The two terms 'lords' and 'gods' probably refer to the same entity [TNTC].

QUESTION—Does Paul concede the existence of these gods and lords, or is he merely saying that the heathen believe they exist?

1. He agrees that the gods and lords do exist [Alf, EBC, Ed, He, Herm, HNTC, Ho, ICC, TH]. Paul's meaning is that gods and lords do exist but they are not the ones the heathen believe in [Ho]. Deut. 10:17 states that Jehovah is God of gods and Lord of lords, so Paul is conceding the existence of rulers in the universe who are subordinate to God [EBC, Herm, HNTC, ICC].
2. He merely concedes that the heathen believe that they exist [AB, EGT, Lns, NIC, NIC2, TG, TNTC]. Galatians 4:8 talks of gods which are not gods. Here Paul has called them 'so-called' gods. To concede their actual reality would be to go against the belief that 'there is no God but one'. They exist only in the minds of heathen worshippers [AB]. There may be beings behind the idols, but any deity or lordship ascribed to them is only 'so-called' [EGT]. Suppose there are such beings, what of it? [Lns].

8:6 yet[a] for-us (there is) one God the Father

LEXICON—a. ἀλλά (BAGD 4. p. 38): 'yet' [AB, BAGD, HNTC; all versions except KJV, LB], 'but' [NIC2; KJV, LB], 'still' [ICC], 'nevertheless' [Lns], 'it would be none the less true that' [He], 'certainly, at least' [BAGD]. It is strongly adversative and contrasts Christians with idol worshippers [NIC2, TNTC]. The God whom Christians worship as Father and Son stands in contrast with the 'many gods' and 'many lords' of the heathen [Alf, NIC2].

QUESTION—What is the significance of the position of ὑμῖν 'to/for us' in the clause, and its dative case

The fronted position of ὑμῖν makes it emphatic [Alf, ICC, Lns, NIC2, TNTC]. The dative case means: 'for us' [He, HNTC, ICC, Lns; all versions except KJV, LB], 'to us' [AB; KJV], 'we know' [LB].

QUESTION—To whom does the word ὑμῖν refer?

It is used in the inclusive sense to refer to 'us Christians' [ICC, TG].

QUESTION—What is the meaning of πατήρ 'Father'?

It means that God is Father both of Jesus and of believers [Gdt, HNTC, NIC, TNTC]. It means that He is the Father of believers [Ed, Ho, My]. 'Father' here is used in the sense of 'Creator', not in the usual Christian sense of Father of Jesus [Herm, TH]. It means that God is Father of Jesus and believers, and of all He has created [Lns].

from whom (are) all-things

QUESTION—What is the meaning of this clause?

It means that God created all things [HNTC, Ho, NIC2, TG]. God is the source of all that exists [NIC], the source of the whole universe and all that is in it [Ho].

and we (are) to him,

QUESTION—What is the meaning of this clause?

It means that we exist to bring honor to God [Ho, NIC], to serve him [HNTC, TNTC], and to fulfill his purposes [NIC2, TNTC]. It means that God is the purpose for which we live [AB, NCBC]. It means that we find our true fulfillment in God [HNTC, TG]. It means that we believe in God, love God and worship God so that our whole life is directed Godward [Lns].

QUESTION—What word is emphatic in this clause?

The word ἡμεῖς 'we' is emphasized [NIC2].

QUESTION—What verb is implied after ἡμεῖς 'we'?

It is implied that it is God for whom we are [AB], for whom we exist [He, HNTC; NASB, NJB, NRSV, REB, TNT], for whom we live [NAB, NIV, TEV].

and (there is) one Lord Jesus Christ

QUESTION—What is the meaning of this clause?

It means that there is only one Lord and he is Jesus Christ, the historical person who administers the universe [Ho]. Mentioned with the Father like this indicates that he is included in the Godhead [TNTC].

through whom (are) all-things

QUESTION—To what does τὰ πάντα 'all things' refer?

It has the same reference as the 'all things' just mentioned above [Ho]: from whom are all things...through whom are all things.

QUESTION—What does δι' οὗ 'through whom' mean?

It means that Jesus is the agent of creation [Ho, TG, TNTC]. God created all things by means of Jesus Christ [NIC2, TG].

and we (are) through him.

QUESTION—What is the meaning of this clause?

It does not mean that we were created as physical beings by Christ [HNTC, Ho, NIC], but that we became sons of God through him [Alf, Gdt, HNTC, Ho, Lns, My, NIC, TNTC, Vn]. Christ redeemed us and brought us to God [HNTC, Ho, NIC]. It means that through Christ we live for God [EBC].

QUESTION—To whom does ἡμεῖς 'we' refer?

It refers to all Christians [TG].

DISCOURSE UNIT: 8:7–13 [AB, EBC, EGT, Gdt, Herm, NIC2, TNTC]. The topic is the obligation of deference to the conscience of a weak brother [AB], freedom to be used with care [EBC], difference in knowledge, with the practical obligations arising from it [Gdt], the criterion: our brother [Herm], the criterion: caring for a brother [NIC2], the weak brother [TNTC]. This section gives specifics to the principle of 8:1–3 that love defines true knowledge [NIC2].

8:7 However[a] this knowledge[b] (is) not in all-people;

LEXICON—a. ἀλλά (LN 89.125): 'however' [LB, NASB, NJB, NRSV], 'but' [He, LN; NIV, REB, TEV, TNT], 'nevertheless' [AB, Lns], 'still' [ICC], 'howbeit' [KJV], 'of course' [NAB], not explicit [HNTC].

b. γνῶσις: 'knowledge'. See this word at 8:1.

QUESTION—What relationship is indicated by ἀλλά 'however' ?

This strong adversative indicates that Paul is now going to qualify what has just been said [NCBC, NIC2]. Paul agrees with the Corinthians only partially. The thesis of the Corinthians was that if you had knowledge everything would be all right. Paul attacks this position by saying that not all possessed it [NIC]. The 'all' of 8:1 was too sweeping since some did not possess knowledge [NCBC].

QUESTION—To what 'knowledge' is Paul referring?

He is referring to the knowledge that there is no idol in the world and heathen gods are imaginary [Ho, TNTC]. Some of the weaker Christians do not yet realize this [TNTC]. He is referring to the concept that food being dedicated to an idol is no different from any other food [AB].

QUESTION—What is the difference between the act of 'having knowledge' of 8:1 and the 'knowledge being in someone' of this verse?

'Having knowledge' refers to theoretical knowledge, while this 'knowledge in someone' refers to practical and emotional knowledge [NIC2]. 'Having knowledge' refers to intellectual awareness, while 'knowledge in someone' refers to an inner illumination [Ed]. 'Having knowledge' is accepting something as valid, while 'knowledge in someone' indicates an inner certainty [AB]. There is no difference between the expression in 8:1 and the expression here [TNTC].

but some by the custom[a] of-the idol until now eat (food) as (being) food-offered-to-an-idol,

TEXT—Instead of συνήθεια 'custom', some manuscripts have συνειδήσει 'conscience'. GNT selects 'custom' with an A rating indicating that the text is certain. Ho, My and KJV select 'conscience'.

LEXICON—a. συνήθεια (LN 41.25) (BAGD 2.a. p. 789): 'custom, habit' [BAGD, LN], '(due to the) custom' [Lns], 'accustomed' [AB, BAGD, He; NASB, NIV, NRSV, REB, TNT], 'used to' [TEV], 'devoted' [NAB], '(through) familiarity (with)' [HNTC]; 'conscience' [KJV] . It is also translated '(false gods) still play such a part (that)' [NJB] 'accustomed to look upon (an idol) as real' [ICC], 'to be used to thinking of (idols) as alive' [LB].

QUESTION—What is the significance of the dative case of τῇ συνείδησις 'by the custom'?

It is a dative of cause and can be translated 'through/because of being accustomed to (idols)' [AB, BAGD, He, HNTC, Lns; LB, NAB, NIV, NJB, NRSV, REB, TEV, TNT].

QUESTION—What is the meaning of the genitive construction τῇ συνηθείᾳ τοῦ εἰδώλου 'the custom of the idol'?

It means the custom connected with the idol [LN]. The custom refers to the habit of thinking of an idol as real [Gdt, ICC]. The custom of attending idol feasts is so engrained that it is impossible for them to get rid of the old feeling [Lns]. When they are eating food offered to idols, they still feel as if they are participating in the worship of idols [ICC]. The thought that food offered to idols has real spiritual power is so engrained in them that they continue to think of it in this way [HNTC]. Their former association with the idol lingers as a present feeling [NIC2]. When they became Christians, they did not cease to believe in the reality of the spiritual beings behind the idols. They still thought of the food as having religious meaning [HNTC].

and their conscience[a] being weak[b] is-defiled.[c]

LEXICON—a. συνείδησις (LN 26.13) (BAGD 2. p. 786): 'conscience' [AB, BAGD, He, HNTC, ICC, LN, Lns; all versions], 'moral consciousness' [BAGD, NIC2], 'moral sensitivity' [LN]. It refers to the ability to discern between right and wrong [TH].

b. ἀσθενής (LN 88.117) (BAGD 2.b. p. 115): 'weak' [AB, He, HNTC, Lns; all versions except LB, NJB], 'tender' [LB], 'vulnerable' [NJB], 'too weak to guide them aright' [ICC], 'morally weak' [BAGD, LN]. This refers to a weakness in faith, which causes the believer, through lack of knowledge, to consider externals to be of primary importance [BAGD].

c. pres. pass. indic. of μολύνω (LN **53.34**) (BAGD 2. p. 527): 'to be defiled' [AB, He, HNTC, ICC, LN, Lns; all versions except LB, TEV], 'to feel defiled' [**LN**; TEV], 'to be stained' [LN], 'to be made impure, to be soiled' [BAGD]. This word is also translated actively: '(it) bothers (them)' [LB].

QUESTION—What is the meaning of a 'weak conscience'?

It may mean that the conscience is too weak to refrain from following the example of others or that it is weak because of a lack of insight about a matter [ICC]. It means a conscience that continues to judge an action according to an old criterion and to make a person feel guilty in spite of his changed attitude toward that kind of action [TG]. It means one that considers an act to be wrong when it is right [Ho]. It means one that is not sure whether an act is right or wrong [BAGD, Ed, Ho, Lns]. It means a failure to fully assimilate emotionally the fact that there is only one God [NIC2].

QUESTION—What is the meaning of μολύνεται 'defiled'?

A conscience is defiled when it has a sense of guilt [EBC, Ho, ICC, My]. It means that a person is spiritually or ritually unfit to worship God [Gdt, TG]. The weak Christian is morally defiled in his own estimation [Ed]. It means that one's relationship with Christ is spoiled and results in his return to idolatry [NIC2].

8:8 But/Now[a] food[b] will-commend[c] us not to God;

LEXICON—a. δέ: 'but' [KJV, NASB, NIV], 'but surely' [ICC], 'but of course' [NJB], 'however' [TEV], 'now' [AB, He, Lns; NAB], 'certainly' [REB], 'just remember that' [LB], not explicit [HNTC; NRSV, TNT].

b. βρῶμα (LN 5.1; 5.7): 'food' [AB, BAGD, He, HNTC, ICC, LN (5.1), Lns; all versions except KJV], 'meat' [LN (5.7); KJV]. Either 'food' or 'eating food' is indicated by this word [TG]. See this word at 3:2.

c. fut. act. indic. of παρίστημι (LN 85.14) (BAGD 1.e. p. 628): 'to commend' [He, HNTC; KJV, NASB, NRSV, TNT], 'to affect one's relation to' [ICC, NIC2], 'to affect one's standing with' [AB, Lns], 'to improve one's relation with' [TEV], 'to make acceptable to' [NJB], 'to bring into the presence of' [REB], 'to bring close/near to' [NAB, NIV, NRSV], 'to bring before (the judgment seat of God)' [BAGD], 'to present oneself' [LN]. This word is also translated with God as the actor: 'God doesn't care' [LB]. In the context, the meaning is 'to bring near' [BAGD, Herm; NAB, NIV, NRSV], 'to present for approval' [ICC, Vn]. The verb is neutral: to come before God for either approval or condemnation [ICC, Lns, Rb], with the resultant implication that neither eating food or not eating food affects our relationship to God [AB, HNTC, ICC, Lns, My, NIC, NIC2].

QUESTION—What relationship is indicated by δέ 'but'?

1. It indicates contrast [EGT, ICC, TNTC; KJV, NASB, NIV, NJB, TEV]: but.
2. It indicates transition [AB, He, Lns, My, NIC2; LB, NAB, REB]: now.

QUESTION—Are these words Paul's, or is he quoting from the position in the letter from the Corinthians?

1. These are Paul's words [AB, Alf, Gdt, Herm, Ho, Lns, My; probably all versions except NRSV]. It is an admitted truth [Ho].

2. These are a quoted from the Corinthian position [EGT, HNTC, NCBC, NIC, NIC2, TNTC; NRSV].
2.1 The whole verse is a quote from the Corinthian position [EGT, NCBC, NIC, NIC2]. The fact that the next verse begins with a warning supports this interpretation so here Paul grants their argument but counters with a warning [NIC, NIC2]: A may be true, but take care lest B.
2.2 The first clause is a quote from the Corinthian position [HNTC, TNTC; NRSV].

neither are-we-worse-off[a] if we-eat not, nor are-we-better-off[b] if we-eat.

LEXICON—a. pres. pass. indic. of ὑστερέω (LN **65.51**): 'to be worse off' [LB, NRSV], 'to be the worse' [ICC, Lns; KJV, NASB, NIV, REB], 'to lack something' [AB], 'to lack an advantage' [**LN**], 'to lack benefits' [LN], 'to lose something' [NJB, TEV, TNT], 'to suffer loss' [NAB], 'to fall behind' [He], 'to go short of something' [HNTC].

b. pres. act. indic. of περισσεύω (LN **65.47**) (BAGD 1.b.α. p. 651): 'to be better off' [LB, NRSV], 'to be the better' [ICC, Lns; KJV, NASB, NIV, REB], 'to gain' [TNT], 'to gain something' [NJB, TEV], 'to gain favor' [NAB], 'to have special advantage' [**LN**], 'to gain an advantage' [HNTC], 'to have a greater benefit' [LN], 'to have an abundance' [AB, BAGD], 'to advance further' [He], 'to abound in, to be rich in' [BAGD]. Here it means: 'to have more divine approval' [BAGD].

QUESTION—With whom is a person not 'worse off' or 'better off'?

1. In both cases, it is with God that a person is not worse or better off [ICC, Lns, My, NIC]. These are matters of indifference to God [NIC].
2. If we eat not, we are not inferior to one who eats, and if we eat, we are not superior to the one who abstains [Ed].

8:9 But[a] be-careful[b] lest-somehow[c] this liberty[d] of-yours

LEXICON—a. δέ (LN 89.124): 'but' [AB, LN, Lns; KJV, LB, NASB, NRSV, REB], 'however' [ICC; NAB, NIV, TEV], 'yet' [He], 'only' [NJB], not explicit [HNTC; TNT].

b. pres. act. impera. of βλέπω (LN 27.58) (BAGD 6. p. 143): 'to be careful' [LB, NIV, NJB, REB, TEV], 'to take care' [BAGD, ICC; NAB, NASB, NRSV, TNT], 'to see to it' [AB, BAGD, Lns], 'to beware' [BAGD, He, HNTC, LN], 'to take heed' [KJV], 'to watch, to look to' [BAGD]. See this word at 3:10.

c. μή πως (LN **89.62**) (BAGD 1.b. p. 519): 'lest somehow' [NASB], 'that not somehow' [AB, BAGD; NRSV], 'lest by any means' [Lns; KJV], 'lest' [HNTC, LN; LB, NAB], 'that not' [He, ICC, **LN**; NIV, REB, TNT], 'so that not, in order that not' [LN], 'that not in any way' [NJB], 'not' [TEV].

d. ἐξουσία (LN **30.122**) (BAGD 1. p. 278): 'liberty' [AB, BAGD, He; KJV, NASB, NRSV, REB], 'freedom' [ICC; LB, NIV, NJB], 'freedom of choice' [**LN**], 'freedom of action' [LN; TEV], 'right' [LN; NAB, TNT], 'authority' [HNTC], 'power' [Lns], 'power to evaluate' [LN]. This word means: 'lawful power or right' [Ho].

QUESTION—What relationship is indicated by δέ 'but'?

It is adversative [AB, Alf, Ed, Gdt, Ho, NIC2]: but. The 'but' indicates that while Paul concedes the validity of the previous verse, he cautions them to be careful how they use their liberty [Ho]. Food does not affect relationship with God, but it can affect relationships with fellow Christians [Ed].

QUESTION—To what 'liberty' is Paul referring?

It is the liberty to eat any kind of food [HNTC]. This is probably a Corinthian buzz word which indicated doing as they pleased without restraint. That this is a Corinthian word is indicated in the way Paul refers to it: 'this liberty of yours' [HNTC, NIC2]. 'Liberty' here refers to eating sacrificial meat [NIC]. It is lawful for those with this knowledge to do as they like, their eating will not harm them [Ho, ICC].

become (an) occasion-to-sin[a] to-the-weak-(ones).[b]

LEXICON—a. προσκόμμα (LN **88.307**) (BAGD 2.b. p. 716): 'occasion to sin' [LN], 'occasion of sin' [NAB], 'that which causes someone to sin, that which provides an occasion for someone to sin' [LN], 'pitfall' [REB], 'stumbling block' [AB, He, HNTC, Lns; KJV, NASB, NIV, NRSV], 'a cause of stumbling' [TNT], 'obstacle to trip someone' [NJB], 'obstacle to the well-being of someone' [ICC], 'hindrance, opportunity to take offense or to make a misstep' [BAGD]. This word is also translated as a verb: 'to make someone fall into sin' [**LN**; TEV], 'to cause someone to sin' [NIC; LB], 'to cause someone to stumble' [BAGD]. A stumbling block is something which causes someone to fall [Ho, NIC2]. In this case the stumbling block would be tempting a person to go against what their conscience was telling them [Alf, NCBC].

b. ἀσθενής: 'weak'. See this word at 8:7.

8:10 For[a] if anyone should-see you the-one having knowledge eating[b] in (an) idol's-temple,[c]

LEXICON—a. γάρ: 'for' [AB, He, HNTC, ICC, Lns; KJV, NASB, NIV, NRSV], 'you see' [LB], not explicit [all other versions].

b. pres. mid. participle of κατάκειμαι (LN 17.23; 23.21) (BAGD 3. p. 411): 'to eat' [LN; LB, NIV, NRSV, TEV], 'to dine' [AB, BAGD, LN; NASB], 'to take part at a banquet' [He], 'to eat a meal' [LN], 'to sit down to a meal' [REB], 'to sit and eat' [ICC, LN], 'to sit eating' [NJB], 'to sit at table' [HNTC; TNT], 'to be at table' [LN], 'to sit at meat' [KJV], 'to recline' [LN, Lns], 'to recline at table' [NAB], 'to recline on a couch at table' [BAGD].

c. εἰδωλεῖον (LN **7.19**) (BAGD p. 221): 'idol's temple' [BAGD, Lns; KJV, NASB, NIV, NRSV, TNT], 'temple of an idol' [**LN**; NAB, NJB, TEV], 'idol temple' [AB], 'idol-shrine' [HNTC], 'heathen temple' [REB], 'pagan temple' [He], 'court of the idol' [ICC], 'temple restaurant' [LB].

QUESTION—What relationship is indicated by γάρ 'for'?
'For' introduces an illustration of how eating food offered to idols could cause someone else to sin [Ed, HNTC, Ho, Lns]. It explains the danger they are to watch out for [NCBC]. It explains how the weak Christian might be led to sin when the strong Christian eats sacrificial meat [NIC2].

QUESTION—What is the significance of changing from second person plural in8:9, to second person singular here?
It is like the same phenomenon in 4:6, 7 and functions to give greater emphasis [NIC2]. It serves to dramatize what Paul is saying [Lns]. One Corinthian with knowledge represents all who have knowledge [NIC].

QUESTION—What is implied by this condition?
This is the first specific mention of what the general problem of 'food offered to idols' involved, and it implies that the knowledgeable believers were attending the banquets in the idol temples. This is apparently the specific question about which the Corinthians were asking. They were asking not about eating food offered to idols, but attending the idol banquets [NIC2].

QUESTION—Is this condition purely hypothetical or does it have reference to an actual occurrence in Corinth?
1. It may have reference to what had or was occurring in Corinth [EBC, Ed, NIC, NIC2, Rb]. Paul's urgency about this matter suggests that although this is a present general supposition, it reflects what was actually going on [NIC2].
2. It is purely hypothetical. It is a condition of expectancy suggesting something that is likely to occur [Lns].

QUESTION—What did this kind of action imply?
After a part of an animal was offered on a pagan altar, the worshippers would eat the rest of it in the temple. They might invite friends to share their meal [TG]. By itself, this kind of action was idolatrous [EGT, Gdt, ICC, My, Rb].

(might) not his conscience being weak be-strengthened[a] to-eat foods-offered-to-idols?

LEXICON—a. fut. pass. indic. of οἰκοδομέω (LN 74.15) (BAGD 3. p. 558): 'to be strengthened' [BAGD, LN; NASB], 'to be made more able' [LN], 'to be fortified' [HNTC], 'to be made bold' [TNT], 'to be emboldened' [KJV, NIV, REB], 'to be bolstered up' [Lns], 'to be built up' [AB], 'to be edified' [He], 'to be influenced' [NAB], 'to be encouraged' [TH; NJB, NRSV, TEV], 'to cause to be hardened' [ICC]. This word is also translated actively: 'to become bold enough' [LB].

QUESTION—What does 'being weak' mean?
It means that he still believes that the idol is real [EGT]. It means that he still believes that the food is a sacrifice to an idol [ICC, NIC2].

QUESTION—What reply is expected to this question?
The negative οὐκ 'not' in a question expects a positive reply [NIC, TH].

QUESTION—What is Paul's purpose in using a positive verb like οἰκοδομέω 'to strengthen' in a scene of potential destruction?

Paul uses this verb to express irony [AB, Alf, BAGD, Ed, EGT, Gdt, He, Lns, My, NIC2, TNTC]. The 'strong' Christians might argue that they are helping the 'weak' by encouraging them to such an action [BAGD, TNTC]. They *encourage* them, a term for edifying the church, to idol worship [AB]. The irony functions to express Paul's sorrow [EGT], his stern warning against possible consequences [AB], or his attempt to shame them [Lns]. He may be using it as a quote from a serious question they had asked in which they see the 'strengthening' of a weak brother's conscience as a good thing [BAGD, HNTC, Lns, TH].

QUESTION—What is the function of this rhetorical question?

It directs their attention to the harm they can do [TNTC].

8:11 So[a] by/because-of[b] your knowledge the weak-one is-destroyed,[c]

LEXICON—a. γάρ: 'so' [LB, NIV, NRSV], 'and so' [TEV], 'then' [AB], 'and then' [NJB], 'for' [HNTC, Lns; NASB], 'and' [KJV], not explicit [He; NAB, REB, TNT]. This word is also translated with implied information: 'this must be wrong, for' [ICC].

b. ἐν (LN 89.76; 89.26): 'by' [HNTC, LN (89.76); NIV, NRSV, TNT], 'through' [ICC, LN; KJV, NASB, NJB], 'because of' [AB, LN (89.26); LB, TEV], 'in connection with' [Lns]. The phrase ἐν τῇ γνώσει 'because of your knowledge' is translated 'for lack of your knowledge' [He], 'this knowledge of yours destroys' [REB].

c. pres. pass. indic. of ἀπόλλυμι (LN 20.31; 21.32): 'to be destroyed' [LN (20.31); NIV, NRSV], 'to be ruined' [LN (20.31); NASB, TNT], 'to be lost' [LN (21.32); NJB], 'to be swept away' [He]. This verb is also translated actively: 'to perish' [AB, HNTC, LN (21.32), Lns; KJV, NAB, TEV], 'to be responsible for causing great spiritual damage' [LB], 'to destroy' [REB], 'to bring ruin to' [ICC]. The present tense indicates that he is now in the act of perishing [Ed, EGT]. He is on the point of perishing [AB]. See this word translated 'perishing' at 1:18.

QUESTION—What relationship is indicated by γάρ 'so'?

1. It indicates the result of 8:10 [Alf, Gdt, HNTC, TNTC; LB, NIV, NRSV, TEV]: might he not be encouraged to eat food offered to idols *and as a result* this man is destroyed. The manuscript reading καί in the sense of 'and so' should be selected in place of γάρ 'for' [Gdt].
2. It explains 8:10 [AB, ICC, NIC2]. 'For' means: 'this must be wrong, for' [ICC].

QUESTION—What word is emphasized in this clause?

The word 'your' is strongly emphasized [TH].

QUESTION—What relationship is indicated by ἐν 'by/because of'?

1. It indicates means [Ed, Gdt, ICC, My, NCBC, TNTC; KJV, NASB, NIV, NRSV, TNT]. It is attempting to share one's knowledge without the weak

Christian really making it his own [Ed]. It is by acting in accordance with one's knowledge that the weak one is destroyed [NCBC].

2. It indicates reason [AB, He, HNTC; LB, TEV]. Because they act according to what they know, they lead their brothers to sin [HNTC].

QUESTION—Does ἀπόλλυται 'is destroyed' refer to eternal or temporary injury?

1. It refers to eternal destruction [Gdt, HNTC, Ho, Lns, My, NIC2]. This verb shows decisively that not the mere eating of food offered to idols is in focus, but real idolatry through eating at the idol feasts. The weak brother is brought back into the practice of idol worship and is eternally lost [NIC2]. In respect to him, Christ suffered in vain [HNTC].
2. It refers to temporary harm [EBC, ICC, NCBC, NIC, TNTC, Vn]. Paul has in mind the retarding of the brother's Christian life and usefulness [NCBC, TNTC]. He calls him a brother so he does not mean eternal destruction but rather the weakening of his faith and spoiling of his Christian life [EBC].

QUESTION—What is the significance of the present participle ὁ ἀσθενῶν 'the one being weak'?

It may mean that he is in a continual state of being weak [EGT, TNTC].

the brother for whom Christ died.

QUESTION—What is the function of this phrase?

Its position serves to emphasize it [NIC2, TH, TNTC]. Paul redefines 'the one being weak' as 'the brother for whom Christ died' [NIC2]. This clinches the argument [Rb, Vn]. Regard for Christ should keep them from doing this [Lns, My]. If Christ died for the weak, the stronger brother should have a proper regard for him [NIC].

8:12 And in-this-way[a]

LEXICON—a. οὕτως (LN 61.9): 'in this way' [AB, LN, My; NIV, REB, TEV, TNT], 'thus' [He, LN, Lns; NAB, NASB, NRSV], 'so' [HNTC, ICC; KJV, NJB], not explicit [LB].

QUESTION—To what does 'this way' refer?

It refers to destroying a brother for whom Christ died [NIC2]. It is described in 8:10–11 [My]. It refers to not acting in a loving way toward the weak brother [NIC].

sinning against the brothers and wounding[a] their conscience when-it-is-weak you-sin against Christ.

LEXICON—a. τύπτω (LN **20.15**) (BAGD 2. p. 830): 'to wound' [AB, BAGD, He, HNTC, Lns; all versions except LB, NJB], 'to harm' [**LN**], 'to injure' [LN; NJB], 'to cause spiritual injury to' [**LN**], 'to give a blow' [ICC], 'to strike, to beat' [BAGD], not explicit [LB].

QUESTION—What is the significance of the change to second person plural?

It may indicate that there were a significant number in Corinth to whom this applied [EBC].

QUESTION—What is meant by 'wounding their conscience'?

It means to make a person feel guilty by making him do something his conscience feels is wrong, or it means to weaken the resolve of his conscience by causing him to go against it [AB]. To wound a conscience is to cause it the pain of regret [Ho]. This describes what is mean by 'sinning against the brothers' [Alf, Ho].

QUESTION—Why does this constitute a sin against Christ?

What is done to Christ's people is counted by Christ as done to himself [Ho, ICC, NCBC, NIC2, Rb, TNTC]. Christ's death is frustrated [EGT, Gdt, Vn]. They regard Christ's death as of little value [NIC]. It shows their lack of love to Christ [Ho].

8:13 Therefore[a] if food makes-to-sin[b] my brother,

LEXICON—a. διόπερ (LN **89.47**) (BAGD p. 199): 'therefore' [AB, BAGD, HNTC, ICC, **LN**; all versions except KJV, LB, NJB, TEV], 'wherefore' [Lns; KJV], 'so then' [LN; TEV], 'so' [LB], 'this/that is why' [He; NJB], 'for this very reason' [BAGD, LN]. The word 'therefore' refers back to the danger of sinning against Christ [Ed, EGT, ICC], or to the whole picture of wounding a brother and sinning against Christ [Gdt, My]. It indicates a conclusion [NIC].

b. pres. act. indic. of σκανδαλίζω (LN 88.304) (BAGD 1.a. p. 752): 'to make sin' [LB, TEV], 'to cause to sin' [BAGD; NAB], 'to cause to fall into sin' [NIV], 'to cause to fall' [AB, BAGD], 'to be the downfall of' [REB], 'to be the cause of downfall/falling' [NJB, NRSV], 'to cause to fall away' [TNT], 'to cause to stumble' [NASB], 'to cause offense to' [He], 'to make to offend' [KJV], 'to offend' [HNTC], 'to put a stumblingblock in someone's way' [ICC], 'to entrap' [Lns], 'to cause to be caught' [BAGD].

QUESTION—What is the significance of this condition?

The indicative emphasizes the reality of the condition: if food really does cause my brother to sin ... [EBC].

by-no-means[a] will-I-eat meat[b] forever,[c]

LEXICON—a. οὐ μή (LN 69.5) (BAGD D.1. p. 517): 'by no means' [LN], 'in no wise' [Lns], 'never' [BAGD], 'certainly not' [AB, BAGD], 'not (eat) any' [LB]. This word is also joined with 'forever' and translated 'never' [AB; NRSV, TNT], 'never again' [HNTC, ICC; NAB, NASB, NIV, REB, TEV], 'never anymore' [NJB]. It is also translated as an adjective: 'no (meat)' [He; KJV]. Οὐ μή is an emphatic negative and coupled with the word 'forever' form a strong expression for 'never' [TNTC].

b. κρέας (LN **5.14**) (BAGD p. 449): 'meat' [AB, BAGD, He, ICC, **LN**; all versions except KJV, LB], 'flesh' [HNTC, Lns; KJV], 'it' [LB]. 'Meat' here refers to that which is offered to idols [ICC, TG].

c. εἰς τὸν αἰῶνα(LN 67.95): 'forever' [He, LN], 'to eternity' [Lns], 'always, forever and ever, eternally' [LN]. This word is also translated as a clause: 'while the earth stands' [KJV], 'as long as I live' [LB].

QUESTION—What is the significance of changing from βρῶμα 'food' to κρέας 'meat'?

It may be because the poor would not eat meat apart from the feasts in honor of the idol. For them therefore, the word 'meat' would have religious connotations [NIC2].

lest I-cause-to-sin my brother.

QUESTION—What is the significance of the repetition of the words τὸν ἀδελφόν μου 'my brother' and σκανδαλίωζω 'to cause to sin'?

They serve to emphasize both that this man was Paul's brother and that he must not cause him to sin [Lns, My].

DISCOURSE UNIT: 9:1–27 [AB, Alf, Ed, GNT, Herm, HNTC, Ho, ICC, Lns, NCBC, NIC, NIC2, TG, TNTC]. The topic is Paul's exercise of his rights [AB], the reconciliation of the opposite Christian conceptions of liberty and love [Ed], the rights of an apostle [GNT], even an apostle will renounce his rights for the sake of the gospel [HNTC], the rights of ministers to an adequate maintenance and the necessity of self-denial [Ho], the great principle of forbearance [ICC], Paul, an illustration of love [Lns], the question of apostolic freedom [NCBC], Paul's example in self-sacrifice [NIC], Paul's apostolic defense [NIC2].

DISCOURSE UNIT: 9:1–22 [Gdt]. The topic is the example of abnegation given by Paul.

DISCOURSE UNIT: 9:1–18 [EBC]. The topic is on giving up Paul's rights as an apostle.

DISCOURSE UNIT: 9:1–14 [TNTC]. The topic is Paul's rights.

DISCOURSE UNIT: 9:1–12a [EBC, TH]. The topic is rights of an apostle.

DISCOURSE UNIT: 9:1–6 [AB, EGT]. The topic is Paul's apostolic freedom [AB], Paul's apostolic status [EGT].

DISCOURSE UNIT: 9:1–2 [NIC2]. The topic is a defense of Paul's apostleship.

9:1 Am-I not free?[a]

TEXT—In some manuscripts the first two questions are reversed. GNT does not mention this alternative. Only KJV and LB reverse them.

LEXICON—a. ἐλεύθερος (LN 37.134) (BAGD 2. p. 250): 'free' [AB, He, HNTC, LN, Lns; all versions except TEV], 'independent, not bound' [BAGD]. This word is also translated as a noun phrase: 'a free man' [TEV], 'a free agent' [ICC].

QUESTION—What is the function of these four rhetorical questions?

They present a challenge to Paul's critics [TG]. They defend Paul's apostleship and actions, such as eating marketplace food [NIC2]. They all contain the Greek negative particle οὐ and therefore expect a positive reply [EBC, NIC2, TG, TNTC].

QUESTION—What does Paul mean by being 'free'?

He is free as every Christian is [EGT, Gdt, Ho, NIC, Rb]. He is free to live according to his convictions about what is right [Ho]. He is free from conforming to the opinions of others [Alf, Ho]. He is free to eat meat offered to idols [Gdt, NIC2]. He is not under obligation to obey the Law of Moses in regard to the things under discussion [EGT]. He is free from superstition, sin, and legalism [TG]. He is not bound to the ceremonial law [NIC]. Paul is free from the obligation of working for his living [TH].

Am-I not (an) apostle?[a]

LEXICON—a. ἀπόστολος: 'apostle'. See this word at 1:1.

QUESTION—What is implied in this question?

The question implies that the Corinthians were questioning his claim to be an apostle (see 1:1, 12; 4:1–5, 8–13, 14–21; 5:1–2) [NIC2]. It implies that Paul has all the prerogatives of an apostle [Ho, ICC, TNTC]. It means that he is claiming equality with the apostles [Ho].

Have-I-seen[a] not Jesus our Lord?

TEXT—Instead of Ἰησοῦν τὸν κύριον ἡμῶν 'Jesus our Lord', some manuscripts have Ἰησοῦν Χριστὸν τὸν κύριονἡμῶν 'Jesus Christ our Lord'. GNT does not mention this alternative. Only KJV includes 'Christ'.

LEXICON—a. perf. act. indic. of ὁράω (LN 24.1) (BAGD 1.a. p. 577): 'to see' [AB, BAGD, He, HNTC, LN, Lns; all versions except LB], 'to actually see' [LB], 'to see face to face' [ICC], 'to catch sight of, to notice' [BAGD].

QUESTION—What is the significance of the change from the negative particle οὐ to the emphatic negative particle οὐχί?

It may indicate that Paul was emphasizing the verb [AB, ICC, TNTC; LB]: have I not actually seen Jesus our Lord?

QUESTION—To what event is Paul referring?

He is referring to Jesus' appearance to him on the road to Damascus [AB, Alf, BAGD, Ed, EGT, Gdt, He, ICC, Lns, My, NCBC, NIC, NIC2, TNTC, Vn]. He may also be referring to Acts 18:9; 27:17, and 2 Cor. 12:2–4 [My]. A qualification for being an apostle is having seen the risen Lord (Acts 1:22; 2:32; 3:15; 4:33) [ICC].

QUESTION—What is the purpose of this and the following question?

They support his claim to being an apostle [EBC, EGT, ICC, NIC2, Rb].

QUESTION—What is the significance of the title Ἰησοῦν τὸν κύριον ἡμῶν 'Jesus, our Lord'?

The title probably has reference to Jesus' resurrection [NIC2, TG], 'our Lord' was what Jesus became through his resurrection [NIC2]. 'Our Lord' points to Jesus as the head of the Church. As such he alone is able to make someone an apostle [Gdt].

Are you not my workmanship[a] in[b] (the) Lord?

LEXICON—a. ἔργον (LN **42.12**) (BAGD 3. p. 308): 'workmanship' [LN], 'result of (my) work' [BAGD, LN; NIV, TEV], 'result of (my) hard work' [LB], 'work' [AB, He, HNTC, Lns; KJV, NAB, NASB, NJB, NRSV], 'handiwork' [REB], 'result of (my) service' [TNT]. This word is also translated as a clause: '(you) who were won over (to him) through (me)' [ICC].

b. ἐν with dative object: 'in' [AB, He, HNTC; all versions except LB, TEV, TNT], 'for' [LB, TEV, TNT], 'to' [ICC], 'in connection with' [Lns].

QUESTION—What is the meaning of ἐν κυρίῳ 'in the Lord'?

1. This phrase goes with 'you' and means: your being in union with the Lord is the result of my work [Ho, TG]. The reference is to their becoming Christians [TG].
2. It refers to the Lord's enablement to do the work [Alf, Gdt, He, ICC, TH]: you are my workmanship 'by the power of the Lord'. It was the result of the Lord working through Paul [TH].
3. This refers to the character of Paul's work, it was done in connection with the Lord [Lns, My].
4. This means that the work was done for Christ [LB, TEV, TNT]: you are the result of my work for Christ.

QUESTION—What is implied by this question?

It implies that the establishing of a church was a work which was worthy of an apostle [ICC, NIC, NIC2].

9:2 If to-others I-am not (an) apostle, yet-at-least[a] I-am to-you;

LEXICON—a. ἀλλά γε 'yet at least' [HNTC, Lns], 'but at least' [ICC], 'yet doubtless' [KJV], 'yet' [BAGD], 'nevertheless' [He], 'at least' [AB, BAGD; NASB, NRSV, REB, TNT], 'at any rate' [NJB], 'certainly' [BAGD; LB, NAB], 'surely' [NIV, TEV]. The γέ 'indeed' strengthens the ἀλλά meaning: 'yet, at least' [Alf, Lns, My].

QUESTION—What is implied by the conditional clause?:

Some did not regard Paul to be an apostle [Herm, NIC]. He is not an apostle in their estimation [Alf, EGT, HNTC, Ho]. These critics were within the Corinthian church [AB, Ed, EGT, Gdt, HNTC, NCBC, NIC2]. Perhaps they were in the party that said 'I am of Cephas' or in the Judaistic party [EGT]. Another view is that they were not members of the Corinthian church [ICC, Lns, My, NIC, TH, TNTC].

for you are the seal[a] of my apostleship[b] in (the) Lord.

LEXICON—a. σφραγίς (LN **73.9**) (BAGD 2.a. p. 796): 'seal' [AB, He, HNTC, Lns; all versions except REB, TEV, TNT], 'proof' [LN; TEV, TNT], 'seal which authenticates' [ICC], 'very seal' [REB], 'certification' [BAGD, **LN**], 'validation, evidence of genuineness' [LN], 'that which confirms, attests, or authenticates, official confirmation' [BAGD], not explicit [LB]. This word is also translated as a verb: '(you) clearly show that (I am an apostle)' [**LN**].

b. ἀποστολή (LN 53.73) (BAGD p. 99): 'apostleship' [AB, BAGD, He, HNTC, ICC, LN, Lns; all versions except LB, NAB, NJB, REB, TEV], 'the fact that I am an apostle' [TEV], 'apostolate' [NAB, NJB, REB], 'office of an apostle' [BAGD], not explicit [LB].

QUESTION—In what way were they a seal?

Σφραγίς indicates 'legally valid attestation' [Herm, NIC2]. This was a mark impressed in wax or clay which either showed ownership of an object or its genuineness [NIC2]. The Corinthians were won to Christ by Paul and thus their existence as Christians showed that he was a genuine apostle [NIC2, TNTC].

QUESTION—What does ἐν κυρίῳ 'in (the) Lord' mean?

1. It modifies the word 'you' [Ed, ICC, TG; LB, TEV]: that you live in union with the Lord shows that I am an apostle.
2. It modifies 'apostleship' [He]: my Christian apostleship.
3. It modifies the entire sentence [Alf, Lns]: you are the seal of my apostleship as enabled by/in connection with the Lord.

DISCOURSE UNIT: 9:3-14 [NIC2]. The topic is Paul's apostolic rights.

9:3 This is my defense[a] to-the-ones judging[b] me.

LEXICON—a. ἀπολογία (LN **33.436**) (BAGD 1. p. 96): 'defense' [AB, BAGD, He, HNTC, **LN**, Lns; all versions except KJV, LB, NJB], 'answer' [ICC; KJV, LB, NJB], 'reply' [BAGD], 'what is said in defense, how one defends oneself' [LN]. This word is also translated as a verb: 'I defend (myself)' [TEV].

b. pres. act. participle of ἀνακρίνω (LN **33.412**; 56.12): 'to judge', 'to sit in judgment' [NIV], 'to examine' [HNTC, Lns; KJV, NASB, NRSV, TNT], 'to hear a case' [LN (56.12)], 'to investigate' [AB], 'to accuse' [He], 'to interrogate' [NJB], 'to call to account' [REB], 'to question someone's rights' [LB], 'to challenge someone's claim' [ICC], 'to criticize' [**LN**; NAB, TEV]. It is a legal term used figuratively of those making judgments about Paul [EBC]. See this word at 4:3.

QUESTION—What does αὕτη 'this' refer to?

1. It refers to what follows [EBC, He, Herm, HNTC, Lns, NCBC, NIC, NIC2, TH; NAB, NASB, NIV, NJB, NRSV, REB, TEV, TNT]: the following is my defense. The position of 'this' at the end of the Greek sentence argues that it refers to what follows [Lns, NIC2].
2. It refers back to what precedes [Alf, Ed, EGT, Gdt, Ho, ICC, My, TNTC, Vn; LB]. 'There you have my answer' [ICC]. 'This' refers to the conversion of the Corinthians to Christ [Alf].
3. It refers to both, illustrating what Paul had said in 8:13 [Rb].

QUESTION—What is the significance of the present tense of τοῖς ἐμὲ ἀνα κρίνουσιν 'to the ones judging me'?

1. The present tense indicates that this examination was going on at Corinth [AB, NIC, NIC2, Rb, Vn]: to those who are judging me.

2. The present tense should be taken as indicating desire [HNTC; NJB, NRSV, REB]: to those who want to judge me.

QUESTION—What was the examination about?

It was about his apostolic authority [He, Ho, NIC2]. It centered around Paul's refusal to accept support for his work which, in the mind of the Corinthians, showed that he was not a true apostle [He, NIC2]. It was about Christian liberty, not about whether or not he was a genuine apostle [Lns]. Some Corinthians did not feel that Paul was devoting himself as much as he should to his work [Ho].

QUESTION—What words are emphasized in this clause?

The words 'me' and 'my' are emphatic [ICC, My, TNTC].

9:4 Have-we not (the) right[a] to-eat[b] and to-drink?[c]

LEXICON—a. ἐξουσία (LN 30.122) (BAGD 1. p. 277): 'right' [AB, BAGD, He, HNTC, LN, Lns; all versions except KJV, LB, NJB], 'rights' [LB], 'every right' [NJB], 'power' [KJV], 'freedom of choice' [BAGD, LN], 'to be free to do as one thinks best' [ICC].

b. aorist act. infin. of ἐσθίω (LN 23.1) (BAGD 1.e.α. p. 313): 'to eat' [AB, He, HNTC, LN, Lns; all versions except LB, NIV, NRSV, TEV], 'to eat at the cost of the churches' [ICC], 'to consume food, to use food' [LN]. This word is also translated as a noun: 'food' [NIV], 'our food' [NRSV], '(to be given) food for one's work' [TEV]. This word is also joined with 'drink' and translated as: 'to be a guest in someone's home' [LB].

c. aorist act. infin. of πίνω (LN 23.34): 'to drink' [AB, He, HNTC, ICC, LN, Lns; all versions except LB, NIV, NRSV, TEV], not explicit [LB]. This word is also translated as a noun: 'drink' [NIV], 'our drink' [NRSV], '(to be given) drink for one's work' [TEV].

QUESTION—What answer is expected to this rhetorical question?

It expects a positive response [BAGD EBC, NIC, NIC2]. There are two negative particles. The first one, μή, expects a negative reply to a question, the second, οὐ, negates the verbs giving something like: 'It can't be that we don't have the right to eat and drink, can it?' As such it is highly rhetorical. The same double negative is used in 9:5 and 9:6 as well [NIC2]. The question is ironical [Ed, EGT, NCBC]. This and the following questions function to impress on the Corinthians that Paul has all the rights of an apostle [NIC2].

QUESTION—To what does 'to eat' and 'to drink' refer?

1. It refers to his right to be supported by the churches [Alf, BAGD, EBC, Ed, EGT, Gdt, He, Ho, ICC, Lns, My, NCBC, NIC2, TG, TH, TNTC, Vn; TEV]. This right is established in what follows, showing that it is the right to be supported by the churches [Ho]. Food and drink stand for material support in general [TG].
2. It refers to the freedom from food restrictions that all Christians have [AB, Herm, NIC]. Here Paul refers to his Christian liberty, while in the following verses he refers to his apostolate [NIC].

3. It refers to both of the above [HNTC]. Paul has the right to eat and drink what he pleases, and to do so at the expense of the congregation [HNTC].

QUESTION—To whom does 'we' refer?

1. It refers to Paul and others [Gdt, Lns, My, NIC2, TH]. It refers to Paul and the other apostles [Lns, TH], to Paul and Barnabas [Gdt, My], and possibly also to Silas and Timothy [Gdt]. It refers to Paul and those who were traveling with him [NIC2]. Paul is not making an exception for himself alone, but for the rights of all the apostles [Lns].
2. It is a rhetorical epistolary plural referring just to Paul and can be translated as 'I' [LB, REB, TEV].

9:5 Have-we not (the) right to-take-along[a] (a) sister[b] (as a) wife[c]

LEXICON—a. pres. act. infin. of περιάγω (LN **15.170**) (BAGD 1. p. 645): 'to take along' [NASB, NIV], 'to take along on a trip' [ICC, **LN**; TEV], 'to take along with oneself' [BAGD], 'to bring along on trip' [LN; LB], 'to take around' [AB; NAB, TNT], 'to take about with one's self' [BAGD; REB], 'to take about' [BAGD, HNTC], 'to lead about/around' [BAGD, Lns; KJV], 'to have with oneself (constantly)' [BAGD], 'to marry' [NAB]. This word is also translated passively: 'to be accompanied by' [BAGD, He; NJB, NRSV]. This word is used because the apostles did not live in one place, but traveled around [Ho, ICC, NIC].

b. ἀδελφή: 'sister' [AB, LN, Lns; KJV], 'Christian sister' [HNTC, ICC]. This word is also joined with 'woman' and translated as an adjective: 'believing (wife)' [LB, NASB, NIV, NRSV], 'believing (woman)' [NAB], 'Christian (wife)' [He; NJB, REB, TEV, TNT], 'Christian sister' [HNTC]. See this word at 7:15.

c. γυνή: 'wife' [AB, He, HNTC, ICC, Lns; all versions except NAB], 'woman' [NAB]. See this word at 5:1.

QUESTION—Does this refer to the right to be married, or the right to have one's wife be supported by the churches?

1. It refers to the right to have their wives supported by the churches [Alf, ICC, Lns, My, NCBC, Rb, TG, TNTC, Vn]. There was no question about the right to be married [TNTC].
2. It refers to the right of the apostles to be married [EGT, NIC; NAB].
3. It refers to both of the above [Ed, He, NIC2, TH].

as also the rest-of (the) apostles and the brothers of-the Lord and Cephas?

QUESTION—Does the term ἀδελφός 'brother' refer to 'blood brother' or to 'fellow believer'?

It refers to 'blood brother' as a male child of the same father [TH]. It refers to the sons of Joseph and Mary [NIC, NIC2, TNTC]. If Cephas is included among the apostles, then so are the Lord's brothers [Ed, TH]. This does not imply that the Lord's brothers were apostles, rather they were persons of eminence [EGT].

QUESTION—To whom does the word ἀπόστολος 'apostle' refer?

As Paul used the 'apostle' in 2 Cor. 15:7, the term was not limited to the twelve [Alf, NIC2, TG]. This refers to those who were apostles in the technical use of the term [NIC]. It does not imply that all of the other apostles were married [EBC, Ho]. All the other apostles were married [Lns].

QUESTION—Who is 'Cephas' and why is he mentioned?

Cephas is Peter, referred to in 1:12 [TG]. He is mentioned separately from the other apostles because he was one of the teachers around whom some of the Corinthians rallied [NIC, NIC2]. It may be because Peter had visited Corinth with his wife [HNTC, NIC2]. Peter was the leader of the apostles and the most notable example [Lns].

9:6 Or[a] have only I and Barnabas not (the) right not to-work?[b]

LEXICON—a. ἤ: 'or' [HNTC, Lns; KJV, NASB, NIV, TEV], 'or is it' [ICC; NRSV], 'or again' [He], 'and' [LB], not explicit [AB; NAB, NJB, REB, TNT].

b. pres. mid. infin. of ἐργάζομαι (LN 42.41) (BAGD 1. p. 307): 'to work' [He, LN, Lns; KJV, NASB, NJB], 'to work for a living' [HNTC, ICC; LB, NAB, NIV, NRSV, REB, TEV, TNT]. This word is also translated as a noun phrase: 'physical work' [AB]. See this word at 4:12.

QUESTION—What is implied by ἤ 'or' ?

It implies that if the truth value of the previous two questions were denied [Alf, Gdt, ICC], the following would be true [Alf]: Or, if you will not grant me the truth of these, then that would mean, etc.

QUESTION—What is implied by ἐργάζεσθαι 'to work'?

'To work' is this context means to gain one's livelihood by his work [Gdt]. Paul supported himself by tentmaking (Acts 18.3), but what Barnabas did is unknown [My]. To the Corinthians, working at a trade was beneath the dignity of the office of apostle [NIC2].

QUESTION—What is the intent of this rhetorical question?

It is the same as the previous question [NIC2]: it can not be that only Barnabas and I do not have the right to refrain from working for our living, can it?

DISCOURSE UNIT: 9:7-15a [EGT]. The topic is the claims of ministers to public maintenance.

DISCOURSE UNIT: 9:7-14 [AB]. The topic is the traditional guarantee of support to God's workers.

9:7 Who ever[a] serves-as-a-soldier[b] at-his-own expense?[c]

LEXICON—a. ποτέ (LN **67.9**) (BAGD 1. p. 695): 'ever' [AB, He, HNTC, **LN**, Lns; NJB, REB, TEV], '(at) any time' [LN; KJV, NASB, NRSV], not explicit [ICC; LB, NAB, NIV, TNT]. Ποτέ is used in rhetorical questions that expect a negative answer [BAGD].

b. pres. mid. indic. of στρατεύω (LN 55.18) (BAGD 1. p. 770): 'to serve as a soldier' [AB, BAGD, He, LN; NASB, NIV, TNT], 'to serve in the army' [BAGD; NJB, REB], 'to do military service' [BAGD; NRSV], 'to go to war' [HNTC], 'to go a warfare' [KJV], 'to go soldiering' [Lns], 'to be on service' [ICC], 'to be a soldier' [LN]. This word is also translated as a noun phrase: '(what) soldier(s) in the army' [LB, TEV], '(what) soldier in the field' [NAB].

c. ὀψώνιον (LN 57.166) (BAGD 1.a. p. 602): 'expense' [AB, BAGD, He; LB, NAB, NASB, NIV, NJB, REB, TNT], 'wages' [AB, BAGD], 'rations' [BAGD; NAB], 'outfit and rations' [ICC], 'charges' [HNTC, Lns; KJV], 'pay' [BAGD, LN], 'compensation' [LN], 'ration-money paid to a soldier, salary' [BAGD]. This word is also translated as a verb: 'to pay the expenses' [NRSV, TEV].

QUESTION—What reply is expected to each of the rhetorical questions in 9:7 and 9:8 and what is their function?

Each question expects a negative reply [NIC2]. The function of the rhetorical questions is to show that just as in daily life a person is supported by his work, so Paul has a right to be supported from his work [NIC2, TNTC]. The questions are pictures of three activities of an apostle: his battle with evil, church planting, and caring for his flock [Ed, Gdt, ICC, Vn].

Who plants[a] (a) vineyard and doesn't eat its fruit?[b]

LEXICON—a. pres. act. indic. of φυτεύω (LN **43.5**): 'to plant' [AB, BAGD, He, HNTC, ICC, **LN,** Lns; all versions except LB], 'to harvest (one's crop)' [LB]. This question is translated 'What farmers do not eat the grapes from their own vineyard?' [TEV]. See this word at 3:6.

b. καρπός (LN 3.33; 43.15) (BAGD p. 404): 'fruit' [AB, BAGD, He, HNTC, LN, Lns; all versions except LB, NAB, NIV, TEV, TNT], 'grapes' [NIV, TEV, TNT], 'yield' [NAB], 'crop' [LN; LB], 'harvest' [LN], 'produce' [ICC].

QUESTION—Who is the person who plants the vineyard?

1. He is the owner of the vineyard [Ho, ICC, Lns, NIC, TNTC; TEV]. He will not only be the first to taste his grapes, but he owns the whole harvest [Lns]. This is a small field and the owner will eat all the harvest [NIC].
2. He is someone who works in another's vineyard [Alf, Gdt]. He eats of the fruit, but only a part of it [Alf]. The entire harvest does not belong to him [Gdt].

Or who tends[a] (a) flock[b] and doesn't drink[c] of its milk?

LEXICON—a. pres. act. indic. of ποιμαίνω (LN 44.3) (BAGD 1. p. 683): 'to tend' [BAGD, HNTC, ICC, LN; NASB, NIV, NRSV, REB], 'to shepherd' [AB, He, LN, Lns], 'to take care of' [LN; LB], 'to pasture' [LN], 'to keep' [NJB], 'to look after' [TNT], 'to herd, to lead to pasture' [BAGD], 'to feed' [KJV]. This word is also translated as a noun: '(what) shepherd(s)' [NAB, TEV].

b. ποίμνη (LN 4.28) (BAGD p. 684): 'flock' [AB, BAGD, He, HNTC, LN, Lns; all versions except LB, TEV], 'sheep' [TEV], 'flock of sheep and goats' [LB], 'cattle' [ICC]. Ποίμνη is a group of sheep or goats [LN].

c. pres. act. indic. of ἐσθίω (LN **23.1**) (BAGD 1.b.β. p. 312): 'to drink' [HNTC, **LN**; LB, NIV], 'to use' [NASB, REB, TEV], 'to partake of' [AB, He], 'to nourish oneself' [NAB], 'to feed on' [NJB, TNT], 'to get a share of' [ICC], 'to get (any of its milk)' [NRSV], 'to eat' [Lns; KJV], 'to get sustenance from' [BAGD]. The verb means 'to eat', thus suggesting that the milk is thought of as food for nourishment [NIC2]. A more general word such as 'use' is recommended [TG, TH].

QUESTION—Does the preposition ἐκ 'from/of' in the phrase 'of its milk' have any meaning of its own or is it merely signaling the accusative case?

1. It signals the accusative case [He, Herm, NIC2; NASB, REB, TEV, TNT]: drink its milk.
2. It means 'some of' [HNTC, ICC, Lns, NIC; KJV, LB, NIV, NRSV]: drink some of its milk. No one person drinks all of the milk [ICC, NIC].

9:8 (It is) not according-to[a] a-human (that) I-say these-things or does-not the-Law[b] also say[c] these-things?

LEXICON—a. κατά (LN 89.8): 'according to' [AB, LN]. The phrase κατά ἄνθρωπον 'according to a human' is translated 'on human authority' [NRSV, TNT], 'with no more than human authority' [HNTC], 'according to human judgment' [NASB], 'according to a human standard' [AB], 'from a human/worldly point of view' [BAGD, ICC; NIV], 'taking up a purely human standpoint' [He], 'in a human way' [BAGD], 'merely human reasons' [NAB], 'on these human analogies' [REB], 'merely worldly wisdom' [NJB], 'to these everyday examples' [TEV], 'the opinions of men' [LB], 'as a man' [KJV], 'in man fashion' [Lns].

b. ὁ νόμος (LN 33.55) (BAGD 4.a. p. 543): 'the Law' [BAGD, He, LN; NASB, NIV, NJB, TEV, TNT], 'God's law' [LB], 'the Divine Law' [ICC], 'the law' [AB, BAGD, HNTC, Lns; KJV, NAB, NRSV, REB].

c. pres. act. indic. of λέγω: 'to say' [AB, He, HNTC; all versions except NAB], 'to state' [Lns], 'to speak of' [NAB], 'to assume' [ICC].

QUESTION—What answer is expected to this rhetorical question?

He is not basing what he says on human authority but on what the Law says [NIC, NIC2, TH, TNTC].

QUESTION—To what does ταῦτα 'these things' refer?

They refer to his illustrations that support the principle that a person who works has a right to a support [Ho, ICC, NIC2].

QUESTION—What is the meaning of κατὰ ἄνθρωπον 'on human authority'?

It means 'based on human judgment' and is in contrast with the Law [EGT, ICC, NIC2, TG]. It means according to human judgment of what is fitting [ICC], in accordance with human practices [EGT], as men commonly take for granted [NIC]. Paul asks if it is necessary to appeal to what men do in support of the principle that work should be rewarded [Ho].

QUESTION—To what specifically does ὁ νόμος 'the Law' refer?

It refers to the first five books of the Old Testament [Ho, NIC2, TH, TNTC]. Sometimes it was used loosely to refer to all of Scripture [TNTC].

9:9 For[a] it-is-written in-the law of-Moses,

LEXICON—a. γάρ (LN 89.23): 'for' [AB, HNTC, LN, Lns; KJV, LB, NASB, NIV, NRSV, REB], 'indeed' [He], not explicit [ICC; all other versions].

QUESTION—What relationship is indicated by γάρ 'for'?

It indicates that Paul will now explain what is written [NIC2]. It answers the previous question, 'Does not the law also say these things? It does, for it is written the law of Moses' [Alf, Ho].

QUESTION—How are the nouns related in the genitive construction ἐν τῷ Μωϋσέως νόμῳ 'in the law of Moses'?

It means the law that Moses wrote or the law that Moses handed down [TH].

QUESTION—What passage is quoted here?

The passage quoted is Deut. 25:4 [EBC, Ho, NIC2].

"You-shall-muzzle[a] not (an) ox[b] (when it is) treading-out-grain."[c]

LEXICON—a. fut. act. indic. of κημόω (LN **44.6**) (BAGD p. 430): 'to muzzle' [AB, BAGD, He, HNTC, ICC, **LN**, Lns; all versions except LB], 'to put a muzzle on' [LB], 'to keep from eating' [LN]. It means to cover an animal's mouth to prevent it from eating [LN]. The future is used idiomatically as an imperative [Lns]: Do not muzzle an ox.

b. βοῦς (LN **4.15**) (BAGD p. 146): 'ox' [AB, BAGD, He, HNTC, ICC, **LN**, Lns; all versions], 'bull' [LN]. The masculine form means a bull or an ox (a castrated bull) [LN].

c. ἀλοάω (LN 43.19) (BAGD p. 41): 'to tread out grain' [He, ICC, LN; LB, NAB, NIV, NRSV, TNT], 'to tread out corn' [KJV, NJB,], 'to thresh (grain)' [AB, BAGD, HNTC, LN, Lns; NASB, REB, TEV]. This means to separate grain from its husk by beating or by being tread on by cattle [LN]. It also means to drag a sledge over grain [NIC, NIC2].

QUESTION—To what activity does this refer?

The stalks of wheat were laid out on the ground. Then a farmer drove an ox around and around on top of the stalks. This separated the grains of wheat from the straw [NIC, TG, TNTC]. After this, the mixture was thrown into the air so that the wind would blow the chaff away while the heavier grain fell straight to the ground [TNTC].

(It is) not the oxen (that) God is-concerned-about[a]

LEXICON—a. pres. act. indic. of μέλει (LN **30.39**) (BAGD p. 500): 'to be concerned about' [BAGD, He, **LN**; NASB, NIV, NJB, TEV, TNT], 'to be concerned for/with' [AB; NAB, NRSV, REB], 'to care about' [HNTC], 'to think about' [LN; LB], 'to take care for' [Lns; KJV], 'to be a care or concern' [BAGD]. This word is also translated as a phrase: 'out of consideration for' [ICC].

QUESTION—What answer is expected to this part of the question and what is Paul teaching?

A negative answer is expected [Lns, NIC, NIC2, TNTC]: God is not concerned about the oxen. Paul is not speaking about the original meaning of that law as though he denied God's concern for animals, but about its application to the present situation [NIC2]. His intent is to teach that the ox is not God's only concern [EBC, Lns], God's primary concern is about men [NIC, NIC2, TNTC]. The answer from the perspective of the writer of Deuteronomy would be 'Yes, God does care about the ox'. But Paul's intent here is to teach that if God cares about animals, how much more does he care about people [AB, Alf, Ho].

9:10 or[a] does-he-speak entirely[b] for-the-sake-of[c] us?

LEXICON—a. ἤ: 'or' [He, HNTC, Lns; KJV, NAB, NASB, NJB, REB, TNT], 'rather' [AB], not explicit [ICC; LB, NIV, NRSV, TEV].

b. πάντως (LN **91.10**) (BAGD 1. p. 609): 'entirely' [NJB, NRSV], 'altogether' [Lns; KJV, NASB], 'simply' [HNTC], 'indeed' [**LN**], 'certainly' [AB, BAGD, LN], 'surely' [ICC; NIV], 'really' [TEV, TNT], 'always' [He], 'rather' [NAB], 'at all, at least, in any event' [LN], 'by all means, doubtless, probably' [BAGD, NIC2], not explicit [LB]. This word is also translated as a verb: 'must (not the saying refer to us)' [REB].

c. διά with accusative object: 'for the sake of' [AB, He; KJV, NAB, NASB, NJB, NRSV, TNT], 'for' [ICC; NIV], 'on account of' [HNTC, Lns], 'about' [LB]. This word is also translated as a verb: 'to refer to (us)' [REB], 'to mean (us)' [TEV]. See this word at 4:6.

QUESTION—What answer is expected to this question?

A positive answer is expected [AB, HNTC, ICC, NIC, NIC2; LB, NAB, NIV, NJB, NRSV, REB, TEV, TNT]: He speaks entirely for us, doesn't he? There is no negative particle in the Greek, the question is neutral [TH].

QUESTION—To whom does 'he speaks' refer?

It refers to God, as seen from the previous verse [AB, EGT, Gdt, He, Herm, HNTC, Ho, ICC, Lns, TG; KJV, NAB, NASB, NIV, NRSV, TEV, TNT]. It refers to the Scripture just quoted [NIC2]: it speaks.

QUESTION—What is the precise meaning of πάντως, 'entirely, definitely'?

1. It means that God was speaking 'entirely' for our sake [Alf, EGT, Gdt, HNTC, Lns, My, NIC; KJV, NASB, NRSV]. In the Law, God did not have oxen in mind, but Christian preachers [HNTC]. The Law concerns oxen only incidentally, it concerns us altogether [Lns]. In every case, a law is given for our sake [NIC]. It doesn't mean that God is concerned exclusively with us, but every law made about animals who serve people must hold good for God's people who serve him [EGT].
2. It means that God was 'certainly' speaking for our sake [AB, BAGD, Ho, ICC, LN, NIC2, Vn; NIV, NJB, REB, TEV, TNT]. Is it for our sake, as it doubtless is, that God says it? [ICC].
3. It means that 'in general' God was speaking for our sake [Ed]. God speaks for our sake in the law generally as well as in every particular command [Ed].

QUESTION—Does 'for our sake' refer to all people or only to apostles and other missionaries?

1. It refers to the apostles and other missionaries [Alf, Ed, EGT, HNTC, ICC, Lns, My, TG, TNTC].
2. It refers to all people [Gdt, Herm, Ho].

Yes[a] it-was-written for-the-sake-of us

LEXICON—a. γάρ (BAGD 4. p. 152): 'yes' [BAGD, HNTC, NIC2; NASB, NIV], 'yes, indeed' [He], 'no doubt' [KJV], 'of course' [LB, REB, TEV], 'you can be sure' [NAB], 'clearly' [NJB], 'surely He was looking beyond them' [ICC], 'indeed' [BAGD; NRSV], 'certainly' [BAGD], 'for' [Lns], not explicit [TNT].

QUESTION—What is the function of this clause?

It signifies that a 'Yes' answer is to be given to the previous question [BAGD, Ed, EGT, Gdt, He, HNTC, ICC, NIC2; LB, NASB, NIV, NJB, NRSV, REB, TEV]. It indicates that the following is the reason why Paul expected an affirmative answer to the question [NIC].

that/because[a] the-one plowing[b] should[c] plow in hope[d]

LEXICON—a. ὅτι: 'because' [AB, ICC; NASB, NIV, TNT], 'because it is right that' [NJB], 'for' [He, HNTC; NAB, NRSV], 'that' [Herm, Lns; KJV], 'to show (us) that' [LB], not explicit [REB, TEV].

b. pres. act. participle of ἀροτριάω (LN 43.4) (BAGD p. 108): 'to plow' [AB, BAGD, HNTC, ICC, LN, Lns; all versions], 'to till the ground' [He].

c. pres. act. indic. of ὀφείλω: 'should' [AB; all versions except NASB, NIV, TNT], 'ought' [HNTC, ICC, Lns; NASB, NIV, TNT], 'must' [He].

d. ἐλπίς (LN 25.59) (BAGD 1. p. 252): 'hope' [AB, BAGD, He, HNTC, LN, Lns; all versions except LB, NAB, NJB], 'expectation' [BAGD; NJB], 'prospect' [BAGD], 'a good prospect' [ICC]. This word is also translated as a verb: 'to expect' [LB, NAB].

QUESTION—What relationship is indicated by ὅτι 'that/because'?

1. It explains in what respect it was written for us [Ed, EGT, ICC, Lns, My, NIC2, TH; LB]: it was written for us, that is, it was written that one should plow in hope. Ὅτι could be translated 'to show that' [Ed, ICC].
2. It indicates the grounds for saying that it was written for us [Ho, NIC].
3. It indicates the reason why the figurative command about the ox was written [Alf, HNTC]: It was written for us, because the workman should be rewarded for his work.
4. It indicates the content of what was written [Herm; KJV]: For us it was written that the one plowing should plow in hope.

QUESTION—What does the plowman hope for?

He hopes that his work will not be useless [NIC]. He hopes to be rewarded [Ho]. He hopes the same as the man in the later stage, that he will have a share of the crop [EBC, EGT, He, ICC, Lns, My, NCBC, NIC2].

and the-one threshing (should thresh) in hope of having-a-share-of[a] (the crop).

TEXT—Instead of ἐπ᾽ ἐλπίδι τοῦ μετέχειν ‘in hope of partaking’, some manuscripts have τῆς ἐλπίδος αὐτοῦ μετέχειν ἐπ᾽ ἐλπίδι ‘in his hope to partake in hope’. GNT does not indicate the alternative. Only KJV follows the alternative reading.

LEXICON—a. pres. act. infin. of μετέχω (LN **57.6**) (BAGD p. 514): ‘to have a share of’ [BAGD, **LN**], ‘to share in’ [AB, BAGD, LN; NASB, REB], ‘to partake’ [Lns], ‘to be a partaker of’ [KJV], ‘to participate in’ [BAGD], ‘to enjoy’ [BAGD]. This word is also translated as a participle: ‘sharing (the crops/produce)’ [NASB, REB], ‘sharing in (the profit/harvest)’ [ICC; NIV], ‘partaking of (the crop)’ [HNTC]. It is also translated as a noun: ‘some share of (the harvest)’ [LB], ‘a share in (the grain)’ [NAB], ‘(having/getting) his share’ [He; NJB, TNT], ‘a share in/of (the crop)’ [NRSV, TEV]. This refers to his share of the crop [Alf, EBC, HNTC, Ho, ICC, NCBC, NIC, NIC2, TG, TH].

QUESTION—What words are emphasized in these two clauses?

The words ‘in hope’ are emphasized [ICC, My, NIC, NIC2] being in emphatic position in the first clause and repeated for emphasis in the second [ICC, NIC, NIC2].

9:11 If we sowed[a] spiritual-(things)[b] among-you,

LEXICON—a. aorist act. indic. of σπείρω (LN 43.6) (BAGD 1.b.β. p. 761): ‘to sow’ [AB, BAGD, He, HNTC, ICC, LN, Lns; all versions except LB], ‘to plant’ [LB]. The aorist implies that it had already happened [Lns, NIC, TNTC].

b. πνευματικός (LN 26.10): ‘spiritual things’ [BAGD, HNTC, LN, Lns; KJV, NASB, NJB], ‘spiritual matters’ [BAGD], ‘spiritual seed’ [AB, He; NIV, TEV, TNT], ‘the seed of spiritual things’ [NJB], ‘seeds of spiritual life’ [ICC], ‘good spiritual seed’ [LB], ‘a spiritual crop’ [REB], ‘spiritual good’ [NRSV], ‘in the spirit’ [NAB]. See this word at 2:13.

QUESTION—To what does τὰ πνευματικά ‘spiritual things’ refer?

It refers to the gospel [BAGD, My, NIC2, TG], or the Christian message [TH]. The same reference is seen in Rom. 15:27 [NIC2]. It refers also to the Word of God [BAGD]. It refers to Christian knowledge, faith, and love [My]. It refers to the fruits of the Spirit [Ho].

QUESTION—What words are emphasized in this clause?

The word ‘we’ is emphasized both here and in the following clause and contrasts with ‘you’ [ICC].

QUESTION—To whom does ‘we’ refer?

It probably refers to the apostles in general [TG]. It refers to apostles or evangelists in general but excludes his readers [TH]. It refers to Paul and his companions [My]. It refers to Paul, Silas, and Timothy who planted the church in Corinth [Gdt]. It refers only to Paul himself [Alf].

(is it) too-much[a] if we reap[b] of-you material-(things)?[c]

LEXICON—a. μέγας (LN **25.207**) (BAGD 2.b.β. p. 498): 'too much' [LB, NAB, NASB, NIV, NRSV, REB, TEV], 'too much to ask' [NAB], 'a great thing' [AB, HNTC; KJV], 'a great matter' [Lns; TNT], 'strange' [**LN**], 'an extraordinary thing' [BAGD], 'outrageous' [He], 'a very outrageous thing' [ICC], 'surprising' [LN]. The query means: 'are we expecting too much?' [BAGD].

b. fut. act. indic. of θερίζω (LN 43.14) (BAGD 2.a. p. 359): 'to reap' [AB, BAGD, He, HNTC, ICC, LN, Lns; all versions except LB, NAB, NJB, REB], 'to expect' [NAB, REB], 'to ask for' [LB], 'to receive' [NJB], 'to lay claim to' [BAGD].

c. σαρκικός (LN 57.6) (BAGD 1. p. 742): 'material things' [EBC, He, HNTC, LN; NASB, NJB], 'material benefits' [NRSV, TEV], 'material harvest' [NAB, NIV, REB, TNT], 'physical harvest' [AB], 'carnal things' [KJV], 'mere food and clothing' [LB], 'worldly benefit from your purses' [ICC], 'bodily things' [Lns], 'belonging to the order of earthly things, material' [BAGD].

QUESTION—What is the function of this verse?

It brings this subject to a conclusion [Herm]. It teaches that the cost of supporting an apostle is a small price to pay for the benefits of the Good News [HNTC].

QUESTION—To what does 'material things' refer?

It refers to the provision of the necessities of life to enable Paul not to have to work for his living [TG]. It refers to things needed to support the body [Ho]. It refers to things such as food, drink, and accommodation [Lns].

QUESTION—How are the nouns related in the genitive construction ὑμῶν τὰ σαρκικά 'of you material things'?

1. It means they will reap material things from them [He, HNTC, ICC; all versions except KJV, LB].
2. It means they will reap their material things [AB, Lns; KJV].

QUESTION—What answer is expected to this rhetorical question?

A negative reply is expected: it is not too much to expect [HNTC, NIC2, TG, TH].

9:12a If others have/share[a] the right[b] of-you,

LEXICON—a. μετέχω (LN 57.6) (BAGD p. 514): 'to have' [NAB, NIV, TEV, TNT], 'to share' [AB, He; NASB, NRSV], 'to share in' [HNTC, LN, Lns], 'to get one's share of' [ICC], 'to be partakers of' [KJV], 'to be given' [NJB], 'to enjoy' [BAGD]. This word is also translated with 'you' as actor: '(you) allow' [REB], '(you) give (food and clothing)' [LB]. See this word at 9:10.

b. ἐξουσία: 'right' [BAGD, Lns; NAB, NASB], 'rights' [NJB, REB], 'rightful claim' [NRSV], 'right of being supported' [AB; NIV], 'right to expect this' [TEV], 'right of maintenance from' [ICC], 'authority'

[HNTC], 'claim' [TNT], 'power' [KJV], 'goods' [He], not explicit [He; LB]. See this word at 9:4.

QUESTION—To whom does ἄλλοι 'others' refer?

It refers to other apostles, other Christian workers [TG], or other evangelists [TH]. It refers to the Judaizers [ICC, Vn]. It does not refer to Paul's enemies, but may include Apollos and other preachers of the Corinthians [NIC]. It probably refers to Apollos and Peter [NIC2].

QUESTION—How are the nouns related in the genitive construction τῆς ὑμῶν ἐξουσίας 'the right of you'?

1. It means 'the right others exert over you' [AB, Alf, BAGD, EGT, Gdt, Herm, Ho, Lns, My, NIC, NIC2, Rb; KJV, NAB, NASB, NJB, NRSV, TEV]: if others share this right they exert over you, do not we still more? This is the right to claim support from the congregation [My, NIC, NIC2].
2. It means 'the right you give to others' [ICC; NIV, REB]: if you give this right to others, do not we still more deserve it? It refers to a right bestowed by the congregation to receive support from that congregation [ICC].
3. It means 'the goods belonging to you' [He]: if others share the goods belonging to you, do not we still more? The word ἐξουσία is a synonym for οὐσία 'substance, goods' and the proper sense of the verb is 'to share' [He].

(do) not we still-more?[a]

LEXICON—a. μᾶλλον (LN 78.28) (BAGD 2.b. p. 489): 'still more' [NRSV,], 'yet more' [He, Lns], 'still better (right)' [ICC], 'more' [LN; NASB, NJB], 'the more' [HNTC], 'rather' [KJV], 'even greater (right)' [LB, NAB, TEV], 'greater (claim)' [TNT], 'all the more' [AB; NIV], 'stronger (claim)' [REB], 'more surely, more certainly' [BAGD], 'more than, to a greater degree, even more' [LN].

QUESTION—What answer is expected to this question?

A positive reply is expected [NIC2, TG]. They owed most to Paul because he founded the Corinthian church [HNTC].

DISCOURSE UNIT: 9:12b–18 [EBC, TH]. The topic is the rights not used.

9:12b But[a] **we did-not make-use-of**[b] **this right,**

LEXICON—a. ἀλλά: 'but' [He, HNTC; NAB, NIV, REB, TEV], 'nevertheless' [ICC, Lns; KJV, NASB, NRSV], 'however' [AB], 'yet' [LB, TNT], 'in fact' [NJB]. This word signals a contrast with his having the right to be supported [NIC2].

b. aorist mid. indic. of χράομαι (LN **42.23**): 'to make use of' [HNTC, **LN**, Lns; NRSV, TEV], 'to use' [AB, LN; KJV, LB, NAB, NASB, NIV], 'to avail oneself of' [ICC; REB, TNT], 'to exercise' [He; NJB]. The aorist probably refers to the time when Paul was in Corinth [NIC2].

but we-endure[a] all-things, lest in-any-way we-should-give hindrance[b] to-the good-news of Christ.

LEXICON—a. στέγω (LN **25.176**) (BAGD 2. p. 766): 'to endure' [AB, BAGD, HNTC, LN; NASB, NRSV, TEV], 'to put up with' [ICC, **LN**; NAB, NIV, NJB, REB, TNT], 'to bear the cost' [He], 'to bear' [BAGD, Lns], 'to stand' [BAGD], 'to suffer' [KJV], 'to not demand payment' [LB].

b. ἐγκοπή (LN **13.148**) (BAGD p. 216): 'hindrance, obstacle' [LN]. The phrase ἐγκοπή δίδωμι 'to give hindrance' is translated 'to hinder' [LN; KJV, NIV], 'to obstruct' [NJB], 'to cause a hindrance to' [AB, BAGD; NASB, TNT], 'to offer a hindrance to' [REB], 'to furnish a hindrance to' [Lns], 'to place/put an obstacle in the way of' [HNTC, **LN**; NAB, NRSV, TNT], 'to set up an obstacle to' [He], 'to cause to be hampered' [ICC]. This word is also translated with 'you' as patient: '(if we did you) might be less interested' [LB].

QUESTION—What is the function of ἀλλά 'but'?

It functions to indicate a parallel with the previous ἀλλά clause and to emphasize it by supplying its positive side: but we did not use this right, but we put up with all things [Lns].

QUESTION—Who is included in 'we'?

It may mean Paul, Silvanus, and Timothy [ICC, Lns].

QUESTION—What does Paul imply by πάντα 'all things'?

He means 'deprivations' [Alf, Ho, ICC], troubles or difficulties [TG], hardships [Alf, HNTC, NIC2]. What he implies can be seen in 4:10–13 [TH]. In 1 Thess. 2:9–10 and 2 Thess. 3:8 Paul says the he worked day and night with his hands so that he might not be a burden to anyone [NIC2].

QUESTION—What did Paul mean by 'not hindering' the Good News about Christ?

He probably was referring to his desire to offer the Good News 'free of charge' and to further exemplify its free nature as seen in 9:18 [NIC2]. If he took pay for his evangelism, he could be accused of preaching for what he could get out of it. Furthermore, his supporters might resent the burden [ICC].

QUESTION—How are the nouns related in the genitive construction τῷ εὐαγγελίῳ τοῦ Χριστοῦ 'the good news of Christ'?

1. It means the good news about Christ [TG, TH; TEV].
2. It means the good news Christ preached and which is about Christ [NIC].

9:13 Know-you not that the-ones performing[a] the-temple-services[b] eat[c] the-things of the temple,[d]

LEXICON—a. pres. mid. participle of ἐργάζομαι (LN 90.47) (BAGD 2.b. p. 307): 'to perform' [AB, BAGD, LN; NASB, TNT], 'to work in' [LB, NAB, NIV, TEV], 'to minister about/in' [KJV, NJB], 'to officiate at/in' [BAGD, HNTC], 'to practice' [BAGD], 'to be engaged in' [He, ICC, Lns; REB], 'to be employed in' [NRSV].

b. τὰ ἱερά (LN **53.9**) (BAGD 2. p. 372): 'the temple service(s)' [He, ICC; NRSV, REB], 'sacred services' [NASB], 'the holy services' [BAGD], 'the temple rites' [AB; TNT], 'the/a temple' [LB, NAB, NIV, NJB, TEV], '(the) holy things' [BAGD, HNTC; KJV], 'the Temple things' [Lns], 'holy activities, activities involving worship' [**LN**].

c. pres. act. indic. of ἐσθίω (LN 23.1): 'to eat' [AB, He, HNTC, LN, Lns; KJV, NASB, REB], 'to get one's food' [NIV, NJB, NRSV, TEV], 'to have one's food (from)' [TNT], 'to be maintained' [ICC], 'to be supported' [NAB], 'to take for one's needs' [LB]. The present tense indicates a general rule referring to God's provision for the priests [Lns].

d. ἱερόν (LN **7.16**): 'temple' [**LN**, Lns; all versions except LB, NASB, REB], 'holy place' [HNTC]. This word is also joined with the words 'the things of the' and translated 'the temple offerings' [AB; REB], 'temple funds' [ICC], 'the portion of the sacrifices which falls to them' [He], 'the food of the temple' [NASB], 'food brought there as gifts to God' [LB].

QUESTION—What reply does the negative particle οὐκ in this question expect?

It expects a positive answer [EBC, Herm, ICC, NIC, NIC2, TG, TH, TNTC; REB, TEV]: Surely you know...

QUESTION—To what practice is Paul referring?

He is referring to the rights of the Levites who officiate at the offerings of sacrifices (see Deut. 18:3–4 and Num. 18:20–24) [AB]. This rule was true of non-Jewish temple priests as well [Herm, HNTC, NIC, NIC2], but here he is probably only referring to Jewish custom [Alf, EGT, Gdt, Lns, NCBC, NIC2].

QUESTION—To whom do the phrases 'the ones performing the temple services' and 'the ones serving at the altar' in the following clause refer?

1. Both refer to priests [Alf, EGT, Ho, My, NIC, NIC2, TH]. The absence of a καί 'and' between the clauses indicates that the two are references to the same group [NIC2, TH]. This can refer only to Jewish priests [Alf, My], or it could refer to priests in whatever religion [NIC].
2. The first may refer to Levites while the second refers only to priests [He].
3. The first refers to both priests and Levites while the second refers only to priests [Gdt, Lns, TG].

QUESTION—What is the meaning of 'eat the things of the temple', and what are they?

It means that they received their support from the temple system [Ho, ICC, My, TG]. The 'things of the temple' would include animal sacrifices, bread placed before the Lord, and portions of harvests [My]. They would also include the tithes and offerings of the people [Gdt, ICC].

the-ones serving[a] at-the altar[b] have-a-share[c] with-the altar?[d]

LEXICON—a. pres. act. participle of παρεδρεύω (LN **35.26**) (BAGD p. 624): 'to serve' [AB, He, ICC; NIV, NJB, NRSV, TNT], 'to serve regularly' [BAGD], 'to serve at the sacrifices' [**LN**], 'to officiate' [REB], 'to work'

[LB], 'to attend' [HNTC; NASB], 'to minister' [NAB], 'to wait (at)' [KJV], 'to offer sacrifices' [TEV], 'to be engaged in waiting (on)' [Lns].

b. θυσιαστήριον (LN 6.114) (BAGD 1.a. p. 366): 'altar' [AB, BAGD, He, HNTC, ICC, LN; all versions], 'altar of sacrifice' [Lns]. This is the altar of burnt offering in the inner forecourt of the Temple [BAGD].

c. συμμερίζω (LN **57.7**) (BAGD p. 778): 'to share with' [BAGD, ICC], 'to partake with' [KJV], 'to get a share of' [LB, TEV], 'to share in' [AB, LN; NIV, NRSV], 'to share' [NAB], 'to have one's share of/with' [He; NASB, TNT], 'to have one's share together at' [HNTC], 'to have one's portion with' [Lns], 'to claim one's share from/of' [NJB, REB], 'to have a share of (what is sacrificed)' [**LN**], 'to have a part of together with others' [LN]. The present tense indicates a general rule referring to God's provision for the priests [Lns].

d. θυσιαστήριον: 'altar' [BAGD, HNTC; KJV, NASB, NJB], 'altar of sacrifice' [Lns], 'altar-sacrifices' [AB], 'the offerings of the altar' [NAB], 'sacrificial offerings' [NRSV], '(share) the sacrifices with the altar' [ICC], 'sacrifice(s)' [REB, TEV], 'food that is brought by those offering it to the Lord' [LB], 'what is offered/sacrificed on the altar' [He; NIV, NRSV]. Here 'altar' signifies the things sacrificed on it [BAGD].

QUESTION—Who is the object of παρεδρεύω 'to serve'?

The object is God [HNTC]: they serve God at the altar.

QUESTION—What is the relationship between this clause and the preceding one?

The second repeats the first in a more specific form [ICC, My, NCBC, NIC2, TNTC]. The second repeats the first in a more general form [HNTC]. Assuming both refer to priests, the clause defines the first by informing us that 'the things of the temple' are 'the altar' or the sacrifice [NIC]. This repetitive structure functions to emphasize the thought [Lns, TH].

QUESTION—Who are the participants in συμμερίζονται 'to have a share'?

1. It means that the priests share the sacrifices with the altar [Ed, EGT, Herm, ICC]. A portion of the sacrifice is burned on the altar and a portion is eaten by the priests [Ed].
2. It means the priests share with each other at the altar [HNTC].

QUESTION—What is the intent of these figures?

A person should be able to live off his/her work [NIC]. They should not have to pay for their food [TG].

9:14 In-the-same-way[a] also the Lord commanded[b] the-ones proclaiming[c] the good-news[d] to-get-their-living[e] from[f] the good-news.

LEXICON—a. οὕτως (LN 61.9): 'in the same way' [HNTC; LB, NIV, NJB, NRSV, REB, TEV], 'in this way' [LN], 'so' [AB, LN; KJV, NASB, TNT], 'likewise' [He; NAB], 'on the same principle' [ICC], 'thus' [LN, Lns].

b. aorist act. indic. of διατάσσω (LN 33.325): 'to command' [LN; NIV, NRSV, TNT], 'to order' [BAGD, He, LN; NAB, TEV], 'to direct' [AB,

BAGD, ICC; NASB, NJB], 'to give instructions' [REB], 'to give charge' [HNTC], 'to ordain' [Lns; KJV]. See this word at 7:17.

c. pres. act. participle of καταγγέλλω (LN 33.204): 'to proclaim' [AB, He, ICC, LN, Lns; NASB, NRSV, TNT], 'to preach' [HNTC; KJV, LB, NAB, NIV, NJB, REB, TEV]. The present tense indicates that they are presently engaged in this activity [Lns]. See this word at 2:1.

d. εὐαγγέλιον: 'good news'. See this word at 4:15.

e. pres. act. infin. of ζάω (LN 23.88) (BAGD 1.c. p. 336): 'to get one's living' [NASB, NJB, NRSV, REB, TEV, TNT], 'to obtain one's living' [BAGD], 'to receive one's living' [NIV], 'to get enough to live on' [ICC], 'to be supported' [LB], 'to live' [AB, BAGD, He, HNTC, LN, Lns; KJV, NAB].

f. ἐκ with genitive object (BAGD 3.g.α. p. 235): 'from' [AB; NASB, NIV, NJB, TEV], 'by' [He, HNTC, Lns; NAB, NRSV, REB, TNT], 'of' [KJV], 'out of' [ICC]. This word is also translated with implied information 'by preaching' [BAGD], '(supported) by those who accept it' [LB].

QUESTION—What is meant by οὕτως 'in the same way'?

In accordance with the way the priests were provided for, so should the apostles be provided for [EGT, My, NIC2].

QUESTION—To whom did the Lord give this command?

1. He gave it to his disciples in general [Gdt, Herm, HNTC, ICC, TG]: the Lord gave his command for those who proclaim the good news. The dative 'to the ones proclaiming' should rather be taken as a benefactive: 'for them' [Gdt, HNTC].
2. He gave it to the ones who proclaim the Good News [Alf, He, Ho, NIC; NASB, TNT]: the Lord gave his command to those who proclaim the good news. The command was given to his ministers themselves so that they would not seek to provide for themselves [Ho]. The Lord was informing preachers of their rights [NIC].

QUESTION—To whom does ὁ κύριος 'the Lord' refer?

It refers to Christ [AB, Alf, EBC, Ed, EGT, Gdt, HNTC, Ho, Lns, My, NIC, NIC2, Rb, TG, Vn; TNT]. This refers to Jesus' words in Matt. 10:10 and Luke 10:7 [Alf, EBC, Ed, Gdt, Lns, NIC2, TH, TNTC, Vn].

DISCOURSE UNIT: 9:15–23 [AB]. The topic is Paul's waiver of his rights.

DISCOURSE UNIT: 9:15–18 [AB, NIC2, TNTC]. The topic is Paul's compulsion to preach free [AB], Paul's apostolic restraint [NIC2], his refusal to exercise his rights [TNTC].

9:15a But[a] I-have-used[b] not any of-these-things.

LEXICON—a. δέ: 'but' [He, HNTC, ICC; all versions except LB, NAB, NJB], 'however' [NJB], 'yet' [Lns; LB], 'as for (me)' [NAB], 'now' [AB]. This word is adversative [NIC2]: but.

b. perf. mid. indic. of χράομαι (LN 42.23): 'to use' [AB, LN; KJV, NAB, NASB, NIV], 'to make use of' [HNTC, LN, Lns; NRSV, TEV], 'to take advantage of' [REB], 'to avail oneself of' [ICC; NJB, TNT], 'to exercise' [He], 'to employ' [BAGD]. This word is also joined with 'any of these things' and translated 'to ask someone for one penny' [LB]. The perfect indicates a completed action with its results continuing to be significant in the present [EBC, EGT, Lns, NIC]. See this word at 7:21 and 31.

QUESTION—To what does τούτων 'these things' refer?

1. It refers to the rights and benefits he has discussed [AB, Alf, Ed, EGT, He, HNTC, Ho, My, NIC2, Vn; NAB, NIV, NJB, NRSV, REB, TEV]. It refers to the rights mentioned in 9:4–6 [NIC2]. It refers specifically to the rights of freedom from dietary restrictions, freedom to marry [Ed], and the right of support from the churches [Ed, Ho, My, TG, Vn].
2. It refers to the various reasons he has given to support his right from 9:4 on [Gdt].

QUESTION—What word is emphasized in this sentence?

The word 'I' is emphatic [He, HNTC, ICC, Lns, NIC2, TNTC]: But I myself have not used any of these things.

DISCOURSE UNIT: 9:15b–23 [EGT]. The topic is Paul's renouncement of his rights for the sake of the gospel.

9:15b And I wrote these-things not in-order-that it-might-be[a] like-this to[b] me;

LEXICON—a. aorist mid. subj. of γίνομαι (LN 13.3) (BAGD I.2.b. p. 158): 'to be' [LN]. This word is also joined with the words 'like this to me' and translated 'to see to it that anything should be done for me' [NAB], 'the maintenance due to preachers should henceforth be granted in my case' [ICC], 'to be done so in my case' [NASB], 'you will do such things for me' [NIV], 'it shall be thus in my case' [Lns], 'it should be done unto me' [KJV], 'in my case things may be done in this way' [HNTC], 'to claim such rights for myself' [TEV], 'to intend to claim it' [REB], 'to claim them' [He], 'to secure such treatment for myself' [NJB], 'I should (avail myself of any of these things)' [TNT], 'they may be applied in my case' [NRSV], 'they may turn out so in my case' [AB], 'to hint that I would like to start now' [LB], 'to have such action taken in my case' [BAGD], 'in order that this might happen to me' [LN (90.56)].

b. ἐν with dative object (LN **90.56**): 'to' [**LN**], 'in relation to, with respect to' [LN]. See other versions in a. above.

QUESTION—What is the function of the aorist ἔγραψα 'I wrote'?

It should be taken as an epistolary aorist, past tense from the readers' viewpoint, but present from the writer's, referring to his present letter [Alf, EBC, EGT, He, HNTC, ICC, Lns, NIC, Rb, TH; LB, NAB, NASB, NIV, NJB, NRSV, REB, TEV, TNT]: I am writing.

QUESTION—To what does ταῦτα 'these things' refer?

It refers to all of the arguments he has been writing in 9:4–14 [HNTC, ICC]. It refers to the argument of chapter 9 [TH].

for[a] (it is) better[b] for-me to-die rather than[c]—no-one will-make-empty[d] my boast.[e]

TEXT—Instead of breaking off in the middle of a sentence, some manuscripts replace οὐδείς 'no one' in the second clause with ἵνα τις 'that anyone' and thus finish the sentence: it would be better for me to die than *that anyone* should make my boasting empty. GNT selects the break with a B rating, indicating that the text is almost certain. Only KJV selects the replacement. It is unclear whether it is a matter of text selection or of smoothing out of the translation for some other versions. The better interpretation is that Paul breaks off his sentence and does not complete it [AB, Alf, EBC, Ed, EGT, He, HNTC, ICC, NIC, NIC2, Rb; NJB, REB, TEV]: it would be better for me to die than—no one will make my boasting empty.

LEXICON—a. γάρ 'for' [AB, He, HNTC, ICC, Lns; KJV, NASB], 'indeed' [NRSV], not explicit [all other versions]. This indicates that what follows is the reason why he is not writing to get their support [Ho, Lns].

b. καλός: 'better' [AB, BAGD, ICC; KJV, NASB, TNT], 'good' [Lns]. This word is also joined with the words 'to me' and translated 'I would prefer' [He], 'I would rather' [HNTC; LB, NAB, NIV, NJB, NRSV, TEV], 'I had rather' [REB].

c. ἤ (LN 64.18) (BAGD 2.a. p. 342): 'than' [AB, BAGD, He, HNTC, LN; KJV, LB, NAB, NASB, NIV], 'or' [Lns], not explicit [REB, TEV]. It is also translated with implied information: 'than that' [NJB, NRSV, TNT], 'than submit to that' [ICC].

d. fut. act. indic. of κενόω (BAGD 2. p. 428): 'to make empty' [BAGD, HNTC; NASB, REB, TNT], 'to turn into empty words' [TEV], 'to make void' [BAGD, ICC, Lns; KJV], 'to deprive of' [He; NIV], 'to deprive one of reason for' [BAGD; NRSV], 'to rob' [NAB], 'to take from' [NJB], 'to nullify' [AB], 'to lose (satisfaction)' [LB]. See this word at 1:17.

e. καύχημα : 'boast' [NAB, NASB, NIV, REB, TNT], 'this boast' [He, HNTC], 'rightful boast' [TEV], 'ground of/for boasting' [NJB, NRSV], 'basis for boasting' [AB], 'glory' [Lns], 'glorying' [KJV]. This word is also translated with implied information: 'satisfaction one gets from preaching without charge' [LB], 'glorying in taking nothing for my work' [ICC]. See this word at 5:6.

QUESTION—What is the function of this sentence?

1. The word ἤ means 'than' and at this point the sentence is broken off without completing it [AB, Alf, EBC, Ed, He, HNTC, NIC, NIC2, TNTC; all versions]: it is better for me to die than—No one will make my boast empty. It functions to emphasize Paul's deep emotion as he writes this [NIC2, TNTC]. The meaning is not changed but the intensity is [HNTC]. It is a figure of speech which adds drama to Paul's words [EBC].
2. The word ἤ means 'or'. [Lns, My]: it is better for me to die, or otherwise, if I remain alive, no one will make my boast empty.

QUESTION—It is better to die than what?

1. It is better to die than be deprived of the reason for his boasting of not accepting help [Alf, Ed, EGT, HNTC, Ho; KJV, NAB, NASB, NIV]. He started out to say 'It is better for me to die than that anyone should deprive me of my boast' but he turned the last clause into a direct statement [Ed, EGT, HNTC].
2. It is better to die than to use his rights to make them support him [ICC, Lns, My; LB, NJB, NRSV, REB, TEV, TNT]: it is better for me to die than that. No one can make my boast empty.

QUESTION—What does τὸ καύχημά μου 'my boasting' refer to?

It refers to the fact that he had never accepted remuneration for his work [Ed, ICC, My, NIC2, Rb]. This boasting must be seen in the light of not hindering the gospel (9:12) and of being able to offer the gospel free of charge (9:18). It was not meant to indicate competition with others who did accept remuneration for their preaching [NIC2].

9:16 For[a] if I-preach-the-Good-News,[b] there-is not for-me (a) right-to-boast;[c]

LEXICON—a. γάρ (LN 89.23): 'for' [AB, HNTC, LN, Lns; KJV, LB, NASB], 'for indeed' [He], 'yet' [NAB, NIV], 'in fact' [NJB], 'even' [REB], not explicit [ICC; NRSV, TEV, TNT].

b. pres. mid. subj. of εὐαγγελίζω (LN 33.215): 'to preach the Good News' [TNT], 'to preach the gospel' [AB, HNTC, Lns; all versions except NRSV, TNT], 'to proclaim the gospel' [NRSV], 'to tell the good news, to announce the gospel' [LN], 'to simply proclaim the Gospel' [He], 'to preach the Glad-tidings' [ICC]. The condition using the present tense assumes that this is Paul's usual activity [EBC, NIC2]. See this word at 1:17.

c. καύχημα (LN **33.372**): 'right to boast' [**LN**; TEV], 'ground for boasting' [HNTC; NRSV], 'basis to boast' [AB], 'something to boast of/about' [BAGD; NASB, NJB, TNT], 'something to be proud of' [He], 'something to glory of' [KJV], 'cause for glory' [Lns], 'subject of a boast' [NAB], 'special credit' [LB], 'glorying' [ICC]. This word is also translated as a verb: 'to boast' [NIV], 'to claim credit' [REB]. See this word at 5:6.

QUESTION—What relationship is indicated by γάρ 'for'?

It indicates the reason why no one could deprive him of his grounds for boasting [NIC, NIC2]. The answer is given negatively by telling what his boast does not consist of. Preaching the gospel is no grounds for boasting, but preaching without taking pay is [NIC2]. Only things that he was free to do or not do could be a grounds for boasting and here it is preaching without charge [Alf, Ho, ICC, My].

QUESTION—Does Paul's use of 'preaching the Good News' here carry implied information?

1. It refers to the act of preaching the gospel [AB, Alf, EBC, EGT, HNTC, Ho, ICC, Lns, My, NCBC, NIC2, TH, TNTC, Vn]. Just to preach the gospel is no basis for boasting [AB].
2. It implies the opposite of his grounds for boasting: 'if I preach the gospel like the rest', i.e., accepting living expenses [NIC].
3. It implies what he boasts about: 'even though I preach the gospel without being paid for it' [TG]. He has just talked about boasting, yet he now says that he really has no reason to boast [TG].

for[a] (an) obligation[b] is-laid[c] on-me;

LEXICON—a. γάρ: 'for' [HNTC, Lns; KJV, NASB, NIV, NJB, NRSV], 'because' [He], 'indeed' [AB], 'after all' [TEV], not explicit [ICC; LB, NAB, REB, TNT]. This indicates the reason for there being no ground for boasting about preaching the gospel [Gdt].

b. ἀνάγκη (LN **71.30**): 'obligation' [NRSV], 'necessity' [BAGD, Lns; KJV], 'the task...as a necessity' [He], 'necessary obligation' [**LN**], 'complete obligation' [LN]. This word is also joined with the words 'is laid to me' and translated 'to be compelled' [NIV], 'to be under compulsion' [AB, BAGD, HNTC; NASB, NJB], 'to be under compulsion and have no choice' [NAB], 'to be under orders' [TEV], 'to simply have to do something' [TNT], 'to be unable to help oneself' [REB], 'to be unable to keep from preaching' [LB], 'a duty which one must perform' [ICC]. See this word at 7:37.

c. pres. mid. indic. of ἐπίκειμαι (LN 76.17) (BAGD 2.c. p. 294): 'to be laid' [BAGD, He; KJV, NRSV], 'to be imposed, to be incumbent' [BAGD], 'to lie' [Lns], 'to be in force, to have power over' [LN]. This word is also joined with 'obligation' and translated as noted in b. above.

QUESTION—Who is the actor of the passive verb ἐπίκειται 'is imposed'?

1. The actor is God [Herm, NIC, NIC2, TH]: God has imposed the obligation on me. God has ordained this destiny since birth [NIC2]. He is under compulsion because he must fulfill God's plan for him which was revealed on the Damascus road [Herm, NIC, NIC2].
2. It refers to Jesus Christ who ordered Paul to do this [Ed, TG]. He is under compulsion because Christ had given him a command which he must obey [Ed, TG].

for[a] woe[b] is to-me if I-preach-the-Good-News not.

LEXICON—a. γάρ: 'for' [AB, HNTC, Lns; NASB], 'because' [ICC], 'yea' [KJV], 'and' [NRSV, TEV], not explicit [all other versions]. This explains the obligation [Alf].

b. οὐαί (LN **22.9**) (BAGD 2. p. 591): 'woe' [AB, BAGD, He, HNTC, Lns; KJV, NASB, NIV, NRSV], 'how terrible' [**LN**; TEV], 'disaster, horror' [LN], 'calamity' [BAGD]. This word is also joined with the words 'is to me' and translated 'how miserable I should be' [TNT], 'I would be utterly miserable' [LB], 'I am ruined' [NAB], 'I should be in trouble' [NJB], 'it would be agony for me' [REB], 'it will be the worse for me' [ICC].

QUESTION—What is implied in the word οὐαί 'woe'?

It implies the punishment of God [EBC, EGT, Gdt, Lns, My, NIC, NIC2, TG, TH]. Paul is remembering Jesus' threatening words about kicking against the pricks (Acts 9:5) [Gdt]. It implies an unspecified disaster of some kind [TNTC]. It implies despair [He], pain, or displeasure [BAGD].

QUESTION—What is the significance of the aorist μὴ εὐαγγελίζωμαι 'I do not preach the Good News'?

The aorist implies a single act: if I were not once to preach the Good News [NIC2].

9:17 For[a] if I-do this willingly,[b] I-have (a) reward;[c] but if unwillingly,[d] I-have-been-entrusted-with[e] (a) task;[f]

LEXICON—a. γάρ: 'for' [HNTC, Lns; KJV, NASB, NRSV], 'you see' [AB], not explicit [all other versions].

b. ἑκών (LN **25.65**) (BAGD p. 247): 'willingly' [BAGD, LN; KJV, NAB], 'of one's own (free) will' [BAGD, HNTC, LN, Lns; NRSV], 'out of willingness' [**LN**], 'voluntarily' [AB; NASB, NIV], 'gladly' [BAGD], 'spontaneously' [ICC], 'by one's own decision' [He], 'of one's own choice' [REB], 'as a matter of choice' [TEV]. This word is also translated as a clause: 'because one wanted to' [TNT], 'one had chosen this work himself' [NJB], 'one were volunteering his services of his own free will' [LB].

c. μισθός (LN 38.14): 'reward' [He, HNTC, LN; KJV, NASB, NIV, NJB, NRSV], 'special reward' [LB], 'pay' [ICC, Lns; REB], 'wage' [AB], 'recompense' [LN; NAB]. This word is also translated as a verb: 'to be paid' [TEV, TNT]. See 'wages' at 3:8.

d. ἄκων (LN **25.67**) (BAGD p. 34): 'unwillingly' [BAGD; NAB], 'against one's (own) will' [KJV, NASB, TNT], 'involuntarily' [AB; NIV], 'under compulsion' [NJB], 'as a matter of duty' [TEV], 'independently of one's own will' [He], 'not of one's own (free) will' [LN, Lns; NRSV], 'without choice' [HNTC], 'not a matter of free choice' [**LN**], 'because one must' [ICC], not explicit [LB]. This word is also translated as a verb: 'to have no choice' [REB].

e. perf. pass. indic. of πιστεύω (LN 35.50) (BAGD 3. p. 662): 'to be entrusted with' [AB, BAGD, HNTC; NAB, NRSV], 'to have something entrusted to one' [ICC, LN, Lns; NASB, NJB], 'to have something committed to one' [He; KJV, NIV], 'to be put into the care of' [LN]. This word is also translated actively: 'God has picked (me) out and given (me)...and (I) have no choice' [LB], 'God has/had entrusted me with' [TEV, TNT], 'I am discharging (a trust)' [REB]. The prefect tense carries the idea of an act completed and remaining in force in the present [EBC].

f. οἰκονομία (LN **42.25**) (BAGD 1.b. p. 559): 'task' [**LN**; NJB, TEV, TNT], 'responsibility' [**LN**], 'commission' [BAGD, LN; NRSV], 'stewardship' [AB, ICC, Lns; NASB], 'charge' [He; NAB], 'trust' [NIV, REB], 'sacred trust' [LB], 'office' [HNTC], 'dispensation' [KJV], 'management (of a household), office' [BAGD]. Paul compares his work as an apostle to a steward who has been given the responsibility to manage a household. As such, he is entitled to no pay [NIC2]. The οἰκονόμοι were household slaves. The master did not ask for the slave's consent when he gave him a responsibility [Lns].

QUESTION—What relationship is indicated by γάρ 'for'?

1. It explains what is meant by saying an obligation is laid upon him [Gdt, Ho, Lns, My, NIC2, TG].
2. It explains why he said 'Woe is me' [Alf].

QUESTION—What is meant by giving these two conditions?

1. The first condition is hypothetical and the second is factual [Alf, Ed, EGT, Gdt, He, HNTC, Ho, ICC, Lns, My, NIC2, TG, Vn]: if I preach of my own decision (but I don't), I would have a reward, but if I preach without having a choice (as is the case), I do it because I have been commissioned to do it. Paul did not take up his ministry by his own decision, so he has no reward for doing his duty [Alf]. Paul is just a steward who cannot demand a payment, not a mercenary who could claim his wages [Ed]. The words ἑκών 'willingly' and ἄκων 'unwillingly' should not be taken as indicating 'cheerfully' and 'reluctantly', but rather 'optionally' and 'obligatorily' [Gdt, Ho]. Since he does not merit a reward for preaching the gospel, the next question means 'But by what then do I merit a reward?' [He, HNTC].
2. The first condition is factual and the second is hypothetical [EBC, NCBC, NIC]: if I preach willingly (and I do), I have a reward, but if I preach unwillingly (but I don't), I still have to preach because I have been commissioned to do it. He preaches freely, not merely fulfilling the commission given to him (Acts 26:16) [EBC]. He receives a reward because he preaches with all his heart and that reward is described in the next verse [NIC]. If he obeys his commission willingly, he will get a reward. If he does so unwillingly, he must still do it, but without a reward [NCBC].

QUESTION—Who is the actor of the passive verb πεπίστευμαι 'I have been entrusted with'?

God is the actor [LN, TG, TH]: God has entrusted me with a task.

QUESTION—What is implied if Paul is 'entrusted with an task'?

It implies that he deserves no pay or reward [Alf, Ed, EGT, Gdt, Lns, My, NIC, NIC2].

9:18 What then is my reward?

QUESTION—Does this belong with the preceding verse or with this verse?

1. It belongs to this verse and begins a new sentence [AB, Alf, Ed, EGT, Gdt, He, Herm, Ho, ICC, Lns, My, NIC, NIC2, TNTC, Vn; all versions]: What then is my reward? The next sentence answers this.

2. It belongs with the preceding verse [GNT, HNTC, TH]. But if I involuntarily fulfill the responsibility entrusted to me, what then is my reward? This balances the construction: If I preach voluntarily, I have a reward. But if I preach involuntarily, receiving a commission from God, what then is my reward? [TH]. The implied answer is that he has no right to a reward [HNTC].

That preaching-the-Good-News I-may-offer[a] the Good-News free-of-charge[b]

LEXICON—a. τίθημι (LN 33.151) (BAGD I.2.a.β. p. 816): 'to offer' [He; NAB, NASB, NIV, NJB], 'to make' [Lns; KJV, NRSV], 'to deliver' [AB], 'to present' [HNTC], 'to explain' [LN], 'to give' [ICC], not explicit [LB, REB, TEV, TNT].

b. ἀδάπανος (LN **57.164**) (BAGD p. 15): 'free of charge' [AB, BAGD, ICC, **LN**; NAB, NIV, NJB, NRSV], 'without cost' [He, LN], 'without charge' [HNTC, Lns; KJV, NASB, TEV, TNT], 'without expense' [LB, REB].

QUESTION—What is the function of this clause?

1. It answers the question of what his reward is [AB, Alf, Ed, EGT, Gdt, He, Herm, HNTC, Ho, ICC, Lns, NIC, NIC2, TNTC, Vn; all versions]: What is my reward? It is that I might offer the Good News free of charge. This can be considered a reward because it gives a basis to his boasting about preaching without charge (9:15) [EBC, TNTC]. It gives him satisfaction [EGT], and pleasure [ICC, Vn]. Preaching without charge is itself his reward, since this means that he has a better chance to see the gospel spread when there can be no complaints that he is doing this for the money [HNTC].
2. It tells the purpose of not receiving a reward [My]: What is my reward? There is none. I do it this way so that I may offer the Good News free of charge.

so-as[a] not to-make-full-use-of[b] my right[c] in the Good News.

LEXICON—a. εἰς: 'so as' [He, HNTC, ICC, Lns; NASB, NRSV], 'and so' [NIV], 'so that' [AB], 'in other words' [REB], 'and' [NAB], 'that' [KJV], not explicit [all other versions].

b. aorist mid. infin. of καταχράομαι (LN 90.13): 'to make full use of' [BAGD, HNTC; NAB, NASB, NRSV], 'to use to the full' [ICC], 'to use up' [AB], 'to abuse' [KJV], 'to make use of' [NIV], 'to employ' [**LN**], 'to use' [LN; NJB], 'to use at all' [Lns], 'to claim' [TEV], 'to take' [TNT], 'to take advantage of' [He], 'to demand' [LB]. This word is also joined with μή 'not' and translated 'to waive' [REB]. The prefix κατά functions to strengthen the meaning of 'to use', that is, 'to use to the full' [AB, BAGD, Gdt, HNTC, ICC, Lns, My; NAB, NASB, NRSV]. The negative of 'to use to the full' is 'to not use at all' [Lns]. The negative of this verb means 'to abuse' or 'to misuse' [He, NIC2; KJV].

c. ἐξουσία: 'right'. See this word at 9:4 and 12.

QUESTION—What is the function of εἰς τὸ μὴ καταχρήσασθαι 'so as not to make full use of'?

1. It indicates purpose [AB, Ed, EGT, He, HNTC, ICC, Lns, My, Rb; NASB, NJB, NRSV]: I make the Good News free of charge in order that I may not make full use of my right.
2. It indicates result [Lns, NIC2, TG]: I make the Good News free of charge with the result that I do not make full use of my right.
3. It indicates restatement [Ho; REB, TNT]: I make the Good News free of charge, that is, I do not make full use of my right.

QUESTION—To what 'right' is Paul referring?

He is referring to the right to be supported by the churches for proclaiming the Good News [ICC, Lns, NIC2].

DISCOURSE UNIT: 9:19–27 [EBC, TH]. The topic is Paul's subjection to others and meeting God's approval.

DISCOURSE UNIT: 9:19–23 [AB, NIC2, TNTC]. The topic is Paul's adaptability for the gospel [AB], his apostolic freedom [NIC2], his service of all people [EBC].

9:19 For[a] being free[b] from[c] all-men I-enslaved[d] myself to-all-men,

LEXICON—a. γάρ: 'for' [He; KJV, NASB, NRSV], 'so' [NJB], 'and' [LB], not explicit [all other versions]. This word is also translated with implied information: 'So far from claiming my full rights, I submit to great curtailments. For' [ICC].

b. ἐλεύθερος (LN 37.134; 87.84) (BAGD 2. p. 250): 'free' [AB, He, HNTC, LN (87.84), Lns; KJV, NASB, NRSV], 'free and independent' [ICC], 'independent' [BAGD]. This word is also translated as a noun phrase: 'not a slave' [NJB], 'free man' [LN (37.134)]. It is also translated as a verb: 'not to be bound' [NAB], 'to be not bound to obey' [LB]. It is also joined with the words 'from all men' and translated 'no man's slave' [TNT], 'a free man, nobody's slave' [TEV], 'free and own no master' [REB], 'free and belong to no man' [NIV]. See this word at 7:21 and 9:1.

c. ἐκ with genitive object (LN **89.121**)(BAGD 1.d. p. 234): 'from' [AB, BAGD, HNTC, ICC, **LN**, Lns; KJV, NASB], 'with respect to' [NRSV], 'in respect of' [He], 'to' [NAB, NIV, NJB], 'free from, independent of, apart from' [LN], not explicit [LB, REB, TEV, TNT].

d. aorist act. indic. of δουλόω (LN **37.27**): 'to enslave' [AB, LN], 'to make oneself a slave/servant' [BAGD, HNTC, ICC, **LN**, Lns; all versions except LB, NJB], 'to become a servant' [LB], 'to put oneself in slavery' [NJB], 'to subject' [BAGD, He], 'to cause to be like a slave, to cause someone to be subservient to, to make a slave of' [LN]. The aorist indicates a past action which governed his specific past actions [NIC2]. He means that he enslaved himself and continues to do so [Alf]. See this word at 7:15.

QUESTION—What relationship is indicated by γάρ 'for'?

It explains Paul's general policy of waiving his rights (9:15–18) [EGT, Gdt, ICC, Lns, My, NIC, TNTC]. He confirms this policy by telling his practical procedures in other matters [My].

QUESTION—From whom or what is Paul free?

1. Since 'all' is masculine gender, it refers to people [AB, Alf, Ed, EGT, He, HNTC, Ho, ICC, Lns, My, NIC, NIC2, TH; all versions except NRSV]: being free from all people. He was free in that he did not have to conform to the ideas of others [Ho, NIC2]. He was free in that he was financially independent of others [EGT, Lns, NIC, NIC2].
2. 'All' is neuter and refers to things: from legal laws concerning means, days, and all external things [Gdt].

QUESTION—What relationship is indicated by the participial construction ἐλεύθερος ὢν 'being free'?

1. It indicates a concessive relationship to the verb 'I have made myself a slave' [all versions except LB, REB, TEV]: although free, I have made myself a slave.
2. It indicates a contrastive relationship [REB, TEV]: I am free, but I have made myself a slave.
3. It indicates a circumstantial relationship [He]: while being free, I have made myself a slave.
4. It indicates a causal relationship [NIC2]: because I am free from all people (financially), I can freely become everyone's slave so that I can gain the more.

QUESTION—In what sense did Paul 'enslave himself to all men'?

He enslaved himself in respect of their prejudices concerning observances which to him were inconsequential [Gdt]. It means 'a servant' in the sense that Christ was, a servant in order to save others (Phil. 2:5–8; Gal. 4:4–5) [NIC2]. He explains this in the following verses [Ho].

in-order-that I-might-win[a] as-many-as-possible;[b]

LEXICON—a. aorist act. subj. of κερδαίνω (LN 57.189) (BAGD 1.b. p. 429): 'to win' [AB, HNTC, ICC; NASB, NIV, NJB, NRSV, TEV], 'to win over' [NAB, REB], 'to win to/for Christ' [LB, TNT], 'to gain' [He, LN, Lns; KJV], 'to gain someone for the Kingdom of God' [BAGD], 'to earn, to make a profit' [LN]. 'To win' implies 'to Christ' or 'to the gospel' [AB, NIC2, TG, TH].

b. πολύς (LN **59.1**) (BAGD II.2.a.α./γ. p. 689): 'as many as possible' [NAB, NIV, NJB, REB, TEV, TNT], 'more' [BAGD; KJV, NASB], 'more men' [Lns], 'more persons' [**LN**], 'more of them' [AB, HNTC, ICC; NRSV], 'the greatest number' [He], 'them' [LB], 'the majority, most; the others, the rest' [BAGD], 'many, a great deal of, a great number of' [LN].

QUESTION—What is the precise meaning of τοὺς πλείονας 'the more'?
It means 'as many as possible' [He, NCBC; NAB, NIV, NJB, REB, TEV, TNT], 'more than I would have otherwise gained' [Ed, EGT, Gdt, ICC, Lns, NIC2, Rb], 'more than those converted by others' [Alf], 'the majority of those to whom I preach' [BAGD, Ho, My, NIC].

9:20 and[a] to-the Jews I-became[b] as[c] (a) Jew, in-order-that I-might-win Jews;

LEXICON—a. καί: 'and' [KJV, NASB], 'that is why' [He], 'thus' [ICC], not explicit [all other versions].
b. γίνομαι (LN 13.48; 41.1) (BAGD II.1. p. 160): 'to become' [AB, BAGD, HNTC, ICC, LN (13.48), Lns; all versions except LB, NJB, REB], 'to make oneself' [NJB], 'to seem (as)' [LB], 'to behave' [LN (41.1); REB], 'to be' [BAGD, He], 'to make oneself like' [BAGD].
c. ὡς (LN 64.12) (BAGD II.3.b. p. 897): 'as' [AB, HNTC, ICC, LN, Lns; KJV, LB, NASB, NRSV], 'like' [BAGD, He, LN; NAB, NIV, REB, TEV], not explicit [NJB, TNT].

QUESTION—What relationship is indicated by καί 'and'?
It is epexegetical and continues the explanation of the previous verse [ICC, Lns, My, NIC2]: and further. Paul now gives specific examples of the principle given in 9:19 [ICC, My, NIC2].

QUESTION—What did 'becoming as a Jew' entail?
It included living according to Jewish customs [Lns, My, NIC2]; using the Jewish forms of instruction [Lns, My]; circumcising Timothy at Lystra (Acts 16:3) [HNTC, ICC, TNTC]; taking a Nazarite vow in the temple (Acts 21:23) [NCBC]; observing the rules of the Jewish law [Ho, NIC, NIC2, TG], but not as a means to be saved [Ho, NIC, NIC2]; observing kosher rules about eating (1 Cor. 8:8; Gal. 2:10–13; Rom. 14:17; Col. 2:16) [NIC2].

to-the-ones under[a] law[b] (I became) as (one) under law,

LEXICON—a. ὑπό with accusative object (LN 37.7) (BAGD 2.b. p. 843): 'under' [AB, BAGD, HNTC, ICC, LN, Lns; all versions except LB, NAB, TEV]. This word is also translated as a verb: 'to be bound by' [NAB], 'to live under' [He], 'to be subject to' [TEV]. It is also joined with the words 'the ones...the law' and translated 'Gentiles who follow Jewish customs and ceremonies' [LB].
b. νόμος (LN 33.55) (BAGD 3. p. 542): 'law' [BAGD, Lns], 'the law' [AB, HNTC; KJV, NAB, NIV, NRSV, REB], 'the Law' [He, LN; NASB, NJB, TNT], 'the Law of Moses' [BAGD; TEV], 'the Mosaic Law' [ICC], not explicit [LB]. See this word at 9:8.

QUESTION—What 'law' is indicated by νόμος 'law' here?
It refers to the Law written by Moses [BAGD, Ed, He, ICC, NIC, TH, TNTC, Vn; NASB, NJB, TEV, TNT]. It refers to the Pentateuch and the traditions of the elders [NCBC].

QUESTION—To whom does τοῖς ὑπὸ νόμον 'to the ones under law' refer?

1. It is another way to refer to the Jews just mentioned in the previous sentence [Alf, EBC, Ed, HNTC, Ho, Lns, My, NIC, NIC2, TG, Vn; REB, TEV, TNT]: To the Jews I became as a Jew, that is, to those under law I became, etc.
2. It refers to both Jews and to Gentiles who had become Jews [EGT, Gdt, ICC]: To the Jews I became as a Jew, to all those under law I became, etc. 'Jews' refers to nationality, while 'those under law' refers to religion and includes proselytes to the Jewish religion [ICC].
3. It refers to Gentiles who followed Jewish customs [LB]: To the Jews I became as a Jew, to Gentiles who live under the law as Jews, I became, etc.

not being under law myself, in-order-that I-might-win the-ones under law;

TEXT—Some manuscripts do not have μὴ ὢν αὐτὸς ὑπὸ νόμον'not being under law myself'. GNT includes it with an A rating, indicating that the text is certain. Only KJV omits it.

QUESTION—What relationship is indicated by the participial construction μὴ ὢν αὐτὸς ὑπὸ νόμου 'not being under law myself'?

The participle indicates a concessive relationship [NIC2; all versions]: though not being under law myself. Paul did not want anyone to mistake his true status in the midst of all his accommodations [AB].

QUESTION—What does Paul mean by this phrase?

He means that he would act as though he were under it, while in reality he was free from the law [Ho]. He means to clarify that his becoming under law was an act of freedom, not obligation, the purpose of which was to win those under law [NIC2]. Paul followed practices that enabled him to be more acceptable to those under the law [TNTC].

9:21 to-the-ones outside-the-law[a] (I became) as outside-the-law,

LEXICON—a. ἄνομος (LN **11.42**; **33.57**) (BAGD 2.a. p. 72): 'outside the law' [HNTC; NRSV, REB], 'outside the Law' [NJB], 'without the Law' [He, LN (33.57)], 'without law' [Lns; KJV, NASB], 'not under the law' [AB], 'not subject to the law' [NAB], 'not having the law' [NIV], not explicit [LB]. This word is also translated as a noun phrase: 'Gentiles' [BAGD, LN (11.42); TEV], 'Gentiles who are outside the Law' [TNT], 'Gentiles who are free from the law' [ICC].

QUESTION—To whom does τοῖς ἀνόμοις'to the ones without the Law' refer?

It is a term that is functionally equivalent to the Gentiles [BAGD, EBC, Ed, EGT, HNTC, ICC, LN, Lns, NCBC, NIC, NIC2, TG, TH, TNTC; TEV, TNT]. It refers to the heathen who had no written revelation to guide them [Ho].

QUESTION—How did Paul become as ἄνομος 'without the Law'?

When Paul was with the Gentiles, he, like them, did not observe Jewish ceremonial laws such as those pertaining to unclean foods [TG]. He was not under Jewish law. For example, he ate whatever he was served without asking questions (10:27) [NIC2]. He quoted Gentile poets, he preached from a text written on a Gentile altar [ICC].

QUESTION—What kind of action is indicated in the implied verb 'I became'?

It refers not to a single act, but to repeated acts and could be translated 'I live' [TH].

not being outside-the-law of-God

QUESTION—In what sense was Paul μὴ ἄνομος θεοῦ 'not without the law of God'?

He was not without the law of God in the sense that he still obeyed the moral law [Ho]. God's laws are not the same as all Jewish laws [TG].

but under-the-law[a] of-Christ, in-order-that I-might-win the-ones outside-the-law;

LEXICON—a. ἔννομος (LN **33.342**) (BAGD p 267): 'under the law' [ICC, LN; all versions except LB, REB, TNT], 'in the law' [Lns], 'within the law' [TNT], 'subject to the law' [AB, BAGD, He, **LN**; REB], 'under law' [LN], 'under legal obligation' [HNTC], 'obedient to the law' [BAGD]. This word is also joined with the words 'of Christ' and translated 'do what is right as a Christian' [LB].

QUESTION—What does Paul mean by being ἔννομος Χριστοῦ 'under the law of Christ'?

He was referring to his obligation to obey Christ [Ho]. He was referring to his obligation to follow Christ's example and obey his commandments [NCBC].

9:22 to the-weak[a] (I became) weak, in-order-that I-might-win the weak;

LEXICON—a. ἀσθενής (LN **74.25**): 'the weak' [He, HNTC, **LN**, Lns; all versions except LB, TEV], 'those who are weak' [AB], 'weak (in faith)' [BAGD, **LN**; TEV], 'the men of tender scruples' [ICC], 'those whose consciences bother them easily' [LB]. See this word at 8.7.

QUESTION—Is there any significance to the fact that Paul omits the word ὡς 'as, like' here?

The omission may be deliberate. Paul may have a different meaning in mind than in the preceding comparisons [AB, Herm, NIC2]. It may indicate that Paul really did become weak (see 2 Cor. 10:10) [AB, NIC2]. He is referring to the majority of believers in Corinth (see 1:26–31). It is to these that he became weak so that he might win them [NIC2].

QUESTION—Are 'the weak' Christians or not?

1. They are Christians [AB, BAGD EBC, HNTC, Ho, ICC, Lns, My, NCBC, NIC, NIC2, TG, TH, TNTC, Vn; TEV]. They were undecided in their views [Ho]. They were very scrupulous about keeping rules and could not readily accept the fact that some rules need no longer be observed [HNTC, ICC]. They could not eat sacrificial meat without feeling guilty. There were many in Corinth in this class [NIC]. They were immature in

faith [Lns, TG], and Christian knowledge [Lns]. Paul lived as though he was limited by the same scruples and superstitions they were bound by [TG].

2. They are not Christians [Alf]. This refers to those who lacked the strength to accept the Good News. The weak Christians of chapter 8 have already been won to Christ [Alf].

QUESTION—If 'the weak' are already Christians, what is the meaning of 'to win'?

It means to seek their spiritual good [NIC], to bring to a more mature belief [HNTC, Lns, TG, TNTC], to win them over to a better understanding of Christian freedom [Ho, NCBC], to win them to full commitment to Christ as Lord [TG]. It may mean to keep within the believing community [HNTC, My, TNTC].

I-have-become all-things to-all-(men), in-order-that by-all-(means)[a] I-might-save[b] some.

LEXICON—a. πάντως (LN 91.10) (BAGD 1., 4. p. 609): 'by all means' [AB, BAGD, He, Lns; KJV, NASB, NRSV], 'by all possible means' [NIV, NJB, TNT], 'by whatever means are possible' [TEV], 'at least' [BAGD, LN; NAB], 'in one way or another' [REB], 'at all events' [HNTC, LN], 'at all costs' [ICC], 'certainly, indeed, at all' [LN], 'whatever a person is like I try to find common ground' [LB].

b. aorist act. subj. of σῴζω (LN **21.27**): 'to save' [AB, He, HNTC, ICC, LN, Lns; all versions except NJB], 'to bring to salvation' [NJB]. See this word at 7:16.

QUESTION—What is the significance of the perfect tense γέγονα 'I have become'?

It has the effect of summing up all the individual acts mentioned previously as aorists and adds the concept that Paul continues in the present to be 'all things to all men' [Ed, ICC, Lns].

QUESTION—How did Paul 'become all things to all men'?

He abstained from things which the scrupulous abstained from so he could help the scrupulous [ICC]. Paul sacrificed his own views and adopted the view of others in matters that were inconsequential to the Christian life [NIC2]. Paul accommodated himself to all according to their circumstances [My].

QUESTION—What is the meaning of the verb σώσω 'I might save'?

It has the same meaning as κερδήσω 'I might win' of 9:19–22: to bring people to believe in Jesus Christ as Savior and Lord [HNTC, NIC2, TG]. His use of 'to save' in this final clause shows that this was the meaning he intended for the verb 'to win' of the previous verses [NIC2].

QUESTION—What is the precise meaning of πάντως 'by all means'?

1. It means 'by all means' or 'in all ways' [AB, Alf, Ed, EGT, He, Lns, NIC, NIC2, Rb, TG, TH, TNTC, Vn; KJV, NASB, NIV, NJB, NRSV, REB, TEV, TNT]: that I might by all means save some.

2. It means 'certainly' or 'surely' [HNTC, Ho, My]: that I might certainly save some.
3. It means 'at all costs' [ICC]: that I might at all costs save some.
4. It means 'at least' [BAGD, Gdt, Herm; NAB]: that I might at least save some.

DISCOURSE UNIT: 9:23–10:22 [Gdt]. The topic is the question considered from the viewpoint of the salvation of the strong themselves.

DISCOURSE UNIT: 9:23–27 [Gdt]. The topic is the example of Paul.

9:23 And[a] I-do all-things for-the-sake-of/because-of[b] the Good News,

TEXT—Instead of πάντα 'all things', some manuscripts have τοῦτο 'this'. GNT selects 'all things' without rating it. KJV and LB select 'this'.

LEXICON—a. δέ: 'and' [He; KJV, NASB, NJB], 'but' [HNTC, ICC], 'now' [Lns], 'in fact' [NAB], not explicit [AB; all versions except KJV, NAB, NASB, NJB].

b. διά with accusative object (LN 90.38; 89.26): 'for the sake of' [AB, BAGD, He, HNTC, LN (90.38), Lns; all versions except LB], 'because of, on account of' [LN (89.26)]. This word is also translated 'for one and the same reason, that I may not keep (the gospel) to myself' [ICC], 'to get (the gospel) to them' [LB].

QUESTION—What does διά mean here?

1. It means 'for the sake of' [EGT, He, Ho, Lns, My, NIC, TG; all versions except LB]: I do it all for the sake of the gospel. 'For the sake of the gospel' means for the promotion of the gospel, for the sake of preaching the gospel [NIC], for the success of the gospel in saving men [Lns], in order to spread the gospel widely and to foster its success [EGT].
2. It means 'because of' [Ed, ICC, Vn]: I do it all because of the gospel. He means 'because the gospel is so precious to me' [ICC]. Because the gospel is so wonderful that it requires self-denial from those who proclaim it [Ed].

in-order-that I-may-become (a) fellow-partaker[a] of-it.

LEXICON—a. συγκοινωνός (LN **57.10**) (BAGD p 774): 'fellow partaker' [NASB], 'partaker (thereof) with (you)' [KJV], 'joint partaker' [Lns], 'one who shares in' [**LN**], 'partner' [AB, BAGD, LN; TNT], 'participant' [BAGD]. This word is also translated as a verb phrase: 'to jointly share in' [BAGD], 'to share in' [NIV, NRSV, TEV], 'to have a share in' [HNTC; REB], 'to share with others' [He, ICC; NJB], 'to receive (a blessing)' [LB], 'in the hope of having a share in' [NAB].

QUESTION—What is meant by becoming a 'fellow partaker of it'?

1. It means that Paul wants to have a share with others in the benefits of the Good News [Alf, BAGD, Ed, EGT, Gdt, He, HNTC, Ho, ICC, Lns, My, NCBC, NIC, NIC2, TNTC; NAB, NASB, NIV, NJB, NRSV, REB, TEV]. Paul places himself in company with those to whom he preaches, and along with them he hopes to share in the final blessings of the gospel

[NIC2]. He wants to partake in the effect of the gospel, the final salvation [Ho, NIC].

2. It means that he wants to share with the Good News [AB, EBC, Vn]. Paul is not thinking of his partnership with believers, but of his partnership with the Good News itself in its working, he proclaims it and it converts men [Vn].

DISCOURSE UNIT: 9:24–27 [AB, Ed, EGT, NIC2, TNTC]. The topic is an athletic analogue [AB], Paul's asceticism [EGT], exhortation and example [NIC2], Paul's self–control [TNTC]. This paragraph functions as a transition to conclude chapter 9 and prepare for a return to the matter of eating at the idol-worshipping feasts (10:1–22). Paul's primary purpose in this paragraph is to emphasize the need for self-control which their demand for their 'rights' denied [NIC2].

9:24 Know-you not that the-ones running[a] in (a) stadium[b] all indeed[c] run, but one wins[d] the award?[e]

LEXICON—a. pres. act. indic. of τρέχω (LN 15.230) (BAGD 1. p. 825): 'to run' [BAGD, He, HNTC, ICC, LN, Lns; KJV, LB, NASB, NIV, TNT], 'to run a race' [AB], 'to take part' [REB, TEV], 'to take part in the race' [NAB, NJB], 'to compete' [NRSV], 'to rush' [LN]. Foot-racing is meant [BAGD].

b. στάδιον (LN **7.55**) (BAGD 2. p. 764): 'stadium' [AB, BAGD, HNTC, **LN**, Lns; NAB, NJB, TNT], 'arena' [BAGD, LN]; 'race' [BAGD, He, ICC; KJV, LB, NASB, NIV, NRSV, TEV], '(at) the games' [REB].

c. μέν (LN 91.6): 'indeed' [LN], not explicit [AB, He, HNTC, ICC, Lns; all versions].

d. pres. act. indic. of λαμβάνω (LN 57.125) (BAGD 2. p. 465): 'to win' [REB, TEV], 'to receive' [AB, BAGD, HNTC, LN, Lns; KJV, NASB, NRSV, TNT], 'to get' [BAGD, ICC; LB, NIV, NJB], 'to gain' [He], 'to obtain' [BAGD], '(the prize) goes to (one man)' [NAB].

e. βραβεῖον (LN **57.120**) (BAGD 1. p. 146): 'award' [NAB], 'prize' [AB, BAGD, He, HNTC, ICC, **LN**, Lns; all versions except LB, NAB], 'first prize' [LB], 'victor's prize' [BAGD], 'reward' [LN]. The prize was a wreath [NIC].

QUESTION—What answer is expected to this rhetorical question?

The question expects a positive reply [Ho, ICC, Lns, NIC, NIC2, TH; LB, NAB, REB, TEV].

Run[a] in-such-a-way[b] that you-may-win[c] (it).

LEXICON—a. pres. act. impera. of τρέχω (LN 15.230) (BAGD 2.a. p. 412): 'to run' [AB, BAGD, He, HNTC, ICC, LN, Lns; all versions]. Here it is used figuratively [BAGD].

b. οὕτως (LN 61.9) (BAGD 2. p. 598): 'in such a way' [HNTC; NASB, NIV, NRSV, TEV], 'in such a manner' [TNT], 'in this way, as follows'

[BAGD], 'like that' [NJB], 'like him, so as' [ICC], 'also' [REB], 'so' [AB, LN, Lns; KJV, LB], 'so as' [NAB], 'therefore' [He].

c. aorist act. subj. of καταλαμβάνω (LN **57.56**) (BAGD 1.a. p. 412): 'to win' [AB, BAGD, HNTC; all versions except KJV, NIV, NRSV], 'to take' [**LN**], 'to acquire' [LN], 'to obtain' [LN; KJV, NRSV], 'to get' [NIV], 'to seize, to make one's own' [BAGD], 'to carry off' [He], 'to secure' [ICC], 'to attain' [BAGD, LN, Lns].

QUESTION—Does οὕτως 'in such a way' refer backward or forward?

1. It refers backward [Alf, Ed, Ho, ICC, Lns, My, TNTC; NJB, REB]: Like the winner of a race, so run that you may win.
2. It refers forward [AB, BAGD, EGT, Gdt, He, Herm, NIC2; NAB]: Run in such a way that you may win the award. Of course, it also depends on the preceding image [NIC2].

QUESTION—What are the points of comparison in this metaphor?

The figure is an athlete running a race and the topic is a believer living the Christian life [TG]. The point of comparison is doing something so as to succeed [Ho, NIC2], exerting all of one's strength [Gdt, HNTC, TNTC], fully resolving to succeed [Ed], the need of greatest self-denial in preparation and the greatest effort in participation [My, NIC2].

QUESTION—Is Paul saying that only one Christian will receive the prize?

No [Gdt, HNTC, ICC, TH], but he is saying that all will not receive it [TH]. There are many winners in the Christian race, but all should run as the one victor of a game runs [Ho]. The point of the metaphor is not that only one receives the prize, but that it is necessary to have self discipline to win the prize [NIC2].

QUESTION—To what does the 'prize' in the Christian life refer?

It refers to future salvation which was made possible by Christ's sacrifice and which all may obtain [My]. The prize is glory [Gdt].

9:25 And[a] every one competing[b] exercises-self-control[c] (in) all-things,

LEXICON—a. δέ: 'and' [He, Lns; KJV, NASB], 'now' [AB, NIC2], not explicit [He, HNTC, ICC; all versions except KJV, NASB]. It indicates transition [AB, He, Lns, My, NIC2; KJV, NASB]: and.

b. ἀγωνίζομαι (LN **50.1**) (BAGD 1. p. 15): 'to compete' [LN], 'to compete in an athletic contest' [**LN**], 'to compete in the games' [ICC; NASB, NIV], 'to engage in a contest' [AB, BAGD, Lns], 'to take part in the contests' [HNTC], 'to strive for the mastery' [KJV], 'to struggle' [LN]. 'The one competing' is translated 'athlete' [He; LB, NAB, NJB, NRSV, REB, TEV], 'competitor' [TNT]. This action was not restricted to the actual race, but began 10 months prior to the race and entailed sustained exercise and self-denial of things that would add to the weight of the body [Gdt]. This activity included running, fighting [Ed, Ho], wrestling [Ho], and any other sport [HNTC].

c. ἐγκρατεύομαι (LN **88.83**) (BAGD p. 216): 'to exercise self-control' [BAGD, **LN**; NASB, NRSV, TNT], 'to practice self-control' [Lns], 'to control oneself' [LN], 'to discipline oneself' [HNTC], 'to submit to self-discipline' [AB], 'to submit to discipline' [TEV], 'to deny oneself' [LB, NAB], 'to go into strict training' [NIV, REB], 'to concentrate completely on training' [NJB], 'to be temperate' [ICC; KJV], 'to place restrictions on oneself' [He]. The present tense indicates a general rule for an athlete [Lns]. This includes self-denial in diet, physical indulgences, and self-discipline [Ho]. This includes the training involved [Gdt, NIC].

they on-the-one-hand now/indeed[a] (do it) so-that they-might-win (a) perishable[b] wreath,[c]

LEXICON—a. οὖν (LN 91.7) (BAGD 5. p. 593): 'now' [Lns; KJV], 'indeed' [Ho, LN], 'verily' [ICC], 'then' [LN; NASB], not explicit [AB, He, HNTC; all versions except KJV, NASB].

b. φθάρτος (LN 23.125) (BAGD p. 857): 'perishable' [AB, BAGD, He, HNTC, ICC, LN, Lns; NASB, NRSV], 'mortal' [LN], 'fading' [REB], 'corruptible' [KJV], 'subject to decay or destruction' [BAGD], not explicit [LB]. This word is also translated as a clause: 'that will not last' [NIV, TEV], 'that withers' [NAB, TNT], 'that will wither away' [NJB].

c. στέφανος (LN **6.192**) (BAGD 1. p. 767): 'wreath' [BAGD, LN; NASB, NJB, TEV, TNT], 'winner's wreath' [AB, BAGD], 'crown' [BAGD, He, HNTC, ICC, LN, Lns; KJV, NIV, NRSV], 'crown of leaves' [NAB], 'garland' [REB], 'a blue ribbon or a silver cup' [LB]. This word is also joined with the word 'receive' and translated 'crowned with a wreath' [**LN**]. This was a wreath of foliage or of precious metal formed to resemble foliage and symbolized victory, honor, or high office [LN]. The wreath was wild olive, ivy, parsley, or laurel [Lns].

QUESTION—What verb is implied in this clause?

The implied verb phrase is 'do it' [AB, HNTC; KJV, NASB, NIV, NRSV, REB], 'do this' [NAB], 'exercise self-control' [Alf], 'go to this trouble' [LB].

but[a] we on-the-other-hand (an) imperishable[b] (one).

LEXICON—a. δέ (LN 89.124): 'but' [AB, He, ICC, LN; all versions except NJB, REB, TNT], 'whereas' [NJB], 'while' [Lns], not explicit [HNTC; REB, TNT].

b. ἄφθαρτος (LN 23.128) (BAGD p. 125): 'imperishable' [AB, BAGD, He, HNTC, ICC, LN, Lns; NAB, NASB, NRSV], 'incorruptible' [BAGD; KJV], 'immortal' [BAGD, LN]. This word is also translated as a clause: 'that will last forever' [NIV, TEV, TNT], 'that will never wither' [NJB], 'that never fades' [REB], 'that never disappears' [LB].

QUESTION—What relationship is indicated by δέ 'but'?

It indicates a contrastive relationship [NIC2; all versions except REB, TNT]. The contrast is between φθάρτος 'perishable' and ἄφθαρτος 'imperishable' [Lns, NIC2, Rb].

QUESTION—What verb should be supplied in this clause?

The verb 'exercise self-control' should be supplied [Alf, TG]: but we exercise self-control to win an imperishable award. The verb switches here to a figurative sense [TG].

QUESTION—To whom does the word ἡμεῖς 'we' refer?

It refers to 'we Christians' [My, TG].

QUESTION—How was it necessary for the Corinthians to exercise self-control?

Paul is concerned about their insistence on their right to eat festive meals in the idol temples [NIC2]. The Christian should not only forego definite sinful activity, but everything else that hinders his spiritual progress [TNTC].

9:26 Therefore[a] I so[b] run not as aimlessly,[c]

LEXICON—a. τοίνυν (LN 89.51) (BAGD p. 821): 'therefore' [LN; KJV, NASB, NIV], 'that is why' [TEV, TNT], 'so' [AB, BAGD; LB, NJB, NRSV], 'so, for my part' [HNTC], 'for my part' [Lns; REB], 'hence' [BAGD, LN], 'for this very reason, so then' [LN], 'accordingly' [ICC], 'indeed' [BAGD, LN], not explicit [all other versions].

b. οὕτως: 'so' [ICC, Lns; KJV], 'in such a way' [NASB], 'that is how' [HNTC; NJB], not explicit [AB, He; all versions except KJV, NASB, NJB].

c. ἀδήλως (LN **30.65**) (BAGD p. 16): 'aimlessly' [BAGD, **LN**; NIV, NRSV], 'without aim' [NASB], 'uncertainly' [BAGD, Lns; KJV], 'on a zigzag course' [AB], 'without a clear goal' [NJB], 'without purpose, unintentionally' [LN]. This word is also translated as a noun phrase: '(like) a man who loses sight of the finish line' [NAB]. It is also translated as a adjective: 'aimless (runner)' [REB], 'aimless (way)' [He]. It is also translated as a clause: 'as if I did not know where I was going' [HNTC], 'as being in doubt about my aim' [ICC]. This word is also joined with the word 'not' and translated positively: 'straight for the finish line' [TEV], 'straight to the goal' [LB], 'with a purpose' [TNT].

QUESTION—What relationship is indicated by τοίνυν 'therefore'?

It indicates a conclusion to the fact that a great deal of effort is necessary to succeed [Ed, Ho], and that an imperishable award awaits one [Ed, EGT, TG]. This applies the preceding metaphors to Paul's own life [NIC2].

QUESTION—What word is emphasized in this clause?

The word 'I' is emphatic: [Alf, HNTC, ICC, NIC2, TH]: I myself. There is an implied 'as you also are to run' [NIC2].

QUESTION—What is the meaning of the figure οὐκ ἀδήλως 'not aimlessly'?

It is a *litotes* (emphatic affirmation by denying the opposite) and means 'with complete certainty' [Lns]. There is no uncertainty about the course or goal [Ho, ICC, NIC2].

I-box[a] in-such-a-way as not beating[b] (the) air;[c]

LEXICON—a. pres. act. indic. of πυκτεύω (LN **50.6**) (BAGD p. 729): 'to box' [AB, BAGD, HNTC, **LN**, Lns; NASB, NJB, NRSV, TNT], 'to fight' [ICC; KJV, LB, NAB, NIV], 'to fight with fists' [BAGD], 'to deliver punches' [He]. This word is also translated as a noun: 'a boxer' [REB, TEV]. This word is used symbolically here [BAGD].

b. pres. act. participle of δέρω (LN 19.2) (BAGD p. 175): 'to beat' [BAGD, HNTC, LN; KJV, NASB, NIV, NRSV, REB, TNT], 'to flay' [Lns], 'to punch' [AB], 'to hit into' [He], 'to strike' [LN]. It is also joined with 'the air' and translated 'to shadowbox' [NAB], 'to shadowbox or play around' [LB], 'to waste one's punches' [TEV], 'to waste blows on the air' [ICC; NJB]. This refers to unskillful boxers who miss their mark [BAGD]. It means to strike repeatedly [LN].

c. ἀήρ (LN **2.2**) (BAGD p. 20): 'air' [AB, BAGD, He, HNTC, ICC, **LN**, Lns; all versions except LB, NAB, TEV], not explicit [LB, NAB, TEV].

QUESTION—What is the point of comparison in these two metaphors?

The point of comparison is purposefulness [HNTC, NIC2, TNTC]: As a runner does not run without a goal (but toward the finish line), so I live my Christian life with a definite goal. As a boxer does not direct his blows at nothing (but at his opponent's body), so I live my Christian life with a definite purpose. The point of comparison is controlled effort [HNTC]: As a runner keeps his direction or a boxer keeps his blows under control, so I live my Christian life under Christ's control.

QUESTION—What is the meaning of the figure 'not as beating the air'?

It is a *litotes* and means 'striking home' or 'delivering a knockout' [Lns]. He tries to make every blow count [TG].

QUESTION—Does the figure refer to a boxing match or to training?

1. It refers to an actual boxing match with an opponent [Alf, EBC, Ed, EGT, Gdt, HNTC, Ho, ICC, Lns, My, TG; NJB, TEV]: I do not box and only beat the air. In a boxing match, one does not shadowbox [NIC2].
2. It refers to training exercises [NCBC, Rb; NAB]: I do not merely shadow-box.

9:27 but[a] I-punish[b] my body

LEXICON—a. ἀλλά: 'but' [AB, HNTC; KJV, NASB, NRSV], 'on the contrary' [He], 'far from it' [ICC], 'no' [NIV], not explicit [Lns; all versions except KJV, NASB, NIV, NRSV]. This word indicates a contrast with the picture of the ridiculous boxer of 9:26 who beats the air [NIC2].

b. pres. act. indic. of ὑπωπιάζω (LN **88.89**) (BAGD 2. p. 848): 'to punish' [NJB, NRSV], 'to punish treating roughly' [LB], 'to harden with blows' [TEV], 'to discipline' [NAB], 'to keep under control' [**LN**], 'to beat' [NIV], 'to beat black and blue' [AB], 'to direct heavy blows against' [ICC], 'to treat roughly' [BAGD; TNT], 'to torment, to maltreat' [BAGD], 'to buffet' [HNTC; NASB], 'to pommel' [He], 'to not spare' [REB], 'to give a black eye' [Lns], 'to exercise self-control' [LN], 'to keep under' [KJV]. This word is used figuratively here of self-imposed discipline [BAGD].

QUESTION—Does this continue the figure of 9:26 or is it a different aspect of training?

1. This continues the figure of 9:26 and identifies his body to be the opponent against whom he boxes [Alf, EBC, Ed, EGT, Gdt, He, Lns, NCBC]. Paul's body is where what is opposed to God lives. He fights to defeat and deny fulfillment to bodily lusts [My].
2. This refers to a different aspect of preparation, the training of the body for a match [HNTC, ICC, NIC, NIC2, TG].

QUESTION—To what does 'body' refer?

It refers to human nature [TG]. It refers to the nature opposed to God (see Rom. 6:6; 7:23) [My]. It refers to his body and his spirit [NIC]. It refers to Paul himself [NIC2]. It referred to the sensual nature and all the evil tendencies of his heart [Ho].

QUESTION—What are the points of comparison in this figure?

The point of comparison is self-discipline or self-control [BAGD, HNTC, LN, NCBC, NIC, NIC2, TG, TNTC; NAB]. Another view is that the point of comparison is the neutralizing of opposition. Paul saw physical support by the Corinthians as an obstacle to his making the Good News free of charge. He neutralized this obstacle by denying himself this right and in this way 'knocking it out' [Lns]. The point of comparison is not literal self-flagellation [NCBC, NIC2]. This referred to the privations Paul imposed on himself such as working with his hands to provide for his own needs [Gdt, NIC2], and such hardships as are specified in 4:11–13 [NIC2]. This discipline was the denial of his rights and liberties lest they hinder his proclaiming of the Good News [NCBC]: as a man denies his body to make it work more efficiently, so Paul denies his rights and liberties in order to better proclaim the Good News.

and I-bring-under-complete-control[a] (it),

LEXICON—a. pres. act. indic. of δουλαγωγέω (LN **35.30**) (BAGD p. 205): 'to bring under complete control' [TEV, TNT], 'to bring under (strict) control' [NJB, REB], 'to master' [NAB], 'to make something a/one's slave' [BAGD, Lns; NASB, NIV], 'to enslave' [BAGD; NRSV], 'to bring into slavery' [HNTC], 'to force to be one's slave' [ICC], 'to hold in subjection' [He], 'to bring into subjection' [AB, BAGD; KJV], 'to make ready for service' [**LN**], 'to train something to do what it should, not what it wants to' [LB].

QUESTION—If this is a figure, what figure is it?

It is the picture of defeating an opponent in battle and then enslaving him. Its purpose was to make permanent the victory won in the battle [Ed]. He departs from the metaphor of athletes and takes up slavery [NIC2]. The point is control or mastery of one thing over another: as a master makes his slave serve his purposes, so Paul's made his body serve his purposes in proclaiming the Good News [NIC2].

lest-somehow[a] having-proclaimed[b] to-others I-myself may-become disqualified.[c]

LEXICON—a. μή πως (LN **89.62**) (BAGD 1.a. p. 519): 'lest somehow' [AB, BAGD], 'lest possibly' [NASB], 'lest in any way' [Lns], 'lest' [HNTC, ICC; KJV], 'otherwise' [LB], 'in/for fear that' [He; NAB, REB], 'so that...(perhaps) not' [BAGD; NIV, NRSV], 'to avoid any risk that' [NJB], 'to keep myself from' [TEV], 'in order that...not' [**LN**], 'not' [TNT].

b. aorist act. participle of κηρύσσω (LN 33.256): 'to proclaim' [NRSV], 'to preach' [AB, He, HNTC, ICC, LN, Lns; all versions except LB, NJB, NRSV, TEV], 'to call others to the contest' [TEV], 'to enlist for the race' [LB], 'to act as herald' [NJB]. See this word at 1:23.

c. ἀδόκιμος (LN 65.13) (BAGD p. 18): 'disqualified' [AB, BAGD; NASB, NJB, NRSV, REB, TEV], 'disqualified for the prize' [NIC2; NIV], 'rejected' [He, Lns; NAB], 'to prove to be rejected' [HNTC], 'not standing the test, unqualified, worthless, base' [BAGD], 'valueless, worth nothing' [LN]. This word is also translated as a noun: 'a castaway' [KJV]. It is also translated 'declared unfit and ordered to stand aside' [LB], 'to fail in the test' [TNT], '(my preaching) should end in my own rejection' [ICC].

QUESTION—Does the verb κηρύξας 'having proclaimed' continue the figure or simply refer to the proclaiming of the Good News?

1. It continues the metaphor [Alf, EBC, EGT, Gdt, ICC, My, Rb, TG; LB, NJB, TEV]: 'having called others to the contest' [TEV]. This figure is that of a herald who would summon the competitors together and explain the rules to be observed in order to qualify for the award [TG]: As the herald summons the competitors to the games and explains the rules, so I summon men to the Christian life and teach them the rules.
2. It is just the normal way of referring to proclaiming the Good News [AB, Herm, HNTC, Lns, NIC2, TH; KJV, NAB, NASB, NIV, NRSV, REB, TNT]: having proclaimed the Good News to others.

QUESTION—What is the figure here?

1. It refers to a contestant who did not observe the rules and was disqualified from competing [TG].
2. It refers to a combatant who competed in the contest but was disqualified from winning the prize [Alf, Ed, Ho, ICC, NIC2, Rb, TNTC]. It refers to an examination of the participants by the umpire at the close of the contest [Ed]. Some think this means that he would lose his salvation [Alf, Gdt, HNTC, Ho, Lns, NIC, NIC2], (see 9:24 and 10:5–12) [HNTC]. Others say that he would not lose his salvation, but would experience loss of reward because of unsatisfactory service [TNTC, Vn] (see 3:15) [TNTC].

www.ingramcontent.com/pod-product-compliance
Lightning Source LLC
Chambersburg PA
CBHW050613300426
44112CB00012B/1484

* 9 7 8 1 5 5 6 7 1 2 0 4 3 *